GCSE Higher Mathematics

A Full Course

L Bostock BSc

A Shepherd BSc

S Chandler BSc

E Smith MSc

Stanley Thornes (Publishers) Ltd

First published in 1992.
This edition published in 1996 by:
Stanley Thornes (Publishers) Ltd
Ellenborough House
Wellington Street
CHELTENHAM GL50 1YW

96 97 98 99 00 / 10 9 8 7 6 5 4 3 2 1

A catalogue record of this book is available from the British Library.

ISBN 0 7487 2647 0

Typeset by Tech-Set, Gateshead, Tyne & Wear
Printed and bound in Great Britain by
BPC Books Ltd, Paulton

CONTENTS

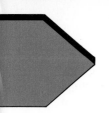

HOW TO USE THIS BOOK
ADVICE TO THE STUDENT

What the Book Contains

This book covers the National Curriculum in Mathematics including Grade A*. It is a reference book, a manual and a practice book, providing detailed explanations, numerous worked examples and a plentiful supply of exercises. This book aims to prepare you for the highest tier of GCSE Mathematics. You are strongly advised to check the syllabus provided by your particular Examining Board as you may not need to study some of the topics we have included. This book can be used either as a complete one or two year course, as a consolidation and top-up book for those of you in your final year of preparation for GCSE, or as a revision course for those of you retaking GCSE and hoping for a better grade.

Self-Assessment

All of you will have done some mathematics so it is unlikely that you will need to cover all the work in this book. However, knowledge and confidence about particular topics will vary from one person to another and, to help assess which topics need to be covered in full, we have provided a self-assessment exercise at the end of each chapter. These exercises are designed to reflect the work contained in the chapter, starting with the basic work and progressing to the harder applications of the topic. Some of you may choose to do the self-assessment exercise before looking at the relevant chapter. If you find that you can do hardly any of the exercise, this indicates that the whole chapter needs to be worked thoroughly. When about half to three quarters of the questions present no problems, it is advisable to read through the chapter, stopping to concentrate only on those areas that do present problems. Those of you who manage at least 80 per cent of the questions without real difficulty can reasonably assume competence in the topics covered by that chapter though some questions within the chapter similar to those that gave difficulty should be worked.

The self-assessment exercises can also be used after working through a chapter to see if the work has been understood, or they can be used later for revision purposes.

Using Exercises

Each chapter contains exercises to test your understanding of the topic being studied and which enable you to practise and consolidate the skills needed to become proficient in mathematics. Many contain large numbers of questions. Individuals vary in the number of questions that they need to work through in order to gain confidence and skill in a particular topic. It is not necessary for you to work every question in every exercise. Once it is obvious to you that you know what you are doing with a particular type of question it is sensible to go on to the next type. There are many worked examples within the exercises. These show how work can be set out. The comments in small type give the thought processes and background information needed. These do not need to be written down.

Investigations and Coursework

Ideas for investigations and practical work are included near the end of several chapters. These vary in difficulty, extent and purpose. Some are suitable for group work and others for individual study. Some are open-ended while others lead to one result only. It is not intended that all of them should be tried. You may find certain of these investigations more interesting than others. Time spent on a few of these investigations will give enjoyment and insight that is not easy to achieve in other ways. It will also give practice in coursework, which forms a part of all GCSE mathematics schemes. Some of the ideas may be suitable for use as part of the GCSE coursework but this must be checked with the appropriate authorities as syllabuses vary in their requirements. Because of the nature of these investigations it is not possible to provide answers. If you are working alone, some competent advice on work done should be sought.

Materials Needed

Apart from ordinary writing paper, you will need a supply of 5 mm squared paper and 2 mm squared graph paper. A small quantity of tracing paper is useful. You will also need a ruler, a protractor, a pair of compasses and a calculator. The calculator should be a scientific one with statistical functions and preferably capable of working in fractions; most of the cheapest scientific calculators have all the functions you will need (and many that you will not). Detailed instructions on the use of calculators are not included in this book as there is no universal standard for the layout of keys or of operation; you will need to consult your manual, and we suggest that you keep the manual with the calculator for reference.

To get the most out of this course you will need access to a computer with graph-drawing software, and database and spreadsheet software with a statistical package. This is not essential but highly desirable. You will find reference in this book to graphical calculators; these are expensive and not essential but if you have access to one it is worth learning how to use it.

Answers and Accuracy

Many problems ask for an answer to a given degree of accuracy, for example a length may be required to be given to the nearest centimetre. When the degree of accuracy is not specified, answers should be given in a form appropriate to the situation – it would be ridiculous to give the distance between London and Paris, say, to the nearest centimetre.

A problem with accuracy can sometimes arise when a value, calculated and given as an answer to the required degree of accuracy, is then used again to calculate a further value. This may be the cause of a difference between the last figure of your answer and that given in the answer in this book. Wherever possible, uncorrected values should be used for further calculation.

One last word about answers – before checking your answer with that given in this book, get into the habit of checking yourself that it is reasonable. For example, if you need to find three-quarters of £288 and come up with £484 as an answer, you should not get as far as even thinking of looking up the answer in the back. However complicated a problem is, you should have some idea of the size of answer expected.

SYMBOLS AND ABBREVIATIONS USED

=	is equal to
≈	is approximately equal to
≠	is not equal to
>	is greater than
<	is less than
⩾	is greater than or equal to
⩽	is less than or equal to
∴	therefore
⇒	gives, giving, implies or implying that
≡	is equivalent to or is congruent with
‖	is parallel to
⊥	is perpendicular to
LHS	left-hand side
RHS	right-hand side
(3 s.f.)	corrected to 3 significant figures
(2 d.p.)	corrected to 2 decimal places
+ve	positive
−ve	negative
△	triangle
∝	is proportional to

WHOLE NUMBERS

NATURAL NUMBERS

The numbers   1, 2, 3, ...   are called the *natural numbers*.
They can be added, subtracted, multiplied and divided.

Number Bonds

The ability to do mental calculations is important. There are many everyday situations where you need to calculate quickly and accurately and, when working on paper with simple numbers, using your brain is quicker than resorting to a calculator.

Mental accuracy and speed depend on knowing the following number bonds:

>   multiplication tables up to 12×12
>   pairs of numbers that add up to 10
>   the sum of any two numbers less than or equal to 10.

By 'know' we mean instant recall; there is only one way to acquire this skill and that is by repeated practice.

The addition facts are needed for subtraction because addition and subtraction are related operations. For example, $8 - 6$ means 'the number that when added to 6 makes 8', i.e. to evaluate $8 - 6$ you need to know that $6 + 2 = 8$.

Similarly you need to know the multiplication facts for evaluating divisions, e.g. $54 \div 6$ is the number of 6s that make 54, so you need to know that $9 \times 6 = 54$.

Adding a String of Numbers

Remember that the order in which numbers are added does not matter, so when adding several numbers together it is sensible to look for pairs of numbers that add up to 10,

e.g.
$$2 + 5 + 7 + 8 + 3 = 10 + 10 + 5$$
$$= 25$$

Note that the result of adding two numbers is called their *sum*.
The *difference* between two numbers is the result of taking the smaller number from the larger number.

Multiplying a String of Numbers

The order in which numbers are multiplied does not matter so, when multiplying several numbers together, we do not have to work from left to right but can first choose to find the product of any two numbers from the string,

e.g. $\qquad 2 \times \overbrace{3 \times 4} \times 5 = 10 \times 12$

$\qquad\qquad\qquad\qquad\quad = 120$

Note that the result of multiplying two numbers is called their *product*.
The result of dividing one number into another is called the *quotient*.

Multiplication and Division by Powers of 10

To multiply a number by   10, 100, ...   we move the figures   1, 2, ...   places to the left,

e.g. $\qquad\qquad 27 \times 100 = 2700 \qquad$ and $\qquad 34 \times 1000 = 34\,000$

To divide a number by   10, 100, ...   we move the figures   1, 2, ...   places to the right,

e.g. $\qquad\qquad 4300 \div 10 = 430.0 \qquad$ and $\qquad 290 \div 100 = 2.90$

$\qquad\qquad\qquad\qquad\quad = 430 \qquad\qquad\qquad\qquad\qquad = 2.9$

(Decimals are fully explained in chapter 2.)

To multiply a number by 500, say, we can first multiply by 5 and then multiply by 100,

e.g. $\qquad\qquad 27 \times 500 = 27 \times 5 \times 100$

$\qquad\qquad\qquad\qquad\quad = 135 \times 100$

$\qquad\qquad\qquad\qquad\quad = 13\,500$

MIXED OPERATIONS

When a calculation involves addition and subtraction only, the order in which the operations are done does not matter. *But it is important to remember that a + or − sign tells you what to do with just the number following that sign;* it has no relevance to any further numbers, e.g. in the calculation $2 - 3 + 5$,   we subtract *only* 3; we do *not* subtract 3 *and* 5.

So $2 - 3 + 5$ can be worked by first adding 2 and 5,

i.e. $\qquad\qquad 2 - 3 + 5 = 7 - 3 = 4$

Similarly, in a calculation involving only multiplication and division, the order in which the operations are done does not matter, but it does matter that you remember that a × or ÷ sign tells you what to do only to the number or bracket immediately after that sign,

e.g. $\qquad\qquad 2 \div 3 \times 6 = 2 \times 6 \div 3$

$\qquad\qquad\qquad\qquad\quad = 12 \div 3$

$\qquad\qquad\qquad\qquad\quad = 4$

When part of a calculation is in brackets, that part must be worked first because the sign before the bracket applies to the whole bracket,

e.g. $\qquad 8 - (3 + 2) = 8 - 5 = 3$

When a calculation involves a mixture of addition, subtraction, multiplication and division then, if there are no brackets,

**multiplication and division
must be done before addition and subtraction**

e.g. $\qquad 2 + 5 \div 3 \times 6 = 2 + (5 \div 3 \times 6)$

$$= 2 + (30 \div 3)$$

$$= 2 + 10$$

$$= 12$$

When a number will not divide into another number exactly, the part left over is called a *remainder*, e.g. $10 \div 3 = 3$, remainder 1 (i.e. $10 = 3 \times 3 + 1$).

To find the remainder when larger numbers are involved, it is sensible to set the calculation out in an organised way. For example, to find the remainder when 127 is divided by 9, we can set the calculation out as follows:

$$\begin{array}{r} 1\,4\ \text{r}\,1 \\ 9\overline{)1\,2^{3}7} \end{array}$$
i.e. $127 \div 9 = 14$, remainder 1

(Check: $14 \times 9 + 1 = 126 + 1 = 127$)

Exercise 1a

This exercise should be used to practise speed and accuracy. Do not use a calculator.

1. Copy this table and fill in the blank squares. You should be able to do it accurately in less than four minutes.

×	1	2	3	4	5	6	7	8	9	10
1										
2										
3										
4										
5										
6										
7										
8										
9										
10										

2. Make another copy of the table but this time write the numbers 1 to 9 in any order across the top and down the side. Now fill in the blank squares. You should be able to do this accurately in less than four minutes.

3. Make another copy of the table in question 1, but this time put a '+' sign in the corner. Use it to test your speed and accuracy of addition.

4. Make another copy of the table in question 2, but with a '+' sign in the corner. Test your speed and accuracy again.

5. Do each of the following calculations in your head and write down the answer.

   (a) 6×9

   (b) 40×30

   (c) $84 + 15$

   (d) 30×70

   (e) 200×40

   (f) 11×12

   (g) $210 \div 30$

   (h) 9×7

   (i) $250 \div 5$

   (j) 9×12

   (k) $56 \div 7$

   (l) $18 + 7$

   (m) $640 \div 8$

   (n) $46 + 16$

   (p) $3600 \div 90$

   (q) $34 + 21$

   (r) 120×12

   (s) $9 + 42$

   (t) $42 \div 6$

   (u) $18 + 27$

6. Write down the answer to each of the following calculations.

   (a) $54 + 31$

   (b) $264 - 18$

   (c) $69 + 27$

   (d) $750 - 28$

   (e) 5×130

   (f) 7×15

   (g) $2 \times 4 \times 3$

   (h) 52×5

   (i) $4 \times 3 \times 5$

   (j) $12 + 5 + 4$

   (k) $182 - 54$

   (l) $132 \div 11$

   (m) $96 - 27$

   (n) $13 + 9 + 7$

   (p) $2 \times 2 \times 3$

   (q) 14×9

   (r) $287 + 155$

   (s) 3×46

   (t) $162 \div 6$

   (u) $147 \div 7$

7. Write down the remainder in each of the following divisions.

   (a) $58 \div 5$

   (b) $36 \div 7$

   (c) $73 \div 4$

   (d) $64 \div 3$

   (e) $93 \div 6$

   (f) $78 \div 8$

   (g) $85 \div 4$

   (h) $106 \div 3$

   (i) $130 \div 9$

   (j) $125 \div 4$

   (k) $103 \div 11$

   (l) $250 \div 6$

   (m) $176 \div 9$

   (n) $143 \div 12$

   (p) $233 \div 9$

   (q) $416 \div 7$

8. Write down the answer to each of the following calculations.

   (a) $2 + 2 \times 3$

   (b) $2 \times 3 + 2 \times 4$

   (c) $3 \times 4 - 2 \times 3$

   (d) $10 - 12 + 5$

   (e) $2 - 7 + 9$

   (f) $4 \div 3 \times 6$

   (g) $6 \times 3 - 8 \div 2$

   (h) $12 \times 4 - 7$

   (i) $8 \times 4 - 3$

   (j) $16 - 21 \div 7$

   (k) $15 + 14 \div 2$

   (l) $3 \div 6 \times 10$

9. Write down the answer to each of the following calculations.

   (a) $5 \times (2 + 7)$

   (b) 130×7

   (c) $(25 - 14) \times 2$

   (d) $12 + 15 + 8$

   (e) $24 \div (5 - 2)$

   (f) $12 + 16 \div 4$

   (g) 200×30

   (h) $(34 + 16) \times 50$

10. (a) Find two numbers whose sum is 6 and whose product is 8.

    (b) Find two numbers whose sum is 15 and whose product is 44.

    (c) Find two numbers whose sum is 12 and whose product is 35.

11. (a) How many 7s can you take away from 45 and what number is left?

    (b) How many 9s can you take away from 100 and what number is left?

    (c) How many 4s can you add to 60 before the total is greater than 100?

12. Starting from 25 count up in 7s until the total is greater than 100. Write down this number.

13. How much change do you get when you buy as many 26 p stamps as possible with £ 2?

14. Eggs are packed into boxes that each hold six eggs. How many boxes are needed to pack 730 eggs?

15. How many pieces of wire, each 9 cm long, can be cut from a 250 cm length of wire?

16. Take any three digit number, where at least two of the digits are different, e.g. 771 is acceptable, but 777 is not. Now write the digits in reverse order and find the difference between the two numbers. Repeat this process with the difference. Continue to repeat with each successive difference until you see a pattern. Try the same process with some other three digit numbers. Comment on your results.

LONG MULTIPLICATION

To multiply 537 by 56 without using a calculator, we break it up into stages:
multiply 537 by 6, then multiply 537 by 50 and add the results.
This is the conventional way to set out a long multiplication calculation:

$$
\begin{array}{r}
537 \\
\times 56 \\
\hline
3222 \quad (\times 6) \\
26850 \quad (\times 50) \\
\hline
30072 \quad (+) \\
\end{array}
$$

LONG DIVISION

To divide 4788 by 37 without using a calculator, we work from the left:

4(thousand) $\div$ 37 $=$ 0, remainder 4(thousand)

then add the remainder to the next figure and divide by 37,

47(hundred) $\div$ 37 $=$ 1(hundred), remainder 10(hundred),

then add the remainder to the next figure and divide again, and so on.

This process is much easier to keep track of if it is set out in the conventional way:

$$
\begin{array}{r}
129 \\
37\overline{)4\ 7\ 8\ 8} \\
3\ 7 \quad\quad \\
\hline
1\ 0\ 8 \quad \text{1st remainder is 10 hundreds} \\
7\ 4 \quad\quad \\
\hline
3\ 4\ 8 \quad \text{2nd remainder is 34 tens} \\
3\ 3\ 3 \quad\quad \\
\hline
1\ 5 \\
\end{array}
$$

i.e. $4788 \div 37 = 129$,   remainder 15

Exercise 1b

Use pen and paper only to evaluate

1. 492×27	**5.** 278×84	**9.** $537 \div 17$	**13.** $905 \div 28$
2. 393×46	**6.** 4878×23	**10.** $699 \div 22$	**14.** $7400 \div 19$
3. 655×82	**7.** 944×153	**11.** $365 \div 31$	**15.** $3899 \div 122$
4. 190×36	**8.** 45×5337	**12.** $850 \div 47$	**16.** $5050 \div 321$

FACTORS

A factor of a number divides into the number exactly leaving no remainder, e.g. the factors of 12 are 1, 2, 3, 4, 6 and 12.

The following tests for divisibility are useful:

> an even number will divide by 2
> a number whose digits add up to a multiple of 3 will divide by 3
> a number ending in 5 or zero will divide by 5
> a number whose digits add up to a multiple of 9 will divide by 9.

Prime Numbers

A prime number has just two distinct factors: 1 and itself, e.g. 5 is a prime number as the only factors of 5 are 1 and 5.

Note that 1 is *not* a prime number (it has only one factor, 1).

Index Notation

The expression 2^4 is an example of index notation.

It means 'four 2s multiplied together',

i.e. $\qquad 2^4 = 2 \times 2 \times 2 \times 2$

The superscript 4 is called the *index* or *power*.

EXPRESSING A NUMBER AS THE PRODUCT OF ITS PRIME FACTORS

To write a number as a product of its prime factors, start by trying to divide by 2 and continue until 2 will no longer divide in exactly. Next try 3 in the same way, then 5 and so on, until a prime number is left as the last factor,

e.g. $\qquad 24 = 2 \times 12 = 2 \times 2 \times 6 = 2 \times 2 \times 2 \times 3 = 2^3 \times 3$

and $\qquad 2100 = 2 \times 1050 = 2 \times 2 \times 525$

$$= 2 \times 2 \times 3 \times 175$$
$$= 2 \times 2 \times 3 \times 5 \times 35$$
$$= 2 \times 2 \times 3 \times 5 \times 5 \times 7$$
$$= 2^2 \times 3 \times 5^2 \times 7$$

Highest Common Factor (HCF)

The highest common factor of two or more numbers is the *largest* number that divides exactly into both of them.

If the numbers are less than 100, the HCF can be found by inspection, e.g. the HCF of 56 and 48 is 8.

If the HCF is not obvious, it can be found by first expressing each number as a product of its prime factors and then picking out the largest product of primes that is a factor of both of them,

e.g. $108 = 2^2 \times 3^3$ and $204 = 2^2 \times 3 \times 17$

Now we can see that $2^2 \times 3$, i.e. 12, is the highest number that is a factor of both 108 and 204.

MULTIPLES

A multiple of a number is any number that contains the first number as a factor, e.g. some multiples of 3 are 3, 6, 24, 300.

Lowest Common Multiple (LCM)

The lowest common multiple of two or more numbers is the *smallest* number that is a multiple of both of them, i.e. each of them is a factor of their LCM.

For example, the smallest number for which 6 and 8 are each factors is 24, so 24 is the LCM of 6 and 8.

If the LCM of a set of numbers is not obvious then it can be found by expressing each number as a product of its prime factors and then picking out the smallest product that includes all the factors of both numbers,

e.g. $108 = 2^2 \times 3^3$ and $204 = 2^2 \times 3 \times 17$

so $2^2 \times 3^3 \times 17$ is the lowest number of which each of 108 and 204 are factors,

i.e. 1836 is the LCM of 108 and 204.

Exercise 1c

1. List all the factors of each number.

    (a) 6   (e) 16   (i) 18

    (b) 8   (f) 20   (j) 36

    (c) 21   (g) 11   (k) 27

    (d) 30   (h) 25   (l) 45

2. Using a ten by ten square, list all the numbers from 1 to 100. Ring all the prime numbers in the square.

3. Starting with the number itself, write down the four lowest multiples of each number.

    (a) 2   (c) 5   (e) 12

    (b) 4   (d) 3   (f) 8

4. Find the highest common factor of each set of numbers.

(a) 2, 3

(b) 4, 6

(c) 8, 12

(d) 36, 45

(e) 24, 51

(f) 26, 65

(g) 12, 15

(h) 12, 18

(i) 6, 12

(j) 48, 110

(k) 39, 13, 26

(l) 12, 36, 42

5. Find the lowest common multiple of each set of numbers.

(a) 2, 3

(b) 4, 6

(c) 3, 5

(d) 4, 18

(e) 6, 15

(f) 4, 10

(g) 12, 15

(h) 18, 24

(i) 15, 18

(j) 24, 36

(k) 9, 12, 18

(l) 12, 16, 24

6. Find the value of

(a) 3^3

(b) $2^2 \times 2^3$

(c) 5^3

(d) $3^2 - 2^3$

(e) 4^3

(f) 2^4

(g) $5^2 - 4^2$

(h) 9^2

(i) $3^3 - 4^2$

(j) 3^4

(k) $(2^3)^2$

(l) $7^2 \times 2^2$

(m) $11^2 + 2^5$

(n) $12^3 \div 3^2$

(p) $(3^3)^2$

(q) $2^3 - 2^2$

7. Express each number as a product of its prime factors and write the answers in index notation.

(a) 136

(b) 720

(c) 216

(d) 450

(e) 84

(f) 528

(g) 726

(h) 314

(i) 784

(j) 405

8. From the set of numbers
$\{1, 3, 4, 5, 6, 8, 10, 11, 15, 17, 21, 27\}$
write down those numbers that are

(a) prime numbers,

(b) multiples of 3,

(c) factors of 60.

9. Find the smallest length of tape that can be cut into an exact number of either 3 m lengths or 8 m lengths or 12 m lengths.

10. Two model trains travel round a double track. One train completes the circuit in 12 seconds and the other completes the circuit in 15 seconds. If they start side by side how long will it be before they are side by side again?

11. A rectangular floor measures 450 cm by 350 cm. What is the side of the largest square tile that can be used to cover the floor without any cutting?

12. What is the smallest sum of money that can be made up of an exact number of £20 notes or of £50 notes?

13. Rectangular tiles measure 15 cm by 9 cm. What is the length of the side of the smallest square area that can be covered with these tiles?

14. A rectangular shaped patio measures 550 cm by 330 cm. What is the largest sized square stone that can be used to pave the area without any cutting?

NEGATIVE NUMBERS

There are many quantities whose values can fall below a natural zero. Temperature is an obvious example.

Measuring in degrees Celsius (°C), 0 °C is the temperature at which water freezes. To describe temperatures below the freezing point of water we use the numbers $-1, -2, -3, \ldots$ These are called negative numbers. Therefore a temperature of -2 °C means two degrees below freezing point.

Most people would call -2 °C 'minus 2 °C' but it is better referred to as 'negative 2 °C' as 'minus' also means 'subtract'.

POSITIVE NUMBERS

To describe temperatures above freezing point we use positive numbers, i.e. $+1, +2, +3 \ldots$

A temperature of 2 °C above freezing point can be written as $+2$ °C and called 'positive 2 °C', although most people would call it simply 2 °C and write it without the $+$ sign. In fact *any number without a symbol in front of it is assumed to be a positive number.*

DIRECTED NUMBERS

Positive and negative numbers are collectively known as *directed numbers.* As well as temperature, they can be used to describe any measurement that goes above or below an obvious zero level, e.g. distance above or below sea-level, time after or before an event.

Directed numbers can also be used to describe quantities that involve one of two possible directions. For example, if a car is travelling along a road at 20 m.p.h. and another car is travelling at 20 m.p.h. in the opposite direction, then we could describe them as moving at $+20$ m.p.h. and at -20 m.p.h. respectively (or as 20 m.p.h. and -20 m.p.h.).

The Number Line

Positive and negative numbers can be represented on a number line.

On this number line, 5 is to the *right* of 3

and we say that   5 is *greater than* 3

or $5 > 3$ where '$>$' means 'is greater than'.

Any number to the right of another number is greater than that second number, i.e. $-1 > -4$ and $6 > -2$

Conversely, any number to the *left* of another number is *less than* the second number. Therefore, using '$<$' to mean 'is less than', we have

$-3 < 1$ and $2 < 6$

Addition and Subtraction of Directed Numbers

If, at midnight, the temperature was 5 °C and if the temperature fell by 7 degrees in the next two hours, then we can represent this mathematically as

$$5\,°C - 7\,°C$$

The resulting temperature can be found by starting at 5 °C and then counting 7 degrees down the temperature scale, giving $5\,°C - 7\,°C = -2\,°C$

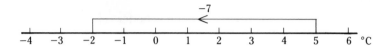

A similar argument applies to any application of directed numbers, so we can abstract the general rule: to take away a positive number, we move to the left along the number line.

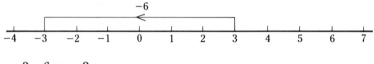

e.g. $3 - 6 = -3$

Extending the argument, to add a positive number move to the right along the number line.

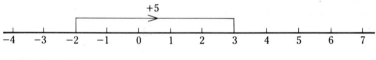

e.g. $-2 + 5 = 3$

The rules for addition and subtraction of negative numbers can also be deduced from temperature problems.

To freeze water we have to reduce its temperature and we can think of this either as adding coldness (negative heat) or as taking away warmth (positive heat), so

                    **adding a negative number
is the same as taking away a positive number,**

e.g. $+(-4) = -(+4) = -4$

If you want to melt an ice cube then you have to take away its frozen state, which means you have to add warmth.

If the temperature of the ice cube starts at −6 °C, then to melt it we have to increase its temperature by 6 °C, i.e. $-(-6\,°C) = +6\,°C$

Therefore,

                    **taking away a negative number
is the same as adding a positive number,**

e.g. $-(-5) = +5$

Exercise 1d

1. Insert > or < between each pair of numbers.

   (a) 3 ⬡ 4
   (b) 5 ⬡ 2
   (c) −1 ⬡ 5
   (d) −3 ⬡ −6
   (e) −2 ⬡ −4
   (f) 0 ⬡ −1

   (g) 2 ⬡ −5
   (h) 6 ⬡ 0
   (i) −15 ⬡ −25
   (j) 0 ⬡ 10
   (k) −7 ⬡ −5
   (l) 12 ⬡ −10

2. Evaluate

   (a) $2-9$
   (b) $-3+2$
   (c) $4-3$
   (d) $-2-7$
   (e) $7-10+6$
   (f) $-3-2+6$
   (g) $5-12+4$
   (h) $8-9-12$
   (i) $-6+2+4$
   (j) $-8+5-2$
   (k) $7-4-6$
   (l) $5+7-9$
   (m) $6+7-8-3+6$
   (n) $-8-6-4+7-3$
   (p) $5-7+9-11$
   (q) $16-20+4-3-6$

Evaluate

(a) $3+(-4)$
(b) $-2-(4-2)-(7-12)$

(a) $3+(-4) = 3-4 = -1$

(b) $-2-(4-2)-(7-12)$
$$= -2-(2)-(-5)$$
$$= -2-2+5$$
$$= 1$$

3. Evaluate

   (a) $-2+(-4)$
   (b) $8+(-4)$
   (c) $3-(-4)$
   (d) $-5-(-4)$
   (e) $-7+(-2)$
   (f) $-2-(-7)$
   (g) $6+(-4)$
   (h) $9-(-6)$
   (i) $3+(-3)-3$
   (j) $7+(-1)-(-4)$
   (k) $(-2)+(-2)+(-2)$
   (l) $4-(-3)+(-6)$

MULTIPLICATION AND DIVISION OF DIRECTED NUMBERS

The rules for multiplication and division of directed numbers are extensions of those for addition and subtraction.

Consider $2\times(-3)$; this means '2 lots of −3' which is −6,

i.e. $2\times(-3) = -6$

The order in which two numbers are multiplied does not matter, so

$$2\times(-3) = (-3)\times 2 = -6$$

Hence when a positive number and a negative number are multiplied, the result is negative.

Now consider $-2 \times (-3)$.

This can be interpreted as meaning 'subtract 2 lots of -3'
i.e. $-2 \times (-3) = -(-6)$ and we know that $-(-6) = 6$

Therefore $\qquad -2 \times (-3) = 6$

so multiplying two negative numbers gives a positive result.

Now consider $-6 \div (-2)$

This means 'the number of (-2)s needed to make -6' which is 3,

i.e. $\qquad -6 \div (-2) = 3$

so dividing a negative number by a negative number gives a positive result.

Lastly consider $-6 \div 2$, which means 'the number of 2s needed to make -6'.

Now to get *negative* 6 we need to multiply 2 by a negative number, so

$$-6 \div 2 = -3$$

A similar argument shows that $6 \div (-2) = -3$, so dividing one number by another with the opposite sign gives a negative result.

We know that multiplying or dividing two positive numbers gives a positive result, so the rules can be summarised as follows.

 **When two numbers are multiplied or divided, then
if the signs are the same (both + or both −), the result is positive,
if the signs are different (one + and one −), the result is negative.**

Exercise 1e

Evaluate (a) $4 + 3(-7)$ (b) $-5 - 6 \div (-2)$

(a) $4 + 3(-7) = 4 - 21 = -17$ Remember, $\times$ and $\div$ before + and −

(b) $-5 - 6 \div (-2) = -5 + 3 = -2$

1. Evaluate

  (a) $2 - 4(-2)$ (g) $8 \div (4 - 6)$

  (b) $4 + 3(-4)$ (h) $12 + 3(-6)$

  (c) $-4 \div -2$ (i) $(-2)^3$

  (d) $(3 - 5) \div (-2)$ (j) $2 \times (-2) \times (-3)$

  (e) $5 - 2 \div (-1)$ (k) $(-4)^2$

  (f) $8 - 3(-5)$ (l) $(-3)^2 \times (-2)^5$

2. Evaluate

  (a) $(-2) \times 3 + 4 \times (-5)$

  (b) $(5 - 8) \div (2 - 5)$

  (c) $(2 - 10) \div (-4 \times 2)$

  (d) $(-2)^2 \times 3 - 10 \div (-2)$

  (e) $(-1)^5 \times (-2)^2 \times 2$

  (f) $(7 - 18) \times (4 + (-2))$

3. There are two numbers, each of which satisfies the condition that when it is multiplied by itself the answer is 25. What are these two numbers?

4. What number has to be multiplied by -6 to get 42?

5. What is the relationship between consecutive numbers in this set?

$$-3, 9, -27, 81, -243$$

6. Consider this list of numbers:

$$-4, 8, -16, 32, -64$$

 (a) What is the relationship between consecutive numbers?

 (b) Keeping the relationship between consecutive numbers the same, extend *each* end of the list by two numbers.

7. Insert $=$ and any of the symbols $+, -, \times, \div$ and brackets, to connect each set of numbers, keeping the numbers in the order given, e.g. for (a) $4 = 1 - (-3)$. (There may be more than one way to connect the numbers.)

 (a) 4   1 -3 (d) 2 -2 4

 (b) 5 -2 7   (e) 1 -2 -3

 (c) 2   3   5   (f) 5 -4 9

8. Find as many ways as you can of connecting the numbers in the following set. They do not have to be kept in the same order.

$$8 \quad -2 \quad 5 \quad 2$$

 (One way is $8 + 2 = -5 \times (-2)$)

TYPES OF NUMBER

Sets of numbers that have properties in common are classified by name.

The *integers* are all the positive and negative whole numbers, and zero,

i.e. $\ldots, -2, -1, 0, 1, 2, \ldots$

(Note that zero is neither positive nor negative.)

The *natural numbers* are the positive whole numbers, $1, 2, 3, 4, \ldots$
These are also called counting numbers, or positive integers.

Even numbers are integers that are exactly divisible by 2,

i.e. $\ldots, -4, -2, 2, 4, 6, \ldots$

All even numbers end with 0, 2, 4, 6 or 8.

Odd numbers are integers that are not exactly divisible by 2,

i.e. $\ldots, -3, -1, 1, 3, 5, \ldots$

All odd numbers end with 1, 3, 5, 7 or 9.

A *prime number* is a positive integer that has only two distinct factors, itself and 1. Note that 1 is not a prime number.

A *square number* is a positive integer for which the number of dots representing the number can be arranged in a square pattern. For example, 25 is a square number because 25 dots can be arranged as a 5 by 5 square. Square numbers are also called perfect squares. A square number can be expressed as the product of two equal factors, e.g. $25 = 5 \times 5$.

A *triangular number* is a positive integer that is equal to the number of dots in any one triangle in this continuing pattern:

So the first four triangular numbers are 1, 3, 6 and 10.

Note that not all numbers fit into one of these categories and we will meet other types of number later in this book.

SEQUENCES

This list of numbers is a sequence: 2, 4, 8, 16 . . .

The numbers are in order, i.e. 2 is the first number in the sequence, 4 is the second number, and so on.

Each number in this sequence is double the previous number, so the sequence can be continued, i.e. 2, 4, 8, 16, 32, 64, . . .   and so on as far as we like.

A sequence is a set of numbers or shapes that has the two general properties illustrated above, i.e. the numbers are in a given order and there is a rule or procedure for continuing the sequence.

Sometimes the rule is given, in which case we can write down as many terms in the sequence as we wish. Sometimes the first few terms of the sequence are given and we have to discover the rule from these.

Each member of a sequence is called a *term* of the sequence.

Exercise 1f

1. Write down the next two terms in each of the following sequences.

    (a) 1, 2, 3, 4, . . .

    (b) −5, −3, −1, 1, 3, . . .

    (c) 1, 3, 6, 10, . . .

    (d) 2, 3, 5, 7, 11, . . .

2. In each sequence in question 1, all the terms are numbers of a particular type. For each sequence write down the name of the type of number.

3. Each of the following sequences is described in words. Write down the first four terms of each sequence.

    (a) the integers in descending order starting with 1

    (b) the prime numbers in ascending order starting with 13

4. For each of the following sequences, the first term and the rule for obtaining the next and subsequent terms is given. Write down the first five terms of the sequence.

    (a) 1; add 2 to the previous term.

    (b) 1; multiply the previous term by −2.

    (c) 96; divide the previous term by −2.

    (d) 1; each term is the sum of all the factors of the number representing its position (e.g. the 10th term is the sum of all the factors of 10, i.e. $1 + 2 + 5 + 10 = 18$).

    (e) 1; the square numbers in order of size.

    (f) 3; subsequent multiples of three.

    (g) 1; the second term is 2 and each subsequent term is the product of the two previous terms.

    (h) 2; the second term is 3 and each subsequent term is the sum of all the previous terms.

Investigations

Some of the suggestions that follow can take a great deal of time. If a computer is available and you have some programming skills, some of these investigations can be taken further. A calculator is essential.

1. *Perfect numbers*

A perfect number is equal to the sum of its factors including 1 but excluding itself. What is the smallest perfect number ? Try to find some more.

2. *Prime primes*

A prime prime number is a prime such that if the right-hand digits are successively removed, the remaining numbers are also prime. For example, 3797 (which is prime) gives 379, 37 and 3, each of which is prime. Try to find some more prime primes.

3. *Palindromes*

A number that reads the same forwards and backwards, e.g. 14641, is called a palindrome. There is a conjecture (i.e. it has not been proved) that if we take any number and reverse the digits and add the two numbers together, then do the same with the result and so on, we will end up with a palindrome.

Try to find some (non-palindromic) two digit numbers for which the palindrome appears after the first sum.

4. *Pandigitals*

A pandigital number contains each of the digits 0, 1, 2, 3, 4, 5, 6, 7, 8, 9 just once.

(a) Try to find a pandigital that when multiplied by one of the digits from 1 to 9 remains pandigital.

(b) Try to find a pandigital that is divisible by every number from 2 to 18.

(c) You will definitely need a computer for this one! There is one pandigital number that is also a prime number. Can you find it ?

Self-Assessment 1

1. Write down the value of (a) $24 + 36 \div 12$
   (b) $4 + 3 \times 6$

2. Find (a) the highest common factor (b) the lowest common multiple, of 12 and 18.

3. Evaluate (a) $5^2 - 2^3$ (b) $4^3 - (-2)^3$

4. Find the value of $7 - 2(5 - 8)$

5. Write down the next two terms in the sequence 2, −6, 18, −54, . . .

6. Using any or all of the figures 2, 3, 5, 6 and 7, write down

   (a) a multiple of 9

   (b) a prime number greater than 20

   (c) an odd number greater than 100

   (d) a number that gives −4 when subtracted from 58.

7. Without using a calculator, evaluate 305×126

8. Find the remainder when 385 is divided by 87.

9. Without using a calculator, write down the value of

   (a) 120×30 (b) $2400 \div 60$ (c) $2 \times 3 \times 2$

10. Find two numbers whose sum is 24 and whose product is 140.

11. Evaluate $12 + 7 + 5 + 8 + 6 + 13$

12. The first two terms of a sequence are 3, 6. Subsequent terms are obtained by subtracting the previous term from the one before it. Write down the next five terms of the sequence.

13. A box measures 12 cm by 15 cm by 9 cm. The box is to be filled with cubes so that no space is left. What is the length of the side of the largest cube that will do this?

FRACTIONS AND DECIMALS

FRACTIONS

The word fraction means part, so part of a quantity is called a fraction of it.

The bottom number in a fraction is called the *denominator*. The denominator gives the fraction its name and describes the number of equal-sized parts into which the whole has been divided.

The top number in a fraction is called the *numerator* and states how many of the equal parts are being considered.

For example, $\frac{3}{5}$ of a bar of chocolate means that the bar has been divided into 5 equal-sized parts and that 3 of these parts are being considered.

Equivalent Fractions

From the diagrams it is clear that $\frac{4}{8}$, $\frac{3}{6}$, $\frac{2}{4}$ and $\frac{1}{2}$ of the circle are all the same part of the circle.

The fractions $\frac{4}{8}$, $\frac{3}{6}$, $\frac{2}{4}$ and $\frac{1}{2}$ are called *equivalent fractions*.

Equivalent fractions are found by multiplying (or dividing) the numerator and the denominator by the same number,

e.g. $$\frac{1}{5} = \frac{1 \times 3}{5 \times 3} = \frac{3}{15} \quad \text{and} \quad \frac{4}{9} = \frac{4 \times 5}{9 \times 5} = \frac{20}{45}$$

When the numerator and denominator are divided by the same number, we get an equivalent fraction with smaller numerator and denominator. This is called simplifying the fraction or *cancelling*.

When the fraction has been simplified to give the smallest possible numerator and denominator, it is said to be expressed in its lowest possible terms,

e.g. $$\frac{15}{75} = \frac{15 \div 5}{75 \div 5} = \frac{3}{15} = \frac{3 \div 3}{15 \div 3} = \frac{1}{5}$$

(This is normally set out as $\dfrac{\overset{1}{\cancel{\overset{3}{\cancel{15}}}}}{\underset{5}{\cancel{\cancel{75}}}} = \dfrac{1}{5}$)

Comparing the Sizes of Fractions

The sizes of $\frac{2}{9}$ and $\frac{1}{6}$ can be compared easily if both are expressed as equivalent fractions with the same denominator. The denominator of the equivalent fractions must therefore be a multiple of both 6 and 9. To keep the numbers involved as small as possible it is sensible to choose the lowest common multiple (LCM) of 6 and 9, which is 18.

Now $\qquad \dfrac{2}{9} = \dfrac{4}{18} \quad$ and $\quad \dfrac{1}{6} = \dfrac{3}{18}$

from which we can see that $\frac{1}{6}$ is smaller than $\frac{2}{9}$.

Mixed Numbers and Improper Fractions

Fractions that are less than a whole unit are called *proper fractions*.

In the diagram below there are one and a half circles. This is written as $1\frac{1}{2}$ circles. $1\frac{1}{2}$ is called a *mixed number* because it contains a whole number and a fraction.

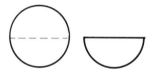

In the diagram, it is clear that $1\frac{1}{2}$ circles is the same as three half-circles, i.e. $\frac{3}{2}$ circles, so $\frac{3}{2} = 1\frac{1}{2}$.

We call $\frac{3}{2}$ an *improper fraction* because the numerator is greater than the denominator.

To change an improper fraction to a mixed number, divide the numerator by the denominator to give the number of units; the remainder is the number of fractional parts,

e.g. $\qquad \dfrac{17}{5} = 3$ and $\dfrac{2}{5} = 3\dfrac{2}{5}$.

To change a mixed number to an improper fraction, multiply the units by the denominator and add the result to the numerator,

e.g. $\qquad 2\dfrac{1}{3} = \dfrac{6+1}{3} = \dfrac{7}{3}$

EXPRESSING ONE QUANTITY AS A FRACTION OF ANOTHER QUANTITY

Many quantities can be divided into equal parts. For instance, there are seven days in a week, so one day is $\frac{1}{7}$ of a week and three days is $\frac{3}{7}$ of a week.

Similarly, 15 minutes can be expressed as a fraction of $1\frac{1}{2}$ hours.
There are 90 minutes in $1\frac{1}{2}$ hours so 15 minutes is $\frac{15}{90}$, i.e. $\frac{1}{6}$, of $1\frac{1}{2}$ hours.

**To express one quantity as a fraction of another,
first express both quantities in the same unit
and then put the first quantity over the second quantity.**

The Meaning of Division

$17 \div 5$ means the number of fives in 17

There are 3 fives in 17 with 2 left over. Now that remainder, 2, is $\frac{2}{5}$ of five, so we can say that there are $3\frac{2}{5}$ fives in 17,

i.e. $$17 \div 5 = 3\frac{2}{5}$$

But $$3\frac{2}{5} = \frac{17}{5}$$

therefore $$\frac{17}{5} = 17 \div 5$$

i.e. $$17 \div 5 = 3 \text{ remainder } 2 \quad \text{or} \quad 17 \div 5 = \frac{17}{5} = 3\frac{2}{5}$$

Exercise 2a

Do not use a calculator for this exercise.

1. Express each of the following fractions as eighths.

   (a) $\frac{1}{2}$ (b) $\frac{1}{4}$ (c) $\frac{3}{4}$

2. Express each of the following fractions as twelfths.

   (a) $\frac{1}{2}$ (b) $\frac{2}{3}$ (c) $\frac{3}{4}$ (d) $\frac{5}{6}$

3. Copy the following, filling in the missing numbers.

   $$\frac{2}{5} = \frac{}{10} = \frac{6}{} = \frac{}{25} = \frac{40}{}$$

4. Express each of the following fractions in its lowest terms.

   (a) $\frac{2}{6}$ (c) $\frac{5}{60}$ (e) $\frac{27}{36}$ (g) $\frac{99}{132}$

   (b) $\frac{3}{9}$ (d) $\frac{16}{56}$ (f) $\frac{48}{84}$ (h) $\frac{25}{115}$

5. Write each of the following improper fractions as a mixed number.

   (a) $\frac{5}{2}$ (c) $\frac{9}{4}$ (e) $\frac{53}{10}$ (g) $\frac{43}{8}$

   (b) $\frac{5}{3}$ (d) $\frac{37}{5}$ (f) $\frac{27}{4}$ (h) $\frac{69}{11}$

6. Write each of the following mixed numbers as an improper fraction.

   (a) $1\frac{1}{4}$ (c) $1\frac{2}{5}$ (e) $2\frac{2}{3}$ (g) $3\frac{2}{5}$

   (b) $2\frac{1}{3}$ (d) $3\frac{1}{4}$ (f) $1\frac{7}{8}$ (h) $6\frac{3}{4}$

7. Evaluate each of the following divisions, giving the answer as a mixed number.

   (a) $25 \div 4$ (e) $33 \div 8$

   (b) $13 \div 3$ (f) $27 \div 6$

   (c) $36 \div 5$ (g) $42 \div 10$

   (d) $50 \div 12$ (h) $17 \div 9$

8. Express both $\frac{5}{7}$ and $\frac{2}{3}$ as equivalent fractions with a denominator of 21.
   Which is larger, $\frac{5}{7}$ or $\frac{2}{3}$?

9. Find equivalent fractions for $\frac{2}{3}$ and $\frac{4}{5}$ that have the same denominator. Hence write down the smaller of $\frac{2}{3}$ and $\frac{4}{5}$.

10. What fraction of one hour is   (a) 1 minute
    (b) 10 minutes   (c) 50 minutes ?

11. In the month of June it rained on 6 days. On what fraction of the total number of days in June did rain fall ?

12. What fraction of the stones in this patio are cracked ?

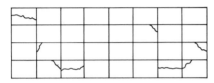

13. A tennis club has 144 members, 63 of whom are junior members, the rest being adult members. What fraction of the members are adult ?

14. Arrange each set of fractions in ascending order of size.

    (a) $\dfrac{2}{3}, \dfrac{1}{2}, \dfrac{3}{5}, \dfrac{11}{30}$ (b) $\dfrac{2}{5}, \dfrac{3}{8}, \dfrac{17}{20}, \dfrac{7}{10}$

15. Arrange each set of fractions in descending order of size.

    (a) $\dfrac{1}{3}, \dfrac{5}{6}, \dfrac{1}{2}, \dfrac{7}{12}$ (b) $\dfrac{7}{10}, \dfrac{3}{5}, \dfrac{17}{25}, \dfrac{3}{4}$

16. Arrange each set of numbers in ascending order of size.

    (a) $\dfrac{14}{5}, 3, 2\dfrac{7}{8}, \dfrac{17}{6}$ (b) $\dfrac{12}{7}, \dfrac{7}{3}, \dfrac{27}{14}, 2\dfrac{1}{6}$

ADDITION AND SUBTRACTION OF FRACTIONS

Fractions of the same kind (e.g. fifths) can be added or subtracted by adding or subtracting their numerators,

e.g. $\dfrac{2}{5} + \dfrac{1}{5} = \dfrac{3}{5}$ and $\dfrac{5}{8} - \dfrac{3}{8} = \dfrac{2}{8} = \dfrac{1}{4}$

Fractions with different denominators must first be expressed as equivalent fractions with a common denominator before they can be added or subtracted.

For example, to evaluate $\frac{3}{4} - \frac{2}{3}$ we note that 12 is a multiple of 3 and of 4 so we express both $\frac{3}{4}$ and $\frac{2}{3}$ as twelfths,

i.e. $\dfrac{3}{4} - \dfrac{2}{3} = \dfrac{3 \times 3}{4 \times 3} - \dfrac{2 \times 4}{3 \times 4} = \dfrac{9}{12} - \dfrac{8}{12} = \dfrac{1}{12}$

When mixed numbers are added or subtracted, it is sensible to add or subtract the units and then deal with the fractions,

e.g. $2\dfrac{1}{2} + 1\dfrac{3}{5} = 3 + \dfrac{1}{2} + \dfrac{3}{5} = 3 + \dfrac{5}{10} + \dfrac{6}{10} = 3 + \dfrac{11}{10} = 3 + 1\dfrac{1}{10} = 4\dfrac{1}{10}$

and $2\dfrac{1}{2} - 1\dfrac{3}{5} = 1 + \dfrac{5}{10} - \dfrac{6}{10} = 1 - \dfrac{1}{10} = \dfrac{9}{10}$

FRACTIONS OF QUANTITIES

To find $\frac{1}{4}$ of the number of tiles on this floor, we need to find $\frac{1}{4}$ of 12, i.e. $12 \div 4$, which is 3.

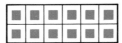

To find $\frac{3}{4}$ of the number of tiles on the floor we need $\frac{3}{4}$ of 12, i.e. $3 \times (12 \div 4)$, which is 9.

Hence to find a fraction of a quantity, multiply by the numerator and divide by the denominator.

MULTIPLYING FRACTIONS

Now $\frac{3}{4}$ of 12   can be written as $\frac{3}{4} \times 12 = \frac{3}{4} \times \frac{12}{1}$

But $\frac{3}{4}$ of 12 $= 3 \times 12 \div 4 = \frac{3 \times 12}{4}$

i.e. $\dfrac{3}{4} \times \dfrac{12}{1} = \dfrac{3 \times 12}{4 \times 1}$

    **Fractions are multiplied by multiplying the
numerators and multiplying the denominators.**

When mixed numbers are multiplied, they must first be changed into improper fractions, e.g.

$$2\frac{1}{2} \times \frac{3}{4} = \frac{5}{2} \times \frac{3}{4} = \frac{5 \times 3}{2 \times 4} = \frac{15}{8} = 1\frac{7}{8}$$

and $1\frac{1}{2} \times 2\frac{2}{3} = \frac{3}{2} \times \frac{8}{3} = \frac{\cancel{3}^{1} \times \cancel{8}^{4}}{\cancel{2}_{1} \times \cancel{3}_{1}} = \frac{4}{1} = 4$

Notice that, in the second example, we simplified the fraction before doing the multiplication. This is sensible, because it is easier to see the numbers that divide exactly into the numerator and denominator when they are expressed as a product of factors, rather than waiting until they are multiplied out.

RECIPROCALS

If the product of two numbers is 1 then each number is called the *reciprocal* of the other.

Now $\frac{2}{3} \times \frac{3}{2} = 1$ so $\frac{2}{3}$ is the reciprocal of $\frac{3}{2}$ and vice versa.

Also $\frac{3}{4} \times \frac{4}{3} = 1$ so $\frac{3}{4}$ is the reciprocal of $\frac{4}{3}$ and vice versa.

Hence the reciprocal of a fraction is found by inverting the fraction. To find the reciprocal of a mixed number, first change it to an improper fraction and then invert it,

e.g. the reciprocal of $1\frac{1}{2}$ is the reciprocal of $\frac{3}{2}$, which is $\frac{2}{3}$

Any number can be written as a fraction, e.g. $3 = \frac{3}{1}$ and $2.5 = \frac{2.5}{1}$

Therefore the reciprocal of 3 is $\frac{1}{3}$, which is $1 \div 3$

and the reciprocal of 2.5 is $\frac{1}{2.5}$, which is $1 \div 2.5$

▶ **The reciprocal of a number is given when 1 is divided by that number.** ◀

DIVIDING BY A FRACTION

Consider $\frac{1}{2} \div \frac{1}{4}$

This means the number of $\frac{1}{4}$s in $\frac{1}{2}$.

From the diagram we see that there are two $\frac{1}{4}$s in $\frac{1}{2}$, i.e. $\frac{1}{2} \div \frac{1}{4} = 2$

Now $1 \div \frac{1}{4}$ is the reciprocal of $\frac{1}{4}$, i.e. $\frac{4}{1}$, so $1 \div \frac{1}{4} = 1 \times \frac{4}{1}$

Hence $\frac{1}{2} \div \frac{1}{4} = \frac{1}{2} \times \frac{4}{1} = 2$

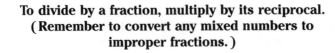

▶ **To divide by a fraction, multiply by its reciprocal. (Remember to convert any mixed numbers to improper fractions.)** ◀

Exercise 2b

Do not use a calculator for this exercise.

1. Find as a fraction in its lowest terms

   (a) $\dfrac{2}{5} + \dfrac{1}{4}$ (e) $\dfrac{1}{3} + \dfrac{1}{5}$

   (b) $\dfrac{1}{4} + \dfrac{7}{10}$ (f) $\dfrac{2}{3} + \dfrac{1}{4}$

   (c) $\dfrac{7}{10} - \dfrac{1}{2}$ (g) $\dfrac{5}{6} - \dfrac{2}{3}$

   (d) $\dfrac{2}{3} - \dfrac{1}{2}$ (h) $\dfrac{3}{8} - \dfrac{1}{7}$

2. Find as a fraction in its lowest terms

   (a) $1\dfrac{2}{3} - \dfrac{5}{6}$ (e) $3\dfrac{1}{4} + 1\dfrac{1}{5}$

   (b) $2\dfrac{1}{2} + \dfrac{1}{3}$ (f) $3\dfrac{1}{3} - 1\dfrac{1}{2}$

   (c) $1\dfrac{1}{2} - \dfrac{2}{3}$ (g) $2\dfrac{1}{4} + \dfrac{4}{5}$

   (d) $2\dfrac{1}{2} + \dfrac{3}{4}$ (h) $2\dfrac{1}{4} - 1\dfrac{2}{3}$

3. Find as a fraction in its lowest terms

   (a) $\dfrac{3}{4} + \dfrac{1}{2} - \dfrac{2}{5}$ (e) $\dfrac{4}{5} - \dfrac{7}{10} + \dfrac{1}{2}$

   (b) $\dfrac{3}{5} + \dfrac{2}{25} - \dfrac{3}{20}$ (f) $4\dfrac{1}{5} - 5\dfrac{1}{2} + 1\dfrac{3}{10}$

   (c) $\dfrac{1}{3} - \dfrac{5}{18} + \dfrac{4}{9}$ (g) $\dfrac{1}{2} + \dfrac{7}{8} - 1\dfrac{1}{4}$

   (d) $\dfrac{2}{3} - \dfrac{1}{5} + \dfrac{1}{2}$ (h) $6\dfrac{1}{3} - 1\dfrac{2}{5} + 1\dfrac{8}{15}$

4. Find

   (a) $\dfrac{1}{4}$ of £24   (g) $\dfrac{2}{7}$ of a week

   (b) $\dfrac{1}{3}$ of 1 hour   (h) $\dfrac{2}{3}$ of 1 minute

   (c) $\dfrac{1}{5}$ of £35   (i) $\dfrac{3}{4}$ of 36 cm

   (d) $\dfrac{1}{9}$ of 27 cm   (j) $\dfrac{5}{8}$ of 36 ft

   (e) $\dfrac{2}{3}$ of £48   (k) $\dfrac{3}{5}$ of 1 year

   (f) $\dfrac{2}{5}$ of 85 kg   (l) $\dfrac{3}{4}$ of £96

5. Find

   (a) $\dfrac{2}{5} \times \dfrac{1}{3}$ (g) $\dfrac{2}{7} \times \dfrac{3}{7}$

   (b) $\dfrac{5}{6} \times \dfrac{1}{4}$ (h) $\dfrac{8}{9} \times \dfrac{3}{40}$

   (c) $\dfrac{7}{8} \times \dfrac{4}{21}$ (i) $\dfrac{3}{7} \times \dfrac{5}{9} \times \dfrac{14}{15}$

   (d) $\dfrac{3}{4} \times \dfrac{16}{21}$ (j) $\dfrac{3}{10} \times \dfrac{5}{9} \times \dfrac{6}{7}$

   (e) $\dfrac{3}{4} \times \dfrac{6}{7}$ (k) $2\dfrac{1}{2} \times \dfrac{7}{10}$

   (f) $\dfrac{2}{5} \times \dfrac{3}{5}$ (l) $4\dfrac{2}{3} \times 2\dfrac{2}{5}$

6. Write down the reciprocal of

   (a) $\dfrac{3}{5}$ (g) 4

   (b) $\dfrac{2}{5}$ (h) 6

   (c) $\dfrac{7}{9}$ (i) $2\dfrac{1}{2}$

   (d) $\dfrac{3}{4}$ (j) $3\dfrac{1}{4}$

   (e) $\dfrac{2}{9}$ (k) $2\dfrac{3}{4}$

   (f) $\dfrac{5}{12}$ (l) $1\dfrac{1}{2}$

7. Find

   (a) $\dfrac{21}{32} \div \dfrac{7}{8}$ (g) $4 \div \dfrac{2}{3}$

   (b) $\dfrac{3}{56} \div \dfrac{9}{14}$ (h) $2 \div \dfrac{2}{5}$

   (c) $\dfrac{8}{75} \div \dfrac{4}{15}$ (i) $18 \div \dfrac{14}{25}$

   (d) $\dfrac{8}{21} \div \dfrac{4}{7}$ (j) $3\dfrac{1}{8} \div 3\dfrac{3}{4}$

   (e) $\dfrac{3}{7} \div \dfrac{9}{14}$ (k) $\dfrac{1}{5} \div 1\dfrac{7}{20}$

   (f) $\dfrac{9}{26} \div \dfrac{60}{52}$ (l) $6\dfrac{4}{9} \div 1\dfrac{1}{3}$

Find $\left(2\dfrac{1}{4} \div \dfrac{3}{14}\right) \times 2\dfrac{1}{7}$

$$\left(2\dfrac{1}{4} \div \dfrac{3}{14}\right) \times 2\dfrac{1}{7} = \left(\dfrac{9}{4} \div \dfrac{3}{14}\right) \times \dfrac{15}{7} \qquad \text{changing mixed numbers to improper fractions}$$

$$= \dfrac{9}{4} \times \dfrac{14}{3} \times \dfrac{15}{7} \qquad \text{inverting } \tfrac{3}{14} \text{ and multiplying}$$

$$= \dfrac{\cancel{9}^3 \times \cancel{14}^{7\,1} \times 15}{\cancel{4}_2 \times \cancel{3}_1 \times \cancel{7}_1} = \dfrac{45}{2} = 22\dfrac{1}{2}$$

8. Find

(a) $\dfrac{5}{8} \times 1\dfrac{1}{2} \div \dfrac{15}{16}$ (c) $\left(\dfrac{3}{5} \div \dfrac{18}{55}\right) \times \dfrac{9}{11}$

(b) $\dfrac{2}{5} \times \dfrac{9}{10} \div \dfrac{27}{40}$ (d) $\dfrac{1}{2} \times \dfrac{3}{5} \div \dfrac{5}{9}$

9. Find

(a) $\left(\dfrac{3}{7} \div \dfrac{8}{21}\right) \times \dfrac{2}{5}$ (c) $2\dfrac{1}{2} \times 2\dfrac{2}{5} \div \dfrac{3}{5}$

(b) $\dfrac{14}{25} \times \dfrac{5}{9} \div \dfrac{7}{18}$ (d) $\left(3\dfrac{1}{3} \div 2\dfrac{1}{6}\right) \times \dfrac{1}{4}$

Find   (a) $\dfrac{\frac{3}{4} + \frac{2}{3}}{\frac{5}{6}}$ (b) $\dfrac{4}{9} + 1\dfrac{1}{2} \div \dfrac{3}{5} - 2\dfrac{1}{3}$

Remember: brackets first, then multiply and divide, lastly add and subtract.

(a) $\dfrac{\frac{3}{4} + \frac{2}{3}}{\frac{5}{6}} = \left(\dfrac{3}{4} + \dfrac{2}{3}\right) \div \dfrac{5}{6} \qquad \text{the fraction line acts as a bracket}$

$$= \left(\dfrac{9}{12} + \dfrac{8}{12}\right) \div \dfrac{5}{6} \qquad \text{bracket first}$$

$$= \dfrac{17}{\cancel{12}_2} \times \dfrac{\cancel{6}^1}{5} \qquad \text{division}$$

$$= \dfrac{17}{10} = 1\dfrac{7}{10}$$

(b) $\dfrac{4}{9} + 1\dfrac{1}{2} \div \dfrac{3}{5} - 2\dfrac{1}{3} = \dfrac{4}{9} + \dfrac{3}{2} \div \dfrac{3}{5} - \dfrac{7}{3} \qquad \text{improper fractions}$

$$= \dfrac{4}{9} + \dfrac{3}{2} \times \dfrac{5}{3} - \dfrac{7}{3} \qquad \text{division}$$

$$= \dfrac{4}{9} + \dfrac{5}{2} - \dfrac{7}{3} \qquad \text{multiplication}$$

$$= \dfrac{8}{18} + \dfrac{45}{18} - \dfrac{42}{18} \qquad \text{addition and subtraction}$$

$$= \dfrac{11}{18}$$

10. Find

(a) $\dfrac{1}{2} + \dfrac{2}{3} \times \dfrac{5}{6}$

(f) $\dfrac{3}{5} \times \left(\dfrac{2}{3} + \dfrac{1}{2} \right)$

(b) $\dfrac{1}{3} - \dfrac{1}{2} \times \dfrac{1}{4}$

(g) $\dfrac{\dfrac{1}{2} - \dfrac{1}{5}}{\dfrac{4}{7}}$

(c) $\dfrac{3}{4} \div \dfrac{1}{2} + \dfrac{1}{8}$

(h) $\dfrac{\dfrac{3}{10} + \dfrac{2}{5}}{\dfrac{7}{15}}$

(d) $\dfrac{2}{3} \times \dfrac{1}{2} + \dfrac{1}{4}$

(i) $\dfrac{\dfrac{7}{8}}{\dfrac{3}{4} + \dfrac{2}{3}}$

(e) $\dfrac{1}{7} + \dfrac{5}{8} \div \dfrac{1}{4}$

The remaining part of this exercise contains a variety of questions involving fractions. Do not use a calculator.

11. How many $2\frac{1}{4}$s are there in $13\frac{1}{2}$?

12. A box holds 1 kg of flour. What fraction of its weight remains after 250 g of flour is used ?

13. The profit made at a jumble sale was £ 270; $\frac{1}{3}$ of this profit was spent on new equipment and then $\frac{1}{4}$ of the remaining profit was spent on paint. What sum of money was left ?

14. What is $\frac{4}{7}$ of $4\frac{2}{3}$ divided by $1\frac{1}{9}$?

15. Which of the following statements are true ?

(a) $3\frac{2}{3} \div 1 = 3\frac{2}{3} \times 1$

(b) the reciprocal of $1\frac{1}{2}$ is $\frac{2}{3}$

(c) $\frac{3}{2} + \frac{1}{2} \div 2 = 1$

(d) $\frac{73}{7} = 1\frac{3}{7}$

16. How many $1\frac{1}{2}$ cm lengths of wire can be cut from a wire that is 35 cm long ? What length is left over ?

17. If it takes $2\frac{1}{2}$ minutes to read 120 lines of text, how long does it take to read one line ?

18. It takes three-quarters of an hour to travel 6 miles in heavy traffic. How long does it take to travel 1 mile ?

DECIMALS

The position of a figure in a number is called its *place value* and it tells us the value of that figure.

Consider the whole number 2058.

Counting from the right, the 8 in the first column represents 8 units, the 5 in the second column is 5 tens. There is 0 in the third column so there are no hundreds and the 2 in the fourth column represents 2 thousands.

Parts of a unit written in the form $\frac{2}{5}$ are properly called *vulgar fractions.*

Parts of a unit can also be written as *decimal fractions* (called decimals for short) by placing a point after the units column and continuing the columns to the right, for example 2.503

The first column after the decimal point represents tenths and this is called the first decimal place,
the second column after the point represents hundredths and is called the second decimal place,
the third column represents thousandths and so on.

Thus the number 2.503 means 2 units, 5 tenths, no hundredths and 3 thousandths.

The number 0.05 means no units, no tenths and 5 hundredths.

Changing Decimals to Fractions

As the positions of the figures after the decimal point tell us their value, it is easy to change from decimals to fractions.

For example, 0.15 means $\frac{1}{10}$ and $\frac{5}{100}$.

Now $\frac{1}{10}$ is $\frac{10}{100}$, therefore $0.15 = \frac{15}{100}$, which cancels to $\frac{3}{20}$.

Similarly, $1.025 = 1\frac{25}{1000} = 1\frac{1}{40}$

Addition and Subtraction of Decimals

Decimals can be added or subtracted in the same way as for whole numbers, provided that tenths are added to tenths and so on. To make sure that this is done it is sensible to write the numbers in a column with the decimal points under one another,

e.g. $1.6 + 3 + 0.05$ is written

$$
\begin{array}{r}
1.60 \\
3.00 \\
+\,0.05 \\
\hline
4.65
\end{array}
$$

Notice that zeros have been added so that each number has the same number of decimal places.

Similarly $3.5 - 1.06$ is written

$$
\begin{array}{r}
3.50 \\
-\,1.06 \\
\hline
2.44
\end{array}
$$

Multiplying and Dividing by 10, 100, . . .

If a number is multiplied by 10, then tens become hundreds, units become tens, tenths become units, hundredths become tenths and so on, i.e. all figures move one place to the left,

e.g. $12.72 \times 10 = 127.2$

If a number is divided by 10, then tens become units, units become tenths and so on, i.e. all figures move one place to the right,

e.g. $12.72 \div 10 = 1.272$

Extending this argument to multiplication by 100, 1000 and so on, we see that

when a number is multiplied by 10, 100, 1000, . . .
the figures move 1, 2, 3, . . . places to the left,

when a number is divided by 10, 100, 1000, . . .
the figures move 1, 2, 3, . . . places to the right.

MULTIPLICATION AND DIVISION OF DECIMALS

Decimals can be multiplied or divided by whole numbers in the usual way,

e.g. $1.3 \times 2 = 2.6$

and $1.3 \times 200 = 1.3 \times 2 \times 100 = 2.6 \times 100 = 260$

Similarly, $2.7 \div 2 = 1.35$ add zeros if necessary, i.e. $\begin{array}{r} 1.35 \\ 2\overline{)2.70} \end{array}$

and $2.7 \div 200 = 2.7 \div 2 \div 100 = 1.35 \div 100 = 0.0135$

Division by a decimal can be changed to division by a whole number, e.g.

$$2.8 \div 0.2 = \frac{2.8}{0.2} = \frac{2.8 \times 10}{0.2 \times 10} = \frac{28}{2} = 14$$

The method used in this example can be extended to give a general rule for division by a decimal.

▶   **To change division by a decimal
to division by a whole number, multiply
both the dividend (the number to be divided)
and the divisor by 10 or 100 or . . . as necessary
to change the divisor into a whole number.**   ◀

The rule for multiplying by a decimal also comes from fractions,

e.g. $1.6 \quad \times \quad 0.02 \quad = \frac{16}{10} \times \frac{2}{100} = \frac{32}{1000} = 0.032$
           (1 d.p.)   (2 d.p.)   (3 d.p.)

Notice that the sum of the numbers of decimal places in the numbers being multiplied together is equal to the number of decimal places in the result. This observation leads to the general rule that

▶   **to multiply by a decimal,
first ignore the point and multiply the numbers
as whole numbers. Then insert the point so that
the number of decimal places in the result
is equal to the sum of the numbers of decimal places
in the numbers being multiplied.**   ◀

CHANGING FRACTIONS TO DECIMALS

The fraction $\frac{3}{8}$ can be interpreted as meaning $3 \div 8$

By placing zeros after the decimal point, this division can be evaluated as a decimal,

i.e.
$$8\overline{)3.000}^{\,0.375}, \quad \text{hence } \tfrac{3}{8} = 0.375$$

Any fraction can be treated in the same way, i.e.

**to change a fraction to a decimal,
divide the numerator by the denominator.**

Exercise 2c

Do not use a calculator for this exercise.

1. Write down the value of the figure 7 in each of the following numbers.
   - (a) 3.07
   - (b) 2.74
   - (c) 73
   - (d) 57.5
   - (e) 30.07
   - (f) 0.007

2. Change each of the following decimals to a fraction in its lowest terms.
   - (a) 0.2
   - (b) 0.5
   - (c) 0.25
   - (d) 0.08
   - (e) 0.001
   - (f) 0.7
   - (g) 1.4
   - (h) 0.125
   - (i) 1.05
   - (j) 0.0025
   - (k) 2.06
   - (l) 5.005

3. Write down the value of
   - (a) $1.6 + 0.3$
   - (b) $2.8 - 1$
   - (c) $1.5 + 3$
   - (d) $1.8 - 0.5$
   - (e) $2.3 + 0.5$
   - (f) $1.6 - 0.2$
   - (g) $3.7 + 8$
   - (h) $4.4 - 1.2$

4. Find the value of
   - (a) $0.24 + 1.7$
   - (b) $0.5 - 0.04$
   - (c) $2.04 - 0.4$
   - (d) $0.09 + 1.57$
   - (e) $2.7 + 0.07$
   - (f) $0.26 - 0.08$
   - (g) $1.77 + 3.9$
   - (h) $2.44 - 1.74$
   - (i) $6.04 + 1.96$
   - (j) $3.74 - 1.27$
   - (k) $0.531 + 1.8$
   - (l) $2.5 - 1.063$

5. Write down the value of
   - (a) 2.5×100
   - (b) 0.066×10
   - (c) $24.4 \div 10$
   - (d) $12 \div 10$
   - (e) $0.35 \div 100$
   - (f) 0.044×100
   - (g) $32 \div 1000$
   - (h) 2.66×1000

6. Write down the value of
   - (a) 0.3×300
   - (b) $1.6 \div 20$
   - (c) 1.2×30
   - (d) 0.7×200
   - (e) $1.5 \div 50$
   - (f) $14.4 \div 120$
   - (g) 400×0.6
   - (h) $0.84 \div 40$

7. Write down the value of
   - (a) $0.3 \div 0.1$
   - (b) $2 \div 0.2$
   - (c) $1.4 \div 0.07$
   - (d) $0.36 \div 1.2$
   - (e) $0.1 \div 0.01$
   - (f) $1.2 \div 6$
   - (g) $2.4 \div 0.06$
   - (h) $25 \div 0.05$

8. Write down the value of
   - (a) 1.2×0.1
   - (b) $(0.1)^2$
   - (c) 45×0.01
   - (d) $(0.01)^2$
   - (e) 2.5×0.05
   - (f) $(0.5)^2$
   - (g) 1.05×0.2
   - (h) $(0.2)^3$

9. Evaluate
   - (a) 2.56×1.2
   - (b) 1.33×0.2
   - (c) 4.5×0.03
   - (d) 0.7×6.3
   - (e) 1.05×0.12
   - (f) 0.06×10.5
   - (g) 6.4×0.05
   - (h) 2.5×0.08

10. Evaluate
    - (a) $8.4 \div 2.1$
    - (b) $3.6 \div 0.12$
    - (c) $4.5 \div 1.5$
    - (d) $0.056 \div 0.8$
    - (e) $1.32 \div 0.11$
    - (f) $5.4 \div 0.18$
    - (g) $0.0144 \div 1.2$
    - (h) $44.4 \div 0.02$

11. Evaluate

    (a) $1.35 - 0.8$ (f) $2.66 + 1.04$

    (b) 1.35×0.8 (g) $144 \div 0.16$

    (c) $121 \div 1.1$ (h) $20 - 0.2$

    (d) $15 + 8.7$ (i) $3.6 + 1.09$

    (e) $(0.2)^5$ (j) 3.7×400

12. Evaluate

    (a) $0.016 \div 80$ (f) 8.1×400

    (b) $52 - 6.99$ (g) $6.9 - 4.09$

    (c) $1.56 \div 0.13$ (h) $1.08 \div 200$

    (d) $0.17 + 1.9$ (i) $(0.4)^3$

    (e) $6 - 4.75$ (j) $0.73 + 4.37$

13. Express each of the following fractions as a decimal.

    (a) $\frac{1}{5}$ (d) $\frac{3}{5}$ (g) $\frac{7}{8}$

    (b) $\frac{1}{8}$ (e) $\frac{3}{20}$ (h) $\frac{6}{25}$

    (c) $\frac{3}{4}$ (f) $\frac{1}{4}$ (i) $\frac{3}{40}$

14. In the number 25.73, calculate twice the value of the figure 7 added to the value of the figure 5.

15. A piece of wire, 12.55 m long is cut into 50 pieces of equal length. How long is each piece?

16. In the number 12.08, take four times the value of the figure 8 away from twice the value of the figure 2.

Recurring Decimals

If we try to express $\frac{1}{3}$ as a decimal, we get 0.333 33 ... and so on for ever, i.e. the figure 3 recurs.

This is called a *recurring decimal* and it is written as $0.\dot{3}$; the dot over the figure 3 indicates that 3 recurs.

Any decimal with a repeating figure or pattern of figures is called a recurring decimal.

Dots are used over the recurring figure, or at each end of the recurring pattern, to abbreviate the writing of such decimals.

For example, $0.\dot{1}2\dot{5}$ means 0.125 125 125 ...

Many fractions give rise to recurring decimals, e.g. $\frac{1}{11} = 0.090\,909\ldots = 0.\dot{0}\dot{9}$

CHANGING RECURRING DECIMALS TO FRACTIONS

We start by noting that $\frac{1}{9} = 0.111\,111\,111\ldots$

then any recurring decimal with one figure in the repeating pattern is a multiple of $\frac{1}{9}$,

e.g. $0.222\,222\,222\ldots = 2 \times 0.111\,111\,111\ldots = \frac{2}{9}$

and $0.666\,666\,666\ldots = 6 \times 0.111\,111\,111\ldots = \frac{6}{9} = \frac{2}{3}$, and so on.

If there are two figures in the repeating pattern, we use the fact that

$$\frac{1}{99} = 0.01\,01\,01\,01\ldots$$

then any recurring decimal with two figures in the repeating pattern is a multiple of $\frac{1}{99}$,

e.g. $0.15\,15\,15\,15\ldots = 15 \times 0.01\,01\,01\,01\ldots = \frac{15}{99}\ (= \frac{5}{33})$

For three repeating figures, we use $\frac{1}{999} = 0.001\,001\,001\,001\ldots$

so $0.125\,125\,125\ldots = 125 \times 0.001\,001\,001\ldots = \frac{125}{999}$

When there are four repeating figures, we use $\frac{1}{9999} = 0.0001\,0001\,0001\ldots$, and so on.

Exercise 2d

1. Express each of the following fractions as decimals.

   (a) $\frac{1}{6}$ (c) $\frac{2}{9}$ (e) $\frac{1}{7}$

   (b) $\frac{2}{3}$ (d) $\frac{5}{6}$ (f) $\frac{1}{30}$

2. Express each of the following recurring decimals as fractions.

   (a) $0.\dot{5}$ (c) $0.\dot{1}\dot{8}$ (e) $0.3\dot{9}\dot{6}$

   (b) $0.\dot{2}\dot{7}$ (d) $0.2\dot{9}\dot{7}$ (f) $0.\dot{1}35\dot{3}$

3. (a) Write down the relationship between $0.666\ldots$ and $0.0666\ldots$

   (b) Hence express $0.0\dot{6}$ as a fraction.

4. Express each of the following decimals as fractions.

   (a) $0.00\dot{2}$ (c) $0.005\dot{5}$

   (b) $0.0\dot{6}\dot{3}$ (d) $0.4\dot{9}\dot{5}$

5. (a) Write down the relationship between $0.2\dot{5}$ and $0.0\dot{5}$

   (b) Hence express $0.2\dot{5}$ as a fraction.

6. Express each of the following decimals as fractions.

   (a) $0.1\dot{2}$ (c) $0.1\dot{4}\dot{5}$

   (b) $0.3\dot{6}$ (d) $0.2\dot{1}0\dot{4}$

ROUNDING NUMBERS

There are many occasions when it is either necessary or desirable to round numbers. For example, it is not possible to measure the length of a dining table exactly and for most purposes a measurement given to the nearest tenth of a centimetre is satisfactory. A statement of the number attending a football match has more impact if it is given to the nearest thousand (rather than the exact figure).

Consider the number 138; to the nearest ten, this is 140.
We write this   138 = 140 to the nearest ten.
However, the number 132 is 130 to the nearest ten.
This is written   132 = 130 to the nearest ten.

Notice that 138 is rounded up to 140 whereas 132 is rounded down to 130.

Now consider 135, which is exactly half-way between 130 and 140. In a case like this the rule is to *round up* to give it to the nearest ten, i.e.   135 = 140 to the nearest ten.

Correcting to a Specified Number of Decimal Places

Giving a number to the nearest tenth, hundredth and so on, is done in the same way.
For example,   1.38 is 1.4 to the nearest tenth.
As tenths are represented by the first decimal place, we write

$$1.38 = 1.4 \quad \text{correct to 1 decimal place (1 d.p.)}$$

Numbers given to the nearest hundredth, thousandth and so on, are said to be correct to 2 decimal places, correct to 3 decimal places and so on.

> **The rule for giving a number
> correct to a specified number of decimal places is:
> look at the figure in the next decimal place.
> If this figure is less than 5, round down.
> If this figure is 5 or more, round up.**

SIGNIFICANT FIGURES

A person's height could be given as 1.73 metres or as 173 cm or as 1730 mm or (although unlikely) as 0.001 73 km.

Each of these measurements has the same degree of accuracy, i.e. each is given to the nearest centimetre. In each number, the figure 1 has a different place value although the figure 1 is the first figure in each number. It is called the *first significant figure.* Similarly, 7 is the second significant figure and 3 is the third significant figure.

> **Reading any number from left to right,**
> **regardless of the decimal point,**
> **the first significant figure is the first non-zero figure,**
> **the second significant figure is the next figure**
> **(which can be zero or otherwise),**
> **and so on for further significant figures.**

For quantities such as length it is sensible to give numbers correct to a specified number of significant figures rather than a given number of decimal places. The rule for giving a number correct to a specified number of significant figures is the same as for correcting to a number of decimal places, i.e. look at the next significant figure; if it is 5 or more then round up, if it is less than 5 then round down.

For example   1.05 ⁞ 9 $=$ 1.06 correct to 3 significant figures   (3 s.f.)
         0.33 ⁞ 3 $=$ 0.33 correct to 2 significant figures
         169 ⁞ 8 $=$ 1700 correct to 3 significant figures
         1.99 ⁞ 9 $=$ 2.00 correct to 3 significant figures

Notice that the corrected number must be the same order of size as the original number. Notice also that zeros are placed after the point when necessary to give the required number of significant figures.

ESTIMATING THE RESULT OF A CALCULATION

Using a calculator makes calculations such as 1.578×16.805 almost trivial. However it is very easy to make mistakes when keying in numbers, so it is essential that you know roughly what answer to expect so that you can check the calculator result for reasonableness.

An estimate for a calculation can be obtained by correcting each number involved to 1 significant figure,

e.g. $1.578 \times 16.805 \approx 2 \times 20 = 40$

A better estimate can be obtained by correcting to the nearest unit,

e.g. $1.578 \times 16.805 \approx 2 \times 17 = 34$

However the first estimate is good enough to act as a check and has the advantage that the numbers involved can easily be multiplied mentally. Note however, that in both cases the numbers have been rounded up, so the estimated answer is greater than the actual product.

Using a Calculator

Most calculators display answers correct to 7 significant figures.
Most problems, however, do not require this degree of accuracy; either the context of the problem will dictate the degree of accuracy needed or it will be specified.

Using a calculator to find 1.578×16.805 correct to 3 decimal places we find that the display gives the result to 7 s.f., but it is not necessary to write all these figures down. As the answer is required correct to three decimal places, we need to copy the result as far as the fourth decimal place only,

i.e. $\qquad 1.578 \times 16.805 = 26.5182\ldots$

$$= 26.518 \qquad (3\text{ d.p.})$$

For an answer correct to 3 s.f. we would copy the number in the display as far as the fourth significant figure,

i.e. $\qquad 1.578 \times 16.805 = 26.51\ldots$

$$= 26.5 \qquad (3\text{ s.f.})$$

Exercise 2e

1. Write down each number to the nearest number given in the bracket.
   - (a) 2177 (ten)
   - (b) 2578 (hundred)
   - (c) 26.87 (unit)
   - (d) 3532 (thousand)
   - (e) 20.73 (unit)
   - (f) 0.479 (unit)
   - (g) 298.2 (ten)
   - (h) 439 (hundred)
   - (i) 139.78 (unit)
   - (j) 905 (ten)
   - (k) 12.58 (unit)
   - (l) 375 (hundred)

2. Write down each number correct to the number of decimal places given in the bracket.
   - (a) 0.6942 (2)
   - (b) 13.479 (1)
   - (c) 0.9999 (2)
   - (d) 2.2525 (3)
   - (e) 0.058 055 (3)
   - (f) 28.75 (1)
   - (g) 40.378 (2)
   - (h) 77.998 41 (3)
   - (i) 0.050 770 2 (5)

3. Write down each number in question 1 correct to 2 significant figures.

4. Write down each number in question 2 correct to 3 significant figures.

5. Express each of the following fractions as a decimal correct to 3 s.f.
   - (a) $\dfrac{2}{3}$
   - (b) $\dfrac{1}{7}$
   - (c) $\dfrac{1}{6}$
   - (d) $\dfrac{2}{9}$
   - (e) $\dfrac{1}{11}$
   - (f) $\dfrac{4}{15}$
   - (g) $\dfrac{5}{13}$
   - (h) $\dfrac{7}{9}$
   - (i) $\dfrac{3}{46}$

6. Write down an estimate for the value of each of the following calculations.
   - (a) 12.5×1.4
   - (b) $54.04 \div 9.89$
   - (c) $23.893 - 4.678$
   - (d) $0.0794 + 0.289$
   - (e) $(0.046)^2$
   - (f) $(0.198)^3$
   - (g) 1.6×3.142
   - (h) $37.88 \div 17.6$

7. Write down an estimate for the value of each of the following calculations.
   - (a) $\dfrac{2.8 \times 3.79}{1.84}$
   - (b) $\dfrac{3.75}{0.94 + 1.8}$
   - (c) $\dfrac{12.06 - 8.62}{125.7}$
   - (d) $\dfrac{2.05 \times 0.3}{0.59}$
   - (e) $\dfrac{2.88 + 3.72}{0.578 \times 37}$
   - (f) $\dfrac{7.08 - 0.7556}{(8.67)^2}$
   - (g) $\dfrac{0.0335 \times 2.09}{1.0956 \times 3.94}$
   - (h) $\dfrac{(0.678)^2}{1.85 - 0.99}$

8. Use a calculator to evaluate each part of questions 6 and 7, giving the answer correct to 3 significant figures.

9. Express each fraction as a decimal correct to 3 decimal places and hence arrange these numbers in ascending order:

$$1.57, \tfrac{5}{3}, 1.49, 1\tfrac{2}{7}, \tfrac{15}{11}$$

10. Arrange these numbers in descending order:

$$0.05, \tfrac{3}{16}, 0.105, \tfrac{2}{13}, \tfrac{6}{25}$$

In each of the following questions, give your answer to the degree of accuracy appropriate to the problem.

11. A path is made by laying 57 paving slabs, each 0.87 m long, end to end. How long is the path?

12. A pile of 16 identical boxes is 2.43 m high. How high is each box?

13. A clock which is running slow takes 1.06 seconds per tick instead of 1 second. How many ticks are there in 10 minutes?

14. What should 4.9 be multiplied by to give 8.428?

15. One wall of a room is 7.28 m long. The floor is covered by square carpet tiles of side 0.52 m. How many tiles fit along the wall?

16. A builders' merchant marks goods net of VAT. The price to be paid is calculated by multiplying the marked price by 1.175. What will be charged for a tin of paint marked at £6.97?

17. Pills, each weighing 0.57 grams, are packed in foil strips each containing 28 pills. Four foil strips are put into a box and 450 of these boxes are put into a carton. What is the weight of pills in a carton?

18. The label on a box of carpet tiles states that each tile measures 45 cm by 45 cm. The tiles are to be placed on a floor to form a square with 12 tiles along a side. How long will the side of the square be?

19. Bricks are packed on pallets, each holding 378 bricks. A lorry is loaded with 15 pallets. If each brick weighs 1.2 kg, what weight of bricks is the lorry carrying?

ROOTS AND POWERS

Square Roots

When a number is expressed as the product of two equal factors, each factor is called a square root of the number.

For example, $4 = 2 \times 2$,   so 2 is a square root of 4
Notice also that $4 = (-2) \times (-2)$, so -2 is also a square root of 4

Any positive number has two square roots, a positive one and a negative one.

A negative number cannot have a square root because a negative number cannot be expressed as the product of two *equal* factors (a negative number results from multiplying a negative number and a positive number).

The symbol $\sqrt{}$ is used for 'square root', so $\sqrt{12}$ means the positive square root of 12, and $-\sqrt{12}$ means the negative square root of 12.

The value of $\sqrt{12}$ can be found from a calculator: $\sqrt{12} = 3.464$ (3 d.p.)
(Check the result by squaring the answer, i.e. $(3.464)^2 = 11.999\ldots = 12$ (4 s.f.).)

Cube Roots

When a number is expressed as a product of three equal factors, each factor is called a cube root of the number.

Some numbers have exact cube roots. The cube root of 8 is 2 since $8 = 2 \times 2 \times 2$

The symbol $\sqrt[3]{\ }$ is used to mean 'the cube root of', e.g. $\sqrt[3]{8} = 2$

Notice that as $2 \times 2 \times 2$ can be written as 2^3,

we have $8 = 2^3 \iff \sqrt[3]{8} = 2$

(The symbol $\iff$ means 'gives and is given by'.)

Similarly, $25 = 5^2 \iff \sqrt{25} = 5$

Extending the argument, the fourth root of a number is the value of the factor such that the product of four of them gives the number,

e.g. $\sqrt[4]{81} = 3$ since $81 = 3^4$

The *n*th root of a number is the factor such that the product of *n* of them gives the number.

MULTIPLYING AND DIVIDING NUMBERS WRITTEN IN INDEX FORM

Now $2^3 \times 2^2 = 2 \times 2 \times 2 \times 2 \times 2 = 2^5$

therefore $2^3 \times 2^2 = 2^{3+2} = 2^5$

We can multiply together powers of the *same number* by adding the powers. (Powers of different numbers cannot be multiplied in this way because the numbers multiplied together are not all the same.)

Also $2^3 \div 2^2 = \dfrac{2 \times 2 \times 2}{2 \times 2} = 2$

Therefore $2^3 \div 2^2 = 2^{3-2} = 2^1 = 2$

We can divide different powers of the same number by subtracting the powers.

Negative Indices

Consider $3^2 \div 3^5$

Subtracting the indices gives $3^2 \div 3^5 = 3^{2-5} = 3^{-3}$

But $3^2 \div 3^5 = \dfrac{3 \times 3}{3 \times 3 \times 3 \times 3 \times 3} = \dfrac{1}{3^3}$

Therefore 3^{-3} means $\dfrac{1}{3^3}$, i.e. 3^{-3} is the reciprocal of 3^3.

▶   **a^{-b} means the reciprocal of a^b**   ◀

For example, $5^{-2} = \dfrac{1}{5^2} = \dfrac{1}{25}$ and $3^{-1} = \dfrac{1}{3}$

The Zero Index

If we consider $3^2 \div 3^2$

subtracting indices gives $3^2 \div 3^2 = 3^0$

But $\qquad\qquad\qquad\qquad 3^2 \div 3^2 = 1, \text{ so } 3^0 = 1$

In general, $\qquad\qquad\qquad a^b \div a^b = 1$

subtracting the indices gives $a^b \div a^b = a^0, \text{ so } a^0 = 1, \text{ i.e.}$

 any number to the power zero is equal to 1

Fractional Indices

Consider $4^{\frac{1}{2}} \times 4^{\frac{1}{2}}$

Adding the indices gives $4^{\frac{1}{2}} \times 4^{\frac{1}{2}} = 4^1 = 4$

This means that 4 is the square of $4^{\frac{1}{2}}$ so $4^{\frac{1}{2}}$ must mean the square root of 4, i.e. $4^{\frac{1}{2}} = \sqrt{4}$

Similarly, $8^{\frac{1}{3}} \times 8^{\frac{1}{3}} \times 8^{\frac{1}{3}} = 8^1, \text{ so } 8^{\frac{1}{3}} = \sqrt[3]{8}$

In general, $a^{1/n}$ means the nth root of a.

Now consider $8^{\frac{2}{3}}$, which can be written as $8^{\frac{1}{3}} \times 8^{\frac{1}{3}}$

i.e. $8^{\frac{2}{3}} = (8^{\frac{1}{3}})^2$ which is 'the square of the cube root of 8'.

Using a Calculator to find Powers and Roots

Note that calculators vary both in the way that keys are marked and in their operation, so consult your instruction book if you do not get the correct results.

To find $(1.7)^4$ by using a calculator with a $\boxed{y^x}$ button, follow this sequence of key strokes.

$\boxed{1}\ \boxed{\cdot}\ \boxed{7}\ \boxed{y^x}\ \boxed{4}\ \boxed{=}$ The display will show 8.3521

To find $\sqrt[4]{1.7}$ first write $\sqrt[4]{1.7}$ as $1.7^{\frac{1}{4}}$

Then if you have a key $\boxed{y^{1/x}}$ use this sequence $\boxed{1}\ \boxed{\cdot}\ \boxed{7}\ \boxed{y^{1/x}}\ \boxed{4}\ \boxed{=}$

If you do not have the key $\boxed{y^{1/x}}$ you can use the key $\boxed{y^x}$ as follows

$\boxed{1}\ \boxed{\cdot}\ \boxed{7}\ \boxed{y^x}\ \boxed{0}\ \boxed{\cdot}\ \boxed{2}\ \boxed{5}\ \boxed{=}$ The display will show $1.1418\ldots$

STANDARD FORM

Very large numbers and very small numbers are more conveniently written in *standard form.*

A number in standard form is written as a number between 1 and 10 multiplied by the appropriate power of 10.

For example $70\,000\,000\,000$ becomes 7×10^{10} when written in standard form,

and $0.000\,000\,004\,5$ becomes 4.5×10^{-9} in standard form.

To express a number in standard form, first place a decimal point between the first and second significant figures to give a number between 1 and 10. Then count to find the power of 10 by which this number should be multiplied (or divided) to restore it to its original size.

For example, to write 5800 in standard form, first place the point between 5 and 8 which gives 5.8; counting then shows that to change 5.8 to 5800, we need to multiply by 10^3

so $5800 = 5.8 \times 10^3$

To write 0.005 03 in standard form, the point goes between the 5 and 0 to give 5.03. To change 5.03 to 0.005 03 we need to divide by 10^3. But dividing by 10^3 is equivalent to multiplying by $\frac{1}{10^3}$, i.e. by 10^{-3}

so $0.005\,03 = 5.03 \times 10^{-3}$

Scientific calculators display very large and very small numbers in scientific notation or engineering notation, but only the power of ten is shown and not the ten itself.

Note that scientific or engineering notation is similar to standard form but the number is not always between 1 and 10.

Try $2\,500\,000^2$ on your calculator: the display will look something like $\boxed{6.25 \qquad 12}$ and this means 6.25×10^{12}

0.0025^2 will give $\boxed{6.25 \qquad -06}$ on the display and this means 6.25×10^{-6}.

Exercise 2f

Do not use a calculator for questions 1 to 6.

1. Find the value of

    (a) 4^2 (e) 2^{-1} (i) 5^{-2}

    (b) 4^{-2} (f) 9^3 (j) 8^{-2}

    (c) 4^0 (g) 5^0 (k) 3^{-3}

    (d) 2^{-5} (h) 3^{-1} (l) 10^0

2. Write each of these numbers in ordinary form

    (a) 1.2×10^3 (e) 9.0704×10^5

    (b) 3.14×10^{-2} (f) 7.605×10^{-4}

    (c) 3.17×10^5 (g) 1.15×10^{-10}

    (d) 9.55×10^{-3} (h) 2.8×10^{12}

Find the value of (a) $\left(\dfrac{1}{3}\right)^{-1}$

(b) $\left(\dfrac{2}{3}\right)^{-2}$

(a) $\left(\dfrac{1}{3}\right)^{-1} = \dfrac{3}{1} = 3$ (b) $\left(\dfrac{2}{3}\right)^{-2} = \left(\dfrac{3}{2}\right)^{2} = \dfrac{9}{4}$

3. Find the value of

(a) $\left(\dfrac{1}{4}\right)^{-1}$ (c) $\left(\dfrac{1}{2}\right)^{0}$ (e) $\left(\dfrac{2}{3}\right)^{-1}$

(b) $\left(\dfrac{5}{2}\right)^{-2}$ (d) $\left(\dfrac{3}{4}\right)^{-3}$ (f) $\left(\dfrac{5}{6}\right)^{0}$

4. Find the value of

(a) $25^{1/2}$ (e) $81^{1/4}$ (i) $64^{1/3}$
(b) $27^{1/3}$ (f) $125^{1/3}$ (j) $121^{1/2}$
(c) $16^{1/4}$ (g) $49^{1/2}$ (k) $625^{1/4}$
(d) $32^{1/5}$ (h) $625^{1/2}$ (l) $144^{1/2}$

Find the value of (a) $4^{3/2}$ (b) $(0.04)^{-5/2}$

(a) $4^{3/2} = (4^{1/2})^{3} = 2^{3} = 8$

(b) $(0.04)^{-5/2} = \left(\dfrac{4}{100}\right)^{-5/2} = \left(\dfrac{100}{4}\right)^{5/2} = (25)^{5/2} = 5^{5} = 3125$

5. Find the value of

(a) $27^{2/3}$ (e) $100^{3/2}$
(b) $32^{3/5}$ (f) $0.25^{1/2}$
(c) $0.01^{1/2}$ (g) $125^{2/3}$
(d) $81^{3/4}$ (h) $36^{3/2}$

6. Find the value of

(a) $\left(\dfrac{1}{9}\right)^{-1/2}$ (e) $125^{-2/3}$

(b) $1000^{-2/3}$ (f) $32^{-2/5}$

(c) $\left(\dfrac{16}{25}\right)^{-1/2}$ (g) $\left(\dfrac{1}{16}\right)^{-1/4}$

(d) $0.01^{-3/2}$ (h) $9^{-3/2}$

7. Use your calculator to find the value of each of the following numbers giving your answer correct to 3 significant figures.

(a) 1.7^{6} (e) 0.67^{5} (i) $1500^{1/2}$
(b) $\sqrt[3]{5}$ (f) $\sqrt[4]{10}$ (j) $1.8^{3/2}$
(c) 2.1^{-4} (g) 1.05^{8} (k) 56^{-3}
(d) $\sqrt[3]{12}$ (h) $\sqrt[5]{4.61}$ (l) 1.09^{-4}

8. Write each of the following numbers in standard form.

(a) $26\,500$ (e) $0.002\,21$
(b) $0.008\,23$ (f) $1\,070\,030$
(c) $204\,000$ (g) 6.2
(d) $0.050\,99$ (h) 4788

If $a = 4.6 \times 10^{4}$ and $b = 2.3 \times 10^{5}$ find, in standard form, the value of
(a) $a \times b$ (b) $a + b$

(a) $a \times b = (4.6 \times 10^{4}) \times (2.3 \times 10^{5}) = 4.6 \times 10^{4} \times 2.3 \times 10^{5}$

$= 4.6 \times 2.3 \times 10^{9} = 10.58 \times 10^{9} = 1.058 \times 10^{10}$

(b) $a + b = (4.6 \times 10^{4}) + (2.3 \times 10^{5})$

$= 46\,000 + 230\,000 = 276\,000 = 2.76 \times 10^{5}$

9. Find, in standard form, the value of
    (a) $(1.2 \times 10^4) \times (5.3 \times 10^6)$
    (b) $(7.2 \times 10^{-4}) \times (1.5 \times 10^3)$
    (c) $(3.6 \times 10^6) \div (1.2 \times 10^4)$
    (d) $(3.3 \times 10^{-3}) \div (6.6 \times 10^{-6})$
    (e) $(1.8 \times 10^3) + (1.2 \times 10^2)$
    (f) $(8.4 \times 10^{-1}) - (9.3 \times 10^{-2})$

10. If $a = 2.4 \times 10^5$, $b = 3.6 \times 10^7$ and
    $c = 2.5 \times 10^{-3}$ find
    (a) $a \times b$ (c) $a + b$ (e) $b \div c$
    (b) $a \div b$ (d) $a \times c$ (f) $a - b$

11. Find the value of each of the following
    (a) $\left(\frac{1}{8}\right)^{-2}$ (c) 6^3
    (b) $\left(\frac{2}{3}\right)^0$ (d) $(2^2)^3$

12. Find the value of each of the following
    (a) $16^{1/2}$ (g) $3^5 \times 3^{-2}$
    (b) 6^{-1} (h) $2^3 \times 3^2$
    (c) $32^{3/5}$ (i) $7^5 \times 7^{-5}$
    (d) $\left(\frac{1}{2}\right)^{-3}$ (j) $\left(\frac{8}{27}\right)^{-2/3}$
    (e) $6^2 \times 6^3$ (k) $(81)^{-3/4}$
    (f) $4^5 \div 4^2$ (l) $\left(\frac{1}{25}\right)^{-1/2}$

13. At a time when Jupiter, Pluto and the Sun are in line, the distances of Jupiter and Pluto from the Sun are respectively 7.88×10^8 km and 5.95×10^9 km.
    What is the distance between Pluto and Jupiter when the two planets and the Sun are in line with
    (a) the planets on opposite sides of the Sun
    (b) the planets on the same side of the Sun ?

Rational and Irrational Numbers

A number that can be written exactly as a fraction is called a rational number; $\frac{1}{2}, \frac{2}{3}, 5$ (i.e. $\frac{5}{1}$) are rational numbers.

Rational numbers can be written either exactly as a decimal or as a recurring decimal, e.g. $\frac{1}{2} = 0.5$ and $\frac{2}{3} = 0.\dot{6}$

Some numbers, such as $\sqrt{2}$, cannot be written exactly as a fraction or as a decimal (the number of decimal places is infinite and there is no recurring pattern in the figures). These numbers are called irrational numbers. All square roots and cube roots that are not exact are irrational numbers.

There are other irrational numbers, one of which is denoted by $\pi (= 3.1415 \ldots)$; π is involved in various circle calculations and is introduced in Chapter 12.

SURDS

When a calculation involves irrational numbers such as $\sqrt{2}$, the only way to give an exact answer is to leave them in the form $\sqrt{2}, \sqrt{5}$ etc.

Square roots in the form $\sqrt{2}$ are called *surds*.

Expressions containing surds can often be simplified.

For example, $\sqrt{20}$ can be simplified because 4 is one of the factors of 20, and 4 has an exact square root,

i.e. $\sqrt{20} = \sqrt{4 \times 5} = \sqrt{4} \times \sqrt{5} = 2 \times \sqrt{5} = 2\sqrt{5}$

A less simple expression such as $\sqrt{3}(2 - \sqrt{3})$ can also be simplified by multiplying out the bracket,

i.e. $\sqrt{3}(2 - \sqrt{3}) = \sqrt{3} \times 2 - \sqrt{3} \times \sqrt{3}$
                     $= 2\sqrt{3} - 3$

A fraction whose denominator contains a surd is more awkward to deal with than one where a surd occurs only in the numerator. There is a way in which the surd can be transferred to the numerator; the process is called *rationalising the denominator*.

Consider, for example, the fraction $\dfrac{2}{\sqrt{3}}$.

The square root in the denominator can be removed if we multiply it by another $\sqrt{3}$; we therefore multiply the top and bottom of the fraction by $\sqrt{3}$ to give an equivalent fraction whose denominator is rational,

i.e. $\qquad \dfrac{2}{\sqrt{3}} = \dfrac{2 \times \sqrt{3}}{\sqrt{3} \times \sqrt{3}} = \dfrac{2\sqrt{3}}{3}$

Exercise 2g

Express in terms of the simplest possible surd.

1. $\sqrt{8}$ 5. $\sqrt{50}$ 9. $\sqrt{72}$
2. $\sqrt{12}$ 6. $\sqrt{45}$ 10. $\sqrt{500}$
3. $\sqrt{32}$ 7. $\sqrt{200}$ 11. $\sqrt{250}$
4. $\sqrt{27}$ 8. $\sqrt{48}$ 12. $\sqrt{18}$

Expand and simplify where possible.

13. $\sqrt{2}(2 - \sqrt{2})$ 17. $\sqrt{3}(5 + \sqrt{27})$
14. $\sqrt{5}(3 + \sqrt{5})$ 18. $\sqrt{5}(\sqrt{6} - \sqrt{5})$
15. $\sqrt{2}(\sqrt{8} - 1)$ 19. $2\sqrt{3}(3 - 2\sqrt{3})$
16. $\sqrt{7}(\sqrt{7} - \sqrt{2})$ 20. $2\sqrt{2}(4 - \sqrt{18})$

Rationalise the denominators.

21. $\dfrac{3}{\sqrt{2}}$ 27. $\dfrac{4\sqrt{3}}{3\sqrt{2}}$

22. $\dfrac{1}{\sqrt{5}}$ 28. $\dfrac{3\sqrt{5}}{5\sqrt{3}}$

23. $\dfrac{1}{\sqrt{8}}$ 29. $\dfrac{15}{\sqrt{15}}$

24. $\dfrac{2}{\sqrt{10}}$ 30. $\dfrac{3}{\sqrt{3}}$

25. $\dfrac{\sqrt{3}}{\sqrt{2}}$ 31. $\dfrac{2\sqrt{7}}{\sqrt{14}}$

26. $\dfrac{\sqrt{5}}{\sqrt{10}}$ 32. $\dfrac{5\sqrt{6}}{3\sqrt{3}}$

33. Simplify
    (a) $\sqrt{12} + \sqrt{3}$ (c) $\sqrt{18} + \sqrt{27}$
    (b) $4\sqrt{5} - \sqrt{20}$ (d) $3\sqrt{3} - \sqrt{12}$

Rationalise the denominators and simplify.

34. $\dfrac{(2 - \sqrt{3})}{\sqrt{3}}$ 37. $\dfrac{(1 - 3\sqrt{2})}{2\sqrt{2}}$

35. $\dfrac{(1 + \sqrt{5})}{\sqrt{5}}$ 38. $\dfrac{(5 + \sqrt{7})}{2\sqrt{14}}$

36. $\dfrac{(4 - 2\sqrt{3})}{\sqrt{2}}$ 39. $\dfrac{(3\sqrt{2} + 2)}{3\sqrt{2}}$

40. Simplify
    (a) $\dfrac{1}{\sqrt{2}} + \sqrt{2}$ (c) $\dfrac{2}{\sqrt{3}} + \sqrt{3}$
    (b) $\dfrac{2}{\sqrt{3}} + \sqrt{3}$ (d) $\dfrac{1}{2\sqrt{5}} + \sqrt{5}$

41. Determine which of the following numbers are rational.
    (a) $(\sqrt{2})(\sqrt{3})$ (e) $(\sqrt{8})^2$
    (b) $\dfrac{\sqrt{2}}{\sqrt{8}}$ (f) $\dfrac{\sqrt{27}}{\sqrt{3}}$
    (c) $0.01\dot{2}$ (g) $\sqrt{1\dfrac{11}{25}}$
    (d) $(\sqrt{5})(\sqrt{2})$ (h) 2π
    (i) $(5 - \sqrt{2})(5 + \sqrt{2})$

Investigations

Trying to Rationalise the Irrational

Once mathematicians discovered that numbers such as $\sqrt{2}$ could not be given an exact rational value, the search was on to find rational numbers that would approximate to the value of the irrational number to any degree of accuracy required. Here are two methods for finding approximations to $\sqrt{2}$.

1. **The Heronian Algorithm**

    To find rational approximations to $\sqrt{2}$:

    Start with any fraction that is roughly equal to $\sqrt{2}$:   say $\frac{7}{5}$

    Next find the fraction which, when multiplied by that fraction ($\frac{7}{5}$) gives 2: $\frac{10}{7}$

    Then find the mean of these fractions, i.e. $\frac{1}{2}(\frac{7}{5}+\frac{10}{7})$: $\frac{99}{70}$

    This fraction, $\frac{99}{70}$, is a better approximation to $\sqrt{2}$ than $\frac{7}{5}$ is.

    (a) Use your calculator to find the number of decimal places to which $\frac{99}{70}$ agrees with $\sqrt{2}$.

    (b) Now repeat the process starting with $\frac{99}{70}$ and you will get an even better approximation to $\sqrt{2}$.

    (c) Can you discover why this algorithm works ?

    (d) Try the process with $\sqrt{3}$ and with some other square roots.

2. **Continued Fractions**

    This process gives successively better approximations to the value of $\frac{1}{2}(\sqrt{5}+1)$.

    Start with $1 + \dfrac{1}{1+1}$ as the first approximation.

    The next approximation is $1 + \dfrac{1}{1+\dfrac{1}{1+1}}$

    The next approximation is $1 + \dfrac{1}{1+\dfrac{1}{1+\dfrac{1}{1+1}}}$

    (a) Find the value of the first three approximations and give the number of decimal places to which they are accurate.

    (b) Continue the pattern to find another two approximations.

    (c) This pattern can obviously be continued indefinitely, hence the name 'continued fraction'. Use reference books to see if you can discover other continued fractions.

    (d) Also with the help of reference books, can you find other methods for evaluating square roots ? Give a brief description of any that you find.

Self-Assessment 2

Do not use a calculator.

1. Find the reciprocal of

   (a) $\frac{3}{4}$ (b) $1\frac{1}{2}$

2. Evaluate

   (a) $1\frac{1}{3} \div \frac{2}{9}$ (b) $1\frac{1}{3} - \frac{2}{9}$ (c) $2\frac{1}{2} \times 1\frac{2}{5}$

3. What fraction of $3\frac{1}{2}$ hours is 45 minutes ?

4. A company has 350 employees. Three-fifths of the employees are female and two-sevenths of these work part-time. What fraction of the employees are female part-time workers and how many of them are there ?

5. Arrange these numbers in ascending order of size; $\frac{2}{3}$, 0.65, $\frac{5}{9}$, 0.7

6. Find the value of $2\frac{1}{2} + \frac{3}{4} \times \frac{4}{7}$

7. Simplify   (a) $\sqrt{18} + \sqrt{98}$ (b) $\sqrt{12} - \dfrac{1}{\sqrt{3}}$

8. In the number 2.057, find ten times the value of the digit 5 multiplied by one quarter of the value of the digit 2.

9. Find the value of

   (a) $1.2 + 0.42$ (d) $3 - 0.67$

   (b) 0.5×0.7 (e) $(0.3)^2$

   (c) $0.1 \div 0.01$ (f) $0.02 \div 0.4$

10. Find the value of

    (a) 2^6 (c) 2^{-4} (e) $27^{2/3}$

    (b) 2^0 (d) $(\frac{2}{5})^{-1}$

11. Write each of these numbers in standard form

    (a) $4\,500\,000$ (b) 0.0024

12. Write each of these numbers correct to 3 significant figures

    (a) 12.678 (b) $0.004\,712$ (c) 9.978

13. Express as a fraction

    (a) $0.\dot{1}2\dot{1}$ (b) $0.0\dot{2}\dot{7}$ (c) $0.4\dot{7}$

BASIC GEOMETRY

POINTS

A point has position but no size. A point has no dimensions.

Only one straight line can be drawn through two chosen points. The straight line joining two points is called a *line segment.* A line has one dimension.

ANGLES

An angle measures the amount of turning.
One complete turn or revolution is divided into 360°.

A quarter of a revolution is called a *right angle.*
A right angle is equal to 90°.

The sign for a right angle is

Half a revolution is two right angles.

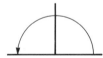

Acute, Obtuse and Reflex Angles

Any angle that is smaller than a right angle is called an *acute* angle.

(When a line turns about a point we shall consider the *anticlockwise* direction as *positive* and the *clockwise* direction as *negative.*)

Any angle that is greater than one right angle and less than two right angles is called an *obtuse* angle.

42

Any angle that is greater than two right angles is called a *reflex* angle.

Lines that meet at right angles are said to be *perpendicular.*

Lines that are in the same direction are called *parallel lines.* They never meet and are always the same distance apart.

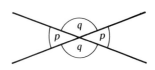

ANGLE FACTS

Vertically opposite angles are equal.

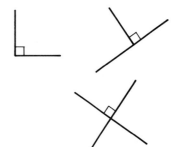

Complementary angles add up to 90°.

$$\widehat{a} + \widehat{b} = 90°$$

$\widehat{a}$ is the complement of $\widehat{b}$

and $\widehat{b}$ is the complement of $\widehat{a}$

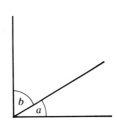

(If we use a to name an angle we will write the size of the angle as $\widehat{a}$ or $\angle a$. Hence $\widehat{a} + \widehat{b} = 90°$ or $\angle a + \angle b = 90°$)

Angles on a straight line add up to 180°.

$$\widehat{a} + \widehat{b} + \widehat{c} = 180°$$

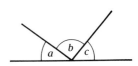

Two angles that add up to 180° are *supplementary* angles.

$$\widehat{a} + \widehat{b} = 180°$$

$\widehat{a}$ is the supplement of $\widehat{b}$

and $\widehat{b}$ is the supplement of $\widehat{a}$

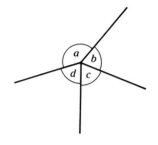

Angles at a point add up to 360°.

$$\widehat{a} + \widehat{b} + \widehat{c} + \widehat{d} = 360°$$

Exercise 3a

1. How many degrees are there
   (a) in half a revolution
   (b) in three-quarters of a turn
   (c) in two complete revolutions
   (d) in two-thirds of a turn ?

2. What angle, in degrees, corresponds to
   (a) $\frac{1}{3}$ of a right angle
   (b) 2 right angles
   (c) 0.4 of a right angle
   (d) 1.7 of a right angle ?

3. How many degrees does the hand of a clock turn through when
   (a) it starts at 2 and stops at 3
   (b) it starts at 2 and stops at 11 ?
   In each case state whether the angle is acute, obtuse or reflex.

4. For each angle in this question
   (a) state whether it is acute, obtuse or reflex
   (b) estimate its size
   (c) check your estimate by using a protractor. (Remember to choose the scale that starts at 0° on the arm of the angle on which you place the base line of the protractor. Using this scale, read off the value at the other arm.)

   (i)

(ii)

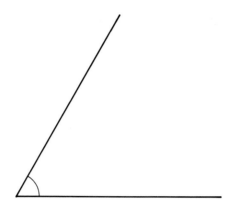

(iii)

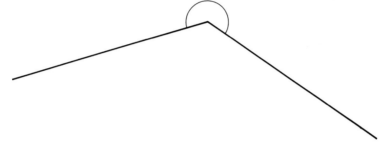

(iv)

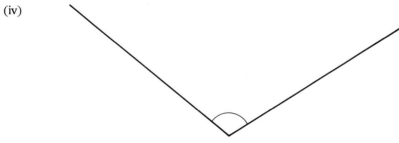

(v)

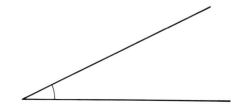

In questions 5 to 10 calculate the size of each angle marked with a letter.

5.

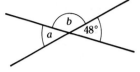

6.

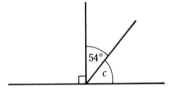

7.

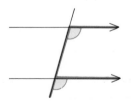

8.

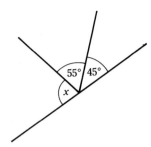

9.

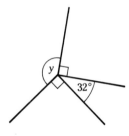

10.

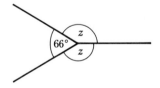

ANGLES AND PARALLEL LINES

When a transversal cuts a pair of parallel lines, various angles are formed.

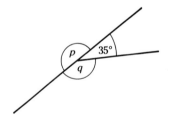

Corresponding angles are equal.
(Look for the letter **F**.)

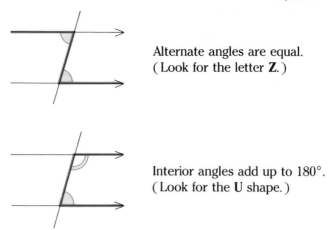

Alternate angles are equal.
(Look for the letter **Z**.)

Interior angles add up to 180°.
(Look for the **U** shape.)

ANGLES OF A TRIANGLE

Draw a large triangle of any shape, using a straight edge to draw the sides. Measure each angle in this triangle, turning your page to a convenient position when necessary. Add the sizes of the three angles.

Draw another triangle of a different shape. Again measure each angle and add them.

Now try this: on a piece of paper draw a triangle of any shape and cut it out. Next tear off each corner and place the three different corners together.

They should look like this:

These experiments suggest that

 the three angles of a triangle add up to 180°.

The three corners of a triangle are called its *vertices* (one corner is a *vertex*).

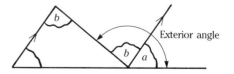

We can also see that it looks as though an exterior angle of a triangle is equal to the sum of the two interior opposite angles.

Exercise 3b

1. In the diagrams below write down the angle that corresponds to the angle marked *x*.

   (a)

   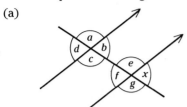

   (b)

   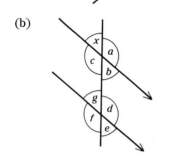

   (c)

   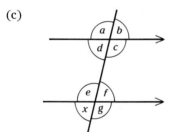

   (d)

   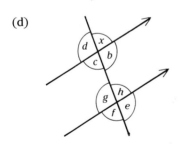

2. For this question refer to the diagrams in question 1.

   (a) In the diagram 1(a) write down the angle that is alternate to *f*.

   (b) In diagram 1(b) write down the angle that is alternate to *d*.

   (c) In diagram 1(c) write down the angle that is alternate to *e*.

   (d) In diagram 1(d) write down the angle that is alternate to *g*.

3. Write down any pairs of interior angles you can find in the four diagrams given in question 1.

   In questions 4 to 12 find the size of each marked angle.

4.

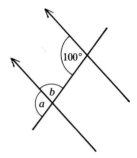

5.

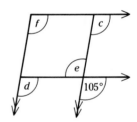

6.

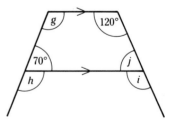

7.

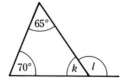

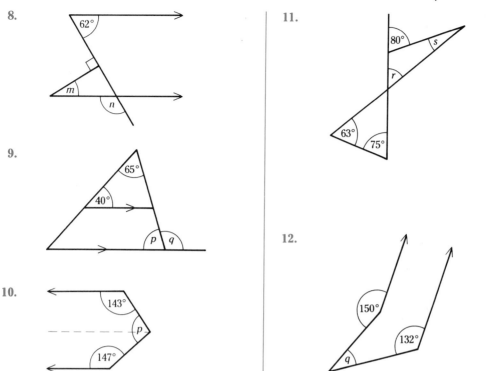

8.

9.

10.

11.

12.

USING CAPITAL LETTERS TO LABEL VERTICES

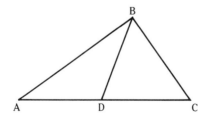

So that we can refer to one particular side, or to one particular angle, we often use capital letters to label the vertices of a figure. In the above diagram we use the letters A, B and C so that we can talk about 'the triangle ABC', which can be abbreviated to '△ABC'. The side joining A and B is called 'the side AB' or just AB, with similar meanings for BC and AC.

The angle at the vertex A is called 'angle A' or $\widehat{A}$ for short.

Sometimes there is ambiguity if we use a single letter. In the above diagram there are three different angles inside triangles at B. We can get over this problem by using the three letters round the arms of an angle to describe it. The three angles inside triangles at B are $A\widehat{B}C$, $A\widehat{B}D$ and $D\widehat{B}C$.

TYPES OF TRIANGLE

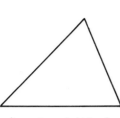

An acute-angled triangle

A right-angled triangle

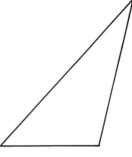

An obtuse-angled triangle

All three of these triangles are examples of *scalene* triangles – in each one the three sides have different lengths.

Some Special Triangles

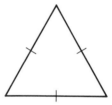

An *isosceles* triangle has two equal sides and the base angles are equal.

An *equilateral* triangle has three equal sides and each angle is 60°.

GENERAL QUADRILATERAL

A quadrilateral is a plane figure bounded by four straight lines.

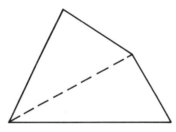

A *diagonal* is a line joining two opposite vertices. Either diagonal divides a quadrilateral into two triangles. The sum of the angles of a triangle is 180° so the sum of the angles of a quadrilateral is twice as big.

 The sum of the interior angles of a quadrilateral is 360°.

At each vertex the sum of the interior and exterior angles is 180°. There are four vertices so the sum of all the exterior and interior angles is

$$4 \times 180° \quad \text{i.e. } 720°.$$

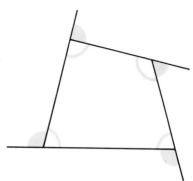

The sum of the interior angles is 360° so

◀ **the sum of the exterior angles of a quadrilateral is 360°.** ▶

Exercise 3c

Find the size of each marked angle.

1.

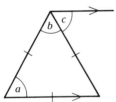

2.

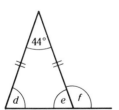

3.

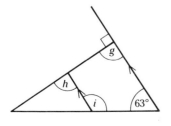

4.

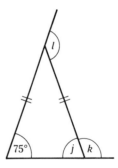

5.

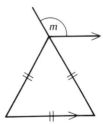

6.

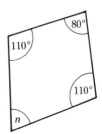

7.

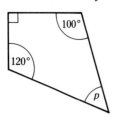

8.

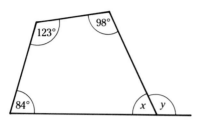

9.

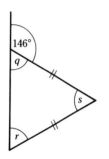

10.

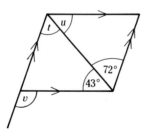

11.

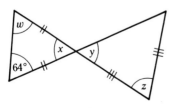

12.

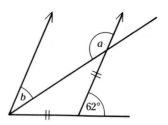

13.

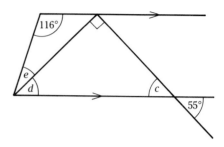

14.

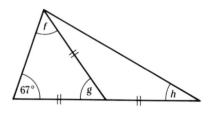

15.

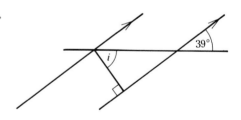

16.

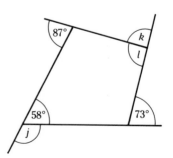

17.

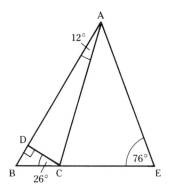

(a) Find the size of (i) $\widehat{ABC}$ (ii) $\widehat{ACE}$ (iii) $\widehat{CAE}$.

(b) Name an isosceles triangle.

(c) What type of triangle is △ADC ?

(d) Is AE parallel to DC ?

18.

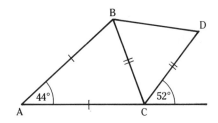

(a) Calculate (i) $\widehat{ABC}$ (ii) each of the angles in △BCD.

(b) What special type of triangle is △BCD ?

19.

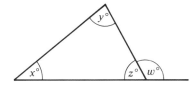

Using the diagram given above, find the sizes of the marked angles when

(a) $x = 48$, $y = 67$

(b) $x = 52$, $w = 108$

(c) $y = 70$, $z = 54$

(d) $y = 58$, $w = 124$

20.

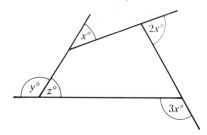

Using the diagram given above, find the sizes of the marked angles when

(a) $x = 42$ \qquad (c) $z = 66$

(b) $y = 138$ \qquad (d) $y = 4x$

21. In △ABC, AB is extended to D to form an exterior angle CBD. If
$\widehat{BDC} = 40°$, $\widehat{BCD} = 38°$ and $\widehat{BAC} = 80°$, draw a diagram to show this information and find the other two angles of △ABC.

22. ABCD is a quadrilateral. $\widehat{A} = 104°$ and $\widehat{B} = 84°$. The diagonal AC cuts $\widehat{DAB}$ in half and AC = AD.
Find $\widehat{BCD}$.

23. In △ABC, AB = AC and $\widehat{ACB} = 66°$. A line is drawn through C perpendicular to AB, to cut AB at D.
Find the angles of △BDC.

24.

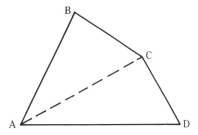

In quadrilateral ABCD, $\widehat{ABC} = \widehat{ACD} = 90°$, $\widehat{BCA} = 60°$ and BC = CD.

(a) Find $\widehat{BAC}$.

(b) Find the angles of △BCD.

(c) BD and AC cut at E. Find the angles of △BEA.

(d) If it is possible, find all the angles of △AED.
If it is not possible, find out what you can about them.

ACCURATE DRAWING OF TRIANGLES

Given One Side and Two Angles

Construct $\triangle ABC$ in which $AB = 7\,cm$, $\hat{A} = 35°$, and $\hat{B} = 40°$.

First make a rough sketch of $\triangle ABC$ and mark all
the given data on your sketch.

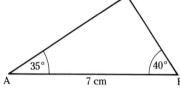

Now draw the line AB, making it
7 cm long. Label both ends.

Then use your protractor to make
and angle of 35° at A.

Next make an angle of 40° at B.
If necessary extend the arms
of the angles until they cross.
The point where they cross is C.

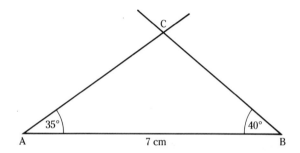

Since $\hat{A} + \hat{B} + \hat{C} = 180°$ we can calculate that $A\hat{C}B = 105°$.
As a check on the construction we can measure $\hat{C}$.

Sometimes it may be necessary to calculate another angle e.g. if $AB = 9\,cm$, $\hat{A} = 53°$
and $\hat{C} = 64°$, the sketch is:

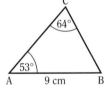

We can draw AB and $\hat{A}$ from the given information but we must calculate $\hat{B}$ before we can
continue. $\hat{C}$ cannot be drawn as we do not know where the point C is.

Given Two Sides and the Angle between those Two Sides

Construct $\triangle PQR$ in which $PQ = 4.5\,cm$, $PR = 5.5\,cm$ and $\hat{P} = 54°$.

First draw a rough sketch and put in all the
measurements.

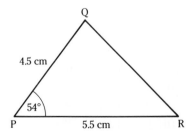

Draw one of the sides whose length you know.
We will draw PR.

P _____ R

Now using a protractor make an angle of 54° at P. Make the arm of the angle quite long.

Use a ruler to set your compasses to the length of PQ.

Then with the point of your compasses at P,
draw an arc to cut the arm of the angle.
This is the point Q.

Finally join R and Q.

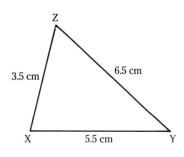

Given the Lengths of Three Sides

Construct △XYZ in which XY = 5.5 cm, XZ = 3.5 cm, YZ = 6.5 cm.

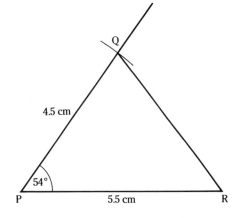

First draw a rough sketch and mark the
measurements on it.

Next draw one side. We will draw XY.

Set your compasses to the length of XZ using a
ruler. With the point of the compasses at X draw a
wide arc.

Next set your compasses to the length of YZ from
a ruler and, with the point at Y, draw another arc
to cut the first arc at Z.

Join ZX and ZY.

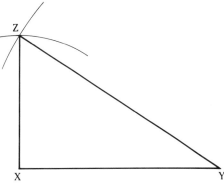

Exercise 3d

Construct the following triangles. Remember to draw a rough diagram first. It may be necessary to calculate the third angle.

1. $\triangle ABC$ in which $AB = 6\,cm$, $\widehat{A} = 50°$, $\widehat{B} = 65°$. Measure BC.

2. $\triangle DEF$ in which $\widehat{E} = 35°$, $EF = 5.5\,cm$, $\widehat{F} = 75°$. Measure DE and DF.

3. $\triangle PQR$ in which $\widehat{P} = 100°$, $PQ = 8.5\,cm$, $\widehat{Q} = 43°$. Measure PR.

4. $\triangle LMN$ in which $\widehat{N} = 73°$, $LN = 4.1\,cm$, $MN = 6.3\,cm$. Measure $\widehat{L}$.

5. $\triangle XYZ$ in which $\widehat{Y} = 65°$, $XY = 3.8\,cm$, $YZ = 4.2\,cm$. Measure XZ.

6. $\triangle ABC$ in which $AB = 7.3\,cm$, $BC = 6.1\,cm$, $AC = 4.7\,cm$. Measure $\widehat{A}, \widehat{B}$ and $\widehat{C}$.

7. $\triangle DEF$ in which $DE = 10.4\,cm$, $EF = 7.4\,cm$, $DF = 8.2\,cm$. Measure $\widehat{D}, \widehat{E}$ and $\widehat{F}$.

8. $\triangle PQR$ in which $\widehat{P} = 72°$, $\widehat{Q} = 53°$, $PQ = 5.1\,cm$. Measure RQ.

9. (a) Try to construct two triangles that fit the following measurements: $\triangle PQR$ in which $\widehat{P} = 60°$, $PQ = 6\,cm$, $QR = 5.5\,cm$.

   (b) Repeat part (a) if $QR = 6.6\,cm$

   (c) Repeat part (a) if $QR = 4.5\,cm$

   What conclusion can you draw from this question ?

10. Construct a quadrilateral ABCD in which $AB = 5\,cm$, $\widehat{A} = 70°$, $AD = 3\,cm$, $BC = 5\,cm$ and $DC = 5\,cm$. Measure AC. Measure all four angles and find their sum.

11. Construct a quadrilateral PQRS in which $PQ = 7\,cm$, $PS = 6\,cm$, $QR = 5.3\,cm$, $\widehat{P} = 65°$ and $\widehat{Q} = 72°$. Measure PR.

12. Construct a quadrilateral WXYZ in which $WX = 6.8\,cm$, $XY = 4.5\,cm$, $\widehat{W} = 90°$, $\widehat{X} = 75°$ and $\widehat{Y} = 125°$. Measure WZ and YZ.

13. Construct a quadrilateral, ABCD, in which $AB = 7.3\,cm$, $AD = 6.4\,cm$, $B\widehat{A}D = 80°$, $A\widehat{B}C = 110°$ and $\widehat{D} = 90°$. Measure BC and DC.

CONSTRUCTING ANGLES WITHOUT USING A PROTRACTOR

Some angles can be made without using a protractor: one such angle is 60°.

Every equilateral triangle, whatever its size, has three angles of 60°. To make an angle of 60° we construct an equilateral triangle but do not draw the third side.

TO CONSTRUCT AN ANGLE OF 60°

Start by drawing a straight line and marking a point, A, near one end.

Next open your compasses to a radius of 4 cm or more (this will be the length of the sides of your equilateral triangle).

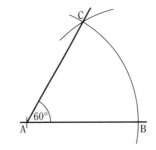

With the point of your compasses on A, draw an arc to cut the line at B, continuing the arc above the line. Move the point to B and draw an arc above the line to cut the first arc at C.

Draw a line through A and C.

Then $\widehat{A}$ is 60°.

△ABC is the equilateral triangle so *be careful not to alter the radius on your compasses during this construction.*

BISECTING ANGLES

Bisect means 'cut exactly in half'.

The construction for bisecting an angle makes use of the fact that, in an isosceles triangle the line of symmetry cuts $\widehat{A}$ in half.

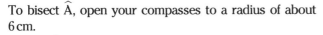

To bisect $\widehat{A}$, open your compasses to a radius of about 6 cm.

With the point on A, draw an arc to cut both arms of $\widehat{A}$ at B and C. (If we joined BC, △ABC would be isosceles.)

With the point on B, draw an arc between the arms of $\widehat{A}$.

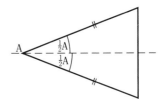

Move the point to C (being careful not to change the radius) and draw an arc to cut the other arc at D.

Join AD.

The line AD then bisects $\widehat{A}$.

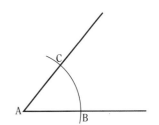

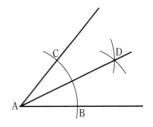

Constructing the Perpendicular Bisector of a Line

To bisect XY, open your compasses to a radius that is about $\frac{3}{4}$ of the length of XY.

With the point on X, draw arcs above and below XY.

Move the point to Y (being careful not to change the radius) and draw arcs to cut the first pair at P and Q.

Join PQ.

The point where PQ cuts XY is the midpoint of XY.

(PQ is the bisector of the angle of 180° at the midpoint of the line XY.)

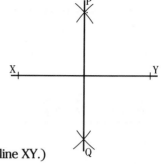

Note. When you are going to bisect a line, draw it so that there is plenty of space for the arcs above *and* below the line.

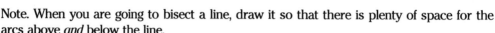

Exercise 3e

Use a ruler and compasses only.

1. Construct an angle of 60°.
   Hence construct an angle of 30°.

2. Construct an angle of 90°.
   (Start with an angle of 180°.)

3. Construct the isosceles triangle LMN in which LM = 6 cm, LN = MN = 8 cm. Construct the perpendicular bisector of the side LM. Explain why this line is a line of symmetry of △LMN.

4. Construct the isosceles triangle PQR, in which PQ = 5 cm, PR = RQ = 7 cm. Construct the perpendicular bisector of the side PR. This line is not a line of symmetry of △PQR; why not?

5. The figure below is a circle whose centre is C, with a line, AB, drawn across the circle. (AB is called a *chord*.)
   This figure has one line of symmetry which is not shown. Make a rough sketch of the figure and mark the line of symmetry. Explain what the line of symmetry is in relation to AB.

6. Construct a triangle ABC, in which AB = 8 cm, BC = 10 cm and AC = 9 cm. Construct the perpendicular bisector of AB. Construct the perpendicular bisector of BC. Where these two perpendicular bisectors intersect (i.e. cross), mark G. With the point of your compasses on G and with a radius equal to the length of GA, draw a circle. This circle should pass through B and C, and it is called the *circumcircle* of △ABC.

7. Construct a square ABCD, such that its sides are 5 cm long. Construct the perpendicular bisector of AB and the perpendicular bisector of BC. Label with E the point where the perpendicular bisectors cross. With the point of your compasses on E and a radius equal to the distance from E to A, draw a circle. This circle should pass through all four corners of the square. It is called the circumcircle of ABCD.

8. Draw a line, AB, 12 cm long. Construct an angle of 60° at A. Construct an angle of 30° at B. Label with C the point where the arms of $\widehat{A}$ and $\widehat{B}$ cross. What size should $\widehat{C}$ be? Measure $\widehat{C}$ as a check on your construction.

9. Construct a triangle, ABC, in which AB is 10 cm long, $\widehat{A}$ is 90° and AC is 10 cm long. What size should $\widehat{C}$ and $\widehat{B}$ be? Measure $\widehat{C}$ and $\widehat{B}$ as a check.

10. Construct a square, ABCD, with a side of 6 cm.

For questions 11 and 12, draw a rough sketch before starting the construction.

11. Construct a quadrilateral, ABCD, in which AB is 12 cm, $\widehat{A}$ is 60°, AD is 6 cm, $\widehat{B}$ is 60° and BC is 6 cm. What can you say about the lines AB and DC?

12. Construct an angle of 120°. Label it BAC (so that A is the vertex and B and C are at the ends of the arms). At C, construct an angle of 60° so that $\widehat{C}$ and $\widehat{A}$ are on the same side of AC. You have constructed a pair of parallel lines; mark them and devise your own check.

Self-Assessment 3

1. How many degrees does the hand of a clock turn through when it starts at 4 and stops at 9?

2. Calculate the size of each angle marked with a letter.

(a)   (b)

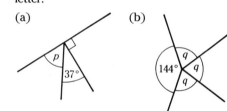

3.

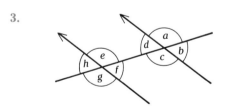

(a) Which angle is alternate to e?

(b) Name a pair of corresponding angles, one of which is d.

(c) Name a pair of interior angles, one of which is c.

(d) Name a pair of vertically opposite angles, one of which is f.

4. Find the size of each marked angle.

(a)

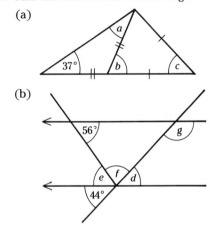

(b)

5. Construct $\triangle$ABC in which AB = 8.4 cm, $\widehat{A} = 38°$ and $\widehat{B} = 72°$. Measure BC.

6. Construct $\triangle$PQR in which PR = 8.2 cm, PQ = 5.7 cm and $\widehat{P} = 65°$. Measure QR.

7. Construct $\triangle$DEF in which DE = 10.4 cm. DF = 8.7 cm and EF = 6.9 cm. Measure $\widehat{D}$ and $\widehat{E}$.

8. Find x and y.

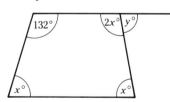

9. Using a ruler and compasses only, construct $\triangle$ABC in which $\widehat{A} = 60°$, $\widehat{B} = 45°$ and AB = 8 cm. Explain how you can check your construction.

SYMMETRY, TRANSFORMATIONS AND PATTERNS

LOCATING A POINT IN A PLANE

The most common way of giving the position of a point in a plane is based on using two fixed perpendicular lines called *the axes of coordinates* or the x and y axes. They meet at a point O, called *the origin*. The scales used on the two axes include both positive and negative numbers.

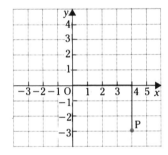

In all the work in this chapter the same scale is used on both axes. Ideally we would always use equal scales but sometimes this is not convenient as, for example, when drawing the graph of $y = x^2$.

Cartesian Coordinates

The position of a point is defined by its Cartesian coordinates. These are its horizontal distance from the y-axis (i.e. in the direction of Ox), followed by its vertical distance from the x-axis (i.e. in the direction of Oy). Distances measured upward or right are positive, while distances measured downward or left are negative. The point P in the diagram above is $(4, -3)$. The x-coordinate is 4 and the y-coordinate is -3.

Although in this book only Cartesian coordinates will be used for problems involving the positions of points, we first take a brief look at another way to locate a point in a plane.

Using One Fixed Line and a Fixed Point on It

The position of a point P is defined by its direct distance from the fixed point O, together with the angle between O*x* and OP.

The position of the point P in the diagram is given as (3, 60°).

(These are called the *polar coordinates* of P.)

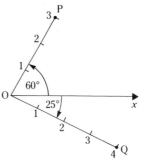

The fixed line is conventionally drawn across the page and anticlockwise rotation is taken as positive. So Q is the point (4, −25°).

Exercise 4a

1. Write down the Cartesian coordinates of each point.

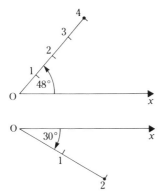

2. Write down the polar coordinates of each point.

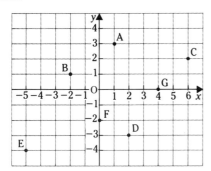

3. Write down the polar coordinates of each point.

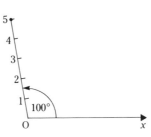

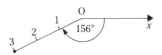

4. Using 5 mm squared paper plot each set of points, join them in order and give the name of the figure so formed.

   (a) (0, 5), (−6, 0), (0, −5), (6, 0)

   (b) (1, 0), (0, 3), (−6, 1), (−5, −2)

   (c) (5, 1), (1, 6), (−3, 1)

   (d) (1, −3), (6, −3), (4, 2), (−1, 2)

SYMMETRY

Line Symmetry

Each of these shapes is symmetrical about the broken line.
If the shape were folded along this *line of symmetry,* one half would fit exactly over the other.

Some shapes have more than one line of symmetry. The examples shown below are symmetrical about each broken line.

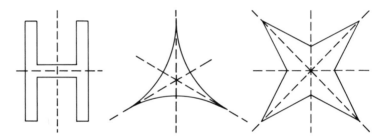

Rotational Symmetry

Some shapes can be rotated about a fixed point to a *new* position and still look the same as before. Such shapes have rotational symmetry, e.g.

This shape needs to be turned through one-third of a revolution before it first looks the same, then two more such turns are needed, i.e. three in total, before it returns to its original position.

The shape has *rotational symmetry of order 3.*

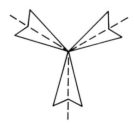

Exercise 4b

1. Some of these shapes have no line of symmetry, some have one line of symmetry and others have more than one. Copy those that are symmetrical and draw all the lines of symmetry.

(a)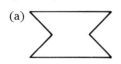

(d)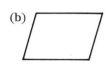

(b)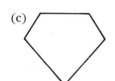

(e)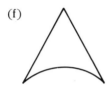

(c)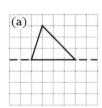

(f)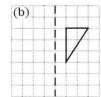

2. On squared paper copy and complete each drawing using the broken lines as lines of symmetry.

(a)

(c)

(b)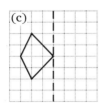

(d)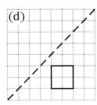

3. State which of the shapes in question 1 have rotational symmetry and give the order of that symmetry.

4. State which of the following shapes have (i) line symmetry only (ii) rotational symmetry only (iii) both

(a)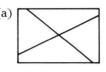

(d)

(b)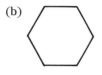

(e)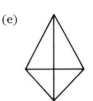

(c)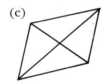

(f)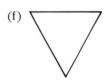

5. On squared paper draw x and y axes and mark each scale from -3 to 8. Plot the given points and join them as instructed. In each case state whether the shape has (i) line symmetry only (ii) rotational symmetry only (iii) both.

(a) A($4, 6$), B($6, 6$), C($5, 1$). Draw AB, BC and CA.

(b) A($2, 2$), B($2, 5$), C($8, 5$) and D($8, 2$). Draw AB, BC, CD, DA, AC and BD.

(c) A($1, -2$), B($4, -1$), C($0, 3$), D($-3, 2$). Draw AB, BC, CD, DA, AC and BD.

6. Draw axes as described in question 5. Plot the points A($6, 6$), B($-1, 6$), C($-3, -1$) and D($-3, -3$).

(a) Draw AB, BC and CD and add points E and F so that ABCDEF forms a figure with one line of symmetry.

(b) Draw the given diagram again and add E and F so that ABCDEF has rotational symmetry only.

TRANSFORMATIONS

A *transformation* is an operation that can change the position and/or the shape and/or size of an object.

We say that a transformation *maps* an object to its image.

Different transformations produce different effects and each of these transformations has a particular name.

Reflection

When an object is reflected in a mirror, the object and its *image* are symmetrical about the mirror line, which is the axis of symmetry.

The object is always 'turned over' to give the image.

Part of the object may be in contact with the mirror line, in which case the image is also in contact.

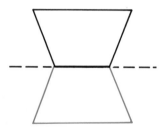

On the other hand, when the object is some distance away from the mirror line, the image and the object are equidistant from the mirror line.

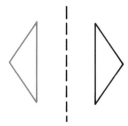

If the mirror line passes through the object it also crosses the image.

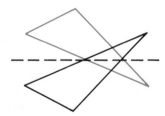

Exercise 4c

1. Use squared paper to copy each diagram (which shows an object and a mirror line). In each case draw the image of the object when it is reflected in the mirror line. Label the vertices of the image as A′, B′, C′, . . . to correspond with the vertices A, B, C, . . . of the object.

(a)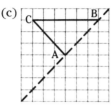

(c)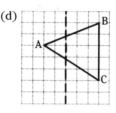

(b)

(d)

2. On squared paper, and using 1 cm for 1 unit, draw axes for x and y, each from −5 to 5. Draw △ABC where A is the point (1, 2), B is (2, 4) and C is (3, 2). Draw

   (a) △$A_1B_1C_1$, the image produced when △ABC is reflected in the x-axis

   (b) △$A_2B_2C_2$, the image of △ABC in the y-axis.

3. On squared paper draw x and y axes graduated from −5 to 5 with 1 cm ≡ 1 unit on each axis. P, Q and R are the points (4, 0), (1, −1) and (5, −1) respectively. Draw △PQR and

   (a) its image $P_1Q_1R_1$ when reflected in the x-axis

   (b) its image $P_2Q_2R_2$ when reflected in the y-axis

4. Using axes graduated from −6 to 8 plot the points A(−3, −4), B(−2, −1) and C(−6, −2) and join them to form △ABC. Draw the following images of triangle ABC.

   (a) $A_1B_1C_1$ by reflection in the x-axis

   (b) $A_2B_2C_2$ by reflection in the horizontal line through (0, −2)

   (c) $A_3B_3C_3$ by reflection in the vertical line through (−1, 0).

5. Using axes graduated from −8 to 8 plot the points A(6, 2), B(6, −1), C(1, −1) and D(1, 2) and join them to form rectangle ABCD. Draw the following images of ABCD.

   (a) $A_1B_1C_1D_1$ by reflection in the x-axis

   (b) $A_2B_2C_2D_2$ by reflection in the y-axis

   (c) $A_3B_3C_3D_3$ by reflecting $A_1B_1C_1D_1$ in the y-axis.

   (d) Describe how to obtain $A_3B_3C_3D_3$ by reflecting $A_2B_2C_2D_2$.

Find the mirror line if △A′B′C′ is the image of △ABC.

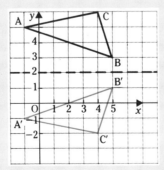

The mirror line is half-way between A and A′ and also half-way between B and B′ (or C and C′).

The horizontal line through the point (0, 2) is the mirror line.

6. Copy each diagram and draw the mirror line.

(a) 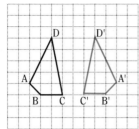   (b) 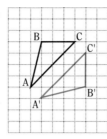   (c)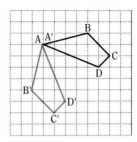

7. Draw △PQR where P is (2, 1), Q is (4, 4) and R is (−2, 4). Draw also △P′Q′R′ where P′ is (2, 1), Q is (4, −2) and R′ is (−2, −2). Given that △P′Q′R′ is the image of △PQR, draw the mirror line.

Translation

Consider the transformations of △ABC shown in this diagram.

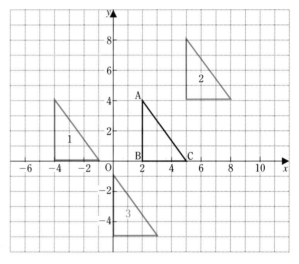

In each of these movements the side AB remains parallel to the *y*-axis and the orientation of the triangle (i.e. the way it faces) is unchanged. Transformations of this type are called *translations*.

Although no mirror is involved the words object and image are still used. A translation can be defined by giving the amount of movement parallel to each of the axes.
In the diagram above, for example, the translations that map triangle ABC to the image triangles are:

for image 1,
   a translation of 6 units to the left parallel to the *x*-axis;

for image 2,
   a translation of 3 units to the right parallel to the *x*-axis
      and 4 units upward parallel to the *y*-axis;

for image 3,
   a translation of 2 units to the left parallel to the *x*-axis
      and 5 units downward parallel to the *y*-axis.

Exercise 4d

1. The diagram below shows six images of the black triangle. Which of the images are given by translation and which by reflection ?

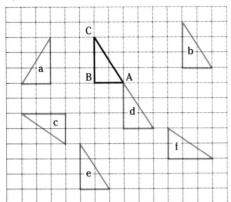

2. On squared paper draw x and y axes, each from -3 to 8 and mark the points A(3, 5), B(2, 1) and C(-1, 4). Mark and label $A_1B_1C_1$, $A_2B_2C_2$, etc., the images of triangle ABC under translations of

   (a) 2 units to the left parallel to Ox and 3 units down parallel to Oy

   (b) 4 units to the right parallel to Ox and 1 unit up parallel to Oy

   (c) 5 units to the right parallel to Ox and 3 units down parallel to Oy.

3. Describe the translation that maps the rectangle ABCD to

   (a) the rectangle $A_1B_1C_1D_1$

   (b) the rectangle $A_2B_2C_2D_2$

   (c) the rectangle $A_3B_3C_3D_3$

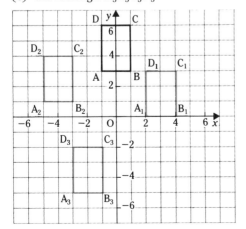

4. Copy the diagram.

   (a) The square ABCD is translated a distance equal to AB and in the direction of AB. Draw the image and label it 1.

   (b) Square ABCD is translated in the direction of AC a distance equal to AC. Draw this image and label it 2.

   (c) Describe the translation that maps 1 to 2.

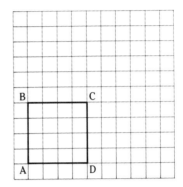

5. Copy the diagram.

   (a) Reflect the triangle labelled A in the x-axis and label the image B.

   (b) Translate B 5 units to the left and 1 unit down. Label the image C.

   (c) Reflect C in the x-axis and label the image D.

   (d) What transformation will map A to D ?

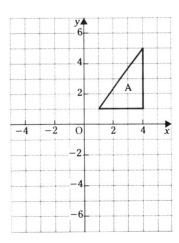

ROTATION

(a)

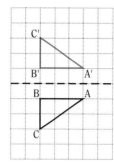

(b)

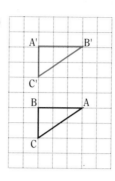

(c)

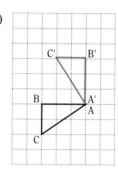

So far a shape has been transformed by reflection, as in (a), and translation, as in (b), but to carry out the transformation in (c) a rotation is needed.

In (c), △ABC is rotated through 90° clockwise ⟳ about A. Or we could say that the rotation is 270° anticlockwise ⟲. The point about which rotation takes place is the *centre of rotation;* in this case A is the centre of rotation.

Exercise 4e

State the angle of rotation when △PQR is mapped to △P'Q'R'.

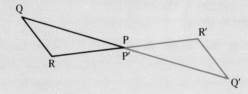

> To see the angle of rotation, consider the angle between *one* line and its image.
> The angle between PQ and its image P'Q' is 180° and for this angle it is not necessary to say whether it is clockwise or anticlockwise.

The angle of rotation is 180°.

Note that, to find the angle between one line and its image, it may be necessary to extend both lines until they cut.

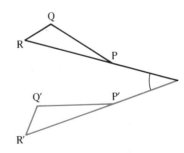

1. State the angle of rotation when △ABC is mapped to △A'B'C'. The centre of rotation is marked with a cross.

   (a)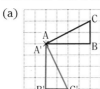

   (b)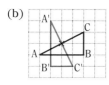

   (c)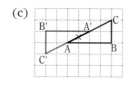

   (d)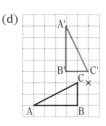

2. Write down the coordinates of A' and B', the images of A and B respectively, when AB undergoes the specified rotation.

   (a) A(1, 0), B(5, 0);
       90° clockwise about (3, 0)

   (b) A(2, 3), B(−1, 0);
       180° about (0, 1)

   (c) A(3, 2), B(3, 4);
       90° anticlockwise about (2, 1)

   (d) A(−1, −1), B(−3, 3);
       270° clockwise about O

3. Copy each diagram and draw the image of △PQR under the given rotation. Label the vertices of the image triangle so that P' is the image of P, etc.

   (a)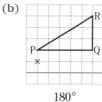

   90° clockwise

   (c)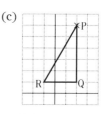

   90° anticlockwise

   (b)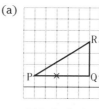

   180°

   (d)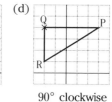

   90° clockwise

Finding the Centre of Rotation

Quite often we can look at an object and its image by rotation and locate the centre of rotation by observation. This is not always possible, however, and then we use the fact that the centre of rotation is the same distance from any one point on the object and the image of that point.

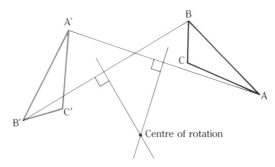

To locate the centre of rotation in this diagram, first we mark the point midway between A and its image A'. Then through this point a line at right angles to AA' is drawn. Any point on this *perpendicular bisector* is equidistant from A and A'. (This fact can be checked by measurement.)

This process is repeated with either B and B' or C and C'. The perpendicular bisectors meet at the centre of rotation.

Exercise 4f

In each diagram the green shape is the image by rotation of the black shape. Trace the diagram and find the centre of rotation.

1.

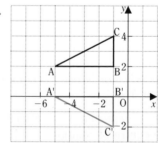

2.

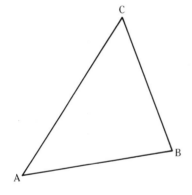

Reflections, translations and rotations all appear in the remaining questions in this exercise.

In questions 3 to 8 name the transformation that maps the black shape to the green one (A′ is the image of A, etc.). Describe each transformation as fully as possible.

3.

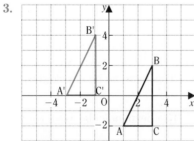

4.

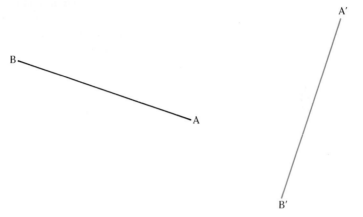

5.

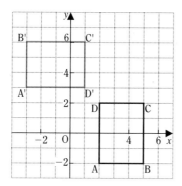

If when a shape is transformed we do not know which point is the image of a particular object point, there may be more than one possible transformation.

In questions 9 to 12 name as many different transformations as you can find that map the black shape to the green one. The number of transformations that you should spot is given in brackets.
(Do not count a rotation of 90° clockwise and a rotation of 270° anticlockwise as different transformations.)

9. (3)

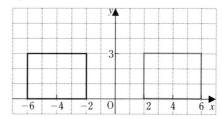

6.

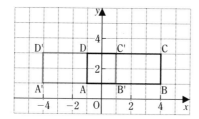

10. (2)

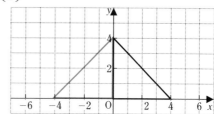

7.

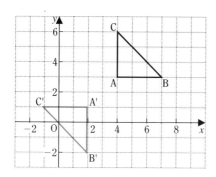

11. (5)

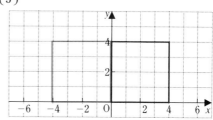

8.

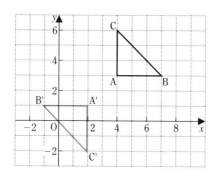

12. (4)

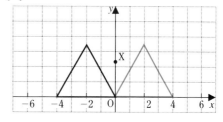

CONGRUENT FIGURES

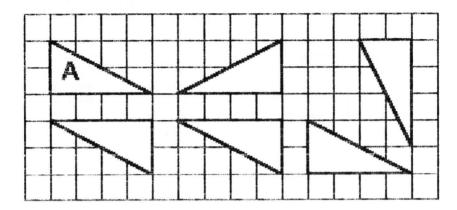

This diagram was drawn on a computer. Triangle A was drawn first and then transformed in various ways to give the other triangles.

All the triangles have exactly the same shape and size and are called *congruent* triangles.

 Two figures with exactly the same shape *and* size are called congruent figures.

(Two figures with the same shape but *different in size* are called *similar* figures.)

Transformations and Congruent Figures

Some transformations leave the size and shape of a figure unchanged, i.e. the object and image are congruent. Reflection produces congruent shapes:

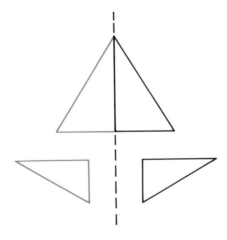

Rotation produces congruent shapes:

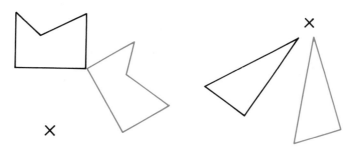

Translation produces congruent shapes:

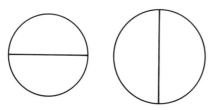

Exercise 4g

In questions 1 to 6 state whether or not the two figures are congruent. If they are congruent, state which transformation has been applied.

1.

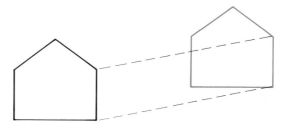

4.

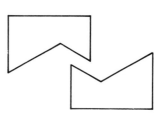

2.

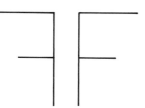

5.

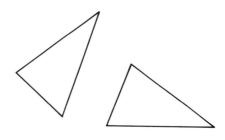

3.

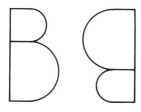

6.

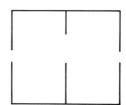

In each of the following questions

(a) describe a transformation, if there is one, that maps the black shape to the green one

(b) state whether or not the object and the image are congruent.

7.

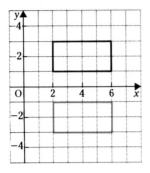

9.

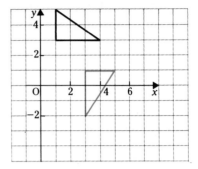

8.

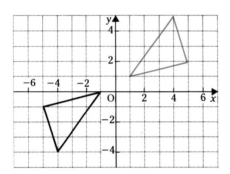

10.

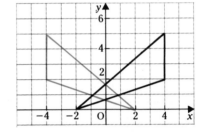

Investigations

1. Using 1 cm as 1 unit on each axis, draw x and y axes from -6 to 6. Mark the points $A(4, 1), B(4, 2), C(2, 1)$ and draw $\triangle ABC$. Draw the line L through the points $(-6, -6)$ and $(6, 6)$.

    (a) When $\triangle ABC$ is reflected in the line L the image is $\triangle A_1 B_1 C_1$. Draw this image and rotate it through $180°$ about O to produce $\triangle A_2 B_2 C_2$.
    Describe the transformation that would map $\triangle ABC$ to $\triangle A_2 B_2 C_2$.

    (b) Rotate $\triangle ABC$ through $180°$ about O and then reflect the image in the line L. Is the final image the triangle $\triangle A_2 B_2 C_2$?

    Do the same comparison with other pairs of reflections and rotations, in each case finding the single transformation that is equivalent to the pair.

    Investigate whether the order in which the transformations are applied affects the result and whether the single transformations themselves are always reflections or rotations.

    Try different vertices for $\triangle ABC$ to see whether these have any effect on your conclusions.

2. (a) Start with two parallel mirror lines, L_1 and L_2, and a triangle ABC as shown. Investigate what happens when $\triangle ABC$ is reflected in L_1, the image $\triangle A_1B_1C_1$ is then reflected in L_2 and this image, $\triangle A_2B_2C_2$, is reflected in L_1 and so on.

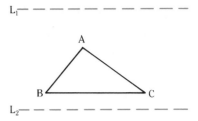

(b) Try a similar sequence of reflections in two non-parallel mirror lines. Start with mirror lines that intersect at P and are inclined at 45°. Investigate the positions of the images of one vertex at a time, relative to P.
Is there a similar relationship when the mirror lines are inclined at a different angle ?

Self-Assessment 4

1. State whether each of the following diagrams has:

   line symmetry, rotational symmetry, both or neither.

   For those shapes that have line symmetry, state the number of lines and for those with rotational symmetry state the order of the symmetry.

(a)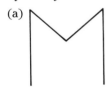

(b)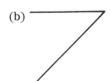

(c)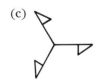

(d)

(e)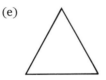

(f)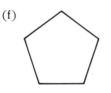

(g)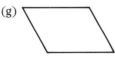

(h)

2. On squared paper, using the side of a square as 1 unit, draw x and y axes scaled from -4 to 7.
Mark the following points, A($-3, 1$), B($1, 4$), C($6, 4$) and D($2, 1$), and draw the quadrilateral ABCD.

   (a) Does ABCD have line symmetry ? If it has, name the mirror line or lines.

   (b) Does ABCD have rotational symmetry ? If it has, give the coordinates of the centre of rotation.

   (c) Repeat the question with C at ($8, 4$) and D at ($4, 1$).

3. (a) Write down the polar coordinates of P.

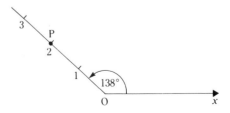

   (b) Sketch the position of the point Q whose polar coordinates are ($3, -55°$).

4. The diagram shows a rectangle PQRS and three of its images. Describe a transformation that maps PQRS to each image.

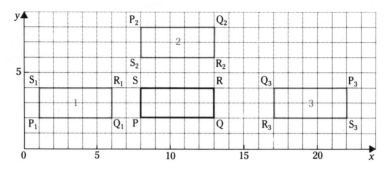

5. Copy the diagram and draw the image given by reflecting the object in each mirror line.

(a)

(b)

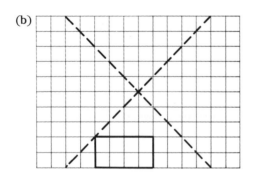

6. On squared paper draw the triangle with vertices at A(4, 2), B(1, 6) and C(2, 0). A second triangle has vertices A$_1$(6, 2), B$_1$(9, 6) and C$_1$(8, 0). Find the mirror line if $\triangle$A$_1$B$_1$C$_1$ is the image of $\triangle$ABC by reflection.

7. In each part state whether or not the two shapes are congruent.

(a)

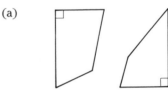

(b)

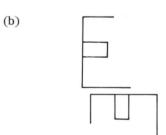

(c)

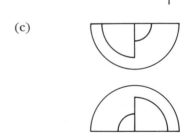

8. Describe the transformations used to produce this border pattern from the element shown.

9. Copy the diagram, in which the green triangle is the image of the black one. Find the angle of rotation and the centre of rotation.

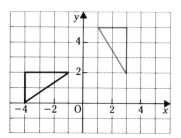

10. Draw on squared paper the triangle whose vertices are the points A(2, 1), B(5, 1) and C(5, 4).

   (a) Draw $\triangle A_1B_1C_1$, which is the image given when $\triangle ABC$ is reflected in the y-axis.

   (b) Draw $\triangle A_2B_2C_2$, the image of $\triangle A_1B_1C_1$ reflected in the x-axis. What single transformation maps $\triangle ABC$ to $\triangle A_2B_2C_2$?

   (c) When $\triangle ABC$ is rotated through 180° about B, the image is $\triangle A_3B_3C_3$. What transformation maps $\triangle A_2B_2C_2$ to $\triangle A_3B_3C_3$?

5 ▷ BASIC MEASUREMENT

BASIC UNITS

Certain quantities, such as length and mass, have a fundamental place in everyday life. Because we need to be able to measure these, it is necessary to have a standard amount of each as a unit.

Length

The metric units of length are based on the metre, which is roughly the length of a man's stride. One metre is written 1 m. So that smaller lengths can be measured conveniently, a metre is divided into 100 parts, each of which is a centimetre (cm). An even smaller unit is given when 1 m is divided into 1000 parts, each of which is 1 millimetre (mm); hence   1 cm = 10 mm.

Clearly it would not be convenient to measure distances between towns in metres so a much larger unit, the kilometre (km), is used, where 1 kilometre is equal to 1000 metres.

▶
$$1\,km = 1000\,m$$
$$1\,m = 100\,cm$$
$$1\,cm = 10\,mm$$
◀

For example:

$$4\,km = 4 \times 1000\,m = 4000\,m \quad \text{and} \quad 376\,m = \frac{376}{1000}\,km = 0.376\,km$$

$$8.7\,m = 8.7 \times 100\,cm = 870\,cm \quad \text{and} \quad 59\,cm = \frac{59}{100}\,m = 0.59\,m$$

$$2.3\,cm = 2.3 \times 10\,mm = 23\,mm \quad \text{and} \quad 472\,mm = \frac{472}{10}\,cm = 47.2\,cm$$

Note that when changing from a large unit to a smaller one there are *more* of the smaller units so we *multiply* by the appropriate factor.
When changing from a small unit to a larger one, there are *fewer* of the large units so we *divide.*

It is useful to recognise the meaning of the prefixes used in front of the basic unit, in this case the metre:

kilo means 'one thousand times as big'
centi means 'one hundredth part of'
milli means 'one thousandth part of'

78

Mass

When a quantity of a commodity is bought, we usually ask for a certain weight but what we really want is a certain *mass.* The *weight* of an object is the pull of gravity on it and this varies from place to place. Weight can be measured by using a spring balance or similar weighing machine.

Weight also depends upon the amount of material in the object. This is the *mass* of the object and it does not vary.

The basic unit of mass is the gram (a very small unit: about the mass of one average-sized crisp). Using some of the same prefixes as for length units gives further units of mass:

1 kilogram (kg) = 1000 grams (g)

1 gram (g) = 1000 milligrams (mg)

A centigram is not in common use.

Because the biggest of the units above, the kilogram, is not a very large one (1 kg is the mass of an ordinary bag of sugar), a much bigger unit is needed to measure, say, building materials. This unit is the tonne where   1 tonne (t) = 1000 kg

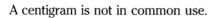

Exercise 5a

Express   (a) 47 tonnes in kilograms   (b) 1227 mm in centimetres.

(a) Change from large unit to smaller unit — multiply.

1 t = 1000 kg

$$47\,t = 47 \times 1000\,kg = 47\,000\,kg$$

(b) Change from small unit to larger one — divide.

1 cm = 10 mm

$$1227\,mm = \frac{1227}{10}\,cm = 122.7\,cm$$

1. Express each quantity in the unit given in brackets.

(a) 4 kg (g)   (e) 5 km (m)   (i) 35 mm (cm)

(b) 81 mm (cm)   (f) 7.3 g (mg)   (j) 5670 kg (t)

(c) 2.1 m (cm)   (g) 21 t (kg)   (k) 140 cm (m)

(d) 2024 g (kg)   (h) 121 mg (g)   (l) 23 m (mm)

Express

(a) 2 m 37 cm in centimetres

(b) 1 kg 79 g in kilograms.

(a) Only the 2 m must be changed into centimetres.

$$2\,m = 2 \times 100\,cm = 200\,cm$$

$$\therefore \quad 2\,m\,37\,cm = 200\,cm + 37\,cm = 237\,cm$$

(b) Change the 79 g into kilograms.

$$79\,g = \frac{79}{1000}\,kg = 0.079\,kg$$

$$\therefore \quad 1\,kg\,79\,g = 1\,kg + 0.079\,kg = 1.079\,kg$$

2. Express each quantity in the unit given in brackets.

(a) 3 cm 5 mm   (mm)

(b) 3 t 250 kg   (kg)

(c) 8 km 36 m   (m)

(d) 3 km 450 m   (km)

(e) 7 m 88 cm   (m)

(f) 9 g 77 mg   (g)

PERIMETER

The total distance round the boundary of a shape is its *perimeter*. When the dimensions of a simple shape are known, its perimeter can be found very easily.

The perimeter of this square is

$$3\,cm + 3\,cm + 3\,cm + 3\,cm = 12\,cm$$

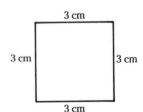

3 cm

3 cm   3 cm

3 cm

▶   **In general the perimeter of a square is given by**
4 × length of one side   ◀

For this rectangle the perimeter is

$7\,\text{cm} + 4\,\text{cm} + 7\,\text{cm} + 4\,\text{cm}$

$= 2 \times 7\,\text{cm} + 2 \times 4\,\text{cm}$

$= 22\,\text{cm}$

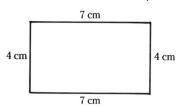

▶ **In general, the perimeter of a rectangle is given by** ◀
$2 \times$ length $+ 2 \times$ breadth

The perimeter of any shape can be found by adding the lengths of all its sides, provided that all these lengths are either given or can be deduced,

e.g.

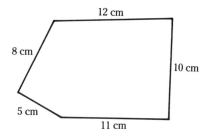

Perimeter $= (5 + 8 + 12 + 10 + 11)\,\text{cm} = 46\,\text{cm}$

Exercise 5b

Find the perimeter of the shape given in each question.

1. A square of side   (a) 6.2 cm   (b) 0.71 m

2. A rectangle measuring   (a) 4.5 m by 3 m
   (b) 11 mm by 6.1 mm

3.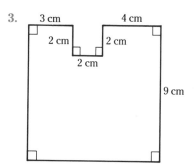

4.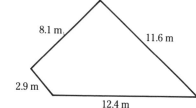

5. A rectangle that measures 10 cm by 16 cm and has a square of side 2 cm cut from each corner.

6. (a) An equilateral triangle of side 7.3 m.
   (b) A rhombus of side 0.42 cm.

Find the perimeter of this shape:

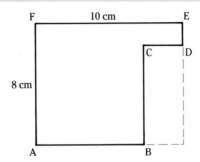

Although there are four sides whose lengths are not given, it is clear that combining some sides gives a known length.

$$AB + CD = FE = 10 \, cm$$

and

$$BC + DE = AF = 8 \, cm$$

The perimeter is given by

$$AB + BC + CD + DE + EF + FA$$

$$= AB + CD \; + \; BC + DE \; + \; EF \; + \; FA$$

$$= \quad 10 \, cm \quad + \quad 8 \, cm \quad + 10 \, cm + \; 8 \, cm = 36 \, cm$$

Find the perimeter of each shape.

7.

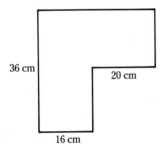

9.

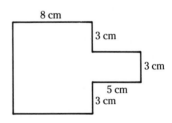

8.

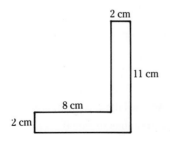

10.

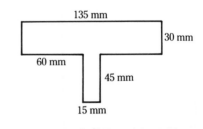

AREA

Counting Squares

The area of a shape drawn on a flat surface is the amount of surface enclosed within the boundary lines.

If the shape is drawn on a squared grid, the area can be assessed by counting the squares inside the boundary.

Exercise 5c

In this exercise, give each area as a number of grid squares.

1. What is the area of each shape ?

(a) 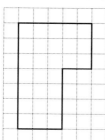   (b) 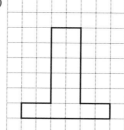   (c)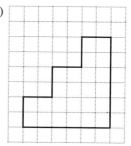

The boundary of a figure may not lie exactly on a grid line. In this case a square is counted if half or more of it is inside the figure but excluded if more than half of it is outside. An area found in this way can only be approximate.

2. Find an approximate value for the area of each shape.

(a)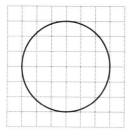

(c)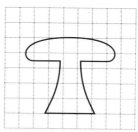

(b)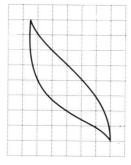

(d)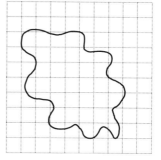

Units of Area

Suppose that the area of a figure is given as 8 squares.
If this is to convey the same size to everybody, the square must be of a standard size which can be clearly defined.

However, large areas are best found from large squares while smaller areas are easier to deal with in smaller squares, so we need a variety of standard squares to measure all types of area.

The side of the square that is useful for working in exercise books is one with a side of 1 centimetre, i.e. 1 cm.

The area of this square is 1 square centimetre, i.e. 1 cm^2

We know that $1 \text{ cm} = 10 \text{ mm}$, so a square of side 1 cm can be divided into 10×10 squares, i.e. 100 squares, of side 1 mm, each with an area of 1 square millimetre, i.e. 1 mm^2

 $$1 \text{ cm}^2 = 100 \text{ mm}^2$$

Now $100 \text{ cm} = 1 \text{ m}$, so a square of side 1 m can be divided into 100×100 squares of side 1 cm and area 1 cm^2.

$$1 \text{ m}^2 = 100 \times 100 \text{ cm}^2 = 10\,000 \text{ cm}^2$$

Similarly, as 1 km is 1000 m, it follows that

$$1 \text{ km}^2 = 1000 \times 1000 \text{ m}^2 = 1\,000\,000 \text{ m}^2$$

Which of the units given above should be used, depends on the kind of area being measured, e.g. the area of a county could be given in km^2, a garden in m^2, a sheet of paper in cm^2 and a small stamp in mm^2.

Another metric unit in which an area of land can be measured is the hectare where

$$1 \text{ ha} = 10\,000 \text{ m}^2$$

CALCULATING AREA

The Area of a Square

A square whose side is 3 cm is made up of 9 squares, each of side 1 cm, as shown,

i.e. the area of a square of side 3 cm is 9 cm^2.

This can be *calculated* using

$$\text{Area} = 3 \times 3 \text{ cm}^2 = 3^2 \text{ cm}^2$$

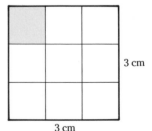

3 cm

3 cm

In general the area of a square is given by

$$\text{area} = (\text{length of side})^2$$

The Area of a Rectangle

A rectangle with a length of 4 m and breadth (or width) of 2 m can be divided into 8 squares of side 1 m, so its area is $8\,\text{m}^2$,

i.e. $\qquad \text{area} = 4 \times 2\,\text{m}^2$

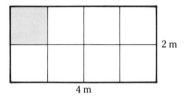

In general, the area of a rectangle is given by

$$\text{area} = \text{length} \times \text{breadth}$$

Note that both sides must be measured in the same unit.

Exercise 5d

Calculate the area of the shape given in each question.

1. A square of side 9 cm.

2. A rectangle of length 14 mm and width 2 mm.

3.

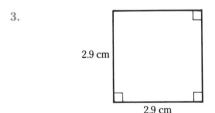

4.

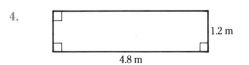

Find the area of a rectangle measuring 1.2 m by 42 cm.

The units must be the same for both sides so change 1.2 m to centimetres.

$1.2\,\text{m} = 1.2 \times 100 = 120\,\text{cm}$

Area of rectangle
$$= \text{length} \times \text{breadth}$$
$$= 120 \times 42\,\text{cm}^2$$
$$= 5040\,\text{cm}^2$$

5.
(a)   (b)

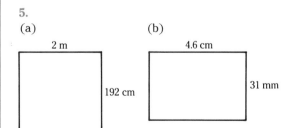

Compound shapes can often be divided into several standard parts whose areas can then be added together or, in some cases, one or more parts can be subtracted from a larger portion.

The diagram shows the floor layout of a workshop. Find the area of the floor.

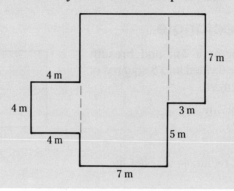

The broken lines split the workshop floor into three sections: a square of side 4 m, a rectangle measuring 7 m by 3 m and a second rectangle whose width is 7 m and whose length is (5 m + 7 m), i.e. 12 m.

Area of square is $4^2 \, \text{m}^2$ $= 16 \, \text{m}^2$

Area of first rectangle is $7 \times 3 \, \text{m}^2$ $= 21 \, \text{m}^2$

Area of second rectangle is $12 \times 7 \, \text{m}^2 = 84 \, \text{m}^2$

Total area of workshop floor is $(16 + 21 + 84) \, \text{m}^2 = 121 \, \text{m}^2$

Find the area shown in each diagram.

6.

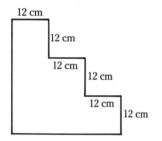

7.

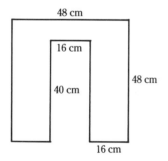

8.

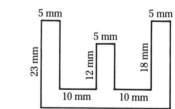

9. This diagram shows the floor plan for a church hall. Find the area of the floor.

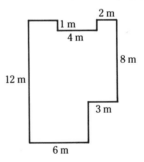

10. A decorative panel is to be set on a wall and the remainder of the wall (shaded in the diagram) will be pebble dashed.
Find the area to be pebble dashed.

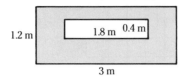

11. A mount for a photograph is in the form of a rectangle measuring 14.5 cm by 20.8 cm. A rectangular hole, 8.9 cm by 15.5 cm, is cut in the card.
Find the area of card left, giving your answer correct to 3 significant figures.

12. A wooden door is made with two glass panels as shown in the diagram. Find
    (a) the area of each panel
    (b) the area of the wood surface visible on one side of the door
    (c) the perimeter of each panel.

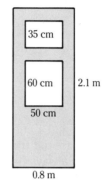

CUBES AND CUBOIDS

The word 'solid' is used rather loosely in this chapter, where 'three-dimensional object' would be a more precise, but clumsier, term. A hollow, closed box, for example, may be called a solid.

The name for a solid whose pairs of opposite faces are parallel rectangles is a *cuboid*. Some of the faces may be square. If all faces are square the cuboid becomes a *cube*.

Drawing Solids

If we look at a three-dimensional object, some of it can be seen but some parts are hidden. It is conventional to use a solid line to draw the parts that are seen and a broken line to show where the hidden parts are.

When a cube is drawn on a flat sheet of paper, only one of its visible faces can be drawn as a square. The other faces look like parallelograms, i.e. their opposite sides are parallel but the angles do not look like right angles.

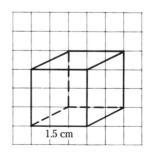

A similar situation applies for cuboids.

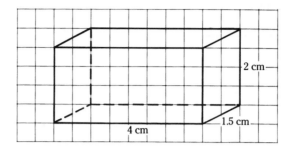

Both for a cube and a cuboid the result of the distortion is that some of the dimensions on the drawing are not true ones and cannot be found by measuring or by counting grid squares. So it is always necessary to mark all lengths on the diagram.

A different way to draw a cube or cuboid is to place one edge in the centre front. Drawn this way none of the angles looks like a right angle and each face is a parallelogram. *Isometric* paper, i.e. a grid of equilateral triangles, provides an easy background for this type of drawing. The advantage is that all the dimensions can be drawn correctly and can be measured from the diagram.

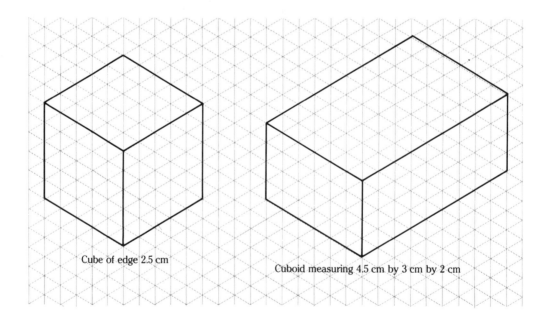

Cube of edge 2.5 cm

Cuboid measuring 4.5 cm by 3 cm by 2 cm

One disadvantage of using isometric paper to draw a cube is that one vertex lies behind another. This does not apply for a cuboid.

THE VOLUME OF A CUBOID

A cuboid can be built up from cubes with edges of length 1 cm. The volume of such a cube is one cubic centimetre, i.e. 1 cm^3.

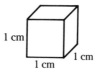

1 cm
1 cm
1 cm

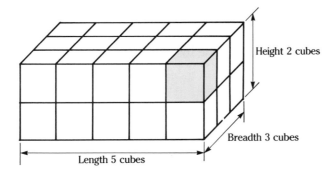

Height 2 cubes

Breadth 3 cubes

Length 5 cubes

The base of this cuboid contains 5 rows (the length)
of 3 cubes (the breadth or width)
and, building upward, there are 2 layers (the height).

The total number of cubes is $5 \times 3 \times 2 = 30$
so the volume of the cuboid is 30 cm^3 (length × breadth × height).

 **In general the volume of a cuboid is given by
volume = (length × breadth × height) cubic units**

Note that the units used for the three dimensions must be the same.

It follows that the volume of a cube is (length of side)^3 cubic units.

Units of Volume

The common units of volume are based on units of length, i.e. mm, cm, m and km.

Consider a cube of edge 1 cm. The cube can be divided into 10 layers each containing 10×10 cubes of edge 1 mm.

100 cubes, each with a
volume of 1 mm^2, in every
one of these layers

 i.e. $1 \text{cm}^3 = 10 \times 10 \times 10 \text{ mm}^3$

Similarly, as $1\,m = 100\,cm$,

$$1\,m^3 = 100 \times 100 \times 100\,cm^3$$

and $$1\,km^3 = 1000 \times 1000 \times 1000\,m^3$$

As before, when changing from a small unit to a larger unit we divide by the appropriate factor, i.e. the number of units is reduced,

e.g. to convert from mm^3 to cm^3, divide by $10 \times 10 \times 10$,
and to convert from cm^3 to m^3, divide by $100 \times 100 \times 100$.

Exercise 5e

How many cubes of edge 2 cm would be needed to form a cube of edge 8 cm ?

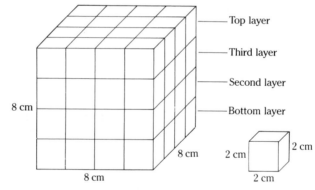

In the bottom layer there are 4×4 cubes, i.e. 16 cubes.

There are 4 layers of cubes altogether.

Therefore 64 cubes are needed.

1. Draw a cube of side 6 cm. How many cubes of side 3 cm would be required to fill it ?

2. How many cubes of side 2 cm would be needed to fill the same space as a cuboid measuring
   (a) 6 cm by 4 cm by 2 cm
   (b) 12 cm by 2 cm by 2 cm ?

3. A cuboid measures 4 cm by 4 cm by 8 cm. If the same space is filled by smaller cubes, how many cubes are needed of side
   (a) 1 cm   (b) 2 cm   (c) 4 cm ?

4. Twenty-four cubes of side 2 cm are arranged to form a cuboid 8 cm high.
   Give a possible length and breadth for the cuboid.

5. Find the volume of each of the following cuboids.

	Length	Breadth	Height
(a)	5 mm	4 mm	3 mm
(b)	6.1 m	3 m	1.2 m
(c)	4 cm	4 cm	4 cm

Find the volume of a cuboid measuring 2 m by 70 cm by 120 mm.
Give the answer in　(a) cm^3　(b) m^3.

(a) All measurements must be in centimetres.

$$\text{Length of cuboid is } 2\,\text{m} = 2 \times 100\,\text{cm}$$
$$= 200\,\text{cm}$$
$$\text{Height of cuboid is } 120\,\text{mm} = 120 \div 10\,\text{cm}$$
$$= 12\,\text{cm}$$
$$\text{Volume of cuboid} = \text{length} \times \text{breadth} \times \text{height}$$
$$= 200 \times 70 \times 12\,\text{cm}^3$$
$$= 168\,000\,\text{cm}^3$$

(b) First convert all measurements to metres.

$$\text{Breadth of cuboid is } 70\,\text{cm} = 70 \div 100\,\text{m} = 0.7\,\text{m}$$
$$\text{Height of cuboid is } 120\,\text{mm} = 120 \div 1000\,\text{m} = 0.12\,\text{m}$$
$$\text{Volume of cuboid} = 2 \times 0.7 \times 0.12\,\text{m}^3 = 0.168\,\text{m}^3$$

Note that the answer to part (b) can also be obtained directly from the answer to part (a) using $168\,000 \div (\,100 \times 100 \times 100\,)\,\text{m}^3$.

6. Express in cm^3
   (a) 0.42 m^3
   (b) 292 mm^3
   (c) 0.0063 m^3
   (d) 73.1 mm^3

7. Express in mm^3
   (a) 6.2 cm^3
   (b) 0.092 m^3
   (c) 0.43 cm^3
   (d) 43 cm^3

Find the volume of each cuboid giving the answer in the unit in brackets.

	Length	Breadth	Height	Unit
8.	2 m	70 cm	60 cm	(cm^3)
9.	0.5 cm	4 mm	3 mm	(mm^3)
10.	3.5 cm	25 mm	20 mm	(cm^3)
11.	1 m	40 cm	700 mm	(m^3)

FURTHER PROPERTIES OF SOLIDS

Capacity

Many three-dimensional objects are used for storing liquid and in these cases what we are usually concerned about is the volume of liquid that can be stored, rather than the volume of the container itself. To avoid any confusion between these two quantities we say that the *capacity* of the container is the volume of liquid it can hold and special units are used. The most common unit of capacity in the metric system is the litre (ℓ); petrol is bought in litres.

A *much* smaller unit, suitable for measuring medicine for example, is the millilitre (mℓ), which is one thousandth of a litre. (A teaspoon holds about 5 mℓ.)

▶ $$1000 \, m\ell = 1\ell$$ ◀

Because capacity is a particular form of volume, there is a relationship between the units of capacity and the units of volume.

▶ $$.\quad 1 \, litre \; = \; 1000 \, cm^3$$
$$1 \, millilitre \; = \; 1 \, cm^3$$ ◀

Strictly speaking, in order to calculate capacity the *inside* measurements of the container should be given. In practice we usually have to *assume* that the given dimensions are internal.

Density

It is often important to know the mass of one unit of volume of the material from which an object is made.
This is sometimes called the *density* of the material, i.e.

▶ $$density \; = \; \frac{mass}{volume}$$ ◀

A jeweller, for example, might need to know that the mass of 1 cm^3 of silver is 10.5 g, i.e. that the density of silver is 10.5 g/cm^3.

Exercise 5f

In all questions on capacity, assume that inside measurements of the container are given.

1. A cake tin has a square base of side 20 cm. The sides are vertical and 6 cm high. Cake mixture is poured into the tin and levelled off 4 cm above the base. Find

    (a) the capacity of the tin

    (b) the volume of cake mixture in the tin.

2. Find the capacity of a water tank measuring 1.2 m by 80 cm by 90 cm

    (a) in cubic centimetres

    (b) in litres.

3. A jug contains exactly 1 litre of liquid. All the liquid is poured into a 9 cm high metal box with a rectangular base, 10 cm by 7 cm. Will any of the liquid spill out and, if so, how much ?

The volume of a gold ingot is $32\,\mathrm{cm}^3$. Given that the density of gold is $19.3\,\mathrm{g/cm}^3$, find the mass of the ingot.

$$\text{Volume} = 32\,\mathrm{cm}^3$$

$$\text{Mass} = 32 \times 19.3\,\mathrm{g}$$

$$= 617.6\,\mathrm{g}$$

For a substance as valuable as gold, the mass would probably not be corrected to 3 significant figures.

Find the mass of each object. Where necessary decide whether or not the answer should be corrected to 3 s.f.

4. A block of brass with volume $14.3\,\mathrm{cm}^3$, given that the mass of $1\,\mathrm{cm}^3$ of brass is $8.5\,\mathrm{g}$.

5. One litre of milk; the density of milk is $0.98\,\mathrm{g/cm}^3$.

6. A cuboid of platinum measuring $12\,\mathrm{cm}$ by $5\,\mathrm{cm}$ by $3.2\,\mathrm{cm}$, given that $1\,\mathrm{cm}^3$ of platinum has a mass of $21.5\,\mathrm{g}$.

7. A $15\,\mathrm{cm}^3$ block of ice of density $0.92\,\mathrm{g/cm}^3$.

KINEMATICS

Kinematics is the study of motion, e.g. how far a moving object goes, how fast it travels and how long it takes.

Speed, Distance and Time

Suppose that a train travels at a steady speed, covering 50 miles in each of 3 consecutive hours, i.e. its speed is 50 m.p.h. The train has travelled 150 miles,

i.e.   distance = speed × time

Now suppose that the train goes 40 miles in each of the first two hours and 70 miles in the third hour. The train has again travelled 150 miles in 3 hours which is the same as if it had kept a steady speed of 50 miles in each hour. The steady speed which achieves the same distance in the same time is called the *average speed*, i.e. the *average speed* of the train is 50 miles per hour.

$$\text{Average speed} = \frac{\text{total distance}}{\text{total time}}$$

$$\text{total distance} = \text{average speed} \times \text{total time}$$

$$\text{total time} = \frac{\text{total distance}}{\text{average speed}}$$

Units of Speed

The common units of speed are

> miles per hour (m.p.h.)
> kilometres per hour (km/h)
> and   metres per second (m/s or $\mathrm{m\,s}^{-1}$)

Other units, such as metres per minute or miles per minute, may occur occasionally.

Note that m is used for miles in 'miles per hour'. Apart from this, m always represents metres.

Exercise 5g

In questions 1 to 5 find the unknown quantity, giving it in the correct unit.

	1.	2.	3.	4.	5.
Distance		80 km	350 miles	120 km	
Average speed	10 m.p.h.		70 m.p.h.	30 km/h	84 km/h
Time	4 h	5 h			$\frac{1}{2}$ h

Express   (a) 80 m.p.h. in miles per minute
          (b) 15 m/s in kilometres per hour.

(a) One minute is $\frac{1}{60}$ of an hour so the number of miles per minute is $\frac{1}{60}$ of the number of miles per hour.

$$80 \text{ m.p.h.} = \tfrac{1}{60} \times 80 \text{ miles per minute}$$

$$= 1.333 \ldots \text{ miles per minute}$$

$$= 1.33 \text{ miles per minute}   (3 \text{ s.f.})$$

(b) First find the number of metres per hour. One hour is 60×60 seconds   so the number of metres per hour is 3600 times the number of metres per second.

$$15 \text{ m/s} = 3600 \times 15 \text{ metres per hour} = 54\,000 \text{ metres per hour}$$

$1 \text{ km} = 1000 \text{ m}$ so the number of km/h is $\frac{1}{1000}$ of the number of metres per hour.

$$54\,000 \text{ metres per hour} = \tfrac{1}{1000} \times 54\,000 \text{ km/h}$$

$$= 54 \text{ km/h}$$

In questions 6 and 7 express each speed in the unit given in brackets.

6. (a) 72 m.p.h.   (miles per minute)
    (b) 9 miles per second   (m.p.h.)

7. (a) 72 km/h   (metres per minute)
    (b) 2.1 m/s   (km/h)

Katie cycled 3 miles in 20 minutes followed by 5 miles in 30 minutes.
Find her average speed in   (a) miles per minute   (b) m.p.h.

$$\text{Average speed} = \frac{\text{total distance}}{\text{total time}}$$

Total distance $= 3$ miles $+ 5$ miles $= 8$ miles

Total time taken $= 20$ minutes $+ 30$ minutes $= 50$ minutes

(a) Average speed $= \frac{8}{50}$ miles per minute

$= 0.16$ miles per minute

(b) Average speed $= 0.16$ miles per minute $= 60 \times 0.16$ m.p.h.

$= 9.6$ m.p.h.

8. Nick drives 70 miles on a motorway in 52 minutes. He then joins a side road and drives the next 20 miles in 38 minutes. Find his average speed in miles per hour.

9. Jenny cycles 4 miles on a hilly road at a steady 8 m.p.h. She covers the next 2 miles on the level in 10 minutes. What is her average speed in miles per hour?

10. A train travels 140 miles in 1 hour 20 minutes. During the first hour the train moves at a steady speed of 108 m.p.h.

   (a) What is the average speed for the whole journey?

   (b) How far does the train travel in the final 20 minutes?

   (c) What is the average speed during the last 20 minutes?

11. An athlete running a cross-country race covers the first 16 miles in 1 hour 20 minutes. Tiring a little, he takes 34 minutes to cover the final 4 miles. Find his average speed in m.p.h.

12. Susan starts a journey by driving 2 miles through a built-up area, taking 18 minutes. Then she covers 12 miles on more open road, in 22 minutes. After that she travels 12 miles on a motorway, taking 14 minutes. Find her average speed in miles per hour

   (a) for the first 40 minutes

   (.b) for the last 36 minutes

   (c) for the whole journey so far.

   After she leaves the motorway she drives to her final destination. The total distance driven is 63 miles at an average speed of 35 m.p.h.

   (d) Find the average speed for the last part of the journey.

Self-Assessment 5

1. Express each quantity in terms of the unit in brackets.

   (a) 588 cm   (m)   (d) 495 kg   (t)

   (b) 588 cm   (mm)   (e) 8 m^2 (cm^2)

   (c) 3.2 g   (mg)   (f) 5 cm^3 (mm^3)

2. Find the perimeter of

   (a) a square of side 4.3 cm

   (b) a rectangle with dimensions 5.1 cm by 22 mm.

3. Find the area of each figure given in question 2.

4. A plane is flying at an average speed of 160 m.p.h.

   (a) How far will it fly in $3\frac{1}{2}$ hours ?

   (b) How long will it take to travel 520 miles ?

5. Three different designs for the layout of a swimming pool are shown in this diagram. Find the area of each plan.

   (a)

   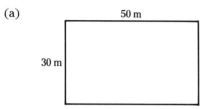

   (b)

   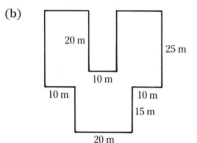

   (c)

   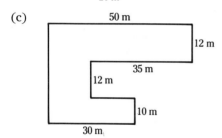

6. John walks 3 miles in 30 minutes and then 2 miles in 25 minutes. What is his average speed in

   (a) miles per minute   (b) m.p.h. ?

7. On 5 mm squared paper sketch a cube of side 4.7 cm. Calculate its volume.

8. A cuboid measuring 6 cm by 9 cm by 3 cm is to be filled with cubes. How many cubes are needed if the edge of the cube is

   (a) 1 cm   (b) 3 cm ?

9. A storage tank is a cuboid whose inside dimensions are: base 0.8 m by 0.65 m and height 0.75 m. It contains water to a depth of 47 cm.

   (a) What is the capacity of the tank ?

   (b) What is the volume of water in the tank ?

10. A bottle contains exactly 750 m ℓ of oil. The oil is poured into a container 12 cm high and with a square base of side 10 cm.

    (a) Will the container hold all the liquid ?

    (b) If the answer to (a) is 'No', how much liquid will be spilt ?

    (c) If the answer to (a) is 'Yes', how much more liquid will the container hold ?

11. What is the density of oak if a block of oak measuring 20 cm by 10 cm by 6.5 cm has a mass of 1.06 kg ?

6 ▷ PERCENTAGES AND THEIR APPLICATIONS

WORKING WITH PERCENTAGES

Per cent means 'in each hundred',
e.g. 23% means 23 out of every 100 items being considered.

It follows that $23\% = \dfrac{23}{100} = 0.23$

Conversely $\dfrac{74}{100} = 74\%$ and $0.69 = 69\%$

▶ **To convert a decimal, or a fraction, to a percentage, multiply by 100.** ◀

A fraction whose denominator is not 100, can be expressed as a percentage if it is first converted to a decimal,

e.g. $\dfrac{3}{4} = 0.75 = 75\%$ and $\dfrac{7}{13} = 0.5384\ldots = 53.8\%$ (3 s.f.)

Some relationships are worth remembering:

$\dfrac{1}{2} = 50\%$ $\qquad \dfrac{1}{4} = 25\%$ $\qquad$ and, in particular, $\qquad 1 = 100\%$

A decimal that is bigger than 1 converts to a percentage bigger than 100%

e.g. $1.34 = 134\%$

Similarly $2\dfrac{1}{2} = 250\%$

If, say 37% of the members of a club are female, it follows that 63% (i.e. 100% − 37%) are not female.

In general, if $x\%$ of a set of items have a particular property, then $(100 - x)\%$ of the items do not have that property.

Exercise 6a

Complete the following table.

	Percentage	Decimal	Fraction
1.	38%		
2.		0.07	
3.			$1\frac{1}{2}$
4.		0.61	
5.	5%		
6.		2.35	
7.			$\frac{9}{10}$
8.	$17\frac{1}{2}\%$		

9. If 23% of the books in a library are reference books, which are not available for borrowing, what percentage of the books can be borrowed?

10. Fourteen per cent of the passengers in a bus are men, 53% are women and the rest are children. What percentage of the passengers are children?

11. On Wednesday afternoons students at a sixth form college choose one physical activity from swimming, table tennis, badminton and gymnastics. If 24% choose swimming, 25% choose table tennis and 37% choose badminton, what is the percentage who choose gymnastics?

12. When a committee took a vote on a motion, 41% voted for the motion and 38% voted against. What percentage abstained?

FINDING A PERCENTAGE OF A QUANTITY

A percentage in itself does not often give practical information unless we also know what it is a percentage of, and what its value is in real terms. For example, if a deposit of 15% is required when buying a TV, the purchaser really wants to know how much money that is, and that depends on the price of the set; or, a school that is instructed to provide places for 5% more children next year needs to know precisely how many extra children there will be, and that depends on the present number of children.

The value of a percentage of a given quantity is

$$\frac{\textbf{percentage}}{\textbf{100}} \times \textbf{given quantity}$$

or   percentage as a decimal $\times$ given quantity

For example, if the price of a TV is £396 then a deposit of 15% is

$$\frac{15}{100} \times £396 \quad \text{or} \quad 0.15 \times £396$$

i.e.   £59.40

and if there are 540 pupils in a school at present, 5% extra places means

$$\frac{5}{100} \times 540 \text{ children or } 0.05 \times 540 \text{ children}$$

i.e.   27 extra children.

Percentage Increase and Decrease

Percentage increases, or percentage reductions, are particularly important in real life. Quoting changes in wages as percentages, for instance, can sometimes be misleading until we find what the value of the change is, in money terms. For example, a 6 % rise in a wage of £ 150 a week is worth £ 9 a week extra, whereas a 10 % rise in a wage of £ 80 is worth only £ 8 extra.

Exercise 6b

Find

1. 13 % of 900 pupils

2. 4 % of 50 m

3. 125 % of 74 kg

4. $12\frac{1}{2}$ % of a population of 40 000

5. 20 % of £ 13.25

6. 78 % of 200 marks

Lynne earns £ 14 from her Saturday job. She decides to save 30 % towards her holiday and to spend 40 % of her pay on clothes. How much money does Lynne

(a) save   (b) spend on clothes ?

(a) 30 % of £ 14 is $0.3 \times £ 14 = £ 4.20$
   Lynne saves £ 4.20

(b) 40 % of £ 14 is $0.4 \times £ 14 = £ 5.60$
   Lynne spends £ 5.60 on clothes.

---

7. A curtain, of length 2.8 m, shrinks by $2\frac{1}{2}$ % when it is washed. How much shorter is the curtain after washing ?

8. The cost of a package holiday for an adult is £ 472. The cost for a child is 70 % of the adult price. If two adults and three children book this holiday, what will the total cost be ?

9. A travelling salesman is paid 5 % commission on each sale with a value up to £ 200. For each sale with a higher value the commission is $7\frac{1}{2}$ %. If he takes two orders, one worth £ 160 and the other worth £ 670, what commission can he expect to receive ?

10. £ 2600 was raised at the village Fun Day. It was decided to give 45 % to Save the Children, 30 % to the RSPB and the remainder to village societies. How much did the village societies receive ?

11. A rug is laid on the floor of a room which measures 2.8 m by 3.5 m. The rug covers 45 % of the floor.
   Find the area of the rug.

12. Of 140 visits made by birds to a bird-table during a six-hour period, 55% were made by blue tits and 35% by chaffinches.
   How many visits were made by blue tits and how many by chaffinches?

The list price of a particular car today is £9650. Next month the price goes up by $7\frac{1}{2}\%$. What will it cost next month ?

Next month's increase is $7\frac{1}{2}\%$ of £9650

$$= £0.075 \times 9650$$

$$= £723.75$$

So next month's price is £9650 + £723.75

$$= £10\,373.75$$

Alternatively,

next month's price is $(100\% + 7\frac{1}{2}\%)$ of £9650

i.e. 1.075 of £9650

$$= £10\,373.75$$

13. A necklace that cost £140 is sold at a profit of 25%. For how much is it sold ?

14. An employee earning £145 a week is offered an increase of 12%. Find

   (a) the cash value of the increase

   (b) the new weekly wage.

15. Each year the population of Far Island, currently 86 000, is increasing by 7% of the population at the beginning of that year. What, to the nearest hundred, will the population be after

   (a) 1 year   (b) 2 years ?

16. Jane and Alice each have a salary of £3600. Jane is offered a rise of 8% for this year, with the same percentage increase next year. Alice's increases are to be 7% for this year and 9% for next year. Who is offered the better deal and by how much over the two years ?

The calculation when a reduction is made is very similar but the change is subtracted from the original value (or the reduction per cent is subtracted from 100%).

17. In their sale, James Brothers offer a 20% discount on the marked price of all goods. Find the sale price of

   (a) a lawnmower marked £145

   (b) a wheelbarrow marked £67.

18. A Speedy-Ace cycle is on sale in two shops. In Jim's Store it is priced at £176, with a discount for cash of $7\frac{1}{2}\%$. Best Wheels are offering 10% off their marked price of £181.60. Which is the better bargain ?

19. A rectangular poster, measuring 34 cm by 48 cm, is reduced by a photocopier which is set to shorten lines by $12\frac{1}{2}\%$. What are the dimensions of the copy of the poster ?

20. A motor bike costs £690 when new. If its value decreases by 10% each year, what is it worth

    (a) after 1 year   (b) after 2 years?

21. Mr Smith's weekly pay is £160 and 18% of this is deducted by his employer for pension contributions.

    (a) How much is left after pension contributions have been deducted?

    (b) Mr Smith is given a $7\frac{1}{2}$% wage increase. If 18% of his new wage is deducted at source, how much is left?

22. A fan heater is priced at £54.
    Store A has it on special offer at £5 off.
    Store B is offering a discount of 5%.
    Which is the better bargain and by how much?

23. Between two elections the size of the electorate in Munton Westside fell by 14%. At the first election 31 765 people were entitled to vote. To the nearest hundred, how many can vote at the second election?

TAXES

Value Added Tax

This is a tax charged on most goods and services. It is calculated at a rate fixed by the Government which (at the time of writing) is $17\frac{1}{2}$%.

The VAT is added to the basic cost.

Income Tax

Income tax is deducted from everyone's *taxable income*, i.e. their earnings over and above the value of their allowances. Usually people pay most of their tax at the *basic rate* of 24% (at the time of writing), although a small amount is paid at the lower rate of 20%, while those earning high salaries have to pay a certain amount of *higher rate* tax.

The rates at which income tax is calculated are announced by the Chancellor of the Exchequer in his Budget. These rates can vary from year to year, as can the allowances that are given before income tax begins to be deducted.

Other Forms of Tax

Direct taxation is applied before any money is spent. Income tax is one example of direct taxation; other direct taxes include capital transfer tax, inheritance tax, capital gains tax and corporation tax.

Indirect taxation takes effect only when money is spent. VAT is an example of an indirect tax because an individual pays only when goods or services are bought. There are other forms of indirect tax: excise duty is a special tax applied to certain goods such as alcohol, tobacco and petrol. These goods also carry VAT. The road fund licence is another indirect tax; every car has to have the licence (payable at regular intervals) before it can be used on public roads.

Exercise 6c

The price of a dining table is given as £860 plus VAT. If the rate of VAT is $17\frac{1}{2}$ %, find the price that a customer must pay for the table.

The value of the VAT is 17.5 % of £860

$$= £0.175 \times 860$$

$$= £150.50$$

The customer pays   £860 + £150.50

$$= £1010.50$$

Alternatively,

The price including VAT is (100 % + $17\frac{1}{2}$ %) of £860

$$= 1.175 \times £860$$

$$= £1010.50$$

Note that the second method gives the inclusive price more quickly and if the amount of VAT is wanted it can be found by subtraction.

In questions 1 to 3 find the total purchase price of the item. Take the rate of VAT as 17.5 %.

1. An electric cooker marked £626 + VAT.

2. A calculator costing £9.60 + VAT.

3. A van marked £5640 + VAT.

4. The price tag on a television gives £289 plus VAT at 15 %. What does the customer have to pay ?

5. In March, Nicki looked at a camera costing £160 plus VAT. The VAT rate at that time was $17\frac{1}{2}$ %. How much would the camera have cost in March ? Nicki decided to wait until June to buy the camera but by then the VAT rate had been raised to 22 %. How much did she have to pay ?

6. An electric cooker was priced in a showroom at £560 plus VAT at 15 %.

   (a) What was the price to the customer ?

   Later in the year VAT was increased to 17.5 %. The showroom manager placed on the cooker a notice which read:

   Due to the increase in VAT this cooker will now cost you £660.10

   (b) Was the manager correct ?

   (c) If your answer is 'Yes', state how the manager calculated the new price.

   (d) If your answer is 'No', give your reason and find the correct price.

7. A wine-merchant buys a certain wine out of bond at a cost of £3.20 a bottle and pays excise duty of 20 %. He adds a mark-up of £1.56 per bottle to what he has already paid to give a price on which VAT at 15% is charged. What does one of his customers pay for a bottle of this wine ?

Ken Watson earns £ 12 500 per year gross and has allowances of £ 5480. How much tax does he have to pay if he pays tax at the lower rate of 20% on the first £ 3500 of his taxable income and tax at the basic rate of 24% on the remainder?

$$\text{Ken's taxable income is gross income} - \text{allowances}$$
$$= £ 12 500 - £ 5480$$
$$= £ 7020$$
$$\text{Tax at the lower rate is 20\% of £ 3500} = £ 0.20 \times 3500$$
$$= £ 700$$
$$\text{Basic rate tax is due on £ 7020} - £ 3500 \quad \text{i.e. on £ 3520}$$
$$\text{Tax due is 24\% of £3520} = £ 0.24 \times 3520$$
$$= £ 844.80$$
$$\text{Total tax payable} = £ 700 + £ 844.80 = £ 1544.80$$

8. Find the taxable income in each of the following cases.

	Gross Income	Allowances
(a)	£ 8600	£ 4230
(b)	£ 12 500	£ 7960
(c)	£ 5860	£ 3470

For each case given above, calculate the income tax payable if a lower rate of 20% is charged on the first £ 3500 and the remainder of the taxable income is charged at a basic rate of

(i) 24%   (ii) 30%   (iii) 33%   (assume that no higher rate tax is due).

A solicitor has an annual salary of £ 44 000 and can claim allowances of £ 9540. The lower rate of income tax is 20% and is payable on the first £ 3500. The basic rate of income tax is 24% and is payable on the next £ 21 600 of taxable income. Higher rate tax of 40% is charged on any taxable income over £ 25 100. Find the total tax payable.

$$\text{Taxable income is £ 44 000} - £ 9540 = £ 34 460$$
$$\text{Lower rate tax on £ 3500 at 20\%} = £ 0.20 \times £ 3500$$
$$= £ 700$$
$$\text{Basic rate tax due on £ 21 600 at 24\% is 24\% of £ 21 600}$$
$$= £ 0.24 \times 21 600$$
$$= £ 5184$$
$$\text{Higher rate tax is due on £ 34 460} - £ 3500 - £ 21 600 \quad \text{i.e. on £ 9360}$$
$$\text{Higher rate tax is 40\% of £ 9360}$$
$$= 0.4 \times £ 9360$$
$$= £ 3744$$
$$\text{Total tax payable} = £ 700 + £ 5184 + £ 3744 = £ 9628$$

9. Lower rate income tax at 20% is payable on the first £3500 of taxable income and a basic rate is payable on the next £21 600. Any taxable income above £25 100 is taxed at a higher rate.

Find the income tax due to be paid in each case.

	Yearly income	Allowances	Basic rate tax	Higher rate tax
(a)	£ 8650	£ 4560	30%	
(b)	£ 34 400	£ 6820	24%	40%
(c)	£ 11 500	£ 7600	30%	
(d)	£ 45 000	£ 8600	33%	50%

National Insurance contributions are paid by employers, employees and the self-employed, to provide various benefits such as retirement pensions, unemployment benefit and health care. The rates are expressed as a percentage of earnings; they are determined by the Government and vary from time to time.

Employees' National Insurance contributions (NI) are calculated at the rates given in the table below.

Gross earnings per month	NI contributions payable
Up to £ 265	nil
Above £ 265 up to £ 1972	2% of £ 265 + 10 % of gross earnings above £ 265
Over £ 1972	£ 176

Use this information to calculate the NI contributions payable on monthly earnings of

(a) £230   (b) £1699   (c) £2000.

(a) NI contribution due on £ 230 per month is zero

(b) NI contribution due on first £ 265 is 2 % of £ 265

$$= 0.02 \times £ 265 = £ 5.30$$

Amount on which 10 % is payable is £ 1699 − £ 265 = £ 1434

NI contribution due is 10 % of £ 1434

$$= 0.1 \times £ 1434 = £ 143.40$$

Monthly contribution is £ 5.30 + £ 143.40 = £ 148.70

(c) NI contribution due on £ 2000 per month is £ 176 (the maximum payable)

Use the National Insurance rates given in the worked example to calculate the National Insurance payable on the given earnings.

10. £ 1000 per month

11. £ 206 per month

12. £ 7600 per year

13. £ 24 000 per year

SAVING

Most people who do not need to spend their money immediately invest it in some form of savings scheme. Money that is invested is lent to an organisation to use until the owner wants it back. The organisation pays interest to the owner for the use of the money.

Some of the best known forms of saving are building society accounts, National Savings and interest-paying bank accounts. Each of these usually pays interest at an annual percentage rate.

Another, increasingly popular, way to save is to make contributions to a pension scheme. Company schemes are often enhanced by contributions made by the employer. Personal pension schemes are taken out by individuals at their own choice; self-employed people make wide use of these.

There are other forms of investment, such as Unit Trusts and Investment Trusts, Equities (these are shares in public companies) and Gilts or Government Stocks. Investments of this type depend upon many different factors, not least upon the general state of the economy.

The Premier Share Account in a building society pays interest of 10% per annum, added to the account half-yearly. If £1000 is invested in this account and the interest is not withdrawn, find the amount in the account at the end of the first year.

Interest for 1st half year is $\frac{1}{2}$ of 10% of £1000 $= 0.5 \times 0.1 \times £1000$

$$= £50$$

The amount in the account at the end of the first half year is £1050

Interest for second half year is $\frac{1}{2}$ of 10% of £1050 $= 0.5 \times 0.1 \times £1050$

$$= £52.50$$

The amount in the account at the end of the first year is £1102.50

Note that if the interest had been paid at 10% per annum *added yearly,* the interest would have been only £100. To provide £102.50, the rate of interest would have had to be 10.25%. This rate is called the *compounded annual rate* (c.a.r.) and is often quoted by building societies along with their ordinary rate. Interest from investments is called *investment income* and is subject to income tax just as earned income is.

In general, tax is deducted by the building society or bank from the gross interest and paid direct to the Inland Revenue, leaving the net interest to be paid to the investor. In this way standard rate tax-payers are not liable to pay any further tax on their interest.

This is why you often see two rates of interest quoted in building society tables in a form such as

$$7\% \text{ p.a. net} = 9.33\% \text{ p.a. gross}$$

(Special arrangements can be made, however, for non-tax-payers to have their interest paid gross.)

Exercise 6d

1. An investment of £400 is made in a building society account. If neither capital nor interest are withdrawn, find the amount in the account at the end of 1 year if the rate of interest is 12% per annum
   (a) added yearly
   (b) added half-yearly
   (c) added quarterly.

2. A savings account pays interest at 8% p.a., added half-yearly. If £1000 is invested, find
   (a) the amount in the account at the end of the first year
   (b) the compounded annual rate.

3. A lump sum of £1000 can be invested for two years. Which of the following accounts provides the better investment?
   (i) A savings account paying half-yearly interest at 7% p.a.
   (ii) An account paying yearly interest of 8% p.a. and making a fixed administration charge of £10 per year.

4. An income bond pays 9% p.a.; the income is payable monthly.
   If £6600 worth of bonds are bought, find the monthly income.

The interest earned on an account can be withdrawn each time it is due, leaving the original *investment* unchanged. In this case the account earns *simple interest.* The more usual system however is for the interest to be added to the original deposit so that it too earns interest during the next year. This is called *compound interest.*

An investment of £580 is made in an account offering a fixed interest rate of 7% per annum. If the interest is left in the account at the end of each year find the total interest earned after three years.

Interest for first year is 7% of £580 $= £0.07 \times 580$
$$= £40.60$$

Amount in account at end of first year is £580 + £40.60
$$= £620.60$$

Interest for second year is 7% of £620.60 $= £43.44$

Amount in account at end of second year is £620.60 + £43.44
$$= £664.04$$

Interest for third year is 7% of £664.04 $= £46.48$

Amount in account at end of third year is £664.04 + £46.48
$$= £710.52$$

The total interest added is £710.52 − £580 $= £130.52$

Note how the *value* of the interest rises year by year even though the *rate* of interest is constant.

5. Find the compound interest earned on
   (a) £200 invested for 2 years at 8% per annum
   (b) £500 invested for 3 years at 10% per annum
   (c) £440 invested for 2 years at 5.25% per annum.

Find the total in the account at the end of the time if

6. £1200 is invested for 4 years at 10% per annum.

7. £850 is invested for 2 years at 6.15% per annun

8. £2000 is invested for 3 years at 6% per annum.

9. In question 6 of this exercise, find the total interest that would be earned if it were withdrawn at the end of each of the four years.

MULTIPLYING FACTORS

The method used above to calculate the compound interest earned becomes tedious if the investment is for a large number of years and the following alternative method can be used.

Suppose that £1000 is invested for 9 years in an account that pays interest yearly at 8% per annum, the interest being left in the account.

Interest for the first year is $0.08 \times £1000$

Amount in account after one year is $£1000 + 0.08 \times £1000 = 1.08 \times £1000$

i.e. $1.08 \times ($ value at beginning of first year $)$

In a similar way the amount at the end of the second year is

given by $1.08 \times ($ value at beginning of second year $)$

$$= 1.08 \times (1.08 \times £1000) = (1.08)^2 \times £1000$$

This is the beginning of a sequence which gives the amount in the account after any number of years, i.e.

after 1 year the amount is $1.08 \times £1000$

after 2 years the amount is $(1.08)^2 \times £1000$

after 3 years the amount is $(1.08)^3 \times £1000$

.
.
.

after 9 years the amount is $(1.08)^9 \times £1000$

Each of these powers of 1.08 is called a *multiplying factor.*

A calculator can be used to find the value of $(1.08)^9$, as follows $\boxed{1}\ \boxed{\cdot}\ \boxed{0}\ \boxed{8}\ \boxed{x^y}\ \boxed{9}\ \boxed{=}$

So the amount after 9 years is $1.9990 \times £1000 = £1999$

This approach can be used in any problem where a fixed rate of increase (or decrease) is applied and compounded,

e.g. if a flat bought for £36000 *appreciates* in value at a constant rate of 3% p.a., after 5 years it will be worth

$$(1.03)^5 \times £36000 = 1.1593 \times £36000$$

$$= £41700 \qquad \text{to the nearest hundred pounds}$$

In the case of a quantity that reduces year by year a similar formula can be established. Suppose that a car, initially worth £12 000, *depreciates* by 10 % per annum. Its value after one year is

$$£12\,000 - 0.1 \times £12\,000 = (0.9) \times £12\,000$$

After 3 years it will be worth $(0.9)^3 \times £12\,000$ and so on.

Exercise 6e

1. Find the value, correct to 4 significant figures, of
   (a) $(1.06)^4$
   (b) $(1.17)^4$
   (c) $(0.87)^6$
   (d) $(0.95)^7$
   (e) $(1.2)^5$

2. A motor cycle bought for £1800 depreciates in value by 10 % per year. Find its value, to the nearest £100, after
   (a) 2 years (b) 5 years.

3. A flat bought for £40 000 appreciates at 4 % each year. What will it be worth after
   (a) 3 years (b) 8 years (c) 20 years ?

4. In 1990 the population of Fabuland was 2.5 million. It is estimated to increase by 4 % yearly. Find, to the nearest hundred thousand, the estimated population in the year 2000.

5. The prices of portable transistor radios have dropped considerably in recent years. Taking the annual price reduction as 12 %, find the present price of a transistor radio if the cost of one 5 years ago was £25.

Compound Growth Tables

These tables give the multiplying factors for various percentage rates over different periods of time. They can be used to find the growth in sums of money, sales, populations, etc.

The table below gives the multiplying factors for rates of growth from 6 % to 15 % over a ten-year period.

Rate of growth p.a.	Number of years									
	1	2	3	4	5	6	7	8	9	10
4 %	1.040	1.082	1.125	1.170	1.217	1.265	1.316	1.369	1.423	1.480
5 %	1.050	1.103	1.158	1.216	1.276	1.340	1.407	1.477	1.551	1.629
6 %	1.060	1.124	1.191	1.262	1.338	1.419	1.504	1.594	1.689	1.791
7 %	1.07	1.145	1.225	1.311	1.403	1.501	1.606	1.718	1.838	1.967
8 %	1.08	1.166	1.260	1.360	1.469	1.587	1.714	1.851	1.999	2.159
9 %	1.090	1.188	1.295	1.412	1.539	1.677	1.828	1.993	2.172	2.367
10 %	1.100	1.210	1.331	1.464	1.611	1.772	1.949	2.144	2.358	2.594
11 %	1.110	1.232	1.368	1.518	1.685	1.870	2.076	2.305	2.558	2.839
12 %	1.120	1.254	1.405	1.574	1.762	1.974	2.211	2.476	2.770	3.106
13 %	1.130	1.277	1.443	1.631	1.842	2.082	2.353	2.658	3.004	3.395
14 %	1.140	1.300	1.482	1.689	1.925	2.195	2.502	2.853	3.252	3.707

The table shows that the multiplying factor for a population growing at 8 % for 8 years is 1.851 and that the multiplying factor for a sum of money growing at 12 % p.a. for 9 years is 2.770.

Exercise 6f

Use the compound growth table opposite for the questions in this exercise, giving answers correct to 3 s.f.

What sum of money will £350 grow to if it is invested for 5 years at 9%?

The table shows that the multiplying factor is 1.539

$$\text{So } £350 \text{ will grow to } 1.539 \times £350$$

$$= £538.65$$

$$= £539 \quad (3 \text{ s.f.})$$

---

1. If £10 is invested for 3 years at 8%, what sum will it amount to?

2. What amount will £20 grow to if it is invested for 6 years at 4%?

3. The population of Brookfield is 1600. If it increases at 7% per year what, to the nearest hundred, will the population be after 10 years?

A sum of money is invested for 7 years at 9% p.a. and grows to £731.20. Find the sum invested.

The multiplying factor is 1.828

When the sum invested is multiplied by 1.828 the result is £731.20
Therefore, when £731.20 is divided by 1.828, the initial sum is given.

The sum invested is given by

$$\frac{£731.20}{1.828}, \text{ i.e. } £400$$

---

4. The population of Broadtown has increased at 7% per year for the past 4 years. If the population is now 29 600, what was it 4 years ago? (Give the answer to the nearest hundred.)

5. The number of magpies nesting in a wood has increased steadily at 14% each year for the last 5 years.
   If the number of magpies is now 231,
   (a) how many were there 5 years ago?
   (b) how many will there be in 5 years time?

6. In Utopia the average weekly wage has grown by a steady 6% p.a. for the last 10 years. If the current figure, to the nearest ten pounds, is £250,
   (a) what was the average weekly wage 10 years ago?
   (b) what should it be in 5 years time?
   Give both answers to the nearest ten pounds.

BORROWING

There are many ways in which money can be borrowed and most people need to borrow at some stage in their lives. Institutions that provide loans charge for the use of their money and the cost of borrowing is often considerable. Some forms of borrowing are more expensive than others, however, and it is wise to understand the language and the systems of the most common forms of lending.

Mortgages

Nearly everybody who wants to buy a house or flat, has to borrow in order to do so. Money borrowed for this purpose is called a *mortgage* and is usually obtained from a building society or bank. The loan is not usually as much as the purchase price of the property; more often it is between 80% and 95% of the price.

This form of loan, being for a large sum, is repayable over a long period of time – anything from 10 to 30 years. As a result the amount of interest charged over the whole term of the mortgage is enormous.
The total payments can be more than four times the value of the property!

What most people are most concerned about is the size of the monthly repayments. These are often quoted as an amount per £1000 borrowed and vary with the interest rate and the number of years over which the loan is to be repaid.

For the duration of the mortgage the deeds of the property are held by the lender, who has certain rights over the property and can impose conditions on how it is used.

Failure to keep up the mortgage repayments can, in extreme circumstances, result in the house being repossessed by the lending institution.

Bank Loans, Credit Sales and Credit Cards

There are so many different names for different loan schemes that it is impossible to mention all of them. Also there are frequent changes in legislation, which can affect the operation, and the cost, of any scheme.

The only things that are unchanging in the sphere of borrowing are that it is not cheap and that it is essential to read the small print. Nevertheless it is worth taking a brief look at the main methods.

Bank loans are straightforward loans of money, which are immediately the property of the borrowers to spend as they please. Before it agrees to a loan, a bank may require some form of credit rating.

A bank loan is repaid by monthly instalments, usually over 2 to 5 years. After mortgages, this is said to be the least expensive way of borrowing.

(If the loan is a large one, some form of security, often a house, is required. Failure to maintain the repayments may result in forfeiture of the security.)

In a *credit sale* the goods belong to the purchaser from the time of purchase. Usually a down payment is required, followed by monthly payments over a period of time (anything from 3 months to 3 years). The total repayments are nearly always more, sometimes a lot more, than the cash price. However, it is not uncommon for interest-free credit to be offered for a limited period on items, particularly cars, when unsold stock is building up.

By law the cost of any form of credit, including mortgages, must be clearly displayed as a percentage called the annual percentage rate (APR).

A *credit card* such as a Visa card can be used to pay for goods and services without using money at the time. Each card-holder is given a credit limit, which is the maximum total amount that can be paid for by using the card. If the card-holder attempts to pay for an item when the credit limit has already been reached, the credit card company will refuse to authorise the payment.

A statement showing all purchases made is sent monthly to the card-holder, who then must pay at least the statutory minimum amount, or any other amount up to the total on the statement. Interest is charged on any part of the amount owed which is not paid.

The rate of interest may look reasonable, as it is quoted as a rate per month; but $2\frac{1}{2}$ % per month is equivalent to about 34 % p.a.!

Other cards, like American Express and some department store cards, operate in a similar way except that the total amount spent in the month must be paid when the bill is presented: payment of part only is not allowed. These are called *charge cards.*

Exercise 6g

A building society offers a twenty-five-year mortgage for monthly repayments of £12.50 per £1000 borrowed.

(a) What are the monthly repayments on a mortgage of £30 000 ?

(b) What is the total of the repayments for the full 25 years ?

(a) The monthly repayment on £1000 is £12.50

The monthly repayment on £30 000 is $30 \times £12.50 = £375$

(b) The total of 12 monthly repayments over each of 25 years is
$$12 \times 25 \times £375 = £112\,500$$

Where appropriate give answers correct to the nearest penny.

1. The Central Building Society offers a twenty-five-year mortgage for monthly repayments of £13 per £1000 borrowed.
   (a) What are the monthly repayments on a mortgage of
   (i) £25 000   (ii) £55 000 ?
   (b) If the monthly repayments are £585, how much has been borrowed ?

2. The repayments on a mortgage of £40 000 are calculated at £12.75 per calendar month for each £1000 borrowed. What amount must be paid
   (a) per month
   (b) per year
   (c) over the full twenty-five-year term ?

3. Wai-Ling Yeung obtains a 95 % mortgage on a flat whose purchase price is £48 000. How much can she borrow and how much must she herself pay initially towards the cost ?

4. The Patel family buy a house costing £70 000. They negotiate an 80 % mortgage on which the monthly repayments are £12.60 for each £1000 borrowed, for 25 years. Find
   (a) the amount borrowed
   (b) the monthly repayments
   (c) the total cost of the house.

5. Winston Armstrong's monthly mortgage interest is £180 when the mortgage rate is 14 %.
   When the mortgage rate falls to 13 % by how much can he reduce his monthly payment ?

The cash price of a washing machine is £360. The credit sale terms are: a deposit of £72 followed by 24 monthly repayments of £15.60. Find

(a) the total credit sale price

(b) the amount that would be saved by paying cash.

(a) Total of monthly repayments is $24 \times £15.60 = £374.40$

$$\text{Total credit sale price} = \text{deposit} + \text{repayments}$$

$$= £72 + £374.40$$

$$= £446.40$$

(b) Amount saved if cash were paid is £446.40 − £360

$$= £86.40$$

6. A second-hand car is offered for sale either for £1700 cash or on credit where the terms are a deposit of 20% and 18 monthly payments of £101. Find

(a) the deposit

(b) the total cost of buying the car on credit

(c) the difference between the cash price and the credit price.

7. The marked price of a motor bike is £1230. A purchaser who pays cash is offered a discount of 5%. The bike can also be bought on credit by paying a deposit of £300 followed by 24 monthly payments of £47.25.

(a) How much does a cash customer pay?

(b) What is the total cost of buying on credit?

8. A department store arranges its own credit terms on any sale over £150. The terms are: a deposit of 25% of the price, the balance to be increased by 20% and then divided by 12 to give the monthly repayments.
If these terms are used to buy a range of kitchen units priced at £2400, find

(a) the deposit

(b) the increased balance

(c) the monthly repayment.

9. Mary James wants to buy a car costing £9800 but cannot afford to pay cash. She has a choice of two methods for buying the car over a period of time; they are

(i) a bank loan for £9800 repayable over 36 months at £327 per month

(ii) a credit agreement requiring a deposit of 25% of the cash price followed by 30 monthly payments of £332.

Which is the cheaper way to buy the car and by how much?

10. The balance shown on Tariq's credit card statement is £193.67. The minimum payment required is either £5 or 5% of the balance, whichever is the greater. How much must Tariq pay?

11. Jayne has a credit limit of £600 on her credit card. At the beginning of the month the balance was nil. During the month she used her card to pay £29.00 for petrol, £320 for a video recorder and £120 for a deposit on a holiday. She then offered her card in payment of a garage bill for £157. The garage checked with the credit card company for authorisation. Was it given? Give a reason for your answer.

EXPRESSING ONE QUANTITY AS A PERCENTAGE OF ANOTHER

We can always express one quantity as a fraction of another quantity and then convert the fraction to a percentage.

For example:
In a test, one pupil scored 39 out of a possible 60 marks. To express this result as a percentage we use

$$\frac{\text{mark}}{\text{total}} \times 100\%$$

i.e. $\dfrac{39}{60} \times 100\% = 65\%$

When counting the number of tiles left in a box, Tom made the total 27, but there were actually only 25. The percentage error is given by

$$\frac{\text{error}}{\text{correct number}} \times 100\%$$

i.e. $\dfrac{2}{25} \times 100\% = 8\%$

A bike that cost £126 was later sold for £80. The percentage loss is given by

$$\frac{\text{loss}}{\text{purchase price}} \times 100\%$$

i.e. $\dfrac{46}{126} \times 100\%$

These examples illustrate the way in which one quantity, A, is expressed as a percentage of another, B,

i.e. $\dfrac{A}{B} \times 100\%$

Examples of what A might represent are: a mark out of a total (first example above), an error (second example above), a profit or loss (third example above), an increase or decrease, part of a larger quantity, etc.

The quantity called B can represent: a total (first example above), a correct value (second example above), an original price (third example) or value, a workforce, etc.

Exercise 6h

> Express 36 g as a percentage of 0.3 kg.
>
> When comparing two quantities in any way, they should be measured in the same unit. So 0.3 kg is converted into 0.3×1000 g, i.e. 300 g.
>
> 36 g as a percentage of 300 g is
>
> $$\frac{36}{300} \times 100\% = 12\%$$

Express the first quantity as a percentage of the second.

1. 30 cm, 50 cm

2. 84 p, £1.25

3. 36 min, 1 h

4. 780 g, 3 kg

5. Find the percentage error if

   (a) a three-metre length of fabric is measured as 3.08 m

   (b) £3.15 is rounded to £3

   (c) the value of 5.1^2 is estimated as 25.

6. Find the percentage mark in each case.

   (a) 14 out of 20

   (b) 34 out of 40

   (c) 111 out of 150

   (d) 84 out of 120.

7. During a bank-holiday weekend 29 people were injured in road accidents and 3 of them died. What percentage of the road casualties died?

8. If 2 litres of water are added to 18 litres of milk, what percentage of the mixture is (a) milk (b) water?

9. A boy saved £1.50 out of his Saturday job wage of £5.50. What percentage of his wage did he save?

10. Nina scored 47 out of 60 in a mental test. What was her percentage mark?

11. In a school of eight hundred and fifty pupils, there are five hundred and ten girls. What is the percentage of boys in the school?

12. A small factory employing sixty-four mechanics makes sixteen of them redundant. What percentage of the original workforce is retained?

13. Jason had sold a number of raffle tickets priced at 2 p each. Everyone who bought a ticket had paid with a 2 p coin. Jason counted the coins and reported that the total number was 54. Unfortunately he had dropped 2 coins without noticing, so they were not included in his total.

    What was the percentage error

    (a) in the number of coins

    (b) in the reported takings?

14. A dealer bought what she believed was an antique silver jug for £420. When she discovered that it was a fake she had to sell it for £180.

    What was her percentage loss? (Remember that the original figure is the purchase price.)

15. If an article bought for £60 is sold for £69, what is the percentage profit?

16. In a sale the price of a television set is reduced from £275 to £225. What is the percentage discount?

17. If Kevin's weekly wage goes up from £80 to £84, what is his percentage pay rise?

18. The value of a bicycle drops in the first year from £240 to £170. What is the percentage depreciation in that year?

FINDING THE ORIGINAL QUANTITY

In all the percentage problems so far examined, the calculation has been direct because the original quantity was known. Now we consider the case when the original quantity has to be found.

Fifty-four per cent of the adults living in a particular street own a car. If 162 adults own a car, how many adults live in this street?

$$54\% \text{ of the total number of adults is } 162$$

i.e.   0.54 of the total number of adults is 162

∴   the total number of adults is $162 \div 0.54$

$$= 300$$

Three hundred adults live in the street.

Exercise 6i

1. In a magazine, 65% of the pages are in colour. If there are 52 coloured pages, what is the total number of pages in the magazine?

2. The number of soft-centred chocolates in a box is 18. If 72% of the chocolates have soft centres, how many chocolates are there in the box?

3. Rita bought a bag of balloons. Sixteen were red and the rest were green. If 64% of the balloons were red, how many were green?

4. When buying a computer and printer, 28% of the total cost was for the printer. The computer cost £540. How much did the printer cost?

5. Questions in a test were allocated 1 mark each. Susan achieved a total of 64%, having correctly answered 16 questions.

   (a) How many questions were there in the test?

   (b) Andrew got 19 questions right. What percentage mark did he get?

6. Of the telephone calls Gary received in one week, 87.5% were from friends. If 9 of the calls were not from friends how many calls did he receive altogether?

A men's outfitter buys in ready-made suits which are sold, with a mark-up of 50%, for £345 each. For what price did the outfitter buy a suit?

We do not know the buying price as a sum of money, but we do know that the mark-up is 50% of the buying price, so the selling price is 150% of the buying price.

$$150\% \text{ of the buying price is } £345$$

i.e. $1.50 \times \text{the buying price} = £345$

So   the buying price $= £345 \div 1.5$

Therefore the outfitter buys a suit for £230.

Similarly if an item is sold at a loss of 28%, the selling price represents (100% − 28%), i.e. 72% of the buying price.

By selling his car for £4550, John Roberts made a loss of 21%. How much did he pay for the car ?

The selling price represents (100% − 21%), i.e. 79%, of his buying price.

79% of the buying price is £4550

i.e. $0.79 \times$ the buying price $= £4550$

∴   the buying price $= £4550 \div 0.79$

To the nearest ten pounds, John Roberts paid £5760 for his car.

Where appropriate, give answers correct to the nearest pound, or the nearest penny.

7. Find the original price in each case.

	Selling price	Profit	Loss
(a)	£1008	12%	
(b)	£445.50		10%
(c)	£920	15%	
(d)	£56		30%
(e)	£252	5%	
(f)	£1200		40%

8. A bookseller buys a book, gives it a mark-up of 30% and sells it for £9.10. What did she pay for the book ?

9. A nearly new, second-hand car is sold for £6440 at a loss of 8%. What was the original purchase price of the car ?

Self-Assessment 6

1. Express
   (a) $3\frac{1}{2}$ as a percentage
   (b) 2.83 as a percentage
   (c) 37% as a decimal
   (d) 135% as a mixed number.

2. Find
   (a) 16% of £40
   (b) 99% of 14 500 people

10. If VAT at 20% is included, the price of a dining-room suite is £1440.
    (a) What is the price without VAT ?
    (b) By what number would you divide the 'VAT inclusive' price in order to find the price before adding VAT, if the rate of VAT is   (i) 15%   (ii) 17.5%   (iii) 22% ?

11. The engine of a particular car was modified. As a result the number of kilometres covered on one litre of petrol increased by 6% to 15.9 km/ℓ.
    What was the petrol consumption before modification ?

12. When water freezes its volume increases by 4%. What volume of water will make 260 cm^3 of ice ?

13. After deductions of 37%, Ron Jackson's take-home pay is £151.20. What is his gross wage ?

3. Two stores sell an identical lawn strimmer at the same basic price of £46.50. Reg's Stores offer a discount of 6% while Right Tools give a reduction of £3. Which store gives the better deal and by how much ?

4. Last quarter my electricity bill was £52.80. This quarter the bill is £59.40. Find the percentage increase.

5. A plumber presented a bill for £254 plus VAT. Find how much the customer has to pay if the rate of VAT is

   (a) $17\frac{1}{2}\%$ (b) 22%

6. Jiten Shah earns £9850 a year and has tax allowances of £4744. How much income tax does she pay at the basic rate of 25%?

7. Copy and complete this bill.

	£
1 bathroom suite	192.00
1 shower unit	126.00
Taps and fittings	88.00
Less $2\frac{1}{2}\%$ trade discount	
Add VAT at 17.5%	
Payment due	

8. 240 boys and 180 girls took an examination. If 65% of the boys passed and 60% of the girls passed, what percentage of the total number of candidates passed?

9. A second-hand car, bought for £6200, depreciates by 8% per year. What is it worth after

   (a) 1 year   (b) 3 years?

10. Express

    (a) 56 marks out of 80 as a percentage

    (b) 72 cm as a percentage of 1.56 m (correct to 3 s.f.).

11. If she sells an article for £45, a dealer loses 10% of the price she paid for the article. At what price would she have to sell to make a gain of 12% on her buying price?

12. The repayments on a 25-year mortgage of £46 000 are calculated at 1.25% per calendar month.

    (a) Find the repayment due
        (i) per month   (ii) per year
        (iii) over 25 years.

    (b) Express the total repayment as a percentage of the original mortgage.

13. Jan has £5000 to invest and decides to pay it into a building society account. The Midtown Building Society can offer an account which pays 10.3% per annum, added yearly. At the Reliant West, there is an account which pays interest quarterly at 10% per annum. If Jan does not intend to withdraw any interest during the year, which account should she choose?

14. A certain factory employs 20 mechanics and 2 supervisors. The mechanics earn £250.80 for a 44-hour week and each of the supervisors is paid £315 weekly.

    (a) Find the total cost per week of employing this labour force.

    As a result of automation, it is found that only one supervisor is needed and that the number of mechanics can be reduced by 40%. The remaining mechanics are given an extra 90 p per hour and their working week is reduced to 40 hours. The supervisor is given a rise of 15%.

    (b) Find the reduction in the total weekly wage bill and express it as a percentage of the total found in part (a).

15. Each week the owner of a corner shop buys one thousand pounds worth of food, marks it up by 10% and turns it over (i.e. sells all of it) in the week. Another retailer spends £1000 on buying furniture. His mark-up is 100% but he only turns his stock over every three months. Who makes the bigger profit over a year?

BASIC ALGEBRA

THE USE OF LETTERS

There are many situations where the value of a number is unknown.

For example, if a textbook costs £14, then the number of these books that can be bought for £490 is unknown without some calculation. If we use the letter x to represent that number of books, then we can express the information given by using mathematical symbols, i.e. $14 \times x = 490$.

As a second example, consider these instructions for the quantity of rice needed for a meal: allow 50 grams per person. In this case both the number of people and the total mass of rice needed are unknown. If we use the letter n to represent the number of people and the letter w for total number of grams of rice, then again we can use mathematical symbols to express the information, i.e. $w = 50 \times n$

Notice that, in both examples, letters are used to represent numbers, not quantities. Thus w is the *number* of grams of rice whereas 'w grams' is the mass of rice.

Letters that are used to represent unknown numbers are sometimes called *variables* because, without further information, they can have a variety of values.

ALGEBRAIC EXPRESSIONS

An algebraic expression is a set of letters and numbers connected by addition, subtraction, multiplication and/or division.

Examples of algebraic expressions are $2 \times x$, $3 - x$, $a + b$, $\dfrac{y}{x}$

It is conventional to omit the multiplication sign so, for example,

$$2 \times x \text{ is written as } 2x \quad \text{and} \quad 2ab \text{ means } 2 \times a \times b$$

The *terms* in an algebraic expression are the parts separated by a $+$ or $-$ sign. A particular term is usually identified by the letter or combination of letters involved.

For example, in the expression $2a - 3xy + 6$, the terms are $2a$, $-3xy$ and 6; they might be identified individually as 'the term in a', 'the xy term' and 'the number term' respectively.

Like terms contain the same letter or combination of letters. Thus $2xy$ and $5xy$ are like terms, whereas $2xy$ and $3x$ are unlike terms.

An expression can be simplified when it contains two or more like terms, as these terms can be combined.

For example, $2x + 5x$ means '2 lots of x' plus '5 lots of x'

so $2x + 5x$ can be written simply as $7x$

In the same way, $5xy - 2xy$ can be simplified to $3xy$.

When simplifying algebraic expressions, remember that, as letters represent numbers, all the ordinary rules of arithmetic apply. Some of the important facts are as follows:

Brackets are dealt with first, then multiplication and division are done before addition and subtraction.

When directed numbers are multiplied or divided, the same signs give a positive result and different signs give a negative result.

When a string of numbers are multiplied, the order does not matter, e.g. $2 \times x \times 3$ is the same as $2 \times 3 \times x$, which can be written as $6x$.

Brackets

If we want to multiply both x and 3 by 4, we can group x and 3 together in a bracket and write $4(x + 3)$,

i.e. $4(x + 3) = 4 \times x \ + \ 4 \times 3 = 4x + 12$

In the same way, $2(2x - 5) = 2 \times 2x \ + \ 2 \times (-5)$
$$= 4x - 10$$

Indices

Indices applied to letters have exactly the same meaning as when applied to numbers.

Therefore, as 3^2 means 3×3, x^2 means $x \times x$

Similarly, $t \times t \times t$ can be written t^3

Also x^{-2} means $1/x^2$, $x^{1/2}$ means $\sqrt{x}$, $x^0 = 1$

Remember that $(a^3)^2$ means $a^3 \times a^3$

Different powers of the same letter can be multiplied by adding the indices,

e.g. $p^3 \times p^5 = p^8$

However, $p^3 \times q^5$ cannot be simplified (apart from omitting the $\times$ sign and writing $p^3 q^5$) because p and q represent different unknown numbers.

Different powers of the same number can be divided by subtracting the indices,

e.g. $\dfrac{p^3}{p^5} = p^{-2}$

Different powers of the same letter cannot be added or subtracted, e.g. $x^2 + x^3$ cannot be simplified because x^2 and x^3 are unlike terms.

Fractions

The four rules ($+$, $-$, $\times$, $\div$) used for numerical fractions are equally valid for fractions involving letters.

For example, we find fractions equivalent to $\dfrac{2a}{4}$ by multiplying or dividing the numerator and the denominator by the same number (or letter),

i.e.
$$\frac{2a}{4} = \frac{6a}{12} = \frac{a}{2} = \frac{ab}{2b} = \frac{a^2}{2a}$$

We can express $\dfrac{2x}{3} - \dfrac{x}{6}$ as a single fraction by finding equivalent fractions with a common denominator and then subtracting the numerators,

i.e.
$$\frac{2x}{3} - \frac{x}{6} = \frac{4x}{6} - \frac{x}{6} = \frac{4x - x}{6} = \frac{3x}{6} = \frac{x}{2}$$

We can simplify $\dfrac{2x}{3} \times \dfrac{x}{6}$ by multiplying the numerators and multiplying the denominators,

i.e.
$$\frac{\overset{1}{\cancel{2}x}}{3} \times \frac{x}{\cancel{6}_3} = \frac{x^2}{9} \quad \text{(Notice that we cancel the common factor 2.)}$$

To simplify $\dfrac{2x}{3} \div \dfrac{x}{6}$ we find the reciprocal of $\dfrac{x}{6}$ and multiply,

i.e.
$$\frac{2x}{3} \div \frac{x}{6} = \frac{2\cancel{x}^1}{\cancel{3}_1} \times \frac{\cancel{6}^2}{\cancel{x}_1} = \frac{4}{1} = 4$$

Exercise 7a

Simplify $3x + 4y + x - 7y$

$3x$ and x are like terms so $3x + x = 4x$; similarly $4y - 7y = -3y$
$$3x + 4y + x - 7y = 4x - 3y$$

1. Simplify
   (a) $2x + 3 + 2 + 5x$
   (b) $3a - 2 + 4a + 6$
   (c) $3x + 5y - 2x$
   (d) $5t - 8 - 2t + 3$
   (e) $4 - 5p - 2 - 3p$
   (f) $a - 4b + 3a$

2. Simplify
   (a) $6 - 2x - 4 - 3x$
   (b) $10 - 5y - 7y - 3$
   (c) $-a + 2b - 3a$
   (d) $5s + t - 2s + 6$
   (e) $4p - q + r + 2q - r$
   (f) $2x + y - z + 3x - 2y$

3. Multiply out the brackets
   (a) $3(x-3)$
   (b) $2(3x+4)$
   (c) $2(3x-2)$

4. Multiply out the brackets
   (a) $5(x-1)$
   (b) $4(3-x)$
   (c) $3(a-2b)$

Simplify (a) $2x-3(4-5x)$ (b) $x-2-(5x-4)$

(a) First we multiply out the bracket; $-3(4-5x)$ means multiply both 4 and $-5x$ by -3. Remember that $(-3)\times(-5x) = +15x$

$$2x-3(4-5x) = 2x-12+15x$$
$$= 17x-12$$

(b) $-(5x-4)$ means subtract $5x$ and subtract -4; remember that $-(-4) = +4$

$$x-2-(5x-4) = x-2-5x+4$$
$$= -4x+2$$
$$= 2-4x$$

---

5. Simplify
   (a) $5x+4(5x+3)$
   (b) $7-3(4-x)$
   (c) $3p+2(4-5p)$
   (d) $x-(2-3x)$
   (e) $8+3(a-8)$
   (f) $b-(5-b)$
   (g) $4(2-t)+2(t-3)$
   (h) $3b-4(2-5b)$
   (i) $3(4-x)-2(1+3x)$
   (j) $-2(x-1)-3(x+1)$
   (k) $-4(c-2)+6(2-c)$

6. Simplify
   (a) $p\times p\times p$
   (b) $2a\times 3a$
   (c) $2x^2\times x$
   (d) $3b\times b^3$
   (e) $4x\times 3y$
   (f) $x^3\div x$
   (g) $a^4\div a^2$
   (h) $y^2\div y^3$
   (i) $p^3\div p^3$
   (j) $4x^2\div 2x$

7. Simplify
   (a) $8x\div 2y$
   (b) $(-x)\times(-2x)$
   (c) $b\times(-b)$
   (d) $8x^3\div 2x$
   (e) $9y^3\div 6xy$
   (f) $(a^2)^3$
   (g) $(1/x)^{-1}$
   (h) $(pq)^0$
   (i) $(1/c)^{-2}$
   (j) $(x^{-1})^2$

8. Simplify
   (a) $3x+x(2+x)$
   (b) $a(a+b)+b(a-b)$
   (c) $x(x-2)-x(2x-4)$
   (d) $a(b-c)-(ab+c)$
   (e) $x^2-3x(4-x)$
   (f) $x^2(1-x^2)-x(1-x)$
   (g) $x-x(1-x)$
   (h) $a(b-c)-b(a-c)$
   (i) $x(x-3)+2(x-3)$
   (j) $4p(q+r)-2p(q-r)$
   (k) $x^3(x+1)-x^2(x-1)$

Simplify   (a) $\dfrac{x}{4} - \dfrac{x-3}{3}$ (b) $\dfrac{x}{4} \div \dfrac{x-3}{3}$

When the numerator and/or denominator of a fraction contains more than one term, it is sensible to place it in brackets.

(a)
$$\frac{x}{4} - \frac{(x-3)}{3} = \frac{3x - 4(x-3)}{12}$$
$$= \frac{3x - 4x + 12}{12}$$
$$= \frac{12 - x}{12}$$

(b)
$$\frac{x}{4} \div \frac{(x-3)}{3} = \frac{x}{4} \times \frac{3}{(x-3)}$$
$$= \frac{3x}{4(x-3)}$$

---

9. Simplify

(a) $\dfrac{x}{2} + \dfrac{2x}{3}$

(b) $\dfrac{2a}{5} - \dfrac{a}{4}$

(c) $\dfrac{y}{3} \times \dfrac{y}{2}$

(d) $\dfrac{2x}{5} \div \dfrac{15}{4x}$

(e) $\dfrac{x}{3} + \dfrac{x-1}{2}$

(f) $\dfrac{x+2}{3} - \dfrac{x-1}{2}$

(g) $\dfrac{x}{3} \times \dfrac{x-1}{2}$

(h) $\dfrac{x}{3} \div \dfrac{x-1}{2}$

(i) $\dfrac{4y}{3} \times \dfrac{15z}{8y}$

(j) $\dfrac{3b}{7} \div \dfrac{9ab}{14}$

(k) $\dfrac{3}{x} \div \dfrac{6}{y}$

(l) $\dfrac{x^2}{2} + \dfrac{x^3}{4}$

(m) $\dfrac{x^2}{2} \times \dfrac{x^3}{4}$

(n) $\dfrac{x^2}{2} \div \dfrac{x^3}{4}$

(p) $\dfrac{2a}{3} - \dfrac{a^2}{4}$

(q) $\dfrac{2(x-1)}{3} - \dfrac{3x}{2}$

10. Find the value of $3x + 2$ when
(a) $x = 4$,   (b) $x = -3$

11. Find the value of $x^2 + 1$ when
(a) $x = 2$,   (b) $x = -1$

12. Find the value of $\dfrac{2x-1}{3}$ when
(a) $x = 5$,   (b) $x = -4$

13. Given the fraction $\dfrac{x+1}{2} - \dfrac{x+2}{3}$
(a) Find its value when $x = 2$.
(b) Simplify the fraction.
(c) Find the value of the fraction found in part (b) when $x = 2$.
(d) Do your answers to (a) and (c) agree? Use a value of x to check your answers to some parts of question 9.

14. Express as one fraction

(a) $\dfrac{x}{5} + \dfrac{3x}{10}$

(b) $\dfrac{x}{5} \div \dfrac{3x}{10}$

(c) $\dfrac{x}{5} \times \dfrac{3x}{10}$

(d) $\dfrac{x-1}{3} \times \dfrac{x}{4}$

(e) $\dfrac{x-1}{3} + \dfrac{x}{4}$

(f) $\dfrac{x}{4} - \dfrac{x-1}{3}$

EQUATIONS

When two *different* algebraic expressions are equal, we have an equation.

For example, $\dfrac{x}{3} = \dfrac{x-1}{2}$ is an equation.

However, $x + x = 2x$ is not an equation because $2x$ is another way of expressing $x + x$, i.e. the two expressions are not different.
($x + x = 2x$ is an example of an *identity.*)

The Solution of an Equation

The solution of an equation is the number or set of numbers which the letters represent in that equation.

A problem can sometimes be solved if we can use algebra to relate the given information to form an equation and then solve it. This chapter started off with a problem which we interpreted as the equation $14x = 490$. This was a simple problem with an obvious solution, but it illustrates the potential of equations as a powerful problem-solving tool. We will start with methods for solving the simplest category of equations.

LINEAR EQUATIONS IN ONE UNKNOWN

Linear equations in one unknown contain just one letter to the power 1, e.g. $2x - 5 = 7$, $5 - 3a = a + 2$ are linear equations, but $x^2 - 2 = 2x$ is not a linear equation.

Sometimes the solution is obvious. For example, if $x + 1 = 3$, then clearly x represents 2 and we say that $x = 2$ is the solution of the equation.
However the solution of $3x + 6 = 2(4 - x)$ is not so obvious and an organised approach is necessary.

The two sides of an equation can be thought of as the contents of the two pans on a pair of scales which are exactly balanced. The equality will remain true (the scales will stay balanced) *provided that we do the same thing to both sides.* The aim is to end up with 'letter' = 'number' and we can achieve this by adding, subtracting, multiplying or dividing by anything except zero, as long as we do it to both sides.

It is sensible to proceed in the following order

1. remove any brackets
2. collect like terms
3. collect letter terms on one side (choose the side where the result will be positive, remembering that $-2 > -3$ and that $-2 < 0$)
4. collect the number terms on the other side.

Therefore to solve $3x + 6 = 2(4 - x)$, we proceed as follows:

Remove bracket $\qquad\qquad\qquad\qquad 3x + 6 = 8 - 2x$

Add $2x$ to both sides $\qquad\qquad\qquad 3x + 6 + 2x = 8 - 2x + 2x$

i.e. $\qquad\qquad\qquad\qquad\qquad\qquad 5x + 6 = 8$

Take 6 from both sides $\qquad\qquad\qquad\qquad 5x = 2$

Divide both sides by 5 $\qquad\qquad\qquad\qquad x = \frac{2}{5}$

As a check, see if the original equation is true when $x = \frac{2}{5}$,

i.e. $\qquad$ LHS $= 3 \times \frac{2}{5} + 6 = 7\frac{1}{5}$,   RHS $= 2(4 - \frac{2}{5}) = 2 \times 3\frac{3}{5} = 7\frac{1}{5}$

Therefore $x = \frac{2}{5}$ is the correct solution.

Exercise 7b

Find x if $5 - 3x = 2$

First we add $3x$ to both sides to give a positive x term.

$$5 - 3x + 3x = 2 + 3x$$
$$5 = 2 + 3x$$
$$5 - 2 = 2 + 3x - 2$$
$$3 = 3x$$

i.e. $\qquad\qquad\qquad x = 1$

1. Solve the equations
   (a) $3x + 2 = 11$
   (b) $2x - 5 = 9$
   (c) $7 - 2x = 3$
   (d) $2x + 6 = 3 - x$
   (e) $x + 5 = 4x - 4$
   (f) $3 - t = 5 - 3t$
   (g) $3x - 2 = 5 - 4x$
   (h) $7 - 5x = 4x - 11$
   (i) $3p - 5 = 7 + 9p$
   (j) $x + 2.5 = 3.6 - x$
   (k) $2t - 1.6 = 4t - 2.8$
   (l) $1.5 - x = 0.7 - 3x$

2. Solve the equations
   (a) $3 - 2(x - 2) = 10$
   (b) $x + 3(2 - x) = 8$
   (c) $5 - (4 - a) = 2a$
   (d) $4x - 3(x + 1) = 7$
   (e) $3(x - 1) = 2(5 - 2x)$
   (f) $6y = 4 - 3(y - 5)$
   (g) $4x - (x - 9) = 0$
   (h) $3(2x - 1) - 2(x - 1) = 0$
   (i) $1 - (3 - 4b) = 0$
   (j) $2(x - 1.5) = 3x$
   (k) $2.6 - (x + 1.3) = 0$
   (l) $7 - 2(x + 3.6) = 1.8$

Solve the equations   (a) $\dfrac{x}{5}+\dfrac{x}{4}=3$ (b) $\dfrac{x+1}{4}-\dfrac{x-1}{3}=1$

Remember that, provided we keep the equality true, we can do anything we choose to an equation. An equation is easier to deal with if it does not contain fractions, so we choose to get rid of them; we can do this by multiplying both sides by the lowest common multiple of the denominators.

(a)

$$\frac{x}{5}+\frac{x}{4}=3$$

Multiply both sides by 20

$$20\left(\frac{x}{5}+\frac{x}{4}\right)=20\times 3$$

i.e.

$$\frac{{}^{4}\cancel{20}}{1}\times\frac{x}{\cancel{5}_{1}}+\frac{{}^{5}\cancel{20}}{1}\times\frac{x}{\cancel{4}_{1}}=60$$

$\Rightarrow$

$$4x+5x=60$$

$$9x=60$$

$\therefore$

$$x=\frac{60}{9}=6\frac{2}{3}$$

(b)

$$\frac{(x+1)}{4}-\frac{(x-1)}{3}=1$$

Multiply both sides by 12

$$12\left[\frac{(x+1)}{4}-\frac{(x-1)}{3}\right]=12\times 1$$

i.e.

$$\frac{{}^{3}\cancel{12}}{1}\times\frac{(x+1)}{\cancel{4}_{1}}-\frac{{}^{4}\cancel{12}}{1}\times\frac{(x-1)}{\cancel{3}_{1}}=12$$

$\Rightarrow$

$$3(x+1)-4(x-1)=12$$

$\Rightarrow$

$$3x+3-4x+4=12$$

$\Rightarrow$

$$7-x=12$$

$\Rightarrow$

$$-5=x,$$

i.e.

$$x=-5$$

3. Solve the equations

(a) $\dfrac{2x}{3}=5$

(b) $\dfrac{2x}{3}=\dfrac{1}{4}$

(c) $\dfrac{x}{3}+\dfrac{2}{5}=\dfrac{1}{2}$

(d) $\dfrac{x}{3}+\dfrac{2x}{5}=4$

(e) $\dfrac{3x}{2}-\dfrac{x}{4}=2$

(f) $\dfrac{x}{2}+\dfrac{1}{3}=\dfrac{x}{3}$

(g) $\dfrac{x+1}{2}+\dfrac{2x-1}{3}=2$

(h) $\dfrac{x+2}{4}=\dfrac{x-1}{3}$

(i) $\dfrac{x+5}{4}=3$

(j) $\dfrac{3a-1}{2}-\dfrac{3-a}{4}=\dfrac{3}{4}$

(k) $\dfrac{2p-3}{7}+\dfrac{3-2p}{14}=0$

(l) $\dfrac{3-b}{5}+3=\dfrac{2b+1}{10}$

The perimeter of a rectangular sheet is 9 m and the length is $\frac{1}{2}$ m more than the width. Find the width of the sheet by forming an equation and solving it.

Let x m represent the width of the sheet.

The length of the sheet is $(x + \frac{1}{2})$ m.

The perimeter is twice the width plus twice the length,

$$\therefore \qquad 2x + 2(x + \tfrac{1}{2}) = 9$$

$$\Rightarrow \qquad 2x + 2x + 1 = 9$$

$$\Rightarrow \qquad 4x = 8$$

so $x = 2$

The width of the sheet is 2 m.

Form an equation from the information given in each problem and then solve the equation. State clearly, either in words or on a diagram, what your letter represents. End your solution by answering the question asked.

Most of these problems are simple enough to answer without the help of an equation: use this to check the validity of your equation.

4. A group of people is divided into three smaller but equal-sized groups. There are 15 people in one of the smaller groups. How many were in the original group ?

5. The perimeter of an equilateral triangle is 81 cm. What is the length of one of the sides ?

6. A twenty per cent increase in my weekly wage will give me an extra £27 a week. What is my present weekly wage ?

7. I asked John to think of a number and then divide it by three. He said that the result was two less than the number he thought of. What number did he think of ?

8. I want to make a rectangular lawn with a perimeter of 60 m so that its length is twice its width. How wide should it be ?

9. The volume of a cardboard box is ten times that of a carton. The box will hold eight cartons with 36 cm^3 of space to spare. Find the volume of one carton.

10. I am ten years older than my sister and I am now twice her age. How old is my sister now ?

11. The length of a rectangle is 6 cm more than its width and its perimeter is 48 cm. Find the length of the rectangle.

INEQUALITIES

The use of letters to represent unknown numbers is not restricted to problems that can be represented as an equation.

For example, suppose that fewer than 50 students enrol for a course at a college.

The number of students enrolling is unknown but if we represent it by x, then using the symbol $<$ to mean 'is less than', we can write

$$x < 50$$

This is an inequality and it is true when x represents any number less than 50, i.e. x represents a range of numbers and this range can be illustrated on a number line.

The open circle at the right-hand end of the range indicates that 50 is not included in the range.

The number of students who enroll cannot be negative so a further inequality is implied, i.e. x must be greater than or equal to zero, which is written $x \geqslant 0$.

The other symbols that are used to represent inequalities are

$>$ means 'is greater than' and $\leqslant$ means 'is less than or equal to'

The range given by $x \geqslant 0$ can also be illustrated on a number line.

The solid circle at the left-hand end of the range indicates that 0 *is* included in the range.

When a variable has to satisfy two inequalities we have a double inequality.

For example x, the number of students enrolling on the course, is restricted in two ways, i.e. $x < 50$ and $x \geqslant 0$ (i.e. $0 \leqslant x$).

Because the values of x lie between two boundaries, these two facts can be combined into one statement, $0 \leqslant x < 50$.

This number line illustrates the double inequality:

THE RANGE IN WHICH A CORRECTED NUMBER CAN LIE

Suppose that the length of a piece of string is given as 23 cm to the nearest centimetre.

The smallest number that can be rounded up to 23 is 22.5, and the largest number that can be rounded down to 23 is just less than 23.5. Therefore the string can have any length from 22.5 cm up to, but not including, 23.5 cm and is not restricted to integer values.

This gives a range of numbers which can be illustrated on a number line.

22.5 is called the *lower bound* of the range
and 23.5 is called the *upper bound* of the range.

If the length of the string is denoted by x cm then we can say that

$$22.5 \leqslant x < 23.5$$

OPERATIONS ON INEQUALITIES

Consider the true inequality $2 < 5$

If we add or subtract the same number on both sides, we find that the inequality remains true, e.g. $2 + 5 < 5 + 5$, $2 - 8 < 5 - 8$

If we multiply (or divide) both sides by the same positive number, we also find that the inequality remains true, e.g. $2 \times 2 < 5 \times 2$

However, multiplication (or division) by a negative number destroys the truth of the inequality, e.g. $2 < 5$ but $2 \times (-2)$ is *not* less than $5 \times (-2)$, i.e.

   **an inequality remains true when
the same number is added to, or subtracted from,
both sides and when both sides are multiplied
or divided by the same positive number.**

However, *multiplication or division by a negative number must be avoided.*

Solving Inequalities

Consider the inequality $3 - 2x \geqslant 5$

The range of values of x for which the inequality is true is not immediately obvious. Finding this range of values of x is called solving the inequality.

Now we can add $2x$ to both sides of $3 - 2x \geqslant 5$

giving $3 \geqslant 5 + 2x$

Subtracting 5 from both sides gives $-2 \geqslant 2x$

Dividing both sides by 2 gives $-1 \geqslant x$

i.e. $x \leqslant -1$ is the solution of the inequality, and it can be illustrated on a number line.

i.e.

```
    |-------|-------|-------●-------|-------|------
       -3      -2      -1       0       1
```

Notice that the procedure for solving inequalities is very similar to that for solving equations; always collect the x terms on the side with the greater number of xs as this avoids ending up with a negative letter term.

Exercise 7c

1. Each of the following numbers is given to the nearest whole number. Illustrate on a number line the range in which the number lies.

   (a) 12   (b) 8   (c) 100

2. Each of the following numbers is correct to 1 decimal place. Illustrate on a number line the range within which the number lies.

   (a) 2.7   (c) 5.0

   (b) 34.4   (d) 1.1

3. Each of the following numbers is correct to 2 significant figures. Use a number line to illustrate the range within which the number lies.

   (a) 2.2   (c) 120

   (b) 0.15   (d) 10

4. Solve each inequality and illustrate the solution on a number line.

   (a) $4x - 5 > 3$ (g) $4x - 1 \geqslant 3$

   (b) $1 + 3x < 4$ (h) $2 + 3x \leqslant 11$

   (c) $7 > 3 + 2x$ (i) $3 - 5x \geqslant 18$

   (d) $1 + 2x > 0$ (j) $4 - 3x \geqslant 2$

   (e) $5 < 7 + x$ (k) $2x - 7 \leqslant 9$

   (f) $3 > 4 - x$ (l) $7 - 5x > 3$

5. Give the largest integer that satisfies each inequality.

   (a) $2x - 3 < 5$ (b) $4 - x \geqslant 2$

6. Give the smallest integer that satisfies

   (a) $5 + 3x \geqslant 14$ (b) $0 < 3 - x$

Find the range of values of x for which   (a) $x \geqslant 2$ and $x > 1$
(b) $x - 2 < 2x + 1 < 5$

(a) If we illustrate both given ranges on a number line, then we can see the values of x where the ranges overlap.

$x \geqslant 2$ and $x > 1$ are both satisfied for $x \geqslant 2$

(b) $x - 2 < 2x + 1 < 5$ represents two inequalities.

i.e. $x - 2 < 2x + 1$ and $2x + 1 < 5$

We solve each inequality and then find the values of x that satisfy both of them.

$x - 2 < 2x + 1$	$2x + 1 < 5$
$\Rightarrow \quad -3 < x$	$\Rightarrow \quad 2x < 4$
i.e. $\quad x > -3$	i.e. $\quad x < 2$

Values of x between -3 and 2 satisfy both the given inequalities, i.e. $-3 < x < 2$

7. Find the range of values of x which satisfy both the inequalities.

   (a) $x \leqslant 1$ and $x < 2$

   (b) $2 + x \geqslant 3$ and $3 - x \geqslant 1$

   (c) $5 > x + 1 > 2$

   (d) $7 \leqslant 3 - x \leqslant 12$

   (e) $10 \geqslant 2x + 6 \geqslant x + 1$

   (f) $3x - 8 < x + 2 \leqslant 2x + 1$

   (g) $x + 4 > 2x - 1 > 3$

   (h) $x - 1 \leqslant 2x \leqslant 4$

8. For each part of question 7 give (i) the smallest integer, (ii) the largest integer, that satisfies each double inequality.

9. Find (i) the smallest integer, (ii) the largest integer, that satisfies each of the following sets of inequalities.

   (a) $x + 1 < 2$ and $x - 1 > -6$

   (b) $x + 4 > 2x + 1 \geqslant 5$

   (c) $x - 1 < 2x - 3 < 7$

   (d) $7 < 1 - x < 2x + 3$

A computer supplier has to sell more than ten computers a week to stay financially viable. The manufacturer can let the supplier have a maximum of 50 computers each week. Use inequalities to represent the number of computers that can be sold each week.

Let the letter n represent the number of computers sold each week.

We know that n is greater than 10 but less than or equal to 50,

i.e. $$n > 10 \quad \text{and} \quad n \leqslant 50$$

We also know that n is a whole number. All this information can be written briefly as

$$10 < n \leqslant 50, \quad \text{where } n \text{ is an integer}$$

Construct an inequality to represent the information about the unknown quantity in each of questions 9 to 13. Remember to state clearly what number your letter represents. If your letter can have only whole number values, this must also be stated.

10. The minimum weight of popcorn that can be bought from a wholesaler is 15 kg.

11. No more than 56 passengers can be carried on a coach.

12. The temperature will remain above $0\,^{\circ}\text{C}$ overnight.

13. I think of a number, double it and then add two. The result is less than one hundred.

14. A teacher is allowed to spend a maximum sum of £50 buying books. There is a delivery charge of £1.50 and a number of books costing £6 each are purchased.

15. A packet of pins contains 250 pins to the nearest 10 pins. What is the largest number of pins possible in a packet?

16. The length of a room is given as 355 cm to the nearest 5 cm. What is the shortest possible length of the room?

FORMULAE

A formula is a set of instructions for solving a problem. For example, the formula for finding the area of a rectangle can be written in words as follows.

   The area of a rectangle is found by multiplying its length by its width.

This formula works for any rectangle, i.e. the length and the width of the rectangle can each be any number of units. Using letters for these unknown numbers, we can express the formula algebraically.

If the length of a rectangle is l units and its width is b units, its area, A square units, is given by

$$A = lb$$

Notice that the letters in the formula represent numbers, i.e. if a rectangle is 12 cm long then l is 12.

Making Formulae

To make an algebraic formula for solving a general problem, we need to be able to express the solution in words. Then we can identify the variable quantities and allocate letters to represent the unknown numbers.

For example, Sam makes earrings and sells them at markets and craft fairs.
Each pair of earrings costs £1 to make and is sold for £2.50.
She keeps her accounts on a computer spreadsheet and needs a formula for the gain or loss made on each occasion.

In words this formula is

The gain made is equal to the difference between the selling price and the cost of each pair, multiplied by the number of pairs of earrings sold less the rent of the sales pitch.

The variables are: the number of pairs of earrings sold, and the rent.

If n is the number sold and £R is the rent, then money made on each pair is £$2.5 -$£1, i.e. £1.50 so the money made on sales is £$1.5 \times n$.

If the gain made is £P, we can now write a formula for P in terms of n and R, i.e.

$$P = 1.5n - R$$

Many people find that making a formula is quite difficult; in this situation it can be helpful to consider a numerical version first. In the problem above, for example, if 20 pairs are sold and the rent is £10, then the gain is given by £$(1.5 \times 20 - 10)$.

Exercise 7d

1. A club has F full-time members and P part-time members. Give a formula for the total number, T, of members.

2. Grit and salt are mixed for salting icy roads. If x tonnes of grit are mixed with y tonnes of salt, to give a total mass, m tonnes, of the mixture, write down a formula for m.

3. Write down a formula for A where $A\,\text{m}^2$ is the area of a square of side a m.

4. Write down a formula for d where d km is the distance travelled by a car moving at a steady speed of s km/h for t hours.

5. The lengths of the sides of a triangle are a cm, b cm and c cm. Write down a formula for p where p cm is the perimeter of the triangle.

6. A greengrocer starts the day with a stock of S boxes of strawberries. During the day he sells T boxes and R boxes are wasted and thrown away. Give a formula for the number of boxes, N, left at the end of the day.

7. Here are the instructions for roasting a chicken.
Roast at a high oven setting for 35 minutes per pound plus 30 minutes.
Give a formula for T where T minutes is the cooking time for a chicken weighing p lbs.

8. Tins of fruit, weighing p grams each, are packed into boxes. If an empty box weighs x grams, find a formula for W when W grams is the weight of a box containing N tins of fruit.

9. A roll of newsprint is L m long. Give a formula for N when N m is the length left on the roll after n pieces, each of length p m, have been cut off the roll.

10. A garage repair bill is made up of the cost of spare parts and labour charges at £20 an hour. Find a formula for T where £T is the bill for a repair needing x hours of labour and y pounds-worth of spare parts.

Find a formula for p where p metres is the perimeter of a rectangle whose length is x metres and whose width is y centimetres.

If p is a number of metres, then the formula for p must also give a number of metres, i.e. the width must be expressed as a number of metres.

$$\text{Width} = \frac{y}{100} \text{ m}$$

The perimeter of a rectangle is equal to twice its length plus twice its width,

i.e.
$$p = 2x + 2\left(\frac{y}{100}\right)$$

$$p = 2x + \frac{y}{50}$$

---

11. One tin of paint weighs W grams and n of these tins are packed into a carton that weighs c grams. Find a formula for K where K kg is the weight of the carton when full of tins.

12. A letter costs x pence to post. Find a formula for C when £C is the cost of posting n such letters.

13. The time, t hours, spent travelling to a job is made up of a train journey taking s hours followed by a walk taking v minutes. Give a formula for t.

14. Give a formula for A where A cm^2 is the area of a rectangle measuring l m by c cm.

15. There are L m of tape on a roll. The length of tape left on the roll after n pieces each of length l cm have been cut from it, is k m. Give a formula for k.

16. A common room contains s sofas that each seat two people and c chairs. Give a formula for N, the total number of people who can be seated.

17. Anne is n years old and she is p years older than Polly who is q years older than Wynne. Wynne is r years old. Give a formula for n.

The remaining questions in this exercise are more difficult. Do not attempt them unless you enjoy being challenged! Where letters are not allocated to variables, state clearly what your letters represent.

18. The terms in a sequence are such that the first term, u_1, is 1^2, the second term is 2^2, the third term is 3^2, and so on. Find a formula for u_n, the nth term of the series.

19. Small and large posters are sold from a market stall. The small posters are sold at £2 each and the large posters are sold at £5 each. Find a formula for the takings from a day's sales.

20. A firm employs casual workers and pays them daily. The number of hours worked each day varies but the rate of pay is a standard £3 per hour. Find a formula for the daily earnings of one casual worker.

21. The first four terms in a sequence are 1, 2, 4, 8. Find a formula for the nth term, u_n, in terms of the $(n-1)$th term, u_{n-1}, of the sequence.

USING FORMULAE

The formula for the area, A square units, of a rectangle is given by

$$A = lb$$

where l units is the length of the rectangle and b units is its width. This formula can be used to find the area of a particular rectangle by substituting numbers for the letters.

For example, for a rectangle 12 cm long and 8 cm wide, $l = 12$ and $b = 8$

Using $A = lb$ gives $A = 12 \times 8 = 96$

Therefore the area of this rectangle is 96 cm^2.

Note that, to use the formula for the area of a rectangle both the length and the width must be expressed in the same unit; if a rectangle is 2 m long and 25 cm wide, then 2 m must be expressed as 200 cm (or 25 cm as 0.25 m). Then we can use $l = 200$ and $b = 25$ which gives the area in cm^2 (or $l = 2$ and $b = 0.25$ giving the area in m^2).

Exercise 7e

In questions 1 to 5, give the numbers that are being substituted for the letters and end each question with a sentence giving the answer. 1(a) is done for you.

1. A length, l cm, of wire is bent into a triangle whose sides are a cm, b cm and c cm long, with the wire along the a cm side doubled.

The formula for l is $l = 2a + b + c$.

Use this formula to find the length of wire used to make each triangle.

(a)

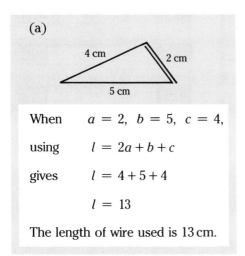

When $a = 2$, $b = 5$, $c = 4$,

using $l = 2a + b + c$

gives $l = 4 + 5 + 4$

          $l = 13$

The length of wire used is 13 cm.

(b)

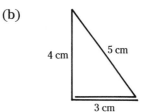

(c)

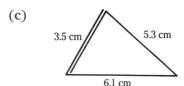

(d)

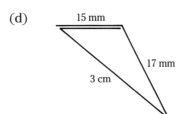

(e)

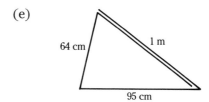

2. The formula for the distance, *d* units, covered when moving at a constant speed of *s* units per hour for *t* hours is $d = st$.

   Use the formula to find the distance moved by

   (a) a car travelling at 75 km/h for 2 hours

   (b) a train moving at 120 m.p.h. for 3 hours

   (c) a bus travelling at 30 km/h for 30 minutes

   (d) a rocket moving at 300 km/h for 10 seconds

   (e) a boat moving at 15 knots (nautical miles per hour) for 30 minutes

   (f) a bullet moving at 100 m/s for 2.83 seconds.

3. Most shops sell goods at a price which includes value added tax (VAT). The amount, £*T*, of this tax can be calculated from the selling price, £*P*, by using the formula

   $T = \dfrac{rP}{100 + r}$ where *r* % is the rate at which VAT is charged.

   Find, to the nearest penny, the VAT charged on

   (a) a calculator sold for £6 when the VAT rate is 18 %

   (b) a suit sold for £120 when the VAT rate is 12 %

   (c) a ream of paper sold for £6.50 when the VAT rate is 20 %

   (d) a packet of pencils sold for 75 p when the VAT rate is 17.5 %.

We do not need to know what a formula is for in order to find the number represented by one of the letters, provided that we are given the numerical values of the other letters.

Given that $v = u - at$, find *v* when $a = -2$, $t = 5$ and $u = 17$

$$v = u - at$$

when $a = -2,\ t = 5,\ u = 17,\quad v = 17 - (-2) \times 5$

$$= 17 - (-10)$$

$$= 17 + 10$$

$$= 27$$

Notice that the negative number has been put in brackets. This is a sensible precaution against mistakes.

---

4. If $S = n(a + b)$, find *S* when

   (a) $n = 6$, $a = 3$ and $b = 6$

   (b) $n = 4$, $a = -3$ and $b = 5$

   (c) $n = 2.4$, $a = 3.6$ and $b = -1.5$

5. If $a = b^2 + c^2$, find the value of *a* when

   (a) $b = 3$ and $c = 4$

   (b) $b = 1.7$ and $c = 2.4$

   (c) $b = -5$ and $c = -12$

6. If $v = \sqrt{(a - 3b)}$, find the value of *v* when

   (a) $a = 27$ and $b = 4$

   (b) $a = 0.18$ and $b = 0.05$

   (c) $a = -1.5$ and $b = -2.6$

7. Given that $f = \dfrac{1}{u} + \dfrac{1}{v}$, find the value of *f* when

   (a) $u = 16$ and $v = 25$

   (b) $u = 0.5$ and $v = 0.8$

   (c) $u = -1.25$ and $v = 0.97$

Sometimes we need to find the value of a letter on the right-hand side of a formula. This can be done by substituting numbers for the letters whose values are known and then solving the resulting equation.

If $v = u + at$, find the value of a when $v = 25$, $u = 11$ and $t = -7$

$$v = u + at$$

when $v = 25$, $u = 11$, $t = -7$, $$25 = 11 + a \times (-7)$$

$\Rightarrow$ $$25 = 11 - 7a$$

add $7a$ to both sides $$25 + 7a = 11$$

take 25 from both sides $$7a = -14$$

$\Rightarrow$ $$a = -2$$

---

8. Given that $y = mx + c$, find
   (a) x when $y = 3$, $m = 2$ and $c = 1$
   (b) x when $y = -3$, $m = 2$ and $c = -5$
   (c) c when $y = 4$, $m = 2$ and $x = 1$
   (d) m when $y = 2.5$, $x = 3$ and $c = 0.4$

9. If $a = \frac{1}{2}(b + c + d)$, find
   (a) b when $a = 3$, $c = 1$ and $d = \frac{1}{2}$
   (b) d when $a = 1.7$, $b = -4$ and $c = 12.5$

10. If $f = \frac{u}{2} + \frac{v}{3}$, find
    (a) u when $f = 5$ and $v = 9$
    (b) u when $f = 2$ and $v = -1$
    (c) v when $f = 0.5$ and $u = 2$
    (d) v when $f = -10$ and $u = \frac{1}{2}$

11. Given that $T = \dfrac{2w - 1.5}{s}$, find s when $T = 3.8$ and $w = 4.8$

In most practical situations we have to supply the formula ourselves.

The area of a rectangle is $36\,\text{cm}^2$ and its length is $9\,\text{cm}$. What is
(a) its breadth   (b) its perimeter?

9 cm   36 cm² b cm

(a) $A = l \times b$

$$36 = 9 \times b$$

$$\frac{36}{9} = b$$

The breadth of the rectangle is $4\,\text{cm}$.

(b) $p = 2l + 2b$

$$p = 18 + 8$$

The perimeter is $26\,\text{cm}$.

In each question find the unknown dimension. Remember that units must be consistent.

12.

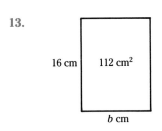

a cm   22.09 cm²

a cm

13.

16 cm   112 cm²

b cm

14.

11 mm

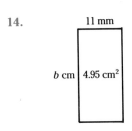

b cm   4.95 cm²

Calculate the values missing from the following table. Each question refers to a rectangle.

	Length	Width	Area	Perimeter
15.		2.6 cm	9.88 cm²	
16.	5.4 cm		648 mm²	
17.		18 mm		86.8 mm

Find the values missing from the following table. Each question refers to a cuboid.

	Length	Breadth	Height	Volume
18.	1 m	4 m		800 cm³
19.	6 cm		8 mm	5760 mm³
20.		35 mm	2 cm	28 cm³

21. Ball-point pens cost x p each. Find a formula for C where £C is the cost of n of these pens. Use the formula to find
   (a) the cost of 50 pens at 25 p each
   (b) the number of pens bought at 30 p each if the total cost is £12.

22. The total charge, £C, for domestic gas bills is made up of a standing charge, £S, and a charge of p pence for each kilowatt hour (kWh) used. Find a formula for C when n kWh are used. Use the formula to find
   (a) the bill when the standing charge is £15.60 and 250 kWh are used at 18.5 p per kWh
   (b) the number of kWh used when the bill is £120, the standing charge is £20 and the cost of each kWh is 2 p.

23. A teacher brings p pieces of paper to a class and gives q pieces to each of the n pupils. There are r pieces over. Give a formula for p in terms of n, q and r.

CHANGING THE SUBJECT OF A FORMULA

The formula for finding the VAT, £T, due on a telephone bill is given by

$$T = \frac{Sr}{100}$$

where £S is the total bill excluding VAT and r% is the rate at which VAT is charged.

This is a formula for finding T, so T is called the *subject of the formula*.

Now suppose we want a formula to find the value of r; this means that we want a formula in the form $r = \ldots$, i.e. a formula in which r is the subject.

We can derive this from $T = \dfrac{Sr}{100}$ by thinking of it as an equation to solve for values of r,

i.e. $$T = \frac{Sr}{100}$$

Multiply both sides by 100 $100T = Sr$

Divide both sides by S $\dfrac{100T}{S} = r$

i.e. $$r = \frac{100T}{S}$$

This process is called *changing the subject of a formula*.

Since changing the subject of a formula involves 'solving' the formula for the required letter, the methods used for solving linear equations apply, i.e. get rid of fractions and brackets; collect the terms containing the required letter on one side; collect all other terms on the other side; divide both sides by the number in front of the required letter.

Exercise 7f

Make a the subject of the formula $s = \frac{1}{2}(a+b+c)$

To make a the subject of the formula, we 'solve' the formula for a.

$$s = \tfrac{1}{2}(a+b+c)$$

Multiply both sides by 2 $2s = a+b+c$

Take c from both sides $2s - c = a+b$

Take b from both sides $2s - c - b = a$

i.e. $a = 2s - c - b$

1. Make the letter in the bracket the subject of the formula.

    (a) $c = x+y$ (x)

    (b) $V = s-t$ (s)

    (c) $C = rT$ (T)

    (d) $r = t+u$ (u)

    (e) $p = \dfrac{x}{y}$ (x)

2. Make the letter in the bracket the subject of the formula.

    (a) $s = a+2b$ (a)

    (b) $b = p+q+r$ (p)

    (c) $v = u+rt$ (u)

    (d) $L = \dfrac{m}{n}$ (m)

3. Change the subject of the formula to the letter in the bracket.

   (a) $d = y - x$ (x)

   (b) $S = 2t - d$ (t)

   (c) $b = \frac{1}{2}(a + c)$ (a)

   (d) $v = u - 3t$ (t)

   (e) $x = \dfrac{3y}{4}$ (y)

   (f) $A = P + \frac{1}{10}I$ (I)

   (g) $V = \dfrac{2R}{I}$ (R)

   (h) $p = q + \dfrac{r}{5}$ (r)

4. Rearrange the formula to make the letter in the bracket the subject.

   (a) $y = c - 2x$ (x)

   (b) $p = 2(q - r)$ (q)

   (c) $p = \frac{1}{4}(s + t)$ (t)

   (d) $C = 2\pi r$ (r)

   (e) $ab - d = c$ (a)

   (f) $c = a(x + b)$ (x)

   (g) $R = 3(P + Q)$ (P)

   (h) $I = \dfrac{PRT}{100}$ (R)

5. (a) Find a formula for the sum, S, of the three consecutive whole numbers n, $n + 1$, $n + 2$.

   (b) Change the subject of the formula found in (a) to give a formula for n, the first of three consecutive whole numbers whose sum is S.

   (c) Find the first of three consecutive whole numbers whose sum is 336.

6. (a) Find a formula for the cost, £C, of taking n children by coach to a swimming pool when the cost of the coach hire is £P and the entry charge is £S for each child.

   (b) Change the subject of the formula found in (a) to give a formula for the number of children.

   (c) Find the number of children that can be taken to the swimming pool for a total cost of £108 when the cost of coach hire is £60 and the entry charge is £1.20 per child.

7. (a) A dealer bought x pens for £y and sold them all for z pence each. His profit was £P. Give a formula for P in terms of x, y and z.

   (b) Make x the subject of the formula.

   (c) Make y the subject of the formula.

Investigation

Test for Divisibility by Three

It is known that if the sum of the digits in a number is divisible by three, then the number itself is also divisible by three. Why does this test work ?

Start with any two-digit number; let the tens digit be a and the units digit be b. The number can then be written as $10a + b$.

What you have to show is that if $a + b$ is a multiple of three, then $10a + b$ is also a multiple of three.

If you can argue successfully that the test works for any two-digit number, try extending your argument to a three-digit number and to a four-digit number.

Now try a similar argument to show why the test for divisibility by nine works.

Self-Assessment 7

1. Simplify $6x - 2(y - 5x)$

2. Solve the equation $4 - (x + 2) = 7$

3. Simplify $\dfrac{2x}{15} \div \dfrac{x}{5}$

4. Illustrate on a number line the values of x for which $3x - 7 < 8$

5. The length of a table is given as 2.56 m correct to three significant figures. If the length of the table is x m, write a double inequality satisfied by x and illustrate it on a number line.

6. Simplify

   (a) $(-2b) \times (-3b)$ (c) $x - x(x - 4)$

   (b) $6p \div 3p$

7. Find the range of values of x for which $x < 2 - x < x + 4$

8. Express $\dfrac{x - 1}{4} + \dfrac{2x + 3}{12}$ as a single fraction.

9. Simplify

   (a) $x^9 \div x^5$ (b) $(w^{-2})^2$

10. Find a formula for W where W kg is the total mass of ballast produced when c kg of sand is mixed with d kg of gravel.

11. Find A when $r = 2$ and $h = 5$ if $A = 3rh$

12. Find f when $v = -1$ and $u = 2$ given that $f = \dfrac{1}{u} + \dfrac{1}{v}$

13. Make p the subject of the formula $r = a(p + q)$

14. The cost of one floppy disc is d pence.

    (a) Find a formula for P if $£P$ is the cost of n of these floppy discs.

    (b) Use your formula to derive a formula for d in terms of P and n.

15. The perimeter of a rectangle is 250 cm, but both the length and the width can vary. If the length of the rectangle is x cm, find a formula for the width, y cm, in terms of x. Hence find a formula for the area, A cm^2, in terms of x.

SOCIAL ARITHMETIC

PERSONAL FINANCE

We all require money to buy food and clothes, to pay the rent or the mortgage, and to settle our electricity or gas bills, etc. When we work, we can get paid in various ways.

Hourly Pay

Many people, such as production workers in a factory, get paid an hourly rate up to an agreed number of hours each week, i.e. their basic working week. Any extra hours are usually paid at a higher overtime rate. This rate may be 'time-and-a-half' or even 'double time', i.e. twice the basic rate.

Commission

Workers such as sales staff and representatives, may be paid a fairly low basic wage, plus a commission on every order they secure. The commission is usually a percentage of the value of the order.

Piece-work

Some workers are paid for the 'amount' of work they do. In a factory, for instance, a person's earnings can be based on the number of components made in a shift. This type of payment is called *piece-work*. Sometimes a worker's earnings are made up partly of a basic wage and partly of a piece-work payment.

Exercise 8a

Last week Sonia Morris worked 50 hours, 14 of which were overtime. If the basic hourly rate is £5 and overtime is paid at time-and-a-quarter, find her gross wage for the week.

Basic working week is $(50 - 14)$ hours $= 36$ hours

Payment for 36 hours at £5 per hour $= £36 \times 5$

$$= £180$$

Overtime rate at time-and-a-quarter is £5 $\times 1.25 = £6.25$

Payment for 14 hours overtime at £6.25 per hour is $14 \times £6.25 = £87.50$

Gross wage for the week is £180 + £87.50

$$= £267.50$$

1. The hourly rate at ABC Electronics for a 38-hour week is £4. Overtime is paid at time-and-a-half.

   (a) One week Sally works 42 hours. Calculate her gross pay.

   (b) In the same week Ian works 45 hours. Find his gross wage.

   (c) The following week Sally works 49 hours. Find her gross wage for this week. How much more does she earn this week than last week?

   (d) Six months later Ian's hourly rate was increased to £4.80. How much would he earn in a week when he worked 48 hours?

2. Jim and George Tranter work in different factories. Jim is paid £5.20 per hour for a basic working week of 35 hours and receives time-and-a-half for any overtime.

   George is paid £5.50 per hour for a basic working week of 39 hours and receives double-time for any overtime.

   Find

   (a) Jim's basic weekly wage

   (b) Jim's overtime rate per hour

   (c) George's basic weekly wage

   (d) George's overtime rate per hour

   (e) which receives the greater gross pay in a week when they both work for 43 hours.

3. Amer Hussein's time-sheet for a week is shown below.

Name Amer Hussein				
Works No. 63				
Week No. 23				
Day	AM		PM	
	in	out	in	out
Monday	8.00	12.00	12.59	4.32
Tuesday	8.02	12.01	1.00	4.30
Wednesday	8.00	12.03	1.00	4.30
Thursday	7.58	12.00	1.15	4.31
Friday	8.00	12.01	1.00	3.32

Use this time-sheet to answer the following questions.

   (a) What time is 'clocking-on' time?

   (b) What time does work normally end for the day?

   (c) How long is the lunch break?

   (d) How long should Amer work   (i) each morning   (ii) each afternoon?

   (e) On which day of the week did Amer have an extended lunch break?

   (f) How long is the basic working week if the time-sheet shows that Amer worked the required time on the Friday?

   (g) Calculate his gross wage when he works a full week if the basic hourly rate is £4.80.

In addition to a basic weekly wage of £45, Eleanor Brett receives a commission of 1% for selling second-hand motor cars. Calculate her gross wage for a week when she sells cars to the value of £18 000.

Basic wage is £45

Commission on £18 000 at 1% is $\dfrac{1}{100} \times £18\,000$

$\qquad\qquad\qquad\qquad = £180$

Gross wage for the week   is £45 + £180

$\qquad\qquad\qquad\qquad = £225$

---

4. Calculate the commission earned on sales of

   (a) £8000 at 5%   (b) £6500 at 2%   (c) £26 000 at $1\frac{1}{2}$%

5. Clive Hannah receives a basic wage of £80 per week and receives a commission of $2\frac{1}{2}$% on all sales over £500. Find his income for a week when he sells goods to the value of £7700.

6. Anne Lewis is paid a basic wage of £60 per week plus a commission of $1\frac{1}{2}$% on her sales over £2000. Find her income for a week when she sells goods to the value of £15 300.

7. Steve Cross sells double glazing. Apart from a basic wage of £40 he is paid commission at the following rates

Up to £1000	none
From £1001 to £5000	5%
Above £5000	3%

Calculate his income in a week when he sells double glazing to a value of £15 500.

Vicki Jones receives a guaranteed weekly wage of £135 plus a bonus of 20 p for every component she completes each day after the first 25. During a particular week the numbers of components she completes are:

Monday 56, Tuesday 47, Wednesday 58, Thursday 46, Friday 52.

Calculate her gross wage for the week.

Guaranteed weekly wage is £135

Bonus payments are paid on (31 + 22 + 33 + 21 + 27), i.e. 134 components

Bonus payment is 134×20 p

$$= £26.80$$

Gross wage for the week is   £135 + £26.80

$$= £161.80$$

---

8. The table shows the number of 24-hour electric plug timers produced by four production workers each day for a week.

	Mon	Tues	Wed	Thurs	Fri
Mrs Adcroft	35	38	34	39	42
Mr Barnard	37	40	37	44	–
Ms Curtis	34	40	42	38	38
Mr Davitt	41	43	41	48	47

The rate of payment is 50 p for each plug up to 20 per day and 65 p for each plug above 20 per day.

(a) How many plugs does each person produce in the week?

(b) For each person find how many plugs are paid for at
    (i) 50 p each
    (ii) 65 p each.

(c) Find each person's income for the week.

(d) On which day of the week does this group of workers produce the greatest number of plugs?

9. Colin Perry wants to earn money to buy a video-recorder costing £216 by washing cars at 80 p a time.

(a) How many cars must he wash?

(b) How many days would it take if he washes 18 cars each day?

10. A team of twelve factory workers assemble front brakes for Volvo cars. For each unit they produce in a day, up to 150 units, the team receives a bonus payment of 40 p; above this figure they receive 45 p. Find the average bonus payment per worker for a week in which the number of units produced is

Mon	Tues	Wed	Thurs	Fri
330	375	354	387	352

11. In a second week, the factory workers described in question 10 assemble over 150 units a day. The bonus payment for the week per worker is £56.95.
How many units do they assemble during the week?

GROSS AND NET WAGES

The amount you earn in a week or a month is called your *gross wage*. Your 'take-home' pay is usually considerably less than this since there can be deductions for income tax, National Insurance contributions (NIC), pension contributions, etc. When all the agreed deductions have been subtracted from your gross wage, what remains is called your *net wage* or *take-home pay*.

National Insurance contributions and income tax, together with the employee's pension contribution, make up the greater part of any deductions (see Chapter 6).

Exercise 8b

Edna Barker earns £190 per week. She pays £14.04 in National Insurance contributions, £11.40 towards her pension fund and her income tax amounts to £25.95. Calculate her take-home pay.

$$\text{Total deductions} = £14.04 + £11.40 + £25.95$$

$$= £51.39$$

$$\text{Net pay} = \text{gross pay} - \text{deductions}$$

$$= £190 - £51.39$$

$$= £138.61$$

Copy and complete the following table, which gives details of the pay earned by several employees of a large company during one week last March.

	Employee	Gross pay	NIC	Income tax	Pension fund	Net pay
1.	Munn	£125	£7.56	£11.00	£7.50	
2.	Squires	£235	£18.43	£38.78		£165.69
3.	Furnell	£183		£24.44	£10.98	£134.24
4.	Waters	£242	£19.78		£14.52	£169.10

5. Sheila Kelly earns £240 per week. She pays 8% National Insurance contributions and 6% for her pension, both calculated on her gross wage. If income tax amounts to £38.12, calculate her net wage.

ELECTRICITY, GAS AND TELEPHONE BILLS

The total cost for all three types of bill is found by adding a fixed or standing charge to the cost of the actual number of units used.

Electricity Bills

The unit of electricity is the kilowatt hour (kWh). It is the amount of electricity used in 1 hour by an appliance with a rating of 1 kilowatt. A 3 kW electric fire would use 1 unit in 20 minutes, whereas a 100 W bulb (1 kW = 1000 W) would burn for 10 hours on the same amount of electricity. The number of units used in any given quarter (of the year) is the difference between the readings at the end and beginning of that quarter.

Gas Bills

Units

The amount of gas used is measured by volume and recorded by a meter in units, each unit being 100 cubic feet. This figure is converted into cubic metres by multiplying by 2.83. Since equal volumes of gas can have different amounts of useful heat, the Gas Boards charge for their gas in the units of heat used throughout the European Community, namely kilowatt hours (kWh). The volume of gas recorded by the meter is converted into kilowatt hours using the formula

$$\text{number of kilowatt hours} = \frac{\text{number of cubic metres} \times \text{calorific value}}{3.6}$$

Tariffs

Various quarterly tariffs are available, each of them consisting of a fixed or standing charge together with a charge for each therm used.

Telephone Bills

The cost of a telephone call depends on three factors:
  (i) the distance between the caller and the person being called,
 (ii) the time of day and/or the day of the week on which the call is being made,
(iii) the length of the call.

These three factors are put together in various ways to give metered units of time, each unit being charged at a fixed rate.

There is a rental charge each quarter, which varies with the system and apparatus being hired, in addition to the charge for the metered units. Value added tax (VAT) is also payable on telephone bills.

Exercise 8c

The electricity meter readings for the Parry household at the beginning and end of the last quarter were 37 459 and 39 007. If electricity costs 7.43 p per unit and there is a standing charge of £11.75, find the cost of electricity for the quarter.

Number of units used is $39\,007 - 37\,459 = 1548$

Cost of 1548 units at 7.43 p per unit is 1548×7.43 p

$$= 11\,501.64\,p$$

$$= £115.02 \text{ (to the nearest penny)}$$

$$\text{Total cost} = \text{standing charge} + £115.02$$

$$= £11.75 + £115.02$$

$$= £126.77$$

Find the quarterly electricity bill for each of the following households.

	Name	Meter reading		Number of units used	Standing charge	Cost per unit
		At beginning of quarter	At end of quarter			
1.	Mr Kilner	22 926	23 792		£13.45	7.66 p
2.	Mrs Dix	35 447	36 413		£18.21	9.88 p
3.	Mr Shaw	18 937	19 784		£17.75	11.5 p

4. (a) Complete the following table which refers to meter readings in the Rehman household for a year.

Date	Meter reading	Number of units used in the specified quarter
9 February	38 294	
8 May		First: 847
10 August		Second: 346
9 November	39 689	Third:
10 February		Fourth: 1015

(b) Find the cost of electricity for the first quarter if the standing charge is £14.66 and electricity costs 9.66 p per unit.

(c) Find the cost of electricity for the third quarter if the standing charge is £13.88 and electricity costs 8.73 p per unit.

(d) Find the total cost of electricity for the year if the standing charge is £15.94 per quarter and the cost of electricity throughout the year is kept fixed at 9.34 p per unit.

Calculate the quarterly gas bill for each of the following households.

Name	Number of kWh used	Standing charge	Cost of gas per kWh
5. Mr Angel	4373	£ 9.40	1.5p
6. Mrs White	9622	£10.55	1.8p
7. Ms Chant	6656	£14.73	1.74p
8. Mr Deats	13 712	£17.21	1.566p

Mrs Khan uses on average 8750 kWh each quarter (91 days). She can pay for this gas using one of two tariffs:

(a) a Credit Tariff, which charges 1.566 p per kWh plus a standing charge of 10.3 p per day

(b) the Domestic Prepayment Tariff, which charges 2.02 p per kWh for the first 1500 kilowatt hours
plus 1.566 p per kWh for additional kilowatt hours
plus a standing charge of £6
Which method of payment should she use ?

(a) If she uses the Credit Tariff

Cost of 8750 kWh at 1.566 p per kWh is 8750×1.566 p

$$= £137.03$$

Standing charge is $£91 \times 10.3$ p

$$= £9.37$$

Total cost $= £146.40$

(b) If she uses the Domestic Prepayment Tariff

Cost of the first 1500 kWh at 2.02 p per kWh is 1500×2.02 p

$$= £30.30$$

Cost of remaining 7250 kWh at 1.566 p per kWh is

$$7250 \times 1.566 \text{ p}$$

$$= £113.54$$

Total cost $= £149.84$

Method (a) costs £3.44 less than method (b). It would therefore be cheaper to pay using the Credit Tariff.

For each of the following customers calculate which tariff is the cheaper and by how much:

		Credit Tariff		Domestic Prepayment Tariff		
Name	Number of kWh used	Standing charge	Cost per kWh	Standing charge	Price per kWh for initial kWh	Price per kWh for further kWh
9. Eyles	12 000	£14	1.58p	£5	1.8p for first 1500	1.59p
10. Yates	15 000	£16	1.70p	£6	2.3p for first 1500	1.73p
11. Fish	11 250	£15	1.82p	£7	2.5p for first 1200	1.82p

John Bateley's telephone account last quarter showed that he had used 1212 metered units. If the rental charge was £21.93, each unit cost 4.85p and the rate of VAT was $17\frac{1}{2}$%, find the total amount due in payment for his telephone account for the quarter.

Cost of 1212 units at 4.85p per unit is 1212×4.85

$$= £58.78 \qquad \text{(to the nearest penny)}$$

Rental charge is £21.93

$$\text{Total (exclusive of VAT)} = £80.71$$

$$\text{VAT at } 17\tfrac{1}{2}\% = £80.71 \times 0.175$$

$$= £14.12$$

$$\text{Total payable} = £94.83$$

Find the quarterly telephone bill for each of the following households.

	Name	Number of units used	Rental charge	Cost per unit	Rate of VAT
12.	Mrs Higgs	495	£18.24	4.8p	17.5%
13.	Ms Hodges	586	£21.16	4.9p	17.5%
14.	Mr Hussain	1392	£28.56	5.2p	17.5%
15.	Miss Bayer	955	£19.12	4.75p	18%
16.	Mr Sweet	1864	£34.76	4.66p	20%

IMPERIAL UNITS

As Imperial units are still part of our everyday vocabulary it is sensible to be familiar with those in common use. These are given below.

Units of length: the inch (in), the foot (ft), the yard (yd), the furlong and the mile

$$1\,\text{ft} = 12\text{ inches}$$

1 inch

$$1\,\text{yd} = 3\,\text{ft}$$

$$1\text{ furlong} = 220\,\text{yd}$$

$$1\text{ mile} = 1760\,\text{yd}$$

Units of area: the square yard, the acre, the square mile (occasionally the square inch and square foot)

Units of volume: cubic feet and cubic yards

Units of capacity: pints and gallons

$$1\text{ gallon} = 8\text{ pints}$$

Units of mass: the ounce (oz), the pound (lb), and the ton; occasionally the stone and the hundredweight (cwt)

$$1\,\text{lb} = 16\,\text{oz}$$

$$1\text{ stone} = 14\,\text{lb}$$

$$1\text{ cwt} = 112\,\text{lb}$$

$$1\text{ ton} = 2240\,\text{lb}$$

Exercise 8d

Express the given quantity in terms of the unit in brackets.

1. 4 ft   (in)

2. $\frac{1}{2}$ lb   (oz)

3. 36 in   (ft)

4. 15 ft   (yd)

5. $6\frac{1}{2}$ stones   (lb)

6. $2\frac{1}{2}$ gallons   (pints)

7. 20 oz   (lb)

8. 12 pints   (gallons)

9. $\frac{1}{6}$ yd   (in)

10. 2 sq ft   (sq in)

11. $\frac{3}{4}$ lb   (oz)

12. 5280 yd   (miles)

13. A dripping tap fills a 1 pint milk bottle in 3 minutes. How many gallons of water drip from the tap in 24 hours ?

14. A rectangular room is 12 ft wide and 15 ft long. What is the floor area in square yards ?

15. A recipe asks for $\frac{1}{2}$ gill of cream. One pint is 20 fluid ounces and 1 gill is $\frac{1}{4}$ pint. How many fluid ounces of cream are required ?

16. One acre is 4840 sq yd. A farmer buys a square field of 40 acres. What is the perimeter of the field ?

EQUIVALENCE BETWEEN METRIC AND IMPERIAL UNITS

In supermarkets it is not unusual to find apples, say, in priced prepacked bags of 500 g or 1 kg but to find loose apples sold by the pound.

This mixture of imperial and metric units in everyday use means that we should all know rough equivalents for corresponding units.

Length: 8 km ≈ 5 miles

                1 metre ≈ 39 inches   (1 m is roughly 1 yd)

                 10 cm ≈ 4 inches

Area: 1 hectare ≈ 2.5 acres

Mass: ·   1 tonne ≈ 1 ton   (1 tonne is slightly less than 1 ton)

                1 kg ≈ 2.2 lb

                100 g ≈ 3.5 oz   (100 g is roughly a quarter of a lb)

Capacity: 1 litre ≈ 1.75 pints

                1 gallon ≈ 4.5 litres

Exercise 8e

The use of rough equivalents cannot give exact answers, so bear this in mind when giving answers.

The cost of posting a first class letter is 26 p for a letter weighing not over 60 g and 38 p for a letter weighing not over 100 g. A letter weighs 1.5 oz on my kitchen scales. What is the value of the stamps I should put on it?

$$3.5\,oz \approx 100\,g$$

$$1\,oz \approx \frac{100}{3.5}\,g$$

so $$1.5\,oz \approx \frac{100 \times 1.5}{3.5}\,g$$

$$= 43\,g \qquad (\text{to the nearest g})$$

A 26 p stamp is enough.

1. The petrol tank on my car holds 12 gallons. How many litres is this?

2. After an excise duty increase, the price of petrol is quoted on the radio as £2.10 a gallon. How much is this per litre?

3. An old dressmaking pattern states that the seam allowance is $\frac{5}{8}$ inch. How many millimetres is this?

4. An old knitting pattern requires twenty 1 oz balls of double knitting yarn. How many 50 g balls are needed to make up this pattern?

5. A farm is advertised for sale as 140 hectares. How many acres is this?

6. Floorboards are sold in units of 30 cm. (30 cm is sometimes called a metric foot!) What length of floorboard should be bought to replace one that is 12 ft long?

7. A recipe for jam requires 20 lb of sugar. How many 1 kg bags of sugar are needed?

8. A particular brand of carpet is priced at £ 8.75 per square yard in a local shop and at £ 9.60 per m^2 in a department store. Which is cheaper?

RATES OF CONSUMPTION

The rate at which quantities are consumed is usually expressed as an amount of one quantity with respect to one unit of another.

Speed is the rate at which a moving object covers distance and it is given as the distance covered in one unit of time, e.g. kilometres per hour (km/h).

Fuel consumption is the rate at which fuel is used. For vehicles it is usually expressed as distance covered on one unit quantity of fuel, e.g. miles per gallon (m.p.g.), kilometres per litre (km/ℓ). It is also often given as litres per 100 km.

When vast quantities of fuel are used the consumption is given as the fuel used in covering a unit of distance or time, e.g. gallons per mile or litres per second.

Coverage of paint, fertilizer, spray, etc., describes how the liquid covers (or should cover) area, so it is expressed in quantity of liquid per unit of area; for example, litres per square metre (ℓ/m^2) or if the quantity used is small, square metres per litre.

Pressure describes the force per unit area when one substance is pressing on another, e.g. air in a car tyre pressing on the inside of the tyre. It can be measured in N/m^2 or lb/in^2.

To change from, say, m.p.g. to km/ℓ, we need to think first about changing one unit, and then about changing the other; m.p.g. is equivalent to $\dfrac{\text{miles}}{\text{gallons}}$ so we *multiply* by the number of kilometres in a mile and *divide* by the number of litres in a gallon.

Exercise 8f

Express a speed of 60 m.p.h. in m/s using 8 km ≈ 5 miles.

$$60 \text{ m.p.h.} = \frac{60 \times 8}{5} \text{ km/h}$$

$$= \frac{60 \times 8 \times 1000}{5} \text{ m/h}$$

$$= \frac{60 \times 8 \times 1000}{5 \times 60 \times 60} \text{ m/s}$$

$$= \frac{80}{3} \text{ m/s} = 26.7 \text{ m/s} \quad (3 \text{ s.f.})$$

i.e. 60 m.p.h. ≈ 27 m/s.

In questions 1 to 6 give answers correct to 3 s.f. when possible. When that degree of accuracy is not possible, give to 2 s.f.

1. Express 40 km/h in m.p.h.

2. Express 70 m.p.h. in km/h.

3. Express 500 litres/second in litres/hour.

4. Express 50 m.p.g. in kilometres/litre.

5. Express 50 m²/litre in sq ft/gallon.

6. Express 4 kg/cm² in lb/sq in.

In questions 7 to 11 use your own judgement, with regard to the context of the question, as to the accuracy required for the answer.

7. The average petrol consumption of a car is 35 m.p.g. The driver puts 25 litres of petrol into the tank. How far can the car be expected to travel ?

8. A bottle of liquid insecticide contains 500 mℓ. The instructions state that it should be diluted in the ratio 2.5 mℓ of insecticide to 2 litres of water and the diluted mixture applied at the rate of 250 mℓ/m². What area will the contents of the bottle treat ?

9. A car manual states that the front tyre pressures should be 3.5 kg/cm², and the pressure gauge at the local garage measures pressure in lb/sq in. What should the gauge read to give the correct pressure ?

10. A petrol pump can deliver petrol at the rate of $\frac{1}{2}$ litre/second. How long does it take to fill a tank that holds 20 gallons ?

11. A firm uses packaging cartons that are cubes of side 2 ft. The full cartons are lifted into containers at the rate of 5 cartons per minute. How long does it take to fill a container measuring 3.5 m by 5 m by 10 m ?

12. To cover an area of 30 m², 2.5 litres of paint are needed.
    Give the coverage in
    (a) ℓ/m²
    (b) litres per square yard.

13. The density of gold is given as 19.3 g/cm³. Using 1 oz = 28.3 g and 1 inch = 2.54 cm, find the density of gold in oz/in³.

TIME AND TIMETABLES

There are two systems for giving the time of day.

One system uses two periods of twelve hours. The first starts at midnight and continues to noon; times within this period are referred to as 'a.m.'. The second period goes from noon to midnight and times are referred to as 'p.m.'.

The other system has one period of twenty-four hours, starting at midnight and continuing through to the next midnight.

Thus 1 hour after noon is 1 p.m. in the first system and 1300 hours (read as 'thirteen hundred hours') or 13.00 in the second system. All times given in the second system have four digits, e.g. 4 a.m. is given as 0400 hours.

Most clocks and watches with dials use the a.m./p.m. system whereas many digital clocks and watches, and timetables, use the 24-hour system.

Exercise 8g

1. Give the equivalent times on a 24-hour clock.

   (a) 8.30 a.m.   (c) 5.42 a.m.

   (b) 8.30 p.m.   (d) 2.36 p.m.

2. Give the equivalent time on a 12-hour clock, using a.m. or p.m.

   (a) 03.00   (c) 08.51

   (b) 19.42   (d) 22.43

Find the elapsed time between 9.20 a.m. and 3.52 p.m.

Method 1
Elapsed time from 9.20 a.m. to noon is

$$12 h - 9 h\ 20 min = 2 h\ 40 min$$

Elapsed time from noon to 3.52 p.m. is 3 h 52 min.

∴ elapsed time from 9.20 a.m. to 3.52 p.m. is

$$2 h\ 40 min + 3 h\ 52 min = 6 h\ 32 min$$

Method 2
9.20 a.m. = 09.20   and   3.52 p.m. = 15.52
Elapsed time is from 09.20 to 15.52

i.e.   6 h 32 min

(Remember that 15.52 means 15 hours 52 minutes.)

---

3. Find the elapsed time between

   (a) 03.20 and 15.08 hours on the same day

   (b) 11.30 a.m. and 5.42 p.m. on the same day

   (c) 20.35 and 09.40 on the next day

   (d) 10.40 a.m. and 7.52 a.m. on the next day.

Here is part of a timetable for trains from Paddington to Bristol and Weston-super-Mare.

Station		1	2	3	4	5	6	7	8	9	10	11
Paddington*	d	00 50	06 35	06 55	07 25	07 35	08 00	08 05	08 35	09 00	09 05	09 35
Slough	d	—	06 48	07 08	07 38	07 48	—	—	08 48	—	—	09 48
Reading C*	d	—	07 03	07 23	07 53	08 03	08 24	08 30	09 03	09 24	09 30	10 03
Didcot	d	—	07 17	07 34	08 06	08 16	—	—	09 16	—	—	10 16
Swindon	a	02 17	07 37	07 54	08 27	08 37	—	—	09 37	—	—	10 37
Chippenham	a	—	07 51	—	08 40	08 50	—	—	09 50	—	—	—
Bath Spa	a	—	08 09	—	08 52	09 02	—	09 16	10 02	—	10 16	—
Bristol Parkway	a	—	—	08 21	—	—	09 12	—	—	10 12	—	11 01
Bristol Temple Meads	a	—	08 25	—	09 07	09 17	—	09 31	10 17	—	10 31	—
Nailsea & Backwell	a	—	—	—	09 25	—	—	10 11	—	—	—	—
Yatton	a	—	—	—	09 32	—	—	10 18	—	—	—	—
Weston-super-Mare	a	—	—	—	09 41	—	—	10 32	10 38	—	11 12	—

Station		1	2	3	4	5	6	7	8	9	10	11	12
Paddington*	d	10 05	10 35	11 00	11 05	11 35	12 05	12 35	13 00	13 05	13 35	13 35	14 00
Slough	d	—	10 48	—	—	11 48	—	12 25	—	—	13 48	13 48	—
Reading C*	d	—	11 03	11 24	11 30	12 03	—	—	13 24	13 30	14 03	14 03	—
Didcot	d	—	11 16	—	—	12 16	—	—	—	—	14 16	14 16	—
Swindon	a	10 55	11 37	—	—	12 37	12 55	—	14 00	—	14 37	14 37	14 49
Chippenham	a	—	11 50	—	—	—	13 08	—	—	—	14 50	—	—
Bath Spa	a	11 17	12 02	—	12 16	—	13 20	—	14 22	—	15 02	—	—
Bristol Parkway	a	—	—	12 12	—	13 01	—	14 12	—	—	—	—	15 14
Bristol Temple Meads	a	11 32	12 17	—	12 31	—	13 35	—	14 37	—	15 17	—	—
Nailsea & Backwell	a	12 11	—	—	13 21	—	14 21	—	15 22	—	16 26	—	—
Yatton	a	12 18	—	—	13 28	—	14 28	—	15 29	—	16 33	—	—
Weston-super-Mare	a	12 34	12 38	—	13 42	—	14 42	—	15 42	—	16 45	—	—

Heavy type indicates through trains and light type indicates connecting trains.

If I catch the 11.05 from Paddington, to go to Weston-super-Mare, do I have to change trains, and if so where? How long should the journey take? (Use the timetable above.)

The 11.05 is in heavy type to Bristol Temple Meads and in light type beyond there, so I have to change trains at Bristol Temple Meads.

Arrival time in Weston-super-Mare is 13.42, so the journey should take

13 h 42 min − 11 h 5 min

i.e.   2 h 37 min

Use the timetable above to answer questions 4 to 9.

4. What is the earliest through train from Paddington to Weston-super-Mare, and how long does it take?

5. Mrs Angelon has an appointment in Swindon at 2.00 p.m. She wants to travel by train from Slough and has to arrive at Swindon at least 15 minutes before 2.00 p.m. What is the time of the latest train she can catch? How long will she have in Swindon before her appointment if the train is on time?

6. Which train from Paddington gives the quickest journey to Weston-super-Mare? Is this a through train?

7. How long do the fastest trains take to go from Paddington to Bristol Temple Meads?

8. How long do the fastest trains take to go from Paddington to Bristol Parkway?

9. Mr Black wanted to go to Bath Spa but mistakenly caught the 09.00 from Paddington instead of the 09.05.

   (a) If Mr Black realises his mistake soon enough he can change trains and still arrive in Bath Spa when he originally intended. Where does he have to make the change and how long should he have to wait there to catch the correct train?

   (b) If Mr Black does not realise that he is on the wrong train soon enough to make the change in (a), where does he next have the opportunity to get off the train?

POSTAGE AND OTHER STEP FUNCTIONS

The table below gives postal rates for inland letters.

Weight not over	First class	Second class	Weight not over	First class	Second class
60 g	26 p	20 p	500 g	£ 1.25	98 p
100 g	38 p	29 p	600 g	£ 1.55	£ 1.20
150 g	47 p	36 p	700 g	£ 1.90	£ 1.40
200 g	57 p	43 p	750 g	£ 2.05	£ 1.45
250 g	67 p	52 p	800 g	£ 2.15	Not
300 g	77 p	61 p	900 g	£ 2.35	admissible
350 g	88 p	70 p	1000 g	£ 2.50	over
400 g	£ 1.00	79 p	Each extra 250 g or		750 g
450 g	£ 1.13	89 p	part thereof 65 p		

Considering just first class post, we see that the cost goes up in steps, depending on the weight. For example, a letter weighing up to 60 g costs 26 p, but when the weight exceeds 60 g the cost jumps to 38 p, and so on.

This graph, showing cost against weight, illustrates the 'step' nature of the postal rates.

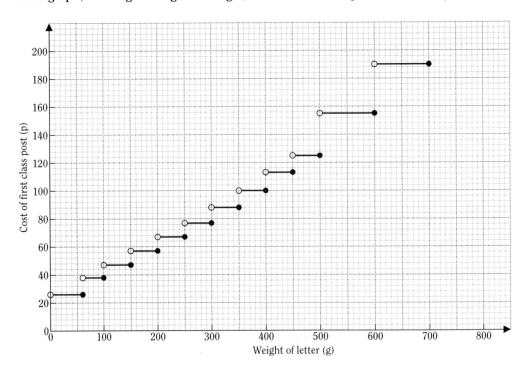

Notice that the 'open' circle at the left-hand end of each line indicates that the point is not included. The closed circle at the right-hand end of each line indicates that the point is included. Many of the charges for services have this 'step' structure. Other examples are parking charges and telephone charges.

Exercise 8h

Use the table for postal rates on the opposite page to find the cost of sending a packet weighing 1.26 kg by

(a) first class letter post   (b) second class letter post.

(a) The cost of the first 1 kg (1000 g) is £2.50
The cost of the remaining 0.26 kg or 260 g is £1.30
The total cost is £3.80

(b) Since the package weighs more than 750 g it cannot be sent by second class letter post.

Use the table on the opposite page to answer questions 1 to 5.

1. Find the cost of first class letter post for a package weighing
   (a) 280 g   (d) 1.44 kg
   (b) 102 g   (e) 4.2 kg
   (c) 396 g

2. Find the cost of second class letter post for a letter weighing
   (a) 75 g   (c) 745 g
   (b) 250 g   (d) 55 g

3. Find the total cost of sending five 80 g letters and three 540 g packages by first class letter post.

4. Find the total cost of sending twelve 72 g letters by first class letter post and six 645 g packages by second class letter post.

5. What is the maximum number of packages weighing 275 g that Nicky Woodman can send by first class letter post if the total bill must be less than £10 ?

6. Draw a graph to show the cost of second class post against weight, similar to that for first class post on the page opposite.

7. A multistorey car-park in a city centre has the following charge tariff:

up to 1 hour	80 p
up to 2 hours	120 p
up to 3 hours	165 p
up to 4 hours	220 p
up to 5 hours	340 p
up to 6 hours	480 p

   each additional hour or part thereof 140 p.

   How much does it cost to park for

   (a) $1\frac{1}{2}$ hours   (c) $4\frac{3}{4}$ hours

   (b) $2\frac{1}{4}$ hours   (d) 8 hours ?

8. Photocopies of particular pages are charged at the following rates:

Number of copies	Cost per copy
1–20	10 p
21–100	8 p
101 upwards	5 p

   (a) Find the total cost of 8 copies of one page and 48 copies of a second page.

   (b) Together with the copies in (a), how many copies of a third page can be made if the money spent is to be less than £7 ?

   (c) If 18 copies are required what is the cheapest way to do it ?

The table below gives the charge rates for inland dialled telephone calls using British Telecom. Calls are charged in whole numbers of seconds, e.g. if a local call of $3\frac{1}{2}$ minutes is made on a Tuesday evening the charge will be for 3.5 minutes at 1.7 pence per minute; i.e. $3.5 \times 1.7\,\text{p} = 5.95\,\text{p}$

	Daytime Mon to Fri 8 a.m. to 6 p.m.	Cheap rate All other times Mon to Fri	Weekends
Local calls	4 p/min	1.7 p/min	1 p/min
Regional calls Up to 35 miles	8.3 p/min	4 p/min	3.3 p/min
National calls	9.8 p/min	5.8 p/min	3.3 p/min
Calls to mobile telephones	£ 1.19 up to 3 minutes	79 p up to 3 minutes	79 p up to 3 minutes

9. Find the cost of a local telephone call lasting 18 minutes at

   (a) 10 a.m. on a Thursday morning

   (b) 7 p.m. on a Wednesday evening

   (c) 11 a.m. on a Sunday morning.

10. Find the cost of a call to another town 100 miles away lasting $4\frac{1}{2}$ minutes at

   (a) 1 p.m. on a Saturday   (b) 3 p.m. on a Monday   (c) 9 p.m. on a Friday

11. Find the cost of a mobile telephone call lasting 2 minutes at the Daytime rate.

12. How much more would it cost to make an 8 minute 22 second telephone call to London, which is 85 miles away, at 10 a.m. on a Tuesday than at 10 p.m. the same day?

INSURANCE

Although all property and people are at risk, relatively few suffer loss. Insurance works by spreading the cost of loss among all who are insured.

Some forms of insurance are legal requirements. For example, any driver using a car or motor cycle on a public road must, by law, be insured for third party risks. Third party risk covers damage caused to other people or their property. Other forms of insurance are sensible precautions against possible loss or damage.

The payment for insurance is called the *premium*. The premium may be given in a form such as £ 2 per £ 100 insured value, or the premium may be quoted as a total amount for a particular insurance. Premiums are usually payable yearly.

Some insurances give a discount if the insured person bears part of the risk. For example a householder may agree to pay the first £50 of any loss. This has the misleading name of 'an *excess*'.

Car insurances usually offer discounts for several consecutive years in which no claims have been made. This form of discount is called a *no claims bonus*.

Exercise 8i

The premium for insuring a building worth £86 000 is £4.30 per £1000 value. Find the premium to be paid.

Premium is £4.30 × 86

= £369.80

The table gives the premiums for insuring buildings and contents as quoted by Northern Star Insurance Co.

	Buildings/ £1000	Contents/ £1000
Area A	£1.80	£ 6.50
Area B	£2.10	£ 8.00
Area C	£2.20	£10.80
Area D	£2.80	£12.90

Use this table to answer questions 1 to 4.

1. Find the premium for insuring a house worth £150 000 (building only) in area D.

2. Find the premium for insuring a house worth £80 000 and its contents worth £9000 in area B.

3. Mr and Mrs Hadinsky live in Area A and value the contents of their house at £12 000. This includes a piano worth £850, a ring worth £700 and a watch worth £350. One condition of the insurance cover is that all items whose value is greater than 5 % of the total insured must be listed.
   (a) Find the premium to be paid.
   (b) State the items that have to be listed.

4. A householder living in area C has a house valued at £75 000 with contents worth £8000. The discount on the buildings premium is 2 % for an excess of £500 and on the contents the discount is 5 % for an excess of £200. Find the premium for insuring house and contents if
   (a) no excess is agreed
   (b) both excesses are agreed.

5. (a) The insurance premium for comprehensive cover on a small family car in Liverpool is £350. Daniel Kirby wants to insure himself to drive such a car but finds that because he is under 25 years of age, there is a 50 % surcharge on the premium. What premium does he have to pay ?

   (b) Three years later, when Daniel is over 25 years old, he no longer has to pay the surcharge and because he has made no claims on his insurance, finds that he is entitled to a 40 % no claims bonus. However, the basic premium has increased to £420. Find the premium he has to pay now.

   (c) Six years later the basic premium is £490 but Daniel pays only £196. What percentage is his no claims bonus now ?

Insurance is only one part of the cost of running a car. In addition there are the annual road fund licence, repairs and maintenance, petrol and, lastly, payment for the vehicle itself. Some people also add in the depreciation of the value of the car.

6. Maya Liang wants to take out a loan to buy herself a second-hand car and decides to estimate what it will cost her for a year. The repayments on the loan are £94 a calendar month. Maya has been quoted £250 premium for insurance. The road tax is £110 and she estimates that she will do 10 000 miles at an average of 40 m.p.g. Petrol is £2.00 a gallon. Maya also estimates that she will need one service costing about £100.

How much does her estimate for 1 year's motoring come to?
How much is this a week?

7. Derek James buys a new car costing £10 000 and decides to work out the cost of running the car for its first year. He includes repayments of £350 per month, depreciation of 25% of the purchase price, £500 for insurance, £110 road tax, a service charge of £200 and £14 a week for petrol.

How much does it cost him each week to run his car?

MONEY

In many respects money is similar to any other commodity. Foreign currencies can be bought and sold in much the same way that cars can be bought and sold. Money can be lent and borrowed in a manner similar to hiring out or renting, say, a scaffold tower.

Exchange Rates

When we shop abroad, prices quoted in the local currency often give us little idea of value so we tend to convert prices into sterling (£). To do this we need to know the exchange rate, i.e. how many units of the local currency are equivalent to one pound sterling.

For example, using an exchange rate of 7.80 French francs (Ff) to £1

means that $£100 = 100 \times 7.80\,\text{Ff} = 780\,\text{Ff}$

and that $78\,\text{Ff} = £\dfrac{78}{7.8} = £10$

A reasonable idea of the cost is given by rounding off the exchange rate to make the arithmetic easy, but skill in mental arithmetic is useful!

For example, a price of 240 Ff could be approximately converted into sterling by rounding $7.80\,\text{Ff} \equiv £1$ to $8\,\text{Ff} \equiv £1$.

Then $240\,\text{Ff} \approx £\dfrac{240}{8} = £30$ to the nearest pound

A more accurate conversion can be made using a conversion graph or a calculator.

Exercise 8j

If £1 is equivalent to 2452 Italian lire (L), estimate the sterling equivalent of

(a) 10 000 L   (b) 500 L.

(a) Approximating the exchange rate to 2500 L = £1 makes the arithmetic easier.

$$10\,000\,L \approx £\,\frac{10\,000}{2500} = £4$$

(b)

$$500\,L \approx £\,\frac{500}{2500} = £\tfrac{1}{5} = 20\,p$$

The following table gives the equivalent of £1 in various currencies.

£	French franc (Ff)	Spanish peseta (pta)	Italian lira (L)	Irish punt (pt)
1	7.64	182	2452	0.97

Use this table (a) to estimate
(b) to calculate (to the nearest penny), the sterling equivalent of

1. 200 Ff
2. 60 Ff
3. 40 pta
4. 3810 pta
5. 900 L
6. 250 pt
7. 3000 L
8. 5354 Ff
9. 450 L

Use the table given above to find how many pesetas are equivalent to 1 Ff.

From the table   7.64 Ff = 182 pta

$$\therefore\ 1\,Ff = \frac{182}{7.64}\,pta$$

$$= 23.82\,pta$$

Use the table given at the beginning of the exercise to make the following conversions. Use your own judgement on how accurately your answers should be given.

10. 100 pta to Ff
11. 100 L to pta
12. 800 pta to L
13. 350 pta to Ff
14. 8.50 pt to Ff
15. 550 pta to pt

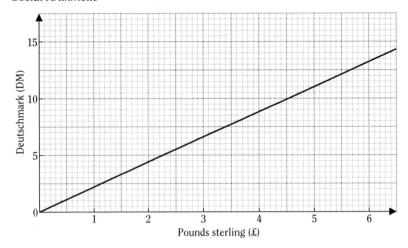

Use this conversion graph to find

16. £3 in DM   **18.** £4.40 in DM   **20.** 12 DM in £

17. £2.50 in DM   **19.** 9 DM in £   **21.** 2.50 DM in £

Buying and Selling Foreign Currency

In the previous section we assumed that there is just one exchange rate between two currencies. For most holiday and business travel purposes it is reasonable to work with a single exchange rate. However, when changing sterling into foreign currency before going on holiday and then changing what is left of that currency back into sterling on return, we find that we have to deal with two exchange rates. High Street banks offering exchange display their rates under two headings: 'Bank Buys' and 'Bank Sells'. (Exchange rates vary slightly from bank to bank in much the same way that the cost of a packet of tea varies from shop to shop.) A typical display of exchange rates looks like this.

	Bank buys	Bank sells
Belgian franc	49.58	45.41
French franc	8.22	7.57
Deutschmark	2.412	2.213
Italian lira	2508	2359
Spanish peseta	198	185
Swiss franc	1.981	1.810
US dollar	1.626	1.498

This means that if we are exchanging French francs and sterling,
the bank will sell us French francs at 7.57 Ff to £1
the bank will buy French francs from us at 8.22 Ff to £1

Hence if we want to change £ 100 into French francs, then we will get

$$100 \times 7.57\,\text{Ff} = 757\,\text{Ff}$$

If we want to change 1220 Ff into sterling then we will get

$$£\,\frac{1220}{8.22} = £\,148.42$$

In addition to the differential exchange rate, banks normally charge a commission on each transaction and this is typically 1 % of the sterling value. Hence our first transaction of changing £ 100 into Ff is subject to a charge of 1 % of £ 100, i.e. £ 1, so the cost of the 757 Ff is £ 101.

Similarly our second transaction is subject to a charge of 1 % of £ 148.42 i.e. £ 1.48. Therefore, for our 1220 Ff we would get £ 148.42 − £ 1.48 i.e. £ 146.94.

Exercise 8k

Use the table on the opposite page to answer the following questions, giving your answers correct to *four* significant figures. In questions 1 to 5 assume that there is no commission.

1. If I change £ 100 into deutschmarks, how many will I get ?

2. If I come back from holiday with 250 DM how much sterling will the bank exchange them for ?

3. What will it cost me in sterling to buy 1 000 000 lire from the bank ?

4. How much will the bank pay me in sterling for US $ 500 ?

5. How many pesetas will £ 500 buy ?

6. A company exporting goods to Belgium is paid in Belgian francs and receives a cheque for 5000 Bf. How much in sterling will the company receive from its bank if the bank charges a commission of $1\frac{1}{2}$ % ?

7. Holiday flats in France are offered for rent at 2000 Ff a week. I rent one for two weeks and pay for it by writing out a cheque in French francs. How much does it cost me in sterling if the bank charges 1 % commission ?

8. Lesley Smith changed £ 100 into US dollars for a business trip, but didn't spend any of the dollars. On return she changed the dollars back into sterling. If 1 % commission was deducted on each transaction, how much did she lose ?

9. A leather bag in an Italian shop is offered for sale at 125 000 L. A tourist, whose lire were bought in England at a charge of $1\frac{1}{2}$ % commission, buys the bag. What is the cost in pounds of the bag to the tourist ?

10. Mr and Mrs Edwards rented a flat in Spain for one week and paid 45 000 pta. On return they were given a refund of 5000 pta. If the bank charged them 1 % commission on currency exchanges, find the cost in pounds of the rental, giving your answer correct to the nearest pound.

11. John bought 500 Swiss francs thinking that the exchange rate was £ 1 to 1.81 f. The exchange rate was in fact £ 1 to 1.87 f. If the bank commission was 1 %, did John pay more or less than he expected and by how much?

SOME MEDIA MISUSES

Sometimes when items appearing in the press or on radio or television contain an element of mathematics, insufficient care is taken to use the correct terminology. What is worse is that there are cases of deliberate misrepresentation in an attempt to make an argument appear to be stronger. It is therefore vital that we do not accept everything we read or hear without carefully considering its true meaning and implications, its accuracy and its honesty.

Here are two examples of careless terminology:

(a) In mathematics the word 'plus' is used only when collecting two quantities together, one on either side of 'plus'. However, advertisements often include phrases such as 'Send in your order today and you will have the chance to win £1000. PLUS Steve Stardust will present the cheque to the winner.' (To express this correctly, although in a less eye-catching way, we could say 'Send in your order today and you will have the chance to win £1000 plus the chance to have it presented by Steve Stardust'.)
This particular misuse is both grammatically and mathematically wrong. Grammar, however, does tend to change with time and no doubt 'plus' will continue to be used in this way. This does *not* mean, though, that the mathematical definition of 'plus' can be changed, so take care.

(b) We often hear a news item saying, for instance, that 'the rate of inflation has fallen by one percentage point'. What is meant is that 'the rate of inflation has fallen by one per cent'. The misuse of 'percentage point' can be very confusing, especially when a decimal point is involved, e.g. if the fall in the rate of inflation is from 4.7 % to 3.7 %.

Keep your eyes and ears open, and see if you can spot more examples of misuse – there are a good many.

Misconceptions

The wrong interpretation of information given in the media can often arise, either from misleading presentation or from misuse of words or from lack of care in reading and considering the information.

Therefore we will now consider the importance of careful reading and thoughtful weighing up of news items with a mathematical content.

Take, for example, the statement 'the rate of inflation is falling'. Some people think that this means that prices are coming down, but it doesn't. Inflation means rising prices; the rate of inflation measures how fast they are rising. If the *rate* goes down it simply means that prices do not rise so quickly – but they still keep on rising.

There are areas where conflicting figures are given to represent what is apparently the same thing. In wage negotiations, for example, the pay of a 'typical employee' might vary considerably; a union official might choose the basic wage of the lowest-paid after all possible deductions, whereas the employer might quote the earnings (including overtime) of a higher-paid employee before any deductions are made. Clearly neither of these is typical and anyone reading only one version would be misled.

These are merely examples of a much wider problem and there are many pitfalls for the unwary in pseudo-mathematical reporting. The best way to avoid any of these is to have a background of precise language, cautious, careful reading and a strong objection to believing everything you hear or read – even in textbooks.

Self-Assessment 8

1. Which is the greater pay packet, and by how much ?

   (a) The payment for 46 hours, including 9 hours overtime, if the basic hourly rate is £4.80 and time-and-a-half is paid for overtime.

   (b) A basic wage of £50 plus commission of $1\frac{1}{2}$ % on sales of £18 000, if the commission is not paid on the first £2500.

2. Phil Strand's telephone account shows that he has used 847 units at 4.80 p per unit. If the rental charge is £21.45 and value added tax at $17\frac{1}{2}$ % is added to the total, find the payment due.

3. (a) The price of petrol is £2.20 a gallon. How much is this a litre ?

   (b) Express 40 m/s in (i) km/h   (ii) m.p.h.

4. A petrol pump can deliver petrol at the rate of $\frac{1}{3}$ litre per second. How long does it take to fill a tank that holds 12 gallons ?
   (1 litre ≈ 1.75 pints)

5. The Budds live in a house valued at £95 000 and have contents valued at £26 000. The Makegood Insurance Co. charge £2.40 per thousand pounds for insuring buildings and £11.20 per thousand for insuring contents. The discount on the building premium is $2\frac{1}{2}$ % for an excess of £500 and on the contents the discount is 5 % for an excess of £250. Find the total premium for insuring house and contents if

   (a) no excess is agreed

   (b) both excesses are agreed.

6. Josie Neumacher converts £550 into US dollars for a holiday in New York. She spent $820 and on her return changed her unspent dollars back into sterling.
   If 1 % commission was charged on each transaction, how much did she receive for the unspent dollars ?
   (The bank buys at $1.69 to the £ and sells at $1.58 to the £.)

QUADRILATERALS, POLYGONS AND TESSELLATIONS

SPECIAL QUADRILATERALS

In Chapter 3 we saw that a general quadrilateral has four sides and the sum of its interior angles is 360°; unless told otherwise, no sides are equal and no angles are equal. However there are several special cases.

Square

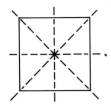

In a square, all four sides are equal and all four angles are right angles. A square has four lines of symmetry.

Rectangle

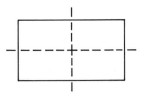

In a rectangle, the opposite sides are equal and all four angles are right angles. A rectangle has two lines of symmetry.

Parallelogram

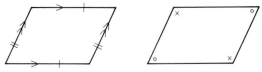

A parallelogram has opposite sides that are equal and parallel, and opposite angles that are equal.

A parallelogram has no lines of symmetry but it does have rotational symmetry of order 2.

Rhombus

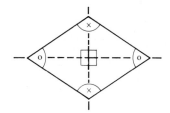

In a rhombus the opposite angles are equal, the opposite sides are parallel and all four sides are the same length.

A rhombus has two lines of symmetry (the diagonals).

Kite

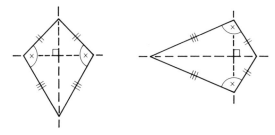

A kite has one pair of opposite angles equal and two pairs of adjacent sides equal.

A kite has one line of symmetry. It has no rotational symmetry.

Trapezium

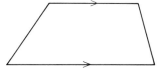

A trapezium has one pair of opposite sides parallel. Usually it has no line of symmetry.

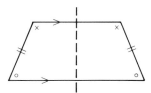

However, in the special case when the two sloping sides are the same length there is one line of symmetry. This is called an isosceles trapezium. Its non-parallel sides are equal and two pairs of adjacent angles are equal.

Exercise 9a

In each question from 1 to 6

(a) name the type of quadrilateral (some may be *general*)

(b) find the size of each marked angle.

1.

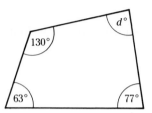

2.

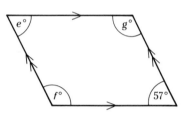

3.

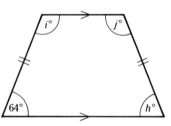

4.

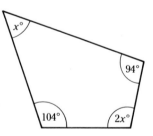

5.

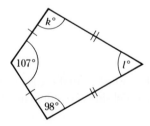

6.

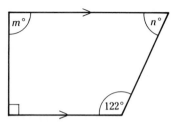

In questions 7 to 12 some of the diagrams contain more than one quadrilateral. Name each quadrilateral and find the size of each marked angle.

7.

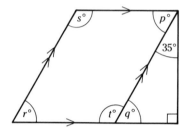

8.

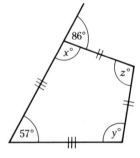

9.

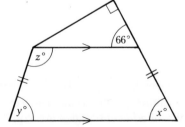

10.

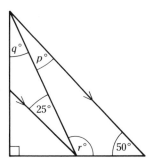

11.

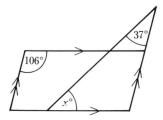

12.

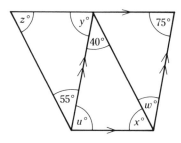

13.

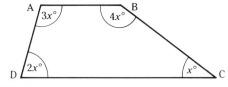

(a) Find the value of *x*.

(b) Prove that ABCD is a trapezium.

14.

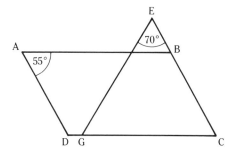

ABCD is a parallelogram. Find the size of

(a) DĈB   (b) EĜC

What sort of triangle is triangle GEC?

15.

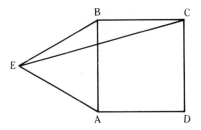

ABCD is a square and ABE is an equilateral triangle. Find

(a) BÂE   (c) BÊC

(b) EB̂C   (d) EĈD.

16. Four rods are placed, in the given order, to make a quadrilateral. Name the special quadrilaterals that can be made if the lengths of the rods are

(a) 5 cm, 10 cm, 5 cm, 10 cm

(b) 5 cm, 5 cm, 10 cm, 10 cm

(c) 5 cm, 5 cm, 5 cm, 10 cm

(d) 5 cm, 5 cm, 5 cm, 5 cm.

17. ABCD is a trapezium with AD parallel to BC. AB̂C = 58° and BĈD = 64°.
BA and CD are produced (i.e. extended) to meet at E.

(a) Calculate the angles in ABCD and △ADE.

(b) What type of triangle is △ADE?

(c) Draw a line through D parallel to AB to meet BC at F. What type of quadrilaterals are EBFD and ADFB?

(d) Join AF. If it is possible, calculate the angles of △ABF. If it is not possible, give a reason.

18. PQRS is a parallelogram. SP̂Q = 72° and RP̂Q = 48°. RP is produced to T so that PT = PQ and SP is produced to meet QT at U.

(a) Find the angles of △s QPT and UPT.

(b) What type of triangle is △UPT?

(c) What type of quadrilateral is PUQR?

(d) What type of triangle is △RQT?

POLYGONS

A polygon is a plane (flat) figure bounded by straight lines.

When all the vertices (corners) of a polygon point outward, the polygon is convex, but if one or more of the vertices point inward, the polygon is concave.

Convex polygon   Concave polygon

Some polygons have names that you already know. They are included in the table given below.

Number of sides	3	4	5	6	8
Name of polygon	triangle	quadrilateral	pentagon	hexagon	octagon

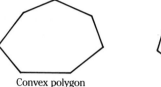

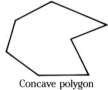

Pentagon   Hexagon   Octagon

The work that follows applies to convex polygons only.

Exterior Angles

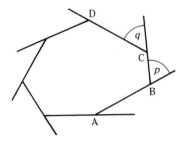

Consider walking around this polygon. Start at A and walk along AB. At B turn through an angle p and walk along BC to C. At C turn through an angle q and walk along CD to D . . . and so on. By the time you get back to A and face along the direction AB you will have turned through one complete revolution, i.e.

**the sum of the exterior angles of any
polygon is 360°**

Exercise 9b

Find the angle marked $x°$

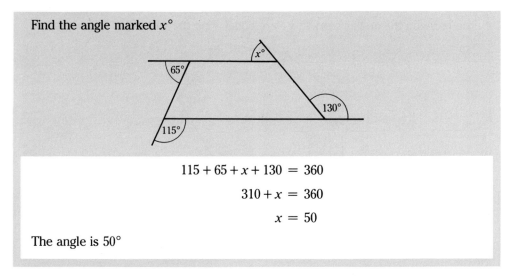

$$115 + 65 + x + 130 = 360$$
$$310 + x = 360$$
$$x = 50$$

The angle is $50°$

In each question find the angle marked $x°$

1.

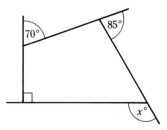

3.

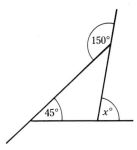

2.

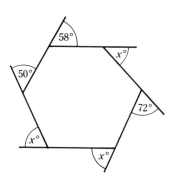

4.

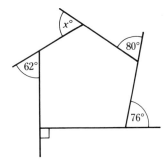

Interior Angles

At any vertex of a convex polygon the sum of the interior and the exterior angles is $180°$. If the polygon has n sides, the sum of all the interior and exterior angles is $n \times 180°$, i.e. $180n°$.

Since the sum of all the exterior angles is $360°$ the sum of all the interior angles is $180n° - 360°$, which can be written $(n - 2)180°$.

Exercise 9c

In the hexagon the angles marked $x°$ are equal. Find the value of x.

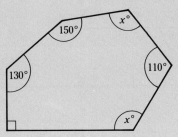

The sum of the interior angles is $180° \times 6 - 360° = 720°$

$$90 + x + 110 + x + 150 + 130 = 720$$
$$480 + 2x = 720$$
$$2x = 240$$
$$x = 120$$

In each question find the angle(s) marked $x°$.

1.

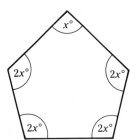

2.

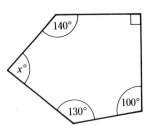

3.

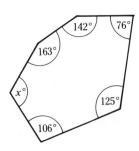

4.

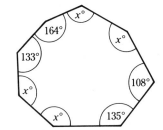

5. Draw a polygon and suppose that it has n sides. Mark a point O inside it and join O to each vertex.

(a) Into how many triangles is the polygon divided?

(b) What is the sum of all the angles in the triangles?

(c) What is the sum of the angles round O?

(d) Use the answers in (b) and (c) to obtain the formula for the sum of the interior angles of an n-sided polygon (already found by a different method on the previous page).

REGULAR POLYGONS

A polygon is regular when its sides are all the same length and its angles are all the same size.

All the polygons shown below are regular.

Square

Pentagon

Hexagon

Octagon

Exercise 9d

> Find the angles of a regular octagon.
>
> An octagon is a polygon with 8 sides.
> To find an exterior angle of a regular polygon we divide 360° by the number of sides, since all exterior angles are equal.
>
> An exterior angle of a regular octagon is
>
> $$360° \div 8 = 45°$$
>
> An interior angle and an exterior angle together make 180°
>
> An interior angle of a regular octagon is
>
> $$180° - 45° = 135°$$

1. Find the size of each exterior angle of a regular polygon with
   - (a) 5 sides
   - (b) 6 sides
   - (c) 7 sides
   - (d) 10 sides
   - (e) 18 sides
   - (f) 20 sides.

2. Find the size of each interior angle of a regular polygon with
   - (a) 9 sides
   - (b) 12 sides
   - (c) 24 sides
   - (d) 36 sides.

3. How many sides has a regular polygon if each exterior angle is
   - (a) 30°
   - (b) 20°
   - (c) 24° ?

4. How many sides has a regular polygon if each interior angle is
   - (a) 120°
   - (b) 156°
   - (c) 162° ?

5. Is it possible for the exterior angle of a regular polygon to be
   - (a) 40°
   - (b) 50°
   - (c) 60°
   - (d) 80° ?

6. Is it possible for the interior angle of a regular polygon to be
   - (a) 90°
   - (b) 135°
   - (c) 170°
   - (d) 180° ?

The remaining questions are mixed problems on polygons.

In questions 7 to 10 find the angle marked $x°$.

7.

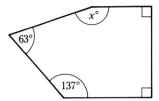

8.

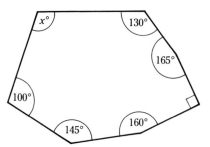

9.

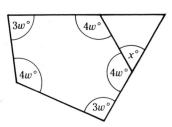

10.

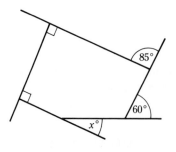

In questions 11 to 14 find the value of x.

11.

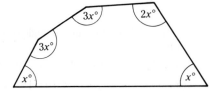

12.

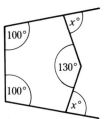

13.

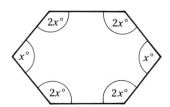

14.

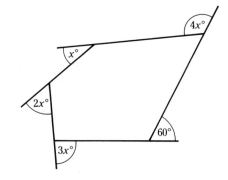

15. ABCD is a regular pentagon. BC and ED are produced (i.e. extended) and meet in F. Find each of the angles in triangle CDF.

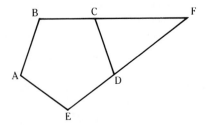

16. (a) Find   (i) an exterior angle,   (ii) an interior angle, for a regular hexagon.

    (b) ABCDEF is a regular hexagon. Find the size of   (i) FÂE   (ii) EÂB   (iii) BÊF   (iv) AÊB.

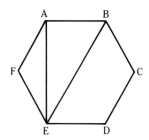

17. The diagram shows a hexagon with just two lines of symmetry. These are marked PQ and RS. Find the values of x, y and z.

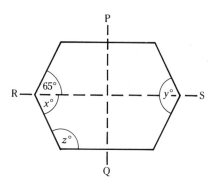

18. ABCDEFGH is a regular octagon and O is equidistant from all the vertices. Find the angles in triangle AOB.

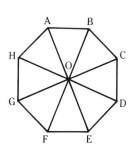

In questions 19 to 21, each polygon is regular. Give answers correct to 1 decimal place where necessary.

19.

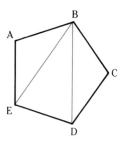

Find

(a) AB̂E   (b) DB̂E.

20.

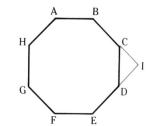

Find the angles in triangle CDI.

21.

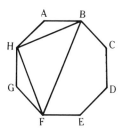

Find

(a) BÂH   (c) AB̂F   (e) HF̂B

(b) AB̂H   (d) HB̂F   (f) FĤB.

What kind of triangle is triangle HBF ?

TESSELLATIONS

Congruent shapes (though not reflections) that fit together, without gaps, to cover a flat surface are said to tessellate. Some examples are given below.

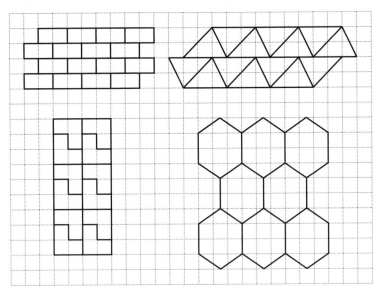

Tessellations can also be made using a combination of regular shapes, for example octagons and squares as shown below.

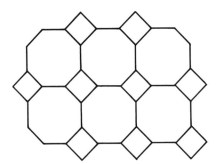

Other interesting shapes that tessellate can be formed by taking a piece away from a square and attaching it to the opposite side, for example

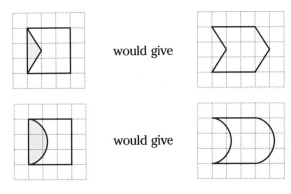

Exercise 9e

1. Use squared paper to show that each of the shapes given below tessellates.

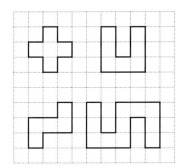

2. Use squared paper to investigate the statement that 'all parallelograms tessellate'. Do you think that the statement is true ? If not, give an example of a parallelogram that will not tessellate.

3. Repeat question 2 for any triangle.

4. Simon has a supply of tiles of the same size and shape. In each case from (a) to (f), can he use them to cover a floor and get a green floor if one side only of each tile is green ?

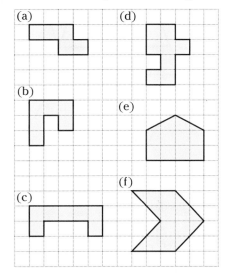

Investigations

1. Draw a series of polygons starting with four sides and increasing the number of sides each time by one. Draw all the diagonals. For each polygon write down

   (a) the number of sides

   (b) the number of diagonals

   (c) the number of intersections of these diagonals.

   Can you find any relationship between your answers to

   (i) (a) and (b)   (ii) (b) and (c) ?

2. (a) Three equal squares can be arranged like this ☐☐☐ and like this ⬜⬜

   Can you find any other arrangements ? Squares must come together along complete edges. How many of each of these arrangements will tessellate ? Show your tessellations on sketches.

   (b) Repeat (a) using 4 squares.

   (c) Repeat (a) using 5 squares, then 6 squares, and so on.

   (d) Can you find any relationship between the number of squares used and
      (i) the number of possible arrangements
      (ii) the number that will tessellate
      (iii) the number that will not tessellate ?

Self-Assessment 9

1. Find the size of each marked angle.

   (a)

   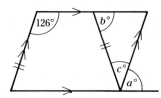

   (b)

   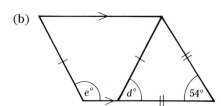

2. Find the interior angle of a regular polygon with 9 sides.

3. The exterior angles of a hexagon are 72°, 59°, 118°, 63°, $x°$ and $x°$. Find the value of x.

4. Is it possible to have a regular polygon with an interior angle of

   (a) 132°   (b) 156° ?

5.

   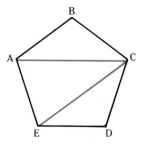

   ABCDE is a regular pentagon. Find the angles in △ACE.

6. Which of the following shapes tessellate ? Illustrate your answers with sketches.

   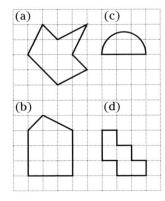

PYTHAGORAS' THEOREM

SQUARES AND SQUARE ROOTS

All scientific calculators have squaring and square root functions and practice in using them is given in Chapter 2. Check the instruction manual if you have any doubt about how to use them.

PYTHAGORAS' THEOREM

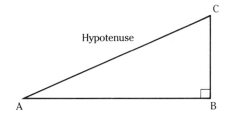

▶ **Pythagoras' theorem states that, in a right-angled triangle, the square of the hypotenuse is equal to the sum of the squares of the other two sides,** ◀

i.e. $$AC^2 = AB^2 + BC^2$$

If any two sides of a right-angled triangle are given, the third side can be found.

Conversely, if the square of one side of a triangle is equal to the sum of the squares of the other two sides, the triangle contains a right angle. The right angle is opposite the longest side.

There are many special triangles where the lengths of the three sides have whole number values. The most important of these are the $3, 4, 5$ triangle and the $5, 12, 13$ triangle, together with multiples of these.

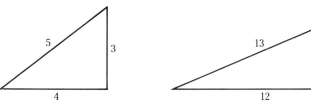

Check that $3^2 + 4^2 = 5^2$ and that $5^2 + 12^2 = 13^2$

Three whole numbers, such that the square of one of them is equal to the sum of the squares of the other two, form a *Pythagorean triad*. Their study leads to many interesting and unexpected results.

Exercise 10a

For each of the following numbers, use a calculator to find   (i) the square   (ii) the square root. Where appropriate, give answers correct to four significant figures.

1. (a) 13.2   (c) 0.9   2. (a) 56.7   (c) 0.82
   (b) 763   (d) 0.006 73   (b) 3370   (d) 0.0005

(a) In triangle ABC, $\hat{B} = 90°$, AB = 56 cm and BC = 37 cm. Find AC.

(b) In triangle ABC, $\hat{B} = 90°$, AC = 8.15 cm and BC = 4.89 cm. Find AB.

Give each answer correct to 3 significant figures.

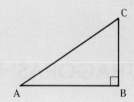

(a) $AC^2 = AB^2 + BC^2$ (Pythagoras)

$\qquad\qquad = 56^2 + 37^2$

$\qquad\qquad = 3136 + 1369$

$\qquad\qquad = 4505$

$\quad AC = \sqrt{4505}$

$\qquad\qquad = 67.119\,\text{cm}$

$\qquad\qquad = 67.1\,\text{cm}$ (3 s.f.)

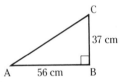

(b) Always write Pythagoras' theorem starting with (hypotenuse)^2 =

$\qquad AC^2 = AB^2 + BC^2$ (Pythagoras)

$\qquad 8.15^2 = AB^2 + 4.89^2$

$\quad 66.4225 = AB^2 + 23.9121$

$\quad 42.5104 = AB^2$

$\qquad\quad AB = \sqrt{42.5104}$

$\qquad\qquad = 6.52\,\text{cm}$

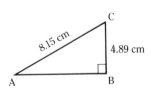

Use the information in the diagrams to find the required lengths, giving your answers correct to 3 significant figures.

3. Find AC.

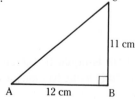

4. Find PR.

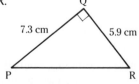

5. Find YZ.

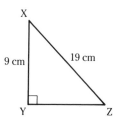

6. Find PQ.

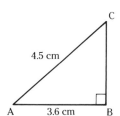

In △ABC, $\hat{B} = 90°$, AC = 4.5 cm and AB = 3.6 cm.
Find BC.

It is worthwhile looking for a 3, 4, 5△ or a 5, 12, 13△ to make the calculation simpler.

AC = 5×0.9 cm

AB = 4×0.9 cm

∴ △ABC is a 3, 4, 5△

∴ BC = 3×0.9 cm

= 2.7 cm

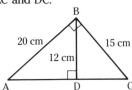

---

7. Find AC and DC.

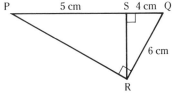

8. Find RS and PR.

It is always sensible to draw a rough diagram and mark the given information on it.

9. In △XYZ, $\hat{X} = 90°$, XY = 3.9 cm and XZ = 4.9 cm.

(a) Find YZ.

(b) YX is extended to W so that XW = 2.5 cm. Find ZW.

10. Are the following triangles right-angled? If so, write down the angle that is 90°.

(a) △ABC in which AB = 11 cm, BC = 61 cm and AC = 60 cm.

(b) △XYZ in which XY = 2.8 cm, YZ = 3.5 cm and XZ = 2.1 cm.

(c) △DEF in which DE = 13 cm, DF = 18 cm and EF = 27 cm.

(d) △PQR in which QR = 570 cm, PR = 950 cm and PQ = 760 cm.

11. In a triangle XYZ, $\widehat{XYZ} = 90°$ and W is the foot of the perpendicular from Y to XZ. XY = 32 cm, YZ = 16 cm and WZ = 7.16 cm.
Find the length of

(a) XZ   (b) WX   (c) WY.

12. In △PQR, PQ = PR = 9 cm and QR = 10 cm. S is the midpoint of QR. Find the height of △PQR.

Find the distance between the points A(1, 2) and B(7, 4).

Draw a diagram to see clearly what is going on.

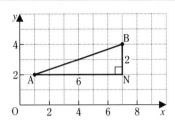

N is the point such that AN is parallel to the *x*-axis and BN is parallel to the *y*-axis. It follows that $A\hat{N}B = 90°$.

AN = $(7-1)$, i.e. 6 units and BN = $(4-2)$, i.e. 2 units

Applying Pythagoras' theorem to $\triangle$ANB

$$AB^2 = 6^2 + 2^2$$
$$= 36 + 4$$
$$= 40$$

∴ AB is 6.32 units   (3 s.f.)

---

13. Find the distance between each of the following pairs of points:

   (a) A(3, 1) and B(6, 7)   (c) P(−2, 2) and Q(9, 5)   (e) P(−3, −3) and Q(9, 6)

   (b) X(1, 2) and Y(10, 9)   (d) A(2, −4) and B(7, 8)   (f) D(−4, 6) and E(2, −5)

PROBLEMS

The first step towards solving any geometric problem should be to draw a clear diagram showing all the information that is given in the question.

If one length is found first and used to find a second length or an angle, use the exact value for the first length or, if that is not possible, use at least 4 significant figures. Unless otherwise stated, all answers should be given correct to 3 significant figures.

Exercise 10b

1. A ship sails 26 nautical miles due north then 34 nautical miles due east. How far is it from its starting point ?

2. Find the length of a diagonal of a square of side 17 cm.

3. Find the length of the side of a rhombus whose diagonals measure 10 cm and 24 cm.

4.

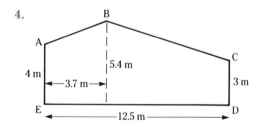

The diagram shows the cross-section of a workshop. Find the length of each sloping edge of the roof.

5.

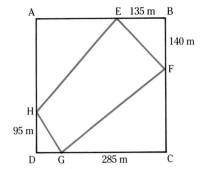

The diagram shows a square field, ABCD, of side 350 m, which has been divided into five enclosures by erecting a fence EFGHE.

Calculate the length of this fence.

6.

A vertical pylon, AB, is 40 m high, and stands on level ground. It is supported by a wire, CD, 38 m long which is attached to a point 7 m from the top of the pylon, the other end being anchored to a point on the ground. How far is this point from the base of the pylon?

7.

ABC is a table top in the shape of an equilateral triangle and AB = 1.2 m. P is the midpoint of AB.

(a) Find the length of CP.

(b) X is a point on CP such that PX = $\frac{1}{3}$CP. Find the length of XB.

8.

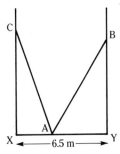

The diagram shows a ladder, AB, resting on horizontal ground, XY, in a narrow street 6.5 m wide. The foot, A, of the ladder is 3.5 m from the base of the vertical wall BY and rests against this wall at a distance 7.5 m above the ground. How long is the ladder?

The ladder is now turned about A so that it rests, at a point C, against a vertical building on the opposite side of the street. How far up this wall does the ladder reach?

9.

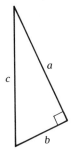

(a) In the diagram, c is the hypotenuse of a right-angled triangle, the other two sides being a and b.
   (i) Find c if a = 3 and b = 4.
   (ii) Find b if a = 5 and c = 13.
   (iii) Find a if b = 24 and c = 25.

(b) (i) Use your answers to (a) to complete the following table

a	b	c
3	4	
5		13
	24	25
9	40	41

   (ii) If the next value of b is 60, find the corresponding values for c and a and complete the fifth row of the table.

   (iii) Add two more rows to the table, following the same pattern.

10.

(a) A carpenter checks that a rectangular window frame is 'square' by measuring the diagonals, which should be the same length. A frame is 185 cm by 105 cm. What should be the length of each diagonal? Give your answer correct to the nearest millimetre.

(b) Use some rectangular objects that you have available, e.g. a picture frame, a door, the cover of a book, etc., to test whether or not they are 'square'.

11.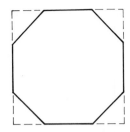

A mirror is in the shape of an octagon. It is formed by starting with a square of side 90 cm and cutting an isosceles triangle from each corner. The two equal sides of each triangle are of length 30 cm.

(a) Find the lengths of the sides of the octagon.

(b) Find the distance of each vertex from the centre of the octagon.

THREE-DIMENSIONAL PROBLEMS

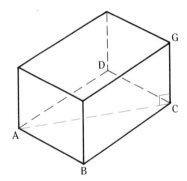

If a line is perpendicular to a plane, then it is perpendicular to any line in that plane. For example, GC is perpendicular to the plane ABCD. Therefore GC is perpendicular to CB, CD and CA.

The following hints may be helpful in drawing a good diagram.

(a) Vertical lines should be drawn vertically on your diagram.

(b) All angles that are 90° in three dimensions should be marked as right angles on the diagram. This is particularly important for those angles that do not *appear* to be 90°.

(c) Lines that are parallel should be shown as parallel on the diagram.

(d) Show sides that cannot be seen by broken lines.

(e) It is often helpful to draw a separate diagram for an individual triangle in which calculations are needed. Mark any right angle.

Exercise 10c

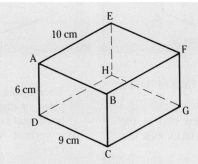

The sketch shows a rectangular box ABCDEFGH measuring 10 cm by 9 cm by 6 cm, where AE = 10 cm, AD = 6 cm and DC = 9 cm.

(a) Calculate the lengths of AC, DG and AG.

(b) What is the length of the longest thin stick that will fit into this box?

(a) To find AC, we use triangle ADC

$$AC^2 = AD^2 + DC^2$$
$$= 36 + 81$$
$$= 117$$
$$AC = 10.81\ldots$$

Similarly

$$DG^2 = DC^2 + CG^2$$
$$= 81 + 100$$
$$= 181$$
$$DG = 13.45\ldots$$

and

$$AG^2 = AD^2 + DG^2$$
$$= 36 + 181$$
$$= 217$$
$$AG = 14.73\ldots$$

Correct to 3 s.f. the lengths of AC, DG and AG are respectively 10.8 cm, 13.5 cm and 14.7 cm.

(b) The length of the longest thin stick that will fit into this box is the length of AG, i.e. 14.7 cm   (3 s.f.).

1. Referring to the box given in the worked example above

   (a) find the length of FC.

   (b) use FC to find the length of FD. How does this compare with the length of AG calculated in the worked example?

2.

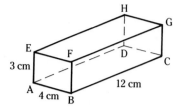

The sketch shows a cuboid. Each of the six faces is a rectangle.

(a) Copy the diagram. Notice that in the drawing the rectangular faces look like parallelograms.

(b) Name all the edges that are equal in length to   (i) AB   (ii) EA   (iii) BC.

(c) Draw triangle EHG and find the length of EG.

(d) Draw triangle EAC and find the length of EC.

3.

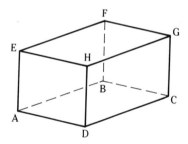

In this cuboid   AB = 12 cm,   AE = 8 cm and   BC = 9.5 cm.

Find   the   length   of   (a) AH   (b) DG   (c) DF.

4. Sketch a cube of edge 6 cm. Find the length of

(a) a diagonal of a face

(b) a diagonal of the cube.

Now imagine that the cube is cut in half to give a cuboid measuring 6 cm by 6 cm by 3 cm. Sketch the cuboid and find the length of

(c) a diagonal of the smallest face

(d) a diagonal of the cuboid.

5.

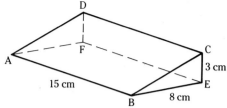

The diagram represents a large wedge-shaped piece of cheese ABCDEF resting on a flat horizontal table. The rectangular face DCFE is vertical. A small mouse approaches the cheese.

(a) Use the information on the diagram to find the distance travelled by the mouse if it walks
   (i) the length of the edge BC
   (ii) in a direct line from A to C across the face ABCD.

(b) Which path gives the mouse the easier climb up the slope? Give a reason for your answer.

6.

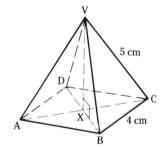

The diagram shows a square-based pyramid VABCD in which V is vertically above X, the centre of the base.

(a) Draw the base ABCD as a square, and find the lengths of AC and AX.

(b) Draw triangle VAX and find the height of V above the base.

7. The coordinates of four points are P(5, 3, 10), Q(9, 3, 7), R(6, 11, 6) and S(−7, 0, −17). Find the lengths of PQ, PR and QS.

Self-Assessment 10

1.

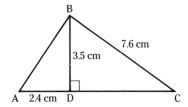

(a) Use the information given on the diagram to find   (i) AB   (ii) DC.

(b) Use your results to determine whether or not triangle ABC is a right-angled triangle.

2. Find the distance between the points A(4, 1) and B(8, −5).

3. In △ABC, $\widehat{B} = 90°$, AC $= 40$ cm and AB $= 24$ cm. Without using a calculator, find BC.

4.

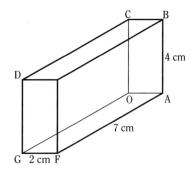

Use the information given in the diagram to find the lengths of

(a) GE   (b) FB   (c) AD.

5. VABCD is a square-based pyramid, V being the vertex. A side of the square is of length 5 cm and each sloping edge is of length 7 cm. Find the height of V above the base.

AREAS AND VOLUMES

CALCULATING AREAS

In Chapter 5 we saw that the area of any shape made up of squares and rectangles can be calculated exactly. For other shapes the method used was to superimpose a squared grid and count squares. The result, however, is only an approximation.

There are a number of such figures for which there is a way to *calculate* the area; these are considered in this chapter.

The Area of a Parallelogram

We know that a parallelogram is a quadrilateral in which both pairs of opposite sides are parallel and equal. Using these properties it is easy to obtain a rectangle equal in area to a parallelogram.

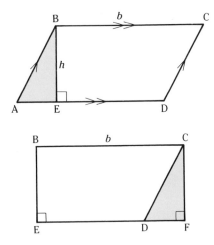

From the given parallelogram ABCD, the shaded right-angled triangle can be cut off and placed with AB along DC as shown. This forms a rectangle EBCF with length b and width h and therefore with an area given by $b \times h$, which is the same as the area of ABCD.

In the parallelogram, h is the perpendicular height; usually we just say *height* because this is understood to mean perpendicular height.

 Area of a parallelogram $=$ base $\times$ height

Note that the side AB of the parallelogram is the *slant height* and is *not* equal to the perpendicular height.

Exercise 11a

Find the area of this parallelogram.

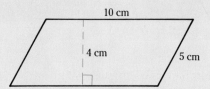

The given length of 5 cm is the slant height and is not needed to find the area.

$$\text{Area} = \text{base} \times \text{height}$$
$$= 10 \times 4 \text{ cm}^2$$
$$= 40 \text{ cm}^2$$

Find the area of each parallelogram.

1.

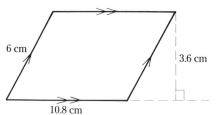

2.

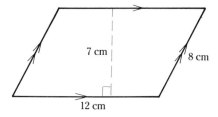

3.

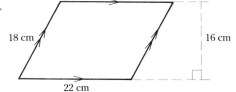

4.

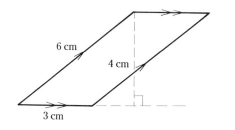

It is not always obvious which side of a parallelogram is the base as it is not necessarily the bottom line. The base may be identified more easily if the parallelogram is viewed from a different direction.

5.

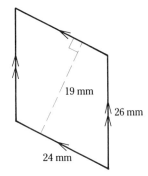

6.

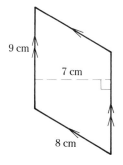

7.

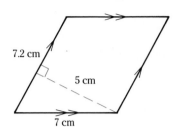

7.2 cm

5 cm

7 cm

8.

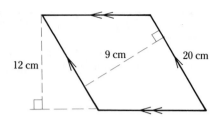

9 cm   20 cm

12 cm

Find the area of parallelogram ABCD.

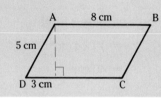

A   8 cm   B

5 cm

D 3 cm   C

First we find the perpendicular height.

In triangle ADE,

$$5^2 = 3^2 + h^2 \quad (\text{Pythagoras})$$

$$h^2 = 25 - 9$$

$$h = 4$$

Area of parallelogram $= b \times h$

$$= 8 \times 4 \text{ cm}^2$$

$$= 32 \text{ cm}^2$$

A   B

5 cm h

D 3 cm E   C

Find the area of each parallelogram.

9.

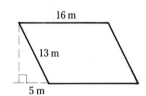

16 m

13 m

5 m

10.

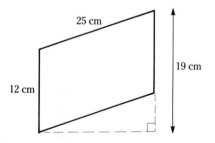

25 cm

12 cm

19 cm

11.

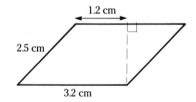

1.2 cm

2.5 cm

3.2 cm

12.

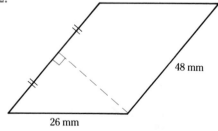

48 mm

26 mm

THE AREA OF A TRIANGLE

Any rectangle or parallelogram can be divided, by drawing a diagonal, into two triangles with the same shape and size and therefore with equal areas.

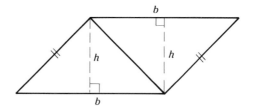

The area of the original rectangle or parallelogram is given by $b \times h$

Therefore the area of a triangle is given by $\frac{1}{2} \times b \times h$ where h is the height of the triangle. As for a parallelogram, height is understood to mean perpendicular height.

▶ **Area of a triangle $= \frac{1}{2} \times$ base $\times$ height** ◀

Exercise 11b

Find the area of each triangle.

1.

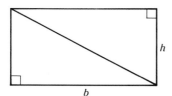

8 cm
12 cm

2.

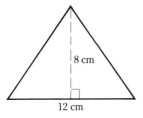

7.4 cm
6 cm

3.

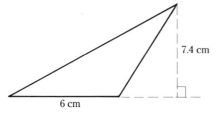

16 cm
12 cm
8 cm

4.

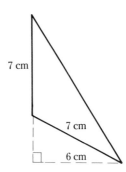

7 cm
7 cm
6 cm

5.

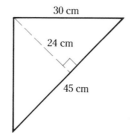

30 cm
24 cm
45 cm

6.

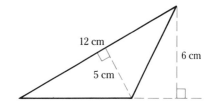

12 cm
6 cm
5 cm

The units must be consistent.

Find the area of a triangle whose base is 12 cm and whose height is 46 mm.

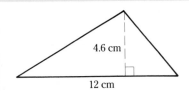

4.6 cm

12 cm

The units must be the same; 46 mm = 4.6 cm

$$\text{Area of triangle} = \tfrac{1}{2} \times 12 \times 4.6 \, \text{cm}^2$$

$$= 27.6 \, \text{cm}^2$$

Alternatively, 12 cm could be expressed as 120 mm and the area found in mm²

Find the area of each triangle   (a) in m²   (b) in cm²

	Base	Height
7.	2.7 m	140 cm
8.	76 cm	0.4 m
9.	0.76 m	230 mm

	Base	Height
10.	7.2 m	47 cm
11.	9.1 cm	58 mm
12.	0.04 m	16 cm

Find the area of a triangle whose vertices are at the points (1, 1), (4, 4) and (7, 0). Take 1 unit on each axis as 1 cm.

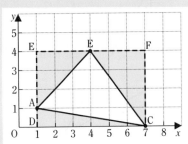

The triangle can be enclosed by the rectangle DEFC as shown.

The area of △ABC can be found from the area of this rectangle less the areas of the three shaded triangles.

$$\text{Area rectangle DEFC} = 6 \times 4 \, \text{cm}^2 = 24 \, \text{cm}^2$$

$$\text{Area} \, \triangle\text{ADC} = \tfrac{1}{2} \times 6 \times 1 \, \text{cm}^2 = 3 \, \text{cm}^2$$

$$\text{Area} \, \triangle\text{BFC} = \tfrac{1}{2} \times 3 \times 4 \, \text{cm}^2 = 6 \, \text{cm}^2$$

$$\text{Area} \, \triangle\text{ABE} = \tfrac{1}{2} \times 3 \times 3 \, \text{cm}^2 = 4\tfrac{1}{2} \, \text{cm}^2$$

$$\therefore \, \text{area} \, \triangle\text{ABC} = (24 - 3 - 6 - 4\tfrac{1}{2}) \, \text{cm}^2$$

$$= 10\tfrac{1}{2} \, \text{cm}^2$$

Taking 1 unit on each axis as 1 cm, find the area of the triangle with the given coordinates.

13. (0, 2), (6, 0), (6, 4)

14. (−2, 1), (3, 2), (5, 6)

15. (3, −3), (6, 1), (−1, 5)

16. (6, 4), (−8, 6), (−3, −6)

The vertices of a quadrilateral are at the points $(2, 4), (6, 0), (-1, 3)$ and $(0, -5)$. Find its area taking 1 unit as 1 cm on each axis.

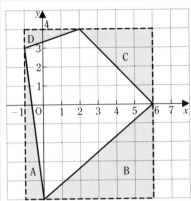

The quadrilateral can be enclosed in a simple rectangle by drawing horizontal or vertical lines through the given points.

Area of quadrilateral $=$ area of rectangle

$-$ area of triangle A

$-$ area of triangle B

$-$ area of triangle C

$-$ area of triangle D

$= (63 - 4 - 15 - 8 - 1\frac{1}{2}) \text{ cm}^2$

$= 34\frac{1}{2} \text{ cm}^2$

In each question find the area of the quadrilateral with vertices at the given points. Take 1 unit on each axis as 1 cm.

17. $(-2, -1), (1, 6), (7, 6), (1, -4)$

18. $(-3, 0), (0, -2), (4, 0), (3, 6)$

19. $(-1, -3), (5, -1), (3, 3), (-1, 4)$

20. $(6, 1), (3, 7), (-2, 6), (0, -3)$

The area of a triangle is 48 mm^2. If its height is 6 mm, what is the length of its base ?

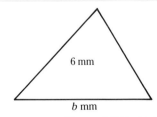

Area $= \frac{1}{2} \times$ base $\times$ height

$48 = \frac{1}{2} \times b \times 6$

$48 = 3b$

$b = 16$

The length of the base is 16 mm.

Find the missing measurement for each triangle. Remember that units must be consistent.

	Area	Base	Height			Area	Base	Height
21.	30 mm^2	10 mm			**23.**	75 mm^2	3 cm	
22.	108 cm^2		6 cm		**24.**	1.28 m^2		64 cm

CALCULATIONS USING CORRECTED NUMBERS

Consider the area of a rectangle with dimensions 12.6 cm by 10.8 cm, each length being correct to 3 s.f.

Because each length is not exact, but lies within a range of values, it follows that the area must also lie within a range of values.

If the length is a cm then $\quad 12.55 \leqslant a < 12.65$
and for the breadth, b cm, $\quad 10.75 \leqslant b < 10.85$

The least possible area is given when both the length and the breadth have their smallest value in the range,

i.e. the lower bound for the area is $12.55 \times 10.75 \text{ cm}^2$
$$= 134.9125 \text{ cm}^2$$

The upper bound can be found by taking the greatest values of the length and breadth,

i.e. the upper bound of the area is $12.65 \times 10.85 \text{ cm}^2$
$$= 137.2525 \text{ cm}^2$$

Note that the area cannot be *equal* to 137.2525 cm^2 as each number in the product is *less than* its upper bound.

So for the area, A cm^2, $\qquad 134.9125 \leqslant A < 137.2525$
or, correct to 3 s.f., $\qquad\qquad\quad 135 \leqslant A < 137$

Using the corrected dimensions (i.e. 12.6×10.8) gives the area as 136.08 cm^2. Comparing this with the values that the area *could* take, shows that a product of numbers, each correct to 3 s.f., does *not* give a result that is correct to 3 s.f. In this case 136.08 cm^2 is correct only to 2 s.f.

This is why, when a previously calculated value is needed for further calculations, it is important *not* to use a corrected value but to use at least 4 significant figures if a result is required correct to 3 significant figures.

Exercise 11c

Find, correct to 3 s.f., the upper and lower bounds of each of the following calculations, given that each number is correct to 3 s.f.

1. 34.4×10.2

2. 1.32×2.68

3. 0.456×1.04

4. 981×523

If division is involved in a calculation, the greatest value occurs when the numerator has its largest value and the denominator its least.

Find, correct to 3 s.f., the range within which the value of $\dfrac{4.2 \times 5.1}{1.6}$ lies. Each number is correct to 2 s.f.

The smallest possible value of the fraction occurs when both numbers in the numerator have their least value and the denominator has its largest value.

So the lower bound is $\qquad \dfrac{4.15 \times 5.05}{1.65} = 12.701 \ldots$

$$= 12.7 \quad (3 \text{ s.f.})$$

The upper bound is $\qquad \dfrac{4.25 \times 5.15}{1.55} = 14.120 \ldots$

$$= 14.1 \quad (3 \text{ s.f.})$$

Note that in this case the fraction cannot be equal to *either* the upper or the lower bound.

If all the given numbers are correct to 2 s.f., find, correct to 2 s.f., the upper and lower bounds of

5. 0.94×1.2

7. $\dfrac{8.3 \times 2.5}{0.24}$

9. $0.025 \div 0.79$

11. 92×14

6. $7.8 \div 1.6$

8. $\dfrac{5.7}{6.3 \times 0.11}$

10. $1.2 \times 0.35 \times 2.1$

12. $1300 \div 46$

For each of the following shapes, the dimensions are given correct to 3 s.f.

(a) Write down the range in which each dimension lies.

(b) Find the upper and lower bounds of the area, to as many decimal places as are given by a calculator.

(c) Correct the upper and lower bounds to 3 s.f. and give the range within which the area, correct to 3 s.f., lies.

13. A rectangle measuring 3.61 cm by 2.57 cm.

14. A triangle with height 25.6 mm and base 19.3 mm.

15. A parallelogram with one pair of parallel sides 8.43 cm long and 5.21 cm apart.

16. A square with side 4.07 cm.

SHAPES WITH EQUAL HEIGHTS AND BASES

Write down the area of each triangle in the diagram below. Take the side of 1 grid square as 1 unit of length.

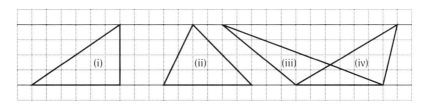

What do you notice about all four bases and all four heights?

From your results you will see that it appears that:

    **triangles with equal bases and equal heights
have equal areas.**

If we look at the formula for the area of a triangle, the above property is obviously true.

As   area $= \frac{1}{2} \times b \times h$ then *all* triangles with base b and height h have the same area.

Considering the formula for the area of a parallelogram gives a similar result, i.e.

    **parallelograms with equal bases and equal heights
have equal areas.**

Exercise 11d

Find the area of the white section of the green and white flag shown in the diagram.

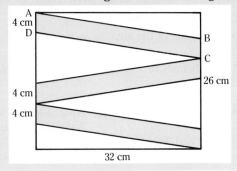

The green sections are all parallelograms with the same height and equal bases.

$$\text{Area of ABCD} = \text{base} \times \text{height}$$
$$= 4 \times 32 \, \text{cm}^2 = 128 \, \text{cm}^2$$
$$\text{Area of green stripes} = 3 \times 128 \, \text{cm}^2$$
$$= 384 \, \text{cm}^2$$
$$\text{Total area of flag} = 32 \times 26 \, \text{cm}^2$$
$$= 832 \, \text{cm}^2$$
$$\text{Area of white section} = (832 - 384) \, \text{cm}^2$$
$$= 448 \, \text{cm}^2$$

Find the area of each shaded section.

1.

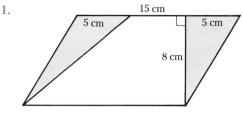

2.

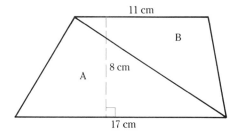

3. The diagram shows a tile pattern. The shaded area is glazed and the remainder is unglazed. Find the unglazed area.

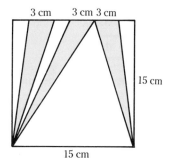

AREAS OF COMPOUND SHAPES

The Area of a Trapezium

A trapezium is a quadrilateral with *one* pair of opposite sides parallel.

Consider the trapezium given in the following diagram. By drawing a diagonal we can divide the trapezium into two triangles.

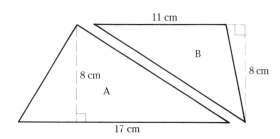

For triangle A the height is 8 cm and the base is 17 cm.
Therefore its area is $\frac{1}{2} \times 8 \times 17 \, \text{cm}^2$.
For triangle B the height is 8 cm and the base is 11 cm.
Therefore its area is $\frac{1}{2} \times 8 \times 11 \, \text{cm}^2$.

The area of the trapezium is the sum of the areas of the triangles,

i.e. $\frac{1}{2} \times 8 \times 17 \, \text{cm}^2 \; + \; \frac{1}{2} \times 8 \times 11 \, \text{cm}^2 = \frac{1}{2} \times 8 \times (17 + 11) \, \text{cm}^2$

and we note that $(17 + 11)$ is the sum of the parallel sides.

Any trapezium can be divided in a similar way into two triangles with equal heights so, in general,

  Area of trapezium $= \frac{1}{2} \times$ height $\times$ sum of parallel sides

Exercise 11e

1. Find the area of each trapezium.

   (a)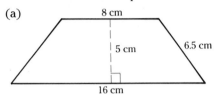

   (b)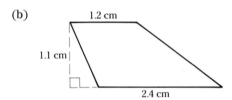

2. Find the area of a trapezium given that

   (a) its parallel sides, which are of lengths 6 cm and 7 cm, are 6 cm apart

   (b) its parallel sides are of lengths 120 cm and 1.5 m and its height is 2.3 m.
       (Remember that units must be consistent.)

The area of a trapezium is 345 cm^2. If the height is 15 cm and the length of one of the parallel sides is 22 cm, find the length of the other parallel side.

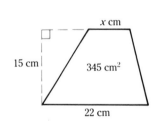

$$\text{Area} = \tfrac{1}{2} \times \text{height} \times (\text{sum of parallel sides})$$

$$345 = \tfrac{1}{2} \times 15 \times (22 + x)$$

$$= 7.5 \times (22 + x)$$

$$\frac{345}{7.5} = 22 + x$$

$$46 = 22 + x$$

$$\therefore \ x = 24$$

The length of the required side is 24 cm.

A trapezium has parallel sides of lengths a cm and b cm, which are h cm apart. Find the unknown dimension.

	a	b	h	Area (cm^2)
3.	14	8		143
4.		6	8	64
5.	15		22	385

The areas of compound shapes can be calculated if they are made up of squares, rectangles, triangles and trapeziums.

The diagram shows the end wall of a bungalow. The wall is entirely brick-built except for the two windows. Find the area of the brickwork.

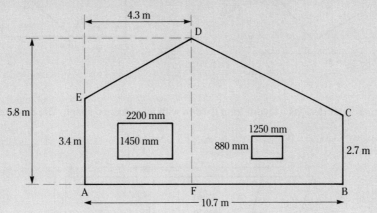

DF divides ABCDE into 2 trapeziums.

Area of AEDF $= \frac{1}{2}(3.4+5.8) \times 4.3 \,\text{m}^2 = 19.78 \,\text{m}^2$

FB $= 10.7 \,\text{m} - 4.3 \,\text{m} = 6.4 \,\text{m}$

Area of FBCD $= \frac{1}{2}(2.7+5.8) \times 6.4 \,\text{m}^2 = 27.2 \,\text{m}^2$

Total area of wall $= (19.78 + 27.2) \,\text{m}^2 = 46.98 \,\text{m}^2$

Take the dimensions of the windows in metres

Area of larger window $= 1.450 \times 2.200 \,\text{m}^2 = 3.19 \,\text{m}^2$

Area of smaller window $= 1.250 \times 0.880 \,\text{m}^2 = 1.1 \,\text{m}^2$

Area of brickwork $= (46.98 - 3.19 - 1.1) \,\text{m}^2 = 42.69 \,\text{m}^2 = 42.7 \,\text{m}^2$ (3 s.f.)

Find the area of each shape. If necessary split the figure into parts whose areas can be calculated.

6.

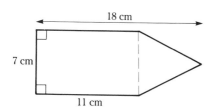

7.

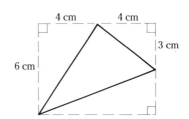

8.

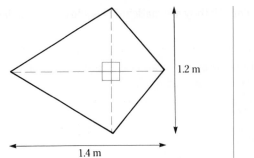

9.

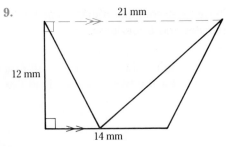

10. A landscape gardener designs a layout for a garden with an awkward shape. The diagram shows his plan.

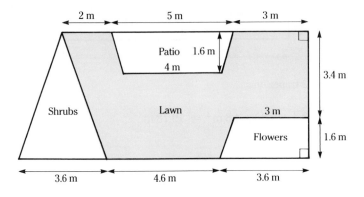

Find the area of the lawn.

11. The front view of a frame tent is shown in the diagram. Find the area of canvas, given that the window and door are made from nylon net.

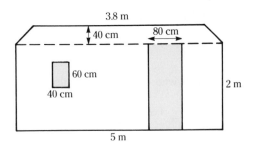

12. The floor of a restaurant is to be carpeted with the exception of the bar area and the dance floor. Find the area of the carpeted section.

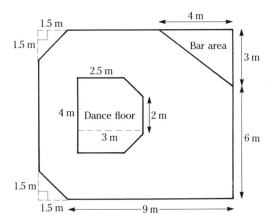

13. The stonework, shown shaded, on the front of an office needs specialist cleaning.

(a) Find the area to be treated.

(b) If the cleaning firm charges £85 for each square metre or part of a square metre, find the cost of the renovation.

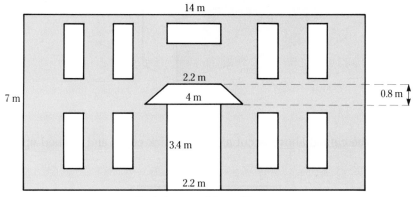

All windows are 2.2 m × 0.8 m

THE SURFACE AREA OF A CUBOID

A cuboid has six faces of which opposite pairs are identical. The total surface area of a cuboid is therefore given by adding the areas of three different faces and doubling the result.

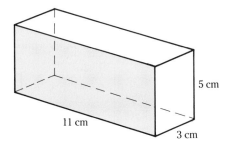

For the cuboid shown,

the area of the top (or the base) is $\quad 11 \times 3\,\text{cm}^2 = 33\,\text{cm}^2$
the area of the front face (shaded) is $\quad 11 \times 5\,\text{cm}^2 = 55\,\text{cm}^2$
the area of an end is $\qquad\qquad\qquad 3 \times 5\,\text{cm}^2 = 15\,\text{cm}^2$

Therefore the total surface area is $\quad 2 \times (33 + 55 + 15)\,\text{cm}^2 = 206\,\text{cm}^2$

This can be seen very clearly if we draw a *net* of the cuboid, i.e. the flat shape obtained when the cuboid is cut along some of its edges and flattened out.

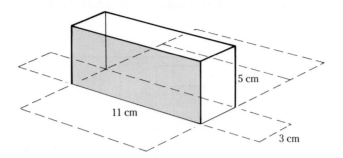

For example if the cuboid above is cut along the thick edges and opened up, this net is produced.

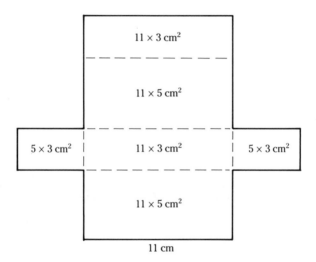

Exercise 11f

In questions 1 and 2 find the surface area and volume of the cuboid given by the net.

1.

2.

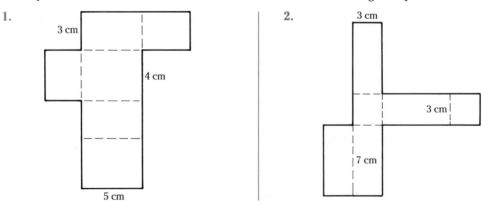

In questions 3 and 4 draw a suitable net for the cuboid with the given dimensions and find the surface area of the cuboid.

3. 7 cm by 4 cm by 3 cm

4. 4 cm by 3.5 cm by 2.5 cm

5. Draw as many different nets as you can for a 3 cm cube. Each net should be in one piece.

6. This net will make a cuboid.

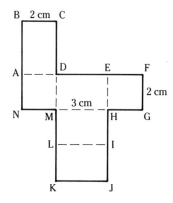

(a) *Sketch* the cuboid and mark its dimensions on the sketch.

(b) Which corners meet with B?

(c) Which edge joins with EF?

7.

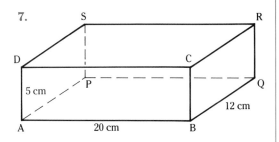

(a) Find the length of BR.

(b) Find the least distance from A to R if the distance is to be measured only along edges of the cuboid.

(c) Draw a net for the cuboid.

(d) Find the least distance from A to R if the distance can be measured anywhere on the surface of the cuboid.

(e) Find the distance from A to R if the points can be joined directly.

8.

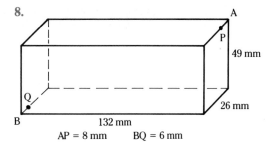

AP = 8 mm   BQ = 6 mm

(a) Using only the given diagram, find what you think is the shortest distance from P to Q on the surface of this cuboid.

(b) Draw a net for the cuboid and again find the shortest distance on the surface from P to Q. (To form the net, start at A and cut along the longest edge first.)

(c) Did you get the same distance both times and which do you think was the better way to find the distance?

9. Which of these nets will make a cuboid?

(a)

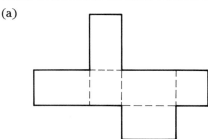

(b)

(c)

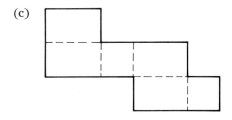

SOLIDS WITH SPECIAL SHAPES

In Chapter 5 the volumes of a cube and a cuboid were investigated. Now we consider ways to calculate the volumes of other solids with interesting shapes.

Prisms

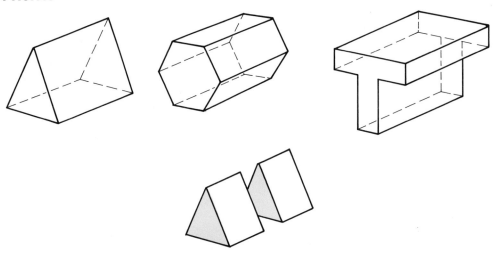

When any one of the solids above is cut through, parallel to the ends, the *cross-section* produced always has the same shape and size as the ends have; the cross-section is said to be *uniform* (i.e. constant). Solids with this property are called *prisms*. One of the simplest prisms is a cuboid; it is called a rectangular prism because its uniform cross-section is a rectangle. Other prisms also are known by their cross-section when this is a simple shape, e.g. the first two solids in the diagram above are a triangular prism and a hexagonal prism.

The Volume of a Prism

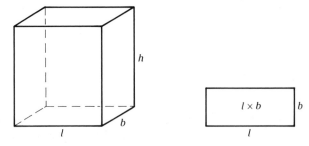

For the rectangular prism shown above, the volume is known to be given by:

$$\text{volume} = \text{length} \times \text{breadth} \times \text{height}$$

Now   breadth × height   gives the area of the uniform cross-section so we can say:

$$\text{volume} = \text{area of cross-section} \times \text{length}$$

This property is true for all prisms, i.e., in general,

volume of a prism = cross-sectional area × length

Note that, if a prism is standing on one of its ends the base is a cross-section, and in this case:

volume = area of base × height

Note also that the term 'right prism' means that the prism can stand upright on its base with its sides vertical, e.g.

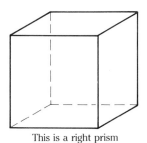
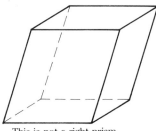

This is a right prism

This is not a right prism

In this book we shall deal only with right prisms.

Pyramids

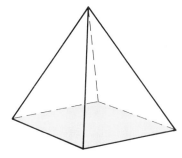

Each of these solids is a pyramid; its shape is given by drawing lines from a single point to each corner of the base.

The first solid has a square base and is called a square pyramid. The second one has a triangular base and can be called a triangular pyramid. It is also known, however, as a *tetrahedron* (a special name that applies only to this shape).

The volume of any pyramid is given by
volume = $\frac{1}{3}$ × area of base × height

(Remember that 'height' means perpendicular height.)

EDGES, FACES AND VERTICES

In examining each of the solids in this chapter we have referred to its edges, its faces and its vertices.

Each flat side is a face; the line where two faces meet is an edge; the point where edges meet is a vertex (i.e. a corner).

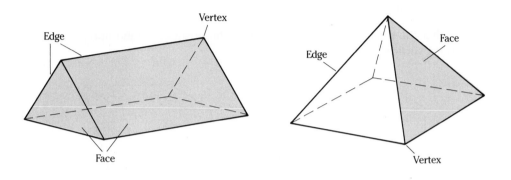

Exercise 11g

Find the volume of this prism.

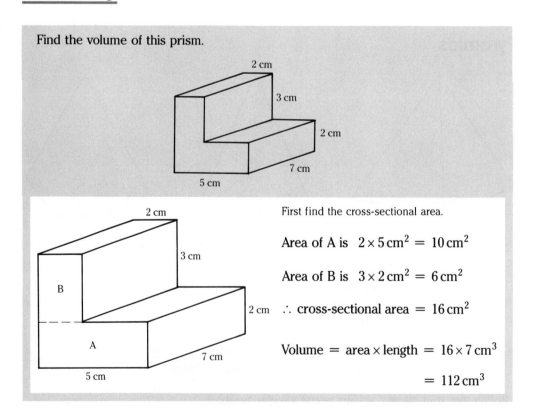

First find the cross-sectional area.

Area of A is $2 \times 5\,\text{cm}^2 = 10\,\text{cm}^2$

Area of B is $3 \times 2\,\text{cm}^2 = 6\,\text{cm}^2$

$\therefore$ cross-sectional area $= 16\,\text{cm}^2$

Volume $=$ area $\times$ length $= 16 \times 7\,\text{cm}^3$

$= 112\,\text{cm}^3$

Find the volume of each of the following prisms.

1.

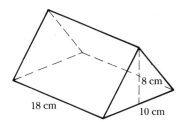

18 cm   8 cm   10 cm

2.

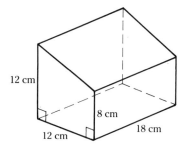

12 cm   8 cm   12 cm   18 cm

3.

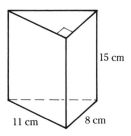

15 cm   11 cm   8 cm

4.

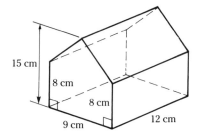

15 cm   8 cm   8 cm   9 cm   12 cm

5.

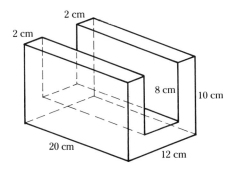

2 cm   2 cm   8 cm   10 cm   20 cm   12 cm

6.

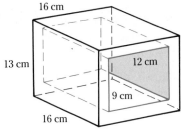

16 cm   13 cm   12 cm   9 cm   16 cm

7. A scout's tent has the shape of a triangular prism. It is 2.6 m long and the triangular end is 2.5 m wide and 1.9 m high.

(a) Find the volume inside the tent.

(b) What is the area of canvas, including the ground sheet, used to make this tent?

8. The uniform cross-section of a water trough is a trapezium 80 cm wide at the top, with a 58 cm wide base; the trough is 45 cm deep and 1.2 m long. Find the capacity of the trough.

9. The volume of a solid with uniform cross-section is 65 cm^3. If the area of its cross-section is 13 cm^2, find its length.

10. A prism of length 12 cm has a square cross-section. The volume of the prism is 108 cm^3. What is the length of a side of its square base?

In questions 11 and 12

(a) sketch a net for the given prism

(b) find the total surface area of the prism (in question 12 you will need to calculate the height of the cross-section).

11.

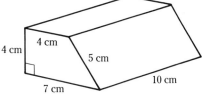

4 cm   4 cm   5 cm   7 cm   10 cm

12.

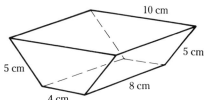

10 cm   5 cm   5 cm   8 cm   4 cm

(a) Find the volume of the pyramid in the diagram, given that its base is rectangular and its height is 9 cm.

(b) Sketch a suitable net, indicating lines that are equal in length.

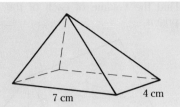

7 cm   4 cm

(a)

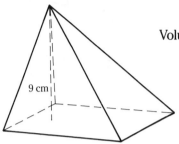

9 cm

Area of base is $4 \times 7 \, \text{cm}^2 = 28 \, \text{cm}^2$

Volume of pyramid is $\frac{1}{3} \times$ base area $\times$ height

$$= \frac{1}{3} \times 28 \times 9 \, \text{cm}^3$$

$$= 84 \, \text{cm}^3$$

(b)

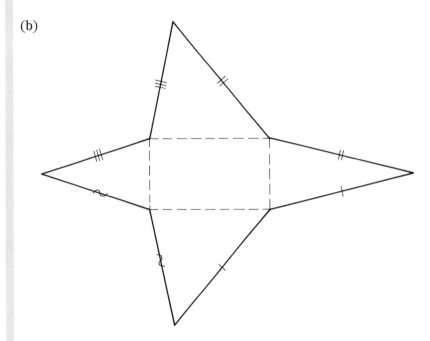

Note that we are not told that it is a right pyramid, i.e. the vertex is not necessarily above the centre of the base.

Other nets are possible but not so straightforward.

In questions 13 to 16 find the volume of each solid.

13. The base of a right pyramid (i.e. the vertex is over the centre of the base) is a square of side 7 cm and its height is 5 cm.

14. The height of a tetrahedron (triangular pyramid) is 6 cm and its base is a triangle of area 24 cm².

15.

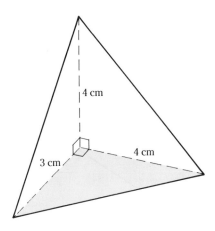

5 cm

9 cm   6 cm

16.

4 cm

3 cm   4 cm

17. Sketch a possible net and find the total surface area of the pyramid given in

(a) question 13

(b) question 16.

18. Sketch each of the following solids and count the number of edges, faces and vertices.

(a) cuboid

(b) triangular prism

(c) square pyramid

(d) tetrahedron

(e) cube

19. (a) Use the facts you collected in question 18 to complete the following table.

Solid	No. of edges (E)	No. of faces (F)	No. of vertices (V)
Cuboid		6	8
Triangular prism	9		
Square pyramid			
Tetrahedron			
Cube			

(b) Can you find a connection between the three numbers in each row of the table ? If you can, write this as a formula relating F, E and V.

(c) If a solid has 10 edges and 6 vertices, how many faces would you expect it to have ? Can you think of a solid with these properties ?

(d) A student added two more solids to the table above. The figures entered were:

E	F	V
8	5	8
11	7	6

Is it possible for either set of numbers to be correct ?

20. This diagram shows a net of a hexagonal prism.

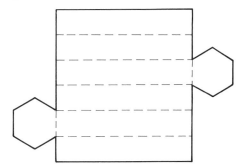

(a) State the number of its faces, edges and vertices

(b) Do your answers check with the formula found in question 19(b) ?

Self-Assessment 11

1. (a) Find the area of a parallelogram with one pair of opposite sides of length 14.7 cm, and 11.3 cm apart.

   (b) Find (i) the height (ii) the area of the parallelogram in the diagram.

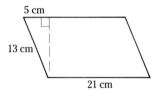

2. Find the area of each triangle.

   (a)

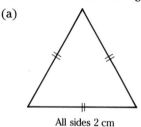

   All sides 2 cm

   (b)

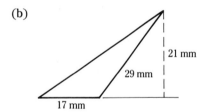

3. On squared paper, using the side of one square to represent 1 cm, draw a triangle with vertices at $(4, -3)$, $(-1, 4)$ and $(3, 6)$. Find its area by enclosing it in a rectangle.

4. In the diagram the side of each grid square represents 1 cm. Find the shaded area. (Look for the quickest method, in which only two separate areas need be calculated.)

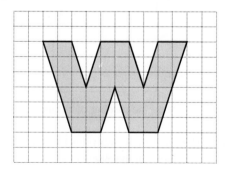

5. Find

   (a) the height of △ABC

   (b) the area of the trapezium shown in the diagram.

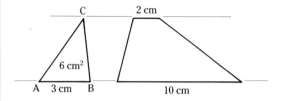

6. The parallel sides of a trapezium are 3.2 cm apart and their lengths are 7.6 cm and 5.3 cm, all measurements being correct to 2 s.f. Find the upper and lower bounds of the area of the trapezium.

7. (a) Find the area of this shape.

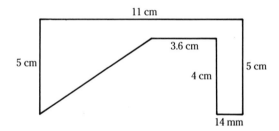

   (b) The floor plan of a conservatory is shown in the diagram. The floor is symmetrical and is to be tiled except for the carpeted area which is shaded. Find the area to be tiled.

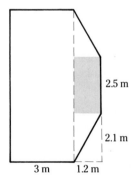

8. (a) Draw a net for the cuboid shown in this diagram.

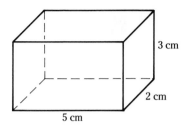

(b) Find the surface area of the cuboid.

9.

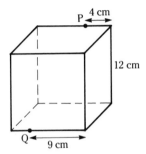

Two points, P and Q, are on the inside of the hollow cube shown in the diagram. A fly is stationary at P. Find how far it moves to get to Q

(a) if it walks only along edges of the cube

(b) if it takes the shortest route on the inside surface of the cube

(c) if it flies directly from P to Q.

10. The dimensions of a cuboid are 3.26 cm by 1.09 cm by 3.10 cm, each correct to 3 s.f. Find the range of values within which the volume lies.

11. The diagram shows a prism and a pyramid, with identical triangular bases and equal heights. Find the volume and surface area of each solid.

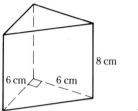 

12. Draw a net for each of the solids given in question 11.

13. The cube shown in the diagram has edges of length 6 cm.

(a) Sketch the section PBR.

(b) Find the lengths of the sides of this section.

(c) Find the area of the section.

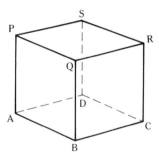

14. For the cube given in question 14,

(a) find the area of △PQB

(b) find the volume of the pyramid PQBR.

12 ▷ CIRCLES, CYLINDERS, CONES AND SPHERES

PARTS OF A CIRCLE

The names of the principal parts of a circle are shown in the diagrams.

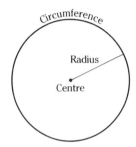
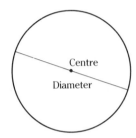

A diameter goes through the centre and is twice as long as the radius.

After measuring the diameter and circumference of a few different circles, it becomes clear that the circumference is given by multiplying the diameter by a number that is a little bigger than 3.

This number cannot be written exactly using figures so is represented by the symbol π.

 Circumference $= \pi \times$ diameter
$C = \pi d \quad \text{or} \quad C = 2\pi r$

The value of π has been calculated to a vast number of decimal places; in fact there is no end to the number of decimal places and no number pattern emerges.
Numbers of this type are called irrational.

In practice no more than three decimal places are usually used and, to this degree of accuracy,

 $\pi = 3.142 \ (3 \ \text{d.p.})$

Even this approximation is not needed very often, as most calculators have a π button which can be used in circle calculations. In all the exercises in this chapter, unless instructed otherwise, use the π button if your calculator has one; if it hasn't, take $\pi = 3.142$. In either case give answers to 3 significant figures whenever it is appropriate.

In situations where only a very rough idea of the circumference of a circle is wanted, taking $\pi \approx 3$ is quite useful. It must be remembered that the result is *less* than the true value however, especially if calculating, say, the length of trim needed to go round a circular table.

CIRCULAR ARCS

Any part of the circumference of a circle is called an *arc*.

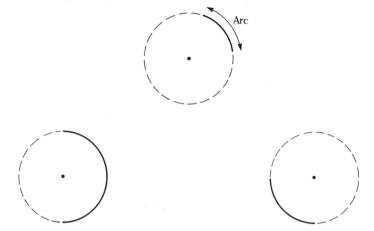

This is a semicircular arc. Its length is half of the circumference of the whole circle.

This is a quadrant arc. Its length is one quarter of the circumference of the whole circle.

The Length of an Arc

In general the length of an arc depends upon the size of the angle at the centre of the circle.

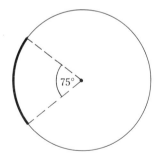

For this arc the angle at the centre is 75°

The complete angle at the centre of the circle is 360°

Hence the length of the arc is $\frac{75}{360}$ of the circumference of the circle, i.e. $\frac{75}{360} \times 2\pi r$

Exercise 12a

1. Use $\pi \approx 3$ to find an approximate value for the circumference of the given circle.

   (a) radius 6 cm   (c) radius 3 m   (e) diameter 8 m

   (b) radius 3.2 mm   (d) diameter 11 cm   (f) diameter 4 mm

For the following questions use a calculator and give answers correct to three significant figures.

2. Find the circumference of a circle of radius

  (a) 38 mm   (c) 10.5 cm

  (b) 4.4 m   (d) 0.25 m

3. Find the circumference of a circle whose diameter is

  (a) 56 cm   (c) 6.3 cm

  (b) 14 m   (d) 9.8 mm

The goal area of a hockey pitch is marked out by a line in the shape of a semicircle of radius 16 yards. Find the length of this line.

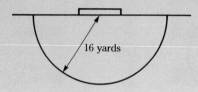

16 yards

$$\text{Circumference of a circle} = 2\pi r$$

The curved goal line is a semicircular arc.

$$\text{Length of line round goal area is } \tfrac{1}{2} \times 2\pi r = \pi r$$

$$= \pi \times 16 \text{ yards}$$

$$= 50.26\ldots \text{ yards}$$

Length of goal line, correct to 3 s.f., is 50.3 yards.

Note that the *perimeter* of the goal area was not asked for, so the base line diameter was not included.

---

4. Find the perimeter of each of the following shapes.

(a)

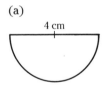

4 cm

(c)

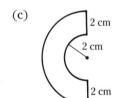

2 cm

2 cm

2 cm

(b)

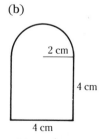

2 cm

4 cm

4 cm

(d)

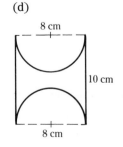

8 cm

10 cm

8 cm

5. A circular flower bed has a diameter of 1.5 m. A metal edging is to be placed round it. Find the length of edging needed and the cost of the edging if it is sold at £6.50 per metre and only a whole number of metres can be bought.

6. A bicycle wheel has a radius of 28 cm.

  (a) What is the circumference of the wheel?

  (b) How far does the wheel travel in one complete revolution?

  (c) If the bicycle travels a distance of 352 m, how many times has the wheel revolved?

  (d) One revolution of the bicycle pedals produces four revolutions of the bicycle wheel. How many revolutions of the pedals make the bicycle travel 106 m?

7. The sides of a square sheet of metal are of length 30 cm. A quadrant of radius 15 cm is cut from each of the four corners. Sketch the shape that is left and find its perimeter.

8. A boy flies a model aeroplane on the end of a wire 10 m long. If he keeps the wire horizontal, how far does his aeroplane fly in one revolution?

9. If the aeroplane described in question 8 takes 1 second to fly 10 m, what is the time taken for 1 revolution? If the aeroplane has enough power to fly for 1 minute, how many revolutions can it perform?

10. A cotton reel has a diameter of 3 cm. If there are 500 turns of thread on the reel, how long is the thread?

11.

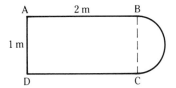

The diagram shows a rectangular breakfast bar with a semicircular flap at the end. Find

(a) the length of BC

(b) the radius of the semicircle

(c) the length of the arc BC

(d) the perimeter of the breakfast bar.

The cross-section of a decorative moulding is a sector of a circle of radius 3 cm. The angle at the centre of the circle is 120°. Find the perimeter of the cross-section.

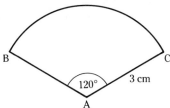

Circumference of a circle $= 2\pi r$

Therefore length of arc BC $= \dfrac{120}{360} \times 2\pi r$

$$= \dfrac{120}{360} \times 2 \times \pi \times 3 \text{ cm}$$

$$= 6.283 \ldots \text{cm}$$

Perimeter of cross-section is   AB + AC + arc BC

$$= (3 + 3 + 6.283 \ldots) \text{cm}$$

$$= 12.3 \text{cm} \qquad (3 \text{ s.f.})$$

12.

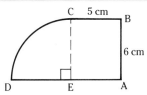

The diagram shows the cross-section of a plinth for a cupboard. Find

(a) the length of EC

(b) the length of the AD

(c) the length of the arc DC

(d) the perimeter of the figure.

13. Find the length of each arc.

(a)

(b)

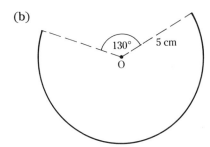

14.

The diagram shows the cross-section of a log splitter. Find the perimeter of the cross-section.

15.

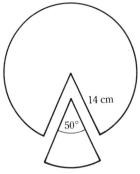

A slice, in the shape of the sector shown, is cut from a cake of radius 14 cm. Find

(a) the length of the curved edge of the slice

(b) the perimeter of the slice

(c) the perimeter of the part of the cake that is left.

16.

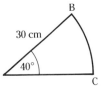

The diagram shows one blade of a fan. Find

(a) the length of the arc BC

(b) the perimeter of the blade.

17.

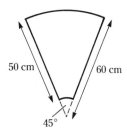

The key-stone of an arch has a cross-section in the shape of a sector of radius 60 cm with a sector of radius 10 cm removed. Find

(a) the length of the inner curved edge

(b) the length of the outer curved edge

(c) the perimeter of the cross-section.

The circumference of a circle is 28 cm.
Find the radius of the circle.

Using $C = 2\pi r$
gives $28 = 2 \times \pi \times r$

$\therefore \qquad \dfrac{28}{2 \times \pi} = r$

So $\qquad\qquad r = 4.456\ldots$

Correct to 3 s.f. the radius is 4.46 cm

---

18. Find the radius of the circle whose circumference is

(a) 44 cm

(b) 121 mm

(c) 831 cm

(d) 550 m

(e) 36.2 mm

(f) 0.3 m

19. A roundabout, which is to be built at a major road junction, has to have a minimum circumference of 192 m. What is the minimum diameter ?

20. The turning circle of a car has a circumference of 63 m. What is the narrowest road in which the car can make a U-turn without going on to the pavement ?

THE AREA OF A CIRCLE

Consider a circle of radius r, and therefore of circumference $2\pi r$.

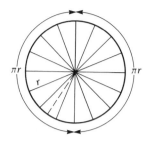

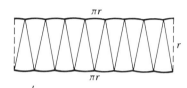

If this circle is cut up into narrow slices (called *sectors*) which are placed together as shown, then a shape that is nearly a rectangle of length πr and width r is produced. The narrower the sectors are, the nearer the shape becomes to a rectangle. The area of the 'rectangle' is $\pi r \times r$, i.e. πr^2, and this is the same as the area, A, of the circle from which it was made. Hence, for a circle of radius r

$$A = \pi r^2$$

The Area of a Sector

A sector of a circle is a portion bounded by an arc and two radii.

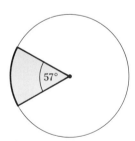

The area of a sector is part of the area of the whole circle and that part is determined by the angle at the centre compared with 360°.

The area, A, of the sector in the diagram is $\dfrac{57}{360}$ of the area of the circle,

i.e.
$$A = \frac{57}{360} \times \pi r^2$$

In general, for a sector with centre angle $x°$,

$$A = \frac{x}{360} \times \pi r^2$$

Exercise 12b

Find the area of

(a) a circle of radius 3.5 cm
(b) a semicircle of radius 5 mm

(a)

Area $= \pi r^2$

$= \pi \times 3.5^2 \text{ cm}^2$

$= 38.48\ldots \text{ cm}^2$

$= 38.5 \text{ cm}^2$ (3 s.f.)

(b)

Area $=$ half area of circle

$= \frac{1}{2} \times \pi r^2$

$= \frac{1}{2} \times \pi \times 5^2 \text{ mm}^2$

$= 39.26\ldots \text{ mm}^2$

$= 39.3 \text{ mm}^2$ (3 s.f.)

1. Find the area of each circle.
   (a)   (c)

   2.1 cm   1.2 m

   (b)   (d)

   9 mm   0.2 m

2. The shape of this flower bed is a semicircle of diameter 6 m.

   Find   (a) its radius   (b) its area.

   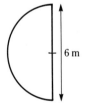

   6 m

3. This diagram shows the cross-section of a window moulding. Find its area.

   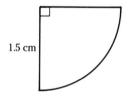

   1.5 cm

4. The floor of a concert hall is square and the stage is a semicircle. Find

   (a) the area of the floor

   (b) the area of the stage

   (c) the total area.

   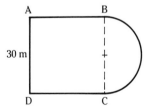

   A   B

   30 m

   D   C

5. The diagram shows a quadrant on one side of a square. Find

   (a) the area of the square

   (b) the area of the quadrant

   (c) the area of the whole figure.

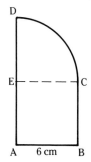

6. Find the area of the shaded shape.

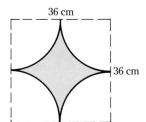

7. Find the area of each shaded shape.

   (a)

   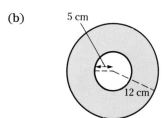

   (b)

   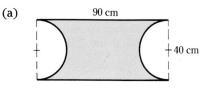

   (c)

   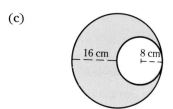

Find the area of this sector.

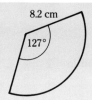

Area of sector is $\dfrac{127}{360}$ of area of circle $= \dfrac{127}{360} \times \pi r^2$

$$= (127 \div 360) \times \pi \times 8.2^2 \text{ cm}^2$$
$$= 74.52\ldots \text{ cm}^2 = 74.5 \text{ cm}^2 \quad (3 \text{ s.f.})$$

---

8. Find the area of each sector.

   (a)

   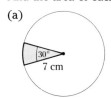

   (b)

   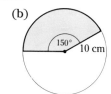

   (c)

   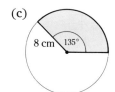

   (d)

   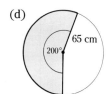

9. This diagram shows the cross-section of a low boundary wall. The cross-section can be divided into a sector of a circle of radius 20 cm and two equal trapeziums. Find each of the areas marked A, B and C, and the total area.

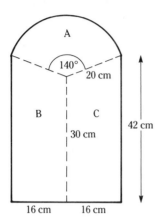

10. A circular bandstand has a diameter of 7 m. The floor is to be sealed.

    (a) Find the area of the floor of the bandstand.

    (b) If one tin of the sealant covers 3 m², how many tins will have to be bought ?

11. A rectangular patio has a circular pond in the middle. Find

    (a) the area of the whole plot

    (b) the area of the pond

    (c) the area of the paved part of the patio

    (d) the circumference of the pond.

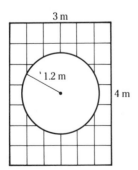

12. The diagram shows the section through a drainage pipe. The bore of the pipe is 14 cm and the wall of the pipe is 11 mm thick. Find

    (a) the area of cross-section of the bore

    (b) the cross-sectional area of the clay from which the pipe is made, i.e. the shaded area.

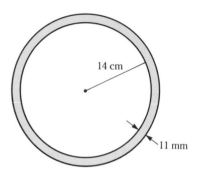

13. The diagram shows a circular engine gasket, of radius 9 cm. The gasket has four circular holes of diameters 5 cm, 5 cm, 6 cm and 8 cm.

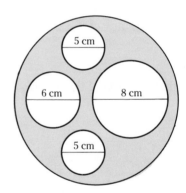

Find, correct to 3 s.f.,

    (a) the area of material removed from the circle to make the gasket

    (b) the area of the gasket.

14. A windscreen wiper blade is 27 cm long and it sweeps through an angle of 156°. What area of the windscreen is cleaned in one sweep ?

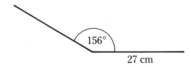

15. A sheet of metal is in the shape of a circle of radius 26 cm. From it is to be cut the largest possible square. Find

 (a) the area of the largest square

 (b) the percentage reduction in perimeter

 (c) the percentage of metal wasted.

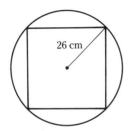

16.

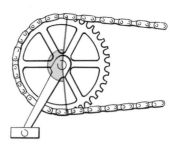

The radius of the chain wheel of a bicycle is 10.4 cm. If the length of chain in contact with the wheel is 34.4 cm, find, to the nearest degree, the angle that this arc forms at the centre of the wheel (shaded in the diagram).

CYLINDERS

Curved Surface Area

Imagine that a thin metal cylinder, without ends, is cut open and the metal flattened. A rectangle is obtained whose width is the height of the cylinder and whose length is equal to the circumference of the cylinder.

The area of the rectangle is therefore $2\pi r \times h$ and this is equal to the area of the curved surface from which it was formed. Hence the area, A, of the curved surface of the cylinder is given by

$$A = 2\pi rh$$

Volume

A solid cylinder has a constant circular cross-section and is therefore a circular prism.

The volume of any prism is given when the base area is multiplied by the height.

Therefore the volume, V, of a cylinder of height h and base radius r is given by $\pi r^2 \times h$, i.e. for a cylinder

$$V = \pi r^2 h$$

Exercise 12c

1. Find the curved surface area of the cylinder whose height, h cm, and radius, r cm, are

    (a) $r = 2$, $h = 6$

    (b) $r = 2.5$, $h = 5.8$

    (c) $r = 30$, $h = 9$

    (d) $r = 5.2$, $h = 7.8$

2. Find the area of the paper label covering the outside of a soup tin (not the top or base) of height 13.6 cm and radius 3.9 cm, given that there is an overlap of 1 cm.

3. A garden roller is in the form of a cylinder of radius 0.24 m and width 0.65 m. What area is rolled by four revolutions of the roller ?

A cylindrical canister is closed (i.e. has a top and a base). It is 18 cm high and the radius of the base is 3 cm. Find the area of the base and the curved surface area.

Hence find the total surface area of the canister.

Area of base $= \pi r^2$
$$= \pi \times 3^2 \text{ cm}^2$$
$$= 28.27\ldots \text{ cm}^2 = 28.3 \text{ cm}^2 \quad (\text{3 s.f.})$$

Curved surface area $= 2\pi rh$
$$= 2 \times \pi \times 3 \times 18 \text{ cm}^2$$
$$= 339.29\ldots \text{ cm}^2 = 339 \text{ cm}^2 \quad (\text{3 s.f.})$$

The total surface area $=$ top $+$ base $+$ curved surface area
$$= (28.27 + 28.27 + 339.29) \text{ cm}^2$$
$$= 395.8\ldots \text{ cm}^2 = 396 \text{ cm}^2 \quad (\text{3 s.f.})$$

3 cm

18 cm

---

4. The radius of a closed cylinder is 2.1 cm and its height is 10 cm.

    Find   (a) the area of its curved surface

    (b) the area of its base

    (c) the total outer surface area.

5. A cylindrical water butt has a diameter of 70 cm and is 92 cm high. It has a removable flat circular lid. What is the outer surface area of the water butt

    (a) without the lid   (b) with the lid on ?

The inside of a cylindrical water tank is 1.26 m high and its radius is 62 cm. Find correct to 3 s.f. the volume inside the tank in cubic centimetres and give the capacity of the tank in litres.

Both dimensions must have the same unit so use   1.26 m $= 126$ cm

Volume inside tank $= \pi r^2 h$
$$= \pi \times 62^2 \times 126 \text{ cm}^3$$
$$= 1\,521\,611 \text{ cm}^3 = 1\,520\,000 \text{ cm}^3 \quad (\text{3 s.f.})$$

$1000 \text{ cm}^3 = 1$ litre

Capacity of tank $= \dfrac{1\,521\,611}{1000}$ litres $= 1520$ litres   (3 s.f.)

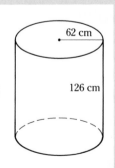

62 cm

126 cm

6. Find the volume of each cylinder whose dimensions are given. Make sure that the units are consistent.

   (a) Radius 1.2 m, height 64 cm.

   (b) Radius 150 cm, height 2 m.

   (c) Radius 0.8 cm, height 22 mm.

7. The internal radius of a cylindrical water tank is 32 cm.

   Find   (a) in cm^3 (b) in litres,
   the amount of water in the tank when the depth of water is 18 cm.

8. A solid cylinder of silver has radius 2 cm and length 6.4 cm.

   (a) Find the volume of the cylinder.

   (b) If one cubic centimetre of silver has a mass of 10.5 g, find the mass of the cylinder.

Find the radius of a cylinder with height 5.3 cm and volume 150 cm^3, giving the answer to the nearest centimetre.

$$V = \pi r^2 h$$

$$\therefore \quad 150 = \pi \times r^2 \times 5.3$$

$$\frac{150}{5.3\,\pi} = r^2$$

$$r^2 = 9.008\ldots$$

$$r = \sqrt{9.008\ldots} = 3.00\ldots$$

To the nearest centimetre the radius is 3 cm.

---

9. The table gives information about a cylinder. Find each missing measurement giving height to 3 s.f. and radius to the nearest whole unit.

	Radius	Height	Volume
(a)	11 cm		1024 cm^3
(b)	3.8 mm		760 mm^3
(c)		1.3 m	17 m^3
(d)		0.12 cm	1.56 cm^3

10. One cubic metre of oil fills a cylindrical drum of radius 40 cm. What is the height of the drum?

11. A rectangular tank measuring 0.6 m by 1 m by 2 m is full of water. The water is all poured into a cylindrical tank and fills it to a depth of 1.5 m. Find

    (a) the volume of the water

    (b) to the nearest centimetre, the diameter of the cylindrical tank.

12. A metal cylinder of length 18 cm and diameter 3 cm is melted down and cast into a cylindrical metal rod of diameter 1 cm. How long is the rod?

13. A cylindrical water butt, of radius 30 cm and height 80 cm, is exactly half full of water. If 60 litres of water are used, what depth of water is left in the butt?

14. A mains water pipe of diameter 1.4 cm delivers water at a rate of 1.2 m/s. How much water comes out per second? (Find how much water there is in a 1.2 m length of pipe.)

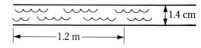

15. A cylindrical jar contains 462 g of marmalade. If the mass of 1 cubic centimetre of marmalade is 1.16 g, find the volume of marmalade in the jar. If the jar is full and its radius is 3.5 cm, find the height of the jar.

16. The diagram shows a spacing collar for a spindle. It is in the form of a metal cylinder with a cylindrical hole drilled through the centre.

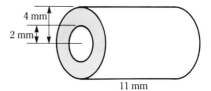

    Use the given dimensions to find

    (a) the volume of metal removed by the drill

    (b) the volume of metal in the collar

    (c) the density of the metal, in g/cm^3, given that the collar has a mass of 3.32 g.

CONES AND SPHERES

The Volume of a Cone

Any solid that has a flat base and which comes up to a point (the vertex) is a pyramid.

The volume of any pyramid is known to be given by $\frac{1}{3} \times$ area of base $\times$ height

A cone is a pyramid with a circular base, therefore the volume, V, of a cone with height h and base radius r, is given by $\frac{1}{3} \times \pi r^2 \times h$, i.e. for a cone

$$V = \tfrac{1}{3}\pi r^2 h$$

In this book we shall deal only with *right* cones, i.e. those where the vertex is vertically above the centre of the base.

The Surface Area of a Cone

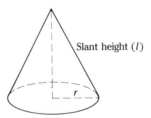
Slant height (l)

r

The surface of a cone without a base is entirely curved and its area is given by a formula which is justified in question 11 in the next exercise, i.e.

Curved surface area of a cone $= \pi \times r \times l$

If the cone also has a base, whose area is πr^2, then the total surface area of the cone is the sum of these two parts.

Total surface area of a cone $= \pi r l + \pi r^2$

The Volume of a Sphere

The volume, V, and the surface area, A, of a sphere of radius r, are given by

$$V = \tfrac{4}{3}\pi r^3 \quad \text{and} \quad A = 4\pi r^2$$

(It is not possible to justify either of these formulae at this stage.)

Exercise 12d

A cone is of height 12 cm and base radius 35 mm.

Find   (a) its volume   (b) its curved surface area.

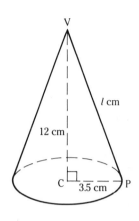

Units must be consistent so use   35 mm = 3.5 cm

(a) $$V = \tfrac{1}{3}\pi r^2 h$$

$$= \frac{\pi \times 3.5^2 \times 12}{3}$$

$$= 153.93\ldots$$

The volume is 154 cm^3 (3 s.f.)

(b) First we need the slant height. Use $\triangle$VCP.

$$l^2 = 12^2 + 3.5^2 = 156.25 \quad \text{Pythagoras}$$

$$\therefore \qquad\qquad l = 12.5$$

$$A = \pi r l$$

$$= \pi \times 3.5 \times 12.5$$

$$= 137.44\ldots$$

The curved surface area is 137 cm^2 (3 s.f.)

1. For each solid cone whose dimensions are given find

   (i) the volume   (ii) the curved surface area   (iii) the total surface area

	Base radius	Height
(a)	14.7 cm	85 cm
(b)	6 cm	13 cm
(c)	98 mm	256 mm

2. A cylindrical pencil has a conical point as shown. Find the volume of the sharpened pencil.

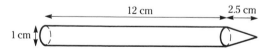

3. A solid cone is 16 cm high and its base radius is 10 cm. The top part of the cone, which is 8 cm high and has a base radius of 5 cm, is cut off. (The portion left is called a *frustum* of a cone.) Find the volume of the frustum.

4. An injection moulding tool for producing plastic cones is a cylindrical metal block with a conical hole drilled in it. The cylinder and the cone have the same radius, 4.6 cm, and length, 11.9 cm. Find the volume of the tool.

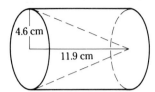

5. A bollard is in the form of a cylinder surmounted by a cone with the same radius. The total height of the bollard is 32 cm, the height of the cylinder is 23 cm and the common radius is 6 cm. Find the volume of the bollard.

Find the volume and surface area of a sphere with radius 14 cm.

$$V = \tfrac{4}{3}\pi r^3$$

$$= \tfrac{4}{3} \times \pi \times 14^3$$

$$= 11\,494.0\ldots$$

The volume is $11\,500\text{ cm}^3$ (3 s.f.)

$$A = 4\pi r^2$$

$$= 4 \times \pi \times 14^2$$

$$= 2463.00\ldots$$

The surface area is 2460 cm^2 (3 s.f.)

---

6. Find the volume and surface area of a sphere whose radius is
   (a) 5 cm   (b) 12 mm   (c) 0.9 m

7. Find the volume of a hemisphere (half of a sphere) with radius 14 mm.

8. Standing in front of the Pepper Pot Café is a model of a pepper pot made up of a cylinder surmounted by a hemisphere. The radius both of the cylinder and the hemisphere is 20 cm and the height of the model pepper pot is 58 cm. Find the volume of the model.

9. Twenty-four tennis balls, each of diameter 62 mm, are packed in a rectangular carton, in layers of 8 as shown.

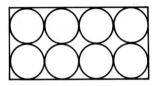

   (a) Find, in centimetres, the dimensions of the smallest possible box.

   (b) Find the volume of the 24 balls.

   (c) What percentage of the volume of the box is occupied by the balls?

10. In a depot, oil is stored in rectangular tanks, each 0.8 m high and with a square base of side 0.7 m. The oil is sold in cylindrical tins of height 25 cm and base radius 5 cm. Find, in cubic centimetres, the volume of oil in

   (a) a full storage tank   (b) a full tin.

   Assuming that no oil is spilt, how many tins can be filled completely from a full tank?

11.

When this cone is cut along the green line and opened out, it gives the sector of a circle as shown.

   (a) Write down
      (i) the length of the curved edge of the sector
      (ii) the circumference of the circle of which it is a part.

   (b) Hence show that the area of the sector is $\dfrac{r}{l}$ of the area of the circle.

   (c) Use the information in (b) to show that the area of the sector, and hence the area of the curved surface of the cone, is given by $A = \pi r l$.

DIMENSIONS OF LENGTH, AREA AND VOLUME

The formulae for finding the lengths, areas and volumes of various objects all contain letters that represent numbers of length units (or area units or volume units). Some of the formulae also contain numbers, and symbols that represent numbers, such as π. An expression that contains only one symbol representing a number of length units is *one-dimensional.* Its value must be given in cm, km, feet, etc.

An expression containing the product of two length unit symbols gives an area. It is *two-dimensional* and its value must be a number of (length)^2 units, e.g. m^2, mm^2.

Three length unit symbols multiplied together (or an area symbol multiplied by a length symbol) give a *three-dimensional* formula. The result is a volume, which is measured in (length)^3 units, e.g. cm^3, m^3.

A number or symbol that does not represent a number of units of length, area or volume, has no effect on the dimension of an expression.

For example, if d is a number of length units and a is a number of area units, then

$$4d \text{ is one-dimensional} \quad (\text{length})$$
$$3d^2 \text{ is two-dimensional} \quad (\text{area})$$
$$\pi a \text{ is two-dimensional}$$
$$2\pi d^3 \text{ is three dimensional} \quad (\text{volume})$$
$$ad \text{ is three-dimensional}$$

Checking dimensions and units helps to identify whether a quantity represents length, area or volume, e.g. a quantity given as $x\,\text{cm}^2$ must be an area.

Applying the same check helps in spotting an incorrect formula. Suppose, for example, that a formula for the volume, V, of an object is given as $V = \frac{1}{3}\pi xy$ where x and y are numbers of length units.

Volume is three-dimensional, whereas $\frac{1}{3}\pi xy$ is only two-dimensional, so the formula cannot be correct.

Exercise 12e

1. State whether each of the following quantities is a length, an area or a volume.
   (a) 10 cm
   (b) 21 cm^3
   (c) 85 cm^2
   (d) 9 km^2
   (e) 630 mm
   (f) 4π mm^3
   (g) 2π cm
   (h) 3 m

2. State whether each of the following quantities should be measured in length, area or volume units.
   (a) The diameter of a circle.
   (b) The region inside a square.
   (c) The space inside a sphere.

3. State whether each of the following quantities should be measured in length, area or volume units.
   (a) A perimeter.
   (b) The amount of air in a room.
   (c) The surface of a cone.

4. The letters a, b and c each represent a number of centimetres. Write down a suitable unit (e.g. cm^2) for the subject of each of the following formulae.
   (a) $N = a + b$
   (b) $R = 4\pi ab$
   (c) $X = 4\pi a^2$
   (d) $Y = \pi a^3$
   (e) $P = 2\pi c$
   (f) $S = abc$

In questions 5 and 6, *a* and *b* represent numbers of length units, *A* and *B* represent numbers of area units and *V* represents a number of volume units.

5. State whether *X* represents a number of units of length, area or volume.

(a) $X = \pi ab$ (e) $X = \dfrac{\pi V}{a}$

(b) $X = a + b$ (f) $X = 2Ab$

(c) $X = \pi B$ (g) $X = a^2 + b^2$

(d) $X = \pi ab^2$ (h) $X = \dfrac{V}{ab}$

6. Some of the following formulae are wrongly constructed. State, with a reason, which are incorrect.

(a) $B = ab$ (d) $V = 2a^2 b$

(b) $A = \pi b^2$ (e) $V = a + B$

(c) $A = a^2 + b^3$ (f) $A = a(a + b)$

7. Peter was asked to find the area of a circle with diameter 18 cm. He wrote down:

$$\text{Area} = 2\pi r$$
$$= 2 \times \pi \times 9 \, \text{cm}^2$$
$$= 56.5 \, \text{cm}^2$$

Louise did not know any circle formulae but she knew that Peter was wrong. How did she know?

8. Emma looked up in her notes to find the formula she was supposed to use to find the volume of a certain solid. What she found was $V = \pi x^? y$ and she couldn't read the index number. She knew that *x* and *y* were units of length. What was the index number?

9. Two lengths are given as *x* cm and *y* cm. Does the expression represent a length, an area, a volume or none of these?

(a) $(x + y)(x - y)$ (c) $\dfrac{x^2 + y^2}{x}$

(b) $x + xy$ (d) $xy^2 - y^3$

Self-Assessment 12

In this exercise give answers that are not exact to 3 s.f. unless a different instruction is given.

1. A square PQRS is drawn inside a circle of radius 16 cm as shown.

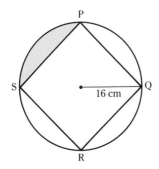

Find the complete perimeter of the shaded part.

2. Referring to the diagram in question 1 find, to the nearest square centimetre,

   (a) the area of the circle

   (b) the area of the shaded part.

3. Find the area of each shaded sector.

   (a)

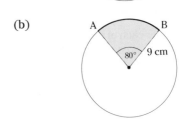

   (b)

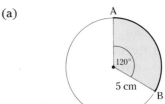

   (c)

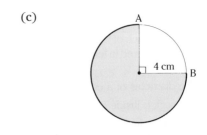

4. Find the length of the arc AB in each part of question 3.

5. Mr Gardener has designed a lawn in the shape of a sector of a circle with radius 2.8 m, as shown in the diagram. He plans to edge the whole lawn with a flexible edging, which is sold by the metre at £4.60 per metre.

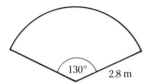

130°
2.8 m

   (a) Find the distance all round the edge of the lawn.
   (b) What will the lawn edging cost ?
   (c) Find the area of the lawn.
   (d) If grass seed is sown at 56 grams per square metre, find how much seed will be needed for the lawn.

6. The concrete foundation for a post is shown in the diagram. It consists of a cylindrical portion surmounting a conical base. Find
   (a) its total surface area
   (b) its volume
   (c) its mass given that the density of concrete is 2360 kg/m³.

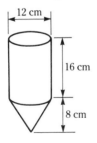

12 cm

16 cm

8 cm

7. Biscuits are sold in cylindrical tins 7 cm high and with a radius of 12 cm. A paper label covers the curved surface of the tin and overlaps by 4 mm. Find the volume of the tin and the area of the label.

8. Sticks of chalk, 8 cm long and 1 cm in diameter, are sold in packets each containing two rows of five sticks. The packet is a cuboid measuring 8.5 cm by 5.5 cm by 2.2 cm. Calculate
   (a) the total volume of ten sticks of chalk
   (b) the volume of the packet
   (c) the percentage of the volume of the packet that is wasted.

9. Twelve identical metal spheres each have a radius of 8 mm.
   (a) Find the total surface area of the twelve spheres.
   (b) Find the volume of all twelve spheres.

   The spheres are melted down and cast, without loss, into a cylindrical rod of diameter 20 mm. What is the length of the rod ?

10. The volume of a solid metal cylinder, A, is 176 cm³. A second cylinder, B, has the same height as A but its radius is twice that of A.
    (a) Cylinder A is melted down and formed into a cuboid whose cross-section is a square of side 4 cm. What is the length of the cuboid ?
    (b) What is the volume of cylinder B ?
    (c) Cylinder B is melted and formed into a circular disc 2 cm thick. Find the radius of the disc.

RATIO AND PROPORTION

RATIO

Ratio is a form of comparison.

'The ratio of 4 g to 12 g' means '4 g compared with 12 g'

A ratio can often be simplified, i.e. expressed in smaller numbers,

e.g.   4 g compared with 12 g is the same as 1 g compared with 3 g
which is the same as   1 compared with 3

Rather than write 'compared with' every time, we use the symbol   :
So 1 compared with 3 is written 1 : 3

Exercise 13a

1. Using the symbol : write each sentence as an equation.

   (a) 16 m compared with 24 m is the same as 2 compared with 3.

   (b) 12 p compared with 48 p is the same as 1 compared with 4.

   (c) 8 kg compared with 14 kg is the same as 4 compared with 7.

2. Write each statement as a sentence.

   (a) 36 p : 18 p = 2 : 1

   (b) 18 g : 20 g = 9 : 10

   (c) 240 : 180 = 4 : 3

   > **Simplify the ratio**
   > (a) £75 : £60   (b) 10 : 18 : 24
   >
   > (a) £75 : £60 = 75 : 60 = 5 : 4
   >   dividing by 15
   >
   > (b) 10 : 18 : 24 = 5 : 9 : 12
   >   (The only number that divides into all three numbers is 2.)

   Simplify each ratio.

3. (a) 32 : 96   (c) 16 : 28

   (b) 7 : 21   (d) 108 : 48

4. (a) 20 : 8 : 32   (c) 14 : 21 : 35

   (b) 9 : 15 : 27   (d) 12 : 30 : 42

5. (a) 35 p : 42 p   (c) 72 g : 150 g

   (b) 18 m : 42 m   (d) £18 : £14

   > **Express in its simplest form the ratio**
   > **4 m : 75 cm**
   >
   > The given units are not the same. It is usually best to change the larger unit to the smaller one.
   >
   > 4 m = 400 cm
   >
   > 4 m : 75 cm = 400 cm : 75 cm
   >
   >   = 400 : 75
   >
   >   = 16 : 3

   Simplify each ratio.

6. (a) 60 p : £1.40   (c) 36 mm : 1.2 cm

   (b) 1.25 kg : 850 g   (d) 45 min : 2 h

7. (a) 950 m : 1.5 km   (c) 550 m : 1.1 km

   (b) £2.40 : 96 p   (d) 40 g : 0.56 kg

8. (a) 3 m : 12 m : 9 m   (c) £28 : £18 : £8

   (b) 15 g : 9 g : 6 g   (d) 12 p : £1 : 72 p

We have seen that some ratios are simplified if both parts are divided by a common factor. To simplify ratios which include fractions we *multiply* both parts by the same number.

Simplify the ratio   (a) $2 : \frac{2}{3}$ (b) $\frac{1}{2} : \frac{2}{3}$

(a) $2 : \frac{2}{3} = 6 : 2$ multiplying by 3

$\phantom{2 : \frac{2}{3}} = 3 : 1$

(b) $\frac{1}{2} : \frac{2}{3} = 3 : 4$ multiplying by 6, the common denominator of 2 and 3

Express each ratio in its simplest form.

9. (a) $2 : \frac{1}{2}$ (c) $\frac{4}{5} : 5$

(b) $3 : \frac{4}{3}$ (d) $4 : \frac{7}{8}$

10. (a) $\frac{1}{5} : \frac{5}{6}$ (c) $\frac{4}{3} : \frac{5}{6}$

(b) $\frac{1}{4} : \frac{1}{7}$ (d) $6 : 4\frac{1}{2}$

In the following problems, express all ratios in their simplest form.

11. A man earns £5500 and pays income tax of £860. What is the ratio of tax to earnings ?

12. A snack bar sells 84 cans of cola and 54 cans of lemonade. Write down and simplify the ratio of the sales of cola to lemonade.

13. There are 280 vehicles in a car park; 42 are vans and the rest are cars. Find the ratio of the number of cars to the number of vans.

14. In a group of 32 students, 18 are female. Find the ratio of
   (a) the number of female students to the number of male students
   (b) the number of female students to the total number of students.

15. One rectangle is 8 cm long by 4.5 cm wide and another one is of length 7 cm and width 5 cm. Taking them in the order given, find the ratio of their
   (a) lengths   (c) perimeters
   (b) widths   (d) areas.

16. Find
   (a) the cost of 11 m² of vinyl flooring at £8.40 per square metre
   (b) the cost of 44 vinyl tiles at £2.40 each
   (c) the ratio of the cost of the vinyl flooring to the cost of the tiles.

17. The diagram shows the design of a garden.

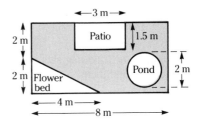

Find the ratio of the areas of
   (a) the patio to the lawn
   (b) the pond to the patio
   (c) the flower bed to the lawn.

Take $\pi \approx 3$.

18.

A solid cone has a base radius of 15 cm and its height is 20 cm. Find the ratio of the surface area of this cone to the surface area of a sphere of radius 15 cm.

RELATIVE SIZES OF RATIOS

One way to compare the sizes of two or more ratios, is to express them as fractions with the same denominator.

Exercise 13b

Which is the larger ratio,
$$4:5 \text{ or } 5:6?$$

First express $4:5$ as $\frac{4}{5}$ and $5:6$ as $\frac{5}{6}$.
Then make the denominators the same;
30 has both 5 and 6 as factors.

$$\frac{4}{5} = \frac{24}{30} \quad \text{and} \quad \frac{5}{6} = \frac{25}{30}$$

So $5:6$ is larger than $4:5$

---

1. Find the larger of the two given ratios.
   (a) $3:4$ or $5:7$ (c) $3:5$ or $2:3$
   (b) $8:5$ or $13:8$ (d) $3:7$ or $4:9$

2. In each of the following sets of ratios, some are equal. Find them.
   (a) $1:\frac{3}{4}$, $8:6$, $20:15$
   (b) $\frac{2}{5}:3$, $4:30$, $\frac{1}{10}:\frac{3}{4}$
   (c) $\frac{2}{3}:\frac{3}{4}$, $240:360$, $8:9$
   (d) $1\frac{1}{2}:2\frac{1}{2}$, $\frac{3}{10}:\frac{1}{2}$, $8:15$

When a ratio is used to describe the scale of a map, the first number in the ratio is very often 1, i.e. the ratio is given in the form $1:n$

Write in the form $1:n$ the ratio
(a) $3:10$ (b) $5\,\text{cm}:2\,\text{km}$

(a) $3:10 = 1:\frac{10}{3} = 1:3.33$
$$(3\,\text{s.f.})$$

(b) $2\,\text{km} = 200\,000\,\text{cm}$
$$5\,\text{cm}:2\,\text{km} = 5:200\,000$$
$$= 1:40\,000$$

---

3. Find each ratio in the form $1:n$, giving n to 3 s.f. where necessary.
   (a) $25:10\,000$ (c) $2:15$
   (b) $5:8$ (d) $8:25$

4. A certain map is drawn so that 5 cm represents 100 km.
   (a) Express this map ratio in the form $1:n$.
   (b) What distance is represented by 17 cm on the map?

5. John is considering which of two road map books to buy. They both have the same page size but map book A uses a scale of $1:10\,000$ while the scale of the maps in book B is $1:50\,000$. John wants the one that gives the larger area of the country on each page. Which should he choose?

If $x:3 = 6:5$, find x.

$x:3 = 6:5$ gives $\dfrac{x}{3} = \dfrac{6}{5}$

$\therefore \qquad\qquad 3 \times \dfrac{x}{3} = 3 \times \dfrac{6}{5}$

$\therefore \qquad\qquad\qquad x = \dfrac{18}{5}$

Hence $x = 3\frac{3}{5}$

Note that if x is the second number in the ratio it is usually easier to reverse both ratios before trying to calculate x,

e.g.   if $3:x = 7:5$

then $x:3 = 5:7$

6. Find x if

(a) $x : 4 = 3 : 5$

(b) $x : 7 = 1 : 2$

(c) $4 : 3 = x : 4$

(d) $3 : 2 = 5 : x$

(e) $7 : 3 = x : 1\frac{1}{2}$

(f) $3 : 7 = 2 : x$

7. In a school the ratio of girls to boys is $5 : 4$. If there are 360 boys how many girls are there? (Let x be the number of girls.)

8. In a certain road there are 16 bungalows. If the ratio of the number of houses to the number of bungalows is $3 : 2$, find the number of houses.

9. The distance 'as the crow flies' between Apton and Bendale is 12 km. The scale of a map of this area is $1 : 250\,000$. What is the distance between Apton and Bendale on the map?

DIVISION IN A GIVEN RATIO

Suppose that £450 is to be divided among Tom, Dick and Harry in the ratio $2 : 3 : 4$. This means that Tom gets 2 portions, Dick gets 3 portions and Harry gets 4. Before the money can be shared out we need to know what one portion is; we divide £450 into $(2 + 3 + 4)$ parts, i.e. 9 parts, so one part is £50. Then Tom gets $2 \times £50 = £100$, Dick gets $3 \times £50 = £150$ and Harry gets $4 \times £50 = £200$. Any quantity can be divided in this way into any number of shares in a given ratio.

The total of the calculated shares should always be checked. In the case above, $£100 + £150 + £200 = £450$, which is correct.

Another type of example occurs when we have to divide a line in a particular ratio.

Consider the point P that divides the line joining A and B in the ratio $5 : 2$. This means that $AP : PB = 5 : 2$.

If P is between A and B, we say that AB is divided internally in the ratio $5 : 2$ and in this case the length of AB must be divided into 7 portions; the length of AP is 5 portions and the length of PB is 2 portions.

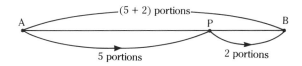

If, on the other hand, P lies on AB produced (or on BA produced) then AB is said to be divided *externally* in the specified ratio. When the ratio is $5 : 2$, P is further from A than from B so P lies on AB produced.

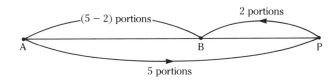

This time the length of AB represents $(5 - 2)$, i.e. 3 portions.

If the specified external ratio were 3 : 8 say, then P would be nearer to A than to B and P would lie on BA produced.

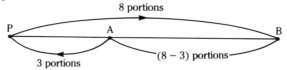

Exercise 13c

1. (a) Divide 48 kg into two parts in the ratio 5 : 1

   (b) Divide 40 minutes into two parts in the ratio 3 : 2

2. (a) Divide 128 g into three parts in the ratio 4 : 3 : 1

   (b) Divide £ 84 into three parts in the ratio 2 : 2 : 3

3. Find the length of AP if P divides the line AB internally in the ratio 3 : 1 and AB is 28 cm long.

4. On a map the direct distance between Lowburgh and Benchurch is 6.5 cm. The village of Winton divides the line joining these towns internally in the ratio 9 : 4. Find the distances on the map between Lowburgh and Winton and between Winton and Benchurch.

5. Two points X and Y are 35 cm apart. Find the lengths of XZ and ZY if Z divides XY

   (a) internally in the ratio 4 : 3

   (b) externally in the ratio 4 : 3

   (c) externally in the ratio 3 : 4

   Illustrate each solution by a line diagram.

6. Teresa weighs 52 kg and Dawn weighs 48 kg. Divide 200 g of chocolate between them in the ratio of their weights.

7. Share 45 sweets among three children in the ratio 3 : 5 : 7

8. A village Fun Day raised £ 3500, which was divided in the ratio 2 : 3 between the Village Hall Fund and Cancer Research. How much was given to Cancer Research ?

9. A garage repair bill came to £ 217. The ratio of the cost of parts to the cost of labour was 3 : 4. What was the labour cost ?

10. Mr Hill decides to give £ 12 000 to his two daughters, to be divided between them in the ratio of their ages. The girls have the same birthday and at present they are 14 and 16 years old. How much money will each daughter receive if the money is given

    (a) today

    (b) in five years' time

    (c) in fifteen years' time ?

    After how many years do you think the daughters would receive equal amounts ?

11. A fruit cake contains flour, sugar, butter and dried fruit. The ratio of the weights of these ingredients is 4 : 2 : 2 : 3. If this cake mixture weighs 1.76 kg, what is the weight of each ingredient ?

12. The angles of a triangle are in the ratio 4 : 5 : 6. Find each angle.

DIRECT PROPORTION

Another word that is used for comparing quantities is *proportion*. For example, if a number of identical books are purchased, the total cost is proportional to the number of books bought; double the number of books and the cost doubles, treble the number and the cost trebles and so on.

Two varying quantities that are always in the same ratio are said to be *in proportion*. This type of relationship is called *direct proportion*.

Solving Problems

A. By the Unitary Method

A machine labels 640 bottles in 4 minutes. How many will it label in 1 hour?

First find the number of labels applied in 1 minute.

In 4 minutes the machine labels 640 bottles

In 1 minute the machine labels $\frac{640}{4}$ bottles

i.e. the machine labels 160 bottles in 1 minute

1 hour = 60 minutes

In 60 minutes the machine labels 160×60 bottles

i.e. 9600 bottles.

In the example above the method used was to find first the 'unit' quantity; in this case the number of labels per minute, i.e. in one unit of time. This way of dealing with proportion problems is called the *unitary method*. It is usually obvious which quantity to take one unit of but, if in doubt, remember that it is the quantity of which different amounts are mentioned. In the example, two different times are mentioned, so we need to find what happens in one unit of time.

B. By the Ratio Method

An alternative method uses direct proportion, i.e. two equal ratios, and is explained by solving the same problem again.

A machine labels 640 bottles in 4 minutes. How many will it label in 1 hour?

Let x be the number of bottles labelled in 60 minutes.

The number of bottles is in direct proportion to the time taken.

$$\frac{x}{60} = \frac{640}{4}$$

$$60 \times \frac{x}{60} = 60 \times \frac{640}{4} = 9600$$

In 60 minutes the machine labels 9600 bottles.

Note that when using this method the ratios should be arranged so that x is in the numerator. In the solution above, for example, it would not be so easy if the ratios were written in the form $\dfrac{60}{x} = \dfrac{4}{640}$

Exercise 13d

Which of the methods on the previous page is used is a matter of personal choice. In this exercise use the method you prefer.

1. A car uses 40 litres of petrol in travelling 280 miles. How much will be used on a journey of 84 miles?

2. Working on his own, a bricklayer building a wall can lay 288 bricks in 4 hours. How many bricks can he lay in $6\frac{1}{2}$ hours?

3. If it costs £9.60 to feed a dog for 11 days, how much will it cost to feed the same dog for 14 days?

4. A wire 33 cm long has a mass of 561 g. What is the mass of 13 cm of this wire?

5. On a hundred-mile trial, a cyclist covers 65 miles in 4 hr 20 min. If she continues at the same speed, how long will she take for the complete course?

6. This recipe is meant to make 12 scones.

240 g flour	40 g sultanas
60 g margarine	75 mℓ milk
24 g sugar	Pinch of salt

   Convert this recipe so that 16 scones can be made.

7. Flying at an average speed of 780 km/h, an aircraft covers 9360 km in a given time. How far can it travel in the same time at an average speed of 720 km/h?

In a mix for making mortar, 70 kg of sand are mixed with 20 kg of cement.

(a) How much sand is needed to mix with 30 kg of cement?

(b) How much cement is needed to mix with 1400 kg of sand?

In the two parts of this question the order of the given and required quantities is reversed. In this situation a different starting point is needed for each part, whichever method is used.

Unitary Method

(a) In this part we work with one unit of cement.

   20 kg of cement are mixed with 70 kg of sand

   1 kg of cement is mixed with $\frac{70}{20}$ kg, i.e. 3.5 kg of sand

   ∴ 30 kg of cement are mixed with 30×3.5 kg, i.e. 105 kg of sand

(b) Now we work with one unit of sand.

   70 kg of sand are mixed with 20 kg of cement

   1 kg of sand is mixed with $\frac{20}{70}$ kg, i.e. $\frac{2}{7}$ kg of cement

   1400 kg of sand are mixed with $1400 \times \frac{2}{7}$ kg, i.e. 400 kg of cement

Ratio Method

To use the ratio method for part (a), where the quantity of sand is to be found, we take x kg as the amount of sand. In part (b) however, the quantity of cement is required so we take this quantity as y kg.

Note that the information in examples of this type is sometimes expressed in a different form e.g. 'sand and cement are mixed in the ratio 7 : 2'. The methods of solution are just the same.

8. If a fan-heater consumes 6 units of electricity in $2\frac{1}{2}$ hours,

   (a) how many units will be consumed in 10 hours

   (b) for how many hours will the heater run on 15 units ?

9. A farmer is using a tractor to plough a square field. He can drive the tractor 13 times across the field in $45\frac{1}{2}$ minutes.

   (a) How long will it take to cross the field 27 times ?

   (b) How many times can he cross the field in $66\frac{1}{2}$ minutes ?

10. For an area of $18\,\text{m}^2$, the amount of a fertiliser required is 675 g.

   (a) How much is needed to fertilise $11\,\text{m}^2$?

   (b) What area will 862.5 g fertilise ?

11. The cost of $14\,\text{m}^2$ of carpet is £176.40.

   (a) How much will $11\,\text{m}^2$ cost ?

   (b) How much carpet can be bought for £113.40 ?

12. Among the ingredients given in a recipe for sponge cake are: 500 g flour, 300 g butter and 4 eggs. The recipe can be adapted to make larger or smaller cakes. If someone wanted to make a cake using 100 g of butter, what decision could be made about the number of eggs ?

13. Copper and tin are mixed in the ratio 3 : 7 to form an alloy.

   (a) How much copper is needed to mix with 42 g of tin ?

   (b) How much tin should be mixed with 15 g of copper ?

   (c) How much of each metal is there in 1 kg of alloy ?

INVERSE PROPORTION

There are some cases where one quantity varies in a way that is linked to another quantity but where an increase in one quantity causes a *decrease* in the other.

Consider, for example, the times that a cyclist would take to cover a distance of 48 miles at various steady speeds.

Speed in miles per hour	4	6	8	12	16
Time taken in hours	12	8	6	4	3

Notice that as the speed goes up the time taken for the journey goes down.
This is an example of *inverse proportion*.
Notice also that speed × time always has the same value.

In general

**the product of
two inversely proportional quantities is constant**

WARNING   Although many quantities are either directly or inversely proportional, a great many more are not. Always be prepared to think carefully before assuming that either of these relationships applies to quantities being considered – or in fact whether there is any relationship at all.

Exercise 13e

> A farmer has enough feed to last his 36 cows 30 days from today. If he buys an extra 12 cows today, how long will the feed last?
>
> *Unitary Method*
>
> $$36 \text{ cows can be fed for } 30 \text{ days}$$
>
> $$1 \text{ cow can be fed for } 30 \times 36 \text{ days} \quad (\text{a longer time})$$
>
> $$48 \text{ cows can be fed for } \frac{30 \times 36}{48} \text{ days}$$
>
> i.e. for $22\frac{1}{2}$ days
>
> *Constant Product Method*
>
> Let x be the required number of days
>
> Then
> $$48 \times x = 36 \times 30 = 1080$$
>
> $$\therefore \qquad x = \frac{1080}{48} = 22\frac{1}{2}$$
>
> The feed will last $22\frac{1}{2}$ days.

1. Which of the following quantities are
   (i) directly proportional
   (ii) inversely proportional
   (iii) not simply related?

   (a) The number of a particular make of ball-point pen bought and the total cost.

   (b) The number of people doing a job and the time taken to finish it.

   (c) The thickness of a pad of notepaper and the number of sheets in it.

   (d) The ages of students and their mathematics marks.

   (e) The length of a trench and the time taken by one man to dig it.

   (f) A woman's age when she married and the number of children she has.

   (g) The steady speed of a car and the time it takes to cover a fixed distance.

   (h) The steady speed of a car and the distance it covers in a fixed time.

2. The length of an essay, typed at an average of 10 words per line, is 204 lines long. How many lines will it occupy if it is retyped at an average of 12 words to the line?

3. A library has funds to buy 280 books that cost £15 each. How many books costing £10.50 could be bought instead?

4. When nine hikers share out their packs of sandwiches equally they get 5 each. If three of the hikers didn't want any sandwiches, how many would each of the others get?

5. A plane takes 4 hours to fly a certain distance at 750 m.p.h.

   (a) How long would the flight take at 800 m.p.h.?

   (b) At what speed should the plane fly to complete the flight in 4 hours 10 minutes?

6. If the students on a course are split into tutorial groups of 8, there will be 15 groups.

   (a) How many groups of 10 would there be?

   (b) If only 6 tutors are available, how many students will be in each group?

7. A supplier delivers a regular quantity of bulk feed to a chicken farm. The quantity lasts for 14 days when there are 500 chickens.

   (a) How long does the quantity last when the number of chickens is 420?

   (b) How many chickens can be fed for 20 days?

8. A contractor estimates that he can carry out the fencing of a large estate in 9 days if he employs 4 labourers.

   (a) How many labourers would be needed to complete the work in 6 days?

   (b) How long would 3 labourers take to do the job?

   Assume that all the labourers work at the same rate!

   The remaining questions in this exercise include cases where there is no simple relationship between the quantities, as well as some involving direct proportion or inverse proportion. Where you think there is no link, briefly explain why.

9. If 2 ounces of flour are needed for 10 pancakes, how many pancakes can be made with 12 ounces of flour?

10. Twelve tins of cat food are enough to feed three cats for four days. For how many days would the same amount of food feed two cats?

11. A baby's weight increased by 3 kg in 6 weeks. By how much did it increase in a year?

12. Carpet to cover a floor of area $9 \, \text{m}^2$ cost £162.

    (a) How much would it cost to cover $15 \, \text{m}^2$ with the same carpet?

    (b) At a cost of £243, what area could be covered with the same carpet?

13. A class of 22 pupils uses 77 exercise books in a term. If the number in the class is reduced to 18, how many exercise books are likely to be used in a term?

14. A group of 6 hikers walk 10 miles in 3 hours. How long would 14 hikers take to walk 10 miles?

15. The seating in a concert room was arranged in 4 rows of 21 chairs. A different arrangement uses the same number of chairs in 7 rows. How many chairs per row are there in the second arrangement?

16. A decorator with twenty years' experience can hang 3 rolls of wallpaper an hour. How long will it take a decorator with ten years' experience to do the same job?

Self-Assessment 13

1. Express in its simplest form the ratio

   (a) 25 p to 80 p

   (b) 45 seconds to $1\frac{1}{2}$ hours

   (c) $65 : 26 : 39$

2. A box of biscuits contains 15 chocolate, 10 cream and 25 plain biscuits.
   What is the ratio of

   (a) chocolate to plain biscuits

   (b) cream biscuits to all the others?

3. Which is the bigger ratio, $1.2 : 1.4$ or $7 : 8$?

4. Express in the form $1 : n$

   (a) the ratio $25 : 375$

   (b) 5 cm to 100 m

5. Find x if

   (a) $3 : 8 = x : 56$

   (b) $2 : 7 = 11 : x$

6. Elaine finds that the ratio of the time she spends watching television to the time she spends doing homework is 3 : 2. If she has 10 hours to herself one weekend, how many hours' homework is she likely to do?

If she doubles her homework time will she double her viewing time that weekend?

7. A hotel bill for £840 is divided between Nick, Gary and Winston in the ratio of their annual salaries. Nick earns £12 500, Winston earns £15 000 and Gary's salary is £7500. How much does each man pay?

8. A pile of 72 identical books weighs 21 kg.

    (a) How many of the same books weigh 35 kg?

    (b) What is the weight of 48 of these books?

9. Thirty-five workmen build a house in 16 days. At the same rate

    (a) how long would it take 28 workmen to build the house

    (b) how many workmen would be needed to build the house in 14 days?

SCALE DRAWINGS

COMPASS DIRECTIONS

Compass directions use the eight points of the compass.

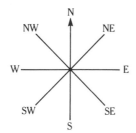

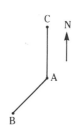

B is south west of A and C is north of A.

Sometimes the direction of one point from another is not exactly one of the eight directions shown above. If it is not, the direction is measured first from north or south, whichever is the nearer, and then towards the east or the west. For example

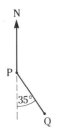

The direction of Q from P is S 35°E

The direction of B from A is N 63°W

Three-Figure Bearings

The modern method of giving the direction of one point from another is to use a three-figure bearing. To find the bearing of B from A, stand at A and look north; then turn clockwise until you are looking at B. The angle you have turned through is the three-figure bearing.

From A, the bearing of B is 210°

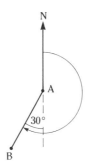

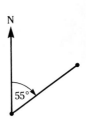

If the angle is less than 100°, it is made into a three-figure bearing by putting a zero in front, e.g. 55° becomes 055°

Exercise 14a

1. Use compass directions to give
   (a) the bearing of each letter from A
   (b) the bearing of A from each of the other letters,

   e.g. the bearing of B from A is N 62°E and the bearing of A from B is S 62°W

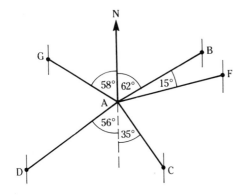

2. Use the diagram in question 1 to write down the three-figure bearing of
   (a) each letter from A
   (b) A from each of the other letters.

3. Draw a rough sketch to illustrate each of the following bearings. Mark an angle in your sketch.
   (a) The bearing of a ship, S, from a lighthouse, L, is 072°
   (b) From town T, the bearing of another town, S, is 330°
   (c) From an aircraft A, the bearing of an airport C, is 126°
   (d) The bearing of the church, C, from the town hall, H, is 215°.

4. Draw diagrams to represent the information given below:
   (a) A town, X, is 50 km from a town Y. The bearing of X from Y is 240°
   (b) A man walks 3 km from A, on a bearing of 285°, to B. Then he walks 3 km due east to C
   (c) ABC is a triangular field. B is 200 m from A on a bearing of 133° and C is 260 m from B on a bearing of 240°
   (d) Ship P is 10 km due east of ship Q. The bearing of ship R from P is 333° and the bearing of R from Q is 046°.

5. Jane starts from A and walks 5 km to B on a bearing of 114°. She then walks 3 km to C on a bearing of 256°. Find $A\hat{B}C$.

6. A is 20 km due west of B. The bearing of C from A is 044° and the bearing of C from B is 314°. Find the angles of triangle ABC.

7.

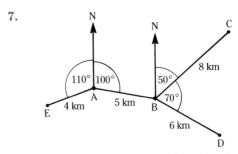

This diagram shows that B is 5 km from A on a bearing of 100°. Describe, in a similar way, the location of
   (a) D from B
   (b) B from C
   (c) A from B
   (d) A from E

8. Use this sketch to answer the questions that follow:

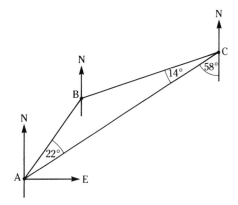

(a) What is the bearing of B from C ?

(b) What is the angle between AC and due east ?

(c) What is the bearing of B from A ?

(d) What is the angle between BC and due north ?

ANGLES OF ELEVATION AND DEPRESSION

The *angle of elevation* is the angle through which you raise your line of view from the horizontal to look up at something.

The *angle of depression* is the angle through which you lower your line of view from the horizontal to look down at something.

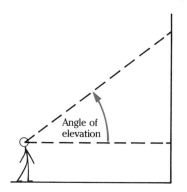

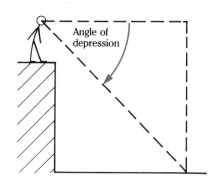

SCALE DRAWINGS

The construction of a scale drawing usually requires the choice of a scale and the calculation of the lengths to be used.

If you are asked to draw a car park that is a rectangle measuring 100 m by 50 m, you cannot draw it full size. To fit it on to your page you will have to scale down the measurements. In this case you could use 1 cm to represent 10 m on the car park. This is called the scale, and can be written 1 cm ≡ 10 m or 1 cm : 10 m. Sometimes the scale is given as a map ratio, e.g. 1 : 50 000. This means that 1 cm represents 50 000 cm, i.e. 1 cm ≡ $\frac{1}{2}$ km. The scale must always be written on any scale drawing.

If you have access to a CAD system you may like to use it to produce some of the scale drawings in the following exercise.

Exercise 14b

In this exercise make measurements correct to the nearest millimetre.

1. Draw a sketch of the following situations.

   (a) From the opposite side of the road, the angle of elevation of the top of the roof of my house is 37°. The horizontal distance from the point where I measured the angle to the point on the ground immediately beneath the ridge of the roof is 12 m.

   (b) From the top of Blackpool Tower, which is 158 m high, the angle of depression of a ship that I can see directly out to sea is 25°.

2. Suggest a suitable scale if you are to make a scale drawing for each of the situations given in question 1.

3.

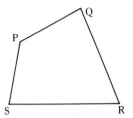

Above is a sketch of a field PQRS in which PQ = 38 m and QR = 52 m.
The field is to be drawn using a scale of 1 cm to 5 m.

   (a) What should be the lengths of PQ and QR on the scale drawing?

   (b) On the drawing SR is 13 cm. How long is the side SR of the field?

4. The map shows part of the north of England. Scale 1 cm : 10 miles
   Trace the map carefully.

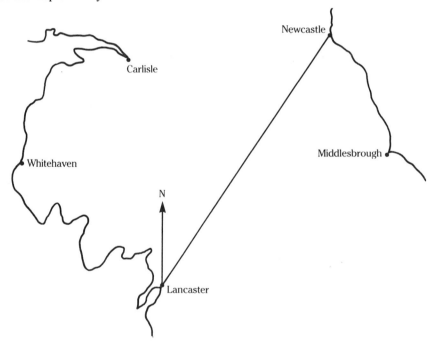

   (a) An aeroplane flies in a straight line from Newcastle to Lancaster.
       (i) What is the distance travelled by the aeroplane?
       (ii) What is the bearing on which the aeroplane flies?

   (b) A helicopter flies from Carlisle to Middlesbrough. How far is this?

   (c) What is the bearing of Newcastle from Whitehaven?

To make a scale drawing start by making a rough sketch of the object you are asked to draw. Mark on the sketch all angles and all full size measurements. Next draw another sketch and put the scaled measurements on this one. (It may be necessary to calculate more angles.) Then do the accurate drawing.

A stained glass window in the town hall is a rectangle with an equilateral triangle on the top. The rectangle measures 10 m wide by 7 m high. Each side of the triangle is equal to the width of the rectangle. Using a scale of 1 cm to 2 metres, make a scale drawing of the window. Use your drawing to find, to the nearest tenth of a metre, the height of the window.

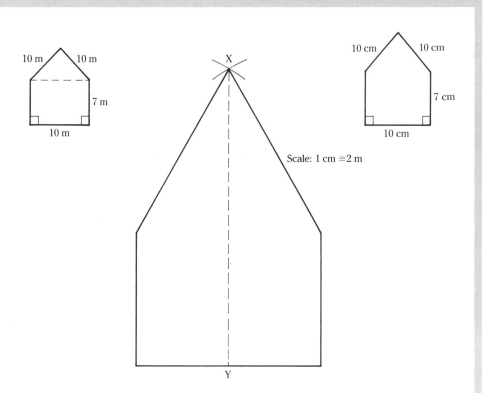

Scale: 1 cm ≡ 2 m

Y is the midpoint of the base.

From the drawing XY measures 7.85 cm, so the height of the window is 15.7 m.

We have chosen a small scale to save space. A more satisfactory scale for this drawing is 1 cm to 1 m.

5. (a) Taking the information given in question 1(a) and using 1 cm to represent 1 m, make a scale drawing to show my position relative to my house. Use your drawing to determine the height of the top of the roof above the ground.

   (b) Use the information given in question 1(b), and a scale of 1 cm : 20 m, to make a scale drawing that will enable you to find the distance from the ship to the base of Blackpool Tower.

6.

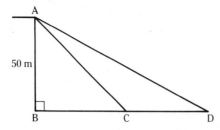

AB represents a vertical cliff 50 m high. C and D are two marker-buoys on the sea such that angle BAC is 40° and angle BAD is 55°. If all four points lie in the same vertical plane draw a scale diagram taking 1 cm to represent 5 m.

(a) What is the angle of depression of D from A?

(b) What is the angle of elevation of A from C?

(c) Measure the lengths of BC and CD, each correct to the nearest millimetre. Hence find the distance of (i) B from C (ii) C from D.

7.

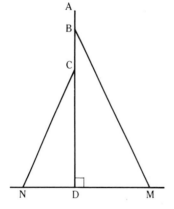

ABCD represents a vertical television mast 75 m high. BM and CN are supporting wires with anchorage points such that NDM is horizontal. ND = 15 m, DM = 30 m, angle BMD = 60° and angle CND = 65°.

(a) Draw a scale diagram using 1 cm to represent 5 m.

(b) Measure the lengths of CN and BM, each correct to the nearest millimetre. What is the length of each supporting wire?

(c) How far is B below the top of the mast?

8. The diagram shows the positions of three British cities: London, Nottingham and Birmingham.

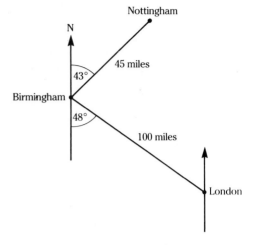

(a) What is the bearing of
  (i) Nottingham from Birmingham
  (ii) London from Birmingham
  (iii) Birmingham from Nottingham?

(b) Using 1 cm to represent 10 miles and the distances given on the diagram, make a scale diagram to show the positions of the three cities.

(c) Join London to Nottingham and measure the length of your line to the nearest millimetre. Hence find the distance from London to Nottingham.

(d) (i) By measuring a suitable angle find the bearing of Nottingham from London.
  (ii) What is the bearing of London from Nottingham?

9. (a) Ship P is 1000 m due south of another ship Q. From P, the bearing of a trawler, T, is 034°, and from Q the bearing of the trawler is 052°. Using a scale of 1 cm to 200 m, make a scale drawing to find the distance of the trawler from P and from Q.

(b) A second trawler, V, lines up 200 m due south of T. Show the position of V on your diagram and find the distance and bearing of Q from V.

10.

N

B•

N   •P

W

Scale 1:4 000 000

This scale drawing shows the positions of Washington (W), Philadelphia (P), and Pittsburgh (B). Trace the diagram carefully.

(a) (i) Measure BP, giving its length to the nearest millimetre.
     (ii) How far is it from Pittsburgh to Philadelphia?

(b) How far is it, in kilometres,
     (i) from Washington to Philadelphia
     (ii) from Washington to Pittsburgh?

(c) (i) What is the bearing of Philadelphia from Pittsburgh?
     (ii) What is the bearing of Pittsburgh from Philadelphia?

(d) By measuring a suitable line on your diagram find
     (i) how far Washington is east of Pittsburgh
     (ii) how far Pittsburgh is north of Philadelphia.

11.

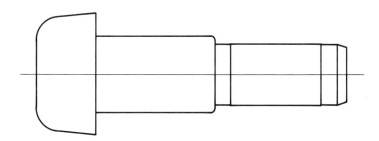

The diagram shows a drawing of a machine pin produced on a CAD program. It is shown here using a scale of 4 : 1. Use the drawing to find the actual measurements of

(a) the length of the pin

(b) the diameter of the thicker part of the shank

(c) the diameter of the narrower part of the shank

(d) the diameter of the head

(e) the thickness of the head.

Self-Assessment 14

1.

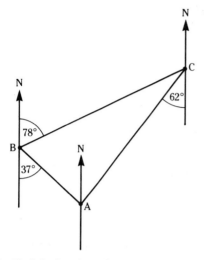

(a) Find the bearing of
    (i) C from B   (ii) A from B
    (iii) B from A   (iv) B from C.

(b) Find the angles in triangle ABC.

2. The bearing of a ship X from a lighthouse Y is 098°. Ship Z is due west of X. The bearing of Z from Y is 240°. Find the angles of triangle XYZ.

3. A triangle ABC is to be drawn to scale. AB = 120 m and AC = 95 m.

(a) Find what the drawn lengths of AB and AC should be if the scale is 1 cm to 10 m.

(b) If the measured length of BC is 10.2 cm, what is the real length of BC ?

4. An aircraft controller observes that the angle of elevation of an approaching aircraft, which is 1.8 km horizontally from the control building, is 20°. Using a scale of 10 cm to represent 1 km, make a scale drawing of this situation and use it to find the height of the aeroplane at this instant.

5. A helicopter flies 12 km on a bearing of 125°. It then changes course and flies 22 km on a bearing of 025°.

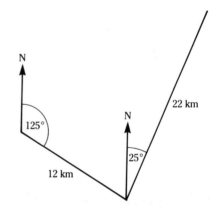

(a) Draw a scale diagram using 1 cm to represent 2 km.

(b) How far is the helicopter due east of its starting point ?

(c) How far is the helicopter due north of its starting point ?

SIMULTANEOUS EQUATIONS AND FORMULAE

COEFFICIENTS

We identify a particular term in an expression by using the letter, or combination of letters, involved.

The number in front of a letter is called the *coefficient*.

For example, for the term $3x$, we say that 3 is the coefficient of x,
      for the term $4pq$, we say that 4 is the coefficient of pq.

If no number is written in front of a term, the coefficient is 1 or -1, depending on the sign of the term,

e.g. in $3 + x - x^2$, the coefficient of x is 1 and the coefficient of x^2 is -1.

SIMULTANEOUS LINEAR EQUATIONS

Sometimes a problem involves two unknown quantities and gives rise to an equation with two variables.

Consider the equation $2x + y = 8$

A solution of this equation is a pair of values of x and y that satisfy the equation. Hence one solution is $x = 2$ and $y = 4$. Another solution is $x = 1$ and $y = 6$. In fact we can give x any value we choose and then find the corresponding value of y, e.g. if $x = 4.5$, then $y = -1$.

Thus a solution to an equation with two unknowns is a pair of values and there is an infinite set of solutions.

If, however, we *also* know that $x + y = 5$
then we find that only one of the solutions of the first equation satisfies the second equation,

e.g. $x = 2$ and $y = 4$ satisfy $2x + y = 8$ but do not satisfy $x + y = 5$ whereas $x = 3$ and $y = 2$ satisfy both equations.

The two equations together form a pair of *simultaneous* equations. In this context, simultaneous means that x and y represent the same numbers in both equations; the solution must be a pair of numbers that satisfies *both* equations.

Solving Simultaneous Equations by Elimination

Consider the equations $2x + y = 8$ [1]

and $x + y = 5$ [2]

We know how to solve an equation with one letter term only, so we will try to eliminate either x or y from these two equations.

Combining the left-hand sides and the right-hand sides of two equations in the *same* way produces another equality.
In this case, subtracting the LHS and the RHS of [2] from the LHS and the RHS of [1] gives

$$(2x + y) - (x + y) = 8 - 5$$

$\Rightarrow$ $x = 3$

Then substituting 3 for x in equation [2] gives $y = 2$.

As a check we see whether $x = 3$ and $y = 2$ satisfy equation [1]

$$\text{LHS of [1]} = 2(3) + 2 = 8 = \text{RHS of [1]}$$

Therefore the solution of the pair of equations is $x = 3$ and $y = 2$

With the equations given above, subtraction made the y terms disappear because they were the same in the two equations. If, in another case, the x terms were the same in both equations, subtraction would eliminate the x terms.

Sometimes one letter can be eliminated by adding the equations. As an example

consider $4x + y = 8$ [1]

and $2x - y = 6$ [2]

[1] + [2] gives $6x = 14$

$\Rightarrow$ $x = \frac{7}{3} = 2\frac{1}{3}$

Substituting $\frac{7}{3}$ for x in [1] gives

$$\tfrac{28}{3} + y = 8$$

$\Rightarrow$ $y = -\frac{4}{3}$

To eliminate a letter from a pair of equations,
***subtract* when the coefficients are the same,**
add when the coefficients are equal and opposite
(i.e. same number but one positive and one negative).

Exercise 15a

1. Solve the following simultaneous equations.

(a) $4x + 3y = 7$
$2x + 3y = 5$

(b) $3a + b = 8$
$a + b = 4$

(c) $4a + b = 17$
$2a + b = 11$

(d) $2x - y = 6$
$3x + y = 14$

(e) $x - y = 2$
$3x + y = 10$

(f) $5x - 2y = 4$
$3x + 2y = 12$

(g) $5x + y = 14$
$3x + y = 10$

(h) $5p + 3q = 5$
$4p - 3q = 4$

(i) $4a + b = 37$
$2a - b = 17$

(j) $2p - 2q = 3$
$3p + 2q = 7$

(k) $9a + 2b = 10$
$a + 2b = 2$

(l) $3s + 7t = 16$
$2s + 7t = 13$

Solve the equations $x + 2y = 7$ and $3x + 2y = 9$

$$x + 2y = 7 \qquad [1]$$
$$3x + 2y = 9 \qquad [2]$$

It is easier to subtract the first equation from the second. A mistake is less likely if the equations are rewritten with equation [2] on top, i.e.

$$3x + 2y = 9 \qquad [2]$$
$$x + 2y = 7 \qquad [1]$$

$[2] - [1]$ gives $\qquad 2x = 2 \quad \Rightarrow \quad x = 1$

Substituting 1 for x in [1] gives $1 + 2y = 7$ so $y = 3$

Checking in [2]: LHS $= 3(1) + 2(3) = 9 =$ RHS

Therefore the solution is $x = 1$ and $y = 3$

2. Solve the simultaneous equations.

(a) $x + y = 5$
$3x + y = 7$

(b) $5x + 2y = 14$
$7x + 2y = 22$

(c) $9x + 5y = 50$
$12x + 5y = 65$

(d) $4a + 3b = 36$
$7a + 3b = 45$

Solve the equations $2x - y = 11$ and $x - y = 8$

$$2x - y = 11 \qquad [1]$$
$$x - y = 8 \qquad [2]$$

The y terms are the same so subtraction eliminates y: $-y - (-y) = -y + y = 0$.

$[1] - [2] \quad \Rightarrow \qquad x = 3$

From [2] $\qquad 3 - y = 8$

$\Rightarrow \qquad y = -5$

Check in [1]: $\quad$ LHS $= 2(3) - (-5)$
$= 6 + 5 = 11 =$ RHS

Therefore $x = 3$ and $y = -5$

3. Solve the simultaneous equations.

   (a) $3x - y = 5$
   $x - y = 1$

   (b) $3x - 2y = 14$
   $x - 2y = 4$

   (c) $3p - 5q = -3$
   $4p - 5q = 1$

Solve the equations $4a - 3b = 5$ and $4a - 5b = 2$

$$4a - 3b = 5 \quad [1]$$

$$4a - 5b = 2 \quad [2]$$

The a terms are the same, so subtraction eliminates a.

$[1] - [2] \quad \Rightarrow \quad -3b - (-5b) = 3$

$\Rightarrow \qquad\qquad\qquad -3b + 5b = 3$

$\Rightarrow \qquad\qquad\qquad\qquad 2b = 3$

$\Rightarrow \qquad\qquad\qquad\qquad b = \frac{3}{2}$

From [1] $\qquad\qquad 4a - 3(\frac{3}{2}) = 5$

$\Rightarrow \qquad\qquad\qquad 4a = \frac{19}{2}$

$\Rightarrow \qquad\qquad\qquad a = \frac{19}{8}$

Check in [2]: LHS $= \frac{19}{2} - \frac{15}{2} = 2 =$ RHS

Therefore $a = \frac{19}{8}$ and $b = \frac{3}{2}$

---

4. Solve the simultaneous equations.

   (a) $x + 3y = 0$
   $x - y = 4$

   (b) $4x - y = 8$
   $4x + 2y = 20$

   (c) $2p + 3q = 0$
   $2p - 5q = -4$

   (d) $2a + 3b = 7$
   $2a - b = -1$

   (e) $3x + 2y = 12$
   $3x - y = 9$

   (f) $2f + r = 8$
   $2f - 4r = 3$

5. In each part of this question, decide which letter to eliminate and then decide whether to add or subtract the equations.

   (a) $a - b = 8$
   $2a + b = 7$

   (b) $2y - 3x = -14$
   $2y + x = 10$

   (c) $3p - 5q = 7$
   $4p + 5q = -14$

   (d) $5t + 3s = 35$
   $5t - 4s = 0$

   (e) $3u + 5v = 17$
   $4u + 5v = 16$

   (f) $3c - d = 10$
   $c + d = -2$

Harder Simultaneous Equations

Sometimes the coefficients of neither of the letter terms are the same. In this case one or both of the equations can be multiplied to produce the same letter term.

Consider the equations $\qquad x - y = 5 \qquad\qquad$ [1]
and $\qquad\qquad\qquad 3x + 4y = 8 \qquad\qquad$ [2]
If we multiply [1] by 4, we get $4x - 4y = 20 \qquad$ [3]

then adding [2] + [3] will eliminate the y terms.

$$x - y = 5 \qquad [1]$$
$$3x + 4y = 8 \qquad [2]$$

[1] × 4 gives $\qquad 4x - 4y = 20 \qquad [3]$

[2] + [3] gives $\qquad 7x = 28 \quad$ so $\quad x = 4$

From [1] $\qquad\qquad y = -1$

Therefore the solution is $x = 4$ and $y = -1$

Note that, alternatively, we could multiply both sides of equation [1] by 3,
which gives $\qquad\qquad 3x - 3y = 15 \qquad\qquad\qquad [3]$
Then [2] − [3] eliminates the x terms.

We chose the first method because mistakes are less likely to be made when adding than when subtracting equations.

Exercise 15b

1. Solve the simultaneous equations.

(a) $2x + y = 7$
$\quad\; 3x + 2y = 11$

(b) $5x - 4y = -3$
$\quad\; 3x + y = 5$

(c) $9x + 7y = 10$
$\quad\; 3x + y = 2$

(d) $5a + 3b = 21$
$\quad\; 2a + b = 3$

(e) $3s - 2t = -2$
$\quad\; s + t = 1$

(f) $5x + 3y = 11$
$\quad\; 4x + 6y = 16$

(g) $4a + 3b = 1$
$\quad\; 16a - 5b = 21$

(h) $2x + 5y = 1$
$\quad\; 4x + 3y = 9$

(i) $7r + 2s = 22$
$\quad\; 3r + 4s = 11$

Sometimes both equations need to be altered before we add or subtract.

Solve the equations $3x + 5y = 6$ and $2x + 3y = 5$

$$3x + 5y = 6 \qquad [1]$$
$$2x + 3y = 5 \qquad [2]$$

[1] × 2 gives $\qquad 6x + 10y = 12 \qquad [3]$

[2] × 3 gives $\qquad 6x + 9y = 15 \qquad [4]$

Then [3] − [4] gives $\qquad y = -3$

From [1] we have $\qquad 3x - 15 = 6$

$\Rightarrow \qquad\qquad\qquad 3x = 21, \quad$ so $\quad x = 7$

Checking in [2] gives LHS $= 2(7) + 3(-3) = 5 =$ RHS

Therefore the solution is $x = 7$ and $y = -3$

2. Solve the simultaneous equations.

(a) $2x + 3y = 12$
$\quad\; 5x + 4y = 23$

(b) $3x - 2y = -7$
$\quad\; 4x + 3y = 19$

(c) $2x - 5y = 1$
$\quad\; 5x + 3y = 18$

(d) $6x + 5y = 9$
$\quad\; 4x + 3y = 6$

(e) $14a - 3b = -18$
$\quad\; 6a + 2b = 12$

(f) $6s - 7t = 25$
$\quad\; 7s + 6t = 15$

(g) $3p + 4q = 5$
$\quad\; 2p + 10q = 18$

(h) $7x - 3y = 20$
$\quad\; 2x + 4y = -4$

(i) $10x + 3y = 12$
$\quad\; 3x + 5y = 20$

The remaining questions are mixed types of simultaneous equations.

3. (a) $x + 2y = 9$
   $2x - y = -2$

   (b) $x + y = 4$
   $x + 2y = 9$

   (c) $2x + 3y = 0$
   $3x + 2y = 5$

   (d) $3x - y = -10$
   $4x - y = -4$

   (e) $3x + 2y = -5$
   $3x - 4y = 1$

   (f) $5x + 2y = 16$
   $2x - 3y = -5$

   (g) $3p + 2q = -4$
   $3p - 4q = 8$

   (h) $a + b = 6$
   $a - b = 1$

   (i) $3s - 5t = 13$
   $2s + 5t = -8$

Solve the simultaneous equations $x = 5 - 2y$ and $4y - x = 7$

$$x = 5 - 2y \qquad [1]$$

$$4y - x = 7 \qquad [2]$$

These equations need rearranging. It is sensible to arrange them so that the letters and the number term are in the same order in both equations; it is not necessary for the letter terms to be on one side and the number term on the other side,

e.g. these two equations could be arranged as $\begin{cases} x = 5 - 2y \\ -x = 7 - 4y \end{cases}$ or $\begin{cases} 2y = 5 - x \\ 4y = 7 + x \end{cases}$

Add $2y$ to both sides of [1] $2y + x = 5$ $\qquad [3]$

[2] + [3] gives $6y = 12$

$\Rightarrow$ $y = 2$

From equation [2] $8 - x = 7$

$8 = 7 + x$

$\Rightarrow$ $x = 1$

Therefore the solution is $x = 1$ and $y = 2$

---

4. Find the values of x and y for which

   (a) $y = 6 - x$ and $2x + y = 8$

   (b) $x - y = 2$ and $2y = x + 1$

   (c) $y = 9 + x$ and $y = 11 - x$

   (d) $x + 4 = y$ and $y = 10 - 2x$

   (e) $y = 4 - x$ and $y = x + 6$

   (f) $x + y = 12$ and $y = 3 + x$

One angle in a triangle is 90° and the difference between the other two angles is 36°. Find the larger of the two unknown angles.

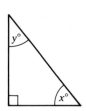

Let $x°$ be the larger angle.

The sum of the three angles is 180°

Therefore $x + y = 90$ $\qquad [1]$

The difference between x and y is 36,

Therefore $x - y = 36$ $\qquad [2]$

[1] + [2] $\Rightarrow$ $2x = 126 \Rightarrow x = 63$

The larger of the two unknown angles is 63°

Form two equations from the information given in each of the following problems. In those cases where the letters are not given, state clearly, either in words or in a diagram, what your letters represent. Solve the equations and end your solution by answering the question asked.

5. A brand of pain reliever comes in two forms of pill; red pills and white pills. Red pills cost x pence each and white pills cost y pence each. A pack containing 10 red pills and 40 white pills costs 250 pence and a pack containing 5 red pills and 30 white pills costs 175 pence. Find the cost of one red pill.

6. The sum of two numbers is 27 and the difference between the two numbers is 15. The larger of the two numbers is x and the smaller number is y. Find the smaller number.

7. When a car travels at a steady speed of v km/h on a flat road, it covers a distance s km in 2 hours. If the same car travels at a steady speed of $2v$ km/h it covers $(s+5)$ km in 2 hours. Find the value of v. (Remember that 'distance $=$ speed $\times$ time'.)

8. The sum of two numbers is 38 and their difference is 12. Find the numbers.

9. One angle in a triangle is 60°. The difference between the other two angles is 45°. What is the size of the largest angle in the triangle ?

10. A rectangle is a cm long and b cm wide. The perimeter of the rectangle is 48 cm and the length is 5 cm more than the width. Find the length of the rectangle.

11. Find two numbers such that twice the first added to the second is 26 and the first added to three times the second is 28.

12. A cup and saucer together cost $2.05. A cup and two saucers cost $2.70. Find the cost of a cup and of a saucer.

13. In 9 years time a father will be twice as old as his son. Three years ago he was four times as old as his son. How old is each of them now ?

14. A motorist drives for two hours at one speed, then for three hours at another speed. The distance she covers is 285 miles. If she had driven for one hour at the first speed and four hours at the second speed, she would have travelled 280 miles. Find the two speeds.

FORMULAE INVOLVING SQUARES AND SQUARE ROOTS

Consider the equation $x^2 = 4$

The solutions of this equation are the values of x which, when multiplied by themselves, make 4, i.e. the square roots of 4.

Now $2 \times 2 = 4$ *and* $(-2) \times (-2) = 4$, so the solutions of $x^2 = 4$ are
$$x = 2 \quad \text{or} \quad x = -2 \quad \text{which is abbreviated to} \quad x = \pm 2$$

Similarly, if $\quad x^2 = 3 \quad$ then $\quad x = \pm\sqrt{3}$

and $\qquad$ if $\quad x^2 = a \quad$ then $\quad x = \pm\sqrt{a}$

Now consider the equation $\sqrt{x} = 5$

To get rid of the square root, we must square both sides.

This gives $\qquad\qquad\qquad x = 25$

Similarly, if $\quad \sqrt{x} = a \quad$ then $\quad x = a^2$

Therefore, when changing the subject of a formula,

> if the letter required is squared, isolate that letter on one side of the formula and take the square root of both sides, remembering that both the positive and the negative square root must be considered;
> if the formula involves a square root, isolate the term containing the square root on one side and then square both sides.

Note that the square of $\sqrt{a+b}$ is $a+b$

Exercise 15c

> If $P = a^2 + b^2$ find a when $P = 2.7$ and $b = 0.9$
>
> $$P = a^2 + b^2$$
>
> When $P = 2.7$ and $b = 0.9$, $\qquad 2.7 = a^2 + (0.9)^2$
>
> i.e. $\qquad\qquad\qquad\qquad\qquad 2.7 = a^2 + 0.81$
>
> $$1.89 = a^2$$
>
> Taking the square root of both sides gives $a = \pm1.37$ (3 s.f.)

1. Given that $V = 4\pi r^2$, find, correct to 3 s.f.
   (a) V when $r = 4$
   (b) V when $r = 2.7$
   (c) r when $V = 16$
   (d) r when $V = 4.87$

2. If $a^2 = b^2 + c^2$, find, correct to 3 s.f.
   (a) a when $b = 4$ and $c = 3$
   (b) a when $b = 1.6$ and $c = 2.1$
   (c) b when $a = 8$ and $c = 4$
   (d) c when $a = 3.5$ and $b = 2.8$

> If $v = \sqrt{u^2 - 5t}$ find u when $v = 12$ and $t = 6$
>
> When $v = 12$ and $t = 6$, $\quad v = \sqrt{u^2 - 5t}$ gives
>
> $$12 = \sqrt{u^2 - 30}$$
>
> We now need to square both sides to get rid of the square root sign.
>
> $$144 = u^2 - 30$$
>
> $\Rightarrow \qquad\qquad\qquad 174 = u^2$
>
> $\therefore \qquad\qquad\qquad u = \pm13.2$ (3 s.f.)

3. If $r = \sqrt{x^2 + y^2}$, find, correct to 3 s.f.
   (a) r when $x = 3$ and $y = 4$
   (b) r when $x = 2$ and $y = 1$
   (c) x when $r = 13$ and $y = 5$

4. If $r = \sqrt{p^2 + q^2}$, find, correct to 3 s.f.
   (a) p when $r = 8$ and $q = 2$
   (b) q when $r = 25$ and $p = 7$
   (c) q when $r = 2.4$ and $p = 1.7$

Make u the subject of the formula $v^2 = u^2 - 2as$

$$v^2 = u^2 - 2as$$

Add $2as$ to both sides $v^2 + 2as = u^2$

i.e. $u^2 = v^2 + 2as$

Take the square root of both sides $u = \pm\sqrt{v^2 + 2as}$

In questions 5 and 6 change the subject of the formula to the letter in the bracket.

5. (a) $c = x^2 + y^2$ (x)
   (b) $a^2 = b^2 + c^2$ (b)
   (c) $p = t + r^2$ (r)
   (d) $g = 2x^2 - y^2$ (y)
   (e) $v = \frac{1}{2}gt^2$ (t)

6. (a) $A = \pi r^2$ (r)
   (b) $V = \pi r^2 h$ (r)
   (c) $x^2 = 5 - y^2$ (y)
   (d) $R = a^3 - at^2$ (t)
   (e) $z^2 = x^2 - y^2$ (y)

Make ℓ the subject of the formula $T = 2\pi\sqrt{\dfrac{l}{g}}$

$$T = 2\pi\sqrt{\frac{l}{g}}$$

Divide both sides by 2π $\dfrac{T}{2\pi} = \sqrt{\dfrac{l}{g}}$

Square both sides $\dfrac{T^2}{4\pi^2} = \dfrac{l}{g}$

Multiply both sides by g $\dfrac{gT^2}{4\pi^2} = l$

i.e. $l = \dfrac{gT^2}{4\pi^2}$

In questions 7 and 8 make the letter in the bracket the subject of the formula.

7. (a) $p = \sqrt{2q}$ (q)
   (b) $x = \frac{1}{2}\sqrt{y}$ (y)
   (c) $q = p\sqrt{r}$ (r)
   (d) $b = \sqrt{a + c}$ (c)
   (e) $v = \sqrt{rt}$ (t)

8. (a) $b = a + \sqrt{c}$ (c)
   (b) $V = \sqrt{3 - t}$ (t)
   (c) $H = \sqrt{x^2 + 4}$ (x)
   (d) $a = \sqrt{b^2 + c^2}$ (c)
   (e) $x = \frac{1}{2}y + \sqrt{z}$ (z)

9. The formula for the volume, V cubic units, of a cylinder whose height is h units and whose radius is r units is given by $V = \pi r^2 h$.

(a) Use the formula to find the volume of a cylinder whose height is 12 cm and whose radius is 5 cm.

(b) Derive a formula for the height of the cylinder in terms of V, π and r.

(c) Find h when $V = 120$ and $r = 6.25$

(d) Make r the subject of the given formula and explain why using $\pm$ is incorrect in this case. Hence find r when $V = 14$ and $h = 2$

(e) Make a check on your answers for (d) by using the given formula to find r when $V = 14$ and $h = 2$

10. The formula for finding the length, d units, of the diagonal of a rectangle a units long and b units wide is $d = \sqrt{a^2 + b^2}$

(a) Find d when $a = 4$ and $b = 8$

(b) Use the formula to find the length of the diagonal of a rectangle that is 1.2 m long and 75 cm wide.

(c) Use the formula to find a when $b = 15$ and $d = 25$

(d) Make a the subject of the formula.

(e) Use the formula found in (d) to find a when $b = 15$ and $d = 25$ How does your answer compare with that for (c)?

LITERAL EQUATIONS

An ordinary linear equation in one unknown contains numbers and the letter representing the unknown, for example, $2x - 3 = 7$

In a literal equation, the numbers also are represented by letters.

For example, $ax - b = c$ is a literal equation in x and to solve it we need to find x in terms of a, b and c.

i.e. $\qquad\qquad ax - b = c$

add b to each side $\qquad ax = c + b$

divide both sides by $a \quad x = \dfrac{c + b}{a}$

Therefore solving a literal equation can be thought of as changing the subject of a formula.

Exercise 15d

Solve the equations for x.

1. $a = x + b$

2. $p = q - x$

3. $a + b = \frac{1}{2}(x + a)$

4. $a - x = 2x$

5. $a(x + b) = c$

6. $\dfrac{a}{b} = \dfrac{x}{c}$

7. $r = \dfrac{ax}{cd}$

8. $p\sqrt{x} = q$

9. $a = x^2 + b$

10. $x^2 + y^2 = r^2$

11. $ax^2 = b$

12. $a = p\sqrt{\dfrac{b}{x}}$

13. $v = \omega\sqrt{a^2 - x^2}$

14. $a + \sqrt{x} = c - d$

Investigation

The number 495

(a) Choose any three digits, not all the same, and then arrange them to make the largest possible three figure number.

(b) Now reverse the digits to give another three figure number and subtract it from the first number.

(c) Using the digits of the numbers given in (b), repeat the process until you find a pattern. (The title of this investigation gives a clue.)

(d) The object of this investigation is to find out whether what you find in (c) always happens with all possible start numbers. One method is to try all the possible numbers, but there are a lot of them! Another method is to find a general formula for the first number and then apply the process to this formula: suppose that the digits, in descending order of size are a, b, c
Remembering that not more than two digits can be the same, what conditions apply to a, b and c ?

(e) Write down a formula for the first number, n_1, in terms of a, b and c.

(f) Write down a formula for the second number, n_2, in terms of a, b and c.

(g) Now find a formula for the third number, $n_1 - n_2$, in terms of a, b and c.

(h) Use the formula found in (g) together with the conditions for a, b and c, to find the possible numbers given by the first subtraction. Now investigate these as the start numbers.

Self-Assessment 15

1. Solve the simultaneous equations
    $x - 2y = 8$ and $x + 2y = 12$

2. Solve the simultaneous equations
    $3x - 5y = -4$ and $x + 2y = 6$

3. Solve for x the equation $a(x - y) = 4y$

4. A pendulum of length l metres takes T seconds to swing from one side to the other and back again.

    The formula for T is $T = 2\pi \sqrt{\dfrac{l}{g}}$

    where $g\,\text{m/s}^2$ is the acceleration due to gravity.

    (a) Find T when $l = 4$ and $g = 10$

    (b) How long does it take a pendulum 6 metres long to swing from side to side when $g = 9.8$?

    (c) Make g the subject of the formula.

5. The formula for finding the length, d cm, of a diagonal of a cuboid whose dimensions are a cm, b cm and c cm is $d = \sqrt{a^2 + b^2 + c^2}$

    (a) Find d when $a = 2.4$, $b = 3.6$ and $c = 1.8$

    (b) How long is the diagonal of a cuboid whose dimensions are 2 m by 2.5 m by 80 cm ?

    (c) The diagonal of a cuboid is 25 cm long. The cuboid is 8 cm long and 12 cm wide. What is its depth ?

    (d) Make a the subject of the formula.

6. If James gives Thomas £3, Thomas will have twice as much money as James. If Thomas gives James £5, James will have twice as much as Thomas. How much money does each boy have ?

THE LANGUAGE OF MATHEMATICS

The further anyone progresses in mathematics, the more vital it becomes to express ideas precisely and accurately. You may so far have taken the view that if *you* know what you mean, and your answer is right, then that is all that matters. Sooner or later, however, some of you will need to communicate more advanced ideas to other people so that *they* know *exactly* what you mean.

The ability to use clear, correct, unambiguous mathematical language cannot be acquired overnight. It depends, first of all, on a frame of mind that sees the necessity for meticulous care in expression, and then it must be developed steadily and consistently until it becomes second nature.

For those who are thinking of taking mathematics further, now is the time to begin to develop the skill of using mathematical language correctly. Because this is done by starting at the beginning, inevitably we shall initially be looking at examples that seem almost too trivial to bother with. This should not deter a student with real mathematical potential, for the introduction to rigour which these simple cases give can create the attitude of mind required to use the language fully.

The language of mathematics is a combination of words and symbols, each symbol being the shorthand form for a word or phrase. When the words and symbols are correctly used, a piece of mathematical reasoning can be read, as prose can, in properly constructed sentences.

You have already used a fair number of symbols but not, perhaps, always with enough care for their precise meaning. As we now take a look at some familiar symbols we find that some can be translated correctly in more than one way.

THE USE AND MISUSE OF SYMBOLS AND WORDS

First consider the elementary symbol $+$.
This can be read as 'plus' or 'and' or 'together with' or 'positive'.

e.g. $3 + 2$ means 3 plus 2 or 3 and 2

The symbol $-$ has a similar variety of translations.

e.g. $5 - 4$ means 5 minus 4
$5 - (-4)$ means 5 minus 'negative 4'

Now consider $\times$ which can be read as 'multiplied by' or 'times' or 'of'.

e.g. 7×5 means 7 multiplied by 5 or 7 times 5

$\frac{1}{100} \times x$ means one hundredth of x

Note.   When 'times' is used for ×, it really means 'lots of', e.g. 3×8 means 3 lots of 8. It is quite incorrect, therefore, to say, 'times 3 by 8' a phrase that teachers often hear, because, clearly it is nonsense to write 'lots of 3 by 8'. (This emphasises that 'times' is not a verb.) If we want to use × as an instruction, we have to use the word 'multiply', e.g. the instruction to 'work out 3×8' is 'multiply 3 by 8'.

The next sign we consider is = which means 'is equal to'. This symbol should be used *only* to link two quantities that are equal in value. Used in this way a short complete sentence is formed, e.g.

$$x = 3 \quad \text{is read as} \quad \text{'}x \text{ is equal to 3'.}$$

It is very easy to slip into the habit of saying 'equals' or 'equal' instead of 'is equal to'. For instance it is not good English to write 'Let $x = 3$' because this really translates to 'Let x is equal to 3'. While this sort of misuse may seem (and, up to this level, is) trivial it can be serious at a more advanced level and is better avoided altogether.

It is also bad practice to use = in place of the word 'is'. For instance, when defining a symbol such as the radius of a circle we should say 'the radius of the given circle is r cm' and *not* 'the radius of the given circle $= r$ cm', because r cm and the radius are not two separate quantities of equal value; r cm *stands for* the radius.

Of course, if the radius is later found to be 4 cm, it *is* then correct to say '$r = 4$'.

Here are some problems followed by solutions which, although sometimes ending with the correct answer, contain nonsense on the way. These solutions have been taken from actual students' work and are examples of very common misuses of language.

You may find it interesting to criticise these solutions.

1. Simplify $2\frac{1}{2} + 1\frac{1}{4} - 2\frac{1}{3}$

$$2\frac{1}{2} + 1\frac{1}{4} = 3\frac{3}{4} - 2\frac{1}{3}$$
$$= 1\frac{5}{12}$$

2. Solve the equation $6x + 5 = 3x + 11$

$$6x + 5 = 3x + 11$$
$$= 3x + 5 = 11$$
$$= \quad 3x = 6$$
$$= \quad x = 2$$

3. Write down the formula for the circumference of a circle.

The formula for the circumference of a circle is $2\pi r$.

4. Make r the subject of the formula $P = r + 2t$

$$P = r + 2t = P - 2t = r$$
$$\therefore \qquad r = P - 2t$$

5. Two angles of a triangle measure 60° and 80°. Find the size of the third angle.

$$60° + 80° = 180° - 140°$$

$$= \text{third angle} = 40°$$

6. Three buns and two cakes cost 54 p and five buns and one cake cost 62 p. Find the cost of one bun and of one cake.

$$\text{Buns} = x\,\text{p} \quad \text{Cakes} = y\,\text{p}$$

$$3x + 2y = 54\,\text{p}$$

$$5x + y = 62\,\text{p}$$

$$10x + 2y = 124\,\text{p}$$

$$7x = 70\,\text{p}$$

$$x = 10\,\text{p} \quad \text{and} \quad y = 12\,\text{p}$$

SYMBOLS THAT CONNECT STATEMENTS

The symbol $\therefore$, meaning 'therefore', introduces a fact, complete in itself, which follows from a previous complete fact. It is correct to write

$$x^2 = 9$$

$\therefore$ $\qquad\qquad x = \pm 3$

It is not correct, however, to use $\therefore$ to link the next two lines

$$3x - 4y - 2x + y$$

$$x - 3y$$

Each of these lines is simply an expression, not a complete fact, and in this case we link the lines by the symbol $\Rightarrow$. This means 'giving' or 'which gives', i.e.

$$3x - 4y - 2x + y$$

$\Rightarrow$ $\qquad\qquad x - 3y$

Note that $\Rightarrow$ can correctly be used as an alternative to $\therefore$, e.g.

$$x^2 = 9 \quad \Rightarrow \quad x = \pm 3$$

but the converse is not necessarily true.

Note also that in the context of Mathematical Logic, the symbol $\Rightarrow$ means 'implies that'.

There are occasions when none of these symbols is absolutely correct, a very simple example being

$$3 = x$$

$$x = 3$$

These two statements give exactly the same information, so neither $\therefore$ nor $\Rightarrow$ is quite right. In this situation it is best to use 'i.e.' ('that is'):

$$3 = x$$

i.e. $\qquad\qquad x = 3$

It is quite common to see the word 'or' where we have used 'i.e.'. Although this is not actually wrong it should be treated with caution because 'or' strongly suggests that an *alternative result* is being given, and not just the same result rearranged.

A similar criticism of bad practice can be levelled at the way some people try to give their reasons for steps in a solution. In the solution of a pair of simultaneous equations, for example, we sometimes see

$$3x - 4y = 5 \qquad \times 2$$

$$2x + 7y = 13 \qquad \times 3$$

$$6x - 8y = 10$$

$$6x + 21y = 39$$

These four lines are disjointed, do not really explain what is happening and cannot be read sensibly in words. It is much better to present this piece of work in one of the following ways:

(a) $\qquad\qquad\qquad\qquad 3x - 4y = 5 \qquad\qquad$ [1]

$$2x + 7y = 13 \qquad\qquad \text{[2]}$$

$$2 \times [1] \quad \Rightarrow \quad 6x - 8y = 10$$

$$3 \times [2] \quad \Rightarrow \quad 6x + 21y = 39$$

After the initial definition of equations [1] and [2] this now reads '2 times equation [1] gives $6x - 8y = 10$' and '3 times equation [2] gives $6x + 21y = 39$'.

(b) $\qquad 3x - 4y = 5 \qquad\qquad\qquad\qquad\qquad\qquad$ [1]

$$2x + 7y = 13 \qquad\qquad\qquad\qquad\qquad\qquad \text{[2]}$$

$$6x - 8y = 10 \quad (\text{multiplying [1] by 2})$$

$$6x + 21y = 39 \quad (\text{multiplying [2] by 3})$$

This version too can be read:
$6x - 8y = 10$; multiplying equation [1] by 2, etc.

Note   In (a) an instruction was given first, describing the operation to be carried out and leading to an equation, whereas in (b) the operation was carried out and then explained.

Either of these approaches can be extended satisfactorily to more advanced mathematics.

MORE USEFUL LINK WORDS

The words and symbols mentioned so far do, in fact, provide sufficient vocabulary to write and read most mathematics at this level, and will continue to be used as the work develops, supplemented by the extra symbols needed for each new area of study.

Even at present, however, variety can be added by a few more words that link or introduce facts.

A traditional, but still useful, one is 'hence' which means 'from this'. It fits nicely into the following type of situation:

> Circle A has a radius of 4 cm and circle B has a radius of 2 cm.
> Hence the area of circle A is four times that of circle B.

It sometimes happens that, in a solution, one line of thought is pursued for a few steps and then a new idea is introduced. This situation is clearly expressed by the word 'now', as in the following example:

$$2x + 3y = 7 \qquad\qquad [1]$$

$$8x - 5y = 11 \qquad\qquad [2]$$

$$4 \times [1] \quad \Rightarrow \quad 8x + 12y = 28 \qquad\qquad [3]$$

$$[3] - [2] \quad \Rightarrow \quad 17y = 17$$

$$\therefore \qquad\qquad y = 1$$

$$\text{In } [1], \ y = 1 \quad \Rightarrow \quad 2x + 3 = 7$$

$$\Rightarrow \qquad\qquad x = 2$$

$\therefore$ the solution of the equations is $x = 2, \ y = 1$.

Now we know that if two lines, whose equations are given, are plotted on the same axes, the coordinates of their point of intersection satisfy both equations.

Hence the lines with equations $2x + 3y = 7$ and $8x - 5y = 11$, meet at the point $(2, 1)$.

SEQUENCES

A great deal of mathematics depends on our perception of patterns. Some are visual or geometric, some numerical or algebraic.

SEQUENCES

A *sequence* is a set of numbers arranged in a particular order, e.g. 2, 5, 8, 11, ...
In this example 11 is the 4th term of the sequence.

If, however, a set of numbers such as 4, 8, 9, 10 are not in any particular order (e.g. could be given as 9, 4, 8, 10 or 8, 10, 4, 9), the numbers are not a sequence.

Notation

We use u_1 to denote the first term of a sequence, u_2 to denote the second term, and so on. If we want to refer to a general term of a sequence, without specifying which term, we call it the nth term and denote it by u_n.

Note that n can have any of the values 1, 2, 3, ..., i.e. n is a positive integer.

Defining a Sequence

A sequence may be defined by giving the connection between one term and the next. This connection can be given in words, e.g. in the sequence above we can see that 3 is added to each term to give the following term.

This can be written as a formula because, if the nth term is u_n, the next term, i.e. the $(n+1)$th term or u_{n+1} is given by $u_{n+1} = u_n + 3$

If the first term is known, then the second term can be found from the formula; the second term can be used to find the third and so on.

The first term of a sequence is 3 and $u_{n+1} = 3u_n - 4$
Write down the next 3 terms of the sequence.

$$u_1 = 3$$
$$u_2 = 3u_1 - 4 = 3 \times 3 - 4 = 5$$
$$u_3 = 3u_2 - 4 = 3 \times 5 - 4 = 11$$
$$u_4 = 3u_3 - 4 = 3 \times 11 - 4 = 29$$

Another way to define a sequence is to relate a term to its position in the sequence, i.e. to n, and give a formula for the nth term. For example, if the nth term is 2^{n+1} then the 1st, 2nd and 3rd terms can be found by replacing n by 1, 2 and 3 respectively, giving $2^2, 2^3$ and 2^4, i.e. 4, 8 and 16.

The nth term of a sequence, u_n, is given by the formula $u_n = 2^n + 1$. Find the third term and the ninth term.

$$u_n = 2^n + 1$$

The third term, u_3, is $2^3 + 1 = 9$

The ninth term, u_9, is $2^9 + 1 = 513$

Finding a Formula for the nth Term

If we are given the first few terms of a sequence then we may be able to find a formula for the nth term in terms of n. One way of trying to spot the relationship is to write out a table, e.g. for the sequence 2, 5, 8, 11, ...

n	1	2	3	4
nth term	2	5	8	11

We can see that we add 3 to the first term to get the second, add another 3 to get the third and so on, so to find the 4th term we start with 2 and add $(4-1)$ threes. To find the nth term we add $(n-1)$ threes; hence the nth term $= 2 + 3(n-1)$
Multiplying out, the nth term $= 3n - 1$

Once a formula has been found it is sensible to check that it does generate the given terms.

Exercise 17a

Give the next two terms in each sequence and state in words the rule you used to find them.

1. 2, 6, 10, 14, ...

2. 20, 17, 14, 11, ...

3. 4, 12, 36, 108, ...

4. 32, 16, 8, 4, ...

5. 1, 2, 4, 7, ...

6. 1, 3, 7, 13, ...

In each question from 7 to 11 the first two terms of a sequence are given and the rule for finding other terms. Write down the next three terms.

7. 2, −4, ...   multiply by −2

8. 2, 4, ...   add 2

9. 4, 2, ...   divide by 2

10. 2, 4, ...   add two more each time

11. 2, 4, ...   add the previous two terms

In each question from 12 to 16 one of the terms of a sequence and the formula for finding the nth term are given. Check that the value of the given term is correct and write down the first four terms and the tenth term.

12. nth term $= 2 + 2n$;   6th term $= 14$

13. nth term $= 2^n$;   5th term $= 32$

14. nth term $= n(n-1)$;   7th term $= 42$

15. nth term $= 3 \times 2^{n-1}$;   7th term $= 192$

16. nth term $= (n-1)^2$;   6th term $= 25$

In each question from 17 to 19, the nth term of the sequence is denoted by u_n and the first term is given. Give the next four terms.

17. $u_1 = 2$, $u_{n+1} = 3u_n$

18. $u_1 = 3, \quad u_{n+1} = u_n + 2$

19. $u_1 = -2, \quad u_{n+1} = u_n - 2$

20. $u_1 = 9, \quad u_{n+1} = \sqrt{u_n + 2}$

21. For the sequences in questions 1 to 4 give u_{n+1} in terms of u_n.

In each question from 22 to 29 find a formula for the *n*th term in terms of *n*; write down the next two terms and the tenth term.

22. 3, 8, 13, 18, ...

23. 1, 4, 9, 16, ...

24. 2, 6, 18, 54, ...

25. $1, \frac{1}{2}, \frac{1}{3}, \frac{1}{4}, \ldots$

26. $1, \frac{1}{2}, \frac{1}{4}, \frac{1}{8}, \ldots$

27. 2, 6, 12, 20, ...

28. 60, 54, 48, 42, ...

29. 3, 9, 19, 33, 51, ...

DIFFERENCES

Sometimes the rule or formula is too difficult to spot; in this case a *difference table* may help us to continue the sequence. The first difference sequence is found by subtracting u_1 from u_2, u_2 from u_3 and so on.

This is a simple example: 1, 2, 5, 10, 17, ...

Terms	1		2		5		10		17		26		37
1st difference		1		3		5		7	→	9	→	11	

We can see that the first difference row will continue with 9 and 11 and hence we can continue the sequence, i.e. 17 + 9 gives 26 and 26 + 11 gives 37.

The sequence is now 1, 2, 5, 10, 17, 26, 37, ...

A less obvious example is 2, 6, 22, 56, 114, ... We find that we need a second difference row before the pattern becomes clear.

Terms	2		6		22		56		114		202		326
1st difference		4		16		34		58		88		124	
2nd difference			12		18		24	→	30	→	36		

In some cases it may be necessary to add a third difference line before being able to see the pattern.

Notice that a difference table does not always help because there are some sequences whose first differences, second differences, and so on, do not show an obvious pattern.

CHOICE OF RULE

If only a few terms are given, we cannot be certain that just one rule is possible.

For instance, if a sequence starts 1, 2, 4, ... we might think that we must multiply each term by 2 to obtain the next and hence get 1, 2, 4, 8, 16, ...

However it is possible that the rule is to add one more each time, in which case we get 1, 2, 4, 7, 11,...

Even if we are given four terms it is sometimes possible to find alternative rules to define the sequence; we give the simplest or most obvious one but you may find a different, equally acceptable, rule.

CONVERGENCE

Considering a sequence such as 2, 5, 8, 11, ... where 3 is being added each time, it is clear that the terms are getting larger and larger. We say that the series *diverges*. On the other hand, if $u_{n+1} = \sqrt{u_n} + 1$ and the first term is 2, then the sequence starts 2, 2.414213..., 2.553773..., 2.598053..., 2.611847..., 2.616121..., and we can see that, slowly but steadily, the terms appear to be getting closer together in value: they are *converging*.

In some sequences terms get larger to start with, then smaller, or vice versa, so as many terms as possible should be checked to make sure that they really do seem to be converging.

Exercise 17b

For the following sequences make difference tables and use them to find two more terms of each sequence.

1. 11, 12, 16, 23, 33, ...

2. 2, 3, 7, 15, 28, ...

3. 11, 17, 33, 71, 143, 261, ...

4. 0, 1, −2, −6, −8, −5, ...

5. 0, −1, 4, 27, 80, 175, ...

For each of the following sequences there are at least two possible rules or formulae for generating it. Find two possibilities and in each case give three more terms.

6. 2, 6, 18, ...   7. 0, 1, 4, ...

8. 3, 6, 12, ...   9. 1, 2, 3, ...

Use any method to continue each of the following sequences for three more terms. Give a rule or formula if possible.

10. 1, 8, 27, 64, ...   11. $\frac{1}{2}, \frac{2}{3}, \frac{3}{4}, \frac{4}{5}, \ldots$

12. 1, 2, 3, 5, 9, ..   13. 0, 3, 8, 15 ...

14. 100, 99, 95, 79, 15, ...

15. 1.3, 2.4, 3.5, 4.6, ...

16. 2, 3, 2, 4, 2, 5, 2, ...

17. 2, 3, 5, 7, 11, ...

18. 1, −2, 4, −8, ...

19. 2, 5, 10, 17, 26, ...

Questions 20 to 27 refer to the sequence 3, 7, 11, 15,...

20. Write down the next two terms and the rule used to obtain them.

21. Give the formula for the nth term in terms of n.

22. Why are there no even terms?

23. Give the first five terms of the sequence formed by multiplying each term of the given sequence by the term following it. (The first term is 3×7, i.e. 21.)

24. Use a difference table on the five terms of the new sequence formed in question 23, to find the sixth and seventh terms.
   Check that you are correct by using the rule given in question 23.

25. Give the first five terms of the sequence formed by adding each term of the original sequence to the term following it.

26. Give the formula for the nth term of the sequence in question 25.

27. (a) The nth term of a sequence is equal to the sum of the first n terms of the given sequence (e.g. the third term $=$ sum of the first three terms $= 3 + 7 + 11 = 21$). Write down the first five terms.

   (b) A new sequence is formed when the nth term of the sequence in (a) is divided by n. Write down the first five terms of this sequence.

   (c) Give a formula for the nth term of the sequence in (b).

(d) Hence give a formula for the nth term of the sequence in part (a).

Investigate whether the terms of each of the following sequences appear to be converging or not. If converging, state what value they seem to be approaching.

28. $u_1 = 2$, $u_{n+1} = u_n + 0.5$

29. $u_1 = 4$, $u_{n+1} = \sqrt{u_n}$

30. $u_1 = 20$, $u_{n+1} = u_n - 2$

31. $u_1 = 3$, $u_{n+1} = u_n^2 - 4$

32. $u_1 = 5$, $u_{n+1} = \frac{1}{2}\left(u_n + \frac{10}{u_n}\right)$

33. $u_n = \dfrac{n}{n+1}$

34. $u_n = \dfrac{2n^2 - 1}{n^2 + 1}$

Fibonacci Sequences

One of the sequences in the first exercise, i.e. 2, 4, 6, 10, ... was generated by starting with two terms and obtaining the rest by adding the previous two terms. This is called a Fibonacci sequence.

The simplest Fibonacci sequence is 1, 1, 2, 3, 5, 8, ... and this crops up in natural objects; for instance, if you count the number of spirals in the seedhead of a sunflower you will find that it is one of the numbers in this sequence, e.g. 55 or 89.

Other Fibonacci sequences can be found by starting with different pairs of numbers.

Pascal's Triangle

```
              1
          1       1
       1       2       1
    1       3       3       1
  1       4       6       4       1
1       5   ...
```

Each number in Pascal's Triangle is formed by adding together the two numbers just above it: for instance, $4 = 1 + 3$
(You may imagine that the triangle is surrounded by zeros, so $0 + 1 = 1$)

The numbers in this arrangement appear in unexpected contexts in mathematics, such as in probability calculations and in expanding brackets.

Exercise 17c

1. Form a Fibonacci sequence from each of the following pairs of numbers. Give six terms.

   (a) 1, 3   (b) 2, 3   (c) 1, 4

2. Form a difference table for the sequence in question 1(a). What do you notice ?

3. (a) Give the first eight terms of the Fibonacci sequence that begins   1, 1, ...

   (b) Form a sequence by expressing each term of the sequence in (a) as a fraction of its following term. Give the first eight terms.

   (c) Give the fractions in (b) as decimals correct to 4 decimal places. What do you notice ?

4. Copy Pascal's triangle. Complete the sixth row and add two more rows.

5. Find 11^0, 11^1, 11^2, ... and compare the figures with the numbers in Pascal's Triangle. How do you explain the discrepancy in the sixth line ?

6. (a) Find the exact value of each of the first four terms of the sequence 9^2, 99^2, 999^2, ...

   (b) Guess the value of the fifth term and check it by calculation.

Using a Computer

If we have a rule or a formula for generating a sequence then it is possible to write a simple program for a computer.

The following programs are in Basic and will run on most machines. They both produce the same sequence.

```
10 PRINT "Rule: Start with 1 and add 4 to each term."
20 PRINT TAB(9); "N" TAB(15); "Nth TERM"
30 X = 1
40 N = 1
50 PRINT N, X
60 N = N + 1
70 X = X + 4
80 IF N < 11 THEN GOTO 50
```

```
10 PRINT "Nth term = 1 + 4(N - 1)"
20 PRINT TAB(9); "N" TAB(15); "Nth TERM"
30 FOR N = 1 TO 10
40 X = 1 + 4*(N - 1)          (or X = 4*N - 3)
50 PRINT N, X
60 NEXT N
```

There may be more refined ways of writing a program but these are simple and self-explanatory and if you have not tried writing a program before, they could act as an introduction. Type RUN (and press Enter) and you should see ten terms of the sequence appear on the screen. Either program can be adapted for other rules and formulae and to give any number of terms. Try producing some of the sequences in Exercise 17a.

These programs can be used to test for convergence, as any number of terms can be calculated for inspection. It is also possible to incorporate a test into the program so that terms will continue to be produced until it is obvious whether or not their values are converging. A program is given here to test the convergence of the sequence where

$$u_{n+1} = \tfrac{1}{2}\left(u_n + \frac{3}{u_n}\right).$$

```
10 B = 1
20 N = 1
30 A = B
40 PRINT N TAB(12); A
50 B = 0.5 * (A+3/A)
60 N = N + 1
70 IF ABS (A − B) > 0.00000001 AND N < 20 GOTO 30
```

Try checking the sequences at the end of Exercise 17b.

Two textbooks that are helpful in this context are:

132 Short Programs for the Mathematics Classroom, published by the Mathematical Association

GCSE BBC Basic Programming for You, by Stephen Doyle, published by Stanley Thornes.

Using a Spreadsheet

A more sophisticated approach to calculating terms is to use a *spreadsheet.* In this case the program is already prepared and all you have to do is to specify the rule or formula and say how many terms you want.

You will need to consult the manual for your particular spreadsheet in order to discover how to enter the numbers and labels and formulae, but the simple use of a spreadsheet is easy if you follow the instructions.

The following sequence was produced on a P.C. but spreadsheets are all very much the same.

To start with you will see the following display.

	A	B	C	D	E	F	G	H
1								
2								
3								
4								

Put N in A1, Nth TERM in A2. These are the *labels*. Then put 1 in B1 and use the fill facility (consult your manual) to add 1 to the previous entry so that 2 appears in C1, 3 in D1 and so on as far as J1.

Now write the formula $4 * B1 - 3$ in B2 and 'fill' this in boxes C2 to J2.

Most of the terms of the sequence should appear on the screen. (The width of the columns may need adjusting to get all ten terms on the screen.)

	A	B	C	D	E	F	G	H
1	N	1	2	3	4	5	6	7
2	Nth TERM	1	5	9	13	17	21	25
3								
4								

The spreadsheet could be used to calculate over two hundred terms if you wished, though you would have to adjust the viewing window to see them all. It could also produce a large number of different sequences at once, using the other rows, but the labelling would need adjusting so that you would know which sequence was which.

SEQUENCES GIVEN BY VISUAL PATTERNS

If we write down the number of dots in each of the squares above we find we have a familiar sequence, i.e. the *square* numbers,   1, 4, 9, 16, ...

Dots can also be arranged in triangles.

The sequence given by the number of dots is   1, 3, 6, 10, ...
These are the *triangular* numbers.

Number sequences are also generated by other visual sequences of arrangements of dots and lines and shapes.

Exercise 17d

In each question from 1 to 4,

(a) add two more diagrams to the sequence

(b) give the associated number sequence

(c) give a rule or a formula for generating the number sequence.

1.

2.

3.

The associated number sequence is given by the *total* number of rectangles of all sizes (including squares) in each diagram.

4.

The associated number sequence is given by the total number of squares in each diagram.

In the following questions it is neither necessary nor helpful to draw the next two patterns. Write down the first five terms of the associated number sequence and give the rule or formula.

5.

The number sequence is given by the number of straight line segments in each diagram (e.g. the second diagram has 12).

6. Cannon balls are piled up in a triangular pyramid. Each ball (apart from those at the bottom) rests on the three underneath.

The number sequence is given by the number of cannon balls in each pile.

7. Each line passes through the centre of the circle.

The number sequence is given by the number of sectors.

8. The lines are positioned to give the maximum number of regions.

The number sequence is given by the number of regions.

9.

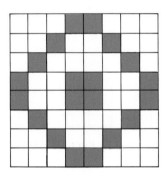

A square pattern is made up of 1 cm green and white square tiles.
The centre four tiles are green.
The middle two tiles on each edge are green and so are the tiles that run diagonally from one group of green edge tiles to the next.
A square of side 8 cm is shown.

(a) Draw and mark the green tiles for a square with a side of
    (i) 6 cm   (ii) 4 cm

(b) Is it possible to draw this pattern in a square of side 7 cm ? What limitations are there on the size of the square ?

(c) Copy and fill in the following table, adding two more columns. If necessary, draw more diagrams.

Length of side in cm	4	6	8		
Number of green tiles			20		
Number of white tiles					

(d) Give the formula for the number of green tiles used in a square of side n cm, where n is even and greater than 2.

(e) How many tiles are there in a square of side n cm ($n \geqslant 4$ and even) ?
How many white tiles are there ?

Investigations

1. Repeat question 3 of Exercise 17c using a different Fibonacci sequence. Investigate further.

2.

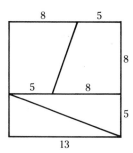

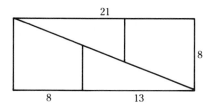

Draw the square above on squared paper, cut out the four pieces and rearrange them as shown to form the rectangle. Find the areas of the square and the rectangle. Explain the discrepancy. (Trigonometry might help.)

The numbers used for the lengths come from the sequence in Exercise 17c, question 3(a). Draw squares and rectangles using other sets of numbers from the same sequence so that a similar situation arises with their areas.

Self-Assessment 17

1. Give the next two terms of the following sequence and a rule for obtaining them. 3, 8, 15, 24, ...

2. Give the first four terms of the sequence whose nth term is $5n - 2$

3. The first term, u_1, of a sequence is 3. Give the next four terms if $u_{n+1} = 2u_n + 1$

4. Give the formula in terms of n for the nth term of the sequence -1, 3, 7, 11, ...

5. Find the value to which the following sequence is converging: $\dfrac{1 \times 3}{4}$, $\dfrac{2 \times 4}{9}$, $\dfrac{3 \times 5}{16}$, $\dfrac{4 \times 6}{25}$, ...

6. Use a difference table to find the next two terms of the sequence 2, 7, 18, 38, 70, ...

7.

(a) Draw two more diagrams in this sequence.
(b) Give the first seven terms of the number sequence given by the number of diagonals in each diagram.

STRAIGHT LINE GRAPHS

PROPERTIES OF A LINE THROUGH TWO POINTS

In Chapter 6 we saw that a point can be located in a plane by means of its coordinate distances from the origin O in the directions of the x and y axes. Now we can investigate various properties of a line that passes through two points with known coordinates.

Consider the line that passes through the points A($2, 4$) and B($5, 8$).

Length

To find the length of the line between A and B, we first make a sketch.

Using Pythagoras' theorem in triangle ABC shows that

$$AB^2 = AC^2 + BC^2$$
$$= (8-4)^2 + (5-2)^2$$
$$= 25$$

i.e. $AB = 5$

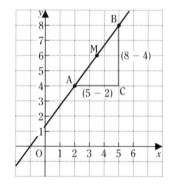

Midpoint

The midpoint, M(x, y), of AB is halfway, in the directions of both Ox and Oy, from A towards B,

i.e. at M, $x = 2 + \frac{1}{2}(5-2) = 3\frac{1}{2}$

which is equal to $\frac{1}{2}(2+5)$

Similarly, $y = 4 + \frac{1}{2}(8-4) = 6$

which is equal to $\frac{1}{2}(4+8)$

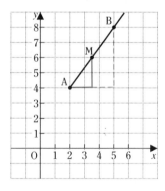

Note that the coordinates of M are the averages of the coordinates of A and B so a quick look at a diagram is often all that is needed to find a midpoint.

Gradient

The *gradient,* or slope, of a line is a measure of how fast the line is rising or falling. It is defined as the rate at which y increases compared with x between *any* two points on that line. Using A($2, 4$) and B($5, 8$) as the two points, the gradient, which is usually represented by m, can be calculated.

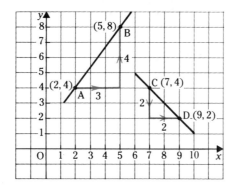

For the line AB $m = \dfrac{y \text{ at B} - y \text{ at A}}{x \text{ at B} - x \text{ at A}} = \dfrac{8 - 4}{5 - 2} = \dfrac{4}{3}$

For the line CD $m = \dfrac{y \text{ at D} - y \text{ at C}}{x \text{ at D} - x \text{ at C}} = \dfrac{2 - 4}{9 - 7} = \dfrac{-2}{2} = -1$

The differences between the y coordinates and the x coordinates must be found in the same order. This may give a negative result, as for the line CD; in these cases the line 'slopes downward'.

Exercise 18a

1. For each pair of points draw a sketch and find the length of the line joining them.

    (a) $(3, 6)$ and $(5, 2)$

    (b) $(-2, 4)$ and $(2, 1)$

    (c) $(5, 1)$ and $(7, 9)$

    (d) $(-3, -4)$ and $(-6, 2)$

2. Write down the coordinates of the midpoint of the line joining each pair of points in question 1.

3. Find the gradient of the line joining each pair of points in question 1.

4. Sketch the line through the points $(-4, 2)$ and $(7, 2)$. At what rate is y increasing? What happens if you try to calculate the gradient? Is there a definite value for m?

5. Sketch the line through the points A($4, -2$) and B($4, 5$). What is the increase in x from A to B? Describe the rate at which y is increasing. What happens if you try to calculate the gradient? Is there a definite value for m?

6. Without drawing a diagram state which, if any, of the lines joining the following points are parallel to the x-axis and which are parallel to the y-axis.

    (a) $(3, 0)$ and $(-10, 0)$

    (b) $(0, -1)$ and $(0, 1)$

    (c) $(99, 0)$ and $(0, 0)$

    (d) $(0, 5)$ and $(5, 0)$

THE EQUATION OF A STRAIGHT LINE

If, for every point on a line, the coordinates satisfy a particular relationship, this relationship is known as the equation of the line.

A Line Parallel to an Axis

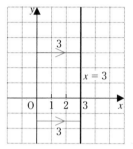

For every point on this line the x coordinate is 3.
The equation of the line is $x = 3$

Any line with equation $x = a$ is parallel to the vertical axis.

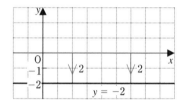

The y coordinate of every point on this line is -2.
The equation of the line is $y = -2$

Any line with equation $y = b$ is parallel to the horizontal axis.

A Slant Line Through the Origin

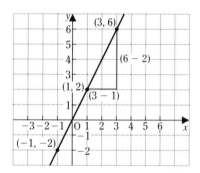

The y coordinate of every point on this line is twice the x coordinate.
The equation of the line is $y = 2x$

Also, considering any two points, we see that the gradient of the line is 2,
i.e. the gradient of the line gives the coefficient of x in the equation of the line.

The equation $y = mx$ represents any straight line through the origin and m is its gradient.

The larger the value of m, the steeper is the line. If m is positive the line rises from left to right and if m is negative the line falls.

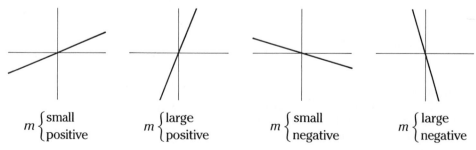

$m \begin{cases} \text{small} \\ \text{positive} \end{cases}$ $m \begin{cases} \text{large} \\ \text{positive} \end{cases}$ $m \begin{cases} \text{small} \\ \text{negative} \end{cases}$ $m \begin{cases} \text{large} \\ \text{negative} \end{cases}$

A General Slant Line

Consider a translation of 3 units upward, applied to the line with equation $y = 2x$. This produces a line where each y coordinate is given by adding 3 to the corresponding x coordinate; therefore its equation is $y = 2x + 3$

The amount of translation is called the y-intercept and this gives the number term, or constant term, in the equation of the line.

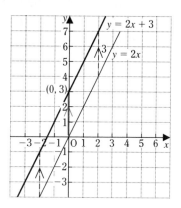

> In general, for a line with a gradient m and y-intercept c,
> the equation is $y = mx + c$.
> If c is positive, the line crosses the y-axis above the origin.
> If c is negative, the line crosses the y-axis below the origin.

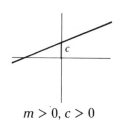   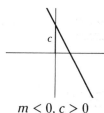   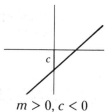   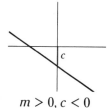

$m > 0, c > 0$ $m < 0, c > 0$ $m > 0, c < 0$ $m > 0, c < 0$

Exercise 18b

1. On squared paper sketch the line with equation
   (a) $x = -5$ (c) $y = -4$
   (b) $y = 1$ (d) $x = 0$

2. Write down the gradient of each line.
   (a) $y = 5x - 1$ (c) $y = x + 3$
   (b) $y = -7x + 3$ (d) $y - 4x = 6$

3. Write down the y-intercept for each line given in question 2 and sketch the line on squared paper.

4. Write down the equation of the line whose gradient and y-intercept respectively are
   (a) 2 and 6   (c) -3 and 2
   (b) 4 and -1 (d) 1 and 0

5. (i) Find the gradient and y-intercept for each of the following lines.
   (ii) Write down the equation of each line.

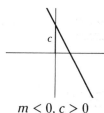

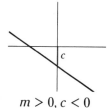

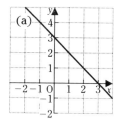

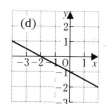

Determine whether the point A is on the line with equation $y = 7 - 2x$ if the coordinates of A are   (a) $(7, 1)$ (b) $(3\frac{1}{2}, 0)$.

Find also the coordinates of the point on this line where $y = -3$

(a) When $x = 7$, $y = 7 - 2(7)$,   i.e. $y = -7$

Therefore the point $(7, 1)$ is not on the line.

(b) When $x = 3\frac{1}{2}$, $y = 7 - 2(3\frac{1}{2})$,   i.e. $y = 0$

Therefore the point $(3\frac{1}{2}, 0)$ is on the line.

When $y = -3$, $-3 = 7 - 2x$,

i.e. $2x = 7 + 3 = 10 \Rightarrow x = 5$

The point where $y = -3$ is $(5, -3)$

Note that $(3\frac{1}{2}, 0)$ is the point where the line crosses the x-axis, so the x-intercept is $3\frac{1}{2}$.

6. Find the y-coordinate of the point on the line $y = 7x - 4$, whose x-coordinate is

   (a) 6   (b) -4 (c) 0

7. Find the x-coordinate of the point on the line $y = 7x - 4$, whose y-coordinate is

   (a) 10   (b) -11 (c) 1

8. Find whether or not the given point lies on the given line.

   (a) $(3, 4)$; $2x + 3y = 18$

   (b) $(1, -8)$; $x - 2y = 15$

   (c) $(0, 5)$; $4x + 3y = 20$

   (d) $(-2, 2)$; $5x - 4y + 18 = 0$

9. Find the x and y intercepts for each line given in question 8 (i.e. find the points where each line crosses the x-axis and the y-axis).

For questions 10 to 12 draw x and y axes, each scaled from -6 to 6.

10. Plot the point $(3, 2)$ and through it draw the straight line with gradient 2.

11. Plot the point $(-2, 1)$ and through it draw the straight line with gradient $-\frac{1}{2}$.

12. Sketch the line passing through the point $(-5, 5)$ and with gradient -2.

Find the equation of the straight line that passes through the point $(-5, 4)$ and has a gradient of -2.

Taking $y = mx + c$ as the equation of the line, the value of m is -2

Therefore the equation of the line is $y = -2x + c$

The point $(-5, 4)$ is on the line so $4 = -2(-5) + c$

$c = -6$

The equation of the line is $y = -2x - 6$

13. Find the equation of the straight line passing through the given point and with the given gradient.

   (a) $(1, 3)$; $\frac{1}{2}$ (b) $(7, -2)$; -1 (c) $(-1, -3)$; 3   (d) $(2, 6)$; $-\frac{1}{2}$.

DIFFERENT FORMS FOR THE EQUATION OF A LINE

The Standard or Gradient Form

So far we have used the equation of a line in the form $y = mx + c$ which we shall refer to as the *gradient form*.

Its advantage is that the gradient and y-intercept can be read from the equation.

The General Form

If the value of m and/or c is a fraction, the equation can be expressed slightly differently.

For example, by clearing the fractions,

$$y = \tfrac{1}{2}x + \tfrac{1}{4} \quad \text{becomes} \quad 4y = 2x + 1 \quad \text{or} \quad 2x - 4y + 1 = 0$$

A typical equation of this type is

$$ax + by + c = 0$$

This is the *general equation* of a line.

Note that, in this form, none of the letters a, b or c has any geometric significance. In particular, c is *not* the y-intercept.

If the equation of a line is given in this general form, it can easily be converted to the form $y = mx + c$ by

(i) isolating the y term on one side,

(ii) dividing each term by the coefficient of y.

The Intercept Form

Consider the equation of a straight line given in the form

$$\frac{x}{a} + \frac{y}{b} = 1$$

When $y = 0$, $x = a$ and when $x = 0$, $y = b$,

i.e. this line crosses the x and y axes at the points $(a, 0)$ and $(0, b)$ respectively.

The y-intercept is b and the x-intercept is a.
Hence the equation of a line expressed in this way is called the *intercept form*.

The advantage of this form is that the line can be drawn immediately through the known points $(a, 0)$ and $(0, b)$.

Parallel Lines

As parallel lines go in the same direction, their gradients are equal,

i.e. if two lines with equations $y = m_1x + c_1$ and $y = m_2x + c_2$ are parallel, then

$$m_1 = m_2$$

If the equations of two lines are given in intercept form, equal ratios of a to b indicate parallel lines.

For example $\dfrac{x}{2} + \dfrac{y}{3} = 1$ and $\dfrac{x}{4} + \dfrac{y}{6} = 1$ represent parallel lines.

Note that $\dfrac{x}{2} + \dfrac{y}{3} = 1$ and $\dfrac{x}{4} - \dfrac{y}{6} = 1$ do *not* represent parallel lines.

Exercise 18c

1. Given that the line with equation $y = 4x + c$ passes through the point $(-1, -5)$, find c and sketch the line.

2. If a line with equation $y = mx - 3$ passes through the point $(2, -1)$, find the gradient and sketch the line.

3. Write down the equation of the straight line that cuts the y-axis at $(0, 4)$ and the x-axis at $(7, 0)$.

> Find the gradient and y-intercept of the line with equation $2y - 6x = 3$. Hence *sketch* the line.
>
> We need the equation in the form $y = mx + c$ so we must isolate y.
>
> $$2y - 6x = 3$$
> $\therefore \qquad\qquad 2y = 6x + 3$
> $\therefore \qquad\qquad y = 3x + 1\tfrac{1}{2}$
>
> The gradient of the line is 3 and the y-intercept is $1\tfrac{1}{2}$
>
>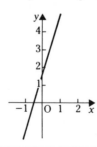

4. Find the gradient and y-intercept for each of the following lines and sketch the line.

   (a) $3y + 6 = x$ (c) $2x + 6y = 12$ (e) $y + 3x + 1 = 0$

   (b) $4y + 3x = 8$ (d) $2x - y - 7 = 0$ (f) $2 + x = 4y$

Sketch, and find the gradient of, the straight line with equation

(a) $\dfrac{x}{3} + \dfrac{y}{2} = 1$ (b) $\dfrac{x}{4} - \dfrac{y}{3} = 1$

(a) The x-intercept is 3,   i.e. the line passes through $(3, 0)$

The y-intercept is 2,   i.e. the line passes through $(0, 2)$

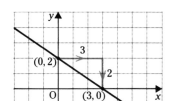

The gradient is $-\dfrac{2}{3}$

(b) $\dfrac{x}{4} - \dfrac{y}{3} = 1$ can be written $\dfrac{x}{4} + \dfrac{y}{-3} = 1$

The x-intercept is 4,   i.e. the line passes through $(4, 0)$

The y-intercept is -3,   i.e. the line passes through $(0, -3)$

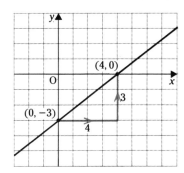

The gradient is $\dfrac{3}{4}$

---

5. Sketch the line representing the given equation. Find the gradient of each line.

(a) $\dfrac{x}{4} + \dfrac{y}{3} = 1$ (d) $\dfrac{x}{3} + \dfrac{y}{6} = 1$

(b) $\dfrac{x}{5} + \dfrac{y}{3} = 1$ (e) $\dfrac{x}{1} - \dfrac{y}{2} = 1$

(c) $\dfrac{x}{4} - \dfrac{y}{2} = 1$ (f) $\dfrac{y}{3} - \dfrac{x}{4} = 1$

6. Without drawing a diagram, state where each line cuts the axes.

(a) $\dfrac{x}{2} + \dfrac{y}{4} = 1$ (b) $\dfrac{x}{12} - \dfrac{y}{9} = 1$

7. Form the equation of the line that crosses the axes at

(a) $(0, 5)$ and $(6, 0)$

(b) $(0, -3)$ and $(4, 0)$

8. Sketch the line with equation $x + y = 1$ and find its gradient.

Find, in the most suitable form, the equation of the straight line that passes through the points $(-5, 0)$ and $(0, 6)$. State the gradient.

The points given are those where the line cuts the x and y axes so the intercept form is best.

The equation of the line is

$$\frac{x}{a} + \frac{y}{b} = 1$$

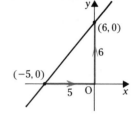

From the given coordinates, $a = -5$ and $b = 6$

Therefore the equation is

$$\frac{x}{-5} + \frac{y}{6} = 1$$

The gradient of the line is $\frac{6}{5}$

Note that the equation can be rearranged as $\dfrac{x}{5} - \dfrac{y}{6} + 1 = 0$ or $6x - 5y + 30 = 0$

Write down the equation, and give the gradient, of the line through each pair of points.

9. (a) $(3, 0)$, $(0, 8)$ (b) $(2, 0)$, $(0, 2)$

10. (a) $(-1, 0)$, $(0, 4)$ (b) $(-3, 0)$, $(0, -7)$

Find the equation of the straight line that passes through the points $(2, 1)$ and $(6, -3)$.

The gradient of the line is

$$\frac{-3 - 1}{6 - 2} = -1$$

Let the equation of the line be

$$y = -x + c$$

The point $(2, 1)$ is on the line so

$$1 = -2 + c$$

i.e. $c = 3$

Therefore the equation of the line is $y = -x + 3$ or $x + y = 3$

(Check: when $x = 6$, $y = -6 + 3 = -3$ which is correct.)

In questions 11 and 12 find the equation of the line through the two given points.

11. (a) $(4, -1)$ and $(3, -6)$ (b) $(3, 2)$ and $(1, 7)$

12. (a) $(-9, -3)$ and $(6, 0)$ (b) $(5, -2)$ and $(-4, 7)$

13. State which of the following equations represent lines that are parallel.

$$y = 2x + 3, \quad y = 4 - 2x, \quad y = 4 + 2x, \quad 2y = x + 1, \quad y = x + 3$$

14. There are two pairs of parallel lines represented in the following set of equations. Which are they and what, for each pair, is the gradient ?

$$2x + y = 2 \quad y = 2x - 4 \quad 3y - 4x = 5 \quad y = 7 - 2x \quad 4x = 3y \quad 2y + x = 1$$

Find the equation of the straight line that is

(a) parallel to the line $y = 5x - 2$ and passes through the point $(-2, 6)$

(b) parallel to the line $3x + 4y = 1$ and cuts the x-axis where $x = -1$

(a) The gradient of the line $y = 5x - 2$ is 5 so the gradient of a parallel line is also 5.

Let the equation of the required line be $y = 5x + c$

The point $(-2, 6)$ is on this line, so

$$6 = 5(-2) + c$$

$$c = 16$$

The equation of the parallel line is $y = 5x + 16$

(b) The gradient of the line is found from the terms $3x$ and $4y$. The equation of any line with the same gradient will therefore contain the same coefficients of x and y.

Let the equation of the required line be $3x + 4y + c = 0$

The line crosses the x-axis at the point $(-1, 0)$

$$\therefore \qquad\qquad 3(-1) + 0 + c = 0$$

i.e. $$c = 3$$

The equation of the required line is $3x + 4y + 3 = 0$

---

15. Give the equations of any three lines that are parallel to the line with equation

(a) $y = 2x - 6$ (b) $5x - 2y - 7 = 0$ (c) $2x = 4 - 3y$

16. Give the equations of the lines that pass through the point $(0, 4)$ and are parallel to the line whose equation is

(a) $y = 4x + 1$ (b) $y + 3x = 6$ (c) $2y - x = 1$

17. Find the gradients and the intercepts on the y-axis of the lines with equations $y = 5 - 2x$ and $y = 5x - 2$. What is the equation of the line that is parallel to the first line and cuts the y-axis at the same point as the second line ?

18. The lines $y = kx + 4$ and $3y = (k + 3)x - 5$ are parallel. Find k.

DRAWING A LINE FROM ITS EQUATION

Consider the line with equation $2x + 3y - 12 = 0$.
The coordinates of three points on the line can be found by making a table as shown, choosing three values of x (we usually include $x = 0$), and then calculating the corresponding values of y from the equation of the line.

x	-3	0	3
y	6	4	2

These three points can now be plotted and the required line drawn through them.

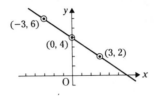

Although only two points are needed in order to draw a particular line, we use a third point as a check. If the three points do not all lie on one line, check the calculations.

Exercise 18d

On graph paper draw each of the following lines. Use 1 cm to represent 1 unit. The range of values of x is given; find the range for y. Find the gradient of each line.

1. $x - 4y = 8$, $0 \leqslant x \leqslant 8$

2. $x + y = 6$, $0 \leqslant x \leqslant 7$

3. $3x + 5y = 15$, $0 \leqslant x \leqslant 6$

4. $2x - y = 3$, $-2 \leqslant x \leqslant 2$

Choosing your own scale and range of values of x, draw on graph paper the line with each of the following equations.

5. $\dfrac{x}{5} + \dfrac{y}{3} = 1$

6. $\dfrac{x}{3} - \dfrac{y}{4} = 1$

7. $\dfrac{x}{4} - \dfrac{y}{2} = 1$

8. $\dfrac{x}{2} - \dfrac{y}{4} = 2$

9. $\dfrac{x}{3} + \dfrac{y}{4} = 1$

10. $x + y = 3$

GRAPHICAL SOLUTION OF SIMULTANEOUS EQUATIONS

The equation of a straight line is a linear equation, i.e. it is made up of an x term, a y term and a number. For every point on the line the x and y coordinates satisfy the equation of the line. If we have two linear equations, each gives a straight line and, unless the lines are parallel, these two lines will cross somewhere.

At their point of intersection the x and y coordinates satisfy both linear equations, i.e. these values of x and y are the solutions of the simultaneous equations that represent the two lines.

Exercise 18e

The value of x that satisfies the pair of equations $x + y = 4$ and $y = 1 + x$ is known to be in the range $0 \leqslant x \leqslant 5$. Solve the equations graphically.

First draw the lines, for $0 \leqslant x \leqslant 5$, representing the two equations.

$x + y = 4$

x	0	4	5
y	4	0	−1

$y = 1 + x$

x	0	2	5
y	1	3	6

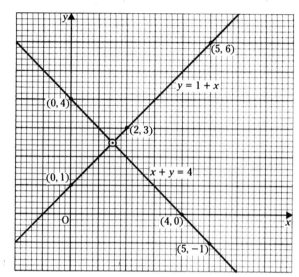

The point where the lines cross has coordinates ($1\frac{1}{2}, 2\frac{1}{2}$).

Therefore the solution of the given pair of equations is

$$x = 1\tfrac{1}{2} \quad \text{and} \quad y = 2\tfrac{1}{2}$$

In questions 1 to 3 the range of values of x and y is given within which the solution of the pair of equations lies. Taking a scale of 2 cm to 1 unit, use graphs to solve each pair of equations.

1. $\left.\begin{array}{l} y = 5 - x \\ y = 2 + x \end{array}\right\}$ $0 \leqslant x \leqslant 5, \quad 0 \leqslant y \leqslant 7$

2. $\left.\begin{array}{l} x + y = 1 \\ y = x + 2 \end{array}\right\}$ $-3 \leqslant x \leqslant 2, \quad -2 \leqslant y \leqslant 4$

3. Try to solve
$\left.\begin{array}{l} x + y = 9 \\ y = 4 - x \end{array}\right\}$ $0 \leqslant x \leqslant 9, \quad 0 \leqslant y \leqslant 9$

Why do you think the method fails?

Use squared paper for questions 4 and 5.

4. Sketch the lines with equations
$$y = 2.4x - 3.1$$
and $y = -3.7x + 2.4$.

Hence show that the value of x that satisfies both equations simultaneously is in the range $0 \leqslant x \leqslant 1$.

5. By sketching the lines represented by
$$2.1x - y = 5.5$$
and $3.8y + 2x = 5.9$

find a range, spanning two integers, within which lies the value of x that satisfies both equations simultaneously. Find a similar range for the corresponding value of y.

STRAIGHT LINE GRAPHS IN PRACTICAL SITUATIONS

In a variety of real-life situations, use can be made of straight line graphs in which the coordinates of points represent practical quantities. A particularly useful application is for converting one set of units to another.

For instance when on holiday abroad it can help if a distance in kilometres can be converted immediately to an equivalent number of miles.

It is also useful to be able to convert between the currencies of different countries.

Exercise 18f

Given that £1 converts to 9.6 Norwegian kroner, draw a graph to convert values up to £100 into kroner.

Use your graph to find

(a) the cost in pounds of a pair of shoes priced at 760 kroner
(b) how many kroner correspond to £46.

$$£1 \equiv 9.6 \, \text{kroner}$$

so

$$£50 \equiv 480 \, \text{kroner}$$

and

$$£100 \equiv 960 \, \text{kroner}$$

Plotting the last two points and $(0, 0)$ gives the required conversion graph.

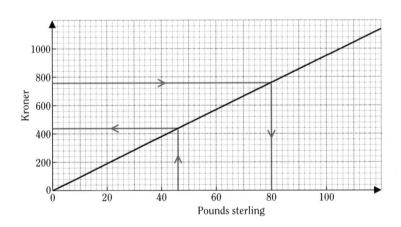

From the graph:

(a) the shoes cost £80

(b) £46 corresponds to 440 kroner.

1. This graph can be used to convert speeds from m.p.h. to km/h and conversely.

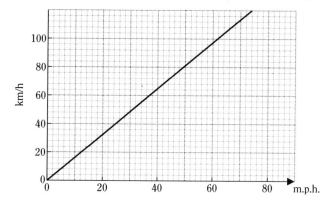

Use the graph to find a speed of:

(a) 52 m.p.h. in km/h   (b) 100 km/h in m.p.h.   (c) 72 m.p.h. in km/h   (d) 52 km/h in m.p.h.

2. The table shows how many US dollars correspond to several amounts of British currency.

Pounds sterling	25	75	112.50
US dollars	42	126	189

Using 4 cm to represent 50 units on both axes, draw a straight line graph through the three points.

Use the graph to convert:

(a) 78 dollars to pounds   (b) £54 to dollars   (c) 140 dollars to pounds   (d) £100 to dollars

3. Some temperatures in degrees Fahrenheit (°F) and the equivalent values in degrees Celsius (°C) are given in the table below.

Temperature in °F	53	115	158
Temperature in °C	12	46	70

Using 2 cm to represent 20 units on each axis, with ranges from 0 to 90 °C and −40 °F to 180 °F, draw the line through the given points and use it to convert

(a) 170 °F into °C   (b) 35 °C into °F

Water freezes at 0 °C. What is the freezing point of water in °F ?

4. This table shows the distances a girl walked in various times.

Time in hours	0	1	$2\frac{1}{2}$	4	5
Distance in kilometres	0	6	15	24	30

Use these results to draw a graph and find the gradient.

(a) What does the gradient represent ?

(b) How far did she walk in 3 hours 45 minutes ?

(c) How long did it take her to walk 21 km ?

5. An examination is marked out of 65. Draw a graph which shows the marks from 0 to 65 as percentages from 0 to 100 %. Use the graph

(a) to express marks of 32 and 57 as percentages

(b) to find the marks given to a candidate who scored 82 %.

THE MEANING OF THE GRADIENT AND THE y-INTERCEPT

For a straight line with equation $y = mx + c$ the gradient, m, tells us the rate at which y is increasing with respect to x (i.e. y compared with x).

This is often abbreviated to

        gradient is the rate of increase of y w.r.t. x

For a straight line graph that results from plotting real quantities, the gradient represents the rate at which the quantity on the vertical axis increases compared with the quantity on the horizontal axis.

Alternatively we can say that the gradient gives the number of units by which the quantity on the vertical axis increases for an increase of one unit in the quantity on the horizontal axis.

The value of the gradient is found, as before, from the coordinates of any two points on the graph *but* as the scales on the two axes are unlikely to be equal, the distances between the two points must be taken from the appropriate scale and not by counting graph squares, i.e.

$$\text{gradient} = \frac{\text{increase in quantity on vertical axis}}{\text{increase in quantity on horizontal axis}}$$

This graph, for example, shows the cost to a householder of consuming different quantities of gas.

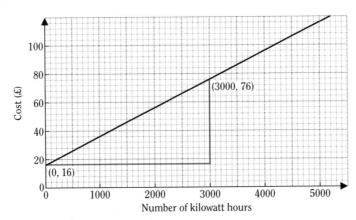

The gradient of the graph is given by

$$\frac{76 - 16}{3000 - 0} = \frac{60}{3000} = \frac{1}{50}$$

It represents the increase in the cost for an increase of one unit of consumption, i.e. £0.02 per kilowatt hour.

The y-intercept is 16 and this represents what the customer has to pay before any gas has been used, i.e. the standing charge is £16.

Exercise 18g

1. For each graph give   (i) the value of the gradient   (ii) a meaning for the gradient.

(a)

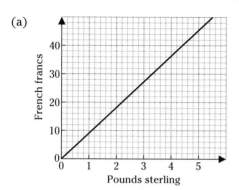

(c)

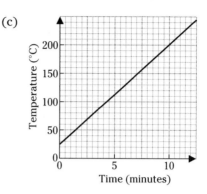

(b)

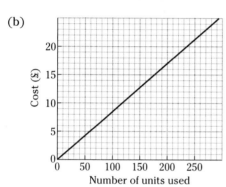

(d)

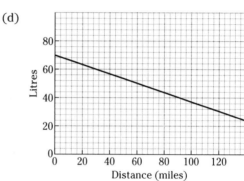

2. This graph shows how the quantity of water in a reservoir varies with time. When full it contains 2 000 000 gallons.

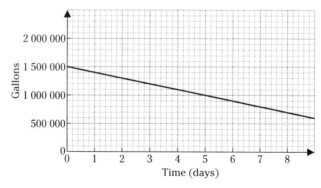

(a) Use the graph to find
   (i) the volume of water in the reservoir after three days
   (ii) after how many days the reservoir is half empty.

(b) What is the gradient of the graph and what does it represent?

(c) What is the value of the intercept on the vertical axis and what does it represent?

3. A householder can choose to buy electricity either on Tariff A or on Tariff B. The graph below shows the costs incurred in using each of these tariffs.

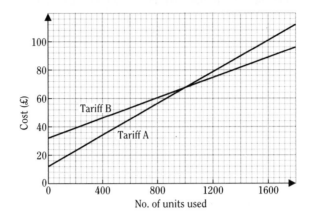

(a) Find the gradient of the line representing each tariff and attach a meaning to each of these values.

(b) Write down the value of the vertical intercept in each case and give it a meaning.

(c) Which is the more economical tariff to choose if the household consumes (i) 560 units (ii) 1400 units ?

4. Details of three families' quarterly telephone bills are given in the table.

Name	No. of units used (n)	Total cost ($£x$)
Smith	500	44
Jones	850	59.40
Robinson	1200	74.80

Represent this information on a straight line graph using 1 cm ≡ 100 units on the horizontal n-axis and   1 cm ≡ £10   vertically.

Use the graph to find   (a) the gradient and vertical intercept

(b) the cost of one unit

(c) the quarterly rental charge.

Self-Assessment 18

1. For the line joining each of the following pairs of points find   (i) the length   (ii) the midpoint (iii) the gradient.

    (a) $(6, -3)$ and $(1, 9)$ (b) $(-2, 5)$ and $(4, -3)$

2. On squared paper sketch the line represented by each equation.

    (a) $y = -5$ (b) $x = 2$ (c) $y = 3x - 4$ (d) $y + x = 5$

3. Find the gradient and y-intercept of each line.

(a)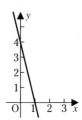

(b)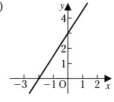

(c)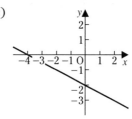

4. Find the equation of the line that
   (a) passes through the point $(4, -1)$ and has a gradient of 2
   (b) has a y-intercept of 4 and an x-intercept of 3
   (c) passes through the origin and is parallel to the line with equation $y = 3x - 1$

5. Find the equation of the line through the points $(-1, 3)$ and $(5, -5)$.

6. On the line given in question 5, find
   (a) x when $y = -1$ (b) y when $x = 8$ (c) the y-intercept

7. Draw, on the same graph, using $-2 \leqslant x \leqslant 4$ and $-1 \leqslant y \leqslant 5$, the lines with equations $y = 2x + 1$ and $3y + x = 10$.

   Use your graph to solve the pair of equations.

8. Given that $\text{\pounds}\,1$ is equivalent to 2.96 Deutschmarks, construct a graph, from 0 to $\text{\pounds}\,100$, to be used for converting between these two currencies.

   Use the graph to give the value of
   (a) $\text{\pounds}\,34$ in DM   (b) 215 DM in $\text{\pounds}$ s

9. This graph shows the cost of producing a magazine as the number of pages in it varies.

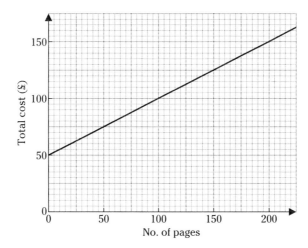

(a) What is the cost of the magazine when it contains 130 pages?
(b) Find the gradient of the graph and say what it represents.
(c) Suggest a meaning for the vertical intercept.

INEQUALITIES IN A PLANE

INEQUALITIES IN TWO DIMENSIONS

In an earlier chapter the inequalities considered involved only one variable; they were discussed in algebraic terms and illustrated by number lines.

Two-dimensional space, with x and y axes, can also be used to illustrate the meaning of inequalities.

For instance, the inequality $x \geqslant 3$ can be illustrated in the xy plane by all the points with an x coordinate equal to or greater than 3.

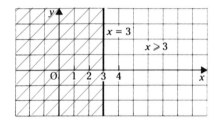

The boundary line, which represents all the points for which $x = 3$, is a solid line to show that it is included in the given inequality. The region to the right of it contains all the points with x coordinates greater than 3. To indicate the region that satisfies an inequality, we usually shade the area we do *not* want, in this case the area to the left of the line $x = 3$. This leaves clear the region we *do* want.

The inequality $x > 3$ is represented by the same area but points on the boundary line are *not* included this time; this is indicated by a broken line.

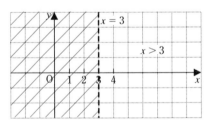

Inequalities involving y can be illustrated in a similar way.

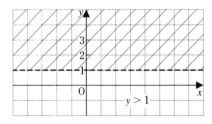

Exercise 19a

Draw on an *xy* plane the region that represents $-2 \leqslant x < 3$ and state whether or not the points $(1,1)$, $(3,2)$ and $(-2,4)$ lie in this region.

$$-2 \leqslant x < 3 \quad \text{gives} \quad -2 \leqslant x \quad \text{and} \quad x < 3$$

The boundary lines of the required region are $x = -2$ (included), $x = 3$ (not included)

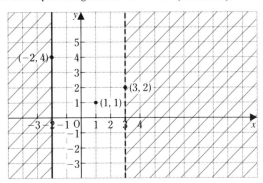

The unshaded region represents $-2 \leqslant x < 3$

$(1,1)$ lies in this region, $(3,2)$ is not in this region, $(-2,4)$ lies in this region.

On an *xy* plane draw diagrams to represent the following inequalities. In each case state whether the point $(-1, 1)$ lies in the given region.

1. $1 < x < 4$

2. $-2 \leqslant x \leqslant 2$

3. $5 \geqslant x > 3$

4. $0 > y > -3$

5. $2 > y > -1$

6. $-5 \leqslant x < 0$

What inequality is represented by the unshaded region?

(a)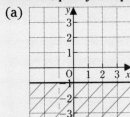

(b)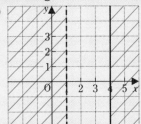

(a) The boundary line is $y = -1$ and is included.

The inequality is $y \geqslant -1$

(b) The boundary lines are $x = 1$ (not included)

and $x = 4$ (included)

The inequality is $1 < x \leqslant 4$

In questions 7 to 12 give inequalities that define each unshaded region.
In each case state whether or not the point $(1, 3)$ lies in this region.

7.

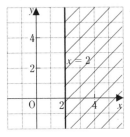

8.

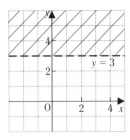

9.

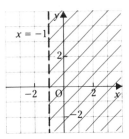

10.

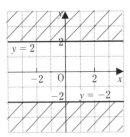

11.

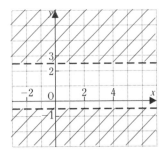

12.

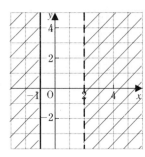

Although in this book we usually shade the region that is not wanted, this is not a hard and fast rule and there may be occasions when the *required* region is shaded. Always check carefully what the shading represents and always *state clearly* on your own work whether the region asked for is shaded or unshaded.

Find inequalities to define each shaded region.

13.

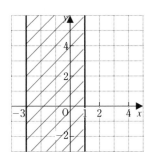

14.

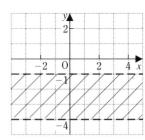

15.

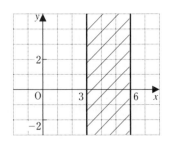

The remaining questions in this exercise use regions of an *xy* plane that are defined by a number of inequalities.

> Draw a diagram to represent the region defined by the set of inequalities
>
> $$-1 \leqslant x \leqslant 2 \quad \text{and} \quad -5 \leqslant y \leqslant 0$$
>
> The boundary lines are $x = -1, \ x = 2, \ y = -5, \ y = 0$
>
>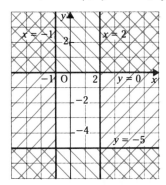
>
> The unshaded region represents the inequalities.

Draw diagrams to represent the regions described by the following sets of inequalities. In each case, draw axes for values of *x* and *y* from −5 to 5.

16. $2 \leqslant x \leqslant 4, \quad -1 \leqslant y \leqslant 3$

17. $-2 < x < 2, \quad -2 < y < 2$

18. $0 \leqslant x \leqslant 4, \quad 0 \leqslant y \leqslant 3$

19. $-4 < x < 0, \quad -2 < y < 2$

20. $-1 < x < 1, \quad -3 < y < 1$

21. $x \geqslant 1, \quad -1 \leqslant y \leqslant 2$

Give the sets of inequalities that describe the unshaded regions.

22.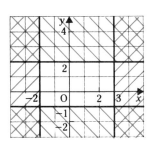

23.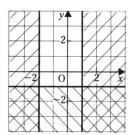

24.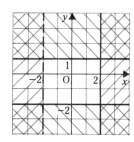

25.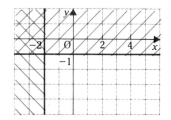

INEQUALITIES INVOLVING TWO VARIABLES

The equation $2x + y = 4$ is represented in the xy plane by a sloping line.

It follows that the inequality $2x + y < 4$ is represented by an area bounded by that sloping line.

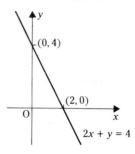

The boundary line divides the space into two regions. To decide which of these regions represents the given inequality we can use a check point that is not on the line.

The easiest point to use is the origin.

When $x = 0$ and $y = 0$, $2x + y = 0$ which is less than 4.
So the origin is in the region that represents $2x + y < 4$.

Alternatively, converting the inequality into the form $y < 4 - 2x$ we see that the required region contains all the points that are *below* the line $y = 4 - 2x$.

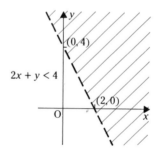

Now we can shade the region that is not required; the boundary line is not included so a broken line is used as before.

Exercise 19b

Leave unshaded the region defined by the inequality $3x - 2y \leqslant 6$

The boundary line is $3x - 2y = 6$
and it is included in the inequality.

x	0	2	4
y	-3	0	3

When $x = 0$ and $y = 0$,
$3x - 2y = 0$ which is less than 6.
So the origin is in the required region
and we shade the area on the other side
of the line.

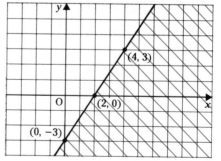

Alternatively $3x - 2y \leqslant 6$ $\Rightarrow$ $2y \geqslant 3x - 6$ $\Rightarrow$ $y \geqslant \frac{3}{2}x - 3$
So the required region is above the line.

The unshaded region represents the inequality $3x - 2y \leqslant 6$

Using x and y axes scaled from -6 to 6, leave unshaded the regions defined by the given inequalities.

1. $x + y < 3$ **3.** $2x + 4y \leqslant 7$ **5.** $x + 2y \leqslant 4$

2. $3x - 2y < 6$ **4.** $2x - y \leqslant 3$ **6.** $3x - 5y > 15$

Find the inequality that defines the unshaded region.

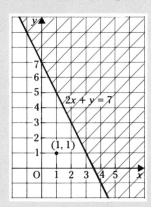

The boundary line, $2x + y = 7$, is solid and is therefore included.

Check a point that is in the unshaded region, e.g. $(1, 1)$

When $x = 1$ and $y = 1$, $2x + y = 3$ which is less than 7

So the inequality is $2x + y \leqslant 7$

Alternatively, writing the equation of the boundary line as $y = 7 - 2x$ and noting that the given region is below the boundary line, we see that the inequality is $y \leqslant 7 - 2x$ or $2x + y \leqslant 7$

Find the inequality that defines each unshaded region.

7.

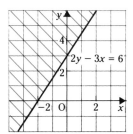

9.

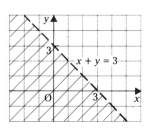

10. First find the equation of the boundary line.

8.

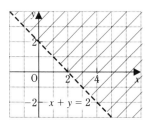

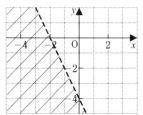

Regions with more than one sloping line boundary can be illustrated in a similar way. Each of the boundary lines is drawn and the unwanted region shaded.

Leave unshaded the region defined by the set of inequalities

$$x+y<4, \quad x\geqslant0 \quad \text{and} \quad x+2y\geqslant2$$

1st boundary line (not included) $x+y = 4$

x	4	0	2
y	0	4	2

2nd boundary line (included) $x = 0$

3rd boundary line (included) $x + 2y = 2$

x	0	2	4
y	1	0	−1

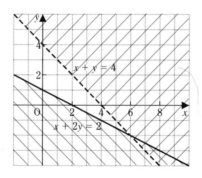

The unshaded region is defined by the given inequalities.

Leave unshaded the regions defined by the following sets of inequalities:

11. $x\geqslant-3, \quad y\geqslant-2, \quad x+y\leqslant3$

12. $y\leqslant0, \quad x\leqslant0, \quad x+y\leqslant-4$

13. $y<3, \quad 2x+3y\geqslant6, \quad y>x-2$

14. $y>x, \quad y<4x, \quad x+y<5$

15. $x\geqslant0, \quad y\geqslant x-1, \quad 2y+x<4$

16. What can you say about the region defined by $x+y>4, \quad x+y<1, \quad x>0 \quad \text{and} \quad y>0$?

17. Do the regions defined by the following sets of inequalities exist ?
    (a) $x+y\geqslant3, \quad y\leqslant2, \quad y\geqslant2x$
    (b) $x+y>3, \quad y<2, \quad y>2x$

Shading a Required Region

In some simple cases you might be asked to shade the region defined by the inequality, instead of leaving it unshaded.

Occasionally, you may be asked to shade the required region when it is defined by several inequalities. If you try to do it by shading the required side of each boundary line, you will find yourself with overlapping shadings, resulting in a confused diagram.

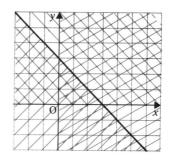

For instance, if $y \geqslant 0$, $x \geqslant 0$ and $x + y \leqslant 3$, the diagram looks like this and the required region disappears in a muddle.

A better method is to do the shading as before so that the required region is left unshaded, then draw a second diagram on which you shade the required area.

1st diagram

2nd diagram
The required region is shaded.

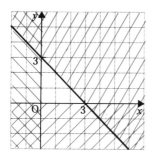

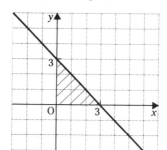

Exercise 19c

Shade the regions defined by the sets of inequalities.

1. $x \leqslant 4$, $y \leqslant 3$, $x + y \geqslant 0$

2. $2x + y \geqslant 4$, $y \leqslant 0$, $x \leqslant 4$

3. $\dfrac{x}{2} + \dfrac{y}{3} \geqslant 1$, $\dfrac{x}{2} - \dfrac{y}{3} \geqslant 1$, $x \leqslant 8$

4. $y \geqslant x$, $y - x \leqslant 2$, $y \leqslant 2$

5. $2y \leqslant 3 - x$, $2y \geqslant x - 3$, $x \geqslant 1$

If you need to use diagrams for solving problems, it is best to leave the required regions unshaded.

Give the inequalities that define the
unshaded region.

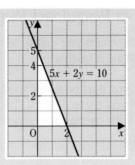

The first two inequalities are $x \geqslant 0, y \geqslant 0$
The 3rd boundary line is $5x + 2y = 10$

Test the point $(1, 1)$
When $x = 1$ and $y = 1$, $5x + 2y = 7$
As $7 < 10$ the 3rd inequality is $5x + 2y \leqslant 10$

In questions 6 to 9, give the sets of inequalities
that define the unshaded regions.

6.

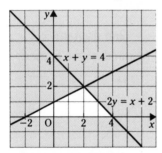

7.

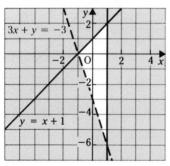

First find the equations of the boundary lines.

8.

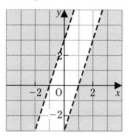

9.

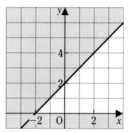

10.

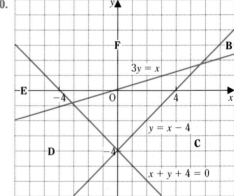

Use inequalities to describe the regions
bounded by green lines.

(a) A   (d) E

(b) B   (e) A + D

(c) C   (f) A + F

11.

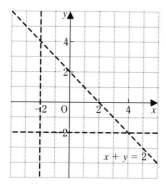

Write down the region, A, B or C, defined by each set of inequalities.

(a) $x + y < 2$, $x < -2$, $y > -2$

(b) $x + y < 2$, $x > -2$, $y > -2$

(c) $x + y < 2$, $x > -2$, $y < -2$

12. Write down the coordinates of the vertices of the unshaded regions.

(a)

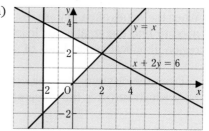

(b)

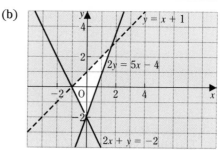

Give the points whose coordinates are integers and that lie in the region given in the diagram.

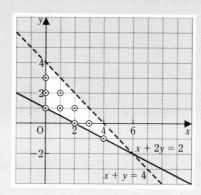

Notice that points on the broken line are *not* in the region.

Points are

$(0,1), (0,2), (0,3), (1,1), (1,2), (2,0), (2,1), (3,0)$ and $(4,-1)$.

13. Draw a diagram and give the coordinates of the points whose coordinates are integers and that lie in the region defined by the inequalities $y \leqslant 3x + 6$, $y > x - 2$, $x + y > -2$ and $x + y \leqslant 3$

14. Draw a diagram and give the points with coordinates that are integers, on the boundaries of the region defined by the inequalities $x \geqslant 2$, $y \geqslant -1$ and $x + y \leqslant 4$

GREATEST AND LEAST VALUES

When the values of x and y are restricted to a specified region of the xy plane, we sometimes need to find the greatest or least value of an expression such as $3x - 2y$ within that region. Practical applications of such situations are given in the next section.

From the diagram, give the coordinates of the vertices of the unshaded region. At which vertex is the value of $x + 2y$ least?

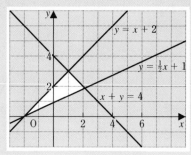

The three vertices are $(1,3)$, $(2,2)$ and $(-2,0)$.

At $(1,3)$ $x + 2y = 1 + 6 = 7$

At $(2,2)$ $x + 2y = 2 + 4 = 6$

At $(-2,0)$ $x + 2y = -2 + 0 = -2$

$\therefore$ $x + 2y$ is least at the point $(-2,0)$.

Exercise 19d

In questions 1 and 2

(a) Find from the diagram the coordinates of the vertices of the unshaded region.

(b) Find the vertex at which the value of the given expression, E, is greatest.

(c) Find the vertex where the value of E is least.

(d) For all the other points in the region whose coordinates are integers, write down the coordinates.

(e) Is the value of E at any of these points greater than its value as found in part (b)?

(f) Is the value of E at any of these points less than its value at the vertex chosen in part (c)?

1.

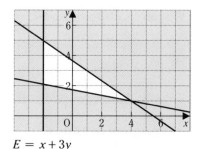

$E = x + 3y$

2.

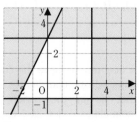

$E = x + y$

The answers to these questions illustrate that, if x and y are integers, the greatest or least values of any expression such as $2x + 3y$ occur at the vertices of a region and not at points within the region. Hence, to find greatest or least values, only the vertex values need be checked. (In cases where the coordinates of the vertices are not integers, greatest or least values of the expression occur at points which are near to the vertices and whose coordinates are integers.)

For the region defined by the set of inequalities $x \geqslant -1$, $y \geqslant -2$ and $x + y < 3$, draw a diagram and find the points with coordinates that are integers, where the value of $2x - y$ is (a) greatest (b) least.

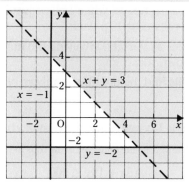

At $(-1, 3)$ $2x - y = -2 - 3 = -5$

At $(-1, -2)$ $2x - y = -2 + 2 = 0$

At $(4, -2)$ $2x - y = 8 + 2 = 10$

(a) $(2x - y)$ is greatest at $(4, -2)$.

(b) $(2x - y)$ is least at $(-1, 3)$.

---

3. In the region defined by $x \geqslant -3$, $y \leqslant x + 1$ and $y \geqslant 2x$, find the point with integer coordinates where the value of $3x - y$ is greatest.

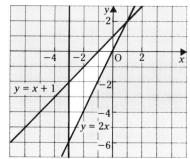

4. In the region defined by $y \geqslant x$, $y + x \geqslant 0$ and $y \leqslant 2.5$ find, by drawing a diagram, the point with integer coordinates at which the value of $2x - y$ is greatest.

5. In the region defined by $y < x + 3$, $3x + y < 6$ and $y \geqslant -1$, find the point with integer coordinates where the value of $3x - 2y$ is greatest.

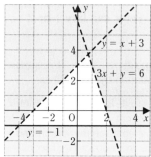

6. In the region defined by $4x + y \leqslant 4$, $y \leqslant 3$ and $x \leqslant 1$ find, by drawing a diagram, the point with integer coordinates at which the value of $x + y$ is greatest. Is there a point at which the value of $x + y$ is least ?

USING INEQUALITIES TO MODEL REAL SITUATIONS

There are many real problems in which quantities have to be limited in some way. These can often be expressed as inequalities if letters are used to represent unknown quantities, numbers, etc. Various facts about these quantities can then be deduced from the inequalities.

Exercise 19e

Peter was given £3 to buy a mixture of white and brown bread rolls. White rolls cost 15 p each and brown rolls cost 19 p each.

(a) Find as many inequalities as you can involving the number of white rolls (x) and the number of brown rolls (y).

(b) If he buys 12 brown rolls find the possible numbers of white rolls that he can buy.

(a) The cost of x white rolls is $15x$ pence and the cost of y brown rolls is $19y$ pence.

Peter cannot spend more than £3, so the total cost of the rolls must not exceed 300 pence

$$15x + 19y \leqslant 300$$

As a mixture of rolls is to be bought, at least one white roll and at least one brown roll are required

$$x \geqslant 1 \quad \text{and} \quad y \geqslant 1$$

If only one brown roll is bought, 281 p is left to buy white rolls. Therefore the greatest possible number of white rolls is the largest number of 15s in 281, i.e. 18.

A similar argument applies to the largest number of brown rolls.

$$x \leqslant 18 \quad \text{and} \quad y \leqslant 15$$

(b) Using $y = 12$ in $15x + 19y \leqslant 300$ gives $15x + 228 \leqslant 300$ i.e. $15x \leqslant 72$

Hence $x \leqslant 4$ (as x must be an integer)

Peter can buy 1 or 2 or 3 or 4 white rolls.

In questions 1 to 3 express the given information by inequalities.

1. A rectangle is to have a perimeter of not more than 20 cm and an area of at least 12 cm². Taking x cm for the length and y cm for the width, write down two inequalities involving x and y (other than $x > 0$ and $y > 0$).

2. In a cash box there are x £1 coins and y 50 p coins. It is known that there are at least twice as many £1 coins as 50 p coins and that the total value of the coins is less than £100.

3. A disc jockey plans to play x pop songs and y rock singles during his programme. A pop song takes 3 minutes of air-time and a rock single takes 4 minutes. The programme must last for less than 45 minutes and there must not be more rock tracks than pop.

4. Barbara is three times as old as Christa and the sum of their ages is less than 20 years. Find

   (a) as many relationships as you can to represent these conditions

   (b) a possible age range for Christa.

When inequalities relating unknown variables are illustrated graphically, further deductions can be made and interesting conclusions drawn.

> The total number of cats and dogs kept in an animal boarding home is limited by regulations to a maximum of 10. There are 2 permanently boarded cats. A cat requires 2 units of accommodation and a dog requires 5. For the home to be operated viably, the total number of units occupied must not be less than 30.
>
> The weekly profit that can be made is £12 for boarding a cat and £10 for a dog.
>
> (a) Find as many inequalities as possible to express the relationship between the numbers of cats and dogs.
>
> (b) Represent these inequalities graphically.
>
> (c) Find the numbers of cats and of dogs for which the profit is greatest.

(a) Let x be the number of cats and y the number of dogs (both x and y must be integers).

Then $$x + y \leqslant 10 \quad \text{and} \quad x \geqslant 2$$

Also, considering the number of accommodation units,

$$2x + 5y \geqslant 30 \quad \text{i.e.} \quad y \geqslant 6 - \tfrac{2}{5}x$$

It is obvious that, in addition, $y \geqslant 0$

(b) The region left unshaded contains all possible values of x and y.

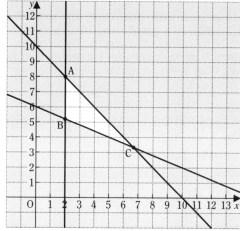

(c) The profit made weekly is £$(12x + 10y)$

We have seen that the greatest value of $12x + 10y$ occurs at, or near, one of the vertices of the unshaded region.

At A $(2,8)$, $12x + 10y = 24 + 80 = 104$

At B, $x = 2$ and $y < 8$ so $12x + 10y < 104$

The point nearest to C, with coordinates that are integers, is $(6,4)$.

At this point $12x + 10y = 72 + 40 = 112$

So the numbers of animals that maximise the profit are 6 cats and 4 dogs.

5. A poultry farmer wants to buy at least 100 ducks and at least 200 hens and can afford to spend up to £600. A duck costs £1.50 and a hen costs £1.00.

  (a) If the farmer buys x ducks and y hens, express this information by using inequalities; illustrate the inequalities graphically and leave unshaded the area in which all the inequalities are satisfied. Take 1 cm for 50 birds on each axis.

  (b) Find the largest possible total number of hens and ducks that the farmer can buy.

6. Sean wants to buy x pencils and y ball-point pens. He wants more than twice as many pencils as pens but needs at least 2 pens.
A pen costs 40 p and a pencil 30 p. Sean has £5 to spend. Illustrate this information graphically using 1 cm to represent 1 pen on one axis and 1 pencil on the other.

  (a) If he buys the maximum possible number of pens, how many pens and pencils does he buy ?

  (b) If he buys the maximum total number of pens and pencils how many of each does he buy ?

7. A developer plans to build some bungalows and some maisonettes on a $4000 \, \text{m}^2$ plot of land. To build a bungalow requires $250 \, \text{m}^2$ of land and 240 days of labour. For a maisonette the requirements are $200 \, \text{m}^2$ of land and 120 days of labour. The developer wants to keep as many as possible of his total labour force employed, so plans to use at least 1800 days of labour.

Use inequalities to express this information and reduce the inequalities to their simplest form. Represent the simplified inequalities on a graph, using 1 cm for 1 unit on each axis.

The developer finds that there is more demand for bungalows than for maisonettes so decides to build at least 5 bungalows. What is the greatest number of dwellings that he can build ?

8. A firework manufacturer is planning a special display pack containing roman candles in two sizes, super and spectacular. The details of each firework are given in the following table.

	No. in pack	Display time (s)	Weight (g)	Profit (£)
Spectacular	p	50	120	1.50
Super	q	25	100	1.00

The pack must contain enough fireworks, set off one after the other, for a display of at least 35 minutes, with at least 20 super candles included. The weight of the pack must not exceed 9 kg.

  (a) Show that $2p + q \geqslant 84$ and $6p + 5q \leqslant 450$

  (b) Illustrate all the given data by a region in the pq plane using 1 cm for 5 fireworks on each axis.

  (c) Find how many of each size of roman candle the pack should contain if the profit is to be maximised.

Self-Assessment 19

For questions 2, 4 and 5, where regions of the *xy* plane are required, sketches on squared paper are adequate.

1. Write down the inequality represented by the unshaded region.

    (a)
    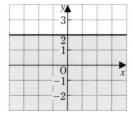

    (b)
    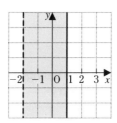

2. Leave unshaded in the *xy* plane the regions that represent the inequalities.

    (a) $1 < x \leqslant 3$ (b) $y < 0$ and $y > 5$

3. Write down the inequalities that define each unshaded region.

    (a)
    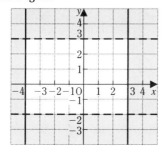

    (b)
    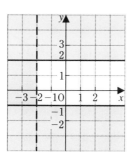

4. *Shade* in the *xy* plane the region representing the set of inequalities

    $$x \geqslant 1 \quad \text{and} \quad 1 < y \leqslant 4$$

5. Leave unshaded the region of the *xy* plane that represents the inequality $y + 2x \geqslant 4$

6. Write down the set of inequalities that define the unshaded region.

    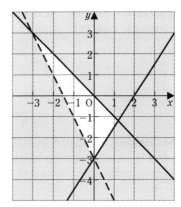

7. Give the coordinates of every point within the unshaded region given in question 6, whose coordinates are integers.

8. Represent by an unshaded region in the *xy* plane, the set of inequalities $2y + x \geqslant 2$, $x - y + 2 \geqslant 0$, $x \leqslant 3$

9. Find the greatest and the least integer values of $2x + 3y$ within the region drawn in question 8.

10. A school library can buy books to the value of £500. Some textbooks costing £8 each and some novels costing £5 each are needed. The number of textbooks bought must be at least twice the number of novels, and at least 20 textbooks must be bought.

    (a) Taking *x* as the number of text books and *y* as the number of novels, express each of these facts as an inequality.

    (b) Using a scale of 1 cm for 10 units on each axis, represent the set of inequalities in the *xy* plane.

    (c) Find the greatest total number of books that can be bought.

TRIGONOMETRY IN RIGHT-ANGLED TRIANGLES

THE USES OF TRIGONOMETRY

Simple trigonometry is concerned with the relationships between the sizes of angles and lengths of sides of triangles.

Trigonometry can be used in a practical way to find, for example, the height of an unclimbable tree PQ.

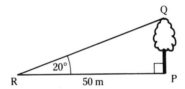

If the distance of a point R from the base of the tree PQ is known and the angle of elevation of the top is found, then the height can be calculated by trigonometry.

RIGHT-ANGLED TRIANGLES

Notation

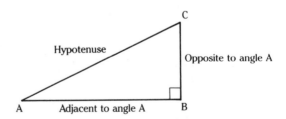

The side AC, opposite the right angle B, is the *hypotenuse*.
BC is the side *opposite* to angle A.
AB is the side *adjacent* to A.

All triangles with a right angle and an angle equal to A are similar.

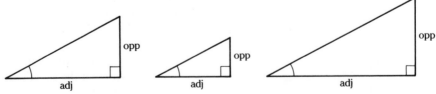

For all these triangles, the ratio $\dfrac{\text{opp}}{\text{adj}}$ is the same.

THE TANGENT OF AN ANGLE

For any given angle the ratio $\dfrac{\text{opp}}{\text{adj}}$ has been calculated and is called the *tangent* of the angle.

(The name is due to the fact that the original definition was based on circle work and was linked with the tangent to a circle. There is no chance of any confusion however.)

In a right-angled triangle,

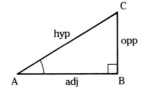

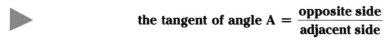

$$\text{the tangent of angle A} = \frac{\textbf{opposite side}}{\textbf{adjacent side}}$$

or, briefly, $\qquad \tan A = \dfrac{\text{opp}}{\text{adj}}$

The values of the tangents of all angles are stored in scientific calculators, e.g. the tangent of 40° can be found by pressing $\boxed{4}\ \boxed{0}\ \boxed{\tan}$. The display shows 0.8390996 . . . , and we write $\tan 40° = 0.8391$ (4 s.f.)

Similarly, if the tangent ratio is known, the angle can be found.

Note that scientific calculators will give angles in various units. Make sure that your calculator is in the correct mode; it should be showing 'deg' on the display.

Using Tangents

Angles are usually given correct to 1 decimal place, tangents to 4 significant figures and lengths to 3 significant figures. Use this convention unless it is inappropriate or you are told to do otherwise.

Using the Tangent Ratio to Find an Angle

When we know the lengths of the sides of a right-angled triangle then, with respect to one angle (not the right angle), the ratio $\dfrac{\text{opp}}{\text{adj}}$ can be calculated. The value of this ratio can then be used to find the size of the angle.

Exercise 20a

Find the tangents of the following angles.

1. 37°
2. 72.6°
3. 6.5°
4. 32.4°

Find the angle whose tangent is 0.78

$\tan X = 0.78$

Press $\boxed{\cdot}$ $\boxed{7}$ $\boxed{8}$ $\boxed{\tan^{-1}}$ The display shows 37.95423 . . .

$$\widehat{X} = 37.95 \ldots °$$

The angle is 38.0° (1 d.p.)

In questions 5 to 8, find the angle whose tangent is given.

5. 0.75   6. 1.457   7. 0.04   8. 3.92

9. Is there any limit to the value of a tangent for which an angle can be found ?

In $\triangle ABC$, $\widehat{B} = 90°$, $BC = 6.2\,cm$ and $AB = 8.9\,cm$. Find $\widehat{A}$.

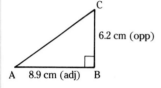

Make a habit of labelling the sides 'opp', 'adj', etc.

$$\tan A = \frac{opp}{adj} = \frac{6.2}{8.9}$$

$$= 0.69662 \ldots \quad \text{press } \boxed{\tan^{-1}}$$

$$\widehat{A} = 34.9° \qquad (\,1\,d.p.\,)$$

Find the marked angle in each of the following triangles.

10.

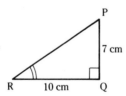

11.

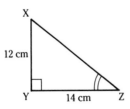

12.

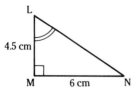

13.

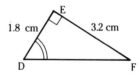

14. In $\triangle ABC$, $\widehat{C} = 90°$, $AC = 56\,cm$ and $BC = 60\,cm$. Find $\widehat{B}$.

15. In $\triangle PQR$, $\widehat{Q} = 90°$, $PQ = 7.2\,cm$ and $QR = 8\,cm$. Find $\widehat{R}$.

16. In $\triangle LMN$, $\widehat{N} = 90°$, $LN = 14\,cm$ and $MN = 12\,cm$. Find $\widehat{M}$.

17. In $\triangle XYZ$, $\widehat{Z} = 90°$, $XZ = 5.34\,m$ and $ZY = 5\,m$. Find $\widehat{X}$.

18. In $\triangle ABC$, $\widehat{B} = 90°$, $\widehat{A} = 45°$ and $AB = 10\,cm$. Without using a calculator, write down the tangent of 45°.

Finding the Length of a Side

If, in a right-angled triangle, we know one side other than the hypotenuse, and an angle, then we can use the tangent ratio to find another side of the triangle.

Exercise 20b

In △LMN, $\hat{L} = 90°$, LM = 9.3 cm and $\hat{M} = 35°$. Find LN.

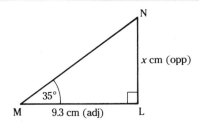

Note that we use the angle opposite to the unknown side. Label the unknown side x cm.

$$\frac{x}{9.3} = \frac{\text{opp}}{\text{adj}}$$

i.e.

$$\frac{x}{9.3} = \tan 35°$$

Multiply both sides by 9.3

$$9.3 \times \frac{x}{9.3} = 9.3 \times \tan 35°$$

$$x = 9.3 \times \tan 35° \quad \text{Press } \boxed{9}\boxed{\cdot}\boxed{3}\boxed{\times}\boxed{3}\boxed{5}\boxed{\tan}\boxed{=}$$

$$x = 6.5119\ldots$$

LN = 6.51 cm (3 s.f.)

In each question from 1 to 4, find the required side.

1. Find DE.

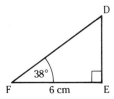

3. Find DE.

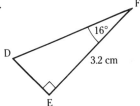

2. Find PQ.

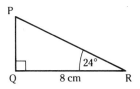

4. Find XY.

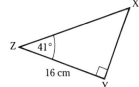

In $\triangle$XYZ, $\hat{Z} = 90°$, $\hat{Y} = 42°$ and ZX $= 9$ cm. Find YZ.

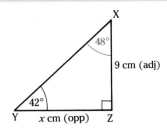

The unknown side is adjacent to the given angle in this case so we need to start by finding the angle *opposite* to the unknown side

$\hat{Y} = 42°$ so $\hat{X} = 48°$

$$\frac{x}{9} = \frac{\text{opp}}{\text{adj}}$$

i.e. $$\frac{x}{9} = \tan 48°$$

$$9 \times \frac{x}{9} = 9 \times \tan 48°$$

$$x = 9.9955 \ldots$$

YZ $= 10.0$ cm   (3 s.f.)

---

5. In $\triangle$JKL, $\hat{K} = 90°$,   JK $= 5$ cm   and $\hat{J} = 61°$. Find KL.

6. In $\triangle$ABC, $\hat{A} = 90°$, $\hat{B} = 39°$ and AC $= 3$ cm. Find AB.

In some of the following questions, the third angle may need to be found.

7. In $\triangle$PQR, $\hat{Q} = 90°$, $\hat{R} = 31.5°$ and QR $= 7.2$ cm. Find QP.

8. In $\triangle$FGH, $\hat{G} = 90°$, $\hat{H} = 16.7°$ and FG $= 13$ cm. Find GH.

9. In $\triangle$DEF, $\hat{F} = 90°$, $\hat{E} = 32°$ and FD $= 6$ cm. Find FE.

10. In $\triangle$ABC, $\hat{A} = 90°$, AB $= 45$ m and $\hat{B} = 34°$. Find AC.

11. A triangular field is to be sown with winter wheat. The farmer needs to know how much seed to buy so he makes a rough survey of the field and draws this sketch, which is not drawn accurately.

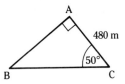

The side AC is measured to the nearest metre and angle C is measured to the nearest degree. Angle A is exactly $90°$.

(a) Find the length of the side AB giving your answer to a sensible degree of accuracy bearing in mind the accuracy of the given measurements.

(b) Which of the following values is the best estimate for the area of the field ?
    (i) $300\,000$ m^2 (ii) $150\,000$ m^2
    (iii) $50\,000$ m^2

Find the height of the cross-section of this prism.

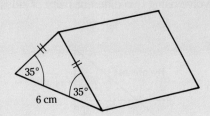

All the information, together with any facts that can be deduced, should be put on to a diagram.

Any isosceles triangle can be divided through the middle into two congruent right-angled triangles.

AD is the height of the cross-section.

Using △ADC,

$$\frac{x}{3} = \tan 35°$$

$$x = 3 \tan 35°$$

$$= 2.100\ldots$$

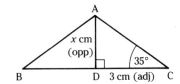

Height of cross-section is 2.10 cm   (3 s.f.)

Note that we named the triangle we used. This is important so that the reasoning can be followed easily.

---

12. A tower PQ is 20 m high.
    Point R is 45 m from Q on level ground.
    What is the angle of elevation of P from R ?

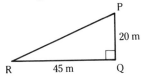

13. The coordinates of A, B and C are (5, 4), (1, 1) and (5, 1) respectively. Find $A\hat{B}C$.

14. From A, John walks 8 km north to B, then east to C. The bearing of C from A is 052°. How far is B from C ?

15. A is the point (6, 5) and O is the origin. Find the angle between the line OA and the *x*-axis.

16. In △ABC, AB = BC, AC = 10 cm and $\hat{A} = 50°$.
    Find the height of the triangle and hence its area.

17. In a circle with centre O, a line of length 12 cm joins two points, P and Q, on the circumference. PQ is 4 cm from O. Find $P\hat{O}Q$.

18. The coordinates of the vertices of a triangle are A(1, 1), B(2, 4) and C(8, 2).

    (a) Find the lengths of AB, BC and AC.

    (b) Show that one of the angles of triangle ABC is 90°.

    (c) Find angle ACB.

SINE AND COSINE

Two more useful ratios involve using two different pairs of sides of a right-angled triangle.

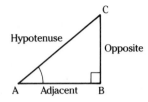

In a right-angled triangle,

$$\text{the sine of angle A} = \frac{\text{opposite side}}{\text{hypotenuse}}$$

$$\text{the cosine of angle A} = \frac{\text{adjacent side}}{\text{hypotenuse}}$$

The sine of angle A is abbreviated to sin A and the cosine of angle A to cos A.

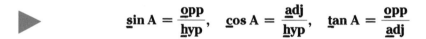

$$\sin A = \frac{\text{opp}}{\text{hyp}}, \quad \cos A = \frac{\text{adj}}{\text{hyp}}, \quad \tan A = \frac{\text{opp}}{\text{adj}}$$

A possible memory aid is the word SOHCAHTOA, whose letters stand for the underlined initial letters above.

Calculations involving the sine or cosine ratio are done in a way similar to those involving the tangent ratio.

Exercise 20c

1. Find the sines of the following angles.
   (a) 76°   (b) 11.3°   (c) 22.5°

2. Find the cosines of the following angles.
   (a) 64°   (b) 31.6°   (c) 3°

3. Find the angles whose sines are given below.
   (a) 0.731   (b) 0.926   (c) $\frac{3}{10}$

4. Find the angles whose cosines are given below.
   (a) 0.12   (b) 0.385   (c) $\frac{4}{9}$

5. For each triangle write down sin A, then find $\widehat{A}$.

   (a)
   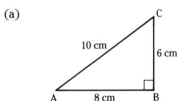

   (b)
   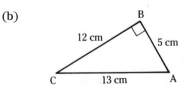

6. Write down cos L for each triangle, then find L̂.

(a)

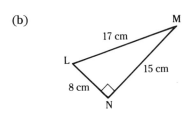

(b)

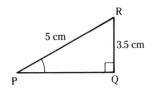

7. In each of the following triangles state which ratio should be used to find the marked angle. The first one is done for you.

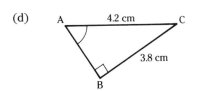

(a) We are given the hypotenuse and the side opposite P, so we use sin P.

(b)

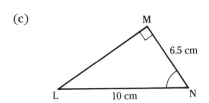

(c)

(d)

8. For each triangle in question 7, calculate the required angle.

9. Is there any limit to the value of a sine ratio or a cosine ratio ?

Questions 10 to 15 involve tangents, sines and cosines. Remember to label the sides 'opp', 'adj' and 'hyp' to help you to decide which ratio to use.

10. In △ABC, B̂ = 90°, AB = 6 cm and AC = 10 cm. Find Â.

11. In △LMN, N̂ = 90°, LN = 5.2 cm and MN = 4.5 cm. Find M̂.

12. In △PQR, Q̂ = 90°, PQ = 3 cm and PR = 6 cm. Find P̂.

13. In △XYZ, X̂ = 90°, XY = 7.3 cm and YZ = 9.8 cm. Find Ẑ.

14. In △DEF, Ê = 90°, EF = 80 m and DF = 112 m. Find D̂.

15. In △EFG, Ê = 90°, EF = 0.65 m and EG = 0.54 m. Find Ĝ.

16. In the triangle with sides 3 cm, 4 cm and 5 cm, the smallest angle is A. Write as fractions, tan A, sin A and cos A.

17. ABC is an equilateral triangle of side 4 cm. D is the foot of the perpendicular from A to BC. Without using a calculator write as fractions in as simple a form as possible (in terms of square roots if necessary).

(a) sin 30°, cos 30° and tan 30°

(b) sin 60°, cos 60° and tan 60°.

(Note that e.g. $\sqrt{8} = \sqrt{4 \times 2} = 2\sqrt{2}$)

18. The measurements are given to the nearest centimetre. Find the smallest possible size of angle F.

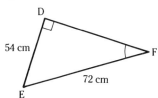

Using Sine and Cosine to Find a Side

Sines and cosines can be used to find the lengths of sides in a similar way to using tangents. It is also possible to find the length of a hypotenuse if suitable information is given.

Exercise 20d

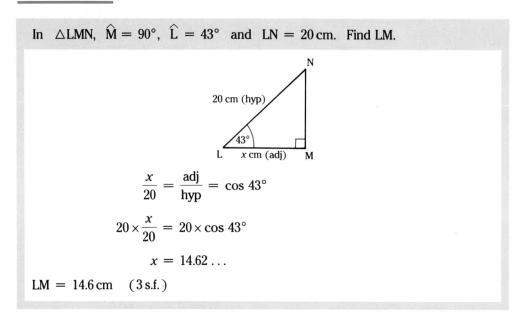

In $\triangle LMN$, $\hat{M} = 90°$, $\hat{L} = 43°$ and $LN = 20$ cm. Find LM.

$$\frac{x}{20} = \frac{adj}{hyp} = \cos 43°$$

$$20 \times \frac{x}{20} = 20 \times \cos 43°$$

$$x = 14.62\ldots$$

LM $= 14.6$ cm   (3 s.f.)

1. In $\triangle ABC$, $\hat{B} = 90°$, $\hat{C} = 57°$ and $AC = 8$ cm. Find AB.

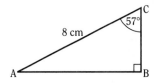

2. In $\triangle PQR$, $\hat{P} = 90°$, $\hat{Q} = 49°$ and $QR = 3.2$ cm. Find PQ.

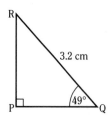

3. In $\triangle ABC$, $\hat{C} = 90°$, $\hat{B} = 36°$ and $BC = 5$ cm. Find CA.

4. In $\triangle PQR$, $\hat{P} = 90°$, $\hat{Q} = 41°$ and $QR = 7.2$ cm. Find PR.

5. In $\triangle LMN$, $\hat{M} = 90°$, $\hat{N} = 16°$ and $LN = 13$ m. Find MN.

6. In $\triangle XYZ$, $\hat{Z} = 90°$, $\hat{X} = 72°$ and $XY = 2.68$ cm. Find ZY.

7. In $\triangle DEF$, $\hat{F} = 90°$, $\hat{E} = 30°$ and $DE = 98$ cm. Find EF.

8. In $\triangle PQR$, $\hat{Q} = 90°$, $\hat{R} = 14°$ and $PR = 12$ cm. Find PQ.

9. In $\triangle BCD$, $\hat{B} = 90°$, $\hat{D} = 25°$ and $CD = 20$ m. Find BD.

10. In $\triangle ABC$, $\hat{C} = 90°$, $\hat{A} = 42°$ and $AB = 9.2$ cm. Find BC.

11. In $\triangle EFG$, $\hat{E} = 90°$, $\hat{F} = 10°$ and $FG = 16$ cm. Find EF.

In △ABC, $\widehat{B} = 90°$, AB = 6 cm and $\widehat{C} = 32°$. Find the hypotenuse.

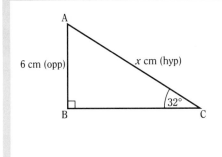

$$\frac{6}{x} = \frac{\text{opp}}{\text{hyp}} = \sin 32°$$

$$x \times \frac{6}{x} = x \times \sin 32°$$

i.e. $x \times \sin 32° = 6$

∴ $x = \dfrac{6}{\sin 32°} = 11.32\ldots$

The hypotenuse is 11.3 cm   (3 s.f.)

In each question from 12 to 17, find the length of the hypotenuse.

12. In   △ABC, $\widehat{A} = 90°$, $\widehat{B} = 31°$ and
AC = 4 cm.

13. In   △DEF, $\widehat{F} = 90°$, $\widehat{D} = 14°$ and
DF = 7 cm.

14. In   △LMN, $\widehat{L} = 90°$, $\widehat{M} = 48°$ and
LM = 10 cm.

15. In   △PQR, $\widehat{R} = 90°$, $\widehat{Q} = 31°$ and
PR = 4.2 cm.

16. In   △ABC, $\widehat{B} = 90°$, $\widehat{C} = 59°$ and
AB = 13 cm. Find AC.

17. In   △PQR, $\widehat{Q} = 90°$, $\widehat{P} = 51°$ and
PQ = 6.5 cm. Find PR.

Problems Involving Sine, Cosine or Tangent

The solution to any problem concerning triangles, involves deciding which of sine, cosine or tangent should be used. When a diagram has been drawn with the information given and required, it becomes clear which pair of sides are involved in relation to an angle and hence which of the three ratios should be used.

Remember that an isosceles triangle can be divided into two congruent right-angled triangles. Also, if more than one triangle appears in the diagram, the triangle you are using should be named.

When a problem involves a circle, the following facts are useful. In the diagram, O is the centre of the circle. A and B are points on the circumference and the line joining them is called a *chord*.

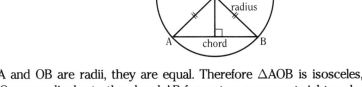

As OA and OB are radii, they are equal. Therefore △AOB is isosceles, and a line drawn from O perpendicular to the chord AB forms two congruent right-angled triangles. We can then use trigonometry to find lengths and angles in either of these triangles.

Exercise 20e

In a circle with centre O, AB is a chord. The radius of the circle is 8 cm and the length of the chord is 12 cm. Find $A\widehat{O}B$.

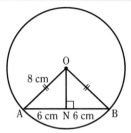

A chord of a circle is a line joining two points on the circumference. OA and OB are radii of the circle, so $\triangle AOB$ is isosceles and can be divided into two right-angled triangles.

Using $\triangle AON$, $\qquad\qquad$ $\sin A\widehat{O}N = \dfrac{6}{8} = 0.75$

$$A\widehat{O}N = 48.59\ldots°$$

$A\widehat{O}B = 2A\widehat{O}N$, $\qquad\qquad$ $\therefore\quad A\widehat{O}N = 97.18\ldots° = 97.2°$ correct to 1 d.p.

1. In a circle with centre O, PQ is a chord of length 12 cm. The chord is 4 cm from O. Find the size of $P\widehat{O}Q$.

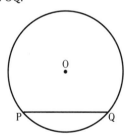

2. In the diagram, C is the centre of the circle. The chord PQ is 12 cm long. Find

   (a) the distance of the chord from the centre of the circle.

   (b) the radius of the circle.

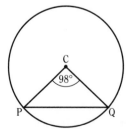

3.

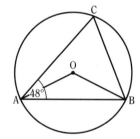

In the diagram, O is the centre of the circle and $\triangle ABC$ is isosceles. $AB = AC = 10$ cm and $B\widehat{A}C = 48°$.

(a) Assuming that AO is a line of symmetry, write down the size of $O\widehat{A}B$.

(b) By dividing $\triangle OAB$ into two congruent right-angled triangles, find
   (i) the distance of O from AB
   (ii) the radius of the circle.

(c) Extend AO to meet BC at D
   (i) Write down the sizes of $O\widehat{D}B$ and $O\widehat{B}D$.
   (ii) Using $\triangle ODB$, find DB.

(d) Using $\triangle ABD$, find DB. Does your answer agree with the result of (c) (ii)?

A plane starts from A and flies 150 km north east to B, then 100 km south east to C.

(a) How far east of A is C ?

(b) How far north of A is C ?

(c) What is the bearing of C from A ?

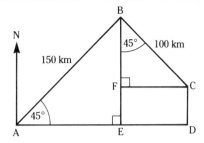

(a) AD is the distance C is east of A.

AD = AE + ED and ED = FC

We need to find AE from △AEB and FC from △BFC.

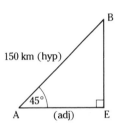

In △AEB, $\widehat{E} = 90°$ and $\dfrac{AE}{150} = \cos 45°$

∴ AE = $150 \times \cos 45° = 106.06 \ldots$

In △BFC, $\widehat{F} = 90°$ and $\dfrac{FC}{100} = \sin 45°$

i.e. FC = $100 \times \sin 45° = 70.71 \ldots$

∴ AD = $106.06 + 70.71 = 176.77 \ldots$

C is 176.8 km east of A, correct to 1 d.p.

(b) CD is the distance C is north of A.

$$CD = BE - FB$$
$$BE = AE = 106.06 \quad \text{△ABE is isosceles}$$
$$FB = FC = 70.71 \quad \text{△FBC is isosceles}$$

∴ CD = $106.06 - 70.71 = 35.35$

C is 35.4 km north of A, correct to 1 d.p.

(c) The bearing is given by $N\widehat{A}C$, so we need to find $C\widehat{A}D$

In △CAD, $\widehat{D} = 90°$

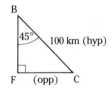

$$\tan CAD = \frac{35.35}{176.77} = 0.1999 \ldots$$

$C\widehat{A}D = 11.30 \ldots °$, ∴ $N\widehat{A}C = 78.70 \ldots °$,

The bearing of C from A is 078.7° (1 d.p.)

When there is more than one triangle in a diagram, state which triangle you are using and which angle is the right-angle. Remember that Pythagoras' theorem can be used to find a third side if two sides are given.

4.

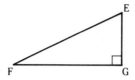

A vertical cliff EG is 30 m high. From a point F, on a level with the foot of the cliff, the angle of elevation of the top of the cliff is 15°.
How far is F from G ?

5.

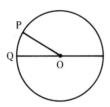

The chairoplane at a fair has a radius, of 10 m.
A point P is 4 m above OQ.
Find angle POQ.

6. From A, Emma cycles 4 miles north east to B, then 6 miles north west to C.

(a) Find BÂC.

(b) How far is C from A ?

(c) What is the bearing of C from A ?

7.

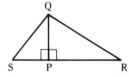

A flagpole PQ is 10 m high. S, P and R are on level ground. From R the angle of elevation of Q is 32°. From S the angle of elevation of Q is 50°. Find the distance from S to R.

8. From a point A on the shore, a boat B can be seen on a bearing of 060°. The bearing from A of a second boat C is 330°. B is 100 m from C and 70 m from A.

Find

(a) BĈA   (b) the bearing of B from C.

9. From A, a ship sails 60 km on a bearing of N 60 °W to B. It then changes course and sails 40 km on a bearing of N 30 °E to C.

(a) How far west of A is C ?

(b) How far north of A is C ?

(c) Find the bearing of C from A.

(d) How far is C from A ?

10.

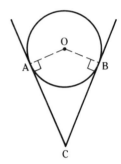

A sphere, of radius 4 cm and centre O, fits into a hollow cone, and BĈA = 46°.
Find

(a) AC   (b) OC   (c) AB.

11.

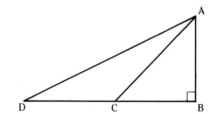

From A the angle of depression of C is 54° and of D is 39°. AB is 24 feet.
Find

(a) BC   (b) DC   (c) AD.

12. The points A(2, 2), B(6, 5), C(8, 1) are joined to form a triangle. Draw lines through A and C parallel to the *x*-axis and draw a line through B parallel to the *y*-axis to form several right-angled triangles.
Use two of these triangles to find ABĈ.

13. The diagram shows a cross-section through an underground water main.

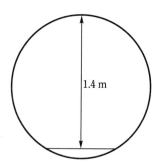

1.4 m

The pipe has a flat platform built into it to make maintenance easier.
The cross-section is a circle whose diameter is 1.5 m.
Find the width of the platform.

14. The diagram shows a section through an underground railway tunnel.

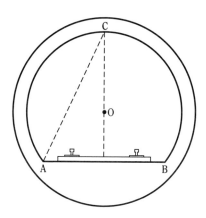

The 'floor' of the tunnel is 2 m wide and the angle of elevation of the highest point (C) from the edge of the floor (A) is 69°.

(a) Draw a diagram showing just the inside wall and floor of the tunnel. Mark the points A, B, C, and O which is the centre of the circle forming the inside wall. Calculate the height of the tunnel.

(b) Join AO and hence find the radius of the circular cross-section forming the inside of the tunnel.

15.

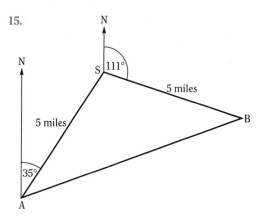

The bearing of ship S from point A is 035° and the bearing of point B from S is 111°. The ship is 5 miles both from A and from B.

Find

(a) AŜB

(b) the distance of B from A

(c) the bearing of B from A.

16.

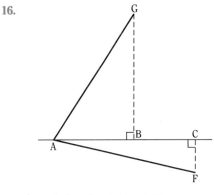

Anne is in a boat A, watching a gannet at G and a fish at F. At the instant when the angle of elevation of G from A is 52°, the angle of depression of F from A is 10° and AG = AF = 30 m, the gannet dives straight at the fish.

Find

(a) AB and AC and hence BC

(b) GB and CF and hence the vertical height of the gannet above the fish

(c) Draw a suitable right-angled triangle and find the angle of slope of the gannet's dive.

The remaining questions in this exercise are three-dimensional problems.

Remember that if a line is perpendicular to a plane then it is perpendicular to any line in that plane. In the following worked example, CG is perpendicular to the plane ABCD. Hence GC is perpendicular not only to CB and CD but also to CA.

In the given cuboid, find

(a) $E\widehat{B}A$ (b) $E\widehat{C}A$

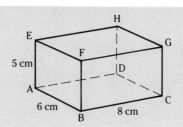

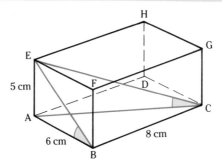

(a) In $\triangle$EAB, $E\widehat{A}B = 90°$

$$\tan E\widehat{B}A = \frac{opp}{adj}$$

$$= \tfrac{5}{6} = 0.83333$$

$$E\widehat{B}A = 39.8° \quad (1\,d.p.)$$

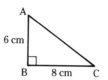

(b) $E\widehat{C}A$ can be found from $\triangle$ECA, as $\widehat{A} = 90°$. However, we only know the length of one side (AE) in $\triangle$ECA, so we need first to find another side. We can use $\triangle$ABC to find AC.

In $\triangle$ABC, $A\widehat{B}C = 90°$

$$AC = 10\,cm \ (3,4,5\triangle)$$

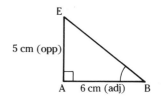

In $\triangle$EAC, $E\widehat{A}C = 90°$

$$\tan E\widehat{C}A = \frac{opp}{adj}$$

$$= \tfrac{5}{10} = 0.5$$

$$E\widehat{C}A = 26.6° \quad (1\,d.p.)$$

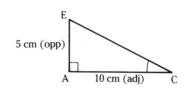

17. Sketch the cuboid given in the worked example.

Find   (a) $F\hat{C}B$ (b) $H\hat{B}F$

18.

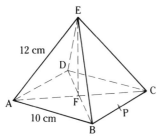

In the square-based pyramid above, P is the midpoint of BC. Find

(a) the lengths of AC and AF

(b) $E\hat{A}F$

(c) EF, first by trigonometry, then by Pythagoras' theorem.
    Do your answers agree ?

(d) $E\hat{P}F$

19.

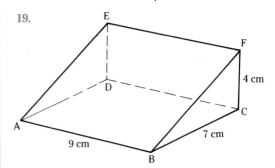

The diagram shows a wedge with three rectangular faces.

Find   (a) FB   (b) $F\hat{B}C$ (c) $F\hat{A}C$

If this wedge is a model of part of a hillside, where should a straight path go, from bottom to top, so that

(d) it is as short as possible

(e) it has as shallow a slope as possible ?

THE ANGLE BETWEEN A LINE AND A PLANE

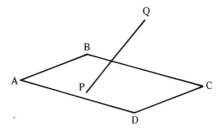

The angle between the line PQ and the plane ABCD is defined as the angle between PQ and its projection on the plane ABCD.
Draw a perpendicular, QN, from Q to the plane. (N is called the foot of the perpendicular.)
Join P to N.

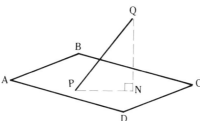

The required angle is $Q\hat{P}N$. (This angle is tucked in under the line.)

The line PN is called the *projection* of the line PQ on the plane.

(If the plane does not look horizontal, it may help you to see which line is the perpendicular if you turn the page and look at the diagram from a different angle.)

Exercise 20f

In the given cuboid name the angle between AG and
(a) the base EFGH   (b) the face ABFE.

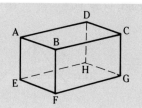

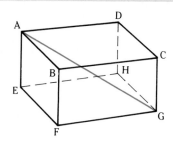

(a) The line from A, perpendicular to the base, is AE.

Join E to G.

$A\hat{G}E$ is the required angle

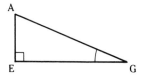

(b) Identify the perpendicular from G to ABFE. This is GF.

Draw AF and AG.

$G\hat{A}F$ is the required angle.

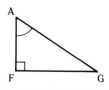

1.

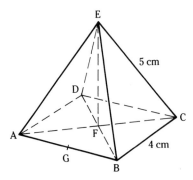

In the square-based pyramid above, G is the midpoint of AB. Name the angle between

(a) AE and ABCD

(b) EG and ABCD.

(c) Calculate the sizes of the angles named in
(a) and (b).

2. Draw the cuboid given in the worked example.
Name the angle between

(a) DF and EFGH   (b) DF and AEHD.

3.

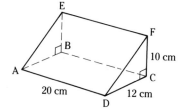

In the wedge above there are three rectangular
faces. Name the angle between

(a) AF and ABCD

(b) EA and BCFE.

(c) Calculate the sizes of the angles named in
(a) and (b).

THE ANGLE BETWEEN TWO PLANES

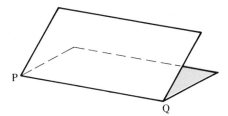

To find the angle between two planes we need to find two lines to act as the arms of the angle.

The two lines, one in each plane, must meet on the joining line, PQ, of the two planes and each must be at right angles to the joining line.

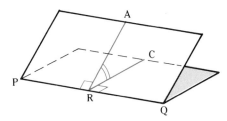

One possible angle is $A\widehat{R}C$.

Notice that any number of pairs of lines can meet at a given point on the joining line but only a pair at right angles to PQ gives the required angle. $D\widehat{E}F$ is *not* a possible angle but $D\widehat{Q}F$ is possible.

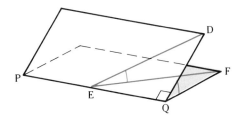

It can be helpful to use a section through a solid when trying to identify the angle between two of its faces. The section, or cut, must be made at right angles to the edge where the two faces meet, cutting this edge at P, say. Then the angle between the faces is the angle at P in the section. For example, in a right pyramid, the angle between the base and a sloping face can be found from a section formed by a cut through the vertex perpendicular to the base.

Exercise 20g

ABCDE is a pyramid of height 5 cm. Its base ABCD is a rectangle in which AB = 6 cm and BC = 8 cm.
Find the angle between the planes EBC and ABCD.

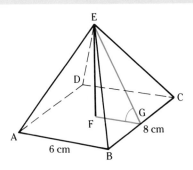

BC is the joining line for the planes. From symmetry, EG and FG are both perpendicular to BC at G.

$\widehat{EGF}$ is the required angle.

In $\triangle EFG$, $\widehat{F} = 90°$

$$\tan G = \frac{opp}{adj}$$

$$= \tfrac{5}{3}$$

$$= 1.66666\ldots$$

$$\widehat{EGF} = 59.0°$$

The angle between the planes is 59.0°

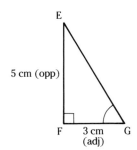

1. Find the angle between the planes EAB and ABCD in the pyramid in the worked example.

2.

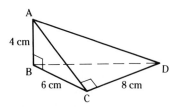

In the pyramid above, all four triangular faces are right-angled. Find the angle between the planes ACD and BCD.

3. In the wedge in Exercise 20f, question 3, find the angle between the planes EFDA and ABCD.

4. In the cuboid in the worked example in Exercise 20f, AE = 4 cm, EF = 5 cm and FG = 7 cm. Find the angle between the planes AFGD and ABCD.

5. In the pyramid in exercise 20f, question 1, find the angle between the planes EBC and ABCD.

6. The cross-section of a prism is a regular hexagon. What is the angle between two adjacent rectangular faces of the prism?

Self-Assessment 20

1. Give the sine, cosine and tangent of 58.4°

2. Find the angle
   (a) whose cosine is 0.382
   (b) whose sine is 0.741

3. In △ABC, find $\hat{A}$.

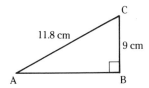

4. In △ABC, $\hat{A} = 90°$, $\hat{C} = 62°$ and AC = 5 cm. Find AB.

5. In △LMN, LN = LM = 7 cm and MN = 6 cm. Find $\hat{M}$.

6. Town P is 30 miles north east of town Q and 20 miles north west of town R.
   (a) How far west of R is Q ?
   (b) How far south of R is Q ?
   (c) Give the bearing of Q from R.

7.

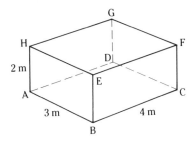

The dimensions of a cuboid are 2 m, 3 m and 4 m.
   (a) Find the angle between a diagonal of the cuboid and the largest face.
   (b) Find the angle between the planes ABFG and CDGF.

8.

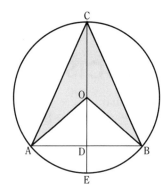

A company logo is in the shape of a symmetrical arrowhead and the designer has set it in a circle of radius 3 cm. The centre of the circle is O and $A\hat{O}B = 100°$.

   (a) Find the distance between A and B.
   (b) Find the length of (i) OD (ii) DE.
   (c) Find $C\hat{O}A$.
   (d) Explain why △AOC is isosceles.
   (e) Find the length of AC.

9.

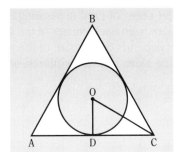

A hole in a child's posting box is an equilateral triangle ABC, of side 5 cm. A cylindrical shape will just push through the hole.
Use triangle DCO to find the radius of the cross-section of the cylinder.

PRODUCTS AND FACTORS

PRODUCTS

We know that $2(x+4)$ means that both terms in the bracket are to be multiplied by 2, i.e. $2(x+4) = 2x+8$

In the same way, $x(x+4)$ means that both terms in the bracket are to be multiplied by x, i.e. $x(x+4) = x \times x + x \times 4 = x^2 + 4x$

Therefore an expression such as $3(x-2)-x(x-4)$ can be simplified by multiplying out the brackets and collecting like terms, i.e.

$$3(x-2)-x(x-4) = 3x-6-x^2-x(-4)$$
$$= 3x-6-x^2+4x$$
$$= 7x-6-x^2$$

THE PRODUCT OF TWO BRACKETS

Consider this problem.

A flat sheet of card measuring 8 cm by 10 cm is made into an open box by cutting out a square from each corner of the sheet and folding up the edges. The area of the base of the box depends on the size of the squares that are cut out, but if we take x cm as the length of the sides of these squares, we can find a formula for the area, A cm^2, of the base.

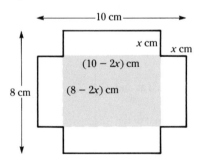

From the diagram, the length of the base is $(10-2x)$ cm and the width is $(8-2x)$ cm, so $A = (10-2x)(8-2x)$

Expressions such as $(10-2x)(8-2x)$ mean that each term in the second bracket is multiplied by each term in the first bracket, i.e.

$$(10-2x)(8-2x) = 10(8-2x)-2x(8-2x)$$
$$= 80-20x-16x+4x^2$$
$$= 80-36x+4x^2$$

The first line of working can be left out, but it is sensible to keep to this order, i.e. multiply

1. the first terms in each bracket
2. the outside terms
3. the inside terms
4. the second terms in each bracket.

Therefore 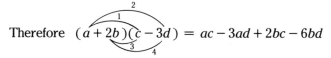 $(a + 2b)(c - 3d) = ac - 3ad + 2bc - 6bd$

Exercise 21a

1. Expand (i.e. multiply out the brackets)

   (a) $x(x-2)$ (g) $2s(2s+5)$

   (b) $3x(2-x)$ (h) $-x(x+2y)$

   (c) $2x(5-3x)$ (i) $2x(x+y)$

   (d) $a(2a-5)$ (j) $-p(2q-3p)$

   (e) $2p(1-p)$ (k) $2a(a-2b)$

   (f) $5a(2-3a)$ (l) $4s(3t-2s)$

2. Expand and simplify where possible

   (a) $2(x+3)+x(x-3)$

   (b) $3x(x-3)-4(2x+6)$

   (c) $4x-x(2+x)$

   (d) $2a(b+c)-2(b+2c)$

   (e) $2x(x-1)-x(2x+1)$

   (f) $-x(2-x)+2x(3-2x)$

3. Expand and simplify where possible

   (a) $(x+2)(x+3)$ (g) $(p+q)(s-t)$

   (b) $(x-2)(x+4)$ (h) $(x-y)(x-2z)$

   (c) $(2x+3)(x-5)$ (i) $(x-2y)(x-3y)$

   (d) $(3x+1)(2x+4)$ (j) $(a+2b)(a-b)$

   (e) $(2x-3)(x-7)$ (k) $(2p-q)(2p+q)$

   (f) $(a+b)(a-c)$ (l) $(3x+2y)(2x+z)$

In question 3 above, some expansions simplify and some do not. The terms in the brackets of those that do simplify involve the same letters. The following expansions all simplify.

4. Expand and simplify

   (a) $(x+4)(x+1)$ (e) $(t+7)(t+3)$

   (b) $(x+1)(x+2)$ (f) $(p+5)(p+2)$

   (c) $(a+1)(a+5)$ (g) $(x+6)(x+8)$

   (d) $(a+3)(a+5)$ (h) $(x+10)(x+3)$

5. Expand and simplify

   (a) $(x-2)(x-3)$ (e) $(s-4)(s-5)$

   (b) $(x-4)(x-3)$ (f) $(x-6)(x-7)$

   (c) $(x-2)(x-5)$ (g) $(p-4)(p-6)$

   (d) $(a-1)(a-4)$ (h) $(t-8)(t-4)$

6. Expand and simplify

   (a) $(x-2)(x+6)$ (f) $(p+3)(p-5)$

   (b) $(x+3)(x-2)$ (g) $(a+3)(a-7)$

   (c) $(x-4)(x+3)$ (h) $(x-4)(x+9)$

   (d) $(x-3)(x+5)$ (i) $(x+7)(x-3)$

   (e) $(t+6)(t-8)$ (j) $(y-2)(y+1)$

Finding the Pattern

In questions 4, 5 and 6 in the last exercise, you may have noticed a pattern linking the simplified answer with the terms in the brackets.

For example, $(x+5)(x+2) = x^2 + (2+5)x + (5)(2) = x^2 + 7x + 10$

$(x-5)(x-2) = x^2 + (-2-5)x + (-5)(-2) = x^2 - 7x + 10$

$(x-5)(x+2) = x^2 + (2-5)x + (-5)(2) = x^2 - 3x - 10$

In each case,

the product of the number terms in the two brackets gives the number term in the expansion,
collecting the number terms gives the coefficient of x.

This means that the simplified expansion can be written down directly, e.g.

$$(x-7)(x+4) = x^2 - 3x - 28$$

When the brackets are slightly more complicated,

e.g. $(2x-3)(4x+1) = 8x^2 + [(2)(1)+(-3)(4)]x - 3 = 8x^2 - 10x - 3$

we see that the x term in the expansion comes from collecting the products of the number term in one bracket with the coefficient of x in the other bracket.

Exercise 21b

Use the pattern above to write down the simplified expansions directly.

1. (a) $(x+4)(x+5)$ (e) $(a+5)(a+7)$
   (b) $(y+1)(y+9)$ (f) $(x-6)(x-2)$
   (c) $(p-4)(p-6)$ (g) $(s+8)(s+3)$
   (d) $(x-3)(x-7)$ (h) $(x+7)(x+9)$

2. (a) $(x-3)(x+7)$ (e) $(x-4)(x+2)$
   (b) $(a+5)(a-4)$ (f) $(s+9)(s-5)$
   (c) $(t-6)(t+3)$ (g) $(b-1)(b+5)$
   (d) $(x+8)(x-6)$ (h) $(x+1)(x-8)$

3. (a) $(x+6)(x-9)$ (e) $(x+4)(x-9)$
   (b) $(b+1)(b+3)$ (f) $(a+5)(a+6)$
   (c) $(y-8)(y-6)$ (g) $(t-7)(t-5)$
   (d) $(x-5)(x+6)$ (h) $(x+3)(x+8)$

4. (a) $(2x+1)(x+3)$
   (b) $(3a+5)(2a+1)$
   (c) $(t-2)(2t-3)$
   (d) $(x-6)(3x-5)$
   (e) $(2x-7)(x-5)$
   (f) $(3y-5)(4y-1)$
   (g) $(5x+2)(4x+3)$
   (h) $(7t+5)(t+2)$
   (i) $(3x-8)(2x-5)$

5. (a) $(3x+5)(x-2)$
   (b) $(2x-7)(3x+1)$
   (c) $(2s+3)(2s-5)$
   (d) $(4x-3)(2x+7)$
   (e) $(3x+1)(3x-1)$
   (f) $(7x-5)(2x+1)$
   (g) $(5x-1)(7x+1)$
   (h) $(3x+1)(5x-1)$
   (i) $(2a+5)(2a-5)$

6. (a) $(5t+3)(3t+2)$
   (b) $(4x-3)(3x+8)$
   (c) $(8x+1)(2x-5)$
   (d) $(5a-3)(2a-7)$
   (e) $(3-x)(2-x)$
   (f) $(5+2y)(1+y)$
   (g) $(12+x)(2-3x)$
   (h) $(2+x)(5-2x)$
   (i) $(6-5y)(4-3y)$

7. (a) $(2x-11)(5x-12)$
   (b) $(2p-3)(3p+10)$
   (c) $(a+12)(10a-5)$
   (d) $(9+4x)(2+9x)$

Squaring a Bracket

$$(x+3)^2 \quad \text{means} \quad (x+3)(x+3)$$

Similarly
$$(x+a)^2 = (x+a)(x+a)$$
$$= x^2 + xa + ax + a^2$$
$$= x^2 + 2ax + a^2 \qquad \text{since } xa \text{ is the same as } ax$$

Therefore
$$(x+3)^2 = x^2 + 6x + 9$$

Also
$$(x-a)^2 = (x-a)(x-a)$$
$$= x^2 - xa - ax + a^2$$
$$= x^2 - 2ax + a^2$$

Therefore
$$(x-5)^2 = x^2 - 10x + 25$$

The Difference Between Two Squares

When two brackets have the same terms but different signs, their product simplifies to just two terms, i.e.

$$(x+a)(x-a) = x^2 - xa + ax - a^2$$
$$= x^2 - a^2$$

This expression is called the difference between two squares.

Collecting together the results of this section we have

$$\blacktriangleright \qquad \boldsymbol{(x+a)^2 = x^2 + 2ax + a^2}$$
$$\boldsymbol{(x-a)^2 = x^2 - 2ax + a^2} \qquad \blacktriangleleft$$
$$\boldsymbol{(x+a)(x-a) = x^2 - a^2}$$

These are important results and should be memorised. Given either the left-hand side or the right-hand side, the other side should be known, e.g. $x^2 - 9$ should be recognised as the expansion of $(x+3)(x-3)$.

Exercise 21c

1. Expand

   (a) $(x+1)^2$ (e) $(x+y)^2$

   (b) $(x+2)^2$ (f) $(a+b)^2$

   (c) $(y+4)^2$ (g) $(p+q)^2$

   (d) $(a+7)^2$ (h) $(x+8)^2$

2. Expand

   (a) $(x-1)^2$ (e) $(x-y)^2$

   (b) $(x-5)^2$ (f) $(a-b)^2$

   (c) $(t-9)^2$ (g) $(y-7)^2$

   (d) $(p-6)^2$ (h) $(x-9)^2$

3. Expand

(a) $(x+1)(x-1)$ (e) $(x+y)(x-y)$

(b) $(x-4)(x+4)$ (f) $(a+b)(a-b)$

(c) $(c+2)(c-2)$ (g) $(x-7)(x+7)$

(d) $(y-5)(y+5)$ (h) $(t-6)(t+6)$

Expand $(2x-5)^2$

$$(2x-5)^2 = (2x)^2 - 2(2x)(5) + 5^2$$
$$= 4x^2 - 20x + 25$$

---

4. Expand

(a) $(3x+1)^2$ (e) $(2a-3)^2$

(b) $(5x-2)^2$ (f) $(3x-1)^2$

(c) $(3y+2)^2$ (g) $(4x+3)^2$

(d) $(2x-1)^2$ (h) $(5p+2)^2$

5. Expand

(a) $(2x-7)(2x+7)$

(b) $(3x-1)(3x+1)$

(c) $(4x+5)(4x-5)$

(d) $(2a+7)(2a-7)$

(e) $(4t-3)(4t+3)$

(f) $(2a+5b)(2a-5b)$

The remaining questions in this exercise involve harder expansions.

Simplify
$$(x+2)(x+7) - 2x(3-x)$$

$(x+2)(x+7) - 2x(3-x)$

$= x^2 + 9x + 14 - 6x + 2x^2$

$= 3x^2 + 3x + 14$

---

6. Simplify

(a) $(x+2)(x+4) + x(x+3)$

(b) $2x(x-2) + (x+1)(x+4)$

(c) $(x-1)(x+4) - x(3-x)$

(d) $(2x+1)^2 + 3x(x+6)$

Expand   (a) $(x-1)(3-x)$

(b) $(ab-c)^2$

(a)

$(x-1)(3-x) = 3x - x^2 - 3 + x$

$\qquad\qquad\quad = 4x - x^2 - 3$

Notice that when the terms in the brackets are not in the conventional places, it is still sensible to keep to the same order when multiplying them.

(b)

$(ab-c)^2 = (ab)^2 - 2(ab)(c) + c^2$

$\qquad\qquad = a^2b^2 - 2abc + c^2$

---

7. Expand

(a) $(2+x)(3-x)$ (g) $(3-2x)(3+2x)$

(b) $(2x-1)(3-x)$ (h) $(3a-6)(2-a)$

(c) $(3-x)^2$ (i) $(2-3x)(2+3x)$

(d) $(x-4)(1-2x)$ (j) $(5x-y)(y-x)$

(e) $(2t+4)(7-3t)$ (k) $(2t+s)(s-3t)$

(f) $(2-3a)^2$ (l) $(2x-y)(y-2x)$

8. Expand

(a) $(xy-z)^2$ (e) $(xy-z)(xy+z)$

(b) $(p+qr)^2$ (f) $(ab+c)(ab-c)$

(c) $(pq-r)^2$ (g) $(ab+cd)^2$

(d) $(a-cb)^2$ (h) $(xy+wz)(xy-wz)$

9. (a) $(4-\sqrt{2})^2$

(b) $(2+\sqrt{3})^2$

(c) $(2+\sqrt{3})(2-\sqrt{3})$

(d) $(1-\sqrt{5})(1+\sqrt{5})$

(e) $(2+\sqrt{7})(2\sqrt{7}-3)$

10. (a) Expand $(3x-a)^2$

(b) Hence find the values of a and q for which $(3x-a)^2 = 9x^2 + qx + 4$

11. Find the values of p and q for which $(x-p)^2 + q^2 = x^2 - 6x + 13$

FACTORISING

So far in this chapter we have started with a product and multiplied it out. It is often necessary to reverse this process, i.e. to express an algebraic expression as a product of factors. This is called *factorising*.

Common Factors

Consider the expression $2x + 6y$

The first term can be written as $2 \times x$ and the second term as $2 \times 3y$

i.e. $\qquad 2x + 6y = 2 \times x + 2 \times 3y$ $\hfill$ [1]

Thus 2 is a factor of each term in the expression, and we say that 2 is a *common factor*.

It is known that $\qquad 2(x + 3y) = 2 \times x + 2 \times 3y$ $\hfill$ [2]

Therefore $\qquad 2x + 6y = 2(x + 3y)$

i.e. we have *factorised* $2x + 6y$ by 'taking out' the common factor.
Note that a factorisation can (and should) be checked by expanding the brackets.

Exercise 21d

1. Factorise

   (a) $3x + 6$ (c) $6a - 9$ (e) $10p - 5$ (g) $6 - 15a$ (i) $12x - 9y$

   (b) $4y - 8$ (d) $2a + 4b$ (f) $8 - 12x$ (h) $2a + 4b$ (j) $8q - 18p$

Factorise   (a) $y^2 + 3y$ (b) $6xy - 4yz$ (c) $x^3 - x^2 + x$

(a) $y^2 + 3y = y \times y + 3 \times y = y(y + 3)$

(b) $6xy - 4yz = 2y \times 3x - 2y \times 2z = 2y(3x - 2z)$

(c) $x^3 - x^2 + x = x \times x^2 - x \times x + x \times 1 = x(x^2 - x + 1)$

Note that the middle step can be done mentally; it is written down here to help explain the thinking involved.

Note also that when an expression has more than one common factor, as is the case in (b), it may be that only one of these factors is noticed. A check for further common factors in the expression in the bracket should reveal any that have been overlooked. The working might then look like this:

$$6xy - 4yz = 2(3xy - 2yz) = 2y(3x - 2z)$$

---

2. Factorise

   (a) $x^2 + 3x$ (c) $y^2 - 2y$ (e) $4a - a^2$ (g) $4b^2 - b$

   (b) $b^2 + 6b$ (d) $3x^2 + 2x$ (f) $x^2 - 4x$ (h) $p - p^2$

3. Factorise

   (a) $3x^2 + 6x + 9$

   (b) $10x^2 - 5x - 20$

   (c) $16 - 12x - 20x^2$

   (d) $5xy - 2xz + 3x$

   (e) $ab - 2ac + 4ad$

   (f) $3y^3 + 6y^2 - 9y$

4. Factorise

   (a) $2x^2 - 4x$

   (b) $5xy + 10xz$

   (c) $x^2 + x^3$

   (d) $8abc - 12bcd$

   (e) $3xy + 6y^2 - 9y$

   (f) $5ab + 10bc - 5bd$

5. Factorise

   (a) $mg - ma$

   (b) $2\pi r + \pi r h$

   (c) $\pi R^2 - \pi r^2$

   (d) $2rh_1 - 2rh_2$

   (e) $\frac{1}{2}mu^2 - \frac{1}{2}mv^2$

   (f) $2\pi rh + \pi r^2$

   (g) $ax^2 - bx^2$

   (h) $\frac{1}{2}ah - \frac{1}{2}bh$

   (i) $\pi r^2 + 4r + r^2$

   (j) $ax^2 + a^2x$

   (k) $P + \dfrac{PRT}{100}$

   (l) $mgh - \frac{1}{2}mv^2$

FACTORISING QUADRATIC EXPRESSIONS

An expression such as $x^2 + 10x + 24$ is called a *quadratic expression in x.* In general a quadratic expression in x contains an x^2 term and usually, but not always, a term in x and/or a number term.

Now we know that the expansion of $(x+4)(x+6)$ gives $x^2 + 10x + 24$
So, from a quadratic such as $x^2 + 5x + 6$ we might expect to find two brackets whose product is $x^2 + 5x + 6$

To be able to do this, we need to be aware of the relationship between what is inside the brackets and the resulting quadratic. We saw on page 333 that when the coefficient of the x^2 term is 1,

> the product of the number terms in the two brackets gives the number term in the expansion,

and

> collecting the number terms gives the coefficient of x.

We also need to know the relationship between the signs in the brackets and the signs in the resulting quadratic. Looking at the examples on page 333 shows that

> positive signs throughout the quadratic come from positive signs in both brackets

> a positive number term and a negative coefficient of x come from negative signs in both brackets

> a negative number term in the quadratic comes from a positive sign in one bracket and a negative sign in the other bracket.

The worked examples in the next exercise show how these facts are used to try to find the factors of a quadratic.

Exercise 21e

Factorise $x^2 + 5x + 6$

The x term in each bracket is x, as x^2 can only be $x \times x$
The sign in each bracket is $+$, so $x^2 + 5x + 6 = (x + \quad)(x + \quad)$

The number terms in the brackets could be 6 and 1 or 2 and 3
The middle term in the quadratic shows that the sum of the number terms is 5

$$x^2 + 5x + 6 = (x + 2)(x + 3) \quad \text{or} \quad (x + 3)(x + 2)$$

Mentally expanding the brackets checks that they are correct.

1. Factorise

   (a) $x^2 + 3x + 2$ (e) $x^2 + 8x + 7$
   (b) $x^2 + 5x + 4$ (f) $x^2 + 16x + 15$
   (c) $x^2 + 6x + 9$ (g) $x^2 + 9x + 18$
   (d) $x^2 + 8x + 12$ (h) $x^2 + 12x + 20$

2. Factorise

   (a) $x^2 - 4x + 3$ (e) $x^2 - 7x + 12$
   (b) $x^2 - 6x + 5$ (f) $x^2 - 8x + 15$
   (c) $x^2 - 2x + 1$ (g) $x^2 - 11x + 30$
   (d) $x^2 - 7x + 6$ (h) $x^2 - 11x + 18$

Factorise $x^2 - 6x - 16$

The x term in each bracket is x; the sign in one bracket is +ve and the sign in the other bracket is −ve, so $x^2 - 6x - 16 = (x + \quad)(x - \quad)$

The numbers could be 4 and 4, 8 and 2 or 16 and 1. Checking the middle term in the quadratic shows that they are 8 and 2, and that the 8 goes with the −ve sign.

$$x^2 - 6x - 16 = (x + 2)(x - 8)$$

Mentally expanding these brackets, or $(x - 8)(x + 2)$, shows that in either order they are correct.

3. Factorise

   (a) $x^2 - x - 6$ (f) $x^2 - x - 12$
   (b) $x^2 + x - 6$ (g) $x^2 - 2x - 24$
   (c) $x^2 - 3x - 4$ (h) $x^2 - 8x - 20$
   (d) $x^2 + x - 20$ (i) $x^2 + 7x - 18$
   (e) $x^2 + 3x - 10$ (j) $x^2 + 7x - 60$

4. Factorise

   (a) $x^2 - 9x + 14$ (f) $x^2 + 6x + 5$
   (b) $x^2 + 3x - 18$ (g) $x^2 - 5x - 14$
   (c) $x^2 + 9x + 20$ (h) $x^2 - 10x + 25$
   (d) $x^2 + 5x - 6$ (i) $x^2 - 15x + 26$
   (e) $x^2 - 3x - 10$ (j) $x^2 + 11x + 24$

FURTHER FACTORISING

When the coefficient of the x^2 term in the quadratic is not 1, then we need to remember that

> the x term in the quadratic comes from the sum of the coefficients formed by multiplying the x term in one bracket by the number term in the other bracket.

It also means that the two brackets do not both start with x, and this may increase the number of combinations of letter term and number term in each bracket that need to be tried.

For example, to factorise $4x^2 - 16x + 15$, we see that the brackets might start with $2x$ and $2x$, or with $4x$ and x. The number terms might be 5 and 3, or 15 and 1. The possibilities are

$$(2x - 5)(2x - 3), (2x - 15)(2x - 1),$$
$$(4x - 5)(x - 3), (4x - 3)(4x - 5), (4x - 15)(x - 1), (4x - 1)(x - 15)$$

We can then try each in turn until the pair that gives the correct middle term is found. In this case it happens to be the first pair, i.e. $4x^2 - 16x + 15 = (2x - 5)(2x - 3)$

After a little practice, you will find that you will get the correct factors fairly quickly.

Standard Results

We saw earlier in this chapter that

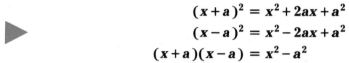

$$(x + a)^2 = x^2 + 2ax + a^2$$
$$(x - a)^2 = x^2 - 2ax + a^2$$
$$(x + a)(x - a) = x^2 - a^2$$

It is now important to recognise the left-hand sides as *factors* of the right. This is particularly important for the difference between two squares, i.e. to recognise that the factors of $a^2 - b^2$ are $(a + b)$ and $(a - b)$.

Exercise 21f

> Factorise   (a) $4x^2 - 9$ (b) $15x^2 + 14x - 8$
>
> (a) $4x^2 - 9 = (2x)^2 - (3)^2$, so comparing with $a^2 - b^2$ gives
> $$4x^2 - 9 = (2x + 3)(2x - 3)$$
> Mentally expanding the brackets confirms that they are correct.
>
> (b) The brackets may start as $(15x \quad)(x \quad)$ or $(5x \quad)(3x \quad)$
> The sign in one bracket is $+$ and the sign in the other bracket is $-$, so the brackets may end with ± 8 and ∓ 1 or ± 1 and ∓ 8 or ± 4 and ∓ 2 or ± 2 and ∓ 4.
> Now we try various combinations until we find the correct one.
> $$15x^2 + 14x - 8 = (5x - 2)(3x + 4)$$

1. Factorise

   (a) $2x^2 - 3x + 1$
   (b) $3x^2 + 8x + 4$
   (c) $3x^2 - 5x + 2$

   (d) $4x^2 + 7x + 3$
   (e) $x^2 - 6x + 9$
   (f) $5x^2 - 17x + 6$

   (g) $2x^2 - 3x - 2$
   (h) $3x^2 + x - 4$
   (i) $7x^2 - 19x - 6$

   (j) $6x^2 - 7x - 10$
   (k) $x^2 - 14x + 49$
   (l) $4x^2 + 17x - 15$

2. Factorise

   (a) $x^2 - 25$
   (b) $x^2 - 1$
   (c) $x^2 - 16$

   (d) $4x^2 - 25$
   (e) $36 - x^2$
   (f) $x^2 - y^2$

   (g) $9x^2 - 4$
   (h) $9a^2 - 1$
   (i) $1 - 36x^2$

   (j) $16a^2 - b^2$
   (k) $9x^2 - 25$
   (l) $36 - 25x^2$

3. Factorise

   (a) $6x^2 + 7x + 2$
   (b) $35x^2 - 24x + 4$
   (c) $9 - 25x^2$

   (d) $8x^2 - 10x - 3$
   (e) $21x^2 + 2x - 8$
   (f) $1 - 9x^2$

   (g) $4x^2 + 12x + 9$
   (h) $4 - 49x^2$
   (i) $5x^2 - 7xy - 6y^2$

   (j) $25x^2 - 20x + 4$
   (k) $15x^2 - 44x + 21$
   (l) $80x^2 - 6x - 9$

HARDER FACTORISING

Quadratic expressions do not always come in the standard order, i.e. the x^2 term followed by the x term with the number term last. In such cases it is sensible to rearrange the terms before factorising.

For example, to factorise $2x + x^2 + 1$, we would start by rearranging the expression so that it is in the standard order,

i.e.
$$2x + x^2 + 1 = x^2 + 2x + 1$$
$$= (x+1)(x+1) = (x+1)^2$$

When the x^2 term is negative and the number term is positive, it is easier to see the factors if the expression is arranged so that the order is: number term, x term, x^2 term.

For example, to factorise $5 - x^2 + 4x$, we start by arranging it as $5 + 4x - x^2$. This order is the reverse of the usual one, so the brackets start with the number term and end with the x term; we see that they are of the form $(\quad - x)(\quad + x)$.

Also the product of the number terms is 5 and their difference is 4, so

$$5 + 4x - x^2 = (5-x)(1+x)$$

Mentally expanding the brackets checks that they are correct.

Sometimes the expression has a common factor, which should be taken out before factorising the quadratic. For example, $2x^3 - 8x^2 + 6x$ has a common factor 2 and a common factor x. If these are taken out first, the quadratic factor can then be factorised, i.e.

$$2x^3 - 8x^2 + 6x = 2x(x^2 - 4x + 3) = 2x(x-3)(x-1)$$

When both the number term and the x^2 term are negative, we can use -1 as a common factor to make factorising the quadratic easier.
For example,

$$5x - x^2 - 6 = (-1)(-5x + x^2 + 6) = (-1)(x^2 - 5x + 6)$$
$$= (-1)(x-3)(x-2)$$
$$= (3-x)(x-2)$$

Finally, it is important to realise that not all quadratic functions factorise.

Consider, for example, $x^2 - x + 1$.

The only possible brackets are $(x-1)(x-1)$ and these do not give the correct x term. Therefore, $x^2 - x + 1$ does not factorise.

To sum up, when factorising a quadratic,

> **arrange the quadratic in standard order or in reverse order,**
> **take out (-1) as a common factor if a positive x^2 term is needed,**
> **look for common factors and take them out,**
> **factorise the quadratic if possible.**

Finally, check your factors by mentally expanding the result.

Exercise 21g

Factorise where possible.

1. (a) $8 + x^2 + 9x$
   (b) $9 + x^2 - 6x$
   (c) $x^2 + 21 + 10x$
   (d) $20 - x - x^2$
   (e) $x - 6 - x^2$
   (f) $x^2 + 15 - 8x$
   (g) $7 + x^2 - 8x$
   (h) $4x + x^2 + 4$

2. (a) $3x^2 - 27x + 24$
   (b) $4x^2 - 24x + 36$
   (c) $x^3 - 6x^2 + 9x$
   (d) $5x^2 - 10x + 5$
   (e) $4 - 8x + 4x^2$
   (f) $2x^2 - 18x - 44$
   (g) $16 + 2x^2 - 18x$
   (h) $ax^2 + 3ax + 4a$

3. (a) $11x - x^2 - 30$
   (b) $2x^2 - 2x + 6$
   (c) $2x^2 - 8$
   (d) $2x^2 + 4$
   (e) $x^2 + 5x + 9$
   (f) $28 - 12x - x^2$
   (g) $2x^2 - 9 + 6x$
   (h) $4x^3 - 6x^2 + 2x$
   (i) $x^2 + 11x + 18$
   (j) $6x^2 + 5x + 1$
   (k) $8x^2 - 2x - 1$
   (l) $6 - 9x + 6x^2$
   (m) $6 - 16x + 8x^2$
   (n) $2x - 5 - 3x^2$

4. (a) $a^2 - (b - c)^2$
   (b) $x^2 - (x - y)^2$
   (c) $3x^2 + 56 - 31x$
   (d) $x^2y^2 - 2xy + 1$
   (e) $3x^3 - 6x^2 + 24x$
   (f) $(a + b)^2 - (a + c)^2$

5. The value of $5.5^2 - 4.5^2$ can be found by multiplying two simple numbers together. What are these two numbers?

6. Describe a way to evaluate $53.4^2 - 46.6^2$ without using a calculator or long multiplication. Hence evaluate $53.4^2 - 46.6^2$.

7. The following table of values of y corresponding to given values of x has to be completed, given that $y = x^2 - 5x + 6$. Now suppose that the square button on your calculator is faulty. Describe a way of finding the required values of y without having to square any numbers. Complete the table.

x	-2	-1.5	-1.25	-1.15
y				

8. Show that 139 is a prime number. Hence find integer values of x and y such that $x^2 - y^2 = 139$.

CHANGING THE SUBJECT OF A FORMULA

Sometimes when changing the subject of a formula, the required letter appears in more than one term. In this case it may be possible to collect the terms containing that letter on one side of the formula and then take it out as a common factor.

For example, to make r the subject of the formula $A = \pi rl + \pi rh$, we see that r is a common factor of the terms on the right-hand side. We can factorise that side to give

$$A = r(\pi l + \pi h)$$

Now we can divide both sides by $(\pi l + \pi h)$, i.e. $\pi(l + h)$, to give

$$\frac{A}{\pi(l + h)} = r, \quad \text{i.e.} \quad r = \frac{A}{\pi(l + h)}$$

When changing the subject of a formula, start by expanding any brackets and eliminating any fractions. Then collect terms containing the required letter on one side and all other terms on the other side.

Exercise 21h

1. Make the letter in the bracket the subject of the formula.
   (a) $T = 2p + ph$ (p)
   (b) $M = Cn - 3C$ (C)
   (c) $g = hl - \pi hr$ (r)
   (d) $V = a^2r + \pi ahr$ (r)
   (e) $r^2 = v(h - a)$ (a)
   (f) $A = 2\pi r(h_1 - h_2)$ (h_1)

2. Solve these literal equations for x (i.e. make x the subject).

   (a) $ax = b - cx$

   (b) $ax - r = bx + q$

   (c) $a - bx = c + dx$

   (d) $x(b - c) = ax + b$

   (e) $a - b(x - a) = ax$

   (f) $x(a - b) = a(b - x)$

Make v the subject of the formula $\dfrac{1}{f} = \dfrac{1}{u} + \dfrac{1}{v}$

First we must eliminate the fractions. We can do this by multiplying both sides by fuv.

$$\cancel{fuv} \times \frac{1}{\cancel{f}} = f\cancel{u}v \times \frac{1}{\cancel{u}} + fu\cancel{v} \times \frac{1}{\cancel{v}}$$

$$uv = fv + fu$$

$$uv - fv = fu$$

$$v(u - f) = fu$$

$$v = \frac{fu}{u - f}$$

---

3. Make the letter in the bracket the subject of the formula.

   (a) $\dfrac{x}{a} + \dfrac{x}{b} = 2$ (x)

   (b) $T = \dfrac{1}{a} + \dfrac{1}{b}$ (a)

   (c) $R = r - \dfrac{1}{p}$ (p)

   (d) $A = P + \dfrac{PRT}{100}$ (P)

   (e) $\dfrac{x+a}{b} = \dfrac{x+b}{a}$ (x)

   (f) $\dfrac{1}{a} + \dfrac{1}{b} = \dfrac{1}{c}$ (c)

   (g) $t = \dfrac{1}{r} - \dfrac{m}{h}$ (m)

   (h) $s = \dfrac{t}{2}(u + v)$ (v)

The formulae in question 4 are a mixture of the types considered in Chapters 7 and 15 as well as those considered here; they are also quite difficult. Remember that a square root can be eliminated by isolating the term containing the square root on one side and then squaring both sides.

It is important to realise that the square of an expression such as $a + b$, is $(a + b)^2$ and, conversely, $\sqrt{(a^2 + b^2)}$ is *not* $a + b$.

4. Make the letter in the bracket the subject.

   (a) $A = \pi r^2 + \pi r h$ (h)

   (b) $v^2 = u^2 + 2as$ (u)

   (c) $s = ut + \frac{1}{2}at^2$ (a)

   (d) $T = \dfrac{2Hh}{H+h}$ (H)

   (e) $A = \pi r \sqrt{(h^2 + r^2)}$ (h)

   (f) $E = \frac{1}{2}m(v^2 - u^2)$ (u)

   (g) $\dfrac{a}{x} + \dfrac{b}{c} = \dfrac{a}{c}$ (x)

   (h) $v = w\sqrt{(l^2 + h^2)}$ (l)

   (i) $\dfrac{a}{\sin A} = \dfrac{b}{\sin B}$ $(\sin A)$

   (j) $x = \dfrac{r}{8}\left[\dfrac{16\rho - 3\sigma}{2\rho + \sigma}\right]$ (σ)

   (k) $\dfrac{R}{w} = \sqrt{\dfrac{4l^2 - 3a^2}{l^2 - a^2}}$ (a)

SIMPLIFYING FRACTIONS

This section extends the work on algebraic fractions covered in Chapter 7 to include cases where brackets have to be expanded and/or quadratic expressions need factorising. Remember that the rules for working with algebraic fractions are the same as those for numerical fractions.

Exercise 21i

Simplify   (a) $\dfrac{2xy}{6y}$ (b) $\dfrac{2a(a+b)}{a+b}$

(a)
$$\frac{2xy}{6y} = \frac{x}{3}$$

(b) Remember that $2a(a+b)$ means $2 \times a \times (a+b)$, i.e. $(a+b)$ is a factor of the numerator. When brackets are placed round the denominator, it is clear that $(a+b)$ is also a factor of the denominator and can therefore be cancelled.

$$\frac{2a\cancel{(a+b)}^{\,1}}{\cancel{(a+b)}_{\,1}} = \frac{2a}{1} = 2a$$

1. Simplify

   (a) $\dfrac{ab}{2b}$ (d) $\dfrac{3pq}{6q}$ (g) $\dfrac{5s^2}{20st}$ (j) $\dfrac{2(p+q)}{p+q}$

   (b) $\dfrac{a^2}{ab}$ (e) $\dfrac{10x}{15xy}$ (h) $\dfrac{x-y}{x(x-y)}$ (k) $\dfrac{a+4}{(a+4)(a-4)}$

   (c) $\dfrac{2ab}{4ac}$ (f) $\dfrac{m^2n}{kmn}$ (i) $\dfrac{st}{s(s-t)}$ (l) $\dfrac{(x+y)(x-y)}{x-y}$

Simplify   (a) $\dfrac{xy-y^2}{4y}$ (b) $\dfrac{2a-8}{a^2-a-12}$

In both of these fractions, the numerator and/or the denominator need factorising before we can see if there are any common factors that can be cancelled.

(a) $\dfrac{xy-y^2}{4y} = \dfrac{y(x-y)}{4y} = \dfrac{x-y}{4}$

(b) $\dfrac{2a-8}{a^2-a-12} = \dfrac{2\cancel{(a-4)}^{\,1}}{\cancel{(a-4)}_{\,1}(a+3)} = \dfrac{2}{a+3}$

2. Simplify

   (a) $\dfrac{4a}{8a-6b}$ (b) $\dfrac{2pq}{p^2-pq}$ (c) $\dfrac{a-b}{a^2-ab}$ (d) $\dfrac{3a-6b}{a^2-2ab}$

3. Simplify

(a) $\dfrac{2p - 4q}{6p - 12q}$

(b) $\dfrac{2a + b}{6ab + 3b^2}$

(c) $\dfrac{x^2 y - xz}{xy - z}$

(d) $\dfrac{a^2 + 2ab}{3a + 6b}$

(e) $\dfrac{x - 4}{x^2 - 6x + 8}$

(f) $\dfrac{a - 2}{a^2 - 6a + 8}$

(g) $\dfrac{ab - 2b}{a^2 - 4a + 4}$

(h) $\dfrac{st + 5t}{s^2 + 7s + 10}$

(i) $\dfrac{2x + 6}{x^2 - x - 12}$

(j) $\dfrac{x^2 + x - 30}{x - 5}$

(k) $\dfrac{3x - 15}{x^2 - 9x + 20}$

(l) $\dfrac{xy - 7y}{x^2 - 9x + 14}$

Simplify $\dfrac{4 - x^2}{x^2 - 3x + 2}$

$$\frac{4 - x^2}{x^2 - 3x + 2} = \frac{(2 - x)(2 + x)}{(x - 2)(x - 1)}$$

Notice that the denominator has a factor $2 - x$ and the numerator has a factor $x - 2$. Now $x - 2 = (-1)(2 - x)$, so we can simplify the fraction.

$$= \frac{\overset{-1}{\cancel{(2 - x)}}(2 + x)}{\underset{1}{\cancel{(x - 2)}}(x - 1)}$$

$$= \frac{-(2 + x)}{(x - 1)} = \frac{2 + x}{1 - x}$$

Notice that we multiplied numerator and denominator by -1 to make the coefficients in the numerator positive.

---

4. Simplify

(a) $\dfrac{x^2 - 9}{x^2 - 2x - 3}$

(b) $\dfrac{x^2 - 5x + 6}{3y - xy}$

(c) $\dfrac{4x - 8}{x^2 - 4}$

(d) $\dfrac{a - a^2}{a - 1}$

(e) $\dfrac{4x^2 - 1}{2x^2 - 3x - 2}$

(f) $\dfrac{2y^2 + 5y - 3}{4y^2 - 1}$

(g) $\dfrac{2 - x}{x^2 - 4x + 4}$

(h) $\dfrac{x^2 - 6xy + 9y^2}{x^2 - 3xy}$

(i) $\dfrac{a^2 - b^2}{b^2 - 2ab + a^2}$

(j) $\dfrac{4y^2 - 7y - 2}{4y^2 - 8y}$

(k) $\dfrac{a - 1}{1 - a^2}$

(l) $\dfrac{3x^2 - xy - 2y^2}{9x^2 - 4y^2}$

Express $\dfrac{2x}{x^2 - 4} \div \dfrac{1}{x - 2}$ as a single fraction.

$$\frac{2x}{x^2 - 4} \div \frac{1}{x - 2} = \frac{2x}{x^2 - 4} \times \frac{x - 2}{1}$$

$$= \frac{2x}{\cancel{(x - 2)}(x + 2)} \times \frac{\cancel{(x - 2)}}{1} = \frac{2x}{x + 2}$$

Express $\dfrac{2x}{x^2-4} + \dfrac{1}{x-2}$ as a single fraction.

$$\frac{2x}{x^2-4} + \frac{1}{x-2} = \frac{2x}{(x-2)(x+2)} + \frac{1}{(x-2)}$$

Remember that, before they can be expressed as a single fraction, each of the fractions needs to be expressed with the same denominator. This common denominator must be a multiple of each original denominator, and it is sensible to choose the lowest common multiple. In this case the LCM is $(x-2)(x+2)$.

$$= \frac{2x + (1)(x+2)}{(x-2)(x+2)}$$

$$= \frac{2x + x + 2}{(x-2)(x+2)}$$

$$= \frac{3x + 2}{(x-2)(x+2)}$$

5. Express as a single fraction and simplify where possible.

(a) $\dfrac{x^2-4}{3} \times \dfrac{6}{x+2}$

(b) $\dfrac{x^2-9}{2} \div \dfrac{x-3}{8}$

(c) $\dfrac{2}{x} + \dfrac{3}{4x}$

(d) $\dfrac{x}{y} - \dfrac{2}{xy}$

(e) $\dfrac{5}{x+3} \times \dfrac{2}{x-2}$,

(f) $\dfrac{5}{x+3} \div \dfrac{2}{x-2}$

(g) $\dfrac{5}{x+3} + \dfrac{2}{x-2}$

(h) $\dfrac{1}{2x} + \dfrac{x-3}{x^2-2x}$

(i) $\dfrac{1}{2x} \div \dfrac{x-3}{x^2-2x}$

(j) $\dfrac{1}{2x} - \dfrac{x-3}{x^2-2x}$

6. Express as a single fraction in its lowest terms.

(a) $\dfrac{1}{x+1} + \dfrac{2}{x^2-1}$

(b) $\dfrac{6}{x^2-2x-8} + \dfrac{1}{x+2}$

(c) $\dfrac{1}{x-1} - \dfrac{x+2}{2x^2-x-1}$

(d) $\dfrac{1}{x^2-4x+3} + \dfrac{1}{x^2-1}$

(e) $\dfrac{10}{2x^2-3x-2} - \dfrac{2}{x-2}$

(f) $\dfrac{x}{x^2+6x+8} + \dfrac{1}{x+2}$

(g) $\dfrac{2}{x^2+4x+3} - \dfrac{1}{x^2+5x+6}$

(h) $\dfrac{1}{x^2+9x+20} + \dfrac{2}{x^2+6x+8}$

(i) $\dfrac{2}{p^2-1} - \dfrac{p}{p^2-2p+1}$

(j) $\dfrac{M}{M^2-4} + \dfrac{M}{M^2-5M+6}$

Investigation

By taking integer values of n greater than 1 show that in each case a triangle with sides of lengths $n^2 + 1$, $n^2 - 1$ and $2n$ gives a right-angled triangle. What familiar Pythagorean triads are produced?

Now show that a triangle with sides $n^2 + 1$, $n^2 - 1$ and $2n$ is *always* right-angled, i.e. do not give n a numerical value.

Show that a triangle with sides of lengths $n^2 + 4$, $n^2 - 4$ and $4n$ also gives Pythagorean triads for integer values of n greater than 2.

Can you find other Pythagorean triads where all three numbers are less than 50?

Self-Assessment 21

1. Expand and simplify
   (a) $4x(3 - 2x)$
   (b) $2(3 - x) - x(x - 8)$
   (c) $(3x - 4)(2x + 3)$
   (d) $(2x - 3)^2$
   (e) $(2a - b)(2a + b)$
   (f) $(12 + x)(4 - 3x)$
   (g) $(2 - \sqrt{5})(2 + \sqrt{5})$

2. Factorise
   (a) $3xy - 9yz$ (d) $4x^2 - 36$
   (b) $2\pi r_1 - 2\pi r_2$ (e) $3x - 2 - x^2$
   (c) $x^2 - 6x + 8$ (f) $9x^2 - 30x + 25$

3. Make v the subject of the formula
   (a) $T = \dfrac{d}{v - u}$ (c) $\dfrac{1}{v} = \dfrac{1}{u} + \dfrac{1}{f}$
   (b) $2vt = a(v + t)$

4. Simplify
   (a) $\dfrac{6}{x - 2} - \dfrac{4}{x^2 - 4}$

   (b) $\dfrac{6}{x - 2} \div \dfrac{4}{x^2 - 4}$

   (c) $\dfrac{1}{2x^2 + 3x - 2} - \dfrac{1}{3x^2 + 7x + 2}$

DRAWING CURVED GRAPHS

GRAPHS FROM TABLES

Graphs are used to give a visual representation of information about two, related, varying quantities.

Before a graph can be drawn it is necessary to know how the quantities vary. Sometimes this information is given in a table, while at other times a formula is given that connects the varying quantities. The following example shows how to draw a clear, informative graph.

The staff at an arboretum collected data for one of their trees. This data is given in the following table:

Age of tree in years	0.8	1.6	2.4	3.8	5	6.8	7.9
Girth of tree in cm	14	19.9	25.1	32.2	38	44.1	47.5

To draw a graph to represent this data we must:

(a) draw axes that intersect at 90° in the bottom left-hand corner of the graph paper
(b) mark the scale used on each axis
    (Put time along the horizontal axis and the girth along the vertical axis.)
(c) name the axes
(d) plot carefully the points representing the data given in the table
    (Use a dot for each point.)
(e) draw a smooth curve to pass through the points
(f) give the graph a title.

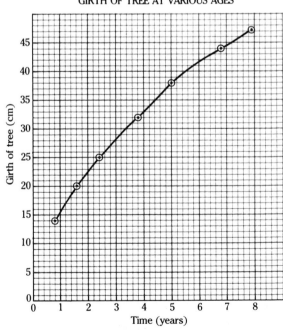

GIRTH OF TREE AT VARIOUS AGES

This graph can be used to find various facts relating the girth (distance round the tree) of the tree to time. For example, when the tree is one year old its girth is 14 cm; the time taken for its girth to double from the time of the first measurement is another 2.2 years, etc.

Examples of graphs appear in many newspapers and periodicals. The best of them give a clear visual impression of the way in which the related quantities vary and allow us to get more information from the graph. The worst graphs are misleading, often because the axes are incorrectly labelled or because the scales are distorted.

Points to Remember when Drawing Graphs

When curved graphs are being drawn the following advice should be kept clearly in mind.

1. Do not take too few points. About eight or ten are usually required.

2. To decide where to draw the *y*-axis look at the range of *x*-values, and vice versa.

3. In some questions you will be given most of the *y*-values but you may have to calculate a few more for yourself. If so, always plot first those points that you were given and, from these, get an idea of the shape of the curve. Then you can plot the points you calculated and see if they fit on to the curve you have in mind. If they do not, go back and check your calculations. Always have a clear idea of the shape of the resulting curve before you begin to draw it.

4. When you draw a smooth curve to pass through the points, always turn the page into a position where your wrist is on the inside of the curve.

Exercise 22a

1. When a sum of money is invested, the interest added to the original value gives an increased value called the amount. The table shows the amount (A) when £100 has been invested for T years at 12% per year compound interest.

T	0	1	2	3	4	5	6	7	8	9
A	100	112	125	140	157	176	197	221	248	277

Draw the graph connecting A and T. Take 2 cm as 1 unit for T and 5 cm as 50 units for A. From your graph find

(a) the amount after (i) $4\frac{1}{2}$ years (ii) $8\frac{1}{4}$ years

(b) the time, in years, in which £100 will double in value.

2. The table shows the weight, W tonnes, which a multi-fibre wire of diameter d centimetres will support before breaking.

d	1.2	1.8	2.2	2.6	2.8	3	3.4	3.8
W	72	162	242	338	392	450	578	722

Draw a graph for values of d from 0 to 4. Take 4 cm as 1 unit for d and 1 cm as 50 units for W. Use your graph to find

(a) the greatest weight that a wire of diameter 2 cm will support

(b) the smallest diameter of wire that will support a load of 500 t.

3. The table gives values for the total external surface area, A cm^2, of a closed rectangular packing case, which has square ends of side b cm.

b (cm)	1	1.5	2	3	4	5	6
A (cm^2)	110	76.5	62	54	59	71.6	90

Draw a graph connecting A and b taking 4 cm to represent 1 unit on the b-axis and 1 cm to represent 5 units on the A-axis. Let 40 (instead of 0) be the lowest value on the A-axis. Use your graph to find

(a) the value of b that gives the lowest value of A

(b) the value of A when b is   (i) 2.2   (ii) 5.3

CONSTRUCTING A TABLE FROM A FORMULA

In each question in the exercise above the data was given in a table. Sometimes, however, a formula connecting the variables is given and from it a table has to be constructed.

Consider a coin that is dropped, from rest, down a vertical mine shaft such that after t seconds it has fallen s metres. Suppose that the formula connecting s and t for the first 6 seconds of the fall is $s = 5t^2$ and a graph is required to show this relationship. Before a graph can be drawn, we must work out some corresponding values of s and t.

Taking half-unit values of t from 0 to 6 gives the values in the following table. Each value of s is calculated correct to the nearest whole number, for example if $t = 4.5$, $s = 5 \times 4.5^2 = 5 \times 20.25 = 101$ to the nearest integer.

t	0	0.5	1	1.5	2	2.5	3	3.5	4	4.5	5	5.5	6
s	0	1	5	11	20	31	45	61	80	101	125	151	180

We plot time (t) along the horizontal and distance (s) on the vertical axis.

When all the points have been plotted, draw a smooth curve through them. The resulting graph is shown in the diagram. From this graph we can find s for any given value of t from 0 to 6, e.g. the distance the coin falls in 3.7 s is 68 m. Similarly, the time to fall 135 m is 5.2 s.

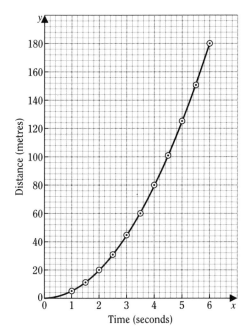

There are graphics programs available for computers that will plot curves and give the coordinates of points of intersection as accurately as anyone could want. There are also graphic calculators that have this facility. There are even pocket calculators on the market which have this facility. If you have access to one of these, you may like to use it to answer some of the following questions. If you explore these graphics capabilities further, you will find that you can do many of the remaining questions in this chapter far more accurately than it is possible to do by drawing.

Exercise 22b

1. A car starts from rest and travels a distance D metres in t seconds, where $D = 40\sqrt{t}$. Construct a table to show the corresponding values of D and t, for values of t from 0 to 10, at unit intervals. Use these values to draw a graph, and use your graph to find

   (a) how far the car travels in the first 4.4 seconds   (b) the time taken to travel 100 m.

2. Draw on the same axes the graphs of $y = x^2$, $y = x^2 + 3$ and $y = x^2 - 3$. Use values of x from -3 to 3 at unit intervals, and at $x = -\frac{1}{2}$ and $x = \frac{1}{2}$, taking 2 cm as 1 unit on the x-axis and 1 cm as 1 unit on the y-axis. Let the scale on the y-axis range from -4 to 12.
   What can you say about the shapes of the three graphs ?
   What can you deduce about the graph of $y = x^2 + C$ for different positive or negative values of C ?

3. Copy and complete the following table, which shows values of $\dfrac{6}{Q}$ for values of Q from 1 to 6 at unit intervals.

Q	1	2	3	4	5	6
6/Q	6		2	1.5		1

   Hence draw the graph of $P = \dfrac{6}{Q}$ within the given range taking 2 cm as 1 unit on both axes.

   Use your graph to write down

   (a) the value of P when $Q = 2.8$ (b) the value of Q when $P = 4.6$

4. Draw the graph of $y = x^3 + 4$ for values of x from -4 to 4 at half-unit intervals. Mark your y-axis from -60 to 70. Use your graph to find

(a) the value of y when $x = 2.7$

(b) the value of x when $y = 40$

(c) the value of y when $x = -1.5$

(d) the value of x when $y = -30$

Make a table to show the values of $x^2 - 3x - 4$ for whole number values of x from -2 to 5. Hence draw the graph of $y = x^2 - 3x - 4$ for this range of values of x.

Use your graph to find

(a) the lowest value of $x^2 - 3x - 4$ and the corresponding value of x

(b) the values of x when $x^2 - 3x - 4$ is   (i) 0   (ii) 4.

x	-2	-1	0	1	2	3	4	5
x^2	4	1	0	1	4	9	16	25
$-3x$	6	3	0	-3	-6	-9	-12	-15
-4	-4	-4	-4	-4	-4	-4	-4	-4
$x^2 - 3x - 4$	6	0	-4	-6	-6	-4	0	6

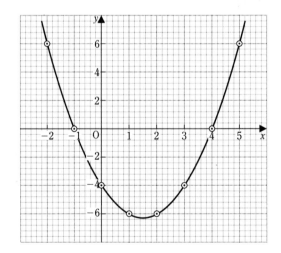

(a) From the graph, the lowest value of $x^2 - 3x - 4$ is -6.25. This occurs when $x = 1.5$

(b) (i) The values of x when $x^2 - 3x - 4$ is 0 are -1 and 4.

(ii) The values of x when $x^2 - 3x - 4$ is 4 are -1.70 and 4.70

Keep the following graphs as you may need them in later exercises.

5. Complete the following table, which gives the values of $x(3-x)$ for values of x in the range -1 to 4 at half-unit intervals.

x	-1	-0.5	0	0.5	1	1.5	2	2.5	3	3.5	4
$3-x$	4			2.5		1.5					-1
$x(3-x)$	-4			1.25		2.25					-4

Hence draw the graph of $y = x(3-x)$ within the given range taking 2 cm as the unit on both axes. Use your graph to write down

(a) the highest value of $3x - x^2$ and the value of x for which it occurs

(b) the values of x where the graph crosses the x-axis

(c) the values of x when $x(3-x) = 1$ (i.e. when $y = 1$).

6. Copy and complete the following table, which gives the values of $(x+1)(x-1)(x-3)$ for values of x between -2 and $+4$.

x	-2	-1.5	-1	-0.5	0	0.5	1	1.5	2	2.5	3	3.5	4
$(x+1)(x-1)(x-3)$	-15	-5.6	0	2.6	3	1.9		-1.9	-3			5.6	15

Hence draw the graph of $y = (x+1)(x-1)(x-3)$ for values of x between -2 and $+4$. Use your graph to find

(a) the values of x where the graph crosses the x-axis

(b) the value(s) of x when y is   (i) 1   (ii) -8

(c) the highest value of $(x+1)(x-1)(x-3)$ within the range $-1 \leqslant x \leqslant 3$ and the value of x for which this highest value occurs.

(d) Are there any values of x for the graph you have drawn for which $(x+1)(x-1)(x-3)$ is greater than the highest value you have given for (c)? If so, give one.

7. Copy and complete the following table, which gives values of $\dfrac{8}{x}$ for values of x from -8 to -1 and from 1 to 8.

x	-8	-7	-6	-5	-4	-3	-2	-1	1	2	3	4	5	6	7	8
$\dfrac{8}{x}$	-1	-1.1	-1.3	-1.6							2.67	2				

Hence draw the graph of $y = \dfrac{8}{x}$ within the given ranges. Use 1 cm to represent 1 unit on both axes.

(a) How many lines of symmetry does this curve have? Show any lines of symmetry on your diagram.

(b) Why is there no point on the graph when $x = 0$?

(c) Use your graph to find the value of y when x is   (i) 4.2   (ii) -3.4

(d) Use your graph to find the value of x when y is   (i) 4.2   (ii) -3.4

8. Copy and complete this table, which gives values of 3^x for values of x from -3 to 3.

x	-3	-2	-1	0	0.5	1	2	3
3^x	0.04		0.33		1.73			27

Hence draw the graph of $y = 3^x$ for the given ranges. Use 1 cm to represent one unit on both axes.

(a) Where does the graph cross the y-axis?

(b) If the x-axis is extended in both directions, will the curve cross the x-axis anywhere? Justify your answer.

(c) Use your graph to find the value of y when x is (i) 1.5 (ii) -1.5

(d) Use your graph to find the value of x when y is (i) 1.5 (ii) 0.5

9. Copy and complete this table, which gives values of 2^{-x} for values of x from -3 to 4.

x	-3	-2	-1	0	0.5	1	2	3	4
2^{-x}		4			0.70			0.125	

Hence draw the graph of $y = 2^{-x}$ for the given ranges. Use 1 cm to represent one unit on both axes.

(a) Where does the graph cross the y-axis?

(b) If the x-axis is extended in both directions, will the curve cross the x-axis anywhere? Justify your answer.

(c) Use your graph to find the value of y when x is (i) 1.5 (ii) -1.5

(d) Use your graph to find the value of x when y is (i) 1.5 (ii) 0.5

(e) How is the shape of this curve related to the shape of the curve in question 8?

CURVE SKETCHING

Quadratic Graphs

The most important family of curves we consider are given by equations of the form

$$y = ax^2 + bx + c \quad (a \neq 0)$$

All these curves have the same basic shape and are called *parabolas*.

If a is positive the vertex is at the bottom and there is no highest point.
On the other hand, if a is negative the vertex is at the top and there is no lowest point.

a is positive

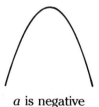

a is negative

Cubic Graphs

All graphs that have equations of the type

$$y = ax^3 + bx^2 + cx + d \quad (a \neq 0)$$

are curves of the same general shape.
They are called *cubic curves*.

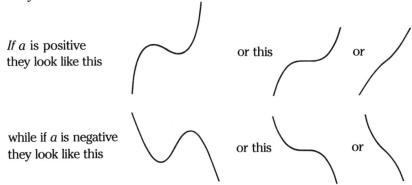

If a is positive
they look like this

or this

or

while if a is negative
they look like this

or this

or

Notice that every cubic curve has a kink in it. Sometimes the kink is a double bend, sometimes the kink is hardly noticeable.

Equations of the Form $\quad y = \dfrac{a}{x}$

Equations of the form $y = \dfrac{a}{x}$ give distinctive 'two part' curves. These are called *reciprocal*
curves. There is no value of y when $x = 0$.

If a is positive
the curve looks like this

while if a is negative
it looks like this

A curve of this type is called a *hyperbola*.

Exponential Graphs

Equations of the form $y = a^x$ and $y = a^{-x}$ give *exponential* curves.
(The exponent is another word for the index or power of a number.)

The shape of
$y = a^x$
looks like this

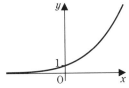

and the shape of
$y = a^{-x}$
looks like this.

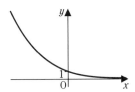

Notice that both curves cut the *y*-axis where $y = 1$
and that the curve does not cross the *x*-axis.

Exercise 22c

Sketch the curve given by the equation $y = x^2 + 8x + 12$

$y = x^2 + 8x + 12$.

The x^2 term is positive, so the vertex is at the bottom and there is no highest value of y.

As $y = (x+2)(x+6)$, $y = 0$ when $x = -2$ and when $x = -6$.

The graph therefore crosses the x-axis at these values of x.

When $x = 0$, $y = 12$

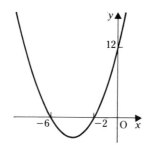

1. Draw a sketch of the curve given by the equation

   (a) $y = (x-3)(x-6)$

   (b) $y = (x-6)(x+4)$

   (c) $y = x(5-x)$

   (d) $y = x^2 + 2$

   (e) $y = x^2 + 7x + 12$

   (f) $y = 15 + 2x - x^2$

   (g) $y = 2x^2 - 13x + 6$

   (h) $y = 2x^2 - 16x + 24$

2. Sketch, on the same axes, the graphs of
   (i) $y = x^2$
   (ii) $y = x^2 - 4$
   (iii) $y = 4 - x^2$

   clearly distinguishing between them.
   Describe a transformation that

   (a) maps the first curve to the second

   (b) maps the second curve to the third.

3.

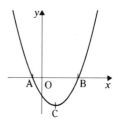

   The sketch shows the graph of

   $$y = x^2 - 2x - 8.$$

   (a) Find the coordinates of A, B and C.

   (b) Find the equation of the straight line joining B and C.

4. Sketch the graph of $y = 3x - x^2$, showing clearly where it crosses the axes.
   On the same axes sketch the graphs of

   (a) $y = x^2 - 3x$

   (b) $y = 6x - 2x^2$

Draw a sketch of the curve given by the equation $y = (x+1)(x-3)(x-5)$.

Since $y = 0$ when $x = -1$, 3 or 5, the graph crosses the x-axis for these values of x.

When $x = 0$, $y = (1)(-3)(-5) = 15$

If $(x+1)(x-3)(x-5)$ is multiplied out, the x^3 term is positive. The sketch we require is therefore of the form

The sketch of the graph of $y = (x+1)(x-3)(x-5)$ is therefore

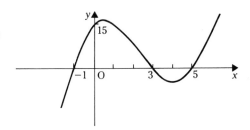

---

5. Draw a sketch of the curve given by the equation

    (a) $y = (x-2)(x-2)(x-6)$

    (b) $y = x(x-4)(x+4)$

    (c) $y = 4x - x^3$

    (d) $y = 2x(9-x^2)$

    In each case give a clear indication of where the graph crosses or touches the axes.

6.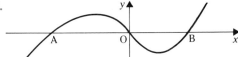

    The sketch shows the graph of $y = x^3 + x^2 - 12x$.

    Find the coordinates of A and B.
    (Hint: factorise the right-hand side.)

7.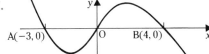

    The equation of the cubic curve shown in the sketch is $y = px + qx^2 - x^3$. The curve passes through the points $A(-3,0)$ and $B(4,0)$. Find the values of p and q.

8.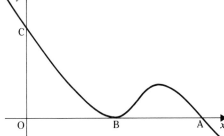

    The sketch shows the graph of $y = (4-x)(x-2)^2$.

    Find the coordinates of A, B and C.

9. Sketch the graph of $y = \dfrac{1}{x}$ for values of x from -10 to $-\frac{1}{10}$ and from $\frac{1}{10}$ to 10.

    (a) What happens to the value of y as the value of x increases beyond 10?

    (b) Is there a value of y for which $x = 0$?

    (c) Is there a value of x for which $y = 0$?

10. Sketch, on separate axes, the graphs of

    (i) $y = \dfrac{8}{x}$ (ii) $y = -\dfrac{8}{x}$. Show clearly the two parts of each curve.

In questions 11 and 12 several possible answers are given. Write down the letter that corresponds to the correct answer.

11. The graph of $y = x(1 - x^2)$ could be

A   B   C   D

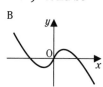
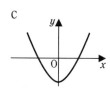
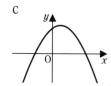
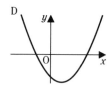

12. The graph of $y = 12 + 4x - x^2$ could be

A   B   C   D

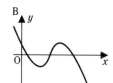

13. For each equation, give the number of the curve that could represent it.

(a) $y = \dfrac{2}{x}$ (b) $y = 3x^2$ (c) $y = 2^x$ (d) $y = x^3$ (e) $y = \dfrac{x}{2}$

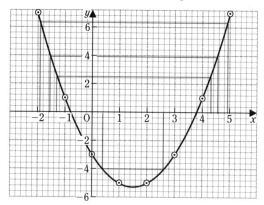

1   2   3   4   5

USING GRAPHS TO SOLVE EQUATIONS

From a single graph it is often possible to solve several different equations.

For example, the graph of $y = x^2 - 3x - 3$, can be used to solve the equations

(a) $x^2 - 3x - 3 = 0$
(b) $x^2 - 3x - 3 = 4$
(c) $x^2 - 3x + 1 = 0$
(d) $2x^2 - 6x - 11 = 0$
(e) $9 + 3x - x^2 = 0$

(a) $x^2 - 3x - 3 = 0$

When this graph crosses the x-axis the value of y is 0, i.e. $x^2 - 3x - 3 = 0$. When $y = 0$ the corresponding values of x are -0.8 and 3.8. These values of x are therefore the solutions of the equation $x^2 - 3x - 3 = 0$.

(b) $x^2 - 3x - 3 = 4$

When $x^2 - 3x - 3 = 4$, $y = 4$; the corresponding values of x are -1.5 and 4.5

Therefore the solutions of the equation $x^2 - 3x - 3 = 4$ are -1.5 and 4.5

(c) $x^2 - 3x + 1 = 0$

To use this graph to solve the equation $x^2 - 3x + 1 = 0$ we must convert the left-hand side to $x^2 - 3x - 3$. This can be done by subtracting 4 from both sides:

$x^2 - 3x - 3 = -4$ i.e. $y = -4$; the corresponding values of x are 0.4 and 2.6

The solutions of the equation $x^2 - 3x + 1 = 0$ are therefore 0.4 and 2.6

(d) $2x^2 - 6x - 11 = 0$

To use the graph to solve $2x^2 - 6x - 11 = 0$ we must convert the left-hand side to $x^2 - 3x - 3$. First we divide both sides by 2 giving $x^2 - 3x - 5.5 = 0$

Now add 2.5 to both sides: $x^2 - 3x - 3 = 2.5$ i.e. $y = 2.5$

When $y = 2.5$, $x = -1.3$ and 4.3

So the solutions of the equation $2x^2 - 6x - 11 = 0$ are $x = -1.3$ and $x = 4.3$

(e) $9 + 3x - x^2 = 0$

First convert the LHS to $x^2 - 3x - 3$ by multiplying both sides by -1

$$-9 - 3x + x^2 = 0 \quad \text{i.e.} \quad x^2 - 3x - 9 = 0$$

Add 6 to both sides $\qquad x^2 - 3x - 3 = 6$

From the graph, when $y = 6$, $x = -1.9$ and 4.9

The solutions of $9 + 3x - x^2 = 0$ are therefore $x = -1.9$ and $x = 4.9$

Exercise 22d

1. The graph of $y = x^2 - 2x - 5$ is given on the right.
   Use it to solve the equations

   (a) $x^2 - 2x - 5 = 0$

   (b) $x^2 - 2x - 5 = 5$

   (c) $x^2 - 2x - 2 = 0$

   (d) $2x^2 - 4x + 1 = 0$

   (e) $1 + 2x - x^2 = 0$

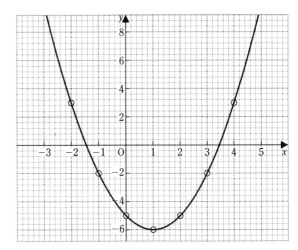

2. Use the graph of $y = x(3-x)$, drawn for question 5 of Exercise 22b, to solve the equations
   (a) $x(3-x) = 0$ (b) $x(3-x) = 2$ (c) $x(3-x) = -3$ (d) $1 + 3x - x^2 = 0$

3. The table gives values of y for certain values of x on the curve with equation $y = 2x^2 - 7x + 7$

x	0	$\frac{1}{2}$	1	$1\frac{1}{2}$	2	$2\frac{1}{2}$	3	$3\frac{1}{2}$	4
y	7	4		1	1	2		7	11

Complete this table.

Remember that $2x^2$ means 'square x first and then double it' e.g. if $x = 2\frac{1}{2}$, $y = 2 \times \frac{25}{4} - 7 \times \frac{5}{2} + 7$

Use the table to draw the graph of $y = 2x^2 - 7x + 7$ for values of x from 0 to 4.
Take 4 cm as 1 unit for x and 2 cm as 1 unit for y.

(a) Use your graph
    (i) to find the lowest value of $2x^2 - 7x + 7$
    (ii) to solve the equation $2x^2 - 7x + 4 = 0$

(b) Suggest a reason why you are unable to use your graph to solve the equation $2x^2 - 7x + 7 = 0$

Draw the graph of $y = x^2 + 4x + 3$ for half-unit values of x from -4 to 0.
Use your graph to find the lowest value of $x^2 + 4x + 3$, and the corresponding value of x.
Draw, on the same axes, the graph of $y = x + 2$. Write down the values of x at the points of intersection of the two graphs. Use your graphs to find the range of values of x for which $x^2 + 4x + 3$ is less than $x + 2$. Find, in its simplest form, the equation for which these values of x are the roots.

x	-4	-3.5	-3	-2.5	-2	-1.5	-1	-0.5	0
$y = x^2 + 4x + 3$	3	1.25	0	-0.75	-1	-0.75	0	1.25	3

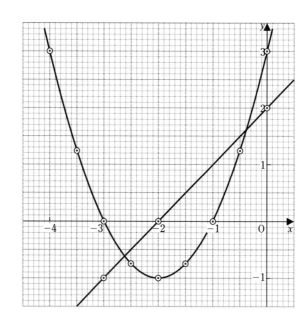

From the graph the lowest value of $x^2 + 4x + 3$ is -1, which occurs when $x = -2$.

The graph of $y = x + 2$ is a straight line so we take only three values of x and find the corresponding values of y.

x	-3	-2	0
$y\,(= x + 2)$	-1	0	2

The graphs intersect when $x = -2.6$ and -0.4

From -2.6 to -0.4 the curve, which has equation $y = x^2 + 4x + 3$, is below the straight line $y = x + 2$

Therefore $x^2 + 4x + 3 < x + 2$ for x greater than -2.6 but less than -0.4

At $x = -2.6$ and $x = -0.4$ the values of y for the curve and for the straight line are equal

i.e. $\qquad\qquad x^2 + 4x + 3 = x + 2$ i.e. $x^2 + 3x + 1 = 0$

The equation $x^2 + 3x + 1 = 0$ therefore has as roots the values of x at the points of intersection of the two graphs.

---

4. Copy and complete the following table, which gives values of $9x - x^2$ for values of x in the range -2 to 10.

x	-2	-1	0	1	2	3	4	5	6	7	8	9	10
$9x - x^2$	-22		0	8	14	18	20		18	14			-10

Using 1 cm as 1 unit for x and 2 cm as 5 units for y, draw the graph of $y = 9x - x^2$
On the same axes draw the graph of $y = 5x - 10$
Write down the range of values of x for which $9x - x^2$ is greater than $5x - 10$
Write down the values of x at the points of intersection of the graphs and the equation for which these values of x are the roots.

5. Simplify $(x + 1)(x - 1)$ and multiply the result by $(x - 3)$. Hence use the graph of $y = (x + 1)(x - 1)(x - 3)$, drawn for question 6 of Exercise 22b, to solve the equations
(a) $x^3 - 3x^2 - x + 1 = 0$ (b) $x^3 - 3x^2 - x + 5 = 0$ (c) $x^3 - 3x^2 + 1 = 0$

6. Use the graph of $y = \dfrac{8}{x}$, drawn for question 7 of Exercise 22b, for this question.

On the same axes draw the graph of $x + y = 8$
(a) Write down the values of x at the points where the graphs intersect.
(b) What equation has these values as its roots?

What graph should be used, together with the graph of $y = x^2$ to solve the equation $x^2 - 2x - 4 = 0$?

Sketch the two graphs for values of x from -4 to 4.

Hence justify the statement that the given equation has one positive root and one negative root. Estimate their values.

Rearranging $x^2 - 2x - 4 = 0$ as $x^2 = 2x + 4$ shows that the equation of the second graph is $y = 2x + 4$.

Two convenient points on the graph of $y = 2x + 4$ are $(0,4)$ and $(-2,0)$.

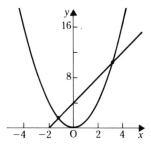

The graphs intersect at two points, therefore the equation $x^2 - 2x - 4 = 0$ has two roots i.e. the values of x at these points. One is positive and the other negative. The negative value is a little below -1 and the positive value just above 3.

7. What graph should be used, together with the graph of $y = x^2$ to solve the equation $2 - 5x - x^2 = 0$? *Sketch* the two graphs for values of x in the range -6 to 2.

Use your sketch to estimate the solutions of the equation $2 - 5x - x^2 = 0$

8. Sketch the graph of $y = \dfrac{10}{x}$ for positive values of x.

(a) What line has to be sketched to solve the equation $\dfrac{10}{x} = x + 2$?

(b) Sketch the line on the same set of axes.

(c) Does the value of x at the intersection of the graphs give all the solutions of $\dfrac{10}{x} = x + 2$?

9. Sketch the graph of $y = x^3$, together with another suitable sketch, to show that the equation $x^3 - 3x + 1 = 0$ has three roots, two of which are positive.

10. Sketch the graph of $y = 2^x$.

(a) What line has to be sketched to solve the equation $2^x = 3x$?

(b) Sketch the line on the same set of axes and give the number of solutions of the equation $2^x = 3x$, stating whether they are positive or negative

11. Investigate the solutions of the equation $x^2 = 2^{-x}$ and give estimates for their values.

TRANSFORMATIONS OF GRAPHS

The graphs of three closely related curves are given below.

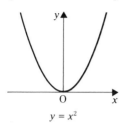

$y = x^2$

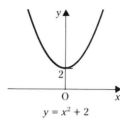

$y = x^2 + 2$

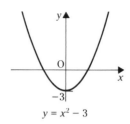

$y = x^2 - 3$

These graphs illustrate that adding a positive or negative value to the right-hand side of an equation of the form $y = f(x)$ has the effect of sliding the graph vertically through that value along the y-axis.

The graphs given below illustrate that replacing x by $x - 2$ moves the whole graph along the x-axis through 2 units to the right, while replacing x by $x + 3$ results in the graph sliding 3 units to the left along the x-axis.

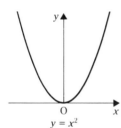

$y = x^2$

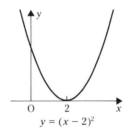

$y = (x - 2)^2$

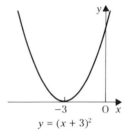

$y = (x + 3)^2$

Similarly, the graphs below show that replacing $f(x)$ with $-f(x)$ reflects the curve in the x-axis, while replacing x with $-x$ reflects the curve in the y-axis.

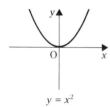

$y = x^2$

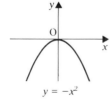

$y = -x^2$

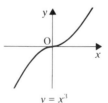

$y = x^3$

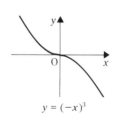

$y = (-x)^3$

In general terms, if the sketch of $y = f(x)$ is given we can obtain sketches of related equations.

(a) The sketch of $y = f(x) + a$ is given by sliding the graph upward a distance a parallel to the y-axis. (If a is negative the graph slides downward.)

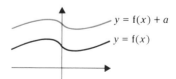

(b) The sketch of $y = f(x - a)$ is given by sliding the graph a distance a in the positive direction of the x-axis. (If a is negative the graph slides to the left.)

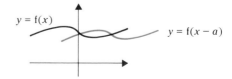

(c) To sketch $y = k\,f(x)$ we stretch the graph by a factor of k in the y-direction.

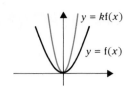

(d) When we sketch $y = f(tx)$, where $t > 1$, the width of the graph is reduced to $\dfrac{1}{t}$ of the original width.

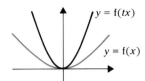

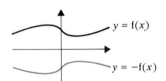

(e) The sketch of $y = -f(x)$ is given by reflecting $y = f(x)$ in the x-axis.

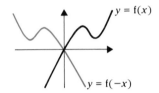

(f) The sketch of $y = f(-x)$ is given by reflecting $y = f(x)$ in the y-axis.

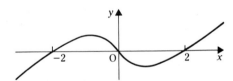

Exercise 22e

1. On separate axes sketch the graphs of
   (a) $y = x^2 + 4$ (c) $y = x^2 - \frac{1}{2}$
   (b) $y = x^2 - 4$ (d) $y = 2(x^2 + 4)$

2. On separate axes sketch the graphs of
   (a) $y = (x - 4)^2$
   (b) $y = (x + 3)^2$
   (c) $y = (x + \frac{1}{2})^2$

3. On separate axes sketch the graphs of
   (a) $y = (x - 6)^2$
   (b) $y = x^2 + 6$
   (c) $y = (x - 6)^2 + 6$

4. Sketch, on separate axes, the graphs of
   (a) $y = x^3$ (d) $y = (x + 3)^3$
   (b) $y = (x - 1)^3$ (e) $y = x^3 + 4$
   (c) $y = x^3 - 3$ (f) $y = \frac{1}{2}x^3$

5. The sketch shows the graph of $y = x^3 - 4x$

Use this diagram to sketch, on separate diagrams, the graphs whose equations are
   (a) $y = x^3 - 4x + 5$
   (b) $y = x^3 - 4x - 4$

6. (a) Sketch the graphs given by the following equations
   (i) $y = x^2$
   (ii) $y = (2x)^2$
   (iii) $y = (3x)^2$
   (b) Sketch the graph of $y = (kx)^2$ where k is a positive number. What difference would it make if k were negative?

7. Sketch, on the same axes, the graphs of $y = x^2$, $y = -x^2$ and $y = -x^2 + 10$, clearly labelling each one.

8. Sketch on the same axes, the graphs of $y = x^2 - 9$, $y = 9 - x^2$ and $y = x^2 - 16$.

9. On the same axes sketch the graphs of $y = 2^x$, $y = 2^x + 1$, $y = 2^x - 2$, $y = 2^{-x}$, $y = 3(2^x)$.

10. Use the sketch of $y = \dfrac{1}{x}$ which is given below to sketch the graphs of

(a) $y = \dfrac{1}{x} - 5$ (c) $y = -\dfrac{1}{x}$

(b) $y = \dfrac{1}{x} + 10$ (d) $y = \dfrac{3}{x} + 1$

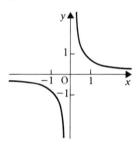

11. On your sketch for questions 10(d) sketch the graph of $y = 3\left(2 - \dfrac{x}{4}\right)$.

(a) Write down, and simplify, the equation that is satisfied by the values of x at the points of intersection of the two graphs.

(b) Use your graph to write down, approximately, the range of values of x for which $\dfrac{3}{x} + 1$ is less than $6 - \dfrac{3x}{4}$.

12. Copy the sketch of the graph $y = f(x)$

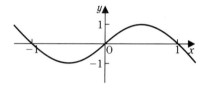

On your copy, sketch the graphs of $y = f(x) + 1$, $y = 2f(x)$, $y = f(x - 1)$, $y = f(x + 1)$.

Self-Assessment 22

1. Draw the graph of $y = x^2 + 5x - 10$ for values of x from -7 to 2. Take 2 cm as 1 unit on the x-axis and 1 cm as 1 unit on the y-axis.

(a) Use your graph to find
   (i) the lowest value of $x^2 + 5x - 10$ and the corresponding value of x.
   (ii) the values of x when
$$x^2 + 5x - 10 = -5$$

(b) What graph should be used, in conjunction with the graph of $y = x^2 + 5x - 10$, to solve the equation $x^2 + 4x - 11 = 0$? By drawing suitable sketches determine how many positive roots this equation has.

2. Sketch, on the same axes, the graphs of $y = \dfrac{12}{x}$ and $y = x^2 + 5$.

How many roots does the equation $x^3 + 5x - 12 = 0$ have? Estimate the integer values between which any root lies.

3. On separate axes, sketch the graphs of
(a) $y = x^3$ (c) $y = -x^3$
(b) $y = (x - 2)^3$ (d) $y = (3 - x)^3$
Show clearly where each graph crosses the axes.

4. Which of the following sketches could represent the graph of $y = 4^{-x}$?

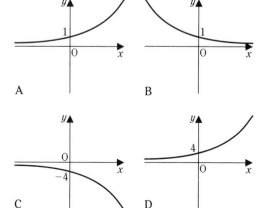

PROBLEM SOLVING

The graphs studied in Chapter 22 can help in the solution of several different types of problem. First we consider some real-life situations.

Exercise 23a

1.

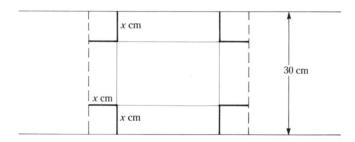

Rectangular pieces are cut from a continuous roll of thin card which is 30 cm wide. Squares of side x cm are removed from the corners of each piece and the sides are folded to form an open rectangular box whose length is twice its width.

(a) What are the dimensions of the base of the box?

(b) Show that the capacity of the box, C cm^3, is given by the equation

$$C = 8x(15 - x)^2$$

(c) Draw the graph of $C = 8x(15 - x)^2$ for values of x between 0 and 15. Use 1 cm to represent 1 unit on the x-axis and 1 cm to represent 500 units on the C-axis. Hence find the maximum capacity of the box and the value of x that provides it.

(d) What percentage of each rectangular piece of card is wasted if it is decided to manufacture rectangular boxes with the maximum capacity?

2. The table shows the capacity, C litres, for jugs that are mathematically similar, but have different heights, H cm.

H (cm)	5	7	8.5	11.25	14.5	18
C (litres)	0.09	0.26	0.46	1.07	2.29	4.38

Draw a graph to represent this data using 1 cm = 1 unit on the H-axis and 4 cm = 1 unit on the C-axis. Use your graph to find

(a) the height of a similar jug with a capacity of   (i) 1.5 litres   (ii) 3.5 litres

(b) the capacity of a similar jug that is   (i) 10 cm high   (ii) 17.5 cm high.

3. The total length, *P* metres, of metal required to make a metal framework of height *h* metres is given by the formula $P = 5h + \dfrac{2}{h}$

   (a) Copy and complete the following table.

h	0.25	0.3	0.4	0.5	0.6	0.7	0.8	0.9	1	1.1	1.2	1.3
P	9.25	8.17	7		6.3	6.36	6.5	6.72		7.32	7.67	8.04

   (b) Plot these points on a graph and join them with a smooth curve. Use 2 cm to represent 0.1 on the *h*-axis and 2 cm to represent 1 unit on the *P*-axis.

   (c) Use your graph to find
      (i) the length of metal required for a framework 1.06 m high
      (ii) the heights of the two frameworks that can be made from 8 m of metal.

   (d) What is the height of the framework that uses the shortest length of metal ?

4. An open rectangular tank with a square base of side *x* m, is to have a fixed capacity of 36 m³. Find, in terms of *x*, an expression for the depth of the tank. If the total external surface area is *A* m², show that

   $$A = x^2 + \frac{144}{x}$$

   Find the values of *A* for whole number values of *x* from 2 to 7 inclusive. Hence draw the graph of $y = x^2 + \dfrac{144}{x}$ for values of *x* between 2 and 7.

   Scale the *x*-axis from 2 to 7 and the *y*-axis from 0 to 80.

   Use your graph to estimate the dimensions of the tank when the total external surface area is least.

5. The graph below shows the price of Brited plc shares at the close of business each week-day over a twelve-week period.

   (a) During which periods is the price of the share rising ?
   (b) During which periods is the price of the share falling ?
   (c) After week 3, when would the best time have been   (i) to buy   (ii) to sell ?
   (d) What do you think is likely to happen to the price of the share during week 13 ?
   (e) 'The price of the share doubled in the first six weeks.' Is this statement true or false ?

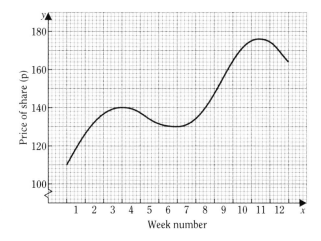

SOLVING QUADRATIC INEQUALITIES

The inequality $x^2 - 2x > 3$ is called a quadratic inequality because it contains an x^2 term.

When a quadratic equation is solved by factorising, the terms are first collected on one side of the equation in the form $ax^2 + bx + c = 0$

A quadratic inequality can sometimes be solved by factorising and it must first be arranged in a similar way.

$$x^2 - 2x > 3 \quad \text{becomes} \quad x^2 - 2x - 3 > 0$$

Factorising $x^2 - 2x - 3$ gives $(x + 1)(x - 3)$ and we see that the graph of the function is a parabola that crosses the x-axis at $x = -1$ and $x = 3$

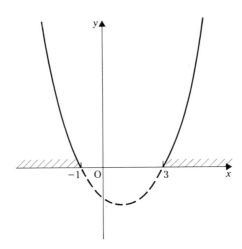

The function is positive (i.e. $x^2 - 2x - 3 > 0$) at points on this parabola that are above the x-axis.
i.e. for values of x that are less than -1, or greater than 3.

So the values of x that satisfy the inequality $x^2 - 2x - 3 > 0$ lie in the ranges

$$x < -1 \quad \text{and} \quad x > 3$$

Note that these two inequalities cannot be combined into one statement because in this case the values of x do not lie *between* the two boundaries.

It is interesting to note that a linear equation has one solution and that the solution of a linear inequality is a range of values of x with one boundary value, whereas a quadratic equation usually has two solutions and the range(s) of values of x that satisfy a quadratic inequality have two boundary values.

Exercise 23b

Find the set of values of x for which $x^2 < 9$

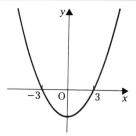

$$x^2 < 9 \quad \text{gives} \quad x^2 - 9 < 0$$

and $$x^2 - 9 = (x - 3)(x + 3)$$

$x^2 - 9 < 0$ when x is between -3 and 3.

i.e. $x^2 < 9$ for $-3 < x < 3$

When a quadratic inequality has no x term it is very important that the above method be used so as to avoid making false statements such as '$x^2 < 9$ therefore $x < 3$'

Find the range(s) of values of x that satisfy each inequality.

1. $x^2 \geqslant 1$

2. $4x^2 < 1$

3. $x^2 - 2 > 7$

4. $5 - x^2 > 1$

5. $(x - 1)(x - 3) \leqslant 0$

6. $x^2 - x - 2 \geqslant 0$

7. $x^2 - 3x - 1 < 3$

8. $x^2 + 2x \leqslant 3$

9. $x^2 + 4 > 5x$

10. $(x - 1)(x - 2)(x + 3) > 0$

APPROXIMATE SOLUTION OF EQUATIONS

Approximate solutions, to any degree of accuracy required, can be found in various ways. One way is to use graphs and this has been discussed in Chapter 22. Other ways are numerical.

Finding a First Approximate Solution

Whichever method is used, for a particular equation we need to start by identifying the number of solutions and roughly what they are. This can be done graphically by using sketch graphs.

Consider the equation $x^3 + x = 3$

To solve this graphically, we can find the points of intersection of two graphs. Because we only want approximate answers we will arrange the equation to give two graphs that can be sketched easily.

In this case we will choose to write the equation as $x^3 = 3 - x$

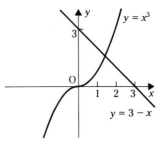

Then from the sketch of $y = x^3$ and $y = 3 - x$
we see that the equation has one solution and that
it is $x \approx 1$

Trial and Improvement

For this method, we first find an interval, usually between two consecutive integers, in
which a single solution lies. This can be done from sketch graphs. For the equation
$x^3 + x = 3$, the sketch graph in the last section shows that there is a solution between
$x = 1$ and $x = 2$

We can illustrate this on a number line:

Next we substitute 1 for x in both sides of the equation and compare values.

When $x = 1$, LHS $= 2$ and this is less than 3 (RHS).

Then we try $x = 2$; LHS $= 10$ and this is greater (a lot) than 3 (RHS).

We can conclude from this that the solution lies closer to 1 than to 2. This fact can be
used to narrow the interval within which the solution lies.

Try $x = 1.2$, LHS $= 1.2^3 + 1.2 = 2.928$ and this is just less than 3

Add this information to the number line:

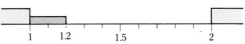

Hence the solution lies between 1.2 and 2, but is closer to 1.2, so we will try 1.3;
when $x = 1.3$, LHS $= 3.49$ and this is greater than 3.

Update the number line:

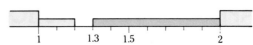

Now we know that the solution lies between 1.2 and 1.3, but is probably closer to 1.2.

If a more accurate solution is required, the interval can be narrowed by trying further
values of x. In this case it is sensible to draw another number line, between 1.2 and 1.3 in
intervals of 0.01

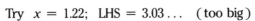

Try $x = 1.22$; LHS $= 3.03\ldots$ (too big)
Try $x = 1.21$; LHS $= 2.98\ldots$ (too small, but nearer)
Try $x = 1.215$; LHS $= 3.008\ldots$ (too big)
$\therefore$ $x = 1.21$ correct to 2 decimal places.

This method can be repeated to give the solution correct to any number of decimal places.

Exercise 23c

1. For each question, draw suitable sketch graphs to find the number of solutions and, to the nearest whole number, an approximate value for the largest solution.

   (a) $x^3 - 2 = x$

   (b) $x^2 + x = 1$

   (c) $\dfrac{10}{x} - x^2 = 2$

   (d) $\dfrac{8}{x} - x = 6$

2. For each of the equations in question 1, given that a and b are integers, write down in the form $a < x < b$ the interval in which the largest solution lies. Use trial and improvement to find this solution correct to three significant figures.

3. Show graphically that the equation $x^3 = 2x$ has three solutions. Use trial and improvement to find the least solution correct to two decimal places.

4. Use suitable sketch graphs to show that the equation $\dfrac{1}{x} = x^2 + 2$ has just one solution.

   Find this solution correct to one decimal place.

5. Use trial and improvement to find the solution, or if there is more than one the largest solution, of each equation. Give answers correct to one decimal place.

   (a) $x^3 + x = 9$

   (b) $x^2 + x + \dfrac{1}{x} = 11$

SOLUTION BY ITERATION

We now examine another way to find solutions of an equation to any degree of accuracy. Starting with an approximate solution, we use it to find a better approximate solution, and then use the better approximation to find an even better approximate solution, and so on. This process is called iteration. There are many iterative methods and we will look at just one of them.

Consider the equation $x^2 - 2x - 9 = 0$

If we want to use iteration to find the largest solution, then the first step is to find an approximate value.

From the sketch of $y = x^2$ and $y = 2x + 9$ we see that the larger solution is approximately 4.

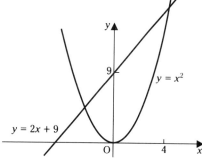

The next step is to rearrange the equation in the form

$$x = (\text{everything else})$$

This can be done in several ways, for example

$$x = \frac{1}{2}(x^2 - 9) \quad \text{or} \quad x(x - 2) = 9 \Rightarrow x = \frac{9}{x - 2}$$

$$\text{or} \quad x^2 = 2x + 9 \Rightarrow x = \frac{2x + 9}{x}$$

For reasons that are explained later we will choose

$$x = \frac{2x + 9}{x} \qquad [1]$$

Equation [1] is now turned into an iteration formula as follows.

If x_n is an approximate value of x, then a better approximation, x_{n+1}, is given by

$$x_{n+1} = \frac{2x_n + 9}{x_n} \qquad [2]$$

Starting with the first approximation, i.e. $\qquad\qquad x_1 = 4$

the iteration formula gives $\qquad\qquad x_2 = \frac{2(4) + 9}{4} = 4.25$

Then we use 4.25 as a better approximation, and repeat the last step,

i.e. $\qquad\qquad x_3 = \frac{2(4.25) + 9}{4.25} = 4.117\ldots$

Next we use 4.117 to get an even better approximation,

i.e. $\qquad\qquad x_4 = \frac{2(4.117) + 9}{4.117} = 4.185\ldots$

Now using 4.185 gives $\qquad\qquad x_5 = \frac{2(4.185) + 9}{4.185} = 4.150\ldots$

At this point it is already apparent that the sequence of numbers generated is closing in to a value between 4.15 and 4.18. We say that the iteration *converges*.
This is enough to justify saying that the largest solution of the equation is
$$x = 4.2 \text{ correct to 1 d.p.}$$
The iteration could be continued to give a more accurate solution if required.

Notice that only four significant figures are used for each approximation; this is enough to give three significant figure accuracy. If solutions are required correct to five significant figures then it is necessary to work to six significant figures.

The advantage of this method is that, once the iteration has started, and provided that it is going to converge, no judgements or decisions have to be made. This makes it ideal for computer programming. Another advantage is that even a fairly wild first approximation may lead to a result; try $x_1 = 5$ as a start in the example above.

The disadvantage is that the method does not always work, i.e. when the first approximation is used, the next approximation may be further from the true value and, as the iteration continues, the approximations get worse. When this happens, and it is obvious, we say that the iteration *diverges*. To illustrate this, consider again the equation $x^2 - 2x - 9 = 0$

This time we will use the rearrangement in the form $x = \dfrac{x^2 - 9}{2}$

This gives the iteration formula as $x_{n+1} = \dfrac{x_n{}^2 - 9}{2}$

Using 4 as the first approximate value gives

$$x_1 = 4$$

$$x_2 = \frac{4^2 - 9}{2} = 3.5$$

$$x_3 = \frac{3.5^2 - 6}{2} = 1.625$$

$$x_4 = \frac{1.625^2 - 9}{2} = -3.179\ldots$$

It is now obvious that the values given by this iteration are getting further away from the true value, i.e. they are diverging.

It is not easy to predict which rearrangement of the equation, if any, will give an iteration formula that converges. At this stage it is sensible to try one and if it does not work, try another one.

Exercise 23d

1. (a) Show that if $x^2 + 7x - 5 = 0$ then $x = 0.5$ is an approximate solution.
   (b) Show that the equation in (a) can be expressed in the form $x = \dfrac{5 - x^2}{7}$
   (c) Hence obtain an iteration formula to give better approximations to the solution near 0.5 and use it five times. To how many decimal places do you think that your answer is correct?

2. (a) Show that 1 is an approximate value for one root of the equation
   $$x^2 - 9x + 6 = 0$$
   (b) By expressing the equation in the form $x = \dfrac{x^2 + 6}{9}$, obtain an iteration formula to give a better approximation to the root of the equation.
   (c) Use the iteration formula to find the root correct to 2 decimal places.

3. For the equation $x^2 - 7x + 2 = 0$,
   (a) write down as many rearrangements as you can find to give the equation in the form $x = (\text{everything else})$
   (b) given that 7 is an approximate value for a root, find which of your rearrangements give iteration formulae that converge. Hence find the value of this root correct to 1 decimal place.

4. (a) An iteration formula is $u_{n+1} = 2 + \dfrac{3}{u_n}$

   Starting with $u_1 = 2$, find the first eight numbers generated by the formula. To what number does the sequence appear to converge?
   (b) Starting with $u_1 = 0$ and using the formula $u_{n+1} = \dfrac{3}{u_n - 2}$, write down the first six numbers of the sequence and the value to which they appear to converge.
   (c) By replacing both u_n and u_{n+1} with x in each formula, show that both formulae give solutions to the same equation. Write down this equation.

5. Use iteration to find both roots of the equation $x^2 + 2x - 5 = 0$, giving answers correct to two decimal places.

6. If x_n is an approximate value for $\sqrt[3]{9}$, then x_{n+1} is a better approximation where
   $$x_{n+1} = \frac{1}{3}\left(2x_n + \frac{9}{x_n{}^2}\right)$$
   (a) Write down an integer that would be a sensible choice for x_1
   (b) Use the iteration formula to find x_4

THE TANGENT TO A CURVE

The graph shows the curve whose equation is $y = \frac{1}{2}x(5 - x)$

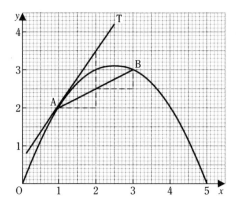

A line joining two points on a curve is a *chord*.

The line AB is a chord of the curve shown.

A line that touches a curve at a point is a *tangent* to the curve at that point.

In the diagram, AT is a tangent to the curve at A.

GRADIENT

The gradient of a straight line is found by taking two points on the line and, moving left to right from one point to the other, evaluating the fraction

$$\frac{\text{distance moved up}}{\text{distance moved across}}$$

When choosing two points on the line, it is sensible to make the distance across a whole number of units.

If the coordinates of the two points are known, the gradient is given by

$$\frac{\text{difference in } y \text{ coordinates}}{\text{difference in } x \text{ coordinates}}$$

In the diagram, the gradient of the chord AB is $\frac{1}{2}$.

When moving along a curve, the gradient changes continuously. Imagine moving along the curve in the diagram, starting from O. When you get to A imagine that you stop following the curve and move on in a constant direction: you will move along the tangent AT.

Therefore

     the gradient of a curve at a point is defined as the gradient of the tangent to the curve at this point

In the diagram, the gradient of the tangent AT is $\frac{3}{2}$, therefore the gradient of the curve at A is $\frac{3}{2}$.

Finding a gradient by drawing and measurement means that the curve must be accurately drawn and then the tangent must be positioned carefully. Using a transparent ruler helps and, as a rough guide, the tangent should be approximately at the same 'angle' to the curve on each side of the point of contact.

Exercise 23e

1.

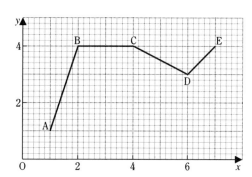

Find the gradient of the line

(a) AB   (b) BC   (c) CD   (d) DE

2. Copy and complete the table for $y = \dfrac{x^2}{10}$

x	0	1	2	3	4	5	6	7	8
y	0	0.1	0.4						

Use a scale of 2 cm for 1 unit on both axes and draw the curve.

(a) P is the point on the curve where $x = 2$ and Q is the point on the curve where $x = 4$. Draw the chord PQ and find its gradient.

(b) Draw, as accurately as possible, the tangents to the curve at the points where $x = 1, 4, 6$.

(c) Find the gradients of the tangents to the curve at the points where $x = 1, 4$ and 6.

3. Copy and complete the table for $y = \dfrac{10}{x}$, giving values of y correct to 1 d.p.

x	1	1.5	2	3	4	5	6	7	8
y	10	6.7	5	3.3	2.5				

Use a scale of 2 cm for 1 unit on both axes and draw the curve for values of x from 1 to 8.

(a) A is the point on the curve where $x = 2$ and B is the point on the curve where $x = 5$. Find the gradient of the chord AB.

(b) Find the gradients of the tangents to the curve at A and B.

(c) Find the gradient of the tangent to the curve at the point where $x = 3$.

UNEQUAL SCALES

In the many practical applications of graphs it is rarely possible to have the same scales on both axes.

If the scales are not the same, care must be taken to read vertical measurements from the scale on the vertical axis and horizontal measurements from the scale on the horizontal axis.

Exercise 23f

The table shows the girth (w cm) of a marrow, n days after being fed with fertiliser.

n	1	2	3	4	5	6	7
w	5	7	10	15	21	31	45

Use a scale of 1 cm for 1 day and 2 cm for 10 cm of girth to draw the graph illustrating this information.

(a) Find the gradient of the chord joining the points where $n = 2$ and $n = 7$ and interpret the result.

(b) Find the gradient of the tangent at the point where $n = 4$ and interpret the result.

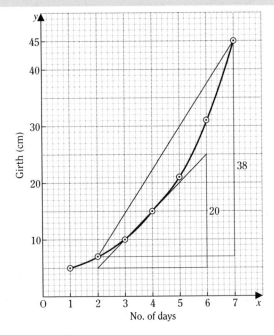

(a) Gradient of chord is $\dfrac{38}{5} = 7.6$. This shows that the girth of the marrow is increasing by an average of 7.6 cm per day over the five-day period

(b) Gradient of tangent $\approx \dfrac{20.5}{4} \approx 5.1$ This shows that the girth of the marrow is increasing by 5.1 cm per day at the time of measurement on the fourth day.

1. The number of ripe raspberries on a particular raspberry plant were picked and counted on Monday, Wednesday, Friday, Saturday and Sunday during one week. The results were recorded and plotted to give the following graph.

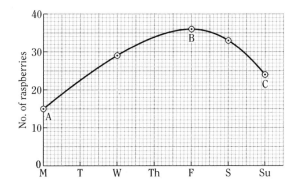

(a) How many ripe raspberries were there on (i) Wednesday   (ii) Saturday?

(b) How many raspberries were probably ripe on Thursday?

(c) Find the gradient of the chord joining the points A and B and interpret the result.

(d) Find the gradient of the chord joining B and C and interpet the result.

(e) On which day did the plant provide the greatest number of ripe raspberries?

(f) Estimate the total number of ripe raspberries picked from this plant during the 7 days.

2. The table shows the population of an Irish fishing village at 10-year intervals from 1900 to 1980.

Year (Y)	1900	1910	1920	1930	1940	1950	1960	1970	1980
No. of people (N)	500	375	280	210	160	120	90	65	50

Using scales of 2 cm ≡ 10 years and 2 cm ≡ 50 people, draw the graph illustrating this information.

(a) Find the gradient of the chord joining the points on the curve where $Y = 1910$ and $Y = 1940$. Interpret your result.

(b) Find the gradient of the tangent to the curve where $Y = 1910$ and interpret the result.

3. The table shows the sales of 'Newvale' jam for 5 months following an advertising campaign.

Month (M)	1	2	3	4	5
Sales (No. of jars)	2000	2500	3500	5000	7000

Using scales of 2 cm ≡ 1 month and 2 cm ≡ 1000 jars, draw the graph illustrating this information.

(a) Find the gradient of the tangent to the curve where $M = 2$ and interpret the result.

(b) Find the gradient of the tangent to the curve where $M = 4$ and interpret the result.

4. Draw the graph of $y = x^3$ for values of x from 0 to 4 using scales of 2 cm for 1 unit on the x-axis and 1 cm for 5 units on the y-axis.

Find the gradient of the curve at the points where

(a) $x = 1$ (b) $x = 3$

THE AREA UNDER A GRAPH

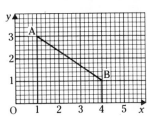

The graph shows the line $y = \frac{1}{3}(11 - 2x)$ drawn for values of x from 1 to 4.

Consider the area enclosed by the section AB of the line, the x-axis, and the lines $x = 1$ and $x = 4$ (these are called *ordinates*).

This is a trapezium and its area is given by

$$\frac{1}{2}(\text{sum of parallel sides}) \times (\text{distance between them})$$

The lengths of the parallel sides are 3 units and 1 unit, and the distance between them is 3 units.

Therefore the area under the line AB is $\frac{1}{2}(3 + 1) \times 3$ square units $= 6$ square units.

Notice that, although 1 cm represents 1 unit on each axis we do not know what those units are, so the area is given as a number of square units.

When the scales on the two axes are different, care must be taken to read vertical lengths in units from the vertical scale and horizontal lengths in units from the horizontal scale.

Exercise 23g

Find the area between the line $y = 20 - 5x$, the x-axis and the ordinate $x = 1$.

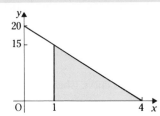

Notice that a sketch of the graph is sufficient to show the area required; an accurate graph is not necessary.

When $x = 1$, $y = 15$

The required area is a triangle of base 3 units and height 15 units.

Therefore area $= \frac{1}{2}(\text{base} \times \text{height})$

$\qquad\qquad = \frac{1}{2} \times 3 \times 15$ square units $= 22.5$ square units

In each case find, in square units, the area enclosed by the x-axis, the given line and the given ordinates.

1. $y = 1 + x$, $x = 0$, $x = 4$

2. $y = 3 + 2x$, $x = 1$, $x = 5$

3. $y = 8 - 2x$, $x = 1$

4. $y = 20 - x$, $x = 4$ and $x = 10$

5. $y = 15$, $x = 5$ and $x = 9$

6. $y = \frac{1}{2}(15 - x)$, $x = 3$ and $x = 12$

Using Trapeziums to Find the Area under a Curve

A curve can be approximated to by a series of straight lines.

To find the area between a curve and the *x*-axis, the area is divided into a convenient number of vertical strips. A chord is drawn across the top of each strip to give a set of trapeziums.

The sum of the areas of these trapeziums is then found and this is approximately equal to the required area.

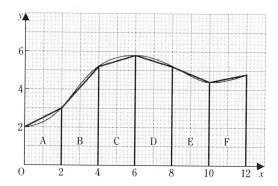

The area under this curve is divided into six strips, each of width 2 units. Drawing the chords across the top of each strip gives six trapeziums.

Reading from the graph,

for trapezium A, the lengths of the parallel sides are 2 units and 3 units and the distance between them is 2 units,

therefore   area A $= \frac{1}{2}$(sum of parallel sides) $\times$ (distance between them)

$$= \tfrac{1}{2}(2 + 3) \times (2) \text{ sq units}$$

$$= 5 \text{ sq units}$$

Finding the sum of the areas of all six trapeziums gives the total area as

$$5 + 8.2 + 11.1 + 11.2 + 9.8 + 9.2 \text{ sq units}$$

$$= 54.5 \text{ sq units}$$

Notice that all the strips are the same width. Although it is not necessary to use equal width strips, it is usually convenient.

Notice also that the area under the curve is only approximately 54.5 square units. A better approximation can be obtained by using more, but narrower, strips.

When using this method we are applying the *Trapezium Rule.*

Exercise 23h

Use five strips to find, approximately, the area under the curve passing through the points given in the table for values of x from 1 to 11.

x	1	3	5	7	9	11
y	2	10	20	25	20	15

A sketch graph is sufficient to give the necessary information.

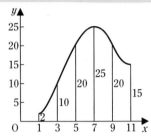

Area $\approx \frac{1}{2}(2+10)(2)+\frac{1}{2}(10+20)(2)+\frac{1}{2}(20+25)(2)+\frac{1}{2}(25+20)(2)$

$$+\frac{1}{2}(20+15)(2) \text{ sq units}$$

$$= 12+30+45+45+35 \text{ sq units}$$

$$= 167 \text{ sq units}$$

Use the trapezium rule to find the area between each of the following curves and the x-axis. Use the given number of *equal width* strips.

1.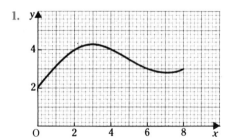

Use (a) two strips (b) four strips
Comment on your answers to parts (a) and (b).

2.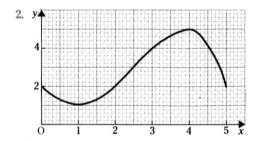

Use five strips.
Comment on the result given by using two strips.

3. A curve passes through the points given in the table.

x	0	1	2	3	4
y	1	2	4	4	2

Use a scale of 1 cm for 1 unit on each axis. Draw the curve for values of x from 0 to 4. Use four strips to find approximately the area between this curve and the x-axis.

4. A curve goes through the points given in the table.

x	0	1	2	3	4
y	1	2	4	4	2

Draw a rough sketch of the curve. Use four strips to find the area under the curve. Is your answer greater than or less than the true value?

5. Sketch the graph of the parabola $y = 3x^2$ from $x = 0$ to $x = 3$.

    (a) Divide the area under the curve into three strips and mark the values of the ordinates on your sketch. Hence find, approximately, the area under your curve.

    (b) Repeat part (a) using six strips.

6. A river is 40 metres wide and its depth was measured from one bank to the other bank at 5-metre intervals across its width. The values obtained are shown in the table.

Distance from bank (m)	0	5	10	15	20	25	30	35	40
Depth (m)	2	5	6	6.5	6	5	4	2.5	1.5

    (a) Draw a rough sketch of the cross-section of the river.

    (b) Use eight strips to estimate the area of the cross-section.

    (c) The speed of the water at this point of the river is measured as 0.25 m/s. How many litres of water pass through this cross-section in one second ?

Self-Assessment 23

1. When a low-loader transports a piece of heavy equipment at a speed of v m.p.h., the cost of a journey of 100 miles is $£\left(\dfrac{6000}{v} + 20v\right)$

    Complete the following table, which shows the cost in pounds (C) for values of v from 10 to 30.

v	10	13	15	18	20	22	25	27	30
C	800	721		693		713		762	800

    Draw a graph to show how the cost varies for speeds between 10 m.p.h. and 30 m.p.h. Take 4 cm to represent 5 m.p.h. on the horizontal axis and £100 on the vertical axis starting at £500.

    Use your graph to estimate   (a) the cost of the journey at a speed of 12.4 m.p.h.

    (b) the speeds at which the journey will cost £780

    (c) the speed at which the cost of the journey is least.

2. Find the range of values of x that satisfy the inequality $x^2 + x - 3 < 3$.

3. Show that there is a root of the equation $x^2 + x - 9 = 0$ between $x = 2$ and $x = 3$

    (a) Use trial and improvement to find this solution correct to 2 d.p.

    (b) Taking 2 as a first approximation, determine which of the following arrangements give an iteration formula that converges to the solution:

    $$x = 9 - x^2 \quad \text{or} \quad x = \frac{9 - x}{x} \quad \text{or} \quad x = \sqrt{9 - x}$$

4. Complete the following table of values for $y = 3x(4 - x)$

x	0	1	2	2.5	3	4
y	0	9				

    Using a scale of 2 cm for 1 unit on the x-axis and 1 cm for 1 unit on the y-axis draw the graph of $y = 3x(4 - x)$.

    (a) Use the graph to find the gradient of the tangent to the curve where
        (i) $x = 2$ (ii) $x = 2.5$ (iii) $x = 3$

    (b) Use the trapezium rule with four equal strips to find an approximate value for the area between the curve and the x-axis.

KINEMATICS AND RATES OF CHANGE

KINEMATICS

Kinematics is the study of motion, and the relationship between speed, distance and time is introduced in Chapter 5.

As a reminder, distance = speed × time and, for a given distance, the average speed is equivalent to the steady speed at which the distance is covered in the same time.

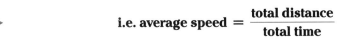 i.e. **average speed = $\dfrac{\text{total distance}}{\text{total time}}$**

Distance-Time Graphs

If an object is moving at a steady speed its motion can be represented in a *distance-time graph* by a straight line.

For example, if an object moves at a steady speed of 2 m/s, then its distance from a fixed point increases by 2 m each second. Plotting this distance against time gives the following graph.

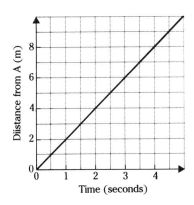

This graph shows that the object travels 8 m in 4 s at a speed of 2 m/s.

Notice that when time is involved in a graph, it is marked on the horizontal axis unless there is a special reason for changing this convention.

Exercise 24a

1. Find the average speed of an object that moves

   (a) 42 m in 6 s

   (b) 144 miles in 8 hours.

2. Find the distance covered by an object that moves in each of the following ways. Make sure that the units are consistent.

   (a) $6\,\mathrm{m\,s^{-1}}$ over 12 s.

   (b) 17 km/h over $3\frac{1}{2}$ hours.

3. Find the time taken by a moving object if it travels

   (a) 15 m at $5\,\mathrm{m\,s^{-1}}$

   (b) 17 km at $3.6\,\mathrm{km\,h^{-1}}$

4. A train travels for 2 hours at 50 m.p.h. and then for 3 hours at 60 m.p.h.

   (a) Find the total distance travelled.

   (b) Find the average speed for the whole journey.

   (c) Find the average of 50 and 60. Does this give the average speed for the journey?

Express $4\,\mathrm{m\,s^{-1}}$ in $\mathrm{km\,h^{-1}}$

$1\,\mathrm{h} = 60 \times 60\,\mathrm{s}$

$1\,\mathrm{km} = 1000\,\mathrm{m}$

In 1 s the object moves 4 m

In 1 h it moves $4 \times 60 \times 60\,\mathrm{m}$

i.e. $\dfrac{4 \times 60 \times 60}{1000}\,\mathrm{km}$

$= 14.4\,\mathrm{km}$

So $4\,\mathrm{m\,s^{-1}} = 14.4\,\mathrm{km\,h^{-1}}$

---

5. Express each speed in the unit indicated.

   (a) $6\,\mathrm{m\,min^{-1}}$ in $\mathrm{m\,s^{-1}}$

   (b) $10\,\mathrm{km\,h^{-1}}$ in m/min

   (c) $30\,\mathrm{km\,h^{-1}}$ in $\mathrm{m\,s^{-1}}$

   (d) $9\,\mathrm{m\,s^{-1}}$ in $\mathrm{km\,h^{-1}}$

6. From each of the following distance–time graphs, give the distance travelled, the time taken and the speed.

   (a)

   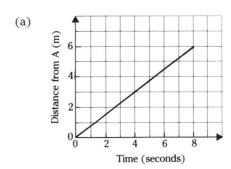

   (b)

   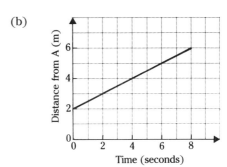

   (c)

   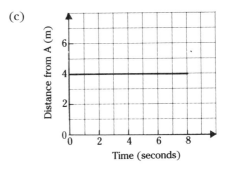

DISPLACEMENT

Distance travelled is independent of the direction in which an object moves.
Displacement is defined as the distance of the object, measured from a given point in a given direction.

$$\overline{\underset{\text{C}}{\quad}\underset{\text{3 m}}{\quad}\underset{\text{A}}{\quad}\underset{\text{4 m}}{\quad}\underset{\text{B}}{\quad}}$$

An object moves from A to B and back to A. The distance it has travelled is 8 m but its *displacement* from A is zero.
If the object carries on moving to C it will have travelled a distance of 11 m but its displacement from A is -3 m.

We use the convention that displacement to the right (or up) is positive and to the left (or down) is negative.

Displacement–Time Graphs

If, in the example described above, the speed is 2 m/s, we can use a displacement-time graph to show the motion.

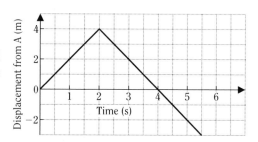

A displacement–time graph can be used to show more complicated motion.

A *Sprinter* train runs between two stations A and B. The motion is shown in the graph below.

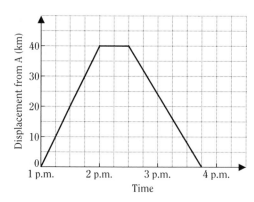

The train runs at a speed of $\dfrac{40}{1}$ km h^{-1}, i.e. 40 km h^{-1}, from A to B, stops at B for half an hour,

then returns to A at $\dfrac{40}{1.25}$ km h^{-1}, i.e. 32 km h^{-1}.

Notice that, at 3 p.m. the displacement from A is 24 km but the distance travelled since 1 p.m. is 56 km.

The graphs of two train journeys can be drawn on the same axes.
Here are two examples.

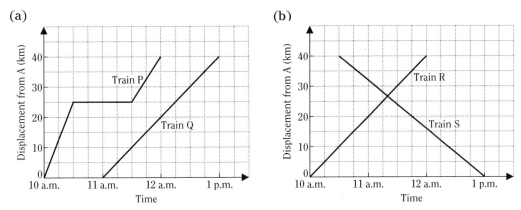

(a)

(b)

In (a), P and Q take the same time to travel from A to B; P travels faster, but stops at an intermediate station. The slope of the graph for P during motion is greater than that for Q. In (b), R is travelling from A to B and S from B to A. They pass 27 km from A, at approximately 11.20 a.m.

Graphs of this type, illustrating a journey made by a person or vehicle, are called *Travel Graphs.*

SPEED AND VELOCITY

Consider a train P travelling from A to B at 60 km/h and another train Q travelling from B to A also at 60 km/h.

Both trains have the same speed but they are travelling in opposite directions so, to specify the motion of either train we have to give the speed *and* the direction of travel.

 The quantity that specifies both speed and direction of motion is called *velocity*.

Taking the direction from A to B as positive, we can give the velocity of P as $+60$ km/h and the velocity of Q as -60 km/h.

Exercise 24b

1. State whether each of the following quantities is a distance, a displacement, a speed or a velocity.

   (a) 30 m.p.h.

   (b) 43 km

   (c) 4 m s^{-1} vertically downward.

   (d) 6 miles due north.

   (e) 3 cm s^{-1} towards the opposite corner of the room.

   (f) 10 km round the M25.

2. In each of the following displacement–time graphs, describe the motion and give the distances, times and velocities in the different sections.

(a)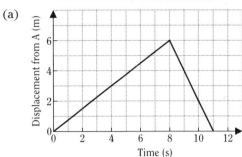

(c)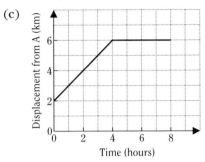

(b)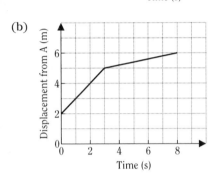

(d)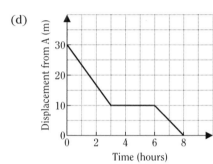

3. Sketch a displacement–time graph to show the following motion, marking in relevant displacements and times.

  (a) A car moves at a steady speed from A to B, a distance of 30 km, in 40 minutes. It stops at B for 30 minutes, then returns to A at $30\,km\,h^{-1}$.

  (b) A train starts from station C and travels to D at a constant speed of 60 m.p.h., taking 50 minutes. A second train starts from C half an hour after the first and takes 40 minutes to get to D.

4.

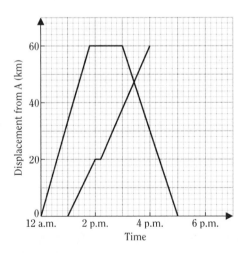

Two trains travel between stations A and B. Describe their movements, giving details of distances, velocities and times. Does one overtake the other or do they pass one another moving in opposite directions ?

5. (a) On graph paper and using scales of 4 cm to 1 hour and 1 cm to 5 km, draw lines to represent the motion of two trains P and Q travelling between two stations A and B, 60 km apart.
Starting at noon, P travels at a steady $60 \, \text{km h}^{-1}$ from A to B, stops there for 18 minutes, then returns to A, taking 72 minutes.
Q starts from A as P reaches B, and reaches B as P reaches A.

(b) At what speed does Q travel?

(c) At what time, and where, do the two trains pass?

(d) Draw an appropriate line on the graph to determine the speed at which Q would have to travel if the two trains were to pass at 1.30 pm. Assume that Q starts from A at the same time as before.

Finding Velocity from a Displacement-Time Graph

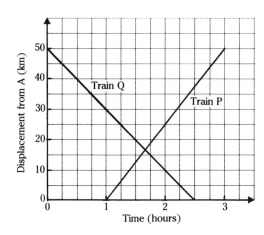

The graph shows two trains moving between stations A and B.

Train P is moving from A to B at $\dfrac{50}{2}$ km/h, i.e. the velocity of train P is 25 km/h.

The gradient of the line representing P's motion is $\dfrac{50}{2}$, i.e. 25, which is the same value as the velocity.

Train Q is moving from B to A at $\dfrac{50}{2.5}$ km/h, i.e. the velocity of Q is -20 km/h because we are taking the direction A to B as positive.

The gradient of the line representing Q's motion is $\dfrac{-50}{2.5}$ and this is the same value as the velocity of Q.

In both cases, the gradient of the line gave the velocity. This is true in general.

  The gradient of a displacement–time graph gives the velocity.

CURVED DISPLACEMENT–TIME GRAPHS

Objects seldom move at a steady speed and a curved graph represents a more realistic situation.

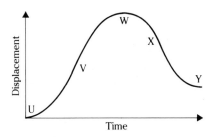

The object starts from rest (the gradient is zero at U) and gradually reaches a maximum speed (the gradient is greatest at V). It slows down again until, for an instant at W, it is at rest, then speeds up in the opposite direction (X) and comes to rest (Y). To find the velocity at a given moment we need the gradient of the curve at this moment and to find this we draw the tangent to the curve at the appropriate point.

The graph below is an accurate plot of the motion from U to W described above. To find the velocity 5 seconds after leaving A we draw, by eye, the tangent to the curve at the point where the time is 5 s. As the calculation depends on the accuracy of measurements taken from a drawing, it is not realistic to expect a result correct to more than one, or at most two, significant figures.

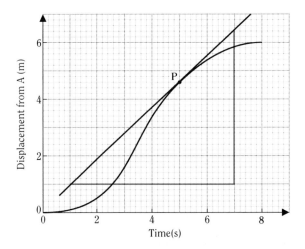

Choose for the base, a line of a convenient, but not too short, length.

The velocity after 5 s is given by the gradient of the tangent at P.

$$\text{Velocity} = \frac{\text{displacement}}{\text{time}}$$

$$= \frac{6.6 - 1}{6} \, \text{m s}^{-1} \quad \text{i.e.} \quad 0.93 \, \text{m s}^{-1} \, (\text{to 2 s.f.})$$

Exercise 24c

1. The graph shows the motion of a stone thrown vertically upward from a point A.

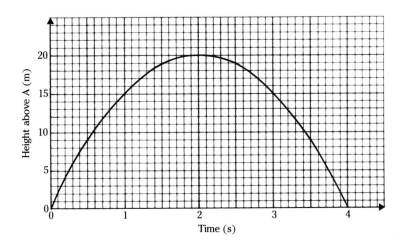

(a) Give the height above A after   (i) 0.5 s   (ii) 1.75 s   (iii) 3.2 s.

(b) When is the stone at its greatest height ?

(c) When is the upward velocity at its greatest ?

(d) After what time does the stone return to A ?

2. The distance, d m, travelled in t s by a marble rolling down a groove, is given in the table.

t	0	1	2	3	4	5
d	0	0.5	2	4.5	8	12.5

(a) On graph paper, using scales of 2 cm to 1 second and 1 cm to 1 m, draw a graph of distance against time.

(b) How far has the marble travelled after 2.5 s ?

(c) Draw a tangent to the curve at the point where $t = 2$ and find its gradient. Hence give an estimate of the velocity of the marble after 2 s.

(d) Estimate the velocity after 3.5 s.

3. A rubber ball is dropped into a swimming pool and sinks to the bottom. The table shows the height, h m, of the ball above the bottom of the pool after t s.

t	0	0.5	1	1.5	2	2.5	3	3.5	4
h	3	2.9	2.7	2.45	2.15	1.8	1.4	0.8	0

(a) Draw a graph to show this information. Use scales of 4 cm to 1 m and 4 cm to 1 s.

(b) How far has the ball fallen through the water after 1.25 s ?

(c) Estimate the velocity of the ball after   (i) 1 s   (ii) 2 s.

VELOCITY-TIME GRAPHS

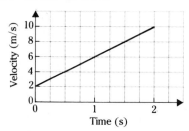

A straight line velocity-time graph represents a different situation from a straight line displacement-time graph. Now the *velocity* is changing by $4\,\mathrm{m\,s^{-1}}$ every second.

Acceleration

The rate of change of the velocity is called *acceleration*. The acceleration of the body above is $4\,\mathrm{m/s}$ per second i.e. $4\,\mathrm{m/s^2}$ or $4\,\mathrm{m\,s^{-2}}$.

In a displacement-time graph the gradient gives the rate of change of the displacement, i.e. the velocity.

In a velocity-time graph the gradient gives the rate of change of the velocity, i.e. the acceleration.

   The gradient of a velocity-time graph gives the acceleration.

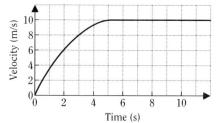

From the graph above we see that the object starts from rest, its velocity going up quickly at first with an acceleration of about $5\,\mathrm{m/s^2}$ (the gradient is approximately 5). The velocity goes on increasing but at a slower rate so that the acceleration decreases until, $6\,\mathrm{s}$ from the start, the velocity becomes constant ($10\,\mathrm{m/s}$) and the acceleration therefore becomes zero.

Note that, if a velocity is decreasing the acceleration is negative and can be called *deceleration*.

Finding Displacements from a Velocity-Time Graph

The object is moving at $3\,\mathrm{m\,s^{-1}}$ for $4\,\mathrm{s}$ and hence covers $12\,\mathrm{m}$.
This is also the number of area units under the line.

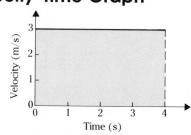

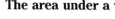   **The area under a velocity-time graph gives the displacement.**

If we have a graph of any other shape it is possible to show that the same relationship still holds.

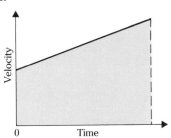 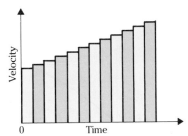

We get a glimpse of the reason for this if we replace a straight line by a series of very small steps so that the area is divided up into narrow rectangles.

In this case the displacement is given approximately by the sum of the areas of all the small rectangles, i.e. by the area of the trapezium. In the case below the area can be broken up into a rectangle, two trapeziums and a triangle.

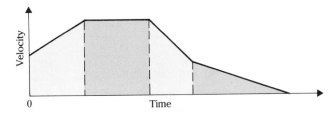

The area under a curved graph can be estimated by the methods described in the previous chapter. The more strips there are the nearer the estimate is to the actual area.

Exercise 24d

1. The graph represents the journey made by a car between two sets of traffic lights.

   (a) What is the acceleration of the car?

   (b) Finds its deceleration.

   (c) What is the steady speed between accelerating and decelerating?

   (d) What distance does it cover while
      (i) accelerating   (ii) decelerating?

   (e) How far is it between the traffic lights?

2. The graph shows the movement of a marble rolled up a groove.

   (a) What is the initial velocity of the marble?

   (b) Finds its deceleration.

   (c) What happens 2 seconds after the start?

   (d) How far up the groove does the marble travel?

   (e) What happens between 2 and 3 seconds after the start?

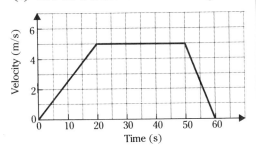 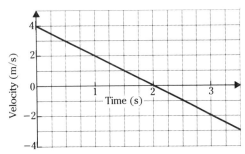

3. The following velocity–time graph shows the motion of a boy on a bicycle.

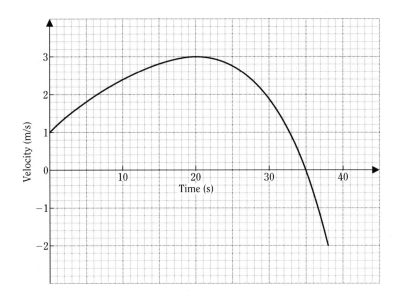

(a) Give the velocity after   (i) 5 s   (ii) 15 s   (iii) 30 s

(b) At what time is the cycle instantaneously at rest ?

(c) At what time is the acceleration zero ?

(d) Give the velocity after 38 seconds. What is the significance of the minus sign ?

4. The table shows the velocity of a child sliding down a giant 'Water Splash'.

Time (s)	0	2	4	6	8	10
Velocity (m s^{-1})	2	3.9	5.4	6.6	7.4	8

(a) On graph paper and using scales of 1 cm to 1 s and 1 cm to 1 m s^{-1}, draw a velocity–time graph.

(b) Divide the area under the graph into strips 1 cm wide and hence find, approximately, the distance travelled in the 10 seconds.

5. The velocity, v m s^{-1}, of a ball at time t is given by

$$v = 8t - \tfrac{1}{2}t^2 + 2$$

(a) On graph paper and using scales of 2 cm to 5 m s^{-1} and 1 cm to 1 s, draw the velocity–time graph for the first 10 s.

(b) Draw a tangent to the curve at the point where $t = 6$ and find its gradient. Hence estimate the acceleration of the ball after 6 s.

(c) Estimate the distance travelled in the first 10 seconds.

(d) Estimate after how many seconds the ball has travelled half this distance.

GROWTH AND DECAY

Kinematics is concerned with changes in motion; similar methods can be applied to changes in other quantities, such as population, temperature or the growth of a tree.

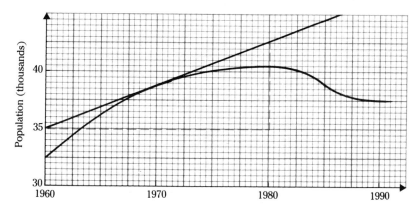

The population of a town is shown in the graph. From it we can find the population at a given time; we can also find the *rate* at which the population is growing by finding the gradient of the curve.

For example, in 1970 the population was 38 800; the gradient then was $\frac{7500}{20}$, i.e. 375, so the population was growing at the rate of 375 a year. In 1980 the gradient was zero, so the population was not growing at all. For a few years after that the growth rate was negative, i.e. the population was decreasing.

Exercise 24e

Use graph paper in this exercise.

1. Interpret the following population graphs, commenting on these points.
   (i) Is the population increasing or decreasing? Is the population constant at any time?
   (ii) Is the growth or decay rate constant or is the rate itself increasing or decreasing?

(a)
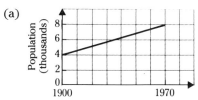

(c)
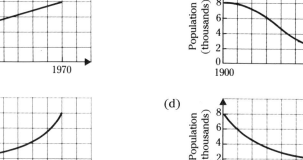

(b)
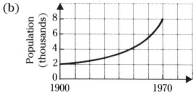

(d)

2. The table gives the population of a small country.

Year	1900	1910	1920	1930	1940	1950	1960
Population (thousands)	230	280	312	334	332	336	343

(a) Draw a graph to show this information, using scales of 1 cm to 5 years and 1 cm to 10 thousand. Start the population scale at 200 thousand.

(b) When was the population at its greatest?

(c) When was the population growth rate at its greatest?

(d) Find, by drawing a tangent, the population growth rate in 1920 and express it as a percentage of the population in that year.

3. The table shows the temperature of water in a saucepan.

Time (min)	0	1	2	3	4	5	6	7	8	9	10
Temp. (°C)	60	51	44	39	35	31.5	29	27	25	24	23

(a) Draw a graph to show this information. Start the temperature scale at 20 °C. Use scales of 2 cm to 5 °C and 2 cm to 1 min.

(b) Find the rate of cooling after 2 minutes.

(c) Find the average drop in temperature over the first 10 minutes. Draw the line on the graph whose gradient gives this quantity.

4. A balloon is blown up so that its volume, $V \text{cm}^3$, after t s is given by the formula

$$V = \frac{4}{3}\pi t^3$$

(a) Draw a graph of V against t for $0 \leqslant t \leqslant 5$, using a scale of 2 cm to 1 unit for t and 1 cm to 50 units for V.

(b) Find the rate at which the volume is increasing after 3 s.

5. The table shows the retail price index at the end of each year from 1978 to 1985.

Year	1978	1979	1980	1981	1982	1983	1984	1985
Index	100	106	123	140	162	171	178	185

(a) Draw a graph to show this information. Choose suitable scales and start the retail price index scale at 100.

(b) Find the rate at which the index is increasing at the end of 1981. Express this rate as a percentage of the index at that time. (This is the *rate of inflation*.)

(c) Repeat part (b) for 1983.

(d) Did the rate of inflation increase or decrease between 1981 and 1983? If the rate of inflation decreases does this mean that prices decrease?

6. The table shows the quantity of an element remaining after radio-active decay.

Time (years)	0	10	20	30	40	50	60	70	80
Quantity (g)	80	67	57	48	40	34	28	24	20

(a) Draw a graph to show this information.

(b) Find the rate of decay after 20 years and express it as a percentage of the amount of the element remaining at that time.

(c) Repeat part (b) for 40 years' decay.

(d) What do you notice about the answers to (b) and (c)?
   Investigate further. Will the element ever disappear altogether?

Self-Assessment 24

1. A train travels 60 km in $1\frac{1}{2}$ hours. What is its average speed?

2. In each case state whether a velocity or a speed is given.

   (a) 2 m/s upward   (b) 16 m.p.h.

3.

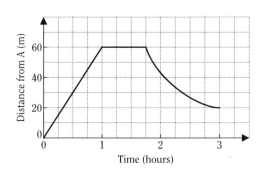

(a) Describe the motion of the train represented on this displacement–time graph.

(b) Give the velocity after $\frac{1}{2}$ hour.

4.

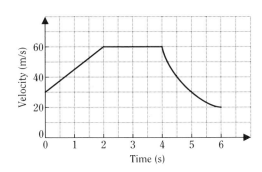

(a) Describe the motion illustrated in this velocity–time graph.

(b) Give the distance travelled in 4 s.

(c) Give the approximate acceleration after 5 s.

5. The table shows the number of people unemployed in a town at the end of each quarter from July 1986 to January 1989.

| Date | 1986 | | 1987 | | | | 1988 | | | | 1989 |
	Jul	Oct	Jan	Apr	Jul	Oct	Jan	Apr	Jul	Oct	Jan
Number unemployed	240	264	278	287	290	288	284	276	265	248	230

(a) Draw a curved graph to show this information. Start the number scale at 220 and use 1 cm to 10. Use 2 cm to 3 months on the horizontal axis.

(b) Give the connection between the rate of change in the number unemployed and the gradient of the graph and/or the area under the graph.

(c) Find the rate of change in the number unemployed in July 1988.

COLLECTING AND ILLUSTRATING DATA

STATISTICS

Statistics is concerned with the collection and analysis of large quantities of information. In this chapter we are going to look at the collection of information and at ways of grouping and illustrating it.

Data is the collective noun for pieces of information.
We require data for all kinds of purposes, e.g. assessing the performance of organisations or products, planning, producing opinion polls.
There are (very roughly) two categories of data: facts and opinions.

Collecting Information

There are various ways of collecting and recording information, the most common being to ask people to fill in forms. If the information is to be of any use then the forms need to be designed carefully. Take the apparently simple request to fill in a name; if a form has just NAME followed by an empty box then anything from a single first name, to all first names plus surname and title, is likely to appear. Thus the exact information required must be considered and then asked for precisely.

Observation Sheets

Some data can be collected directly by counting or measuring and the data can then be recorded on an observation sheet. Some methods for doing this are more efficient than others.
Consider, for example, recording the results of a count of the number of occupants in each car going into a town centre in the morning rush hour. This could be done simply by writing down the numbers as they are observed, e.g. 1, 3, 1, 1, 2, 1, 4, ...
A little forethought would indicate that, because there are only a few possibilities, the results could be recorded in a simple table using tally marks, e.g.

Number of occupants per car	1	2	3	4	5	6 or more
	IIII	I	I	I	I	I

Notice that tally marks are easier to total if they are grouped in fives. This can be done several ways, e.g. ⵀ or ⊠

Questionnaires

When data is required from individuals, the best method is to use a form with the information required written on it. The advantage of this is that each person is asked for the same information in the same way.

We have already seen that a request for precise information, e.g. name, weight, should be asked for unambiguously. Some data however is not precise, e.g. eye colour, opinion about a proposed road development.

It is sensible to ask for such information in predetermined categories. For example, a question asking for eye colour could be in the form

Tick the box that most closely corresponds to the colour of your eyes:

       Brown ☐   Hazel/Green ☐   Blue ☐

A question asking for an opinion could be in the form:

Private cars should be banned from city centres.

       Agree ☐   Disagree ☐   Undecided ☐

FREQUENCY TABLES

The following list of figures shows the number of occupants in each car travelling towards London on the M4. The numbers were recorded for each car passing the observation point during a ten-minute period so they are in random order.

```
1  2  1  4  2  1  1  2  1  2  4  1  5  3  1  2  1  1  2  1  4  3
5  2  3  1  1  2  2  1  3  1  1  1  4  2  1  5  1  2  3  1  2  1
2  1  2  3  3  1  2  4  1  3  1  2  1  3  2  1  5  3  6  2  1  1
3  2  4  1  6  3  3  3  2  3  3  1  1  2  4  1  2  4  4  1  1  3
3  4  3  2  4  3  2  3  1  1  2  1  2  1  3  2  1  1  1  1  4  2
```

Data in this form is called raw data. Before any sense can be made of this data, it needs to be sorted into categories.

There are six categories here: 1, 2, 3, 4, 5 and 6 occupants.

Using a table, each item can be recorded under its appropriate category using tally marks. The total number of items in a category is the *frequency*.

Number of occupants per car	1	2	3	4	5	6	
Tally	卌 卌 卌 卌 卌 卌 卌 卌 卌 卌 ||	卌 卌 卌 卌 卌 |||	卌 卌 卌 卌 卌 ||| ||	卌 卌 卌 卌 ||	||||	||	
							Total:
Frequency	42	28	22	12	4	2	110

This is called a frequency table.

Bar Charts

The frequency table above can be illustrated by a bar chart.

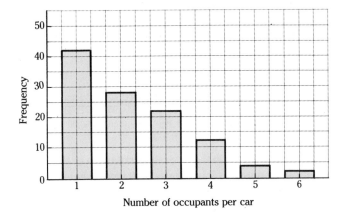

Notice that each bar covers one category, so all bars are the same width. The height of each bar gives the frequency of that category.

Lines can be used instead of bars, in which case the diagram is sometimes called a line graph. An example of a line graph is shown in Chart 1 on page 410.

GROUPING DATA

The following list of numbers gives the bill in pounds of each of the first 50 people going through the express check-out in a supermarket.

15.60	5.95	31.22	3.02	6.60	24.70	15.45	32.50	12.45	4.43
12.65	10.09	52.86	12.88	2.53	31.79	9.86	25.79	18.28	32.05
14.87	24.65	15.70	8.65	4.42	17.20	8.53	0.45	0.95	4.44
7.45	5.82	45.20	2.70	10.04	15.70	32.20	12.43	36.75	32.50
16.87	3.78	0.56	33.67	9.67	25.50	33.06	7.56	2.63	45.80

These figures range from 0.45 to 52.86 and there are 49 different values. Arranging them in order of size would not give much more clarity, but organising them into groups would give a better idea of the pattern of these bills.

We will group them as follows:

0.01–10.00,   10.01–20.00,   20.01–30.00,   30.01–40.00,   40.01–50.00,   50.01–60.00

Counting the number of bills in each group gives this frequency table.

Bill (£)	0.01–10.00	10.01–20.00	20.01–30.00	30.01–40.00	40.01–50.00	50.01–60.00
Frequency	20	14	4	9	2	1

Now we can draw this bar chart.

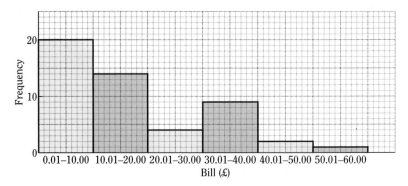

Notice that we can now see a pattern in the overall distribution of the bills, e.g. bills between £0.01 and £10 were most frequent and bills over £40 were a small proportion of the total number. We cannot tell from the bar chart what the distribution of bills is within a group however, e.g. it is not possible to judge whether more than half of the bills between £10.01 and £20 are less than £15. Therefore grouping data enables overall patterns to be seen but detail is lost.

Using Computer Databases

Computer database programs are powerful data-processing tools. Whan data is entered into a database, the program can sort the data into, say, numerical or alphabetical order. Most programs have several further functions, for example grouping the data and producing a variety of diagrams including bar charts.

Exercise 25a

1. The bar chart shows the numbers of different pets kept by households in a block of flats.

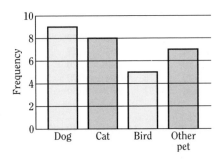

   (a) How many dogs are owned by households in the flats ?

   (b) How many birds are owned by households in the flats ?

   (c) Copy and complete the following frequency table.

Type of pet	Dog	Cat	Bird	Other pet
Frequency				

   (d) How many pets are there altogether ?

   (e) Do any of the households have two dogs ?

2. The passengers getting onto a bus during its journey were placed in one of four categories: man (M), woman (W), boy (B), girl (G). This list shows the information as it was collected.

M W W W B G W M G G G M B M G M

B G B B M M G B W W W W M M W M

(a) Make a frequency table from this information.

(b) Draw a bar chart illustrating the information.

(c) How many males were on the bus and how many females ?

(d) How many more girls than boys were there on the bus ?

(e) How many passengers are there altogether ?

3. This bar chart comes from an analysis of the sizes of shoes sold in the children's shoe department of a large store.

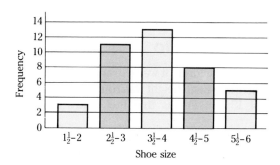

Use the bar chart to answer these questions.

(a) Which group of shoe sizes is the most common ?

(b) Which group of shoe sizes is the least common ?

(c) Can you tell from the bar chart how many people take size 5 shoes ?

(d) How many pairs of shoes are included in this distribution ?

4. The marks gained by students in an examination are given below. They have been extracted from a database and are in numerical order.

30	39	47	52	56	59	63	69	79	86
30	40	47	52	56	59	63	70	79	86
31	42	48	53	57	60	64	72	80	87
31	44	48	53	57	60	65	74	81	87
38	45	49	55	58	61	65	75	85	88
39	46	51	56	59	62	68	77	86	89
39	46	51	56	59	62	68	79	86	89

(a) What are the lowest and highest marks ?

(b) Form a frequency table using the groups 30–39, 40–49, 50–59, 60–69, 70–79 and 80–89.

(c) Draw a bar chart to illustrate this information. For the heights of the bars use 1 cm to represent one pupil.

(d) Which group contains the greatest number of students ?

(e) How many more students were in the group with the highest marks than in the group with the lowest marks ?

CONTINUOUS DATA

The number of occupants in a car is a whole number (2.5 people is not possible!).

On the other hand, a person's height is not an exact whole number of centimetres. An adult's height is likely to be between 150 cm and 200 cm and could be marked anywhere along this section of a tape measure.

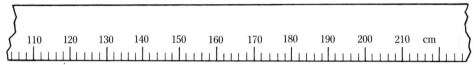

Because height can be anywhere on a continuous scale, it is not possible to have a gap in the scale and say that no person's height can be in that gap.

A collection of heights is an example of *continuous data*.

Grouping Continuous Data

This is a list of the heights of 55 children. It was extracted from a database which has sorted the heights into numerical order. Each height was rounded *up* to the next whole centimetre, so a recorded height of 131 cm means that the child's height, h cm, is in the range $130 < h \leqslant 131$

131	134	136	137	139	141	142	144	145	147	149
132	134	136	137	139	141	142	144	145	148	150
132	134	136	138	140	142	143	144	146	148	150
133	135	136	138	140	142	143	144	147	149	152
133	135	137	139	140	142	144	145	147	149	153

The heights given range from 131 cm to 153 cm.

This information needs grouping to make more sense of it, so we will use groups of width 5 cm, ending the first group at 135 cm and so on. This gives five groups which, using h cm for the actual height, can be written

$$130 < h \leqslant 135, \quad 135 < h \leqslant 140, \quad 140 < h \leqslant 145, \quad 145 < h \leqslant 150, \quad 150 < h \leqslant 155$$

Notice that all groups have the *same width*.
Notice also that a height which is more than 135 cm belongs in the second group whereas a height of 135 cm belongs in the first group.

Looking down the list of heights we see that there are 10 children whose heights are in the first group, 15 children whose heights are in the second group, and so on, and a frequency table can be produced.

Height, h cm	Frequency
$130 < h \leqslant 135$	10
$135 < h \leqslant 140$	15
$140 < h \leqslant 145$	17
$145 < h \leqslant 150$	11
$150 < h \leqslant 155$	2
Total	55

Bar Charts for Continuous Data

We can use the frequency table above to draw a bar chart.

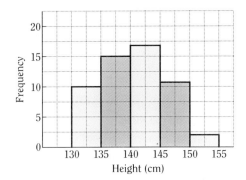

Notice that the horizontal axis gives the heights on a continuous scale, like part of a tape measure, so *there are no gaps between the bars*.

**A bar chart illustrating continuous data
has no gaps between the bars.**

Exercise 25b

1. State whether the following sets of data are discrete (i.e. can take distinct values only) or continuous.

   (a) The populations in parliamentary constituencies.

   (b) The journey times to work of employees at a factory.

   (c) The number of heads showing when four coins are tossed.

   (d) The lengths of sticks of spaghetti in a packet.

   (e) The weights of parcels sent by parcel post.

   (f) The capacities of hand-blown glass bottles.

   (g) The diameters of ball bearings produced by a machine.

   (h) Shoe sizes.

2. Emma kept a record of the time she had to wait for the bus to work each morning for four weeks. The results are shown in this frequency table.

Time, t (in minutes)	Tally	Frequency
$0 \leqslant t < 5$	卌 ||	7
$5 \leqslant t < 10$	卌 ||||	9
$10 \leqslant t < 15$	|||	3
$15 \leqslant t < 20$	|	1

   (a) On how many mornings did Emma have to wait for 15 minutes or longer ?

   (b) How often did Emma wait less than 5 minutes ?

   (c) On how many mornings did Emma record the length of her wait ?

   (d) Did Emma ever have to wait for 20 minutes ?

3. Here is a frequency table showing the times, in minutes, taken by a group of commuters to travel from home to work on a particular morning.

Time, t (in minutes)	Frequency
$0 < t \leqslant 10$	2
$10 < t \leqslant 20$	9
$20 < t \leqslant 30$	5
$30 < t \leqslant 40$	4
$40 < t \leqslant 50$	2
$50 < t \leqslant 60$	1

Copy and complete this bar chart, using the table.

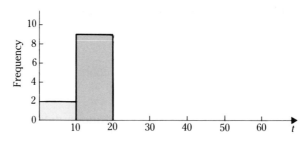

4. Use the bar chart on page 399 to answer the following questions.

   (a) How many children had a height over 145 cm ?

   (b) How many children had a height less than or equal to 140 cm ?

   (c) In which group did the heights of most children lie ?

   (d) How many children had a height of 138 cm ?

5. This is a list of the weights, each correct to the nearest kilogram, of 100 adults. The list is in numerical order.

47	50	52	54	60	63	63	64	66	66	68	69	70	70	72	78	79	80	90	104
48	51	53	55	60	63	63	64	66	67	68	69	70	71	73	78	80	82	92	110
49	51	53	58	61	63	63	65	66	67	68	70	70	71	73	78	80	83	94	112
49	51	53	58	62	63	64	65	66	68	69	70	70	72	74	79	80	85	95	115
49	52	54	59	62	63	64	65	66	68	69	70	70	72	75	79	80	88	100	118

   (a) What is the smallest recorded weight ?

   (b) If a person's weight is recorded as 60 kg, what is the range in which their actual weight, w kg, lies ?

   (c) Copy and complete this frequency table.

Weight, w kg	Frequency
$39.5 \leqslant w < 59.5$	
$59.5 \leqslant w < 79.5$	
$79.5 \leqslant w < 99.5$	
$99.5 \leqslant w < 119.5$	
Total	

   (d) How many people have a weight less than 79.5 kg ?

   (e) Explain why it is not possible to obtain from the table the number of people whose weights are greater than 100 kg.

PIE CHARTS

Bar charts are good for showing the overall pattern of the distribution of the numbers of items in each group. However to show the *proportion* that each group is of the whole, we use a diagram called a *pie chart*.

A pie chart is a circle cut into slices so that the size of each slice represents the proportion of each group to the whole.

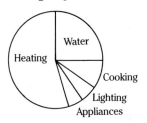

This pie chart shows what proportion of the total fuel consumption is used for different purposes in an average house.

The slice representing hot water is a quarter of the circle, so one quarter of the fuel is used to provide hot water.

Constructing Pie Charts

This frequency table summarises the number of videos out on rental, by recommended viewing classification.

Classification	U	PG	12	15	18	
Frequency	24	16	9	25	36	Total: 110

To construct a pie chart we first find the number in each category as a fraction of the total. For the U classification this is $\frac{24}{110}$ (i.e. 21.8%). Therefore this slice occupies $\frac{24}{110}$ of the circle and its angle is $\frac{24}{110}$ of 360°, i.e. 79° to the nearest degree. Doing this for the other slices gives this table.

Classification	U	PG	12	15	18
Fraction of total	$\frac{24}{110}$	$\frac{16}{110}$	$\frac{9}{110}$	$\frac{25}{110}$	$\frac{36}{110}$
Angle	79°	52°	29°	82°	118°

Note that when angles are calculated to the nearest degree the total is not always exactly 360°. Note also that tables sometimes give each category as a percentage of the total; the percentage is then used to find the angle.

We can now draw the pie chart.

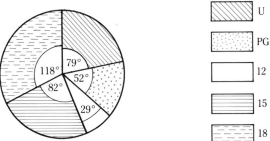

Notice that the size of each slice can be indicated either by giving the angle at the centre or, as is more usual in officially prepared pie charts, the percentage of the total that the slice represents. Also a key is needed when the slices are not labelled.

Interpreting Pie Charts

When a pie chart is marked to show the size of each slice and if the total number of items represented is also given, then the number of items represented by each slice can be found. If the size of each slice is not given, all we can do is to estimate what fraction of the total is represented by that slice.

For example, this slice represents 4.5% of an annual budget of £2 500 000 allocated to promotions.

4.5%

Therefore, 4.5% of £2 500 000 is spent on promotion,

i.e. £0.045 × 2 500 000 = £112 500

Exercise 25c

For questions 1 to 3 draw a pie chart to represent the information.

1. A box of 60 coloured balloons contains the following numbers of balloons of each colour:

Colour	Red	Yellow	Green	Blue	White
Number of balloons	16	22	10	7	5

2. Ninety people were asked how they travelled to work and the following information was recorded:

Transport	Car	Bus	Train	Motorcycle	Bicycle
Number of people	32	38	12	6	2

3. Three hundred people were asked whether they lived in a flat, a house, a bedsit, a bungalow or in some other type of accommodation and the following information was recorded:

Type of accommodation	Flat	House	Bedsit	Bungalow	Other
Frequency	90	150	33	15	12

4.

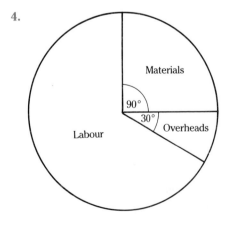

This pie chart shows the costs involved in making a television set. The total cost is £180.

(a) What fraction of the total cost is the cost of materials ?

(b) What fraction of the total cost is the cost of overheads ?

(c) What is the cost of materials ?

(d) What is the cost of overheads ?

(e) What are the labour costs ?

5. This pie chart shows the different methods of transport used by the children of Wiley School.

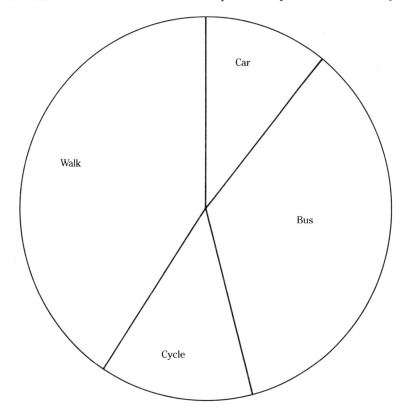

(a) Measure the angle at the centre of the circle for each sector and write each angle as a fraction of a complete revolution (e.g. $48° = \frac{48}{360}$ of a revolution).

(b) If there were 1080 children in the school how many would walk ?

(c) If there were 540 children in the school how many would arrive by bus ?

(d) If there were 630 children in the school how many would cycle ?

(e) What percentage of the children arrived by car ?

6. This pie chart shows the age distribution of the population of Green Island, in years, in 1991:

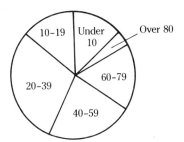

(a) Estimate the *percentage* of the population in the age groups
    (i) under 10 years   (ii) 60–79 years.

(b) State which groups are of roughly the same size.

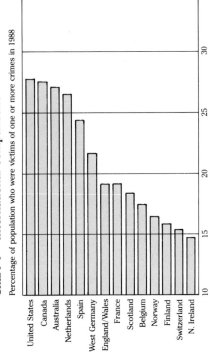

Chart 2   Victims of personal crime

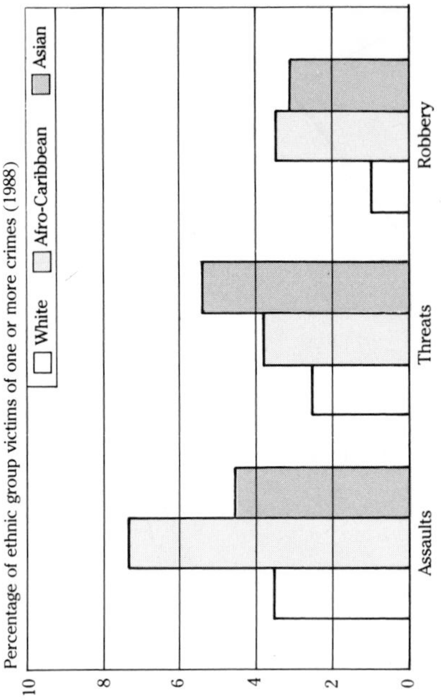

Percentage of ethnic group victims of one or more crimes (1988)

Source: The British Crime Survey 1988 (Home Office Research Study No 111)

Chart 4   International comparisons

Percentage of population who were victims of one or more crimes in 1988

Percentage of respondents

Source: Experience of crime across the world. J. Van Dijk, P. Mayhew, M. Killas (Kluwer 1990)

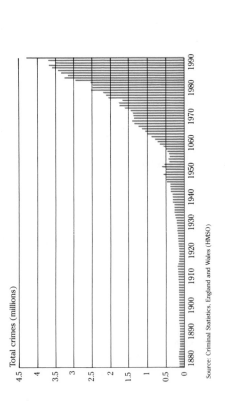

Chart 1   Crimes recorded by police (1876–1990)

Total crimes (millions)

Source: Criminal Statistics, England and Wales (HMSO)

Chart 3   Recorded and unrecorded crime

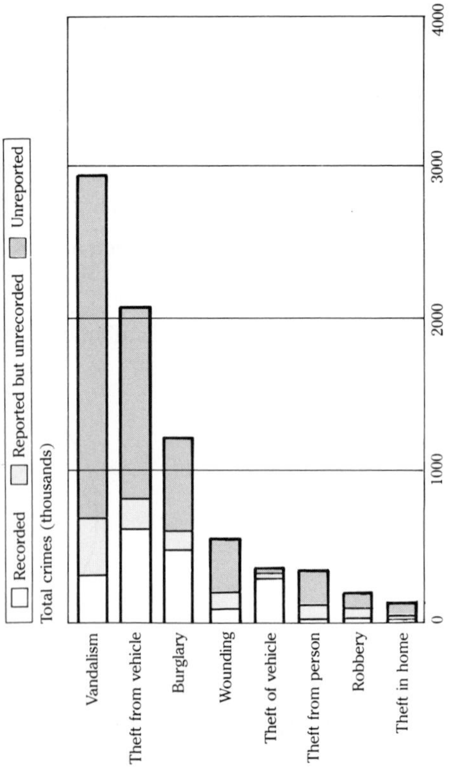

Total crimes (thousands)

Source: The British Crime Survey 1988 (Home Office Research Study No 111)

Chart 5 Risk of assault by age and gender

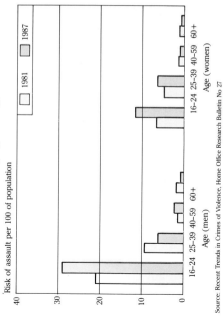

Risk of assault per 100 of population

| | 1981 | 1987 |

Age (men): 16-24 25-39 40-59 60+

Age (women): 16-24 25-39 40-59 60+

Source: Recent Trends in Crimes of Violence. Home Office Research Bulletin No 27

Chart 6 Crimes recorded by the police (1990)

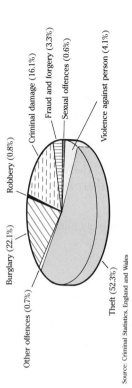

Criminal damage (16.1%)
Fraud and forgery (3.3%)
Sexual offences (0.6%)
Robbery (0.8%)
Burglary (22.1%)
Other offences (0.7%)
Violence against person (4.1%)
Theft (52.3%)

Source: Criminal Statistics, England and Wales

Chart 7 Crimes measured by British Crime Survey (1987)

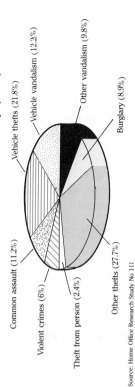

Vehicle thefts (21.8%)
Vehicle vandalism (12.2%)
Common assault (11.2%)
Other vandalism (9.8%)
Violent crimes (6%)
Theft from person (2.4%)
Burglary (8.9%)
Other thefts (27.7%)

Source: Home Office Research Study No 111

This question refers to the charts above.

7. Charts 1, 2, 3, 4 and 5 are all bar charts and they show the variety of ways in which bar charts can be drawn, e.g. horizontally (chart 4), showing two or more sets of information (charts 2, 3 and 5).

(a) Use chart 1 to find the approximate number of crimes reported to the police in 1980 and in 1990. Hence find the percentage increase in reported crimes from 1980 to 1990.

(b) Use chart 3 to find the approximate number of recorded thefts from vehicles and the number of unreported thefts from vehicles.

(c) Use chart 5 to find which age group of the population is most at risk of assault. Who is more likely to be assaulted, a twenty-year old male or a seventy-year old female ?

(d) What percentage of crimes recorded by the police in 1990 were fraud and forgery ? Combine this information with the information found in (a), to find the actual number of recorded fraud and forgery crimes in 1990.

(e) What percentage of the Asian ethnic group were victims of assault in 1988 ?

(f) Which country had the smallest percentage of the population as criminal victims in 1988 ?

(g) Which category of crime formed the smallest percentage of all crimes measured by the British Crime Survey in 1987 ?

SCATTER DIAGRAMS

Sometimes we need to investigate whether a relationship exists between two attributes. For example, is there a relationship between a person's height and shoe size, or between the cost of a book and the number of pages in it ?

In other situations it may appear that two quantities are linked by a linear relationship. A purchaser may think, for example, that the secondhand value of a particular model of a car is directly related to the mileage it has done.

To test hypotheses such as these, points can be plotted on a graph. If there is a direct relationship, the points should lie on a straight line. Because we can expect there to be slight variations in any practical situation, the points will be scattered a little. If there is not a direct relationship, the points will be very scattered.

A graph in which the plotted points do not lie *exactly* on a straight line is called a *scatter diagram*.

For example, this table lists the heights and the shoe sizes of 12 women.

Height (cm)	158	160	161	163	164	166	166	167	168	170	171	174
Shoe size (continental)	37	36	38	39	37	40	38	37	39	42	41	40

Plotting the points gives this graph.

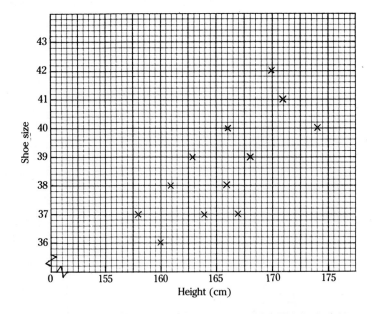

Now we can see that taller people tend to have larger feet but the relationship between height and shoe size is not strong enough to say that there is a direct (i.e. linear) relationship.

Line of Best Fit and Correlation

Looking again at the scatter graph opposite, we can see that the points are scattered loosely about a straight line, which we can draw by eye. This is called *the line of best fit*.

When drawing this line, the aim is to get the points evenly distributed about the line, so that the sum of the distances from the line to points that are above it, is roughly equal to the sum of the distances from the line to points that are below it. This may mean that none of the points lies on the line. It is sensible to use a transparent ruler.

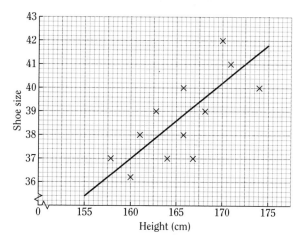

The less scatter there is about the line, the stronger is the relationship between the two quantities. We use the word *correlation* for the strength of the relationship.

In the diagram above, the line slopes upwards, i.e. shoe size tends to increase with height. We call this *positive* correlation.

The scatter graph in the worked example on the next page shows that the price of cars tends to decrease as their mileage increases.
The line of best fit slopes downwards, and we say that there is *negative* correlation.

If the points are close to the line, there is a strong correlation. In this case it is reasonable to use the line to predict the value of one quantity, given the other.

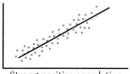
Strong positive correlation

If the points are loosely scattered about the line, there is moderate correlation. Any predictions made from the line would be rough estimates (very rough if the points were widely scattered).

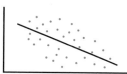
Moderate negative correlation

Sometimes the points are so scattered that there is no obvious line and we say that there is no correlation.

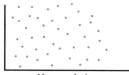
No correlation

Exercise 25d

The prices and mileages of secondhand *Sarrion* cars were checked with a number of dealers and the data obtained is shown in the table.

Price (£)	6100	3300	850	8350	5400	3400	5950
Mileage	26 500	68 900	92 000	16 800	52 600	81 700	43 400

Plot the information on graph paper and draw the best line you can to fit these points.

(a) Do you think there is a reasonable correlation between the mileage and the secondhand value of Sarrion cars ?

Use the line to estimate

(b) the price of a Sarrion that has 18 000 miles on the clock
(c) the mileage of a Sarrion that costs £3200.

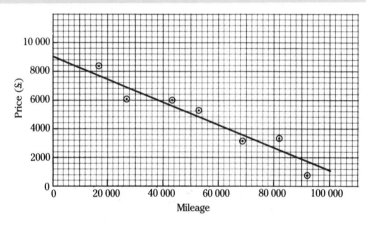

(a) The correlation is quite strong.   (b) £7600   (c) 73 000

The scatter of the points is about £ 200 above and below the line, so these estimates are subject to an error of about ±£ 200.

In each question, plot the information on a graph using the suggested scales where given. If the correlation is good enough to justify doing so, draw a line of best fit. Then answer the specific questions.

1. This table shows the number of bad oranges per box after different delivery times.

No. of bad oranges	0	2	5	4	2
No. of hours in transit	4	10	18	14	6

Use 1 cm ≡ 2 hours and 1 cm ≡ 1 orange

How many bad oranges could be expected after a 12-hour delivery ? Give an indication of the margin of error of your answer.

2. A breeder of exotic fish carried out a survey over eight years to investigate the average weight of koi carp at various ages. The data he collected are given in the table.

Age of koi (years)	1	2	3	4	5	6	7	8
Average weight (g)	90	230	495	610	1050	1090	1280	1560

Use 1 cm ≡ 1 year and 1 cm ≡ 200 g

(a) Do you think that a mistake was made in calculating one of the average weights ? If so, which weight is suspect ?

(b) What might a 9-year-old koi be expected to weigh ?

(c) If the line were extended to 20 years, could it be used to estimate the weight of a 20-year-old koi ? Give a reason for your answer.

3. This table shows the heights and weights of 12 people.

Height (cm)	150	152	155	158	158	160	163	165	170	175	178	180
Weight (kg)	56	62	63	64	57	62	65	66	65	70	66	67

Use 2 cm ≡ 5 cm for height, starting the scale at 145 cm, and 2 cm ≡ 5 kg, starting the scale at 55 kg.

(a) Comment on the correlation between the heights and weights.

(b) Carlos weighs 65 kg. What can you say about his height ?

4. This table shows the number of rooms and the number of people living in each of 15 houses.

Number of rooms	3	4	4	5	5	5	6	6	6	6	7	7	7	8	8
Number of people	3	2	5	4	2	1	6	2	3	4	4	5	3	2	6

Cheryl lives in a house with four other people. Is the house likely to have more than four rooms ?

5. Use the scatter graph on page 413 to give a likely range for the height of a woman whose shoe size is 40.

HISTOGRAMS

When a bar chart is constructed so that the *area* of each bar is proportional to the number of items in that group, it is called a histogram.

Most bar charts are histograms but some are not. Looking at the bar chart on p. 399, we see that it is a histogram because each group covers the same span (5 cm) so the bars are all the same width. Hence the area of each bar is proportional to its height. In this case, therefore, the height of each bar is proportional to the number of items in the group. Chart 4 on p. 404, however, is not a histogram because, although the bars are the same width, the percentage scale does not start at zero; so the height, and therefore the area, of a bar is not proportional to the percentage in the group.

A *frequency polygon* can be formed by plotting the middle point on the top of each bar of a histogram and joining these in order.

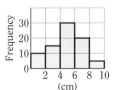
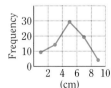

Varying Width Bars

Consider the following frequency table, which shows the results of a survey on the annual pay of part-time workers.

Pay (£)	0–1999	2000–3999	4000–5999	6000–9999	10 000–19 999
Frequency	20	36	25	14	5

The spans of the groups are not equal; the first three groups each span £ 2000, the fourth group spans £ 4000 (twice that of each of the first three) and the fifth group spans £ 10 000, which is five times that of the first three groups.

To construct a histogram we must make the *area* of each bar represent the frequency of items in the group.
We do this by making

> the width of a bar the same as the group it represents

> the height of a bar equal to $\dfrac{\text{frequency}}{\text{width of group}}$; this fraction is called the *frequency density.*

We can choose the unit that denotes the width of the bars. For this example, we could use £ 1 as the unit of width, but this would give very small values for the frequency densities. As the width of the narrowest group is £ 2000, we will choose this as our unit of width.
Adding two more rows to the table helps organise the calculations to find the frequency density for each group.

Pay (£)	0–1999	2000–3999	4000–5999	6000–9999	10 000–19 999
Frequency	20	36	25	14	5
Group width (in units of £ 2000)	1	1	1	2	5
Frequency density i.e. frequency per £ 2000 of income.	20	36	25	7	1

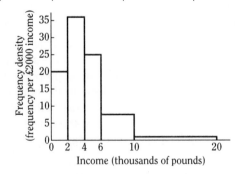

Note that the wider bars are not sub-divided by vertical lines at the intermediate scale marks.

Notice that labelling the vertical axis 'frequency density' is not enough in itself; we must also give the units involved.

Exercise 25e

1. The frequency table shows the distribution of 200 people attending a film show.

Age, n years	$0 \leqslant n < 20$	$20 \leqslant n < 30$	$30 \leqslant n < 40$	$40 \leqslant n < 50$	$50 \leqslant n < 60$	$60 \leqslant n < 100$
Frequency	20	40	50	60	10	20

A histogram is to be constructed to illustrate the data; using 1 year as the unit of width, what is the frequency density of   (a) the first group   (b) the sixth group   (c) the fifth group?

In question 2 and 3, illustrate the frequency tables by (a) a histogram (b) a frequency polygon.

2. The table gives the distribution of marks of 30 children in a test:

Mark	0–39	40–59	60–79	80–99
Frequency	8	8	10	4

3. The table shows the distribution of the times taken by 40 children to complete an obstacle race:

Time (t seconds)	$0 \leqslant t < 40$	$40 \leqslant n < 50$	$50 \leqslant n < 60$	$60 \leqslant n < 70$
Frequency	8	15	7	10

Make a frequency table from the histogram below which shows the distribution of the ages of people boarding buses at the bus station between 0830 and 0900 one morning.

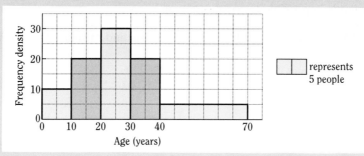

Age, n years	$0 \leqslant n < 10$	$20 \leqslant n < 20$	$20 \leqslant n < 30$	$30 \leqslant n < 40$	$40 \leqslant n < 70$
Frequency	10	20	30	20	15

Notice that the frequency is given in the form of the *area* that represents 5 people.

For questions 4 to 6 make a frequency table from the histogram.

4.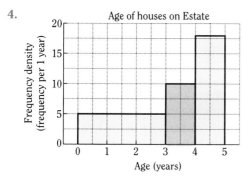

5.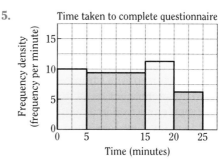

6.

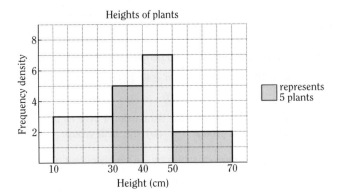

SAMPLING

There are many situations where it is impossible or impractical to gather information on all items in a survey.

For example, a light-bulb manufacturer will want information about the life of the bulbs. He cannot test them all to destruction because he would not then have any bulbs to sell! As another example, imagine trying to get information about the weights of all the wild rabbits in the country; it is impossible to weigh them all.

In situations like these, we take just some of the items and measure them, i.e. we take a *sample*.

Choosing a Sample

How the sample is chosen needs some thought because we want to be confident that the information gathered from a sample is likely to reflect the information that we would get if it were possible to use all the items. (Notice the use of the word 'likely' in the last sentence – however carefully a sample is chosen we can never be certain that it gives the same information as would all the items.)

There are two factors to consider when choosing a sample:
>   How big should it be ?
>   How should the items to be included in the sample be selected ?

Consider the size of the sample first. Commonsense would say 'as many as possible' although the light-bulb manufacturer would say 'as few as possible'. Questions in the next exercise explore the reliability of different sized samples.

The items chosen for a sample should, as far as possible, be selected to be representative of known characteristics of the total items. For example if it is known that there are twice as many men employed in a factory as women, then a sample of employees should contain twice as many men as women. If there are no known characteristics of the total, then the sample should be chosen so that any one item is as likely to be picked as any other. This is called a *random sample*.

To get a random sample from a group of non-identical items, we start by allocating a number to each item.

Suppose that we want a random sample of 5 cards from the suit of clubs from an ordinary pack of playing cards. We start by numbering the cards from 1 to 13.

The cards chosen for the sample can then be selected by any method that produces numbers at random.

One method is to use tickets 9 small pieces of paper) numbered 1 to 13. These can be folded, put in a box and thoroughly mixed; five tickets are then drawn out. The cards whose numbers correspond to those on the tickets withdrawn form the sample.

The main disadvantage of the 'raffle' technique is that it is very time consuming unless the total number of items involved is really small. Another problem is that we cannot be certain that the choice is really random; it may be influenced by subtle personal preferences such as the shape of a particular folded ticket.

USING RANDOM NUMBERS

Using a mechanical process to choose the numbers avoids any chance of human preference introducing bias.

Most scientific calculators have a function that generates random numbers. On a Casio calculator, the key is marked Ran # and produces numbers between 0 and 1, each to 3 d.p. Using this function five times gave the numbers 0.719, 0.664, 0.423, 0.618, 0.115.
As these are random numbers between 0 and 1, we can think of each of them as representing the item which is that fraction of the way through the list of 13 cards,

i.e.   0.719 represents the 0.719×13 th card on the list, and so on.

Now $0.719 \times 13 = 9.347$ and, as there is no such thing as a 9.347th card, we round up to the next integer, 10.
These calculations are always rounded up because this ensures that 1 is the lowest number that will occur and 13 is the highest.

Using the other numbers generated gives

$0.664 \times 13 = 8.632 \Rightarrow 9$
$0.423 \times 13 = 5.499 \Rightarrow 6$
$0.618 \times 13 = 8.034 \Rightarrow 9$ (this is a repeat, so we need another random number)
$0.115 \times 13 = 1.495 \Rightarrow 2$
$0.003 \times 13 = 0.039 \Rightarrow 1$

We now have 5 different numbers; 10, 9, 6, 2, 1. Therefore the cards numbered 1, 2, 6, 9, and 10 are the members of the sample.

Note that using a 3 d.p. random number generator in this way will not produce a random sample if the selection is from a list of more than 100 items,   e.g. $0.001 \times 3000 = 3$, so item 2 out of a list of 3000 has no chance of selection. (The random number generator in a computer usually produces 7 decimal places so the problem will not arise unless the list is greater than 10 million.)

The advantage of using random number generators is that they are quick and easy to operate, particularly if a computer program is used.

There is one major disadvantage; the numbers produced are not really random numbers because the sequence repeats after a given number of steps. For this reason they are sometimes called pseudorandom numbers.

Use of Random Number Tables

If the use of random number generators is not considered acceptable, or they are unavailable, published tables of random numbers can be used.

These tables consist of lists of the digits 0 to 9 in random order.

The digits are arranged in rows and columns,

e.g.

5956	0827	8682	7958	0381	3185
2608	4397	4522	6363	2032	4740
0550	9879	3274	1666	7375	6793
6743	1502	6553	2651	2757	9540
7372	3469	4466	2211	0605	5948
0556	4336	2795	2035	6840	6863 ...

There is no significance in any particular division of the digits into rows and columns; it simply makes the tables easier to read.

By choosing a starting point at random, we can read either across the rows or down the columns to get a string of random digits.

To get our five random numbers from the list of 13, we need two-figure numbers between 01 and 13. Starting at the fourth figure in the second row, and reading across in groups of two, gives

84,   39,   74,   52,   26,   36,   32,   03,   24,   74,   00,   55,   09,   87,   93, ...

Discarding duplicates and all numbers larger than 13 leaves 03, 09, ...

We have to continue nearly to the end of the second row in the lower block of numbers before finding five numbers between 1 and 13, so although this method is easy and direct, it can be a lengthy process (as this example shows); also it does not use all the numbers.

These problems can be overcome by using the first five numbers and treating them as two-figure decimals in the same way as the calculator numbers are used,

i.e. $\qquad 0.83 \times 13 = 10.92 \Rightarrow 11,$
$\qquad 0.39 \times 13 = 5.07 \Rightarrow 6, \text{ and so on.}$

Note that if random number tables are used to select more than one sample, it is important that a *different* starting point is used each time.

Exercise 25f

Explain how you would select a random sample of four bottles of wine from a rack of 123 bottles using the following random numbers.

4 3 8 8 2 3 9 6 7 3 2 9 2 0 0

First number the bottles in the rack from 001 to 123.

We cannot select four three-figure numbers in the range 001 to 123 from this set, so we will use the decimal number method. We can start anywhere in this list.

Use groups of three digits as the three decimal places of a number between 0 and 1. Multiply each by 123 and then round up to the next integer.
Starting at the beginning of the list, the sample is those bottles with the following numbers:

$$0.438 \times 123 = 53.8\ldots \Rightarrow 54$$
$$0.823 \times 123 = 101.2\ldots \Rightarrow 102$$
$$0.967 \times 123 = 118.9\ldots \Rightarrow 119$$
$$0.329 \times 123 = 40.4\ldots \Rightarrow 41$$

1. Use the list of random numbers of page (414) to select two numbers

   (a) between 1 and 50, starting with the second digit in the first row

   (b) between 1 and 670, starting with the fourth digit in the first row

   (c) between 1 and 2500, starting with the third digit in the first row.

2. There are 450 students enrolled at colleges of further education in Wessex for a one-year evening course in keyboard skills. Describe how you would select 10% of these students to make a random sample.

3. The response to a competition resulted in 76 correct entries but there were only 10 prizes. The correct entries were numbered 01 to 76 and the 10 prize winning entries were selected by taking two-digit random numbers from a random number table and, if the number was greater than 76, subtracting 76 and using the resulting number. Explain why this method does not give each entry an equal chance of being selected.

4. This diagram shows twenty rods of varying lengths.

   (a) Choose a sample of three rods which you think are representative of the twenty rods. Measure and write down their lengths. Find the mean length of the rods in your sample. (Reminder: the mean length is the sum of the individual lengths divided by the number of rods.)

   (b) Repeat part (a) 4 times. (It does not matter if a rod is included in more than one sample.)

   (c) Number the rods 01 to 20 and then repeat (a) and (b) but this time use random numbers (from a table or calculator) to select the samples.

   (d) Compare the sample means obtained from the random samples with those of the samples that you selected.

   (e) Measure all the rods and find the mean length of the twenty rods. Which method of selecting samples do you consider to be better? Justify your answer.

STRATIFIED SAMPLING

One of the disadvantages of random sampling is that it may not be representative. Suppose, for example, that there are 200 girls and 50 boys who are members of a junior tennis club. A random sample of these members will not necessarily contain numbers of girls and boys in the same proportion. This does not matter if the gender of a member has no effect on the problem being investigated, e.g. eye colour. If the problem has any relationship to gender, e.g. height, a sample that contains girls and boys in the same proportion as the members of the club is more likely to reflect this aspect of the members.

We now define exactly what is meant by a representative sample.

    A representative sample has numbers of each distinct group in the same proportion as their numbers in the complete set.

A stratified sample produces a representative sample by first dividing the set into groups. Then random numbers are used to select members from each group in numbers proportional to their occurrence in the whole set.

To produce a stratified sample of 25 from our 200 girls and 50 boys, we need first to find the number of girls and the number of boys required for the sample.

The sample size as a fraction of the total group is $\frac{25}{250}$, i.e. $\frac{1}{10}$

so we need $\frac{1}{10}$ of the 200 girls, i.e. 20 girls

and $\frac{1}{10}$ of the 50 boys, i.e.   5 boys

We then use random numbers to select this number of girls and boys from the respective lists.

There are many ways of dividing a set into groups and which particular groups are chosen will depend on the nature of the investigation. For the members of the junior tennis club, division into age groups might be appropriate for investigating attitudes towards pocket money, while division into groups according to height might be appropriate for an investigation into provision of club strip.

The advantage of stratified sampling is that it ensures proper representation of each group and still keeps an equal chance of selection for each member of the population. The disadvantage is that division of a population into groups is not always easy or clearcut. For example, if the population is all people living in Greater London, the proportion of this population who are under the age of 20 can only be, at best, an informed guess. If the members of the tennis club are divided into good and average players, human judgement is needed to place an individual in one group. Situations like these can introduce bias into the sample.

Exercise 25g

A consignment of 3560 bottles of water is delivered to a restaurant. The number of bottles of each type of water is given in the table.

Category	Still	Carbonated	Lemon-flavoured	Lime-flavoured
Number	1280	1980	55	245

How many bottles of each type of water should be selected to give a representative sample that is 5% of the consignment?

For a 5% sample, we need 5% of the bottles of each type.

5% of 1280 = 64
5% of 1980 = 99
5% of 55 = 2.75 = 3 to the nearest whole number
5% of 245 = 12.25 = 12 to the nearest whole number

Rounding each calculation to the nearest whole number gives a total of 178 bottles for the sample. We need to check that this is 5% of the total number of bottles delivered.

The number delivered = 3560, and $\frac{178}{3560} = 0.05$
$= 5\%$ of the number delivered.

Sometimes the rounding process does not give the correct total. If this happens, and the total is too small, the largest decimal part that would normally be rounded down is rounded up instead, and so on until the correct total is reached. If the total is too large then the opposite procedure is adopted.

We need 64 bottles of still water, 99 bottles of carbonated water, 3 bottles of lemon-flavoured water and 12 bottles of lime-flavoured water.

1. The table shows the number of students enrolled in each department of a college.

Department	Catering	Academic	Engineering	Sport	Technology
Number of students	590	280	770	60	520

How many students should be chosen from each department to get a 10% representative sample?

2. There are 180 pupils on the register at Lower Hill Primary School. The table shows the number of pupils in each year.

Year	1	2	3	4	5	6
Number	34	33	29	28	35	21

How many students need to be selected from each year to give

(a) a 10% representative sample

(b) a representative sample of 30 pupils?

3. A farmer grew the same variety of potatoes in four different fields. The table shows the yield, in tonnes, from each of these fields.

Field	A	B	C	D
Yield (tonnes)	250	220	140	90

(a) What weight should be selected from each field to give a representative sample of one tonne?

(b) The purpose of the sample is to try to quantify the number of damaged potatoes in the whole crop. What other method of sampling could be used? Give reasons for your choice.

4. For some coursework, Gary decides to investigate the attitudes to wearing school uniform in his school. He decides to choose a sample. How should he choose his sample so that his results are reasonably reliable? Give as many reasons for your choice as possible.

Questions 5 and 6 refer to this problem.

A university education department wants some information about pupils in the first year of secondary schools. It is decided to gather the information from 10 per cent of the pupils. Here are some ways in which those pupils can be selected. There are no definitive answers to the questions that follow; they invite you to consider some of the reasons why the sample may not be representative.

5. A list of all secondary schools in the country can be obtained and the pupils in the first tenth of these schools selected.

(a) If the list is in alphabetical order, are pupils in religous schools likely to be fairly represented? (Think carefully about the names of religous schools.) What other factors about this method of selection are likely to make the sample unrepresentative?

(b) If the list is in order of education authority, is the choice of schools from just a few geographical areas likely to be representative?

(c) Does this method of selecting a sample take account of independent schools?

(d) How do the differing arrangements for the age at which children change school affect this method of selection?

6. The list of schools could be sorted into categories such as single-sex, church schools, etc. One tenth of the schools in each category could then be selected. (This is called a stratified sample.)

(a) This method of selection is likely to give a more representative sample than the first method, but what can be done about a school in more than one category?

(b) What other drawbacks can you think of?

(c) Another method of selection that overcomes the difficulty of categorising schools is to select one tenth of the pupils from every secondary school in the country. Can you suggest ways in which one tenth of the pupils in the first year of a school can be easily chosen so that any one pupil is as likely as any other to be selected?

7. This question investigates the reliability of sample size. You will need about an hour of spare time and an ordinary pack of playing cards. If you are using this book in a class, you will find it helpful to work in a group of 3 or 4.

(a) If four cards are chosen at random, how many hearts should there be for these four cards to be representative of the proportion of hearts in the full pack?

(b) Shuffle a full pack of playing cards thoroughly and then deal out the top four cards. This is a sample of size four. Write down the number of hearts.

(c) Replace the cards dealt for the first sample and then repeat (b).

(d) Repeat the process several more times. (You will need at least 30 samples.) Keep track of your results in a table like this one:

Sample no.	1	2	3	4	5	...
No. of hearts						

(e) Use your table to copy and complete this frequency table.

No. of hearts	0	1	2	3	4
Frequency					

(f) From your frequency table, find the relative frequency (i.e. frequency over total number of samples) of samples that do represent the proportion of hearts in the whole pack. Hence give an estimate of the probability that a sample of size four represents the proportion of hearts in the pack.

(g) Now repeat parts (b) to (e) using a sample of 20 cards.

(h) A sample of 20 cards should contain 5 hearts to represent exactly the proportion of hearts in the complete pack. If we allow 4, 5 or 6 hearts in a sample as 'good enough' to be representative, find the relative frequency of such samples. Hence estimate the probability that a sample of size 20 gives a representative proportion of hearts in the pack.

Investigations

1. In this investigation you are invited to criticise a questionnaire and to consider the design of some questions.

A student designed this questionnaire to gather evidence for a project on the acceptability of school uniform to the pupils in a school.

1. Name (as it appears in the register) _____

2. Age _____

3. Sex _____

4. Religion (please tick the correct box)

           Christian ☐   Muslim ☐   Jewish ☐   Other ☐

5. School uniform should be worn by every pupil in the school.
Tick the box which most closely matches your opinion.

           Agree ☐   Neither agree nor disagree ☐   Disagree ☐

(a) One problem associated with requests for personal information is a reluctance to tell the truth. Are any of the above questions likely to generate untruthful answers ? Can you re-word them so that a truthful answer is more likely ?

(b) What problems do you think question 4 will pose ?

(c) Why do you think question 4 is there ?

(d) Do you think that a different result would come from this survey if question 5 was worded 'School uniform should be abolished' ?

(e) Do you think that there should be more categories from which to choose a response to question 5, e.g. Agree/Disagree strongly ?

(f) Why do you think that questions 2 and 3 are included ?

(g) Design a questionnaire to find peoples' views on whether uniform should be worn by bank counter staff. Remember that it is rarely possible to foresee all the problems, so any questionnaire that you design should be tried out on a few people and then adapted if necessary.

(h) Find a questionnaire (either one you have had to fill in or one from a magazine) and criticise it for suitability of questions and purpose.

2. If you are interested and have the time to follow through the ideas in this investigation, you will gain some insight into the problems involved in sampling. Your answers should be supported with reasons. Find some books on the subject to help research your ideas.

   A company that distributes fresh fruit, imports 50 000 peaches. They need to have some idea of their quality, particularly how many are likely to be damaged or bad. Suppose that they are prepared to accept a consignment if they think that not more than 5 per cent of the peaches are damaged. There are various ways in which they can come to a decision.

   (a) They could make sure that every peach is inspected. The obvious advantage of doing this is that they would be certain about the proportion of bad peaches. What are the disadvantages ? List as many as you can think of.

   (b) They could inspect a sample of, say, 50 peaches. Suppose that this sample contained 8 damaged peaches, and on this evidence they decided to accept the whole consignment. Is it possible that their decision resulted in accepting a consignment in which considerably more than 5 per cent were damaged ? On the other hand suppose that the sample had 20 damaged peaches; assuming that they rejected the consignment on this evidence, could they have rejected a 'good' consignment ?

   (c) Based on the evidence from a sample, is there likely to be any cost involved in either accepting a 'bad' consignment or rejecting a 'good' consignment ?

   (d) If consignments are delivered every day for four months, can you give an intuitive idea of the proportion of consignments that are incorrectly accepted or rejected on the evidence from a sample of about 50 peaches ?

   (By intuitive, we mean an intelligent guess based on experience – it is not intended that you should try to understand the theory involved.)

Self-Assessment 25

1. A list of the number of heads obtained when five coins were tossed repeatedly is given below.

   0 3 1 0 3 2 4 2 4 2 5 0 1 3 2 5 4 3 2 2 3 3 3 2 2 4 1 1 3 2 5 3 2 4 3 1 3 2 2 0

   Form a frequency table and then draw a bar chart to illustrate this information.

2. Here is a list showing the times, in seconds, taken by a group of people to calculate 125×36 in their heads. The list has been sorted into numerical order.

   7 9 10 15 23 24 24 27 29 30 30 31 32 33 34 35 35 36 39 42 45 46 47 47 49 50 50 55 56 58 59 60 60 61 62 68 70 72 79 80 88 90 95 110 125 159

   Use groups $0 \leqslant t < 20$, $20 \leqslant t < 40$, $40 \leqslant t < 60$, $60 \leqslant t < 80$, $80 \leqslant t < 100$, and $100 \leqslant t < 160$ to make a frequency table.
   Illustrate this information by drawing   (a) a histogram   (b) a frequency polygon.

3. Use the data in question 1 to draw a pie chart showing the percentage of tosses that resulted in 0, 1, 2, 3, 4, or 5 heads.

4. The table shows the score obtained on a verbal reasoning test (VR) and on a pattern recognition test (PR) by twelve different people.

VR score	15	12	20	17	10	13	18	12	18	5	9	14
PR score	6	2	8	5	2	6	8	7	9	4	8	9

(a) Draw a scatter graph to illustrate this information and use it to comment on the degree of correlation between the two scores.

(b) Draw a line of best fit.

(c) If Clarrie got a score of 19 on the verbal reasoning test, what can you say about her likely score on the pattern recognition test ?

5. A manufacturer has 3 machines that produce the same component. Machine A produces 3860 components each day, Machine B produces 2040 components each day and Machine C produces 4820 components each day.

(a) A sample of 5% of the day's production is examined for quality. How many components is this ?

(b) How many components from each machine should be examined to give a stratified sample?

(c) Why is a stratified sample necessary?

QUADRATIC EQUATIONS

THE EFFECT OF MULTIPLYING BY ZERO

If any number is multiplied by zero, the result is zero, e.g. $6 \times 0 = 0$, and in fact, whatever number x represents, $x \times 0 = 0$

Further, the only way in which we can get zero when we multiply two numbers is if at least one of the numbers is zero.

Therefore if $\quad a \times b = 0$

then $\quad$ either $a = 0$ and/or $b = 0$

Hence, given that $p(q-3) = 0$

then we know that either $p = 0$ and/or $q - 3 = 0$, i.e. $q = 3$

QUADRATIC EQUATIONS

When a quadratic expression has a value, we have a quadratic equation.
For example, $x^2 = 4$, $2x^2 - 5x + 6 = 2$ and $x^2 - 3x + 2 = 0$ are quadratic equations.

Solution by Factorisation

Consider the equation $x^2 - 3x + 2 = 0$

If the left-hand side can be expressed as the product of two factors, we have the situation where the product of two numbers is zero. We can then argue that one or the other of these factors is zero;

i.e. $\qquad$ if $\qquad x^2 - 3x + 2 = 0$

then factorising gives $\quad (x-1)(x-2) = 0$

Therefore, $\quad$ either $x - 1 = 0$ or $x - 2 = 0$

i.e. $\qquad$ either $\quad x = 1$ or $\qquad x = 2$

The values of x that satisfy an equation are called the *roots* of the equation, e.g. 1 and 2 are the roots of the equation above.

Any quadratic equation can be rearranged so that it is in the form $ax^2 + bx + c = 0$

If the left-hand side can be factorised, then the equation can be solved since one or other of these factors must be zero.

Notice that, in general, a quadratic equation has two roots.

Sometimes, the left-hand side has two identical factors,

e.g. $4x^2 + 12x + 9 = 0$ gives $(2x+3)^2 = 0$

In this case there are two equal roots and we say that the equation has a *repeated root*.

Many problems give rise to quadratic equations.
For example, a flat piece of card measuring 10 cm by 8 cm has a square cut from each corner and the sides are folded up to make an open box with a base of area 24 cm^2.

The length of the side of the squares is not given. To find it we take x cm as that length.

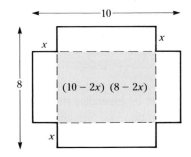 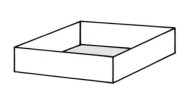

From the diagram we see that the area, A cm^2, of the base is given by

$$A = 80 - 36x + 4x^2$$

As the area of the base is 24 cm^2, $A = 24$.

This gives the quadratic equation $24 = 80 - 36x + 4x^2$

Rearranging in standard order gives $4x^2 - 36x + 56 = 0$

Factorising gives $4(x^2 - 9x + 14) = 0$

$\Rightarrow$ $4(x-7)(x-2) = 0$

Now 4 is not zero, so either $x - 7 = 0$ or $x - 2 = 0$

Therefore the roots of the equation are $x = 7$ and $x = 2$

Not all the roots of an equation always give reasonable solutions to a problem so they need checking.

From the diagram it is clear that squares of side 7 cm cannot be removed from the four corners, but squares of side 2 cm can.
Therefore the cut-out squares have sides of length 2 cm.

Exercise 26a

1. Find the values of x for which
   (a) $(x-1)(x-3) = 0$
   (b) $x(x-2) = 0$
   (c) $(2x-1)(x-4) = 0$
   (d) $(x-3)(x+1) = 0$
   (e) $3x(x-7) = 0$
   (f) $(3x-2)(x+2) = 0$
   (g) $(x+3)(x+5) = 0$
   (h) $x(3x+4) = 0$
   (i) $(2x-3)(2x+3) = 0$

2. Solve the equations
   (a) $x^2 - 5x + 4 = 0$
   (b) $x^2 - 7x + 10 = 0$
   (c) $x^2 + 3x + 2 = 0$
   (d) $x^2 + 7x + 12 = 0$
   (e) $x^2 + 6x - 7 = 0$
   (f) $x^2 + x - 6 = 0$
   (g) $x^2 - 5x - 24 = 0$
   (h) $x^2 - 3x = 0$
   (i) $x^2 - 9 = 0$

3. Find the values of x for which
   (a) $2x^2 + 17x + 8 = 0$
   (b) $3x^2 - 11x + 6 = 0$
   (c) $6x^2 - x - 2 = 0$
   (d) $2x^2 + 5x - 12 = 0$
   (e) $5x^2 + 27x + 10 = 0$
   (f) $6x^2 - 11x - 2 = 0$

4. Solve the equations
   (a) $2x^2 - 10x + 12 = 0$
   (b) $3x^2 - 9x = 0$
   (c) $12x^2 + 20x + 8 = 0$
   (d) $5x^2 - 15x + 10 = 0$
   (e) $8x^2 + 20x - 12 = 0$
   (f) $8x^2 - 4x = 0$

Solve the equation $(4x - 5)(x - 2) = 1$

Note that this equation does not end with $= 0$, so we start by expanding the brackets and then collecting all terms on the LHS in standard order.

$$(4x - 5)(x - 2) = 1$$
$$4x^2 - 13x + 10 = 1$$
$$4x^2 - 13x + 9 = 0$$
$$(4x - 9)(x - 1) = 0$$

Therefore either $4x - 9 = 0$ or $x - 1 = 0$, i.e. $x = \frac{9}{4}$ or $x = 1$

---

5. Find the values of x for which
   (a) $x^2 - x = 30$
   (b) $25 = 4x(5 - x)$
   (c) $10 = 7x - x^2$
   (d) $9 = 6x - x^2$
   (e) $x(x + 1) = 12$
   (f) $(x - 5)(x + 2) = 18$

6. Solve the equations
   (a) $x^2 - x - 20 = 0$
   (b) $x^2 = 4x - 4$
   (c) $9x^2 - 1 = 0$
   (d) $3x^2 - 12x = 0$
   (e) $3 - 12x^2 = 0$
   (f) $4 + 11x + 6x^2 = 0$
   (g) $5x + 2 = 3x^2$
   (h) $4x^2 = 25$
   (i) $x(x - 1) = x + 3$

7. Peter is 4 years older than his brother Adam.
   (a) If Adam is x years old, write down Peter's age as an expression containing x.
   (b) If the product of Adam's age and Peter's age is 140, use (a) to form an equation involving x and then solve it.
   (c) How old is Peter ?

8. The width of a rectangle is 3 cm less than its length.
   (a) If the rectangle is x cm wide, write down its length as an expression involving x.
   (b) Write down an expression in terms of x for the area of the rectangle.
   (c) Given that the area of the rectangle is 54 cm^2, write down an equation in x and then solve it.
   (d) How long is the rectangle ?

Solving a Quadratic Equation by Completing the Square

Not all quadratic expressions factorise so we cannot expect to solve all quadratic equations by factorisation.

Consider the equation $x^2 + 6x - 1 = 0$

Now $x^2 + 6x - 1$ does not factorise.

If we rewrite the equation as $x^2 + 6x = 1$ then, by adding 9 to both sides of the equation, it becomes

$$x^2 + 6x + 9 = 10$$

The left-hand side is now the expansion of $(x+3)^2$, i.e. the equation can be written $(x+3)^2 = 10$ and can then be solved by taking the square root on each side.

i.e. $\qquad (x+3) = \pm\sqrt{10}$

giving $\qquad x = -3 \pm \sqrt{10}$

Note that the number we added, i.e. 9, is given by $(\frac{1}{2} \text{ of } 6)^2$,

i.e. $\qquad \frac{1}{2}(\text{coefficient of } x)^2$, and this is true for all such cases.

So to solve the equation $x^2 + 2px = q^2$ we add p^2 to both sides giving

$$x^2 + 2px + p^2 = q^2 + p^2$$

This process is called *completing the square*.

Exercise 26b

Solve the equations, giving answers correct to 3 s.f. where necessary.

1. (a) Show that $x^2 - 6x - 4$ can be written in the form $(x - a)^2 = b$.
   Give the values of a and b.
   (b) Hence solve the equation $x^2 - 6x - 4 = 0$.

2. (a) $(x + 2)^2 = 9$ (c) $(x - 3)^2 = 6$
   (b) $(2x + 1)^2 = 4$ (d) $(x + 1.5)^2 = 8$

3. (a) $x^2 + 4x = 5$ (c) $x^2 + 8x + 3 = 0$
   (b) $x^2 - 6x = 7$ (d) $x^2 - 4x + 1 = 0$

4. Try to solve the equation $x^2 - 2x + 2 = 0$. Explain why it is not possible and deduce what you can about the values of x for which $x^2 - 2x + 2 = 0$.

SOLVING A QUADRATIC EQUATION BY FORMULA

If we solve the general quadratic equation $ax^2 + bx + c = 0$ by completing the square, we get

$$x = \frac{-b \pm \sqrt{b^2 - 4ac}}{2a}$$

This is called the *formula* for solving quadratic equations. It gives the solutions of the equation for any given values of a, b and c.

Notice that the equation *must* be arranged in standard order before using the formula.

Notice also that if $b^2 - 4ac$ is negative, it does not have a real square root. In this case the equation has no real solutions.

There are many calculators available that will solve a quadratic equation when the values of a, b and c are entered. If you have one, it is well worth learning how to use it (consult the manual).

Checking Solutions to a Quadratic Equation

Whichever method is used to solve a quadratic equation, it is sensible to check the solution.

The formula gives the two values of x as

$$\frac{-b}{2a} + \frac{\sqrt{b^2 - 4ac}}{2a} \quad \text{and} \quad \frac{-b}{2a} - \frac{\sqrt{b^2 - 4ac}}{2a}$$

so the sum of the two roots is $\left(\dfrac{-b}{2a}\right) + \left(\dfrac{-b}{2a}\right) = -\dfrac{b}{a}$

i.e.

the sum of the calculated roots should be equal to $-\dfrac{b}{a}$

Suppose for example that $x^2 - x + 6 = 0$ is solved by factorising incorrectly as $(x + 3)(x - 2) = 0$ to give the roots -3 and 2.

The sum of these roots is $-3 + 2 = -1$ and $-\dfrac{b}{a} = -\dfrac{(-1)}{1} = 1$ which is not equal to the sum of the calculated roots.

This shows that a mistake has been made.

Exercise 26c

Solve the equation $x^2 - 7x - 3 = 0$ giving solutions correct to 2 decimal places.

$$x^2 - 7x - 3 = 0$$

$$a = 1, b = -7, c = -3$$

$$x = \frac{-b \pm \sqrt{b^2 - 4ac}}{2a}$$

$$x = \frac{-(-7) \pm \sqrt{(-7)^2 - 4(1)(-3)}}{2(1)}$$

$$= \frac{7 \pm \sqrt{49 + 12}}{2} = \frac{7 \pm \sqrt{61}}{2} = \frac{7 \pm 7.8102}{2}$$

$$\therefore x = \frac{7 + 7.810}{2} \quad \text{or} \quad \frac{7 - 7.810}{2} = 7.405 \text{ or } -0.405$$

$$= 7.41 \text{ or } 0.41 \quad (2 \text{ d.p.})$$

Check: Sum of roots is $7.41 + (-0.41) = 7$ and $-\dfrac{b}{a} = -\dfrac{(-7)}{1} = 7$

1. Use the formula to solve the following equations, giving answers correct to 2 decimal places.
   (a) $x^2 + 6x + 3 = 0$
   (b) $x^2 + 4x - 3 = 0$
   (c) $x^2 - 6x + 6 = 0$
   (d) $x^2 + 9x + 12 = 0$
   (e) $x^2 + 3x - 5 = 0$
   (f) $x^2 + 7x - 2 = 0$
   (g) $x^2 + 7x + 2 = 0$
   (h) $x^2 - 4x - 9 = 0$

2. Use the formula to solve the following equations, giving answers correct to 3 significant figures.
   (a) $x^2 - 4x + 2 = 0$
   (b) $x^2 - 5x - 5 = 0$
   (c) $2x^2 + 7x + 2 = 0$
   (d) $3x^2 + 7x + 3 = 0$
   (e) $5x^2 + 9x + 2 = 0$
   (f) $2x^2 - 7x + 4 = 0$
   (g) $4x^2 - 7x + 1 = 0$
   (h) $3x^2 + 5x - 3 = 0$

3. Solve these equations, giving answers correct to 2 decimal places. Remember that the equations must be arranged in standard order before using the formula.
   (a) $3x^2 + 2 = 9x$ (d) $3x^2 + 4x = 1$
   (b) $6x^2 - 9x = 4$ (e) $4x^2 = 4x + 1$
   (c) $2x^2 = 5x + 5$ (f) $3x = 1 - 2x^2$

4. Solve these equations by factorising if possible. If factors cannot be found easily then use the formula. Where necessary give solutions correct to 2 decimal places. Some of these equations do not have real solutions; in this case say so.
   (a) $2x^2 + 3x - 2 = 0$
   (b) $3x^2 + 6x + 2 = 0$
   (c) $6x^2 + 7x + 2 = 0$
   (d) $2x^2 + 3x + 3 = 0$
   (e) $3x^2 - 8x + 2 = 0$
   (f) $3x^2 - 8x - 3 = 0$
   (g) $3x^2 - 14x + 15 = 0$
   (h) $5x^2 - 3x + 1 = 0$
   (i) $2x^2 + 9x = 5$
   (j) $x^2 - 9x - 2 = 0$

HARDER EQUATIONS AND PROBLEMS

Some equations involving fractions reduce to quadratic equations when they are simplified.

Consider, for example, the equation $\dfrac{2}{1-x} - \dfrac{4}{x} = 3$

Multiplying both sides by $(1-x)$ and by x gives

$$\frac{2}{1-x} \times x(1-x) - \frac{4}{x} \times x(1-x) = 3 \times x(1-x)$$

i.e. $2(x) - 4(1-x) = 3(x)(1-x)$

Expanding the brackets gives $2x - 4 + 4x = 3x - 3x^2$

Collecting all terms on the left-hand side gives $3x^2 + 3x - 4 = 0$

This is now a quadratic equation in standard order and any method of solution can be tried.

Problem Solving

Problems can often be expressed in terms of a quadratic equation and hence solved. It is important, however, to realise that the solutions of an equation may not all give reasonable answers to the problem, so this must be checked.

Many people, though, would be delighted to get to the point where solutions need checking. It is often getting started that is difficult, so here are some hints on problem solving.

1. Make sure that you understand the problem, i.e. that you know what all the words mean and that you know what has to be found.
   - Identify the information that is given in the problem; if the problem is about an object, draw a diagram and put all the information that you can on the diagram.
   - Decide what is unknown and use letters to identify unknown quantities. If you have a diagram, put the letters on it.
   - If there is more than one unknown, are there any conditions linking them ? If there are, write them down. (This will often help to reduce the number of unknowns.)

2. Look for relationships between the unknowns and the given information. To help find such relationships, try going through the following sequence.
   - Can you use your experience of solving a similar problem ?
   - Can you think of a related, but simpler problem, having the same kind of unknown, that you can solve ? You may then be able to work up from there.
   - Are there any other facts that may be useful ?
   - Try replacing given information/unknowns with simple numbers and see if this helps you to spot a method.

Exercise 26d

(a) Rewrite the equation $\dfrac{8}{x-1} - 2 = \dfrac{15}{x+2}$

in the form $ax^2 + bx + c = 0$.

(b) Hence solve the original equation without using a calculator.

(a) $\dfrac{8}{x-1} - 2 = \dfrac{15}{x+2}$

Multiply *every* term by $(x-1)$ and by $(x+2)$

$$\dfrac{8}{x-1} \times (x-1)(x+2) - 2 \times (x-1)(x+2) = \dfrac{15}{x+2} \times (x-1)(x+2)$$

$$8(x+2) - 2(x^2 + x - 2) = 15(x-1)$$
$$8x + 16 - 2x^2 - 2x + 4 = 15x - 15$$
$$-2x^2 + 6x + 20 = 15x - 15$$
$$0 = 2x^2 + 9x - 35$$

i.e. $2x^2 + 9x - 35 = 0$

(b) Factorising $2x^2 + 9x - 35 = 0$

gives $(2x - 5)(x + 7) = 0$

Then, either $2x - 5 = 0$ or $x + 7 = 0$

i.e. $x = 2\tfrac{1}{2}$ or $x = -7$

---

1. Without using a calculator, solve the equations

(a) $x - \dfrac{4}{x} = 3$

(b) $x + \dfrac{10}{x} + 7 = 0$

(c) $x + 2 = \dfrac{15}{x}$

(d) $\dfrac{2}{x-1} + \dfrac{2}{x+2} = 1$

(e) $\dfrac{4}{x} + \dfrac{5}{x+2} = 1$

(f) $\dfrac{6}{x} + \dfrac{3}{x+1} = 4$

(g) $\dfrac{8}{x+2} + \dfrac{7}{2x-1} = 3$

(h) $\dfrac{1}{x-3} - \dfrac{1}{x-1} = \dfrac{1}{4}$

(i) $\dfrac{3}{x-1} + \dfrac{2x}{x-2} = 0$

2. Solve the equations, giving answers correct to 2 decimal places.

(a) $x + \dfrac{2}{x} = 11$

(b) $x - \dfrac{5}{x} = 3$

(c) $x + \dfrac{2}{x} = 7$

(d) $\dfrac{3}{x+2} - \dfrac{1}{x+4} = 2$

(e) $\dfrac{2}{x+5} + \dfrac{3}{x-2} = 4$

(f) $\dfrac{2}{x} = 4 - \dfrac{1}{x+1}$

(g) $x + \dfrac{3}{x} = 9$

(h) $\dfrac{4}{x+1} - \dfrac{3}{x+2} = 2$

(i) $\dfrac{3}{x+1} = 5 - \dfrac{2}{x+2}$

In a right-angled triangle, one side is 3 cm shorter than the hypotenuse and the other side is 5 cm shorter than the hypotenuse. Find the lengths of the three sides of the triangle.

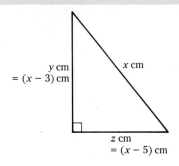

The lengths of all three sides are unknown, so we will let them be x cm, y cm and z cm, as shown. We are told that y is 3 less than x, i.e. $y = x - 3$, and that z is 5 less than x, so $z = x - 5$

Using Pythagoras' theorem, $x^2 = (x-3)^2 + (x-5)^2$

$$x^2 = x^2 - 6x + 9 + x^2 - 10x + 25$$

$$0 = x^2 - 16x + 34$$

Using the formula with $a = 1$, $b = -16$, $c = 34$ gives

$$x = \frac{-(-16) \pm \sqrt{(-16)^2 - 4(1)(34)}}{2}$$

$$= \frac{16 \pm \sqrt{120}}{2}$$

$$= \frac{16 \pm 10.954}{2}$$

$\therefore x = 13.48$ or 2.52   (2 d.p.)

If $x = 13.48$, then $y = 13.48 - 3 = 10.48$ and $z = 13.48 - 5 = 8.48$

If $x = 2.52$ then both y and z are negative. A length cannot be negative, so $x = 2.52$ does not give a solution to this problem,

i.e. the lengths of the sides are 13.5 cm, 10.5 cm and 8.5 cm, correct to 1 d.p.

3. The area of a rectangle is 45 cm^2 and one of its sides is 4 cm longer than the other side. Find the width of the rectangle.

4. The area of a rectangle is 40 cm^2 and its perimeter is 26 cm. Find the lengths of its sides.

5. In a right-angled triangle, one side is 2 cm shorter than the hypotenuse and the other side is 3 cm shorter than the hypotenuse. Find the length of the hypotenuse.

6. The area of a triangle is 40 cm^2 and its base is 8 cm longer than its perpendicular height. Find the length of the base.

If the price of apples increases by 10 p per kilogram, £ 3 buys 1 kilogram less. What is the price per kilogram of apples at present ?

What has to be found is the price of apples per kg before the increase.

Also unknown is
  the number of kg that can be bought for £ 3 at this price
  the number of kg that can be bought for £ 3 at the increased price.

Let the price per kg before the increase be x pence
then the price per kg after the increase is $(x + 10)$ pence.

If y kg can be bought for £ 3 at x pence per kg, then $y = \dfrac{300}{x}$

If z kg can be bought for £ 3 at $(x + 10)$ pence per kg, then $z = \dfrac{300}{x + 10}$

We know, from the problem, that 1 kg is the difference between the quantities that can be bought at the two prices, i.e. $y - z = 1$

$$\therefore \qquad \frac{300}{x} - \frac{300}{x + 10} = 1$$

Multiply each of the three terms by x and $x + 10$

$$300(x + 10) - 300x = x(x + 10)$$
$$300x + 3000 - 300x = x^2 + 10x$$
$$x^2 + 10x - 3000 = 0$$
$$(x + 60)(x - 50) = 0$$

$\therefore x = 50$ or -60

The price of apples is not negative, so $x = 50$ is the only solution that satisfies the problem.

The price of apples before the increase is 50 pence per kg.

---

7. David's father is two years older than his mother and his mother's age is the square of his own age. The sum of all three ages is 80 years. How old is David ?

8. The sum of a number and its reciprocal is 9. Find the number correct to 3 significant figures.

9. When the mass of fertiliser in a bag is reduced by 50 grams, I need to buy 10 more bags to get 36 kg of fertiliser. What was the mass before the reduction ?

10. The difference between five times a number and its square is 3. Show that this statement can be expressed as two different equations. Hence find four numbers for which it is true.

The remaining questions are harder.

11. The members of a club hire a coach for the day for £ 210. When seven members withdraw the remaining people who go on the trip have to pay an extra £ 1 each. How many people originally agreed to go ?

12. When the average speed of a car increases by 10 km/h, the time it takes to travel 105 km reduces by 15 minutes. Find the average speed of the car before the increase.

13. A length is cut from a piece of wire 36 cm long and bent into a rectangle whose length is three times its width. The remaining piece of wire is bent into a square. If the combined area of the rectangle and square is 37 cm² find the width of the rectangle.

SIMULTANEOUS EQUATIONS, ONE QUADRATIC, ONE LINEAR

To solve a pair of equations in two unknowns, one equation having terms such as x^2, y^2 and/or xy we use a substitution to eliminate one of the letters. From the linear equation we find one letter in terms of the other and then substitute this expression in the quadratic equation. This is illustrated in the next worked example.

Exercise 26e

Solve the equations $x^2 + 3y^2 = 21$ and $x + y = 5$

$$x^2 + 3y^2 = 21 \qquad \text{[1]}$$
$$x + y = 5 \qquad \text{[2]}$$

From [2], we can choose to express either x or y in terms of the other; we will choose x as it is slightly easier to substitute an expression for x^2 than one for $3y^2$.

From [2] $\qquad\qquad\qquad x = 5 - y \qquad\qquad\qquad$ [3]

Substituting $5 - y$ for x in [1] gives

$$(5 - y)^2 + 3y^2 = 21$$

This is a quadratic equation in one unknown, which we can solve.

$$25 - 10y + y^2 + 3y^2 = 21$$

i.e. $\qquad\qquad 4y^2 - 10y + 4 = 0$

$$2y^2 - 5y + 2 = 0$$
$$(2y - 1)(y - 2) = 0$$

$\therefore \ y = \frac{1}{2}$ or 2

From [2], when $y = \frac{1}{2}$, $x = 4\frac{1}{2}$ and when $y = 2$, $x = 3$

---

1. Solve the equations

   (a) $x^2 + y^2 = 5$
   $\qquad x + y = 3$

   (b) $\qquad xy = 5$
   $\qquad x + y = 6$

   (c) $10 - x^2 = y^2$
   $\qquad\quad y = 2 - x$

2. Do not solve these equations but decide whether it is easier to substitute for x or for y, given that $x + y = 3$ and

   (a) $x^2 - 3y = 4$ $\qquad$ (b) $y^2 = 5x$

3. Solve the equations

   (a) $\qquad xy = 12$
   $\qquad 2x - y = 10$

   (b) $x + 3y = 14$
   $\qquad\quad xy = 8$

   (c) $\qquad y^2 = 4x$
   $\qquad x - y = 0$

4. Solve, where possible, the equations given in question 2. Give answers correct to 2 decimal places where necessary.

5. Solve these equations. (Think carefully which letter to substitute for, so that algebraic manipulation is kept to a minimum. All these equations result in quadratics that factorise.)

(a) $x^2 = y + 3$
     $2x - 3y = 8$

(b) $\dfrac{3}{x} + \dfrac{6}{y} = 4$
     $x + y = 5$

(c) $x^2 + xy + y^2 = 7$
     $2x + y = 4$

Self-Assessment 26

1. Solve the equations using factorisation.

(a) $x^2 - 5x + 4 = 0$

(b) $3x = x^2 - 10$

(c) $2x^2 + 6x + 4 = 0$

2. Use the formula to find, correct to two decimal places, the values of x for which

(a) $2x^2 + 9x - 12 = 0$

(b) $x^2 - 4x - 13 = 0$

3. What number must be added to each of the following expressions to make them into perfect squares ?

(a) $x^2 + 6x$ (c) $x^2 - 9x$

(b) $4x^2 + 5x$ (d) $x^2 - \frac{1}{2}x$

4. Find the values of a and b if the equation $x^2 - 8x + 10 = 0$ is expressed in the form $(x - a)^2 = b$. Hence solve the equation.

5. Solve the equations
   $xy = 5$ and $2x - y = 3$

6. Use the formula to find the largest root of the equation $2x^2 - 7x - 2 = 0$ giving the answer correct to four significant figures.

7. In a right-angled triangle one of the sides containing the right angle is 7 cm longer than the other and is 1 cm shorter than the hypotenuse. If the length of the shortest side is x cm, form an equation in x and solve it to find the lengths of the three sides.

6. The product of two positive numbers is 221 and their difference is 4.
   What is the smaller number ?

7. I want to build a rectangular playing area. I have enough edging bricks to make the perimeter 42 m and enough paving stones to cover an area of 108 m². Is it possible to build the playing area using all the materials without having to buy more ? If it is, give the length and width of the area.

8. Solve the equation

   $\dfrac{1}{x} + \dfrac{1}{2x - 1} = 4$

   giving your answers correct to 2 decimal places.

9.

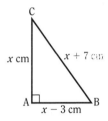

Give the lengths of the sides of the triangles that it is possible to draw from the information given in the diagram.

10. (a) Solve the equation $x^2 + 8x - 15 = 0$ giving your answers correct to 2 decimal places.

(b) Find the values of a and b such that $x^2 + 8x - 15 = (x + a)^2 + b$

(c) Copy this sketch of the graph of $y = x^2$

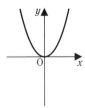

On your copy sketch the graph of $y = x^2 + 8x - 15$, showing clearly how your answers to parts (a) and (b) relate to your sketch.

ENLARGEMENT AND SIMILARITY

ENLARGEMENTS

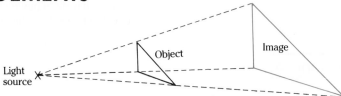

When a projector throws an image on to a screen, the image is the same shape as the object but larger. If each side of the image is twice as long as the corresponding side of the object, then we say that the *scale factor* is 2.

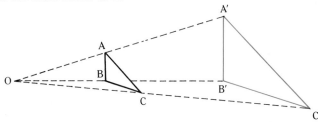

The point O, corresponding to the light source, is called the *centre of enlargement*. Lines drawn from O through AA', BB' and CC' are *guide lines* and, when the scale factor is 2, OA' = 2OA, OB' = 2OB and OC' = 2OC.

The same idea can be used to enlarge any shape. Suppose we wish to enlarge a given quadrilateral so that the lengths of the enlarged version are three times those of the original.

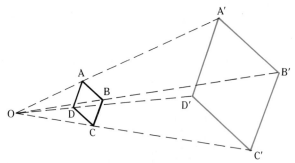

First mark O, the centre of enlargement, at any convenient point. Then draw the guide lines from O through the vertices of the object. The amount by which we extend the guide lines depends on the size of the image required. In this case we want the lines on the image to be three times as long as the corresponding lines on the object, i.e. OA is extended to A' so that OA' = 3OA, OB to B' so that OB' = 3OB and so on.
Note that all the lengths are measured from O.

If the scale factor is less than 1 it is unnecessary to extend the guidelines beyond the vertices of the original figure. For example, if triangle ABC is enlarged using a scale factor of $\frac{1}{2}$ then A′ is the point on OA such that $OA' = \frac{1}{2}OA$. Similarly $OB' = \frac{1}{2}OB$ and $OC' = \frac{1}{2}OC$.

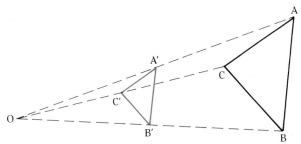

Notice that a scale factor that is less than 1 produces an image that is *smaller* than the object, although the word enlargement is often still used to describe this transformation.

Exercise 27a

1. (a) A source of light O is placed behind a rectangular picture ABCD, held vertically. It casts a shadow A′B′C′D′ on the wall. What is the scale factor ?

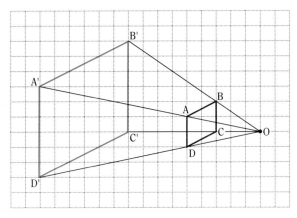

(b) A powerful floodlight at ground level casts a shadow on a nearby building, of a free-standing end-wall of a house that is being demolished. The two walls are parallel. Find the scale factor.

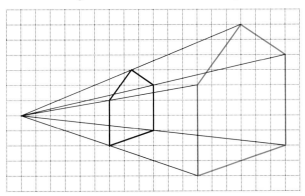

2.

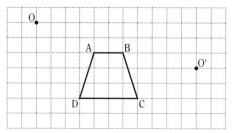

(a) Copy the diagram on squared paper. Using O as the centre of enlargement and a scale factor of 2, draw the enlargement of ABCD. Label the vertices A'B'C'D'. Check that the enlarged shape has sides twice as long as the original.

(b) Repeat part (a) but this time use O' as the centre of enlargement. Is it true that the enlarged shape has sides twice as long as the original ? What is the effect on the image of changing the centre of the enlargement ?

3. Repeat question 2 using a scale factor of

(a) 3   (b) $\frac{1}{2}$ (c) $1\frac{1}{2}$ (d) $\frac{3}{4}$

4.

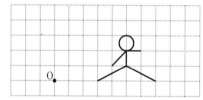

Copy the figure on squared paper allowing plenty of space above and to the right. Use O as the centre of enlargement and, on the same diagram, draw an enlarged figure using a scale factor of   (a) $1\frac{1}{2}$ (b) 3

5. Plot the points A(3, 5), B(6, 2), C(3, −1) and D(0, 2). Join them to give the quadrilateral ABCD.

(a) Using the point E(3, 2) as the centre of enlargement and a scale factor of 2, draw the enlargement of ABCD. Label the vertices A_1, B_1, C_1, D_1 and write down their coordinates.

(b) Repeat part (a) but this time using B as the centre of enlargement and a scale factor of $\frac{1}{3}$. Label the vertices A_2, B_2, C_2, D_2 and write down their coordinates.

(c) How does the length of A_1D_1 compare with the length of A_2D_2 ?

In questions 6 and 7, the green figure is an enlargement of the black figure. Copy the diagram on squared paper. Draw the guide lines for the enlargement. The point where these lines meet is the centre of enlargement. Give the coordinates of this point, and the scale factor of the enlargement.

6.

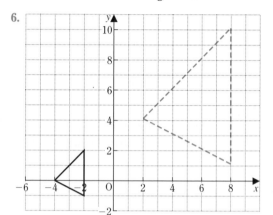

7.

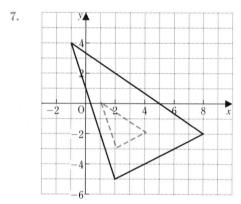

8.

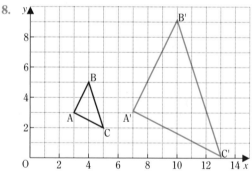

$\triangle A'B'C'$ is an enlargement of $\triangle ABC$. Copy the diagram on to squared paper, draw the guidelines through the corresponding vertices of the two triangles and give the coordinates of the point where they meet. What special point is this ?

SIMILAR FIGURES

Two figures are similar if they have the same shape, but not necessarily the same size, i.e. one figure is an enlargement of the other.

Enlarging a figure does not alter the angles. It does change the lengths of the lines, but all the lengths change in the same ratio, i.e. if one line is trebled in length, all lines are trebled in length.

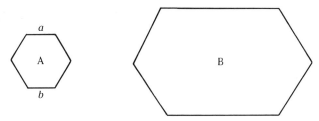

Suppose that a hexagon, A, is enlarged, the sides marked a and b being four times as long, while the other sides are doubled in length. The resulting hexagon, B, contains the same angles as A but the two shapes are obviously different. Not all the lengths have changed in the same ratio. The hexagons are not similar.

Similar Triangles

When we have a pair of similar triangles, corresponding angles are equal and corresponding sides are in the same ratio.

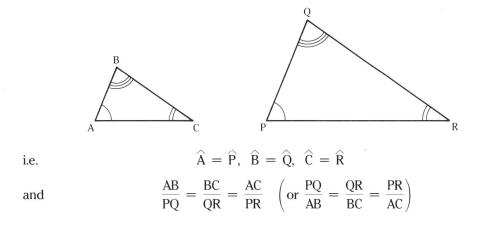

i.e. $\hat{A} = \hat{P}, \ \hat{B} = \hat{Q}, \ \hat{C} = \hat{R}$

and $\dfrac{AB}{PQ} = \dfrac{BC}{QR} = \dfrac{AC}{PR} \ \left(\text{or} \ \dfrac{PQ}{AB} = \dfrac{QR}{BC} = \dfrac{PR}{AC} \right)$

To prove that two triangles are similar, we must show that

either   the three angles of one triangle are equal to the three angles of the other triangle

i.e.

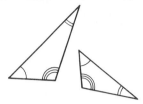

or   the corresponding sides of each triangle are in the same ratio

i.e.

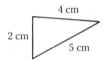 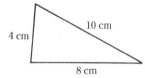

or   there is one pair of equal angles and the sides containing these angles are in the same ratio

i.e.

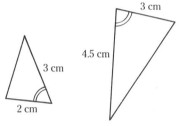

Exercise 27b

State whether or not triangles ABC and XYZ are similar.

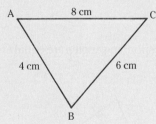 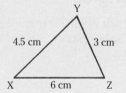

$$\frac{AB}{YZ} = \frac{4}{3} = 1.333 \quad \frac{BC}{XY} = \frac{6}{4.5} = 1.333 \quad \text{and} \quad \frac{AC}{XZ} = \frac{8}{6} = 1.333$$

The three pairs of corresponding sides are in the same ratio.

$\therefore \quad \triangle s \begin{smallmatrix} ABC \\ ZYX \end{smallmatrix}$ are similar

Note that we write the letter Z immediately beneath the letter A because these angles are equal. Using this convention helps us to name the pairs of corresponding sides correctly.

In questions 1 to 6 state whether or not the two triangles are similar. Where appropriate give brief reasons.

1.

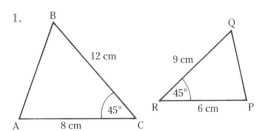

6.

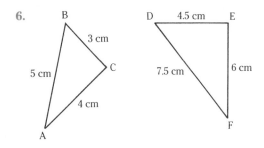

2.

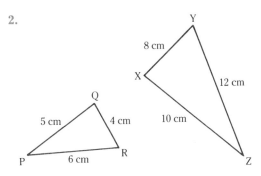

In △s ABC and DEF, $\widehat{A} = \widehat{E}$ and $\widehat{B} = \widehat{D}$. AB = 4 cm, DE = 3 cm and AC = 6 cm. Find EF.

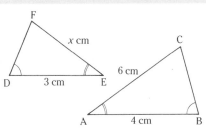

$$\triangle s \; \frac{EDF}{ABC} \; \text{are similar}$$

We put the triangle with the unknown side on top

$$\frac{FE}{CA} = \frac{ED}{AB} = \frac{DF}{BC}$$

$$\frac{x}{6} = \frac{3}{4}$$

$$\overset{1}{\cancel{6}} \times \frac{x}{\cancel{6}_1} = \frac{3}{\cancel{4}_2} \times \cancel{6}^{3} \;\; \Rightarrow \;\; x = \frac{9}{2} = 4.5$$

so   EF = 4.5 cm

3.

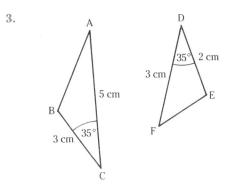

In questions 7 and 8, state whether the pairs of triangles are similar. If they are, find the required side.

4.

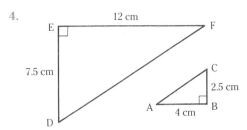

7. Find PR

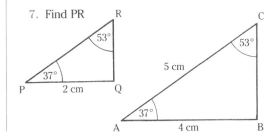

5.

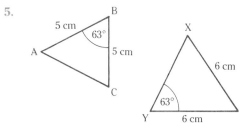

8. Find PR.

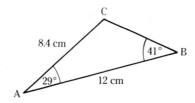 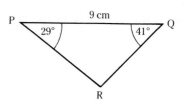

9. In △s ABC and XYZ, $\widehat{A} = \widehat{X}$ and $\widehat{B} = \widehat{Y}$. AB = 6 cm, BC = 5 cm and XY = 9 cm. Find YZ.

10. In △s ABC and PQR, $\widehat{A} = \widehat{Q}$ and $\widehat{C} = \widehat{R}$. AC = 8 cm, BC = 4 cm and QR = 9 cm. Find PR.

11.

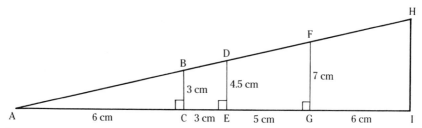

Show that

(a) △s ABC, ADE, and AFG are all similar.

(b) Find the values of $\dfrac{BC}{AC}, \dfrac{DE}{AE}$ and $\dfrac{FG}{AG}$

(c) If △s $\dfrac{ABC}{AHI}$ are similar   (i) what is the value of angle AIH ?   (ii) what is the length of HI ?

12.

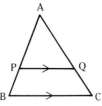

If PQ is parallel to BC show that △APQ is similar to △ABC.

13.

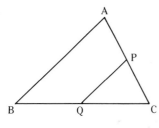

In △ABC, P is the midpoint of AC and Q is the midpoint of BC. Show that △ABC is similar to △PQC.

14.

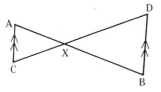

AB and CD are two straight lines that intersect at X in such a way that AC is parallel to BD. Show that △ACX is similar to △BDX.

In △ABC, P is a point on AB and Q is a point on AC such that AP = 2 cm, PB = 3 cm, AQ = 3 cm and QC = 4.5 cm. Show that PQ is parallel to BC.

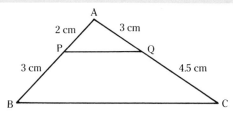

First show that △s $\frac{APQ}{ABC}$ are similar

$$\frac{AP}{AQ} = \frac{2}{3}, \quad \frac{AB}{AC} = \frac{5}{7.5} = \frac{50}{75} = \frac{2}{3}$$

and $\hat{A}$ is common to △APQ and △ABC

Since there is one pair of equal angles and the sides containing those angles are in the same ratio △s $\frac{APQ}{ABC}$ are similar

$$\therefore A\hat{P}Q = A\hat{B}C$$

With respect to PQ and BC these are corresponding angles.

$$\therefore \text{ PQ is parallel to BC}$$

15. In △ABC, P is a point on AB and Q is a point on AC such that $\frac{AP}{AB} = \frac{3}{4}$ and $\frac{AQ}{AC} = \frac{3}{4}$

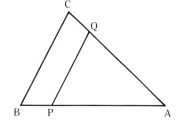

(a) Show that △APQ is similar to △ABC.

(b) Hence show that PQ is parallel to BC.

(c) If $\hat{A} = 65°$ and $A\hat{P}Q = 58°$ find $B\hat{C}A$.

16.

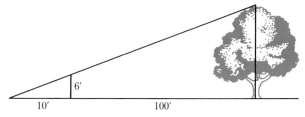

Sally wishes to find, with a little help from a 6 foot pole, the height of an oak tree that stands on level ground. She walks away from the base of the tree, with the Sun directly behind her, until she reaches a point 100 ft from its base. At this point she stands the pole on the ground and finds that the top of the shadow of the pole coincides with the top of the shadow of the tree at a point a further 10 feet away. How tall is the tree ?

17.

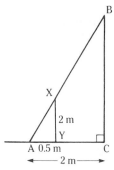

AB is a ladder leaning against a vertical wall BC, with its foot A on level ground such that AC = 2 m. XY is a straight pole placed so that it is vertical, with one end X touching the ladder and the other end Y resting on the horizontal ground. If AY = 0.5 m and XY = 2 m, find BC and hence find the length of the ladder.

18.

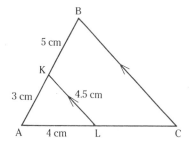

K and L are points on the sides AB and AC respectively of triangle ABC such that KL is parallel to BC.

(a) Show that △AKL and △ABC are similar

(b) If AK = 3 cm, KB = 5 cm, AL = 4 cm and KL = 4.5 cm, find BC and AC.

(c) Write down AK : KB and AL : LC.

19.

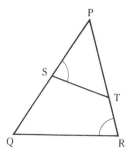

In △PQR, S is a point on PQ and T is a point on PR such that $\widehat{PST} = \widehat{PRQ}$.

(a) Show that △s $\genfrac{}{}{0pt}{}{PST}{PRQ}$ are similar.

(b) If PS = 3 cm, SQ = 2 cm, QR = 6 cm and PR = 4 cm find ST and TR.

20.

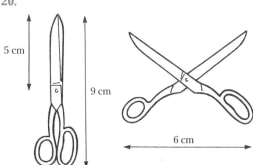

A closed pair of scissors is 9 cm long, the pivot being 5 cm from the points. The maximum that Paul can open the scissors using his thumb and first finger is 6 cm. When he does this, what is the distance between the points.

THE INTERCEPT THEOREM

From questions 15 and 18 in the last exercise we see that

 if a line is drawn parallel to one side of a triangle it divides the other two sides in the same ratio

This result is called the intercept theorem, and can be quoted.

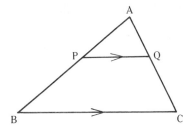

For example, if in triangle ABC, PQ is parallel to BC,

then $\dfrac{AP}{PB} = \dfrac{AQ}{QC}$ (intercept theorem)

so if PB = 6 cm, AQ = 3 cm and QC = 4 cm,

$\dfrac{AP}{6} = \dfrac{3}{4}$ and we can find the length of AP.

Exercise 27c

In each question from 1 to 4, all the measurements are in centimetres. Find x.

1.

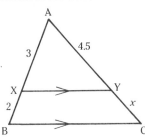

2.

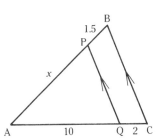

3.

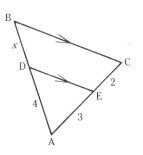

4.

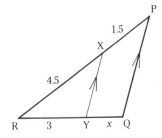

5. In $\triangle XYZ$, PQ is parallel to YZ. If XP = 12 cm, PY = 3 cm and XZ = 10 cm, find QZ.

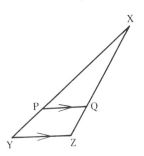

6. In triangle ABC, D is a point on AB and E is a point on AC such that DE is parallel to BC. If AC = 6 cm, AE = 4.5 cm and BD = 2 cm, find AD.

AREAS OF SIMILAR FIGURES

Exercise 27d

1. These four rectangles are similar.

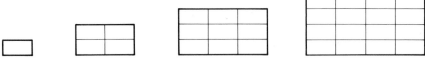

(a) Write down the ratio of the lengths of their bases.

(b) Write down the ratio of their heights.

(c) By counting rectangles, write down the ratio of their areas. Is there a relationship between the ratio you get in (c) and the ratios you got in (a) and (b)?

(d) What is the ratio of the lengths of the diagonals of the four rectangles?

2.

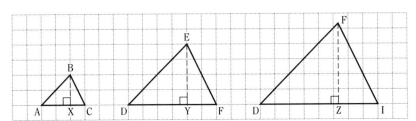

In triangle ABC   the length of the base, AC, is 3 units

the perpendicular height, BX, is 2 units

the area of $\triangle ABC$ is $\frac{1}{2} \times 3 \times 2$, i.e. 3 square units.

(a) Write down the length of   (i) DF   (ii) EY.

(b) What is the area of $\triangle DEF$?

(c) Write, as a fraction in its lowest terms, the value of   (i) $\dfrac{AC}{DF}$ (ii) $\dfrac{AC^2}{DF^2}$ (iii) $\dfrac{\text{area } \triangle ABC}{\text{area } \triangle DEF}$

(d) Triangles ABC and GHI are similar.

Find the value of   (i) $\dfrac{AC}{GI}$ (ii) $\dfrac{AC^2}{GI^2}$ (iii) $\dfrac{\text{area } \triangle ABC}{\text{area } \triangle GHI}$

Hence find the area of triangle GHI and use your result to find the perpendicular height, HZ, of triangle GHI.

3. The parallelograms are similar. First find the length of HG and then find the area of each figure.

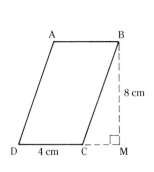

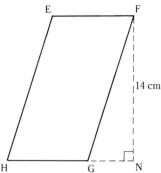

Do your results justify the statement that

the ratio of the areas of similar figures is equal to the ratio of the squares of corresponding sides ?

The results of the previous exercise lead us to the conclusion that

    the ratio of the *areas* of similar figures is equal to the ratio of the *squares* of corresponding lengths.

For example, if the linear scale factor is 4, the area scale factor is 4^2 i.e. 16.

Exercise 27e

1. For each pair of similar figures write down the ratio of their areas. The first one is done for you.

(a)

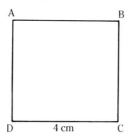

DC and SR are corresponding sides and $\dfrac{DC}{SR} = \dfrac{4}{3}$

$$\therefore \quad \frac{\text{area ABCD}}{\text{area PQRS}} = \frac{4^2}{3^2} = \frac{16}{9}$$

(b)

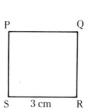

(c)

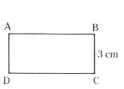 

(d)

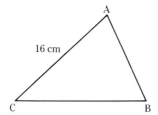 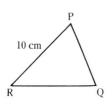

2. My lounge door is 800 mm wide and a picture of the door is 20 mm wide. Find the ratio of the area of the picture of the door to the area of the actual door.

3. Find the value of $\dfrac{AB}{PQ}$ for each of the following pairs of similar figures. The first one is done for you.

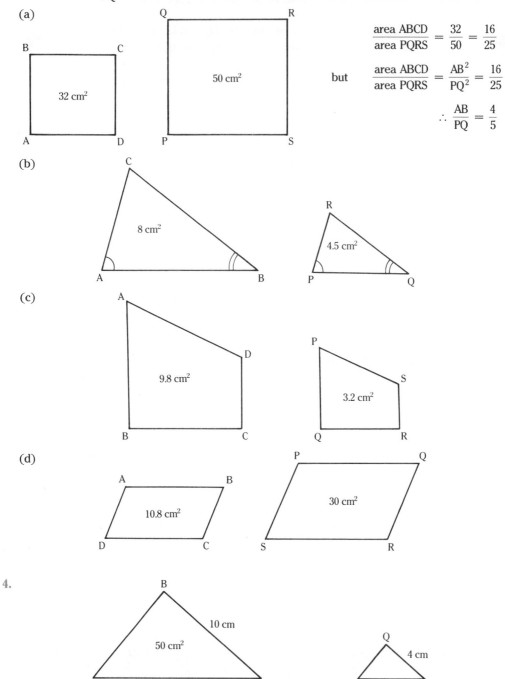

(a)

$$\dfrac{\text{area ABCD}}{\text{area PQRS}} = \dfrac{32}{50} = \dfrac{16}{25}$$

but $\quad\dfrac{\text{area ABCD}}{\text{area PQRS}} = \dfrac{AB^2}{PQ^2} = \dfrac{16}{25}$

$$\therefore \quad \dfrac{AB}{PQ} = \dfrac{4}{5}$$

(b)

(c)

(d)

4. Triangles ABC and PQR are similar. Use the information in the diagrams to find the area of triangle PQR.

5. Rectangles ABCD and WXYZ are similar. If BD = 4 cm, XZ = 7 cm and area ABCD = $4.8\,cm^2$, find the area of WXYZ.

6.

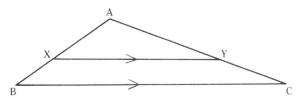

XY is parallel to BC. If AY = 8 cm, YC = 6 cm and the area of △ABC is $98\,cm^2$, find the area of △AXY.

7. The scale factor of a map is 1 : 50 000.
    (a) What is the area scale factor ?
    (b) What distance, in m, is represented by 1 cm on the map ?
    (c) What area, in m^2, is represented by $1\,cm^2$ on the map ?
    (d) A field is represented on the map by an area of $2.5\,cm^2$. Find the area of the field in m^2.

8.

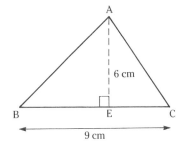
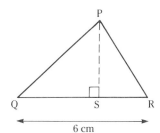

Triangles ABC and PQR are similar. Use the information given in the diagrams to find the area of triangle PQR.

The remaining questions are harder and, in some, it may be necessary first to show that some triangles are similar.

9.

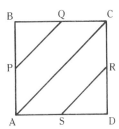

P, Q, R, S are the midpoints of the sides AB, BC, CD, DA of a square field ABCD. The field is divided into four smaller fields by erecting fences PQ, AC and SR. If the area of ABCD is $8000\,m^2$ find
    (a) the area of the triangular field PBQ
    (b) the area of the trapezoidal field ACRS.

10. The scale of a map is 1 : 10 000. On the map, the area representing a plot of land is $3\,\text{cm}^2$. Find the area of the field in m^2.

11. ABC is a triangle with X a point on AB and Y a point on AC such that XY is parallel to BC. If $AY = 3\,\text{cm}$, $YC = 5\,\text{cm}$ and $XB = 3\,\text{cm}$, find

   (a) AX

   (b) $\dfrac{\text{area } \triangle\text{AXY}}{\text{area } \triangle\text{ABC}}$

   (c) $\dfrac{\text{area } \triangle\text{AXY}}{\text{area trapezium XYCB}}$

12.

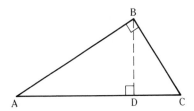

Triangle ABC has a right angle at B and BD is perpendicular to AC. The area of $\triangle$BDC is $4\,\text{cm}^2$ and the area of $\triangle$ABD is $5\,\text{cm}^2$. Find the ratio of the area of $\triangle$BCD to the area of $\triangle$ABC and hence find the value of BC : AC.

13.

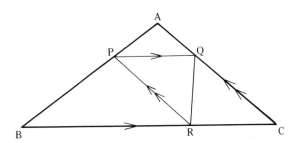

In the diagram, which represents a framework for a factory roof, PQ is parallel to BC and PR is parallel to AC. $AQ = 2\,\text{m}$, $QC = 6\,\text{m}$, $AP = 3\,\text{m}$ and $PQ = 4\,\text{m}$.

   (a) Calculate

      (i) PB

      (ii) BR

      (iii) $\dfrac{\text{area } \triangle\text{APQ}}{\text{area } \triangle\text{ABC}}$

      (iv) $\dfrac{\text{area } \triangle\text{BPR}}{\text{area } \triangle\text{ABC}}$

   (b) If the area of triangle APQ is $x\,\text{m}^2$, express in terms of x
      (i) area $\triangle$ABC   (ii) area $\triangle$BPR.

14. A triangular field ABC is bounded by hedges. Three trees D, E and F grow within these hedges such that D lies on BC, E lies on AC and F lies on AB. Fences are erected to enclose triangle DEF. FE is parallel to BC and DF is parallel to AC. If $AE = 30\,\text{m}$, $AF = 40\,\text{m}$, $BF = 120\,\text{m}$ and $BC = 200\,\text{m}$ find

   (a) EC, EF and BD

   (b) (i) $\dfrac{\text{area of enclosure AEF}}{\text{area of field ABC}}$ (ii) $\dfrac{\text{area of enclosure BDF}}{\text{area of field ABC}}$

   (c) $\dfrac{\text{CE}}{\text{EA}}$ and $\dfrac{\text{CD}}{\text{DB}}$. Is DE parallel to AB ?

VOLUMES OF SIMILAR SHAPES

Exercise 27f

1.

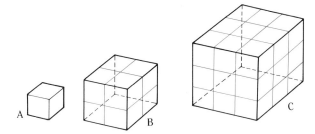

The diagram shows three cubes.

(a) Write down the ratio of the lengths of their bases.

(b) By counting the number of cubes equal in size to cube A, write down the ratio of their volumes.

Is there a relationship between your answers to (a) and (b)?

2.

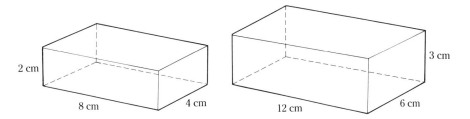

The diagram shows two similar rectangular boxes.

(a) Write down the ratio of their
   (i) longest edges   (ii) widths   (iii) heights.

(b) How many cubes of side 1 cm are needed to fill each box completely? Write down the ratio of their volumes.

Is there any relationship between the ratios in (a) and (b)?

3. The diagram shows three similar cylindrical cans.

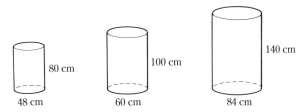

(a) Write down the ratio of
   (i) their heights   (ii) their base radii.

(b) Express the capacity of each can as a multiple of π. Hence find the ratio of their capacities.

Is there a relationship between your answers to (a) and (b)?

We conclude that

> **the ratio of the *volumes* of similar objects is equal to the ratio of the *cubes* of corresponding lengths.**

A student is to make a scale model of a building. The building is 20 m high and she decides to make the model 30 cm high.

(a) Express, in its simplest form, the ratio of the height of the building to the height of the model.

(b) If the total surface area of the model is 6480 cm^2 find the total surface area of the building.

(c) If the volume of the building is 16 000 m^3 find the total volume of the model.

(a) Height of building is 20 m

$$= 2000 \, \text{cm}$$

$$\frac{\text{height of building}}{\text{height of model}} = \frac{2000}{30} = \frac{200}{3}$$

(b) $$\frac{\text{surface area of building}}{\text{surface area of model}} = \frac{200^2}{3^2}$$

i.e. $$\frac{\text{surface area of building}}{6480} = \frac{40\,000}{9}$$

∴ surface area of building is $$\frac{40\,000 \times 6480}{9} \, \text{cm}^2$$

$$= \frac{40\,000 \times 6480}{9 \times 10\,000} \, \text{m}^2$$

$$= 2880 \, \text{m}^2$$

(c) We wish to find the volume of the model and so we arrange our fraction with this unknown quantity on the top.

$$\frac{\text{volume of model}}{\text{volume of building}} = \frac{3^3}{200^3}$$

i.e. $$\frac{\text{volume of model}}{16\,000} = \frac{27}{8\,000\,000}$$

∴ the volume of the model is $$\frac{16\,000 \times 27}{8\,000\,000} \, \text{m}^3$$

$$= 0.054 \, \text{m}^3$$

$$= 54\,000 \, \text{cm}^3$$

For the remainder of this exercise, objects referred to in the same question are mathematically similar. Always try to arrange to have the unknown quantity on the top.

4. The sides of two cubes are in the ratio 2 : 5. What is the ratio of their volumes ?

5. Two cones have volumes in the ratio 64 : 27. What is the ratio of

   (a) their heights   (b) their base radii ?

6. Three similar jugs have heights 8 cm, 12 cm and 16 cm. If the largest jug holds 4 pints, find the capacities of the other two.

7. The cost of the baked beans needed to fill a cylindrical can 10 cm high is 8p. What is the cost of the beans needed for a similar can standing 15 cm high ?

8. A wax model has a mass of 1 kg. Find the mass of a similar model which is twice as tall and made from metal ten times as heavy as the wax.

9. A toy manufacturer produces model buses that are similar in every way to the actual bus. If the ratio of the door area of the model to the door area of the actual bus is 1 : 2500 find

   (a) the ratio of their lengths

   (b) the ratio of the capacity of their fuel tanks

   (c) the width of the model, if the actual bus is 240 cm wide

   (d) the area of the front window of the actual bus if the area of the front window of the model is 6 cm^2.

The radius of one sphere is 20% more than the radius of another. Find, to the nearest whole number, the percentage difference in

(a) their surface areas   (b) their volumes.

If the radius of the smaller sphere is r, the radius of the other sphere is 120% of r

i.e. $1.2r$

$\therefore$ $\qquad \dfrac{\text{larger radius}}{\text{smaller radius}} = \dfrac{1.2r}{r} = \dfrac{1.2}{1}$

(a) $\dfrac{\text{surface area of larger sphere}}{\text{surface area of smaller sphere}} = \dfrac{1.2^2}{1^2}$

$\qquad\qquad\qquad = 1.44$

i.e. larger surface area is $1.44 \times$ smaller surface area

$\qquad\qquad = 1.44 \times 100\%$ of smaller surface area

$\qquad\qquad = 144\%$ of the original surface area

The percentage difference in their surface areas is 44%

(b) $\dfrac{\text{volume of larger sphere}}{\text{volume of smaller sphere}} = \dfrac{1.2^3}{1^3} = 1.728$

$\therefore \qquad\qquad$ larger volume $= 1.728 \times$ smaller volume

$\qquad\qquad\qquad = 172.8\%$ of the smaller volume

The percentage difference in their volumes, to the nearest whole number, is 73%.

10. The radius of a spherical snowball increases by 60%. Find, correct to the nearest whole number, the percentage increase in

    (a) its surface area   (b) its volume.

11. The volume of a cone increases by 100%, the ratio of its height to its base radius remaining constant. Find the percentage increase in

    (a) its height   (b) its base radius
    (c) its surface area.

12. A spherical orange has a diameter of 8 cm. If its peel is 1 cm thick, find, correct to the nearest whole number, the percentage of the volume of the orange that is thrown away as peel.

13. The edge of a wooden cube is 50% longer than the edge of a metal cube. If the volume of the metal cube is 405 cm^3, what is the volume of the wooden cube ?

Self-Assessment 27

1.
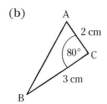

The green triangle is an enlargement of the black triangle. Copy the diagram on squared paper. Find the coordinates of the centre of enlargement and state the scale factor.

2. State whether or not the given pairs of triangles are similar.
    (a)
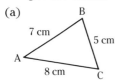

    (b)
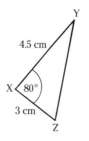

3. Are the given pairs of triangles similar ? Give reasons for your answer.
    (a)
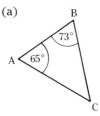

    (b)
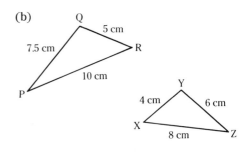

4.
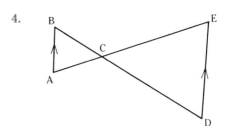

    (a) Show that △s ABC and CDE are similar.

    (b) If AB = 7 cm, BC = 6 cm, AC = 4 cm and CE = 6 cm find CD and DE.

5. Use the information in the diagram to find the lengths of

   (a) YC   (b) BC.

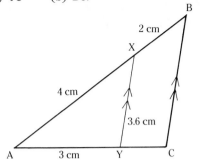

6. The lengths of the edges of two cubes are in the ratio $2 : 3$.

   (a) What is the ratio of
      (i) their surface areas
      (ii) their volumes ?

   (b) If an edge of the larger cube is 12 cm what is the length of an edge of the smaller cube ?

   (c) If the total surface area of the smaller cube is $54 \, cm^2$ what is the total surface area of the larger cube ?

   (d) If the volume of the larger cube is $108 \, cm^3$, what is the volume of the smaller cube ?

28 ▷ GEOMETRIC PROOF AND CONGRUENT TRIANGLES

CONCLUSIONS BASED ON SAMPLES

Most of the properties of figures which have been used up to now have been based on drawing and measuring a number of examples. When this process gives the same result every time we have said that 'this suggests that' we have found a general result.

For example, to investigate the sum of the angles in a triangle a number of triangles were drawn and in each case the three angles were measured and added. The total always came to about 180°, suggesting that the sum of the angles of *any* triangle is 180°.

However this is really jumping to a conclusion which could be invalid for several reasons. The lines enclosing the triangle have a thickness, which affects the measurement of the angles; protractors are not always completely accurate; different people's judgements of the size of an angle can vary and there is always the possibility that the sum of the angles in a triangle *not* drawn and measured could be different from 180°. In fact there is no justification for saying anything more definite than 'it seems likely that the three angles of any triangle add up to 180°'

DEDUCTIVE PROOF

Geometry can be given a logical structure in which, starting from simple accepted facts, other properties can be deduced without resort to trying individual samples. This forms the basis for deductive proof.

Suppose that we start by accepting that
vertically opposite angles are equal
and that, for a pair of parallel lines with a transversal, corresponding angles are equal.

Using just these two facts we can *prove* that
alternate angles are equal.

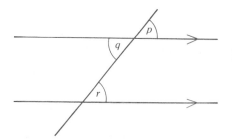

In the diagram $\hat{p} = \hat{q}$ (vertically opp. angles)

$\hat{p} = \hat{r}$ (corresponding angles)

$\Rightarrow \hat{q} = \hat{r}$

This is true for *any* pair of parallel lines and angles of *any* size so we have proved that
alternate angles are always equal

Note that the symbol ⇒ means 'implying that' or 'implies' and indicates a logical deduction from stated facts. Now this fact can be used in proving further facts. As an example we will *prove* that in any triangle the sum of the interior angles is 180°.

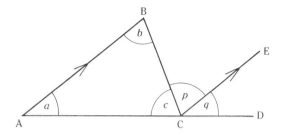

If △ABC is any triangle, AC is extended to D and CE is drawn parallel to AB, then

$$\hat{p} + \hat{q} + \hat{c} = 180° \quad \text{(angles on a straight line)}$$

$$\hat{p} = \hat{b} \quad \text{(alternate angles)} \qquad [1]$$

$$\hat{q} = \hat{a} \quad \text{(corresponding angles)} \qquad [2]$$

⇒ $$\hat{a} + \hat{b} + \hat{c} = 180°$$

i.e. the sum of the interior angles of *any* triangle is 180°.

Statements [1] and [2] above, when added give

$$\hat{p} + \hat{q} = \hat{a} + \hat{b}$$

This proves another useful fact about angles in a triangle i.e. an exterior angle of a triangle is equal to the sum of the two interior opposite angles.

Because this proof does not involve measuring angles in a particular triangle it applies to *all* possible triangles, thus closing the loophole that there may exist a triangle whose angles do not add up to 180°.

Notice how this proof uses the property proved in the first example, i.e. this proof follows the previous proof. The angle sum property of triangles can now be used to prove further properties.

Euclid was the first person to give a formal structure to Geometry. He started by making certain assumptions, such as 'there is only one straight line between two points'. Using only these assumptions (called axioms), he then proved some facts and used those facts to prove further facts and so on. Thus the proof of any one fact could be traced back to the axioms.

This method of proof is called deductive proof because one fact is deduced from another.

However when *you* are asked to give a geometric proof you do not have to worry about which method to use or which property depends on which; you can use *any* facts that you know in any order.

One aspect of proof is that it is an argument used to convince other people of the truth of any statement, so whatever facts you use must be clearly stated.

Therefore it is a good idea to marshal your ideas before starting to write out a proof. This is most easily done by marking right angles, equal angles and equal sides etc. on the diagram.

The exercises in this chapter give practice in writing out a proof.

For the next exercise the following facts are needed:

> vertically opposite angles are equal
>
> corresponding angles are equal
>
> alternate angles are equal
>
> interior angles add up to 180°
>
> angle sum of a triangle is 180°
>
> an exterior angle of a triangle is equal to the sum of the interior opposite angles
>
> an isosceles triangle has two sides of the same length and the angles at the base of those sides are equal
>
> an equilateral triangle has three sides of the same length and each interior angle is 60°.

Exercise 28a

1.

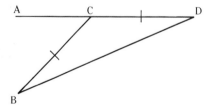

Prove that $A\widehat{C}B = 2C\widehat{D}B$.

2.

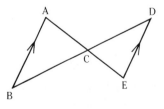

Prove that $A\widehat{C}D = A\widehat{B}C + D\widehat{E}C$.

3.

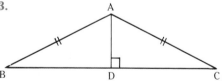

Prove that AD bisects $B\widehat{A}C$.

4.

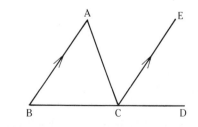

CE bisects $A\widehat{C}D$ and CE is parallel to BA. Prove that △ABC is isosceles.

USE OF A COUNTER EXAMPLE

We saw in the last section that drawing a few triangles and measuring the angles led us to say that 'it looks as though' the angles of any triangle add up to 180°. At that stage we had a *hypothesis,* which we then *proved* to be true for any triangle.

It is also important to be able to show that certain hypotheses are in fact false.

Suppose that students were asked to investigate the relationship between the number of lines drawn across a circle and the number of regions that the circle is divided into by those lines.

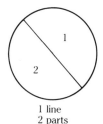

1 line
2 parts

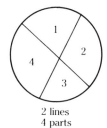

2 lines
4 parts

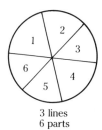

3 lines
6 parts

John drew these three drawings, which led him to the hypothesis that *n* lines drawn across a circle give 2*n* regions.

Jocelyn however, drew the lines this way, showing that 3 lines can give 7 regions, and that John's hypothesis is false.

Jocelyn used a *counter example* to disprove the hypothesis.

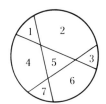

Now consider the hypothesis 'the product of two irrational numbers is itself irrational'. This can be shown to be untrue using this counter example: $\sqrt{2}$ and $\sqrt{8}$ are both irrational, but $\sqrt{2} \times \sqrt{8} = \sqrt{16} = 4$, which is rational.

You may like to see if you can find a counter example to disprove each of the following hypotheses.

(a) All prime numbers are odd.
(b) The square root of a positive number is always smaller than the number.
(c) If the side of a square is *x* cm long, the number of units of area of the square is always different from the number of units of perimeter.
(d) The diagonals of a parallelogram never cut at right angles.

Not every hypothesis can be *either* proved *or* shown to be false. In mathematics there are several in this category that are well known, one being 'Fermat's last theorem'.
This states that, although there are whole number values of *a, b* and *c* for which $a^2 + b^2 = c^2$, there are no whole number values for which $a^3 + b^3 = c^3$,
or in fact for which $a^n + b^n = c^n$ where *n* is any integer greater than 2.
No one has yet proved this to be true for all values of *n*; on the other hand no one has found a counter example.

CONGRUENT TRIANGLES

Any two triangles that have exactly the same shape and size are called *congruent triangles*.

Two triangles are congruent if they satisfy any one of four conditions.

(i) The three sides of one triangle are equal to the three sides of the other triangle. (SSS)

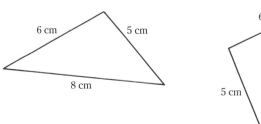

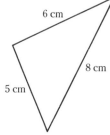

(ii) Two angles and one side of one triangle are equal to two angles and the corresponding side of the other triangle. (AAS)

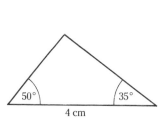

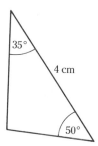

(iii) Two sides and the included angle of one triangle are equal to two sides and the included angle of the other triangle. (SAS)

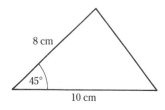

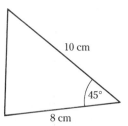

(iv) There is a right angle in each triangle and the hypotenuse and one side of one triangle are equal to the hypotenuse and one side of the other triangle. (RHS)

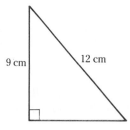

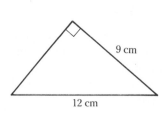

Each of these conditions is based on the information needed to fix the size and shape of a unique triangle. Question 9 in Exercise 3d showed that when the lengths of two sides and the size of one angle were given it was sometimes possible to draw two triangles with these measurements. This did not happen, however, if the given angle was *between* the two given sides; in this case the triangle was defined unambiguously. It is for this reason that condition (iii) above specifies the *included* angle.

Exercise 28b

In each question state whether or not the two triangles can be proved to be congruent. Give a brief reason for your answer, e.g. SAS.

1.
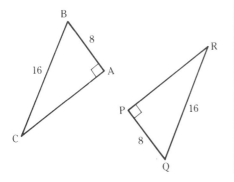

2.
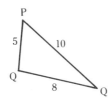

3.
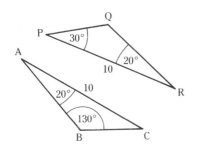

4.
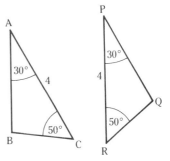

5.
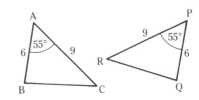

6.
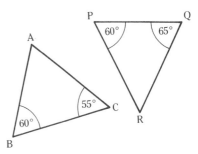

7.
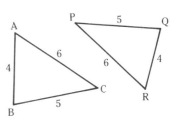

8.
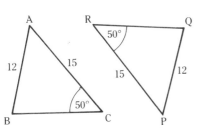

We do not need to know actual measurements in order to prove that triangles are congruent. If it can be shown that a correct combination of sides and angles are equal in two triangles, those triangles must be congruent.

AC and BD are diameters of a circle with centre O. Prove that triangles AOB and COD are congruent.

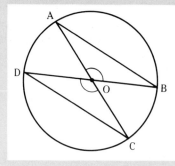

In △s AOB and COD

$$AO = CO \quad (\text{both radii})$$

$$BO = DO \quad (\text{both radii})$$

$$A\hat{O}B = C\hat{O}D \quad (\text{vertically opp. angles})$$

$$\therefore \triangle s \begin{array}{c} AOB \\ COD \end{array} \text{ are congruent (SAS)}$$

9.

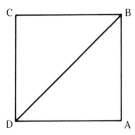

ABCD is a square. Prove that triangles ABD and CDB are congruent.

11.

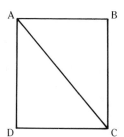

The diagram shows the rectangular outer frame, ABCD, of a door with a diagonal brace AC. Prove that △ABC and △CDA are congruent.

10.

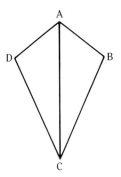

ABCD is a kite in which AD = AB and CD = BC. Prove that △ADC and △ABC are congruent.

12.

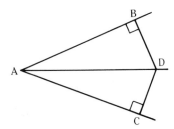

Part of the mechanism for a pair of governors in an engine is shown in the diagram. AD bisects $B\hat{A}C$, DB is perpendicular to AB and DC is perpendicular to AC. Prove that triangles ABD and ACD are congruent.

13.

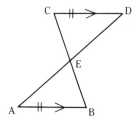

A portion of the framework for a roof truss is shown in the diagram. The girders AB and CD are equal and parallel. Prove that △ABE is congruent with △ECD.

14. ABCD is a parallelogram. Prove that triangles ADB and CBD are congruent.

15.

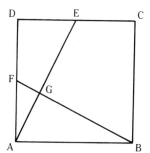

A child's puzzle is made from a wooden square, cut into four pieces as in the diagram. E is the midpoint of DC and F is the midpoint of AD. Show that △ADE and △BAF are congruent.

Using Congruent Triangles

Once two triangles have been shown to be congruent, i.e. they are alike in all respects, it follows that the other pairs of corresponding sides and angles are equal. This often provides a means of proving that certain angles are equal or that certain lines have the same length.

Exercise 28c

In the diagram, D is the midpoint of AC, and AE and CF are both perpendicular to BF. By showing that triangles AED and CFD are congruent, prove that AE = CF.

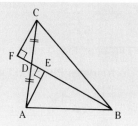

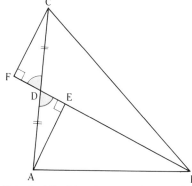

In triangles AED and CFD

$$A\hat{E}D = C\hat{F}D \quad (\text{both } 90°)$$

$$A\hat{D}E = C\hat{D}F \quad (\text{vert. opp. angles})$$

$$AD = CD \quad (\text{D bisects AC})$$

$$\therefore \triangle s \begin{matrix} AED \\ CFD \end{matrix} \text{ are congruent (AAS)}$$

Note that the triangles are written so that corresponding vertices are lined up. In this way the remaining pairs of corresponding sides and angles can be identified easily.

$$\therefore \qquad AE = CF$$

1.

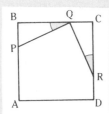

The diagram shows the end frame of a garden swing. BD bisects $A\hat{B}C$; BE and BF are equal. Show that triangles BED and BFD are congruent and hence that ED = FD.

2.

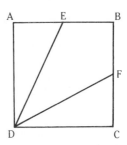

The pattern on a square tile, ABCD, is shown in the diagram. E and F are the midpoints of AB and BC. By proving that two triangles are congruent, show that DE = DF.

3. ABCD is a rectangle and E is the midpoint of AB. Join D to E and C to E and prove that DE and CE are equal in length.

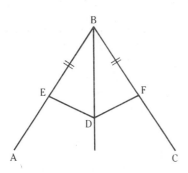

Three components for making a doll's house can be cut from a square board ABCD. P, Q and R are points such that BP, CQ and DR are all equal. Show that $P\hat{Q}R = 90°$.

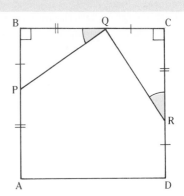

First prove that △s PBQ and QCR are congruent.

In triangles PBQ and QCR

    PB = QC   (given)

    $P\hat{B}Q = Q\hat{C}R$

        = 90°   (angles in a square)

    BQ = CR   (BC = CD, QC = RD)

∴ △s $\begin{matrix} PBQ \\ QCR \end{matrix}$ are congruent (SAS)

⇒ $B\hat{Q}P = C\hat{R}Q$

In △QRC $Q\hat{R}C + C\hat{Q}R = 90°$ (angles of △ total 180°)

∴ $B\hat{Q}P + C\hat{Q}R = 90°$

But $B\hat{Q}P + P\hat{Q}R + C\hat{Q}R = 180°$ (angles on a straight line)

∴ $P\hat{Q}R = 90°$

4.

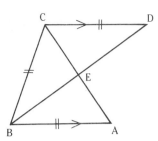

In the diagram, CD is parallel to BA and CD = CB = BA.   Show that △CDE is congruent with △BAE and hence prove that CA bisects BD.

5.

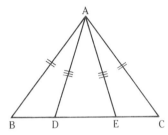

ABCDE represents a roof truss.   AB = AC and   AD = AE.   Prove that   BD = EC. (Consider triangles ABD and ACE.)

6. AB is a straight line. Draw a line AX perpendicular to AB. On the other side of AB, draw a line BY perpendicular to AB so that BY is equal to AX. Prove that $A\hat{X}Y = B\hat{Y}X$.

7. Taking the definition of a parallelogram as a quadrilateral with both pairs of opposite sides parallel, prove that

  (a) the opposite angles of a parallelogram are equal.

  (b) the opposite sides are equal.

  (c) the diagonals bisect each other.

8. Taking the definition of an isosceles triangle as a triangle with two equal sides, prove that the angles opposite to these sides are equal.

9. Taking the definition of a rhombus as a parallelogram with equal adjacent sides, prove that the diagonals of a rhombus bisect each other at right angles.

10. Taking the definition of a kite ABCD as a quadrilateral in which   AB = BC   and   CD = DA,   prove that BD bisects the angles at B and D.

Self-Assessment 28

1. From the following triangles, select any pairs that are congruent. Give the reason for your decision in the form (AAS) etc.

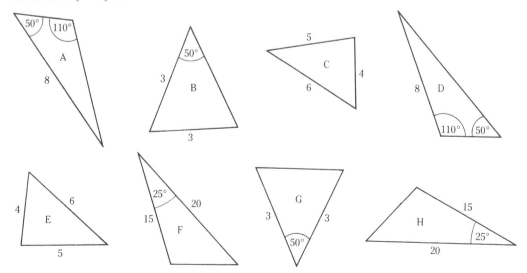

2. Each pair of triangles is congruent. Find the named side or angle.

(a)

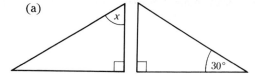

(b)

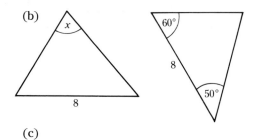

(c)

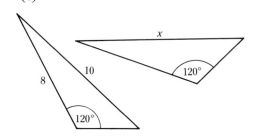

(d)

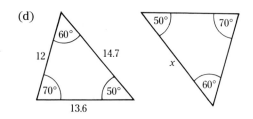

3. In a quadrilateral ABCD, AB = DC and AD = BC. Prove that triangles ABD and CDB are congruent.

4.

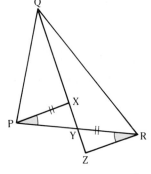

Given that PX = RZ and XP̂Y = ZR̂Y, find two congruent triangles and hence prove that Y is the midpoint of PR.

5.

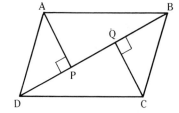

ABCD is a parallelogram. AP is perpendicular to BD and CQ is perpendicular to BD. Prove that AP = CQ.

ANGLES IN A CIRCLE

PARTS OF A CIRCLE

The basic terms used in circle work, i.e. centre, radius, diameter, circumference, arc and sector, are defined in Chapter 12. In this chapter we make use of further parts of a circle.

A line joining two points on the circumference is a *chord*. A chord divides a circle into two parts which are called segments; the larger part is the *major segment* and the smaller is the *minor segment*.

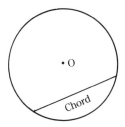 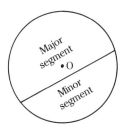

A segment should not be confused with a *sector*, which is a region of a circle bounded by two radii and an arc.

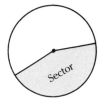

Subtended Angles

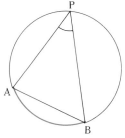

If A, B and P are three points on the circumference of a circle with centre O, then we say that

 angle APB is *subtended* either by the arc AB or by the chord AB

Alternatively we can say that

 both the arc AB and the chord AB *subtend* the angle APB *at the circumference*

The arc and chord also subtend the angle AOB *at the centre.*

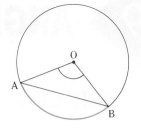

Note that a chord can subtend an obtuse angle at the circumference.
In such a case the angle is in the minor segment.

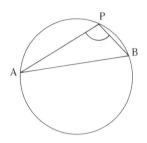

Exercise 29a

Use this diagram to answer questions 1 to 6.

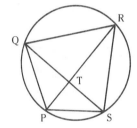

Use this diagram for questions 7 to 12.

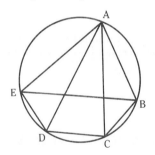

1. Which chord subtends $P\widehat{R}Q$?

2. Name an angle subtended at the circumference by the arc PS.

3. State whether or not the region bounded by QT, PT and the arc PQ is a sector of the circle.

4. The chord QS divides the circle into two segments. Does the point R lie in the minor or the major segment ?

5. Which arc subtends $P\widehat{Q}R$?

6. Name two angles that are subtended by RS.

7. Which arc subtends $A\widehat{D}C$?

8. Which arc subtends $B\widehat{E}D$?

9. Which arc subtends $E\widehat{A}D$?

10. Which angle is subtended by
    (a) arc CB   (b) arc EC ?

11. Which angle is subtended by
    (a) arc EB   (b) chord DA ?

12. Name two angles subtended by the arc AB.

13. Draw a circle with a radius of about 5 cm and mark any two points A and B on the circumference. Taking any other three points P, Q and R on the circumference on the same side of AB, draw angles $A\widehat{P}B$, $A\widehat{Q}B$ and $A\widehat{R}B$. Measure these angles.
What do you observe ?

14.
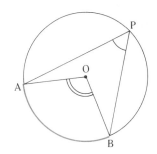 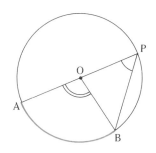 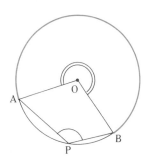

In each of the diagrams above, the arc AB subtends an angle $A\widehat{P}B$ at the circumference and also subtends angle $A\widehat{O}B$ at the centre. Copy the diagrams, using a radius of at least 5 cm (the angles need not be copied exactly).
Measure $A\widehat{P}B$ and $A\widehat{O}B$ in each case. What do you observe ?

PROPERTIES OF ANGLES IN A CIRCLE

Angles in the Same Segment

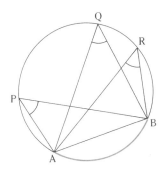

In this diagram the angles $A\widehat{P}B$, $A\widehat{Q}B$ and $A\widehat{R}B$ are all subtended at the circumference by the arc AB.
These angles are referred to as *angles in the same segment*.

If question 13 in Exercise 30a is repeated with other circles and other points, the same conclusion is reached each time suggesting that, in general

 angles in the same segment are equal.

The Angle Subtended at the Centre

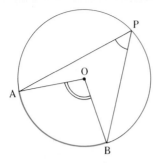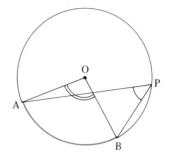

Repeating question 14 in Exercise 30a with different circles and angles gives the same result every time indicating that, in general

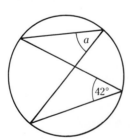 **the angle subtended at the centre of a circle by an arc is twice any angle subtended at the circumference by the same arc.**

Now the angle subtended at the centre by a semicircular arc is always 180°.
It follows that any angle subtended at the circumference by a semicircular arc is 90°.

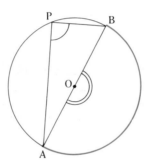

Any angle in a semicircle is a right angle.

Exercise 29b

Find the angles denoted by the letters.

1.

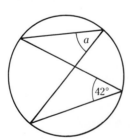

2.

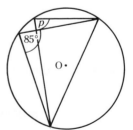

3.

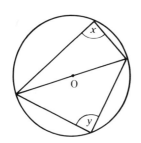

4.

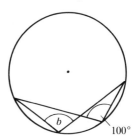

In each diagram find the angle denoted by *p*.

(a)

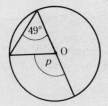

(b)

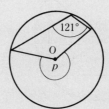

(a) $p = 2 \times 49°$

    $= 98°$ ($\angle$ at centre $= 2 \times \angle$ at circumference)

(b) $p = 2 \times 121°$

    $= 242°$ ($\angle$ at centre $= 2 \times \angle$ at circumference)

Note that in (b) the arc subtending angle *p* at the centre of the circle is more than half the circumference, so *p* is a reflex angle.

Find the angles denoted by the letters.

5.

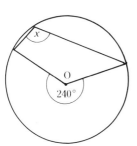

7.

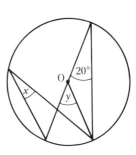

6.

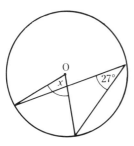

8.

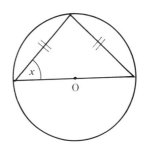

9.

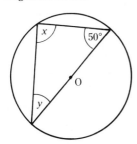

11.

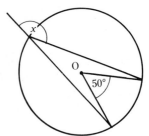

10.

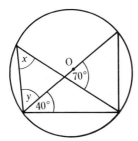

12.

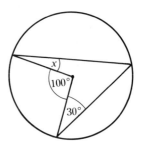

THE PERPENDICULAR BISECTOR OF A CHORD

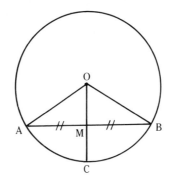

In the diagram above, the radius OC passes through M, the midpoint of the chord AB.
Therefore △OAM and △OBM are congruent.
(AM = BM, OM is common and the two radii OA and OB are equal.)
Hence OM̂A = OM̂B = 90°. (AMB is a straight line.)

A radius that passes through the midpoint of a chord is perpendicular to the chord.

and conversely

the perpendicular bisector of a chord passes through the centre of the circle.

Exercise 29c

A chord AB of a circle with centre O, is 10 cm long.
The midpoint of AB is the point C and OC is of length 3 cm.
What is the radius of the circle ?

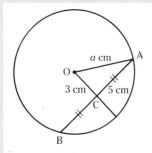

OC produced is a radius of the circle.

As OC bisects chord AB, $O\hat{C}A$ is $90°$

In $\triangle OCA$

$$AC = \tfrac{1}{2}AB = 5\,\text{cm}$$

$$OA^2 = OC^2 + AC^2 \quad (\text{Pythag.})$$

$$a^2 = 3^2 + 5^2$$

$$a = \sqrt{34}$$

$$= 5.830\ldots$$

Correct to 3 s.f. the radius of the circle is 5.83 cm.

1. The distance of a chord PQ from the centre of a circle is 5 cm. If the radius of the circle is 13 cm, find the length of PQ. (Remember that 'distance' means perpendicular distance.)

2. A chord of length 32 cm is at a distance of 12 cm from the centre of a circle. Find the radius of the circle.

3. A chord AB of a circle centre O, radius $3\sqrt{3}$ cm, is $2\sqrt{15}$ cm long. Find, without using a calculator, the distance of AB from O. Give your answer in the form $a\sqrt{b}$.

4.

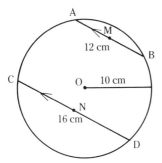

The diagram shows a circle with centre O and radius 10 cm. AB and CD are two parallel chords with midpoints M and N. The lengths of AB and CD are 12 cm and 16 cm respectively. Find the distance between M and N.

5.

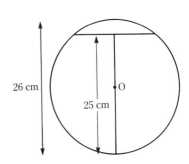

A logo is being designed in a circle with diameter 26 cm. The basic outline is a symmetrical T-shape with a height of 25 cm. How wide is the cross-piece of the T ?

These questions may require the use of any or all of the properties of angles in a circle that have been given in this chapter, as well as the methods of deductive proof explained in Chapter 29.

In each question from 6 to 9, find the angles denoted by the letters.

6.

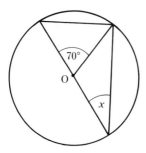

7.

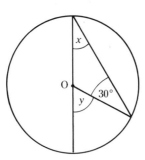

8.

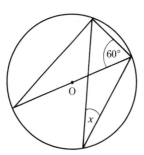

9.

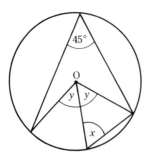

10.

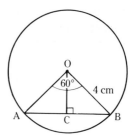

Find, correct to 3 s.f., the length of OC. Give a reason for each step in your calculation.

11.

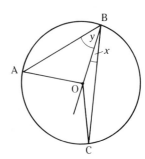

Prove that △AOB and △COB are both isosceles. Hence show that AÔC = 2(x + y)

Note that, in question 11, use is *not* made of the conclusion, based on drawing and measurement, given on page 477. The solution to question 11 *proves* that this conclusion is true in every case.

12.

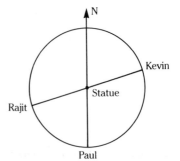

Three boys are walking round a circular pond learning to use a compass. Paul stands so that a statue in the centre of the pond is due north. Rajit and Kevin line up with the statue as shown. Paul sees Kevin on a bearing of 028°. On what bearing is Kevin from Rajit?

CYCLIC QUADRILATERALS

A quadrilateral with all four vertices lying on the circumference of a circle is called a cyclic quadrilateral.

One important property of a cyclic quadrilateral is that its opposite angles are supplementary, i.e. add up to 180°.

It is easy to see why this is so if we remember that an angle at the centre of a circle is twice the angle subtended at the circumference by the same arc.

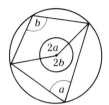

$$2\widehat{a} + 2\widehat{b} = 360°$$

$$\therefore \widehat{a} + \widehat{b} = 180°$$

▶ **The opposite angles of a cyclic quadrilateral are supplementary.** ◀

A further property is

▶ **an exterior angle of a cyclic quadrilateral is equal to the opposite interior angle.** ◀

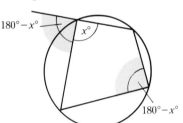

Again a simple diagram shows why this is true.

Exercise 29d

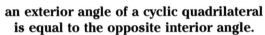

Find the angle denoted by a

$$\widehat{a} + 106° = 180° \quad (\text{opp. } \angle \text{ s of cyclic quad.})$$

$$\widehat{a} = 180° - 106° = 74°$$

1. Copy each diagram, shade the interior angle opposite to the given exterior angle and state its value.

(a)

(b)

Find the angles denoted by the letters.

2.

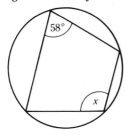

3.

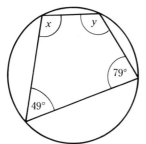

4.

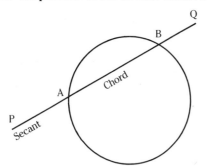

5.

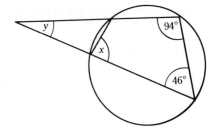

6.

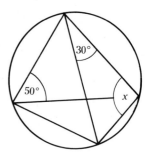

7.

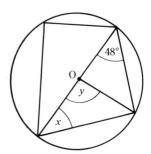

THE TANGENT TO A CIRCLE

When a straight line cuts a circle at two distinct points, A and B say, the line is called a *secant* and the part AB of the secant within the circle, is a chord.

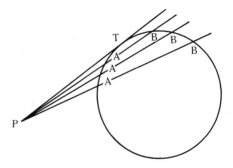

If the secant PQ rotates about the point P then, as PQ approaches the edge of the circle, the positions of A and B move closer together until they coincide at T say.

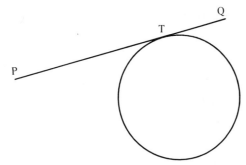

When this position is reached, the line PQ *touches* the circle and is called a *tangent* to the circle. The point T where PQ touches the circle is called the *point of contact*.
The distance PT is called *the length of the tangent* from P to the circle.

PROPERTIES OF TANGENTS

First Property

For any position of the secant PQ, we know that the chord AB is perpendicular to the radius drawn through the midpoint of the chord. Applying this fact as A and B get closer together, we can deduce that, when A and B coincide,

 a tangent to a circle is perpendicular to the radius drawn at the point of contact.

Exercise 29e

The length of a tangent drawn from A to a circle of radius 3.7 cm and centre O, is 8 cm. Find the length of OA.

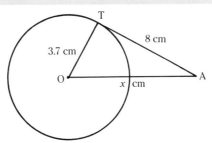

$$O\hat{T}A = 90° \qquad (\text{tangent} \perp \text{to radius})$$
$$x^2 = OT^2 + AT^2 \qquad (\text{Pythagoras in } \triangle OTA)$$
$$= (3.7)^2 + (8)^2$$
$$= 77.69$$

$$\therefore \ x = 8.81 \quad (3 \text{ s.f.})$$

The length of OA is 8.81 cm (3 s.f.)

In questions 1 to 6, O is the centre of the circle and PT is the tangent at T. Find the marked unknown quantities.

1.

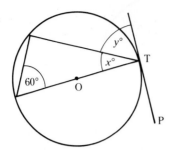

5.

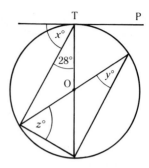

2.

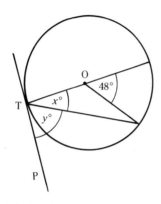

6.

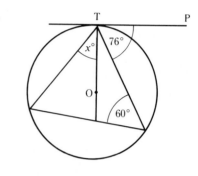

Find the marked angles.

3.

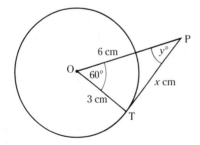

7.

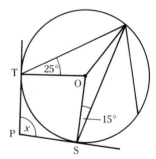

4.

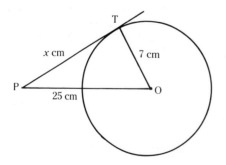

8.

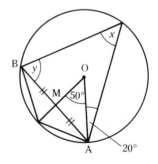

The following questions provide an opportunity to apply the ideas of formal proof to problems involving tangents.

The tangent from a point P to a circle with centre O touches the circle at T. TA is a diameter and AP cuts the circumference at the point B. If B bisects AP prove that the angle BTP is 45°.

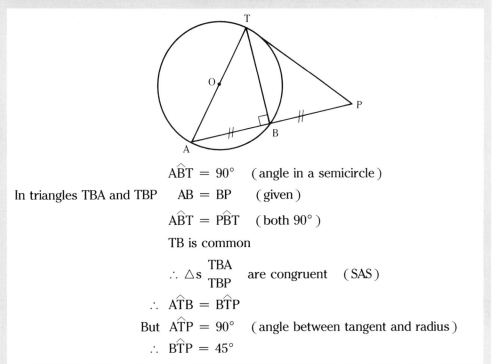

$$A\widehat{B}T = 90° \quad (\text{angle in a semicircle})$$

In triangles TBA and TBP $\quad AB = BP \quad (\text{given})$

$$A\widehat{B}T = P\widehat{B}T \quad (\text{both } 90°)$$

TB is common

$$\therefore \triangle s \begin{matrix} \text{TBA} \\ \text{TBP} \end{matrix} \quad \text{are congruent} \quad (\text{SAS})$$

$$\therefore A\widehat{T}B = B\widehat{T}P$$

But $A\widehat{T}P = 90° \quad (\text{angle between tangent and radius})$

$$\therefore B\widehat{T}P = 45°$$

---

9. AB and BC are tangents to the circle, touching it at A and C. Show that △AOB and △COB are congruent.

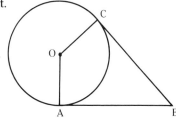

10. R is a point on the circumference of a circle with a diameter PQ. Another circle is drawn with PR as a diameter. Prove that QR is a tangent to this circle.

11. A and B are two points on the circumference of a circle with centre O. Another circle, with centre P, passes through A and B such that $P\widehat{A}O$ is a right angle. Prove that PB is a tangent to the circle with centre O.

12. M is the midpoint of a chord AB of a circle with centre O. A tangent drawn to the circle from a point P touches the circle at T. If PT is parallel to AB, prove that TM, or TM produced, passes through O.

13. A pulley is in a horizontal plane with its centre fixed at a point O. A loop of rope, longer than the circumference of the pulley, is passed round the pulley, pulled tight, and fastened to a point P on a level with O. If Q and R are the points where the rope leaves the pulley, prove that the lengths of PQ and PR are equal. (Hint. Draw a plan and join OP.)

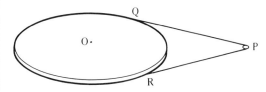

Second Property

In question 13 of the last exercise, it was proved that

> **two tangents drawn to a circle from the same point
> are equal in length.**

Note that the same proof also shows that the angles $O\hat{P}Q$ and $O\hat{P}R$ are equal,
i.e. OP bisects the angle between the tangents.

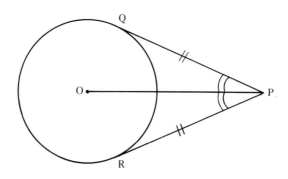

Exercise 29f

PT and PS are tangents to the circle with centre O. $T\hat{O}S = 110°$.

(a) Find $T\hat{P}S$ (b) What type of quadrilateral is TOSP ?

(a)

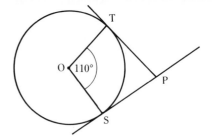

$P\hat{T}O = 90°$ (radius $\perp$ to tangent)

$P\hat{S}O = 90°$

But $P\hat{T}O + T\hat{O}S + P\hat{S}O + T\hat{P}S = 360°$ (angles in quadrilateral)

$\therefore T\hat{P}S = 360° - 290° = 70°$

(b) TOSP has two pairs of equal adjacent sides but the opposite sides are not
parallel.

Therefore TOSP is a kite.

In these questions PT and PS are tangents to a circle with centre O.

1.

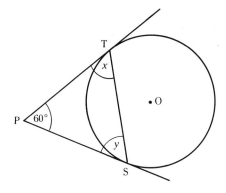

Find the angles marked *x* and *y*.
What type of triangle is PTS ?

2.

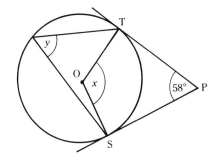

Find the angles marked *x* and *y*.

3.

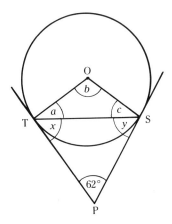

Find the size of each marked angle.

4.

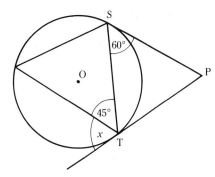

Find the angle marked *x*.

5.

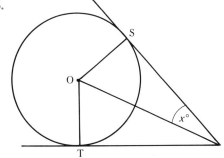

TP = 12 cm, OP = 13 cm

(a) Find the radius of the circle.

(b) Express $S\widehat{O}T$ in terms of $x°$.

6. A children's game involves catching a ball in a hollow cone. This diagram shows a section through the centre of the ball and cone. The sloping sides of the cone are tangents to the ball as shown.

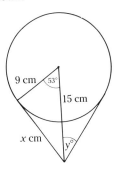

Find

(a) the angle marked $y°$ at the vertex of the cone

(b) the slant height, *x* cm, of the cone.

The Alternate Segment Property

PT is part of the tangent PQ to a circle and TR is a chord; the angle PTR is referred to as the angle between the tangent and the chord at the point of contact. The segment that is shaded is called the *alternate segment* with respect to the angle PTR, as it is on the side of the chord opposite, or alternate, to the angle.

(Similarly, for the part QT of the tangent, the unshaded segment is alternate with respect to the angle QTR.)

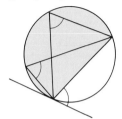 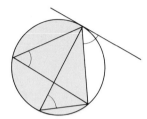 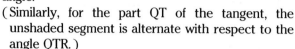

If, in a number of different diagrams, the angle between a tangent and a chord is compared with *any* angle in the alternate segment, the results suggest that

**the angle between a tangent and
a chord drawn from the point of contact
is equal to any angle in the alternate segment.**

This is known as *the alternate segment theorem*.

Exercise 29g

1. Copy each of the following diagrams and shade the alternate segment relative to the angle *x*.

   (a) 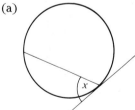   (b) 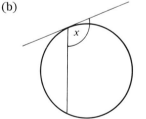   (c)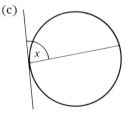

2. Copy each of the following diagrams and shade any angle that is in the alternate segment relative to the angle *x*.

   (a) 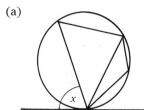   (b)    (c)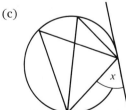

Find the sizes of the angles marked *x* and *y*.

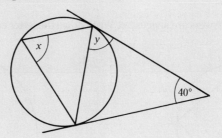

$$y = 70° \quad \text{(base angle of isosceles triangle)}$$
$$x = y \quad \text{(alternate segment theorem)}$$
$$\therefore \ x = 70°$$

These questions may require any of the properties given in this chapter concerning angles in circles. Find each marked angle.

3. (a)

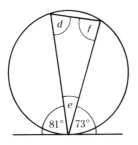

(b)

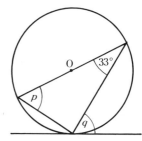

4. (a)

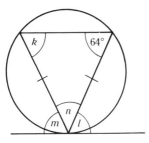

(b)

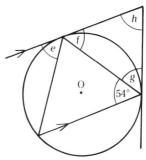

5. (a)

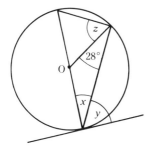

(b)

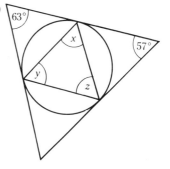

Self-Assessment 29

In questions 1 to 3 several answers are suggested. Write down the letter corresponding to the correct answer.

1.

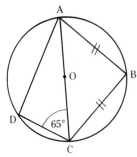

AOC is a diameter of the circle with centre O. AB = BC and $A\widehat{C}D = 65°$. The size of angle BAD is

A 115°   **B** 90°   **C** 70°   **D** 155°

2.

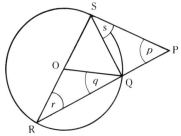

PS is a tangent to the circle with centre O. Which statement is true ?

A $\widehat{p} = \widehat{q}$ **C** $\widehat{p} = \widehat{s}$

B $\widehat{r} = \widehat{p}$ **D** $\widehat{s} = \widehat{r}$

3.

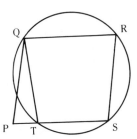

PQRS is a parallelogram. Which of these statements is true ?

A $T\widehat{Q}R + Q\widehat{R}S = 180°$

B $P\widehat{Q}R + R\widehat{S}T = 180°$

C $Q\widehat{T}S + Q\widehat{R}S = 180°$

D $Q\widehat{P}S + Q\widehat{R}S = 180°$

4.

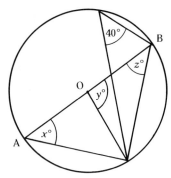

AOB is a diameter of the circle with centre O. Find the values of x, y and z.

5.

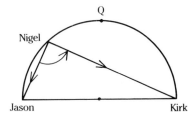

Jason and Kirk are standing at opposite ends of the diameter of a semicircular lawn. Nigel walks part of the way round the curved edge to the position shown in the diagram. He faces Jason directly and then turns to face Kirk. Through what angle does Nigel turn ? If he walks on to the position marked Q and again turns from facing Jason to facing Kirk, does he turn through a larger angle ?

6.

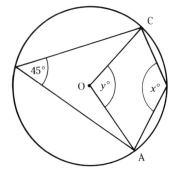

(a) Find x and y.

(b) Explain why a circle drawn on AC as diameter must pass through O.

7.

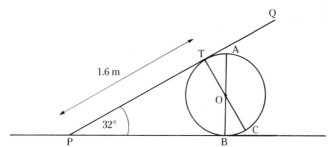

A scaffold pole PTQ rests against an oil drum with centre O as shown. Find

(a) TÔA   (b) TĈA   (c) PB

8.

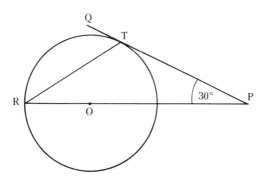

PQ is a tangent at T to the circle with centre O and TP̂O is 30°. Giving a reason for each step in your calculations, find the size of

(a) PÔT   (b) OR̂T   (c) RT̂Q

9.

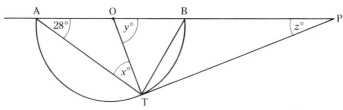

PT is a tangent to the semicircle with centre O. AOBP is a straight line. If TÂO = 28° find the values of x, y and z.

10.

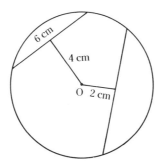

A chord of length 6 cm, drawn in a circle with centre O, is 4 cm from O. If another chord is drawn 2 cm distant from O, what is its length ?

LOCI

'Locus' is the Latin word for 'position' or 'place' but in mathematics it is used to mean not just one point, but a set of points whose positions satisfy a given rule.

Every point on a locus must obey the given conditions or rule and every point that obeys the rule lies on the locus.

Consider the rule that a point P on a sheet of paper is to be 3 cm from a fixed point O (also on the paper). A few possible positions can be marked to give an idea of the shape of the complete locus. Mark as many positions of P as you need to deduce the shape of the locus.

It can now be seen that the locus is the circle, centre O, radius 3 cm.

It is sometimes helpful to think of a locus as the path traced out by a moving point.

For example, suppose that a goat is tethered by a rope with one end fixed at O. If the goat moves so that the rope is always taut, the path is a circle.

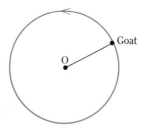

In two dimensions a locus can be a set of separate points, a set of lines or curves, or a region.

The plural of locus is *loci*.

Exercise 30a

One end of a chain 2 m long is attached to the collar of a dog and the other end to a ring that can slide on a fixed rail 4 m long. Assuming that the dog's collar remains 0.5 m from the ground, sketch the locus of the point of attachment on the collar.

To find a region, find its boundary first, in this case by thinking of the chain as being taut. Mark a few possible positions.

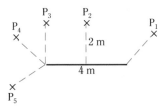   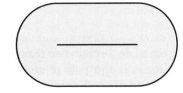

The boundary is part of the locus so it is drawn with a solid line, not a broken one.

Sketch the locus in each of the following questions. In some cases the sketch will have to be approximate but if a straight line or a circle is involved it should be described where possible, e.g. by giving the centre and radius of the circle.

1. The end of a hand of a clock.

2. (a) A ball thrown vertically upwards.

   (b) A ball thrown up at an angle.

3. The needle on a record as it rotates on the turntable.

4. A bicycle is ridden in a straight line along a level road.

   (a) A point on the saddle.

   (b) A point on the rim of the bicycle wheel.

   (c) The midpoint of a spoke.

5. A lower corner of an up-and-over garage door.

6. A goat tethered by a rope 6 m long to a point in the centre of a field.

7. A dog on a long rope, tethered to a tree trunk. The dog walks clockwise round the tree, keeping the rope taut.

8. A point that is equidistant from two fixed points A and B whose distance apart is 6 cm.

9. A point that is always 2 cm from a fixed line.

10. A point that is equidistant from two fixed intersecting lines AB and AC.

11. A door handle on an opening door.

12.

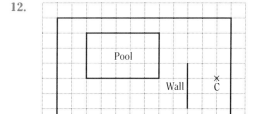

The diagram shows a swimming pool and a wall in a garden. Carol is sitting behind the wall at point C. Alan is walking about on the other side of the wall in such a way that Carol is unable to see him. Copy the diagram and shade the locus of the point representing Alan.

STANDARD LOCI

The more important loci previously discussed are now listed.

1. The locus of a point that moves in such a way that it is always at a fixed distance *r* from a fixed point C, is called a circle. C is the centre of the circle, and *r* is its radius.

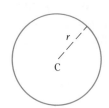

2. If a point moves so that it is at a constant distance from a line through two fixed points A and B, its locus is the pair of straight lines drawn parallel to AB and distant *d* from it.

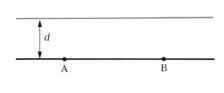

3. The locus of a point that is equidistant from two fixed points A and B, is the perpendicular bisector of AB.

4. The locus of a point that is equidistant from two fixed intersecting lines XOY and ZOW, is the pair of bisectors of the angles between the fixed lines. These bisectors are always at right angles to each other.

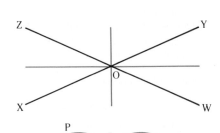

5. The locus of a point P at which two fixed points A and B subtend a given angle $x°$, i.e. angle APB $= x°$, is the pair of arcs of circles.

In particular, if $x = 90$, the locus is the pair of semicircles.

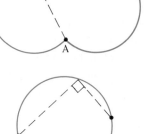

When drawing a locus accurately, draw a rough sketch and use it to find the shape of the locus and to calculate any necessary information. The accurate drawing should be as simple and as clear of unnecessary clutter as possible.

Exercise 30b

For each question sketch the locus of P and then draw the locus accurately, using whatever instruments are appropriate. If the locus is a region, draw the boundary accurately and shade the region lightly. If possible describe the locus briefly.

1. AB is a chord of length 6 cm of a circle, centre O, radius 5 cm, and P is the midpoint of AB. AB moves round the circle.

2.

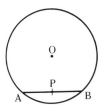

AB is a chord of variable length in a circle centre O, radius 5 cm, and P is the midpoint of AB. AB moves so that it is always parallel to its original position.

3. A is a fixed point. P is such that AP < 4 cm.

4. A and B are fixed points 8 cm apart. P is a point such that AP ≤ BP.

5.

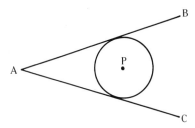

P is the centre of a circle that touches AB and AC.

6. A is a fixed point. P is the centre of a circle of radius 6 cm that passes through A.

7. A and B are two fixed points, 10 cm apart. P is the point such that angle APB = 90°.

8. P is such that it is less than 4 cm from a fixed line.

In the square ABCD, AB = 8 cm. Find all possible positions of a point E that is 6 cm from A and also equidistant from B and C. Measure EB.

The locus of a point 6 cm from A is a circle and the locus of a point equidistant from B and C is the perpendicular bisector of BC. E lies at the intersection of these two loci.

From this sketch we see that there are two positions for E. An accurate drawing may be made from which EB can be measured.

EB = 5.3 cm or 13.1 cm.

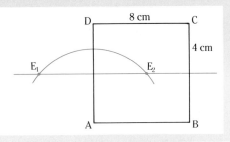

In the following questions, a rough sketch and an accurate drawing are required.

9. In triangle PQR, PQ = 10 cm, $\hat{Q} = 90°$ and $\hat{P} = 50°$. Find a point T within the triangle such that T is equidistant from PQ and QR, and T is 7.5 cm from P. (There may be more than one possible position for T.) Measure TQ.

10. ABCD is a rectangle such that AB = 8 cm and BC = 12 cm. Find all the possible positions of a point E, if E is 5 cm from AB and 8 cm from D. Measure EC in each case.

11. ABCD is a rectangular enclosure where AB = 8 m and BC = 16 m. A donkey is tethered by a rope 9.5 m long attached to the corner A. The owner has divided the enclosure into two sections by a line that is the perpendicular bisector of AC and has planted the part further from A with cabbages. Sketch a diagram and shade the planted region that the donkey can reach.

(a) Use an accurate drawing to find the length of the straight line boundary of this region.

(b) How long a rope *should* the donkey have?

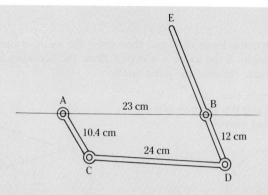

This linkage is a simplified version of a windscreen wiper mechanism. A and B are fixed points and AC rotates through 360° about A. C is linked to a point D on the wiper.

(a) Sketch the loci of C and D.

(b) Using an accurate drawing, find the extreme positions of D. Hence find the angle through which the wiper turns.

(a) The locus of D is part of a circle, radius 12 cm.

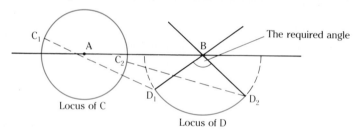

$$C_1D_1 = C_2D_2 = 24\,\text{cm}$$

(b) Draw the line AB, circle and semi-circle. With compasses set at a radius of 24 cm, use trial and error to find D_1 and D_2. It should become clear that C_1AD_1 and AC_2D_2 are straight lines. We have used a scale of 1 cm to 6 cm to save space but this is too small for accuracy. A better scale to use is 1 cm to 2 cm.

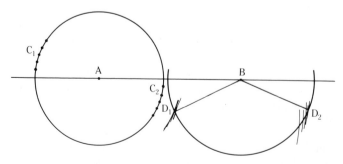

The angle turned through is 130°

12.

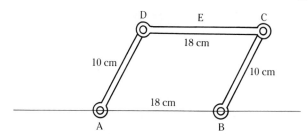

In the linkage above, A and B are fixed points. DA rotates about A. D starts on AB and AD turns through 180°. Sketch and describe the locus of

(a) D

(b) C

(c) E, the midpoint of DC.

(d) Sketch the locus of F, the midpoint of AC and make an accurate drawing to find four possible positions of F.

13.

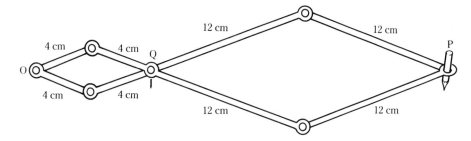

This linkage is a pantograph, which is used in drawing. O is a fixed point. If Q is moved round a drawing of a square, the mechanism moves the pen at P so that it draws a shape. Describe the shape. How does it compare with the original drawing ?

14.

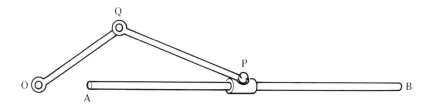

In this linkage, OQ is constrained to rotate about O, which is a fixed point. A sleeve P is linked to Q. P is free to slide along the fixed bar AB.

OQ = 5 cm, QP = 10 cm, OA = 3 cm and AB = 16 cm.

(a) Sketch the locus of Q.

(b) Sketch the locus of P as OQ rotates.

(c) Make an accurate drawing and mark four possible positions of Q and the corresponding positions of P. Find the greatest and least distances of P from O.

LOCI IN THREE DIMENSIONS

The ideas and methods developed to deal with loci in two dimensions can be extended to three dimensions.

In three dimensions a locus can be a line or a surface or a region contained by a surface. The locus of the possible positions of a fly trapped in a box is the space enclosed by the box.

Two other examples of loci in three dimensions are given below.

The locus of a point that is at a given distance r from a fixed point A, is a sphere, centre A, radius r.

The locus of a point P that is equidistant from two fixed points A and B is the plane bisecting AB at right angles. (Only part of this plane is shown in the diagram. Two possible positions of P are shown, marked P_1 and P_2.)

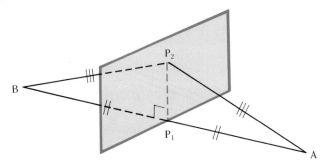

The questions in the next exercise refer to loci in two and three dimensions.

Exercise 30c

For each question give either a sketch or a full description of the locus of P, or both if it helps to make the situation clear.

1. A door measures 1 m by 2 m, and it rotates through 80° as it opens. P is the top outer corner.

2. A square table 1 m high can be placed anywhere in a room. P is a point on a corner of the table.

3. P is the end of a rod PQ, of length 80 cm. The rod can swing in any direction about the fixed point Q, though P never rises above the level of Q.

4. P is 4 cm from a fixed plane.

5. Q is the centre of a sphere of radius 4 cm. The distance of P from the surface of the sphere is

   (a) 6 cm, (b) 2 cm, (c) 4 cm.

6. P is 2 cm from the curved surface of a cylindrical tube of radius 1 cm.

7. P is a bee that flies no more than 40 m from its hive and no more than 1 m from the ground, which is level.

8. Two sticklebacks have their nests 1 m apart. When the two fish meet they fight but the one nearer its own nest will win. P is a point at which neither is dominant.

The rest of this exercise consists of harder mixed questions. Unless told otherwise work in two dimensions.

9. P is the centre of a circle that touches a fixed line at a given point T. The circle and the line are in the same plane. Sketch and describe the locus of P in each of the following cases.

   (a) Two dimensions: the radius of the circle can be of any size.

   (b) Three dimensions: the radius of the circle is 5 cm.

10. Draw accurately △ABC in which AB = 12 cm, BC = 10 cm and CA = 8 cm.

    (a) Draw the locus of a point equidistant from A and B.

    (b) Draw the locus of a point equidistant from B and C.

    (c) The two loci cut at D. How do you expect DA, DB and DC to compare with one another in length? Check by measuring.

    (d) Draw a circle, centre D, radius DA. (This is the *circumcircle* of △ABC.)

11. (a)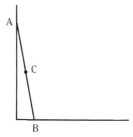

    A square WXYZ is rolled along a fixed line. Sketch and describe the locus of X.

    (b) Repeat the question for an equilateral triangle XYZ.

12.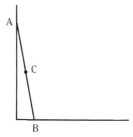

    A ladder AB is propped at a very steep angle against a wall. It slides down, its ends staying in contact with the wall and the floor, until it is flat on the floor. C is the midpoint of AB.

    Sketch the locus of   (a) A   (b) B   (c) C.

13.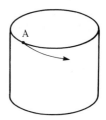

    A spider crawls from top to bottom down the outside of a cylinder in such a way that its path is always at 30° to the horizontal.

    (a) Sketch or describe the locus of the spider in three dimensions.

    (b) If the curved surface of the cylinder were unrolled and flattened out, sketch the spider's path.

    (c) The height of the cylinder is 6 cm and the radius 8 cm. How long is the spider's path?

    (d) If the radius of the cylinder were 1 cm, how would the length of the path differ from that found in (c)?

14.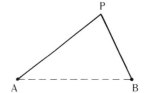

    A and B are two fixed points 6 cm apart. P is a point such that AP + BP = 10 cm. Plot as many positions of P as convenient and find the shape of the locus of P. (This locus may also be drawn by using a thread 10 cm long and fixing the two ends to A and B. Put the pencil into the loop of the thread and move the pencil, keeping the thread taut. This method works better on a larger scale.)

15. In three dimensions, A and B are two points 16 cm apart.

    (a) Describe the locus of a point that is always 10 cm from   (i) A   (ii) B.

    (b) Describe the locus of a point that is always 10 cm from both A and B.

16. (a) P moves so that the sum of its distances from two fixed perpendicular lines is 8 cm. Use graph paper to draw the locus of P.

(b) Draw the locus of P if the two fixed lines are at 60° to each other. (Use isometric paper.)

17. AOB and COD are two lines that cut at 60°. The locus of a point P that is equidistant from AB and CD is the pair of lines XY and ZW.

(a) Find angle XOZ.

(b) If P is also 8 cm from O find all four possible positions of P. Give the distances between adjacent positions of P.

Investigations

1. Up-and-over garage doors, mechanical weighing machines and similar mechanisms have interesting linkages controlling movement. Investigate as many as you can find, drawing the locus of a point on a moving part, e.g. a garage door, giving both a sketch and an accurate drawing where possible.

2. In Exercise 30c, question 11, a square and a triangle were rolled along a straight line and the locus of a vertex was considered. This situation can be further investigated.

(a) Other polygons or circles can be rolled.

(b) The locus of a point other than a vertex can be traced. The point can even be inside the figure.

(c) The figure can be rolled on a curve or inside a square.

Self-Assessment 30

Assume that all the questions refer to two-dimensional situations unless you are told otherwise.

1. A circle of radius 2 cm rolls round the inside of a square of side 6 cm. Describe the locus of the centre of the circle.

2. A is a fixed point. Illustrate the locus of P if

(a) $4 \text{ cm} < AP < 6 \text{ cm}$

(b) $AP \geqslant 3 \text{ cm}$.

3. Point P lies within a square ABCD of side 6 cm so that it is 5 cm from B and 3 cm from CD.

Use an accurate drawing to find how far P is from A.

4. In three dimensions, A and B are fixed points 8 cm apart and C is the midpoint of AB. Describe the locus of point P if it is

(a) 5 cm from B

(b) equidistant from A and B

(c) both 5 cm from B and equidistant from A and B.

5.

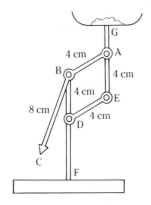

The diagram shows the linkage in a miniature weighing machine with a tray at G on which an object can be placed. C is a heavy pointer, BDF, GAE and ABC are rigid, $A\hat{B}C = 150°$ and F is fixed to a heavy base. The linkage is freely jointed at A, B, D and E. With nothing on the tray, BC is vertical. When an object is placed on the tray, the tray descends a short distance. Describe the locus of

(a) A   (c) C

(b) E   (d) the midpoint of BE.

31 TRIGONOMETRY IN ANY TRIANGLE

TRIGONOMETRIC RATIOS

In trigonometry in Chapter 20 we confined ourselves to right-angled triangles. Many triangles do not have right angles and some have one angle that is obtuse. We therefore need to modify the definitions of sine, cosine and tangent so that they cover angles of all sizes.

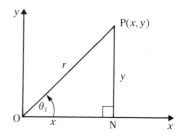

We start with a right-angled triangle and impose a coordinate system on it. P is the point (x, y), so $ON = x$ and $PN = y$. Let the length of OP be r.

In the diagram above, $\tan \theta_1 = \dfrac{y}{x}$, $\sin \theta_1 = \dfrac{y}{r}$ and $\cos \theta_1 = \dfrac{x}{r}$.

(θ is a Greek letter pronounced 'theta'.)

Now think of this diagram in a different way: OP is a line (of length r) that starts from the x-axis and can rotate through as large an angle as we wish.

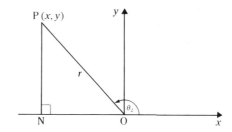

We will continue to use the same definitions i.e. $\tan \theta_2 = \dfrac{y}{x}$ and so on.

We see that x is now negative while y is still positive, so $\tan \theta_2$ is negative, $\sin \theta_2$ is positive and $\cos \theta_2$ is negative.

If $\theta_1 = 60°$ and $\theta_2 = 120°$ we can see that
$\tan \theta_2 = -\tan \theta_1$, $\sin \theta_2 = \sin \theta_1$, $\cos \theta_2 = -\cos \theta_1$

It is useful to remember that, if θ is obtuse,

$$\sin \theta = \sin(180° - \theta)$$
$$\cos \theta = -\cos(180° - \theta)$$
$$\tan \theta = -\tan(180° - \theta)$$

493

Exercise 31a

1. Find (a) sin 30°   (b) sin 150°

2. Find (a) cos 39°   (b) cos 141°

3. Find the following ratios.
   (a) sin 140°   (d) sin 162°
   (b) tan 98°   (e) tan 110°
   (c) cos 162°   (f) cos 142°

4. Do not use a calculator in this question.

   Use $\sin \theta = \sin(180° - \theta)$
   and $\cos \theta = -\cos(180° - \theta)$
   to complete the following statements.
   (a) If sin 60° = 0.866, sin 120° =
   (b) If cos 72° = 0.309, cos 108° =
   (c) If sin 135° = 0.7071, sin 45° =
   (d) If cos 132° = −0.6691, cos 48° =

5. Investigate the sine, cosine and tangent of
   (a) 0°   (b) 90°   (c) 180°

6.

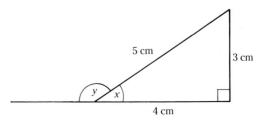

   Without using a calculator write down as a fraction
   (a) sin x   (c) sin y
   (b) cos x   (d) cos y

Find the angle between 90° and 180° for which
(a) the cosine is −0.6   (b) the sine is 0.72

(a) cos θ = −0.6

       θ = 126.9°

Press ⬚· ⬚6 ⬚+/− ⬚cos⁻¹

A negative cosine gives an angle between
90° and 180°

(b) sin θ = 0.72

       θ = 180° − 46.05...°

         = 133.9° (1 d.p.)

Press ⬚· ⬚7 ⬚2 ⬚sin⁻¹

The display shows an angle between 0° and 90°

---

7. Find the angle between 0° and 180° for which
   the cosine is
   (a) 0.6   (c) −0.7345
   (b) −0.3   (d) 0.7345

8. (a) There are two angles between 0° and
        180° that have a sine of 0.5. What are
        these angles?
   (b) Repeat (a) for a sine of 0.765

9. Find the angle between 90° and 180° for
   which the sine is
   (a) 0.345   (b) 0.65

10. How many angles are there, from 0° to 180°,
    for which
    (a) the sine is 0
    (b) the cosine is 0
    (c) the tangent is 0?

NON-RIGHT ANGLED TRIANGLES

In a right-angled triangle we can use sine, cosine and tangent as defined in Chapter 20 to calculate sides and angles directly. In a triangle that does not contain a right angle we need other relationships in order to calculate these quantities.

Notation

In $\triangle$ABC the side opposite angle A is usually marked a, the side opposite angle B is marked b and so on.

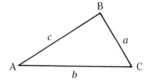

THE SINE RULE

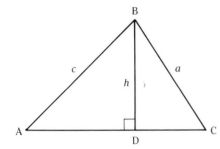 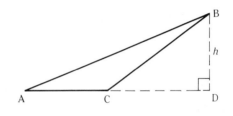

In $\triangle$ABD, $\widehat{ADB} = 90°$ so $\sin A = \dfrac{h}{c}$ $\Rightarrow$ $h = c \sin A$

In $\triangle$BDC, $\widehat{BDC} = 90°$ so $\sin C = \dfrac{h}{a}$ $\Rightarrow$ $h = a \sin C$

Comparing the expressions for h we see that $a \sin C = c \sin A$

Dividing both sides by $\sin C$ and $\sin A$ gives $\dfrac{a}{\sin A} = \dfrac{c}{\sin C}$

Repeating this with a perpendicular drawn from C to AB gives $\dfrac{a}{\sin A} = \dfrac{b}{\sin B}$, so

$$\frac{a}{\sin A} = \frac{b}{\sin B} = \frac{c}{\sin C}$$

It is sometimes useful to rearrange this as

$$\frac{\sin A}{a} = \frac{\sin B}{b} = \frac{\sin C}{c}$$

This is called the *sine rule* and can be used to find the side of a triangle by selecting the two parts that fit the given information.

Exercise 31b

In $\triangle ABC$, $\widehat{A} = 72°$, $\widehat{B} = 31°$ and AC = 4 cm. Find BC.

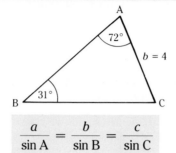

Sine rule

$$\frac{a}{\sin A} = \frac{b}{\sin B} = \frac{c}{\sin C}$$

We are concerned with A and B only so ignore c and sin C.

$$\frac{a}{\sin 72°} = \frac{4}{\sin 31°}$$

$$a = \frac{4}{\sin 31°} \times \sin 72° \qquad \text{Multiplying both sides by sin } 72°$$

$$= 7.386\ldots$$

$\therefore$ BC = 7.39 cm   (3 s.f.)

Look at the triangle and check that this is a reasonable answer. Is the smallest angle opposite the smallest side?

---

1. Find AC.

2. Find BC.

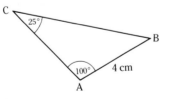

3. In $\triangle ABC$, $\widehat{B} = 56°$, $\widehat{C} = 23°$ and AB = 6 cm. Find AC.

4. In $\triangle ABC$, $\widehat{A} = 132°$, $\widehat{C} = 21°$ and BC = 12 cm. Find AB.

5. In $\triangle LMN$, $\widehat{L} = 60°$, $\widehat{M} = 34°$ and LN = 3.8 cm. Find MN.

6. In $\triangle ABC$, $\widehat{A} = 56°$, $\widehat{B} = 37°$ and AB = 6 cm. Find BC and AC.

(Notice that you will need to find $\widehat{C}$ first.)

7.

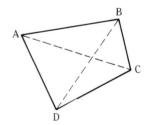

In a survey of a field ABCD, the following measurements were taken: BD = 100 m, $D\widehat{B}C = 32°$, $B\widehat{D}C = 40°$, $B\widehat{D}A = 36°$ and $A\widehat{C}D = 45°$.

Find the lengths of

(a) BC   (b) CD   (c) AD.

(More than one triangle is involved so state which triangle you are using.)

THE COSINE RULE

Suppose that we need to find angle A in this triangle.

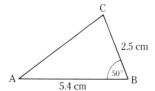

Using the sin formula gives $\dfrac{2.5}{\sin A} = \dfrac{5.4}{\sin C} = \dfrac{AC}{\sin 50°}$

Whichever pair we try to use from these equations, there are two unknown quantities, so we cannot use the sine rule.

There is, however, another relationship between the sides and angles in any triangle.

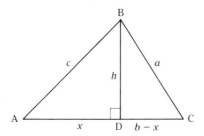

In $\triangle$CBD, $\hat{D} = 90°$, and Pythagoras' theorem gives

$$a^2 = h^2 + (b - x)^2 \quad \text{so} \quad a^2 = h^2 + b^2 - 2bx + x^2 \qquad [1]$$

In $\triangle$ABD, $\hat{D} = 90°$ $\qquad\qquad$ so $\quad c^2 = h^2 + x^2$ $\qquad\qquad\qquad$ [2]

[1] − [2] gives $\qquad\qquad a^2 - c^2 = b^2 - 2bx \quad \text{so} \quad a^2 = b^2 + c^2 - 2bx \qquad$ [3]

But in $\triangle$ABD, $\cos A = \dfrac{x}{c}$ so $x = c \cos A$

Substituting for x in [3], gives

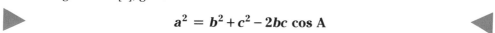

$$a^2 = b^2 + c^2 - 2bc \cos A$$

This is called the *cosine rule* and, although we have not proved this, it is also valid when $\hat{A}$ is obtuse.

Notice that it starts off as if it were Pythagoras' theorem $(a^2 = b^2 + c^2)$ but it is then modified.

Similarly,

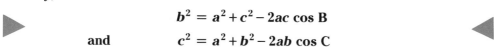

$$b^2 = a^2 + c^2 - 2ac \cos B$$

and $\qquad\qquad c^2 = a^2 + b^2 - 2ab \cos C$

Make sure that you have understood the *pattern* of the formula so that you can adapt it for use with other letters. Note that the first letter and the angle letter are the same in each case.

The cosine rule can be used directly to find the third side of a triangle when two sides are given and the angle between the sides is known.

Exercise 31c

Write down the version of the cosine rule that involves the marked angle. The first one is done for you.

1.

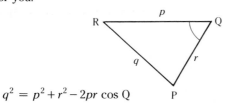

$$q^2 = p^2 + r^2 - 2pr \cos Q$$

3.

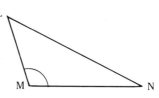

2.

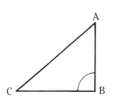

4.

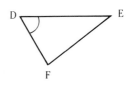

In $\triangle ABC$, $\widehat{A} = 65°$, $AC = 7$ cm and $AB = 5$ cm. Find BC.

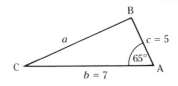

$$a^2 = b^2 + c^2 - 2bc \cos A$$
$$= 7^2 + 5^2 - (2 \times 7 \times 5 \times \cos 65°)$$
$$= 49 + 25 - (70 \times 0.4226)$$
$$= 74 - 29.58\ldots$$
$$= 44.41\ldots$$
$$a = \sqrt{44.41} = 6.664$$

$\therefore BC = 6.66$ cm (3 s.f.)

---

5. In $\triangle ABC$, $\widehat{A} = 45°$, $AB = 5$ cm and $AC = 6$ cm. Find BC.

6. In $\triangle ABC$, $\widehat{B} = 72°$, $BC = 8$ cm and $BA = 10$ cm. Find AC.

7. In $\triangle CDE$, $\widehat{C} = 102°$, $CD = 10$ cm and $CE = 12$ cm. Find DE.

8. In $\triangle PQR$, $\widehat{R} = 32°$, $PR = 1.4$ m and $QR = 2.2$ m. Find PQ.

9. A village has three features; the church C, the shop S and the bridge B. $CB = 120$ m, $SB = 86$ m and $S\widehat{B}C = 78°$. Find how far the church is from the shop.

10. (a) Make cos A the subject of the formula
$$a^2 = b^2 + c^2 - 2bc \cos A$$
(You may find the manipulation easier to manage if you write x in place of cos A.)

   (b) Write down the version of the formula with cos B as the subject.

Using the Cosine Rule to Find an Angle

If the lengths of all three sides are known, the cosine rule can be used to find an angle. There are two methods.

The values for a, b and c can be substituted into the appropriate version of the formula, e.g. if $\widehat{C}$ is required, then use $c^2 = a^2 + b^2 - 2ab \cos C$

Alternatively, make $\cos C$ the subject of the formula so that

$$\cos C = \frac{a^2 + b^2 - c^2}{2ab}$$

Exercise 31d

In $\triangle ABC$, $AB = 6\,cm$, $BC = 8\,cm$ and $AC = 11\,cm$. Find $\widehat{B}$.

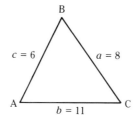

The formula containing $\widehat{B}$ starts with b.

$$b^2 = a^2 + c^2 - 2ac \cos B$$

Let x represent $\cos B$

$$11^2 = 8^2 + 6^2 - (2 \times 8 \times 6 \times x)$$
$$121 = 64 + 36 - 96x$$
$$121 + 96x = 100$$
$$96x = -21$$
$$x = -\tfrac{21}{96}$$

i.e. $\cos B = -0.21875 \ldots$

$\widehat{B} = 102.6°$ (1 d.p.)

In this exercise, use either the method given in the worked example above or use the formula with the cosine as the subject.

1. In $\triangle ABC$, $AB = 7\,cm$, $BC = 8\,cm$ and $AC = 9\,cm$. Find $\widehat{A}$.

2. In $\triangle PQR$, $PQ = 6\,cm$, $QR = 5\,cm$ and $RP = 9\,cm$. Find $\widehat{P}$.

3. In $\triangle LMN$, $LM = 13\,cm$, $MN = 10\,cm$ and $NL = 22\,cm$. Find $\widehat{M}$.

4. In $\triangle DEF$, $DE = 4.3\,m$, $EF = 3.2\,m$ and $DF = 6.2\,m$. Find $\widehat{E}$.

5. In △ABC, AB = 7.3 cm, AC = 4.6 cm and
    BC = 6.1 cm. Find

    (a) $\hat{B}$ (b) $\hat{C}$.

6. In △PQR, QR is twice as long as PQ and PR is
    1.5 times as long as PQ. Taking the length of
    PQ as x cm, find $\hat{R}$.

7. Point A is 32 m due north of B, and C is 19 m
    from A and 21 m from B, to the east of AB. Find
    the bearing of C from B.

8. Gary is drawing a map showing three towns
    P, Q and R. He knows that PQ = 32 km,
    QR = 46 km and RP = 38 km but he
    would find the map easier to draw if he knew
    the angles.
    Find all three angles of the triangle PQR.

CHOOSING WHICH FORMULA TO USE

1. If the triangle is isosceles, it can be divided into two
    right-angled triangles and right-angled triangle methods can
    be used.

2. If two angles and a side are given, either of the other two
    sides can be found using the sine rule, first finding the third
    angle if necessary.
    The sine rule is easier to use than the cosine rule and should
    be considered first.

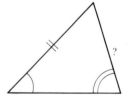

3. If two sides and the included angle are given, the cosine rule
    will give the side opposite the angle.

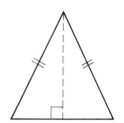

4. If three sides are given, the cosine rule will give any one of the
    angles.

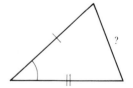

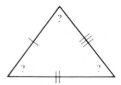

Exercise 31e

In each of the questions from 1 to 6 write down 1, 2, 3 or 4 from the list of methods above and, where appropriate, the version of the sine or cosine rule to be used to find the required side or angle.

These questions may also be used to give extra practice in calculation.

1. In △CDE, DE = 6 cm, $\hat{E}$ = 87° and $\hat{C}$ = 45°. Find CD.

2. In △LMN, LM = 6 cm, $\hat{L}$ = 87° and LN = 5.4 cm. Find MN.

3. In △PQR, PQ = 6 cm, QR = 5.4 cm and RP = 3.5 cm. Find $\hat{Q}$.

4. In △ABC, AB = BC = 5.2 cm and $\hat{B}$ = 34°. Find AC.

5. In △XYZ, XZ = 6 cm, $\hat{Z}$ = 32° and $\hat{X}$ = 90°. Find XY.

6. In △FGH, GH = 6 cm, $\hat{G}$ = 62° and $\hat{H}$ = 71°. Find FH.

Pythagoras' theorem may be useful in some of these questions.

7.

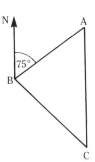

The bearing of town A from town B is 075° and the distance is 30 km. C is due south of A and its bearing from B is 120°. Find the distance of C from A.

8.

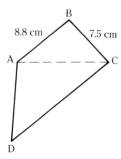

In the quadrilateral, AB is parallel to DC, AB = 8.8 cm, BC = 7.5 cm and AC = 12 cm.

(a) Find A$\hat{B}$C.

(b) If B$\hat{D}$C = 36°, find BD.

9.

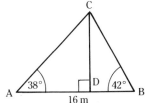

A pole CD stands on level ground. Points A and B are on opposite sides of the pole, 16 m apart. The angles of elevation from A and B of the top of the pole are 38° and 42° respectively. Find

(a) AC   (b) the height of the pole.

10. Starting from A, a ship sails 10 km on a bearing of 060°, to B, then 12 km due east to C.

(a) Find how far C is from A.

(b) Find the bearing of C from A.

11.

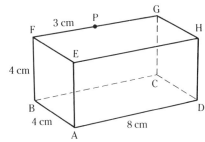

The diagram shows a cuboid. Find

(a) PB   (c) PC   (e) A$\hat{P}$D

(b) PA   (d) PD   (f) P$\hat{C}$A

(g) In each part from (a) to (f) state which two congruent triangles were used.

12.

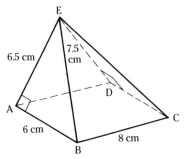

The base ABCD of this pyramid is a rectangle. The vertex E is immediately above a point on AD, so $\widehat{EAB} = \widehat{EDC} = 90°$. AE $= 6.5\,\text{cm}$ and ED $= 7.5\,\text{cm}$. Find

(a) $\widehat{AED}$

(c) EC

(b) EB

(d) $\widehat{BEC}$.

13.

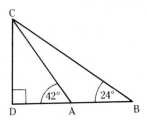

From two points A and B on horizontal ground the angles of elevation of the top C of a pole are 42° and 24° respectively. AC = 25 m. Find AB.

If A and B are on opposite sides of the pole but the rest of the information is the same as before, how far apart are A and B ?

14.

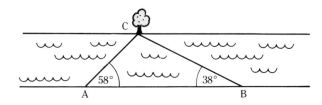

A base line AB of length 60 m is marked out on a river bank and the position of a tree C on the opposite bank is surveyed. It is found that $\widehat{CAB} = 58°$ and $\widehat{CBA} = 38°$.

(a) Find CA.

(b) Hence find the width of the river.

THE AMBIGUOUS CASE

If two sides and an angle opposite one of those sides are given, then the sine rule gives the angle opposite the other side. Because there can be two possible values for this in some cases, as can be seen from the diagrams below, the calculations are more complicated.

In $\triangle ABC$, AB $= 6\,\text{cm}$, AC $= 4\,\text{cm}$ and $\widehat{B} = 40°$.

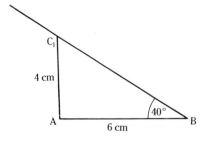
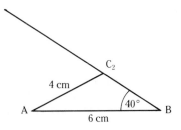

Exercise 31f

In $\triangle PQR$, $\hat{P} = 46°$, $PQ = 5\,cm$ and $QR = 6\,cm$. Find $\hat{R}$.

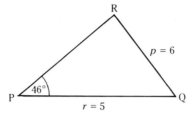

To find an angle we use the sine rule the other way up

$$\frac{\sin P}{p} = \frac{\sin R}{r}$$

We want R at the beginning of the formula so rearrange it

$$\frac{\sin R}{5} = \frac{\sin 46°}{6}$$

$$\sin R = \frac{\sin 46°}{6} \times 5$$

$$= 0.5994$$

There are two possible values of R between $0°$ and $180°$

$$\hat{R} = 36.8° \quad \text{or} \quad 180° - 36.8° \text{ i.e. } 143.2°$$

Now consider the angles of the triangle as a whole: it is not possible for $\hat{R}$ to take such a large value as $143.2°$ because the *sum* of the angles is only $180°$

$$\therefore \hat{R} = 36.8° \quad (1 \text{ d.p.})$$

Another useful check is to make sure that the smallest angle is opposite to the smallest side and so on.

1. Find the two angles between $0°$ and $180°$ for which the sine is
   (a) 0.6   (b) 0.45   (c) 0.512

2. In $\triangle ABC$, $\hat{B} = 56°$, $AC = 5\,cm$ and $BC = 3\,cm$. Find $\hat{A}$.

3. In $\triangle ABC$, $\hat{A} = 45°$, $BC = 10\,m$ and $AB = 12\,m$. Find $\hat{C}$.

4. In $\triangle PQR$, $\hat{P} = 62°$, $QR = 8\,cm$, $PR = 9\,cm$ and $\hat{Q}$ is obtuse. Find $\hat{Q}$.

5. In $\triangle LMN$, $\hat{M} = 29°$, $LN = 4\,cm$ and $LM = 6\,cm$. Find the two possible values of $\hat{N}$ and sketch the two possible triangles.

6. A student surveyor has collected the following information about a triangular field ABC:

$$AB = 72\,m, \quad BC = 109\,m \quad and \quad \widehat{C} = 41°.$$

He wishes to know the size of $\widehat{A}$.

(a) Has he enough information to find $\widehat{A}$? If the answer is yes, find it. If the answer is no, give possible values of $\widehat{A}$.

(b) Another student surveyor measured the same field and got $AB = 64\,m$, $BC = 109\,m$ and $\widehat{C} = 41°$. Is it possible to find a value for $\widehat{A}$ from these measurements ?

7. Amy is making a map of her local area. She knows that the monument M is $460\,m$ away from her house, H; the sports centre, S, is $406\,m$ from the monument, and $\widehat{HSM} = 70°$. Find $\widehat{SHM}$.

8. As part of a technology project Dena needed to have a triangle cut from a metal sheet. She sketched the triangle, labelled it ABC and marked these measurements on it: $AB = 32\,cm$, $BC = 20\,cm$, $\widehat{A} = 35°$. The sheet metal cutters sent it back saying that not enough information was provided. Explain why.

THE AREA OF A TRIANGLE

Until now, to find the area of a triangle we have needed to know the base and the perpendicular height. Now we can establish a formula that uses any two sides and the included angle.

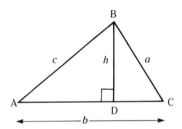

Area of $\triangle ABC = \frac{1}{2}$ base $\times$ height

The height is h and in $\triangle ABD$, $\sin A = \dfrac{h}{c} \quad \Rightarrow \quad h = c \times \sin A$

$\therefore$ area of $\triangle ABC = \frac{1}{2} \times b \times c \sin A = \frac{1}{2} bc \sin A$

In a similar way we can show that the area is $\frac{1}{2} ac \sin B$ or $\frac{1}{2} ab \sin C$

Again, learn the *pattern*.

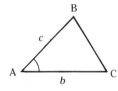

Area $= \frac{1}{2} bc \sin A$

The area of a triangle is half the product of two sides multiplied by the sine of the angle between them.

Exercise 31g

In △PQR, $\hat{P}$ = 43°, PQ = 9 cm and PR = 7 cm. Find the area of the triangle.

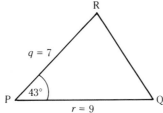

Area = $\frac{1}{2}qr$ sin P

$= \frac{1}{2} \times 7 \times 9 \times$ sin 43° cm²

= 21.48 cm² = 21.5 cm² (3 s.f.)

Find the area of each of the following triangles.

1. In △ABC, AB = 5 cm, AC = 6 cm and $\hat{A}$ = 48°

2. In △ABC, AB = 12 cm, BC = 10 cm and $\hat{B}$ = 121°

3. In △PQR, QR = 6.8 cm, RP = 3.8 cm and $\hat{R}$ = 76°

4. In △LMN, LM = 7 cm, $\hat{L}$ = 32° and $\hat{M}$ = 41°. Find

   (a) LN

   (b) the area of the triangle.

5. Find the area of an equilateral triangle of side 10 cm.

6. From A a spotter plane flies 60 km on a bearing of 032° to B, then from B 75 km roughly south east to C. The plane then flies 92 km back to A.

   (a) Find the bearing of C from A.

   (b) Find the area of the triangle enclosed by the path of the plane.

   (c) Suppose that the rough direction of the route from B to C had not been specified. What other possible answer could there be to part (a) ?

7.

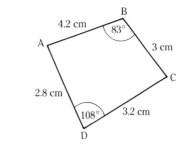

Find the area of quadrilateral ABCD.

8.

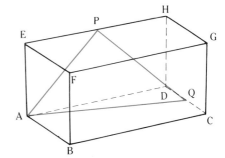

The cuboid in the diagram is such that AB = AE = 4 cm and EH = 6 cm. P and Q are midpoints of EH and DC. A triangular shape PAQ is being made to fit inside the cuboid.

   (a) Find the lengths of the sides of △PAQ.

   (b) Find P$\hat{A}$Q.

   (c) Find the area of △PAQ.

Self-Assessment 31

1. Find (a) sin 123° (b) cos 135°

2. Angle A is obtuse. Find $\hat{A}$ if
   (a) sin A = 0.453
   (b) cos A = −0.213

3. In △ABC, $\hat{A}$ = 72°, $\hat{B}$ = 34° and BC = 10 cm. Find AC.

4. In △ABC, $\hat{A}$ = 72°, AC = 7 cm and AB = 6.3 cm. Find BC.

5. In △LMN, $\hat{L}$ = $\hat{M}$ = 47° and LM = 8 cm. Find LN.

6. In △DEF, DE = 6 cm, EF = 7 cm and FD = 11 cm. Find $\hat{E}$.

7. Find the area of the triangle in question 4.

8. On a map, P is 4.7 cm due north of Q and R is 5.5 cm on a bearing of 125° from P. Find QR.

9. David wrote down what he thought was enough information to draw △ABC accurately; the measurements he had were AB = 3 cm, AC = 4 cm and $\hat{C}$ = 42°.
   How many triangles can be drawn with these measurements ?
   Sketch them and find $\hat{B}$ in each case.

32 ▶ VECTORS

A vector quantity is one that has both *magnitude* (i.e. size) and *direction*.

The simplest example of a vector is *displacement*, i.e. change of position. Both the distance moved and the direction are needed to describe it.

We can describe a displacement as, for example, 10 km on a bearing of 065°, or as the result of moving 4 m parallel to a wall followed by 3 m at right angles to the wall.

In either case the displacement can be represented by a directed line, i.e. a line with an arrow.

Other examples of vectors are
      force, e.g. 5 newtons acting downward
and   velocity, e.g. 4 m.p.h. due north.
      (Speed is the word used when no direction is given, so speed is *not* a vector.)

An example of a quantity that is not a vector is the mass of an object: it has magnitude but no direction. The word *scalar* is used for quantities of this kind.

We will use displacement to illustrate the properties of vectors. Once these have been grasped they can be applied to all other examples of vectors.

Notation

A directed line representing a vector can be drawn on squared paper.

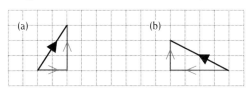

In (a) the displacement is 2 units to the right (+ve) and 3 units up, and is written $\begin{pmatrix} 2 \\ 3 \end{pmatrix}$

In (b) the displacement is 4 units to the left (−ve) and 2 units up, and is written $\begin{pmatrix} -4 \\ 2 \end{pmatrix}$

Note that the top number represents the movement parallel to the *x*-axis
and   the bottom number the movement parallel to the *y*-axis.

We can identify the vector either by using the capital letters indicating its end points, with an arrow over the top, ($\overrightarrow{AB}$), or by a small letter in heavy type (**a**) or, if handwritten, a small letter with a line underneath i.e. a̲.

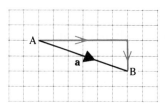

e.g.
$$\overrightarrow{AB} = \mathbf{a} = \underline{a} = \begin{pmatrix} 6 \\ -2 \end{pmatrix}$$

A small a is sometimes used to indicate the magnitude of **a** (i.e. the length of the line representing **a**) so the way in which the letter is written is important.

As vectors are usually independent of position, a line representing **a** can appear in different positions in a diagram.

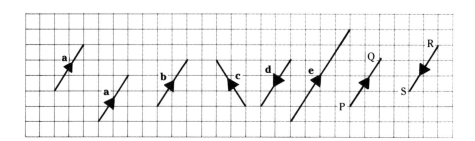

Two vectors are equal if they are in the same direction and have the same length, so **b** = **a**; but **c** ≠ **a** as the lines for **a** and **c** point in different directions, even though **a** and **c** are the same length.

Now **d** and **a** are the same length but are in opposite directions and we say that **d** = −**a**. The vectors **e** and **a** are in the same direction but the line representing **e** is twice as long as the line representing **a**. In this case we say that **e** = 2**a**.

Notice also that $\overrightarrow{PQ}$ = **a**, $\overrightarrow{RS}$ = −**a**   and $\overrightarrow{RS}$ = −$\overrightarrow{PQ}$

a and **e** are parallel vectors; **a** and **b** are equal vectors.

a and **c** are equal in magnitude but are *not* equal vectors.

The Magnitude of a Vector

The magnitude of **a** is usually written |**a**| and is given by the length of the line representing the vector. In this case using Pythagoras' theorem gives $|\mathbf{a}| = \sqrt{4+9} = \sqrt{13}$

In the diagrams in this chapter, unless otherwise indicated, the side of each square is of unit length.

Exercise 32a

1. State whether each of the following quantities is a vector or a scalar.

   (a) The length of a mat.

   (b) A velocity of 7 km per hour due east.

   (c) An acceleration of $1\,\text{m s}^{-2}$ downwards.

   (d) The flight of a bird in a straight line from bird-table to window-sill.

   (e) The mass of a bag of sugar.

   (f) The time it takes to read this sentence.

   (g) The flight path of an aeroplane.

   (h) The force needed to move a lift.

2.

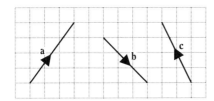

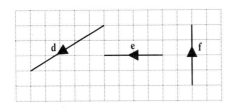

Give in the form $\begin{pmatrix} p \\ q \end{pmatrix}$ the vectors shown in the diagram above.

3. On squared paper, draw directed lines to represent the following vectors.

   (a) $\mathbf{a} = \begin{pmatrix} 4 \\ 5 \end{pmatrix}$ (d) $\mathbf{d} = \begin{pmatrix} -4 \\ -5 \end{pmatrix}$

   (b) $\mathbf{b} = \begin{pmatrix} 2 \\ -5 \end{pmatrix}$ (e) $\mathbf{e} = \begin{pmatrix} 0 \\ 2 \end{pmatrix}$

   (c) $\mathbf{c} = \begin{pmatrix} -6 \\ 1 \end{pmatrix}$ (f) $\mathbf{f} = \begin{pmatrix} -3 \\ 0 \end{pmatrix}$

4. Draw the vectors **a**, **b** and **c** where

   $\mathbf{a} = \begin{pmatrix} -2 \\ 4 \end{pmatrix}$, $\mathbf{b} = \begin{pmatrix} 6 \\ 3 \end{pmatrix}$ and $\mathbf{c} = \begin{pmatrix} 4 \\ -8 \end{pmatrix}$

   (a) Which vectors are parallel ?

   (b) Which two vectors are perpendicular ?

   (c) Find to which, if any, of **a**, **b** or **c** the following vectors are parallel.

   (i) $\begin{pmatrix} -3 \\ 6 \end{pmatrix}$ (ii) $\begin{pmatrix} 3 \\ 6 \end{pmatrix}$ (iii) $\begin{pmatrix} 3 \\ -6 \end{pmatrix}$

   (iv) $\begin{pmatrix} -1 \\ -2 \end{pmatrix}$ (v) $\begin{pmatrix} -2 \\ -1 \end{pmatrix}$ (vi) $\begin{pmatrix} 8 \\ -4 \end{pmatrix}$

5. Draw lines representing the following vectors and find the magnitude of each.

   (a) $\mathbf{a} = \begin{pmatrix} 3 \\ 4 \end{pmatrix}$ (d) $\mathbf{d} = \begin{pmatrix} -5 \\ 12 \end{pmatrix}$

   (b) $\mathbf{b} = \begin{pmatrix} -4 \\ 0 \end{pmatrix}$ (e) $\mathbf{e} = \begin{pmatrix} 2 \\ 1 \end{pmatrix}$

   (c) $\mathbf{c} = \begin{pmatrix} 0 \\ 6 \end{pmatrix}$ (f) $\mathbf{f} = \begin{pmatrix} -3 \\ -2 \end{pmatrix}$

   Leave the answers to (e) and (f) in square root form.

ADDITION OF VECTORS

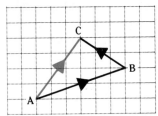

If we start at A and move to B and then move from B to C, the two displacements combined give the total displacement from A to C.

We write $\qquad \overrightarrow{AB} + \overrightarrow{BC} = \overrightarrow{AC}$

$\overrightarrow{AC}$ is called the *resultant* of $\overrightarrow{AB}$ and $\overrightarrow{BC}$.

Now, $\overrightarrow{AB} = \begin{pmatrix} 6 \\ 2 \end{pmatrix}$, $\overrightarrow{BC} = \begin{pmatrix} -3 \\ 2 \end{pmatrix}$ and $\overrightarrow{AC} = \begin{pmatrix} 3 \\ 4 \end{pmatrix}$

It can be seen that combining the left–right moves, 6 and −3, gives 3 and combining the up–down moves, 2 and 2, gives 4, so $\begin{pmatrix} 6 \\ 2 \end{pmatrix} + \begin{pmatrix} -3 \\ 2 \end{pmatrix} = \begin{pmatrix} 3 \\ 4 \end{pmatrix}$

Hence we can add vectors that are in the form $\begin{pmatrix} p \\ q \end{pmatrix}$ by adding elements in corresponding positions.

Any number of vectors can be added,

e.g.

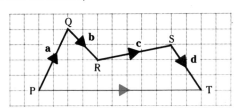

$$\mathbf{a} + \mathbf{b} + \mathbf{c} + \mathbf{d} = \begin{pmatrix} 2 \\ 4 \end{pmatrix} + \begin{pmatrix} 2 \\ -2 \end{pmatrix} + \begin{pmatrix} 5 \\ 1 \end{pmatrix} + \begin{pmatrix} 2 \\ -3 \end{pmatrix} = \begin{pmatrix} 11 \\ 0 \end{pmatrix}$$

(We could also write this as $\overrightarrow{PQ} + \overrightarrow{QR} + \overrightarrow{RS} + \overrightarrow{ST} = \overrightarrow{PT}$)

Multiples of Vectors

Now $\mathbf{a} + \mathbf{a} = 2\mathbf{a}$, so if $\mathbf{a} = \begin{pmatrix} x \\ y \end{pmatrix}$ then $2\mathbf{a} = \begin{pmatrix} 2x \\ 2y \end{pmatrix}$

and if $\mathbf{a} = \begin{pmatrix} 3 \\ -1 \end{pmatrix}$, then $3\mathbf{a} = \begin{pmatrix} 9 \\ -3 \end{pmatrix}$

In the same way, $-\mathbf{a} = -1 \times \mathbf{a} = \begin{pmatrix} -3 \\ 1 \end{pmatrix}$

Subtraction of Vectors

If $\mathbf{b} = \begin{pmatrix} -2 \\ 3 \end{pmatrix}$ then $-\mathbf{b} = \begin{pmatrix} 2 \\ -3 \end{pmatrix}$.

Furthermore, if $\mathbf{a} = \begin{pmatrix} 6 \\ 4 \end{pmatrix}$ then $\mathbf{a} - \mathbf{b} = \begin{pmatrix} 6 \\ 4 \end{pmatrix} - \begin{pmatrix} -2 \\ 3 \end{pmatrix}$

but $\mathbf{a} - \mathbf{b} = \mathbf{a} + (-\mathbf{b}) = \begin{pmatrix} 6 \\ 4 \end{pmatrix} + \begin{pmatrix} 2 \\ -3 \end{pmatrix} = \begin{pmatrix} 8 \\ 1 \end{pmatrix}$

i.e. $\begin{pmatrix} 6 \\ 4 \end{pmatrix} - \begin{pmatrix} -2 \\ 3 \end{pmatrix} = \begin{pmatrix} 8 \\ 1 \end{pmatrix}$

So we can subtract vectors by subtracting corresponding elements.

Exercise 32b

1. $\mathbf{a} = \begin{pmatrix} 4 \\ 2 \end{pmatrix}$ and $\mathbf{b} = \begin{pmatrix} -3 \\ 4 \end{pmatrix}$

   Draw on squared paper diagrams to represent

   (a) $\mathbf{a}$ (d) $\mathbf{a} + \mathbf{b}$ (g) $-\mathbf{a}$

   (b) $\mathbf{b}$ (e) $\mathbf{b} + \mathbf{a}$ (h) $-3\mathbf{b}$

   (c) $2\mathbf{a}$ (f) $\frac{1}{2}\mathbf{a}$ (i) $-\frac{1}{2}\mathbf{a}$

2.

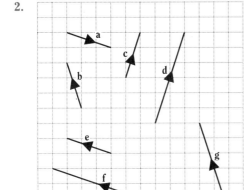

   (a) Find as many relationships as you can between the vectors in the diagram.

   (b) Give pairs of unequal vectors that are equal in magnitude.

   (c) Give each vector in the form $\begin{pmatrix} p \\ q \end{pmatrix}$

3.

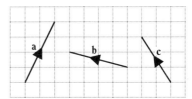

   Draw diagrams to illustrate

   (a) $\mathbf{a} + \mathbf{c}$ (d) $\mathbf{a} + \mathbf{c} + \mathbf{b}$

   (b) $\mathbf{c} + \mathbf{a}$ (e) $\mathbf{b} + \mathbf{c} + \mathbf{a}$

   (c) $\mathbf{a} + \mathbf{b} + \mathbf{c}$ (f) $\mathbf{c} + \mathbf{b} + \mathbf{a}$

   (g) What conclusion do you draw from comparing the diagrams?

   (h) Find other possible orders in which to add $\mathbf{a}, \mathbf{b}$ and $\mathbf{c}$. Do you get the same result as before?

4. If $\mathbf{a} = \begin{pmatrix} 2 \\ -3 \end{pmatrix}$ and $\mathbf{b} = \begin{pmatrix} -4 \\ -4 \end{pmatrix}$ find

   (a) $2\mathbf{a}$ (d) $3\mathbf{a} + \mathbf{b}$ (g) $-\mathbf{a}$

   (b) $-\mathbf{b}$ (e) $-3\mathbf{b}$ (h) $\mathbf{a} + 7\mathbf{b}$

   (c) $\mathbf{a} + \mathbf{b}$ (f) $\frac{1}{4}\mathbf{b}$ (i) $4\mathbf{a} + 4\mathbf{b}$

5. $\mathbf{x} = \begin{pmatrix} 3 \\ 6 \end{pmatrix}$, $\mathbf{y} = \begin{pmatrix} -2 \\ 3 \end{pmatrix}$ and $\mathbf{z} = \begin{pmatrix} 4 \\ -6 \end{pmatrix}$

   Find, in the form $\begin{pmatrix} p \\ q \end{pmatrix}$,

   (a) $\mathbf{x} - \mathbf{y}$ (d) $\mathbf{x} - \mathbf{y} + \mathbf{z}$

   (b) $\mathbf{y} - \mathbf{x}$ (e) $2\mathbf{x} - 3\mathbf{y}$

   (c) $\mathbf{x} + \mathbf{y} - \mathbf{z}$ (f) $\frac{1}{2}\mathbf{z} - \frac{1}{3}\mathbf{x}$

   Draw diagrams to illustrate (a) and (c).

VECTOR DIAGRAMS

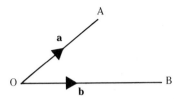

Given two vectors **a** and **b** we can draw diagrams to represent combinations of **a** and **b**.

To represent **a** + **b** we draw **a**, *followed* by **b**; we do this by drawing AC parallel and equal to OB. Alternatively we can draw **b** followed by **a**.

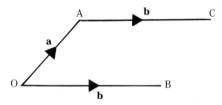
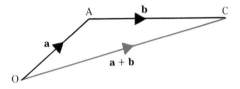

Now we can see that $\overrightarrow{OC} = \mathbf{a} + \mathbf{b}$

To represent **a** − **b** we need to draw **a** followed by −**b**, or −**b** followed by **a**

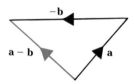
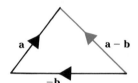

If we draw △AOB and label it as shown, the line BA represents **a** − **b** because

$$\overrightarrow{BA} = \overrightarrow{BO} + \overrightarrow{OA}$$
$$= -\mathbf{b} + \mathbf{a}$$
$$= \mathbf{a} - \mathbf{b}$$

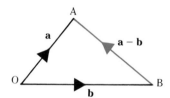

Exercise 32c

1.

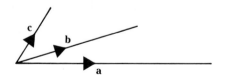

Sketch diagrams to illustrate

(a) **a** − **b**   (d) **c** − **a**

(b) **a** − **c**   (e) **a** − **b** + **c**

(c) **b** − **a**   (f) **b** − **a** − **c**

2.

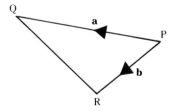

What vector, in terms of **a** and **b**, is represented by

(a) $\overrightarrow{RQ}$ (b) $\overrightarrow{QR}$

3.

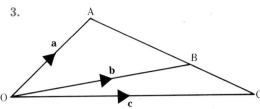

What vector, in terms of **a**, **b** and/or **c**, is represented by (a) $\overrightarrow{AB}$ (b) $\overrightarrow{BC}$ (c) $\overrightarrow{AC}$?

4.

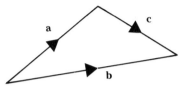

(a) Give **c** in terms of **a** and **b**.

Draw lines to represent

(b) **a** + **b**   (c) **a** + **b** + **c**

(d) What is **a** − **b** + **c**?

If N is the point that divides LM in the ratio $1:5$, express in terms of **a** and **b**   (a) LN   (b) ON.

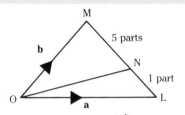

In the diagram we see that $\overrightarrow{LM}$ is equivalent to $\overrightarrow{LO}$ followed by $\overrightarrow{OM}$.

(a) $\overrightarrow{LM} = \overrightarrow{LO} + \overrightarrow{OM}$

$\qquad = -\mathbf{a} + \mathbf{b} = \mathbf{b} - \mathbf{a}$

$\overrightarrow{LN} = \frac{1}{6}\overrightarrow{LM}$

$\qquad = \frac{1}{6}(\mathbf{b} - \mathbf{a})$

(b) $\overrightarrow{ON} = \overrightarrow{OL} + \overrightarrow{LN}$

$\qquad = \mathbf{a} + \frac{1}{6}\mathbf{b} - \frac{1}{6}\mathbf{a} = \frac{5}{6}\mathbf{a} + \frac{1}{6}\mathbf{b}$

5. ABC is a triangle and D is a point on BC such that BD : DC = 2 : 1.

If $\overrightarrow{AB} = \mathbf{b}$ and $\overrightarrow{AC} = \mathbf{c}$, find, in terms of **b** and **c**, (a) $\overrightarrow{BD}$ (b) $\overrightarrow{AD}$

6.

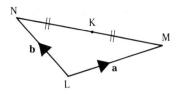

$\overrightarrow{LM} = \mathbf{a}$, $\overrightarrow{LN} = \mathbf{b}$ and K is the midpoint of MN

Express in terms of **a** and **b**

(a) $\overrightarrow{MN}$

(b) $\overrightarrow{MK}$

(c) $\overrightarrow{LK}$ using △LKM

(d) $\overrightarrow{NM}$

(e) $\overrightarrow{NK}$

(f) $\overrightarrow{LK}$ using △LKN

7. $\overrightarrow{AB} = \begin{pmatrix} 6 \\ -9 \end{pmatrix}$ and C divides AB in the ratio 1 : 2

(a) What fraction is $\overrightarrow{AC}$ of $\overrightarrow{AB}$?

(b) Find $\overrightarrow{AC}$ and $\overrightarrow{CB}$ in the form $\begin{pmatrix} a \\ b \end{pmatrix}$

8. A and B are the points $(1, 4)$ and $(3, 2)$ respectively and O is the origin.

If $\mathbf{a} = \overrightarrow{OA}$ and $\mathbf{b} = \overrightarrow{OB}$ find, in terms of **a** and **b**, the vector $\overrightarrow{AM}$ where M is the midpoint of AB.

9.

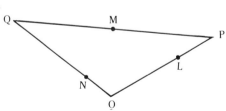

M is the midpoint of PQ, L divides OP in the ratio 2 : 1 and N divides OQ in the ratio 1 : 3

$\overrightarrow{OP} = \mathbf{a}$ and $\overrightarrow{OQ} = \mathbf{b}$

Express in terms of **a** and **b**

(a) $\overrightarrow{OM}$

(b) $\overrightarrow{OL}$

(c) $\overrightarrow{ON}$

(d) $\overrightarrow{LN}$

GEOMETRY USING VECTORS

We can see from the previous exercise that relationships between the positions of points can be described in vector form. This means that it is possible to investigate geometry using these methods.

Useful conclusions can be drawn from very simple vector relationships.

1. If we find that two vectors $\overrightarrow{AB}$ and $\overrightarrow{AC}$ are equal to one another, i.e. $\overrightarrow{AB} = \overrightarrow{AC}$, then B and C are the same point.

2. If $\overrightarrow{XY} = 2\overrightarrow{RS}$, then two facts emerge: XY is twice the length of RS and, also, XY is parallel to RS.

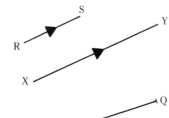

3. If $\overrightarrow{PQ} = 2\overrightarrow{PR}$, then P, Q and R all lie on one straight line and R is the midpoint of PQ.

4. If we obtain two different versions of the same vector they must in fact be the same e.g. if $5\mathbf{a} + h\mathbf{b} = k\mathbf{a} + 3\mathbf{b}$ then k must be 5 and h must be 3 (provided that $\mathbf{a}$ and $\mathbf{b}$ are not parallel, for then $\mathbf{a}$ could be written in terms of $\mathbf{b}$).

The worked examples below illustrate the possibilities.

Exercise 32d

In $\triangle ABC$, P and Q are the midpoints of AB and AC respectively. Prove that $PQ = \frac{1}{2}BC$ and that PQ is parallel to BC.

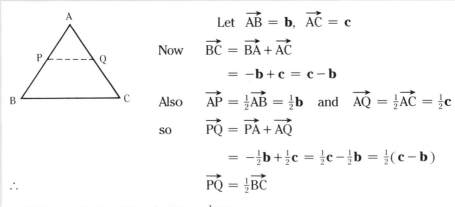

Let $\overrightarrow{AB} = \mathbf{b}$, $\overrightarrow{AC} = \mathbf{c}$

Now $\overrightarrow{BC} = \overrightarrow{BA} + \overrightarrow{AC}$

$\quad = -\mathbf{b} + \mathbf{c} = \mathbf{c} - \mathbf{b}$

Also $\overrightarrow{AP} = \frac{1}{2}\overrightarrow{AB} = \frac{1}{2}\mathbf{b}$ and $\overrightarrow{AQ} = \frac{1}{2}\overrightarrow{AC} = \frac{1}{2}\mathbf{c}$

so $\overrightarrow{PQ} = \overrightarrow{PA} + \overrightarrow{AQ}$

$\quad = -\frac{1}{2}\mathbf{b} + \frac{1}{2}\mathbf{c} = \frac{1}{2}\mathbf{c} - \frac{1}{2}\mathbf{b} = \frac{1}{2}(\mathbf{c} - \mathbf{b})$

$\therefore \qquad \overrightarrow{PQ} = \frac{1}{2}\overrightarrow{BC}$

$\therefore$ PQ is parallel to BC and $PQ = \frac{1}{2}BC$

This proves the **midpoint theorem,** which states that the line joining the midpoints of two sides of a triangle is parallel to the third side and half its length. This result may be quoted in solving problems.

1.

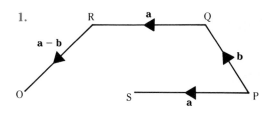

In the diagram above, $\overrightarrow{PQ} = \mathbf{b}$, $\overrightarrow{PS} = \mathbf{a}$, $\overrightarrow{QR} = \mathbf{a}$ and $\overrightarrow{RO} = \mathbf{a} - \mathbf{b}$

(a) Find $\overrightarrow{QS}$ and $\overrightarrow{SO}$ in terms of $\mathbf{a}$ and $\mathbf{b}$.

(b) What type of quadrilateral is QROS ?

(c) Do O, S and P lie in a straight line ?

2.

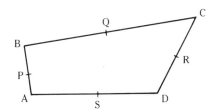

In the quadrilateral ABCD, $\overrightarrow{AD} = \mathbf{p}$, $\overrightarrow{BC} = 2\mathbf{p}$ and $\overrightarrow{AB} = \mathbf{q}$. L and M divide AB and DC respectively in the ratio $1:3$. Find in terms of $\mathbf{p}$ and $\mathbf{q}$

(a) $\overrightarrow{AL}$ (c) $\overrightarrow{DM}$

(b) $\overrightarrow{DC}$ (d) $\overrightarrow{LM}$

(e) What conclusions can you draw about the lines AD, LM and BC ?

3.

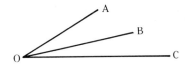

P, Q, R and S are midpoints of the sides AB, BC, CD and DA of a quadrilateral.

$\overrightarrow{AB} = \mathbf{b}$, $\overrightarrow{AC} = \mathbf{c}$ and $\overrightarrow{AD} = \mathbf{d}$

Find in terms of $\mathbf{b}$, $\mathbf{c}$ and $\mathbf{d}$

(a) $\overrightarrow{DC}$ (c) $\overrightarrow{DQ}$ (e) $\overrightarrow{SP}$

(b) $\overrightarrow{RS}$ (d) $\overrightarrow{RQ}$

(f) Hence show that PQRS is a parallelogram.

4.

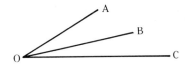

$\overrightarrow{OA} = 2\mathbf{x} + 3\mathbf{y}$
$\overrightarrow{OB} = 3\mathbf{x} + 2\mathbf{y}$
$\overrightarrow{OC} = 4\mathbf{x} + \mathbf{y}$

Show that A, B and C are collinear (i.e. lie on a straight line). How does B divide AC ?

5. $\mathbf{a}$ and $\mathbf{b}$ are non-parallel vectors. In each case find the values of h and k.

(a) $h\mathbf{a} + 2\mathbf{b} = 6\mathbf{a} - k\mathbf{b}$

(b) $(h+2)\mathbf{a} - k\mathbf{b} = 2\mathbf{a} + 3\mathbf{b}$

(c) $\mathbf{a} + h\mathbf{a} - 3\mathbf{b} = 4\mathbf{a} + \mathbf{b} - k\mathbf{b}$

(d) $k\mathbf{a} + 6\mathbf{b} = \frac{1}{2}h\mathbf{a} - k\mathbf{a} - k\mathbf{b}$

> Two parallel vectors are such that $\mathbf{x}$ is parallel to $\mathbf{y}$; $\mathbf{x} = 2\mathbf{a} + h\mathbf{b}$ and $\mathbf{y} = 3\mathbf{a} - 6\mathbf{b}$. Find h.
>
> As $\mathbf{x}$ is parallel to $\mathbf{y}$, $\mathbf{x}$ is a multiple of $\mathbf{y}$ so the coefficients of $\mathbf{a}$ and $\mathbf{b}$ are in proportion
>
> $$\frac{2}{3} = \frac{h}{-6}$$
>
> $$h = -6 \times \frac{2}{3}$$
>
> $$= -4$$

6. $\mathbf{p}$ and $\mathbf{q}$ are parallel vectors. Find h in each case.

(a) $\mathbf{p} = h\mathbf{a} + 3\mathbf{b}$, $\mathbf{q} = \mathbf{a} + 8\mathbf{b}$

(b) $\mathbf{p} = 4\mathbf{a} - 3\mathbf{b}$, $\mathbf{q} = 3\mathbf{a} + h\mathbf{b}$

(c) $\mathbf{p} = (1-h)\mathbf{a} + h\mathbf{b}$, $\mathbf{q} = 2\mathbf{a} + 3\mathbf{b}$

(d) $\mathbf{p} = \mathbf{a} + (h-1)\mathbf{b}$, $\mathbf{q} = (h+1)\mathbf{a} + 3\mathbf{b}$

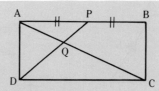

ABCD is a rectangle. P is the midpoint of AB.
AC and PD meet at Q.
Find the ratio in which Q divides AC.

We need to find $\overrightarrow{AQ}$ as a fraction of $\overrightarrow{AC}$, so we start by writing $\overrightarrow{AQ}$ as $h\overrightarrow{AC}$.
We also do not know where Q is on PD, so we start with $\overrightarrow{PQ} = k\overrightarrow{PD}$.
Now if we can find two different versions of $\overrightarrow{AQ}$, we can equate coefficients and find h.

Let $\overrightarrow{AQ}$ be $h\overrightarrow{AC}$, $\overrightarrow{PQ}$ be $k\overrightarrow{PD}$, $\overrightarrow{AB}$ be **b** and $\overrightarrow{AD}$ be **d**

then $\overrightarrow{AP} = \frac{1}{2}\overrightarrow{AB} = \frac{1}{2}\mathbf{b}$

and $\overrightarrow{PD} = \overrightarrow{PA} + \overrightarrow{AD} = -\frac{1}{2}\mathbf{b} + \mathbf{d}$

Now $\qquad\qquad \overrightarrow{AQ} = \overrightarrow{AP} + \overrightarrow{PQ} = \frac{1}{2}\mathbf{b} + k\overrightarrow{PD}$

$$= \frac{1}{2}\mathbf{b} + k\left(-\frac{1}{2}\mathbf{b} + \mathbf{d}\right)$$

$$= \frac{1}{2}\mathbf{b} - \frac{1}{2}k\mathbf{b} + k\mathbf{d}$$

$$= \left(\frac{1}{2} - \frac{1}{2}k\right)\mathbf{b} + k\mathbf{d} \qquad\qquad\qquad [1]$$

Also $\qquad\qquad \overrightarrow{AQ} = h\overrightarrow{AC} = h(\overrightarrow{AB} + \overrightarrow{BC})$

$$= h(\mathbf{b} + \mathbf{d}) \qquad\qquad (BC = AD)$$

$$= h\mathbf{b} + h\mathbf{d} \qquad\qquad\qquad\qquad [2]$$

Comparing [1] and [2] gives $\frac{1}{2} - \frac{1}{2}k = h$

and $\qquad\qquad\qquad\qquad\qquad\qquad k = h$

so $\qquad\qquad\qquad\qquad\qquad \frac{1}{2} - \frac{1}{2}h = h$

$$\frac{1}{2} = \frac{3}{2}h$$

$$h = \frac{1}{3}$$

i.e. Q is one-third of the way along AC

$\therefore$ Q divides AC in the ratio $1 : 2$

7.

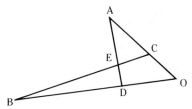

C and D divide OA and OB respectively in the ratio 1 : 2. AD and BC cut at E. $\overrightarrow{OA} = \mathbf{a}$ and $\overrightarrow{OB} = \mathbf{b}$; $\overrightarrow{CE} = h\overrightarrow{CB}$ and $\overrightarrow{DE} = k\overrightarrow{DA}$

Find in terms of **a**, **b**, h and k

(a) $\overrightarrow{OD}$ (b) $\overrightarrow{OC}$ (c) $\overrightarrow{CB}$ (d) $\overrightarrow{DA}$ (e) $\overrightarrow{CE}$ (f) $\overrightarrow{DE}$

Express $\overrightarrow{OE}$ in terms of **a** and **b**   (g) using your expressions for (b) and (e)

(h) using your expressions for (a) and (f).

(i) Hence find h and k and the ratio in which E cuts AD.

8.

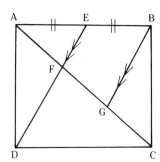

ABCD is a square. $\overrightarrow{AD} = \mathbf{p}$ and $\overrightarrow{AB} = \mathbf{q}$. E is the midpoint of AB and ED cuts AC at F. G is on AC such that BG is parallel to ED. $\overrightarrow{CG} = h\overrightarrow{CA}$ and $\overrightarrow{BG} = k\overrightarrow{ED}$

Find in terms of **p**, **q**, h and k

(a) $\overrightarrow{AE}$ (c) $\overrightarrow{BG}$ (e) $\overrightarrow{CG}$, use (d)

(b) $\overrightarrow{ED}$ (d) $\overrightarrow{CA}$ (f) $\overrightarrow{CG}$, use (c)

(g) Use your expressions for (e) and (f) to find h and k.

(h) In what ratio does G divide CA ?

9.

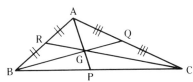

In △ABC, R and Q are midpoints of AB and AC respectively. $\overrightarrow{AB} = \mathbf{b}$ and $\overrightarrow{AC} = \mathbf{c}$. CR and BQ cut at G. AG meets BC at P.
$\overrightarrow{BG} = h\overrightarrow{BQ}$ and $\overrightarrow{CG} = k\overrightarrow{CR}$.

Find in terms of **b**, **c**, h and k

(a) $\overrightarrow{AR}$ (c) $\overrightarrow{BQ}$ (e) $\overrightarrow{CG}$ (g) $\overrightarrow{AG}$, using (e)

(b) $\overrightarrow{AQ}$ (d) $\overrightarrow{CR}$ (f) $\overrightarrow{BG}$ (h) $\overrightarrow{AG}$, using (f)

(i) Hence find the values of h and k. In what ratio does G divide BQ ?

POSITION VECTORS

In general, vectors are not fixed in position but if we wish to describe the position of one point relative to another we can fix the vector and say that the *position vector* of P relative to Q is **p**.

This is particularly useful if there are several points whose positions relative to the origin need to be given.

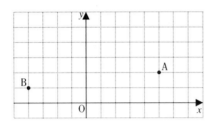

Relative to O, the position vector of A is $\begin{pmatrix} 5 \\ 2 \end{pmatrix}$

and the position vector of B is $\begin{pmatrix} -4 \\ 1 \end{pmatrix}$

Notice that the *coordinates* of A and B are $(5, 2)$ and $(-4, 1)$.

Translations

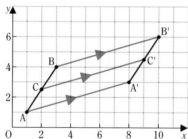

The translation that maps AB to A′B′ can be described by the vector $\overrightarrow{AA'}$, i.e. $\begin{pmatrix} 7 \\ 2 \end{pmatrix}$

Notice that this is the same as $\overrightarrow{BB'}$ or $\overrightarrow{CC'}$ because any point on the line AB is translated in the same way. $\overrightarrow{AA'}$ is *not* a position vector.

Exercise 32e

In the next two exercises, all the position vectors are given relative to the origin O. The position vector of P is $\overrightarrow{OP}$.

1.

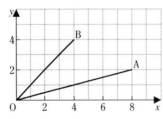

C and D are the midpoints of OA and OB respectively.

Give the position vectors of

(a) A   (b) B   (c) C   (d) D

(e) the midpoint of AB.

2. Draw axes for values of x and y from -3 to 7 and mark the following points whose position vectors are given.

   (a) A, $\begin{pmatrix} 6 \\ 3 \end{pmatrix}$

   (b) B, $\begin{pmatrix} 3 \\ -1 \end{pmatrix}$

   (c) C, $\begin{pmatrix} -2 \\ 1 \end{pmatrix}$

   (d) D, $\begin{pmatrix} 1 \\ 5 \end{pmatrix}$

   (e) Join ABCD to form a quadrilateral. What type of quadrilateral is it ?

   (f) Give the position vector of the midpoint of AC.

3. Draw axes for values of x and y from -5 to 5. A is the point $(3, 4)$.

   (a) Reflect the line OA in the x-axis. The image of A is A_1. Give the vector OA_1.

   (b) Reflect OA in the y-axis. The image of A is A_2. Give the position vector of A_2.

   (c) Rotate OA through $180°$ about O. The image of A is A_3. Give the vector OA_3.

   (d) Translate OA by 2 units to the right. The image of O is O_1 and of A is A_4. Give the position vectors of O_1 and A_4 and give the vector $\overrightarrow{AA_4}$.

   (e) If B is the midpoint of OA, the image of B under the translation described in (d) is B_1. Give the position vector of B_1. Give the vectors $\overrightarrow{OO_1}$, $\overrightarrow{AA_4}$ and $\overrightarrow{BB_1}$.

A translation is described by the vector $\begin{pmatrix} 2 \\ -3 \end{pmatrix}$. A, B and C are the points $(2, 1)$, $(1, 5)$ and $(-2, 2)$. Find the images of A, B and C under the given translation.

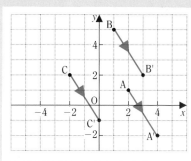

From the diagram,

the image of A is $(2+2, 1-3)$, i.e. $(4, -2)$,

the image of B is $(1+2, 5-3)$, i.e. $(3, 2)$

the image of C is $(-2+2, 2-3)$, i.e. $(0, -1)$

---

4. Draw axes for values of x and y from -8 to 8. In $\triangle PQR$, P, Q and R are the points $(0, 4)$, $(1, 3)$ and $(-1, 1)$ respectively.

   (a) P_1, Q_1 and R_1 are the points $(3, 8), (4, 7)$ and $(2, 5)$ respectively. Give the vector describing the translation that maps $\triangle PQR$ to $\triangle P_1Q_1R_1$.

   (b) $\triangle PQR$ is mapped to $\triangle P_2Q_2R_2$ by the translation given by the vector $\begin{pmatrix} -3 \\ 1 \end{pmatrix}$. What vector describes the translation that maps $\triangle P_1Q_1R_1$ to $\triangle P_2Q_2R_2$.

   (c) What is the connection between the two vectors in part (b) and the vector in part (a) ?

5. Draw axes as for question 4. In $\triangle ABC$, A, B and C are the points $(1, 1), (4, 2)$ and $(3, 6)$ respectively.

   (a) Find the image $A_1B_1C_1$ of ABC under the translation described by $\begin{pmatrix} 4 \\ 2 \end{pmatrix}$

   (b) Find the image $A_2B_2C_2$ of ABC under the translation described by $\begin{pmatrix} -6 \\ 1 \end{pmatrix}$

   (c) Find the image $A_3B_3C_3$ of ABC under the translation described by $\begin{pmatrix} 0 \\ -4 \end{pmatrix}$

   (d) Find the vector describing the translation that maps $\triangle A_1B_1C_1$ to $\triangle A_2B_2C_2$.

BASE VECTORS

Any vector in a plane can be made out of multiples of any two *base vectors*.

Any pair of vectors can be used as base vectors as long as they are not parallel.

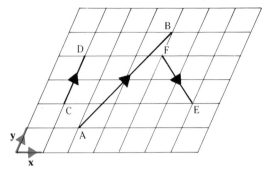

If **x** and **y** are used as base vectors then, for example,

$\overrightarrow{AB} = 2\mathbf{x} + 4\mathbf{y}$, $\overrightarrow{CD} = 2\mathbf{y}$ and $\overrightarrow{FE} = 2\mathbf{x} - 2\mathbf{y}$

The most useful base vectors to use for work with coordinates are the unit vectors parallel to the x and y axes. They are written **i** and **j**.

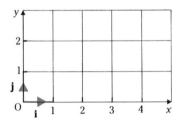

If A is the point $(3, 2)$, then $\overrightarrow{OA} = 3\mathbf{i} + 2\mathbf{j}$ and if B is $(-4, 1)$ then $\overrightarrow{OB} = -4\mathbf{i} + \mathbf{j}$

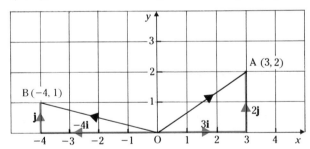

Exercise 32f

1. Give in terms of **i** and **j** the position vectors of each of the following points.

   (a) A(6, 3)   (d) D(5, 0)

   (b) B(7, −4)   (e) E(0, 4)

   (c) C(−1, −3)   (f) G(0, −5)

2. Write down the coordinates of each of the points whose position vectors are given below.

   (a) A, $2\mathbf{i} - 4\mathbf{j}$ (c) C, $-7\mathbf{i}$

   (b) B, $6\mathbf{i} + 4\mathbf{j}$ (d) D, $3\mathbf{j}$

3. $\mathbf{a} = 5\mathbf{i} - 6\mathbf{j}$, $\mathbf{b} = 8\mathbf{i} + 2\mathbf{j}$ and $\mathbf{c} = 4\mathbf{i}$
   Express each resultant vector in terms of
   $\mathbf{i}$ and $\mathbf{j}$. The first one is done for you.

   (a) $\mathbf{a} + \mathbf{b} = (5\mathbf{i} - 6\mathbf{j}) + (8\mathbf{i} + 2\mathbf{j})$
   $= (5 + 8)\mathbf{i} + (-6 + 2)\mathbf{i}$
   $= 13\mathbf{i} - 4\mathbf{j}$

   (b) $3\mathbf{a}$ (d) $\frac{1}{2}\mathbf{b}$

   (c) $\mathbf{a} - \mathbf{c}$ (e) $3\mathbf{a} - 2\mathbf{b} + \mathbf{c}$

4. A, B, C and D have position vectors $2\mathbf{i} + 3\mathbf{j}$,
   $5\mathbf{i} + 7\mathbf{j}$, $3\mathbf{i} + 8\mathbf{j}$ and $4\mathbf{j}$ respectively.
   Show, using vectors, that ABCD is a
   parallelogram.

5. P, Q and R have position vectors $2\mathbf{i} - 4\mathbf{j}$,
   $6\mathbf{i}$ and $-\mathbf{i} + 3\mathbf{j}$ respectively.
   $\triangle$PQR is mapped to $\triangle$P'Q'R' by a translation
   described by the vector $-3\mathbf{i} + \mathbf{j}$
   Give the position vectors of P', Q' and R'.

6. The unit vectors pointing north and east are $\mathbf{n}$
   and $\mathbf{e}$ respectively. The units are kilometres.

   (a) A man walks 3 km north and then 4 km
   east. Give his journey in terms of $\mathbf{n}$ and $\mathbf{e}$.

   (b) If he retraces his route, give his return
   journey in terms of $\mathbf{n}$ and $\mathbf{e}$.

7.

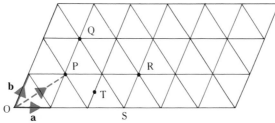

Using $\mathbf{a}$ and $\mathbf{b}$ as base vectors, the position vector of P is $\mathbf{b} + \mathbf{a}$. Find, in terms of $\mathbf{a}$ and $\mathbf{b}$,
the position vector of   (a) Q   (b) R   (c) S   (d) T.

PRACTICAL USES FOR VECTORS

The properties of vectors that we have found have come from investigating displacements
because they are the easiest vectors to visualise. All vector quantities, e.g. force and
velocity, behave in the same way.

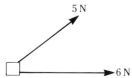

For example, if two forces act at a point on a body we can find
one *resultant* force that would have the same effect as the
two forces combined.

We can represent the forces as vectors in a
diagram and use vector addition to combine them.

$\overrightarrow{AC}$ represents the resultant force acting on the
body and its magnitude and direction can be found
if required.

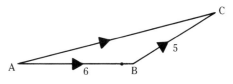

Exercise 32g

1.

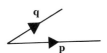

$\mathbf{p}$ and $\mathbf{q}$ are two forces acting on a body.
Draw a diagram to show the resultant force
$\mathbf{p} + \mathbf{q}$.

2.

(a) Draw a vector diagram to show the two
forces and their resultant.

(b) Find the magnitude of the resultant force.

3.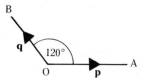

p and q represent two forces acting on a body. The magnitude of each is 3 newtons.

(a) Draw a vector diagram to show the resultant force.

(b) Give the magnitude of the resultant force.

(c) Draw a diagram with the resultant force alone acting on the body. Indicate the direction of the force.
(Remember that the resultant force will act through the same point as the two given forces.)

4. A boat on a river has two velocities, one due to the boat being rowed across the river at $4\,\mathrm{m\,s}^{-1}$, the other due to the current carrying it down the river at $3\,\mathrm{m\,s}^{-1}$.

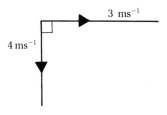

Use a vector diagram to find

(a) the magnitude of the resultant velocity

(b) the angle between the resultant velocity and the direction of the current.

Sometimes we are given the resultant of two vectors and one of those vectors. The methods already used can be adapted to find the unknown second vector.

Two forces have a resultant force of magnitude 9 N on a bearing of 150°. The first of the forces has magnitude 6 N and its direction is due south. Find the magnitude of the second force.

First sketch the given forces separately.

First force

6 N

Resultant

30°

9 N

Now draw a combined diagram. $\vec{AC} + \vec{CB} = \vec{AB}$ so $\vec{CB}$ represents the second force.

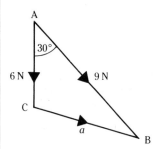

In $\triangle ABC$, $b = 6$ and $c = 9$

$$a^2 = b^2 + c^2 - 2bc\,\cos A$$
$$= 36 + 81 - (2 \times 6 \times 9 \times \cos 30°)$$
$$= 117 - 93.53 = 23.47$$
$$a = 4.844$$

∴ the magnitude of the second force is 4.84 N (3 s.f.)

We could if required find another angle of the triangle and hence find the direction in which the second force acts.

5. The sum of two vectors **a** and **b** is a resultant vector **c**. Vector **a** is of magnitude 8 and is parallel to the positive direction of the x-axis.

    (a) If **c** is of magnitude 13, parallel to the upward direction of the line $y = x$, draw a sketch of the vector triangle showing **a**, **b** and **c**. Find the magnitude and direction of **b**.

    (b) If **c** is of magnitude 13, direction unknown, and **b** is parallel to the upward direction of the y-axis, find
    (i) the direction of **c**
    (ii) the magnitude of **b**.

6. A body is acted upon by two forces P and Q, which are equivalent to a resultant force of 8 N. Force P is of magnitude 6 N at an angle of $60°$ to the resultant. Find the magnitude and direction of the force Q.

7. A boat, whose speed through still water is 3 m/s, is rowed across a river flowing at 2 m/s. Scale drawings may be used to answer the following questions.

    (a) If the boat is pointed upstream at $60°$ to the bank, in what direction does the boat actually move ?

    (b) The boat needs to travel straight across at right angles to the bank. In what direction should it be rowed ?

    (c) The boat is pointed upstream at $60°$ to the bank but the current speed has changed. If the boat moves across at right angles to the bank, what is the speed of the current ?

8. In 1931, Francis Chichester flew alone in his Gypsy Moth plane across the Tasman Sea. He was out of sight of land for many hours at a time and had to work out what course to set. He had a compass, a speedometer to give his air-speed, a slide-rule with trigonometric functions and a book of six-figure trigonometrical tables. He *estimated* the wind speed and then, without writing anything down, solved one problem after another of the following type.
He wished to fly north west. His speed in still air was 80 m.p.h. and he estimated the wind speed to be 20 m.p.h. in the direction $282°$. In what direction should he steer the plane ?

Self-Assessment 32

1. If $\mathbf{a} = \begin{pmatrix} 3 \\ -2 \end{pmatrix}$ draw diagrams to represent **a**, 2**a** and $-\mathbf{a}$.

2. $\mathbf{a} = \begin{pmatrix} 3 \\ 5 \end{pmatrix}$ and $\mathbf{b} = \begin{pmatrix} -4 \\ 1 \end{pmatrix}$

    Find $\mathbf{a} + \mathbf{b}$ and $\mathbf{a} - \mathbf{b}$.

3. Which of the following quantities are vectors ?

    (a) A speed of 30 m.p.h.

    (b) A force of 30 N upward.

    (c) A change of position of 45 km due east.

4. Which of the following vectors are parallel ?

    $$\begin{pmatrix} 4 \\ -2 \end{pmatrix}, \quad \begin{pmatrix} -6 \\ -3 \end{pmatrix}, \quad \begin{pmatrix} -8 \\ 4 \end{pmatrix}, \quad \begin{pmatrix} 3 \\ 6 \end{pmatrix}$$

5. Draw a diagram on squared paper to show points A and B whose position vectors are $\begin{pmatrix} -1 \\ 5 \end{pmatrix}$ and $\begin{pmatrix} 3 \\ 3 \end{pmatrix}$ respectively.

    What is the position vector of the midpoint of AB ?

6. A and B are the points $(4, 5)$ and $(-3, 6)$. A and B are mapped to the points A′ and B′ by the translation described by the vector $\begin{pmatrix} -2 \\ -1 \end{pmatrix}$. Give the points A′ and B′.

7. **i** and **j** are unit vectors parallel to the x and y axes respectively. $\mathbf{a} = 2\mathbf{i} + 5\mathbf{j}$ and $\mathbf{b} = 3\mathbf{i} - 4\mathbf{j}$.
Give $\mathbf{a} + \mathbf{b}$ and $\mathbf{a} - \mathbf{b}$.

8. Find $|\mathbf{a}|$ where $\mathbf{a} = \begin{pmatrix} 5 \\ -12 \end{pmatrix}$

9.

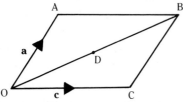

If OABC is a parallelogram and D is the midpoint of OB,

(a) find $\overrightarrow{OD}$ in terms of $\mathbf{a}$ and $\mathbf{c}$.

(b) show that ADC is a straight line and that AD = DC.

10.

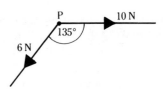

Two forces act on a body P as shown in the diagram. Use a scale drawing to find the magnitude of the resultant force and the angle its line of action makes with the line of action of the 10 N force.

11. Under its own steam, a boat moves through the water at 4 km h^{-1}. The boat is steered due north but the current makes it actually move north east at 4.5 km h^{-1}. Find the speed of the current.

To understand this chapter you need to be familiar with the work on straight-line and curved graphs and with the various methods for solving quadratic equations, including completing the square.

Rules

Consider each of the following situations, which should be familiar by now.

- The cooking time for a chicken is 30 minutes per pound plus 30 minutes. So the number of minutes cooking time for a chicken weighing 3 lb is given by $30 \times 3 + 30$, i.e. 120.

- The equation of a straight line is $y = 4 - 3x$. Hence the y-coordinate of the point on the line where $x = -2$ is given by $4 - 3(-2)$, i.e. 10.

- The formula for the area of a circle is $A = \pi r^2$, so if a circle has a radius of 5 cm, its area, in cm^2, is given by $\pi(5)^2$, i.e. 78.5 to 3 s.f.

- The nth term of a sequence is $\dfrac{n}{n+1}$, so the 10th term is $\dfrac{10}{10+1}$, i.e. $\dfrac{10}{11}$.

The feature that is common to all these situations is that, starting with one number, we apply a rule to get another number.

In this chapter we are going to look at some general aspects of such rules and study two particular forms.

Terminology and Notation

A rule that changes one number into another number is called a *function*. The function 'double' can be illustrated by this flow chart,

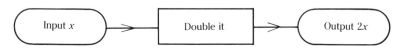

The letter f is used to represent a function.

The *result* of applying a function to x, is denoted by $f(x)$. [We say 'f of x'.]

Therefore, when f is the function 'double', we write $f(x) = 2x$

Similarly, if $f(x) = x^2$, then the function is 'square'.

Further, if $f(x) = 2x - 3$, then $f(2)$ means the result of applying f to the number 2, i.e. $f(2) = 2(2) - 3 = 1$

The set of numbers that we put into a function is called the *domain* of the function.

The set of numbers that result from using the function is called the *range* of the function.

Exercise 33a

1. Describe the given functions in words.

(a) $f(x) = 3x$ (c) $f(x) = x + 1$

(b) $f(x) = \dfrac{1}{x}$

2. Draw a flow chart to illustrate the functions

(a) $f(x) = x^2 + 3$ (c) $f(x) = x^3$

(b) $f(x) = 3 - 2x$

3. Given that $f(x) = (x-4)^2$, find

(a) $f(2)$ (c) $f(4)$

(b) $f(-1)$ (d) $f(0)$

4. If $f(x) = (x-2)(x+1)(x-3)$, find

(a) $f(2)$ (d) $f(-4)$

(b) $f(-2)$ (e) $f(1)$

(c) $f(0)$ (f) $f(0.5)$

5. If $f(x) = \dfrac{1}{x}$, $x \neq 0$,

(a) find $f(3)$, $f(0.01)$, $f(-4)$

(b) explain why this function cannot be applied to zero.

If $f(x) = x^2 - 3x$ find the values of x for which $f(x) = 4$

We need the value of x that gives an output of 4, i.e. the value of x that makes $x^2 - 3x$ equal to 4, so we need to solve the equation $x^2 - 3x = 4$

$$x^2 - 3x = 4$$

$$\Rightarrow \qquad x^2 - 3x - 4 = 0$$

$$\Rightarrow \qquad (x-4)(x+1) = 0$$

$$\therefore \; x = 4 \; \text{ or } \; x = -1$$

6. Find the value(s) of x for which the function has the given value.

(a) $f(x) = 2x - 7$, $f(x) = 3$

(b) $f(x) = \dfrac{1}{x}$, $f(x) = 8$

(c) $f(x) = x^2$, $f(x) = 25$

(d) $f(x) = x + \dfrac{1}{x}$, $f(x) = 2$

7. The function f is given by $f(x) = 5 - x$.

(a) Find $f(-2)$, $f(0)$, and $f(3)$

(b) Which value of x gives zero for $f(x)$?

(c) Does the value of $f(x)$ increase or decrease as the value of x increases?

GRAPHICAL REPRESENTATION

Consider the function $f(x) = 4x - 2$

If we write $y = f(x)$ then the equation $y = 4x - 2$ can be used to give a graphical representation of $f(x)$.

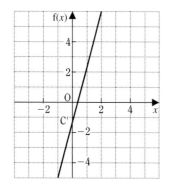

Now $y = 4x - 2$ is the equation of a straight line with gradient 4 and *y*-intercept -2.

The vertical axis can be labelled either $f(x)$ or y, since $y = f(x)$. A graphical representation like this gives a picture of how $f(x)$ changes in value as the value of x varies.

In this case the graph shows that as x increases in value the corresponding values of $f(x)$ also increase.

Remember that, if the graph of $y = f(x)$ is known, then the graphs of simple variations of the function can be drawn easily using transformations, i.e.

$y = f(x) + a$　is a translation by a units upward when　$a > 0$

$y = f(x - a)$　is a translation by a units to the right when　$a > 0$

$y = f(-x)$　　is a reflection in the y-axis

$y = -f(x)$　　is a reflection in the x-axis

$y = af(x)$　　is a one-way stretch by a factor a parallel to the y-axis

$y = f(ax)$　　is a one-way contraction by a factor $\dfrac{1}{a}$ parallel to the x-axis

Exercise 33b

Draw a sketch graph to represent each of the following functions.

1. $f(x) = 2x$

2. $f(x) = x + 1$

3. $f(x) = -x^2$

4. $f(x) = \dfrac{1}{x}, x \neq 0$

5. $f(x) = x^3 + 2$

6. $f(x) = x^2 + 2$

7. $f(x) = 1 - x^2$

8. $f(x) = 1 + \dfrac{1}{x}, x \neq 0$

9. $f(x) = (x - 3)^2$

10. Sketch the graph of $f(x) = x^2 + 1$. On the same axes, sketch the curves

    (a) $y = f(x) + 2$　　　　(c) $y = f(2x)$

    (b) $y = f(x + 2)$　　　　(d) $y = 2f(x)$

QUADRATIC FUNCTIONS

Any function of the form given by $f(x) = ax^2 + bx + c$ is called a quadratic function.

From the earlier work on graphs, we know that the graph of a quadratic function has a distinctive shape, called a parabola.

If a is positive,
the parabola has a lowest point (called its vertex),
so the quadratic function has a least value.
(It has no greatest value.)

If a is negative,
the parabola has a highest point (also called its vertex),
so the quadratic function has a greatest value.
(It has no least value.)

All these parabolas have a line of symmetry which is a vertical line through the vertex.

Finding the Greatest or Least Value

The greatest, or least, value of any quadratic function can be found without recourse to an accurate plot of the graph.

If a quadratic function factorises, we can use the line of symmetry of its graph to find the greatest or least value at the turning point. This method is illustrated in the following worked example.

Find the greatest value of the function given by $f(x) = 3 - 2x - x^2$

$$f(x) = 3 - 2x - x^2 = (3 + x)(1 - x)$$

We can now sketch the curve $y = f(x)$ using the following information. The coefficient of x^2 is negative, so the curve $y = f(x)$ has a greatest value. The curve crosses the x-axis where $x = -3$ and where $x = 1$

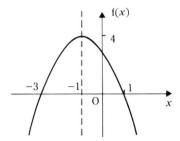

The curve has a line of symmetry that cuts the x-axis midway between $x = -3$ and $x = 1$, i.e. where $x = -1$. Therefore the greatest value of $f(x)$ occurs when $x = -1$, i.e. the greatest value of $f(x)$ is $f(-1)$.

Greatest value is $f(-1) = 3 - 2(-1) - (-1)^2 = 3 + 2 - 1 = 4$

If the quadratic does not factorise, we can use the method of completing the square.

Suppose, for example, that $f(x) = x^2 - x - 5$

We can change $x^2 - x$ into a perfect square by adding $\frac{1}{4}$, i.e.

$$x^2 - x + \tfrac{1}{4} = (x - \tfrac{1}{2})^2$$

Therefore we can rewrite $x^2 - x - 5$ as $x^2 - x + \tfrac{1}{4} - 5 - \tfrac{1}{4} = (x - \tfrac{1}{2})^2 - \tfrac{21}{4}$

Whatever the value of x, the value of $(x - \tfrac{1}{2})^2$ is greater than or equal to zero because it is a square. Hence, whatever value x has,

$$f(x) \geqslant -\tfrac{21}{4} \quad \text{and} \quad f(x) = -\tfrac{21}{4} \quad \text{when} \quad (x - \tfrac{1}{2})^2 = 0$$

i.e. $f(x)$ has a least value of $-\tfrac{21}{4}$, and it occurs when $x = \tfrac{1}{2}$

Note that this method *must* be used if you are asked to *prove* that a quadratic function has a greatest/least value. (The graphical method *assumes* the existence of a greatest or least value.)

Exercise 33c

1. State whether f(x) has a greatest or least value. Find this value and the value of x at which it occurs, when f(x) is

   (a) $(x-3)(x-5)$

   (b) $(2x-1)(2x-5)$

   (c) $(3-x)(4+x)$

   (d) $(2x+7)(x+2)$

   (e) $(x-3)^2$

   (f) $(x-9)(4-3x)$

Express in the form $r(x+p)^2+q$ (a) $2x^2-4x+7$ (b) $9-4x-x^2$

(a) $2x^2-4x+7$

We start by taking out the factor 2 from the x^2 and x terms, i.e.

$$2x^2-4x+7 = 2(x^2-2x)+7$$
$$= 2(x^2-2x+1)+7-2$$

Notice that 1 was added inside the bracket to make that a perfect square but, because the bracket is doubled, we have to subtract 2 from the number term.

$$\therefore \qquad 2x^2-4x+7 = 2(x-1)^2+5$$

Notice that $r=2$, $p=-1$ and $q=5$

(b) $9-4x-x^2$

In order to complete the square the x^2 term must be positive, so we take out the factor -1

$$9-4x-x^2 = 9-(x^2+4x)$$
$$= 9-(x^2+4x+4)+4$$
$$= 13-(x+2)^2$$

Notice that this function is now in the form $13-(\,0$ or $+$ve number$)$ so it has a greatest value of 13, when $x=-2$.

---

2. Express each function in the form
   $$r(x+p)^2+q$$

   (a) x^2-3x+2

   (b) x^2+3x+2

   (c) x^2+3x-2

   (d) $3x^2+6x+5$

   (e) $3x^2-6x-5$

   (f) $2x^2-x+6$

   (g) $5-2x-x^2$

   (h) $5+2x-x^2$

   (i) $7+8x-2x^2$

3. Use your results from question 2 to give the greatest or least value of each function and the value of x at which it occurs; hence sketch the graph of the function.

4. The function f is given by f(x) $= x^2+3x+7$

   (a) Show that f(x) has a least value and find it.

   (b) Sketch the curve $y=$ f(x)

   (c) Use your sketch to explain why there are no values of x for which f(x) $= 0$

CUBIC FUNCTIONS

Any function of the form $y = ax^3 + bx^2 + cx + d$ is called a cubic function.

We know, from Chapter 22, that the graph of a cubic function looks like this

when a is positive

or this

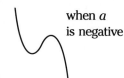

when a is negative

THE FUNCTION $f(x) = \dfrac{1}{x}$

The graph of the function $f(x) = \dfrac{1}{x}$

has a distinctive two-part shape.

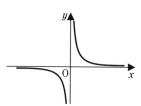

The shape and position of the curve for variations of this function, which is called a reciprocal function, can often be deduced using transformations of graphs,

e.g.   for $g(x) = \dfrac{1}{1+x}$, we see that $g(x) = f(x+1)$

We know that $f(x+1)$ represents a shift of the curve $y = f(x)$ by one unit to the left,

i.e.   the graph of $g(x) = \dfrac{1}{1+x}$ looks like this

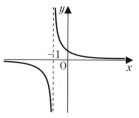

EXPONENTIAL FUNCTIONS

A function of the form $f(x) = a^x$ is called an *exponential* function.

The graph of this function is shown in the diagram.

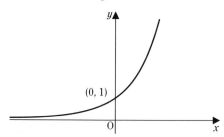

The important features of this curve are that it cuts the y-axis where $y = 1$, *whatever the value of a*, and that it does not cross the x-axis.

Exercise 33d

The diagram shows the graph of the curve with equation $y = a^x + b$.
Use the graph to estimate the values of a and b.

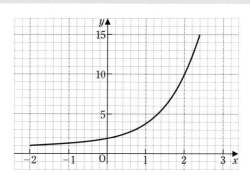

From the graph, when $x = 0$ (i.e. where the curve crosses the y-axis),

$$y = 2$$

Substituting these values into $y = a^x + b$ gives $2 = 1 + b$,

i.e. $\qquad\qquad b = 1$

If we substitute the coordinates of any other point on the graph into the equation of the curve, this will give an equation from which we can find a.

When $x = 1$, $y = 4$, $\qquad$ so $\;4 = a^1 + 1$

$$\text{i.e. } a = 3$$

We can only reliably read values of x and y to 2 significant figures from this graph; therefore results can only be reliable to at most 2 significant figures; i.e. the values found are (good) estimates.

Therefore estimates for a and b are 3 and 1 respectively.

---

1. Given that $y = ax^3 + bx$, use the graph to estimate the values of a and b.

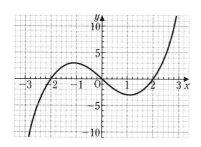

2. Given that $y = \dfrac{a}{x} + b$, use the graph to find estimates for a and b.

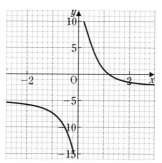

3. Identify the curve that could represent each of the following functions.

   (a) $f(x) = 3x^2$ (b) $f(x) = \dfrac{1}{(x-3)}$ (c) $f(x) = 2(3^x)$ (d) $f(x) = 3^{-x}$

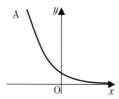 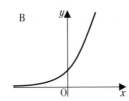 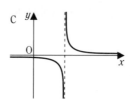 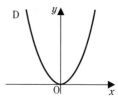

TRIGONOMETRIC FUNCTIONS

We have used sines, cosines and tangents of angles in triangles and so tend to think of them in relation to acute and obtuse angles only. However, $\sin x°$ has a value for any value of x and so have $\cos x°$ and $\tan x°$, as you will see if you use your calculator to find, say, $\sin 256°$.

The Graph of $f(x) = \sin x°$

If values of $\sin x°$ are found for values of x from 0 to 360 at intervals of 15 units, and then plotted against the corresponding values of x, this graph is obtained.

This curve has a distinctive shape: it is called a *sine wave*.

Note that when we write $\sin 45°$, 45 is the number of degrees. Similarly, for $\sin x°$ remember that x is a number so that it is correct to write either $0° \leqslant x° \leqslant 180°$ or $0 \leqslant x \leqslant 180$. We have chosen the latter.

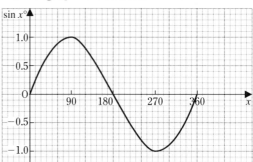

The Graph of $f(x) = \cos x°$

If the values of $\cos x$ are found for the same values of x, the resulting graph looks like this.

Notice that the cosine curve looks quite different from the sine curve for angles between 0° and 360°.

However, if both curves are drawn for a larger range of angles, the relationship between the curves becomes obvious. This relationship is explored in the next exercise.

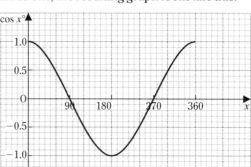

Exercise 33e

1. (a) Draw a sketch of the curve $y = \sin x°$ for $0 \leqslant x \leqslant 360$

   (b) On the same diagram sketch the curve $y = -\sin x°$

2. On the same set of axes for values of x between 0 and 360 sketch

   (a) $y = \cos x°$ (c) $y = \cos(x - 90)°$

   (b) $y = 2 \cos x°$

   Compare your sketches for 1 (a) and 2 (c); what do you notice?

3. (a) Draw a sketch of the curve $y = \cos x°$ for $0 \leqslant x \leqslant 360$

   (b) On the same diagram sketch the curves
   (i) $y = 1 + \cos x°$ (ii) $y = -\cos x°$

4. (a) Draw a sketch of the curve $f(x) = \sin x°$ for $0 \leqslant x \leqslant 360$

   (b) From your sketch, find the values of x for which $f(x) = 0$

   (c) On the same axes draw a line to show how the value(s) of x can be found for which $f(x) = 0.4$

5. (a) Draw a sketch of the curve $f(x) = \cos x°$ for $0 \leqslant x \leqslant 360$

   (b) For what values of x is $f(x) = 0$?

   (c) On the same axes draw lines to show how the values of x can be found for which
   (i) $f(x) = 0.5$ (ii) $f(x) = -0.8$

6. For the domain $0 \leqslant x \leqslant 360$, give the range of

   (a) $f(x) = \sin x°$ (b) $f(x) = \cos x°$

7. Draw the graph of $y = \sin x°$ for $0 \leqslant x \leqslant 720$ using the following steps.

   (a) Make a table of values of $\sin x°$ for values of x from 0 to 720 at intervals of 30 units. Use a calculator and give values of $\sin x°$ correct to 2 d.p.

   (b) Draw the y-axis on the left-hand side of a sheet of graph paper and scale it from -1 to 1 using 2 cm to 0.5 units. Draw the x-axis and scale it from 0 to 720 using 1 cm to 60 units

   (c) Plot the points given in the table made for (a) and draw a smooth curve through them.

8. Draw the graph of $y = \cos x°$ for $0 \leqslant x \leqslant 720$ using the same sequence of steps as in question 7.
   Compare the graphs of $y = \sin x°$ and $y = \cos x°$. What do you notice?

9. For values of x between 0 and 360 and on the same diagram sketch the graphs of

   (a) $y = \sin x°$

   (b) $y = \sin(x + 30)°$

   (c) $y = \sin(x + 90)°$

10.

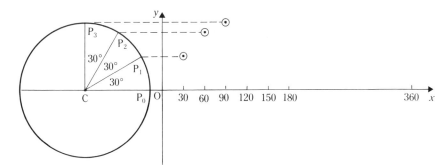

Copy this diagram on graph paper. Make the radius of the circle 6 cm. Scale the x-axis from 0 to 360 using 1 cm to 30 units.

(a) Starting at P_0, mark positions of P at 30° intervals right round the circle. (P_0 to P_3 is shown.)

(b) Draw a line from each position of P parallel to the x-axis, stopping the line above (or below) the point on the x-axis corresponding to the angle that CP makes with CP_0. Mark the end of the line with a circle. The first four lines are drawn in the diagram.

(c) Draw a smooth curve through the marked points. What is this curve?

You will need access to a graphics calculator or a computer with graph drawing software for questions 11 to 13. If you can print out the results, do so and keep them.

11. Set the range to $-360 \leqslant x \leqslant 360$ and $-2 \leqslant y \leqslant 2$

   (a) Draw the graph of $y = \sin x°$ and then superimpose the graph of $y = \sin 2x°$

   (b) Describe the transformation that maps the first curve to the second.

   (c) Clear the screen and repeat (a) and (b) for $y = \sin x°$ and $y = \sin 3x°$?

   (d) *Without drawing the graphs,* describe the transformation that maps the curve $y = \sin x°$ to the curve $y = \sin \frac{1}{2}x°$

12. Set the range to $0 \leqslant x \leqslant 1080$

   (a) Draw the graph of $y = \sin x°$

   (b) What is the range of values of $\sin x°$?

   (c) *Sketch* the graph of $y = \sin x°$ for $-360 \leqslant x \leqslant 4 \times 360$

13. Repeat question 11 for $y = \cos x°$

The Sine and Cosine Functions

The last exercise shows that $f(x) = \sin x°$ is never greater than 1 and never less than -1,

i.e. for all values of x, $-1 \leqslant \sin x° \leqslant 1$

Also the curve has a basic pattern, which repeats at intervals of 360 units.

The function $f(x) = \cos x°$ has the same properties. In fact if the curve $y = \sin x°$ is translated 90 units to the left, we get the curve $y = \cos x°$

The Graph of $y = \tan x°$

If values of $\tan x°$ are plotted against values of x for $0 \leqslant x \leqslant 360$, the resulting graph looks like this.

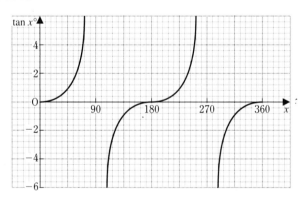

This shows that the function given by $y = \tan x°$ has properties that are different from those of the sine and the cosine functions, namely

   $\tan x°$ has no greatest or least value

   the graph of $y = \tan x°$ does have a repeating pattern, but it repeats at intervals of 180 units

   the graph has 'breaks' in it: these occur at 90 and every 180 step from there along the x-axis.

(Try this on your calculator: find $\tan 89°$, $\tan 89.9°$, $\tan 89.99°$, $\tan 89.999°$, $\tan 89.999999°$, $\tan 90°$. Why do you think the last one gives 'error'?)

Trigonometric Functions

The functions $f(x) = \sin x°$, $f(x) = \cos x°$, $f(x) = \tan x°$, are collectively known as trigonometric functions.

Summarising the work above, the graphs of these functions are

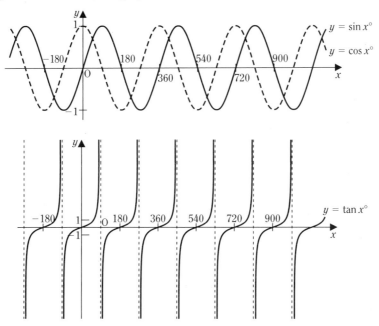

Exercise 33f

1. Sketch the graph of $y = \tan x°$ for $0 \leqslant x \leqslant 360$. On the same axes, sketch the graph of
   (a) $y = 1 + \tan x°$
   (b) $y = \tan(x - 90)°$

2. Sketch the curves $y = \cos x°$ and $y = \tan x°$ for $0 \leqslant x \leqslant 360$. Hence give the number of values of x between 0 and 360 for which $\cos x° = \tan x°$. Estimate these values of x. (If you have access to appropriate graph drawing facilities, find these values correct to the nearest degree.)

3. The diagram shows a sequence of right-angled triangles.

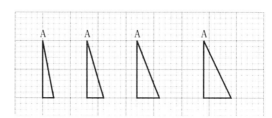

   (a) Continue this sequence and use it to complete the following table.

$\tan A$	0.2															
$\widehat{A}$																

   (b) What can you deduce about the value of $\tan A$ when $\widehat{A}$ is less than or equal to 45° ?

   (c) Describe what is happening to the values of $\tan A$ as $\widehat{A}$ increases in value.

4. The height of water, h metres, above the mean
   water level in an estuary, t hours after midnight,
   is given by $h = \sin(30t)°$ and is illustrated
   by the graph. Trace this graph.

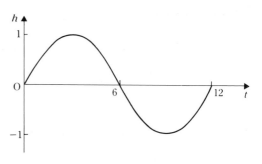

   (a) Use your copy to estimate the times at
       which the water level is 0.7 m below the
       mean water level, i.e. estimate the values of
       t for which $\sin(30t)° = -0.7$.

   (b) Draw an appropriate line to estimate the

       values of t for which $\sin(30t)° = 1 - \dfrac{t}{6}$

5. Mark the x-axis every 90 units and then use *sketch* graphs for values of x between 0 and 360 to find
   exactly the values of x for which
   (a) $\sin x° = -\sin x°$ (b) $\cos x° = 2 \cos x°$

6. Use sketch graphs to find approximate values of x between 0 and 180 for which
   (a) $\cos x° = \cos(x - 90)°$ (b) $1 + \sin x° = \tan x°$

7. Sketch the graphs of $y = \cos x°$ and $y = \dfrac{x}{10}$ for $0 \leqslant x \leqslant 90$. Hence show that there is one

   solution of the equation $x = 10 \cos x°$ between 0 and 20.

   (a) If x_n is an approximate root of the equation then x_{n+1} is a better approximation, where
       $x_{n+1} = 10 \cos x_n°$. Use this iteration formula, with $x_1 = 10$ to find x correct to 2 decimal
       places.

   (b) If the values of x are not restricted to those between 0 and 90, how many solutions does the
       equation have?

8. Sketch the graph of $y = 5 \cos x°$ for $-90 \leqslant x \leqslant 180$. On the same set of axes, sketch the
   graph of $x - 10y - 10 = 0$. Hence show that $x = 50$ is an approximate root of the equation
   $10 - x + 50 \cos x° = 0$
   Draw an accurate plot of the graphs for $42 \leqslant x \leqslant 54$ at intervals of 1 unit to find a better
   approximation to this root.

9. (a) What graphs need to be drawn to solve graphically the equation $50 \cos x° = x - 10$?

   (b) To what equation is the solution given by the value of x at the intersection of the graphs
       $y = \cos x°$ and $100y + x - 1 = 0$?

10. The approximate number, n, of hours of daylight in London is given by the formula
    $n = 12 - 5.5 \cos d°$ where d is the number of days after 21 December.

    (a) Calculate the number of hours of daylight
        (i) when $d = 120$ (ii) when $d = 240$ (iii) on 14 February   (iv) on 5 April

    (b) What are the values of d when day and night are of equal length?

    (c) On which dates will there be 15 hours of daylight?

    (d) Why is the formula only a rough approximation to reality?

Investigation

You will need access to a graphics calculator or computer.

Sketch the graph of $f(x) = x^2 + 1$

(a) What can you say about the value of $f(x)$ when $x = 0$?

(b) Describe what is happening to the value of $f(x)$ as x increases from -10 to 0

(c) What happens to the value of $f(x)$ as x increases from 0 to 10 ?

(d) What is happening to the value of $\dfrac{1}{x^2 + 1}$ as

    (i) x increases from -10 to 0,   (ii) x increases from 0 to 10 ?

(e) What can you say about the value of $\dfrac{1}{x^2 + 1}$ when $x = 0$?

(f) Use the information from (d) and (e) to sketch the graph of $y = \dfrac{1}{x^2 + 1}$

(g) Check your sketch by using a graphics calculator or computer.

Use a similar approach to deduce the shape of the curve $y = \dfrac{1}{x^2 - 1}$

Try drawing sketch graphs of $\dfrac{1}{f(x)}$ when $f(x) = \sin x°$, and when

$f(x) = (x-1)(x-2)^2$

Check your attempts by using a graphics calculator or computer.

Self-Assessment 33

1. If $f(x) = x^3 - 2$ find $f(2), f(0)$ and $f(-1)$ and sketch the graph of the function.

2. Show that the function given by
   $f(x) = 4 - x - x^2$ has a greatest value of 4.25 and find the value of x that gives this value of $f(x)$.

3. Find the values of x for which $f(x) = -3$ when $f(x) = x^2 - 4x$

4. Find the values of a and b for which
   $x^2 + 2x + 4 = (x + a)^2 + b$

5. Sketch the graph of $f(x) = \cos x°$ for values of x from 0 to 720

6. On the same axes and for $0 \leqslant x \leqslant 360$, sketch the graphs of $f(x) = \sin x°$ and $f(x) = \sin(x + 45)°$

7. On the same axes, sketch the graphs of $y = \cos x°$ and $y = \tan(x - 45)$ for $0 \leqslant x \leqslant 90$. For how many values of x in this range is $\cos x° = \tan(x - 45)°$?

8. Use the result of question 4 to sketch the graph of $f(x) = x^2 + 2x + 4$. On the same set of axes, sketch the curves $y = f(x) + 3$, $y = -f(x)$ and $y = 4 - f(x)$

PROBABILITY

EXPERIMENTAL PROBABILITY

If you throw an ordinary dice there are six possible scores, namely 1, 2, 3, 4, 5 or 6.

The act of throwing the dice is called an *experiment*.
The score that you get is called an *outcome* or *event*.
The set $\{1, 2, 3, 4, 5, 6\}$ is called the set of all possible outcomes.

The probability of obtaining a particular score is the number of ways of getting that score divided by the total number of possibilities.

For example, the probability of scoring 3 is $\frac{1}{6}$, since out of the six equally likely outcomes, only one is 'successful', i.e. is a 3.

We write $\qquad P(3) = \frac{1}{6}$

and $P(1 \text{ or } 2 \text{ or } 3 \text{ or } 4 \text{ or } 5 \text{ or } 6) = 1$ since the outcome *must* show one of these scores.

Similarly, the probability of scoring a 7 is 0, for out of the six equally likely scores, not one of them is 7.

When we get the result we seek, we say that the outcome is a successful event.

Generally

$$P(\text{successful event}) = \frac{\textbf{number of successful outcomes}}{\textbf{total number of possible outcomes}}$$

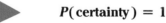 $P(\textbf{certainty}) = \textbf{1}$

$P(\textbf{impossibility}) = \textbf{0}$

If A stands for a particular event, the probability of A happening is written $P(A)$, and

$$0 \leqslant P(A) \leqslant 1$$

The probability that an event A does not happen is written $P(\overline{A})$, and

$$P(\overline{A}) = 1 - P(A)$$

In some experiments an event can happen more than once.

For example, since there are four Jacks in an ordinary pack of 52 playing cards

$$P(\text{a Jack}) = \frac{4}{52} = \frac{1}{13}$$

Similarly, if a bag contains 7 white discs and 9 black discs

$$P(\text{choosing a white disc}) = \frac{7}{16}$$

and $\qquad P(\text{choosing a black disc}) = \frac{9}{16}$

Exercise 34a

A card is drawn at random from a pack of 52 playing cards. What is the probability that the card is

(a) red
(b) a king
(c) a red jack, queen or king
(d) a card that is lower than 8 ? (An ace is higher than 8.)

(a) There are 26 red cards in the pack

$$\therefore \qquad P(\text{red}) = \tfrac{26}{52} = \tfrac{1}{2}$$

(b) There are 4 kings in the pack

$$\therefore \qquad P(\text{king}) = \tfrac{4}{52} = \tfrac{1}{13}$$

(c) Since there are 2 red jacks, 2 red queens and 2 red kings in the pack

$$P(\text{red jack, queen or king}) = \tfrac{6}{52} = \tfrac{3}{26}$$

(d) Similarly, $P(\text{lower than 8}) = \tfrac{24}{52} = \tfrac{6}{13}$

1. (a) What is the probability that, if a dice is rolled, the score is 5 or 6 ?

(b) Roll a dice 20 times and record the number of times a 5 or 6 is scored.

Work out the fraction

$$\frac{\text{number of times 5 or 6 is scored}}{\text{number of times dice is rolled}}$$

Roll it another 20 times and find the value of this fraction for the 40 outcomes. Carry on another 20 times, and another 20, and so on. Does the fraction, correct to two decimal places, settle down to a steady value ? How does this value compare with the answer you got for part (a) ?

2. A two-figure number is written down at random. Find the probability that

(a) the number is greater than 44

(b) the number is less than 100.

3. (a) What is the probability that the next person you meet was born in one of the summer months June, July or August ?

(b) Conduct an experiment. Ask at least 100 people:
In which month were you born ?

Calculate the fraction

$$\frac{\text{number born in June, July or August}}{\text{total number of people you have asked}}$$

Compare your answers for (a) and (b).

4. A letter is picked at random from the English alphabet. Find the probability that

(a) the letter is a vowel

(b) the letter comes in the first half of the alphabet

(c) the letter is one that appears in the word PROBABILITY.

A pin-board is marked as shown and a pin is stuck into the board at random. Find the probability that

(a) the pin is stuck into the shaded area
(b) the pin is not stuck into the shaded area.

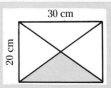

Area of board $= 20 \times 30 \, \text{cm}^2$

Area of triangle is $\frac{1}{2}$ base $\times$ perpendicular height $= \frac{1}{2} \times 30 \times 10 \, \text{cm}^2 = 150 \, \text{cm}^2$

(a) $P(\text{pin in shaded area}) = \frac{150}{600} = \frac{1}{4}$

(b) The unshaded area is $(600 - 150) \, \text{cm}^2 = 450 \, \text{cm}^2$

$\therefore \qquad\qquad P(\text{pin in unshaded area}) = \frac{450}{600} = \frac{3}{4}$

5. A rectangular board measuring 30 cm by 40 cm is marked as shown in the diagram. A pin is stuck into the board at random. Find the probability that

(a) the pin is stuck into the shaded area

(b) the pin is stuck into the unshaded area.

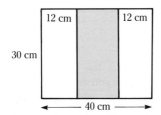

6. When Fiaz drops a coin on the board shown in the diagram its centre is equally likely to fall anywhere on the board. Find the probability that the centre of the coin falls

(a) on the shaded area

(b) on the unshaded area.

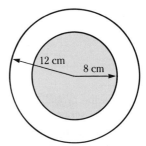

The probability of drawing a diamond from a pack of 52 playing cards is $\frac{13}{52}$, i.e. $\frac{1}{4}$. What is the probability of drawing a card that is not a diamond ?

$P(\text{card is not a diamond}) = 1 - \frac{1}{4} = \frac{3}{4}$

7. A bag contains black, blue and red counters. The probability of drawing a red counter is $\frac{2}{5}$. If Ali draws a counter from this bag what is the probability that it is not red ?

8. In a raffle 750 tickets are sold. If you buy 10 tickets what is the probability that

(a) you will win first prize

(b) you will not win first prize ?

9. A letter is chosen at random from the letters of the word SUCCESSION. What is the probability that the letter is

(a) N   (b) S   (c) a vowel   (d) not S ?

10. A bag contains a set of snooker balls (i.e. 15 reds and 1 each of white, yellow, green, brown, blue, pink and black). What is the probability that one ball removed at random is

(a) red   (c) black
(b) not red   (d) not red or white ?

11. A bag of sweets contains 4 caramels, 3 fruit centres and 5 mints. If one sweet is taken out, what is the probability that it is

   (a) a mint   (b) a caramel   (c) not a fruit centre ?

Of a class of 21, 10 altogether learn French, 6 learn both French and German and 6 learn neither. What is the probability that a pupil chosen at random learns only German ?

We can represent this information on a diagram. Suppose that the left-hand circle represents those pupils studying French and that the right-hand circle represents those studying German. Six study neither so are placed outside both circles. If 10 learn French and 6 learn both languages then 4 study only French. Since the total is 21 the number studying only German is 5.

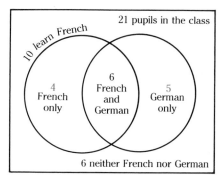

$$P(\text{pupil picked at random studies only German}) = \tfrac{5}{21}$$

12. A group of 50 television addicts were asked if they watched BBC and/or ITV. The replies revealed that 21 watched both channels but 9 watched only ITV. What is the probability that one of these people chosen at random watches only BBC ?

13. Of the 24 pupils in a class 20 have a television set and 12 have a video recorder. If every pupil has at least one of these items what is the probability that a pupil chosen at random has both ?

14. In a group of 30 children, all but 5 had a dog or a cat or both. If 18 kept a dog and 5 of these also kept a cat, what is the probability that one pupil, chosen at random,

   (a) keeps both a dog and a cat

   (b) keeps only a cat ?

15. During November, 36 cars were taken to a Testing Station for an MOT certificate. The results showed that 8 had defective brakes and lights, 10 had defective brakes, and 13 had defective lights. If one car had been chosen from these at random what is the probability that

   (a) it had defective brakes

   (b) it had defective lights

   (c) it passed the test ?

The Expected Number of Successes

The converse of what we have considered in the last exercise is also important. If we know the probability that an event will occur we can find the expected number of successes for a given number of trials. In general

    likely number of successes is equal to the number of trials × probability of success

So, for example, since the probability of getting a head when a fair coin is tosssed is $\frac{1}{2}$, we would expect to get about 250 heads when a coin is tossed 500 times. (We are of course very unlikely to get exactly 250 heads, but there should be roughly that number of heads if the coin is not biased.)

Exercise 34b

In a television audience if one person is picked at random the probability that it is a man is $\frac{3}{8}$. There are 360 people in the audience. How many are likely to be men ?

$$\text{Number of men} = 360 \times \tfrac{3}{8}$$
$$= 135$$

1. A dice is rolled 180 times. How many times would you expect to get

   (a) 5   (b) an even number   (c) 1, 2 or 3 ?

2. A card is drawn at random, 260 times, from an ordinary pack of 52 playing cards. How many times would you expect to get

   (a) an Ace   (c) a black card

   (b) a heart   (d) a red 7 ?

3. The probability that it will rain in Sunbrook on any given day in August is $\frac{2}{7}$. How many rainy days can you expect if you go to Sunbrook for 14 days in August ?

4. In a car park there is a probability of $\frac{3}{8}$ that a car picked at random is British made. There are 184 cars in the car park. How many of them

   (a) are British made

   (b) are not British made ?

5. The probability that you will get a yellow disc when you draw a disc at random from a box is $\frac{2}{5}$. How many yellow discs will you expect to get if you do this with each of 40 such boxes ?

6. At a school canteen, the estimated probabilities that a pupil asks for milk, cola or squash are $\frac{3}{12}$, $\frac{5}{12}$ and $\frac{4}{12}$ respectively. Next week it is estimated that there will be 1800 pupil customers. How many of each type of drink does the canteen expect to sell ?

7. An opinion poll used a sample of 1000 randomly selected voters to find voting intentions in a general election. Of these voters, 360 said that they would vote Conservative at the next general election and 75 said that they would vote for the Raving Looney party.

   (a) If a voter is selected at random from the sample, what is the probability that he/she stated an intention to vote Conservative ?

   (b) If there are 20 000 000 voters in the general election, how many are likely to vote
   (i) Conservative   (ii) Raving Looney
   assuming that candidates for each party are standing in all constituencies ?

ADDITION OF PROBABILITIES

If we select a card at random from a pack of 52, the probability of drawing a king is $\frac{4}{52}$ and the probability of drawing a black ten is $\frac{2}{52}$.

There are 4 kings and 2 black tens so if we want to find the probability of drawing either a king or a black ten there are 6 cards that we would count as 'successful'.

$$\therefore \qquad P(\text{king or a black ten}) = \frac{6}{52}$$

Now $\qquad P(\text{king}) = \frac{4}{52}$ and $P(\text{black ten}) = \frac{2}{52}$

i.e. $\qquad P(\text{king or black ten}) = P(\text{king}) + P(\text{black ten})$

We *add* the probabilities if there are several mutually exclusive possibilities (i.e. separate and independent possibilities) that we count as successful.

Sometimes two events are not completely separate, i.e. mutually exclusive. Consider, for example, the probability of drawing either a red card or a king. There are 26 red cards and 4 kings, but 2 of the kings are also red cards. There are therefore a total of 28 possible successful cards.

$$P(\text{red card or king}) = \frac{28}{52} = \frac{7}{13}$$

If two events are not mutually exclusive we cannot add the separate probabilities.

Exercise 34c

1. A card is drawn at random from an ordinary pack of 52. What is the probability that the card is
   (a) a red ace   (b) a black king
   (c) a red ace or a black king?

2. Joy rolls an ordinary dice. What is the probability that the number shown is
   (a) 2   (b) 3 or 4   (c) 2, 3 or 4?

3. A card is drawn at random from the 12 court cards (jacks, queens and kings). What is the probability that the card is
   (a) a black jack
   (b) a red queen
   (c) either a black jack or a red queen?

4. Graham is looking for his house key. The probability that it is in a pocket is $\frac{5}{9}$, while the probability that it is in the car is $\frac{1}{3}$. What is the probability that
   (a) the key is either in a pocket or in the car
   (b) the key is somewhere else?

5. When Mrs Greene goes shopping the probability that she returns by bus is $\frac{4}{7}$, in a taxi $\frac{1}{7}$, on foot $\frac{3}{14}$. What is the probability that she returns
   (a) by bus or taxi   (b) by bus or on foot?

6. Karl has a bag containing some coloured discs. When a disc is drawn from the bag the probability of getting a red disc is $\frac{2}{5}$, a blue disc $\frac{2}{7}$ and a yellow disc $\frac{1}{4}$. Karl offers the bag to Sandra who draws one disc. Find the probability that the colour of this disc is
   (a) red or blue
   (b) blue or yellow
   (c) red, blue or yellow
   (d) some other colour.

7. Sengha rolls an ordinary dice. What is the probability that the number on the dice is
   (a) an even number
   (b) a prime number
   (c) either even or prime?

POSSIBILITY SPACE FOR TWO EVENTS

Any two-dimensional array that shows all the possible outcomes is called a *possibility space*.

When two coins are tossed the possible outcomes are   HH, HT, TH, TT

Each outcome is equally likely so $P(2\text{ heads}) = \frac{1}{4}$

By listing the possible equally likely outcomes the required probability can be found. However if two dice are rolled there are many possible outcomes. We must set out the list in an organised way so that there is no risk of missing any.

We can list the outcomes in the following table using crosses.

First dice

	1	2	3	4	5	6
1	×	×	×	(×)	×	×
2	×	×	(×)	×	×	[×]
3	×	(×)	×	×	[×]	×
4	(×)	×	×	[×]	×	×
5	×	×	[×]	×	×	×
6	×	[×]	×	×	×	×

Second dice

The table shows that there are 36 possible outcomes.

To find the probability of getting a total score of 5, ring the crosses that indicate a total score of 5, i.e. $1+4, 2+3,$ and so on.

Hence $P(5) = \frac{4}{36} = \frac{1}{9}$

Similarly, we can find the probability of scoring, say, 8. Put squares around the outcomes that total 8. Thus $P(8) = \frac{5}{36}$

Exercise 34d

In each question from 1 to 3, draw a possibility space to show the outcomes when two ordinary dice are rolled. Use this possibility space to find the required probabilities. Use different marks such as a ring or a square, or different colours, for the first two parts of each question.

1. Find the probability that
   (a) the sum of the two numbers is 7
   (b) the difference between the scores is 2
   (c) the sum is 7 and the difference is 2.

2. Find the probability that
   (a) the sum of the two numbers is 7 or more
   (b) the difference between the two numbers is 3 or less
   (c) the sum of the two numbers is 7 or more and their difference is 3 or less.

3. Find the probability that
   (a) prime numbers appear on both dice
   (b) at least one prime number appears
   (c) only one prime number appears.

4. A four-sided spinner has the numbers 1 to 4 marked on it. It is spun twice and the two scores are noted. Draw a possibility space table to show the outcomes. Find the probability that

(a) the total score is even

(b) the two separate scores are both even

(c) the product of the scores is even.

5. I have two bags each containing four hyacinth bulbs and I know that each bag contains a pink, a blue, a yellow and a white bulb. If I take one bulb at random from each bag, find the probability that

(a) the hyacinths will be the same colour

(b) the hyacinths will be of different colours.

DEPENDENT EVENTS

In the questions in the previous exercise the second outcome (e.g. rolling a dice a second time) is not influenced by the result of the first outcome. Sometimes however (e.g. when picking discs from a bag without replacement) the second outcome depends on what happened first. We cannot use possibility spaces to solve this new type of question.

Exercise 34e

A bag contains 5 red discs and 8 white discs.

(a) A disc is drawn at random from the bag. What is the probability that it is red ?

(b) If a red disc is drawn first and not replaced what is the probability that the next disc drawn from the bag is also red ?

(a) There are 5 red discs out of 13,

therefore $P(\text{1st disc red}) = \frac{5}{13}$

(b) There are now 4 red discs left out of a total of 12 discs,

therefore $P(\text{2nd disc red}) = \frac{4}{12} = \frac{1}{3}$

1. (a) A card is drawn from a pack of 52 playing cards. What is the probability that it is black ?

(b) If the first card is black and a second card is drawn from the remaining 51 cards, what is the probability that the second card is red ?

2. A bag contains 4 blue beads and 6 yellow beads. A bead is drawn at random from the bag.

(a) What is the probability that the bead is
(i) blue   (ii) yellow ?

(b) If a yellow bead is drawn first and not replaced, what is the probability that the next bead drawn is
(i) blue   (ii) yellow ?

3. A small dairy herd consists of 14 Guernseys and 8 Jerseys. The cows gather at the gate and, when the gate is opened, come through in random order.

(a) What is the probability that the first through is
(i) a Jersey   (ii) a Guernsey ?

(b) If the first through is a Jersey what is the probability that the second one through is
(i) a Jersey   (ii) a Guernsey ?

(c) If the first through is a Guernsey what is the probability that the second one through is
(i) a Jersey   (ii) a Guernsey ?

PROBABILITY TREES

Suppose that we have seven discs in a bag, three of which are black and the remainder white. When a disc is drawn at random the probability that it is black is $\frac{3}{7}$ and the probability that it is white is $\frac{4}{7}$.

We can show this in a diagram.

If we have drawn a black disc, and do not put it back, there are two black discs and four white discs left. The probabilities of drawing a black or a white disc are now $\frac{2}{6}$, i.e. $\frac{1}{3}$, and $\frac{4}{6}$, i.e. $\frac{2}{3}$.

Similarly, if a white disc is drawn first, the diagram showing the probabilities for the colour of the second disc is

These three diagrams can be combined in one diagram, called a *tree diagram*.

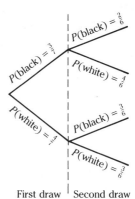

First draw ┊ Second draw

We can use the tree diagram to find the probability that, say, two black discs are drawn. Follow the path along the branches for 'black disc first' and 'black disc second' and multiply together the probabilities on these two branches, i.e.

$$P(\text{two black discs}) = \tfrac{3}{7} \times \tfrac{2}{6} = \tfrac{1}{7}$$

Similarly

$$P(\text{two white discs}) = \tfrac{4}{7} \times \tfrac{3}{6} = \tfrac{2}{7}$$

The reason for multiplying the two probabilities together can be seen if we consider drawing two of the seven discs on a large number of occasions, say 350 times. We would expect to get a black disc on $\frac{3}{7} \times 350$, i.e. 150 occasions.

On $\frac{1}{3}$ of these occasions, i.e. on 50 occasions, we would expect to get another black disc.

$$P(\text{two black discs}) = \tfrac{50}{350} = \tfrac{1}{7}$$

Exercise 34f

In this exercise, the first object is not replaced before the second object is drawn.

> A bag contains 12 counters; 5 are red and the remainder are blue. Two counters are drawn at random without replacement. Find the probability that
> (a) both are red   (b) both are blue.
>
> Are the answers to parts (a) and (b) the same if the first counter is placed back in the bag before the second counter is removed?
>
>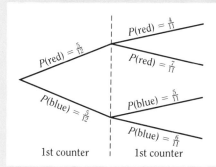
>
> (a) $P(2 \text{ red}) = \frac{5}{12} \times \frac{4}{11} = \frac{5}{33}$
>
> (b) $P(2 \text{ blue}) = \frac{7}{12} \times \frac{6}{11} = \frac{7}{22}$
>
> No, because if the first counter is replaced, the probability that the second counter is red is $\frac{5}{12}$ and the probability that it is blue is $\frac{7}{12}$.

1. A bag contains 5 green beads and 6 blue beads. Two beads are withdrawn at random.

   (a) Find the probability that the first bead is green.

   (b) If the first bead is green find the probability that the second bead is blue.

   Draw a probability tree to show the probabilities when two beads are withdrawn and find the probability that

   (c) both beads are blue

   (d) the first bead is blue and the second bead is green.

2. Nine cards are numbered 1 to 9 and two cards are drawn at random. Draw a probability tree to show the probabilities of drawing odd or even cards. Find the probability that

   (a) the first card is even

   (b) both cards are even

   (c) both cards are odd

   (d) the first card is even and the second card is odd

   (e) the first card is odd and the second card is even

   (f) one card is odd and one card is even in any order. (Use your answers to parts (d) and (e) to answer part (f).)

3. A hand of 13 cards contains 5 red cards and 8 black cards. Two cards are drawn at random from the hand.

   (a) What is the probability that the first card is black?

   (b) If the first card is black what is the probability that the second card is black?

   (c) Draw a probability tree and use it to find the probability that both cards are red.

4. Ann Taylor breeds pugs. She has 6 fawn pug puppies and 9 black pug puppies. They are struggling in the pen and, when the gate is opened, they come out one at a time in random order.

   (a) What is the probability that the first is fawn?

   (b) If the first is fawn what is the probability that the second is black?

   Find the probability that

   (c) one of the first two puppies is fawn and one is black

   (d) the first three out are all fawn.

Simplified Tree Diagrams

We do not always need to draw every possible branch of the tree diagram. If, for instance, in throwing a dice three times, we are interested only in the number of times a 6 is thrown, the tree diagram need have only two branches per throw. One branch is for 'throwing a 6', the other is for 'throwing a number other than 6'.

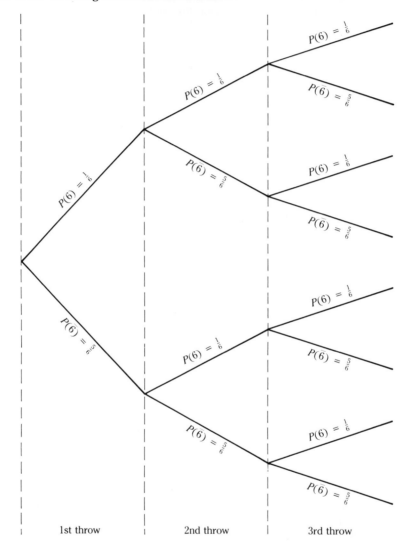

| 1st throw | 2nd throw | 3rd throw |

We have seen (Exercise 34f, question 2(f)) that the required outcomes are sometimes given by following more than one path along the branches.

As the outcomes from each path are mutually exclusive, we *add* the probabilities resulting from the separate paths.

  We *multiply* the probabilities when we follow a path *along* the branches of the probability tree and *add* the results of following several paths.

Exercise 34g

In this exercise, objects are not replaced before the next object is drawn.

Two dice are rolled. What is the probability of getting an even number on one dice and a 3 on the other ?

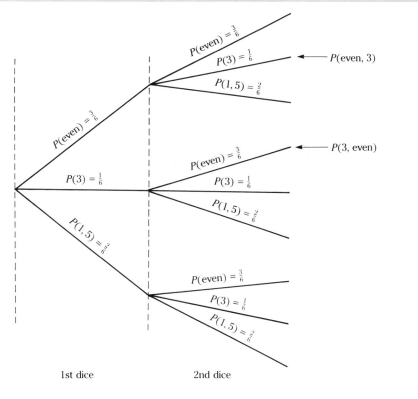

$$P(\text{ an even number and 3 in any order }) = \tfrac{3}{6} \times \tfrac{1}{6} + \tfrac{1}{6} \times \tfrac{3}{6}$$

$$= \tfrac{1}{12} + \tfrac{1}{12}$$

$$= \tfrac{1}{6}$$

1. A hand of cards contains nine cards, four of which are diamonds and the rest spades. Two cards are drawn at random. Draw a tree diagram to show the probabilities and find the probability that

   (a) one card is a diamond and the other is a spade

   (b) the two cards belong to the same suit.

2. Josie has a bag containing eighteen building blocks. Eleven of them are blue and seven are yellow. Two blocks are withdrawn at random from the bag. Draw a probability tree and use it to find the probability that

   (a) the first block is yellow and the second one is blue

   (b) one is yellow and the other is blue

   (c) the two blocks are the same colour.

3. Jane has 8 white handkerchiefs and 5 coloured handkerchiefs in a drawer. She takes out two handkerchiefs in the dark. What is the probability that exactly one of them is white ?

4. A coin is tossed three times. Draw a tree diagram to show the possibilities and use it to find the probability of getting

   (a) a head and two tails   (b) exactly one tail   (c) at least one head.

5. In a game of chance on a machine a player can win with a probability of $\frac{1}{3}$, lose with a probability of $\frac{2}{5}$, or draw. Another game is allowed after a draw, but not otherwise.

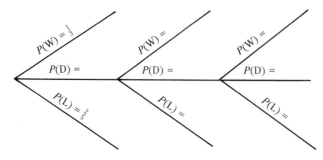

   (a) The partly completed tree diagram shows all the possible outcomes for up to three games. Copy the diagram and fill in the missing probabilities.

   (b) Find the probability that Aziz will win after   (i) one game   (ii) exactly two games (iii) exactly three games.

   (c) What is the probability that Joanne can continue playing after three games ?

6. On the way home Larry passes through three sets of traffic lights. The probability that the first set is green when he reaches them is $\frac{3}{5}$, the probability that the second set is green is $\frac{2}{3}$ and the probability that the third set is green is $\frac{3}{4}$. Draw a probability tree and use it to find the probability that he has to stop at

   (a) just one set of traffic lights

   (b) at least one set of traffic lights

   (c) exactly two sets of traffic lights.

7. The probabilities that Alice, Bernard and Cindy can solve a problem are respectively $\frac{1}{2}, \frac{2}{3}$ and $\frac{1}{4}$. Find the probability that

   (a) all three can solve it

   (b) just two out of the three can solve it

   (c) only one of them can solve it.

   The remaining questions are mixed problems and some of them are quite difficult.

8. In a geography test a group of one hundred pupils were given marks out of 60. The table shows the number achieving the various marks.

Marks	1–10	11–20	21–30
Frequency	4	16	20

Marks	31–40	41–50	51–60
Frequency	24	27	9

   (a) State the probability that a pupil chosen at random will have a mark
      (i) from 41 to 50 inclusive
      (ii) greater than 50
      (iii) 20 or less.

   (b) A second group of one hundred pupils was tested and ten scored more than 50 marks. If one pupil is chosen at random from each of the groups, find the probability that
      (i) both will have scored more than 50
      (ii) just one of them will have scored more than 50.

9. Each of the following draws is from a set of four cards that are numbered 1, 3, 6, 8.

   (a) One card is drawn at random. Find the probability that the number on the card is a prime number.

   (b) Two cards are drawn at random. Find the probability that the numbers on both cards are multiples of 3.

   (c) Two cards are drawn at random. Find the probability that the sum of the two numbers is 9.

10. At a disco, thirty tickets numbered 1 to 30 are placed in a drum. A ticket drawn from the drum wins a prize if its number is a multiple of 5. A ticket, once drawn, is not replaced. Two tickets are drawn in succession. Find the probability that

    (a) the first ticket wins a prize

    (b) the first ticket does not win a prize but the second does.

    Three tickets are drawn in succession.

    (c) What is the probability that no ticket wins a prize ?

    (d) What is the probability that at least one ticket wins a prize ?

11. Tim and Cath play a game using a dice. Tim tosses it and records the score. If he throws a one or a two he tosses it again. Tim wins if on either the first throw or the second he scores 5 or 6. If he does not, then Cath wins.

    (a) What is the probability that Tim wins ?

    (b) Who is more likely to win, Tim or Cath ?

12. In a sideshow at a fête, a player is required to roll balls towards five channels marked with the scores 1 to 5.

1	3	5	4	2

    The probabilities of achieving the various scores are

    $$P(1) = \tfrac{1}{10} \qquad P(5) = \tfrac{2}{5}$$
    $$P(3) = \tfrac{1}{5} \qquad P(4) = \tfrac{1}{5}$$

    (a) Calculate the probability of scoring 2

    With two balls, find the probability of achieving a total score of

    (b) 10   (c) 3   (d) 4.

    With three balls, find the probability of achieving a total score of

    (e) 15   (f) 3.

13. A biased dice is such that the probability of throwing a six is $\tfrac{1}{3}$, and the probability of scoring each of the other numbers is $\tfrac{2}{15}$. I have two biased dice and two fair dice.

    If I throw   (a) two biased dice

    (b) one fair dice and one biased dice, calculate the probability of obtaining a total score of

    (i) 12   (ii) 11.

14. The probability that Alex passes his driving test on his first attempt is $\tfrac{2}{5}$ and the probability that he passes on his second or subsequent attempts is $\tfrac{3}{5}$. Find the probability that Alex passes his driving test on his third or fourth attempt.

RELATIVE FREQUENCY

We have assumed that if you toss a coin it is equally likely to land head up or tail up so that $P(\text{a head}) = \tfrac{1}{2}$.

Coins like this are called 'fair' or 'unbiased'.

Most coins are likely to be unbiased but it is not necessarily true of all coins. A particular coin may be slightly bent or even deliberately biased so that the chances of getting a head or a tail are not equal.

The only way to find out if a particular coin is unbiased is to collect some information about how it behaves when it is tossed. We can do this by tossing it several times and recording the results.

Tossing a bent coin gave these results.

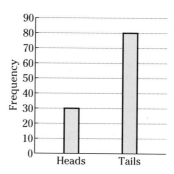

For this coin we have 30 heads out of 110 tosses.
We say that the *relative frequency* of heads with this coin is $\frac{30}{110}$.

We can use the relative frequency of heads as an estimate for the probability of a head with this coin, i.e.

$$P(\text{a head}) \approx \frac{\text{number of heads}}{\text{total number of tosses}} = \frac{3}{11}$$

The approximation gets more reliable as the number of tosses gets larger, but on this evidence it looks as though this coin is more likely to give a tail than a head.

Exercise 34h

Do not find the probabilities. Decide whether evidence is needed to determine the relative frequency or whether theoretical probability can be used to find the probability that

1. a new drug will cure migraine

2. a new 2p coin lands head up

3. next Christmas will be a white Christmas

4. when an ordinary pack of cards is cut, the next card is the two of clubs

5. a sweet removed from a bag containing 6 toffees and 4 chocolates is a toffee

6. there will be fog at Heathrow Airport next Saturday

7. a chipped dice will show six.

Investigations

1. Pick out two cards from a shuffled pack of 52 playing cards. Write Y if you have at least one ace, king, queen or jack. Write N otherwise. Replace the cards, shuffle the pack and do the same thing again. Repeat this at least 100 times.

   Work out the relative frequency of $Y = \dfrac{\text{number of } Y\text{s}}{\text{total number of outcomes}}$

   Work out the theoretical probability that at least one card out of two cards drawn at random is an ace, king, queen or jack and compare this with your relative frequency.

   Repeat this procedure for other selections of your own choice from the pack. Do your results convince you that the theoretical results give a good indication of what is likely to happen?

2. A company runs the following promotional offer with tubes of sweets.

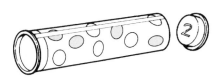

Each lid has a number 1, 2, 3, 4, 5 or 6 printed inside.

Collect 4 lids with the same number and get a free T-shirt.

What are the chances of getting four numbers the same if you just buy four tubes?

What is the most likely number of tubes that you need to buy to get four identical lids?

(a) We could answer these questions by collecting evidence, i.e. buying tubes of these sweets until we have four lids with the same number on them, and repeating this until we think we have reliable results.
What are the disadvantages of this approach?

(b) We can avoid the disadvantages of having to buy tubes of these sweets by simulating the situation.
First we assume that any one of the numbers 1 to 6 is equally likely to be inside a lid.
Now you can toss a dice to simulate the number you would get if you bought a tube, and carry on tossing it until you get four numbers the same. You will need several tally charts, one for each simulation, to keep a record of the number of tosses needed to get four numbers the same, and one summary tally chart to record the number of tosses needed on each occasion.

This shows the start of the simulation.

Sample Tally Chart for one simulation

Score	1	2	3	4	5	6	Total
Tally	/	///	/	//	////	/	12

Summary Tally Chart

Number of tosses needed to get 4 numbers the same	4	5	6	7	8	9	10	11	12	13	14	15	16	...
Tally									/					

Self-Assessment 34

1. A card is drawn at random from an ordinary pack of 52 playing cards. What is the probability that it is

   (a) a red 3   (b) the Ace of spaces ?

2. If a person enters the library, the probability that it is a woman is $\frac{2}{5}$ and the probability that it is a man is $\frac{3}{10}$. What is the probability that the next person to come in to the library is

   (a) a man or a woman

   (b) neither of these ?

3. The six faces of a dice have the first six prime numbers marked on them. This dice and an ordinary dice are rolled together. Draw a possibility space to show the possible outcomes and use it to find the probability that the total score is

   (a) odd   (c) a multiple of 3

   (b) prime   (d) more than 12.

4. A dice is rolled 360 times. How many times would you expect to get

   (a) 6   (b) 1 or 2 ?

5. Jim takes a CD at random from his collection of 8 jazz CDs and 14 pop CDs.

   (a) What is the probability that it is
       (i) a jazz CD   (ii) a pop CD ?

   (b) If a jazz CD is drawn first and not replaced, what is the probability that the next CD selected is
       (i) a jazz CD   (ii) a pop CD ?

6. A hand of 13 cards contains 7 red cards and 6 black cards. Two cards are drawn at random from the hand. Draw a probability tree and use it to find the probability that

   (a) both cards are red

   (b) the cards are of different colours.

NOTATION FOR TRANSFORMATIONS

In the earlier chapter on transformations, if we wished to refer, for example, to a reflection in the line $x = 1$, or a rotation of 90° anticlockwise about the origin, we had to describe it in full. If we wish to refer to the transformation several times, a symbol to denote it is useful.

For example we can use Y to denote a reflection in the y-axis. Then the image of a triangle (called P) under this reflection is named Y(P).

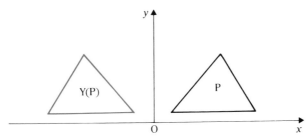

Exercise 35a

> R_1 is the rotation of 90° anticlockwise about O. The object P is △ABC with vertices
> A(1,1), B(4,1) and C(4,5).
> Draw P and R_1(P)

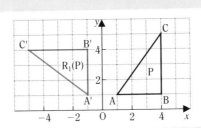

In this exercise,

R_1 is a rotation of 90° anticlockwise about O
R_2 is a rotation of 180° about O
R_3 is a rotation of 90° clockwise about O

X is a reflection in the x-axis
Y is a reflection in the y-axis
T is a translation defined by the vector $\begin{pmatrix} 2 \\ 3 \end{pmatrix}$

For each question, draw x and y axes, each for values from −6 to 6.

1. P, Q and R are the points (2,1), (5,1) and (5,3).
   Draw △PQR and label it A. Then draw and label the following images of A

   (a) R_1(A)   (b) R_2(A)   (c) R_3(A).

2. P is the triangle with vertices $(-5,0)$, $(-3,0)$ and $(-3,2)$.

   Q is the triangle with vertices $(1,0)$, $(3,0)$ and $(1,2)$.

   R is the triangle with vertices $(-2,-6)$, $(0,-6)$ and $(0,-4)$.

   Draw and label

   (a) T(P)   (b) T(Q)   (c) T(R).

3. A, B and C are the points $(-2,1)$, $(-4,1)$ and $(-2,5)$.

   Draw △ABC and label it Q.

   Draw and label the following images

   (a) X(Q)   (b) Y(Q).

4. L is a reflection in the line $x + y = 2$ and M is a reflection in the line $y = x + 2$. The object A is the triangle with vertices $(1,2)$, $(4,2)$ and $(4,4)$.

   Find

   (a) L(A)   (b) M(A).

5. N is a rotation of 90° anticlockwise about $(1,1)$.

   R is a rotation of 90° clockwise about $(0,-1)$. The object B is the triangle with vertices $(-2,1)$, $(-5,1)$ and $(-2,2)$.

   Find   (a) N(B)   (b) R(B).

COMPOUND TRANSFORMATIONS

If we reflect the object P in the *x*-axis and then reflect the resulting image in the *y*-axis, we are carrying out a compound transformation. The letters defined in Exercise 37a can be used to describe the final image.

The first image is X(P). The second image is Y(X(P)) but the outer set of brackets is not usually used and it is written YX(P).

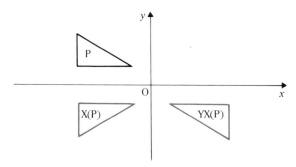

Notice that the letter X, denoting the transformation used first, is nearer to the object P. We work outwards from the bracket containing the object.

For example, YT(P) means translate P first and then reflect the image in the *y*-axis, whereas TY(P) means reflect P in the *y*-axis and then translate the image.

Notice that YT(P) is not the same as TY(P).

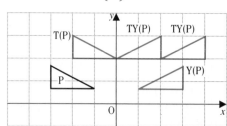

Exercise 35b

In this exercise,

R_1 is a rotation of 90° anticlockwise about O
R_2 is a rotation of 180° about O
R_3 is a rotation of 90° clockwise about O

X is a reflection in the *x*-axis
Y is a reflection in the *y*-axis
T is a translation defined by the vector $\begin{pmatrix} 2 \\ 3 \end{pmatrix}$

A, B and C are the points $(3,1)$, $(5,1)$ and $(5,4)$. Draw $\triangle$ABC and label it P.
Draw and label $R_1(P)$, $XR_1(P)$ and $YR_1(P)$.

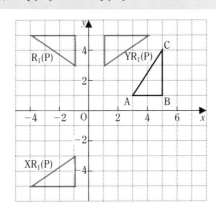

In each of the following questions draw *x* and *y* axes, each for values from −6 to 6.

1. P, Q and R are the points $(1,3)$, $(3,3)$ and $(1,6)$. Draw $\triangle$PQR and label it A. Draw and label

   (a) $R_3(A)$ (c) $X(A)$
   (b) $XR_3(A)$ (d) $R_3X(A)$.
   (e) Describe the single transformation that will map A to $R_3X(A)$.

2. L, M and N are the points $(-2,1)$, $(-4,1)$ and $(-2,5)$. Draw $\triangle$LMN and label it P. Draw and label

   (a) $R_1(P)$
   (b) $R_2R_1(P)$
   (c) $R_3R_1(P)$.
   (d) What is the single transformation that will map P to $R_2R_1(P)$?
   (e) What is the single transformation that will map $R_2R_1(P)$ to $R_1(P)$?

3. A, B and C are the points $(-5,2)$, $(-2,2)$ and $(-5,4)$. Draw $\triangle$ABC and label it P. Draw and label

   (a) $X(P)$ (d) $Y(P)$
   (b) $YX(P)$ (e) $XY(P)$.
   (c) $R_2(P)$
   (f) Is $YX(P)$ the same triangle as $XY(P)$?
   (g) Is $R_2(P)$ the same triangle as $XY(P)$?
   (h) What single transformation is equivalent to a reflection in the *x*-axis followed by a reflection in the *y*-axis?

4. L, M and N are the points $(-3,0)$, $(-1,0)$ and $(-1,3)$. Draw $\triangle$LMN and label it Q. Find

   (a) $T(Q)$ (c) $X(Q)$
   (b) $XT(Q)$ (d) $TX(Q)$.
   (e) Describe the single transformation that will map $X(Q)$ to $XT(Q)$.
   (f) Describe the single transformation that will map $XT(Q)$ to $TX(Q)$.

EQUIVALENT SINGLE TRANSFORMATIONS

We have seen that if we reflect an object P in the x-axis and then reflect the image X(P) in the y-axis we get the same final image as if we had rotated P through 180° about O. YX(P) is the same as R_2(P) and the effect of YX is the same as the effect of R_2. Referring to the images we can write   YX(P) = R_2(P) and, referring to the transformations,   YX = R_2.

In the following exercise notice that X^2 = XX,   i.e. the transformation X is used twice in succession.

The Identity Transformation

If an object is rotated through 360° or translated using the vector $\begin{pmatrix} 0 \\ 0 \end{pmatrix}$, the final image turns out to be the same as the original object. This operation is called the *identity transformation* and is usually denoted by I.

Exercise 35c

In this exercise

R_1 is a rotation of 90° anticlockwise about O
R_2 is a rotation of 180° about O
R_3 is a rotation of 90° clockwise about O
X is a reflection in the x-axis
Y is a reflection in the y-axis

T is a translation defined by the vector $\begin{pmatrix} 2 \\ 3 \end{pmatrix}$

Z is a reflection in the line $y = x$
W is a reflection in the line $y = -x$
I is the identity transformation.

In each question draw x and y axes, each for values from -6 to 6. Use 1 cm for 1 unit.

1. A is a reflection in the line $x = -1$ and B a reflection in the line $y = 2$. Label as G the triangle PQR where P is the point (1,4), Q(4,6) and R(1,6).
   (a) Find A(G), B(G), AB(G) and BA(G).
   (b) Give the single transformations given by AB and BA. Is AB equal to BA ?
   (c) Find A^2(G) and B^2(G).

2. S is a reflection in the line $x = 1$. U is a reflection in the line $y = 2$. V is a rotation of 180° about the point (1,2). Label with A the triangle PQR where P is the point (1,1), Q is (3,1) and R is (3,-2).
   (a) Draw S(A), U(A), SU(A) and US(A).
   (b) Are SU and US the same transformation ?
   (c) Is it true that   V = SU ?

3. Label with P the triangle ABC where A is the point (1,2), B is (4,2) and C is (1,4).
   (a) Draw R_1(P), $R_1{}^2$(P), R_2(P), $R_2 R_1$(P) and R_3(P). Complete the following statements
      (i) $R_1{}^2$ =
      (ii) $R_2 R_1$ =
   (b) Draw whatever images are needed and complete the following statements
      (i) $R_3{}^2$ =
      (ii) $R_2 R_3$ =
      (iii) $R_3 R_2$ =

P is the triangle with vertices $(2,1)$, $(5,1)$ and $(2,3)$.
Find $Y(P)$ and $Y^2(P)$. Name the single transformation that is equal to Y^2.

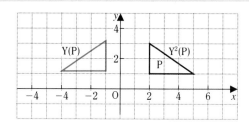

$$Y^2(P) = P$$
$$\therefore \qquad Y^2 = I$$

For each question draw x and y axes, each for values from -6 to 6. Use $1\,cm$ to 1 unit.

4. P is the triangle with vertices $(2,1)$, $(5,1)$ and $(5,5)$.

   (a) Find $R_1(P)$, $R_2(P)$, $R_3(P)$, $R_1R_3(P)$ and $R_3R_1(P)$.
   Name the single transformation which is equal to R_1R_3 and to R_3R_1.

   (b) Complete the following statements with a single letter.
   (i) $R_2{}^2 =$ (ii) $R_2R_3 =$ (iii) $R_1R_2 =$

5. Q is the triangle with vertices $(-2,1)$, $(-5,1)$ and $(-4,5)$.

   (a) Find $X(Q)$, $Y(Q)$, $XY(Q)$, $R_2(Q)$ and $X^2(Q)$.

   (b) Complete the following statements with a single letter.
   (i) $X^2 =$ (ii) $XY =$

6. N is the triangle with vertices $(1,3)$, $(1,6)$ and $(5,6)$.

   (a) Find $Z(N)$, $WZ(N)$, $Z^2(N)$, $XZ(N)$, $YZ(N)$ and $IZ(N)$.

   (b) Complete the following statements with a single letter.
   (i) $WZ =$ (iii) $XZ =$ (v) $IZ =$
   (ii) $Z^2 =$ (iv) $YZ =$

7. M is the triangle with vertices $(3,2)$, $(5,2)$ and $(5,6)$.

   (a) Find $R_1(M)$, $X(M)$, $X^2(M)$, $XR_1(M)$ and $R_1X(M)$.

   (b) Complete the following statements with a single letter.
   (i) $X^2 =$ (ii) $XR_1 =$ (iii) $R_1X =$

   (c) Is the statement $XR_1 = R_1X$ true or false?

8. L is the triangle with vertices $(3,1)$, $(4,4)$ and $(1,4)$.

   (a) Find $I(L)$, $XI(L)$, $YI(L)$, $IX(L)$ and $IY(L)$.

   (b) Simplify XI, YI, IX and IY.

9. P is the rectangle with vertices $(-2,-2)$, $(-5,-2)$, $(-5,-4)$ and $(-2,-4)$.

   (a) Find $I(P)$, $ZI(P)$, $WI(P)$ and $W^2(P)$.

   (b) Simplify ZI, WI and W^2.

10. Q is the rhombus with vertices $(-3,-3)$, $(-4,-1)$, $(-3,1)$ and $(-2,-1)$.

    (a) Find $R_1(Q)$, $R_2R_1(Q)$ and $R_1R_2R_1(Q)$.

    (b) Simplify R_2R_1 and $R_1R_2R_1$.

    (c) Is it true that $R_1R_3 = R_3R_1 = R_2{}^2$?

    (d) In which quadrant does the image of Q lie when R_2 is applied 13 times?

Self-Assessment 35

In this exercise
R_1 is a rotation of 90° anticlockwise about O
R_2 is a rotation of 180° about O
R_3 is a rotation of 90° clockwise about O
X is a reflection in the *x*-axis
Y is a reflection in the *y*-axis

T is a translation defined by the vector $\left(\begin{smallmatrix} -2 \\ 2 \end{smallmatrix}\right)$
Z is a reflection in the line $y = x$
W is a reflection in the line $y = -x$
I is the identity transformation

1.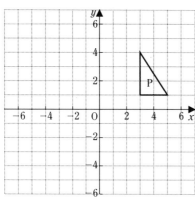

Copy the diagram and use your copy to draw and label the following images

(a) X(P)   (c) R_1(P)   (e) T(P)
(b) Y(P)   (d) R_2(P)

2.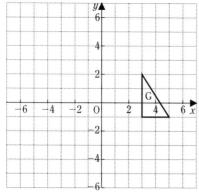

Copy the diagram and use your copy to draw and label

(a) YX(Q)   (c) R_2(Q)
(b) XY(Q)   (d) R_1R_2(Q)
(e) Is YX(Q) the same triangle as XY(Q)?
(f) Is R_2(Q) the same triangle as YX(Q)?
(g) Is R_1R_2(Q) the same triangle as R_3(Q)?

3.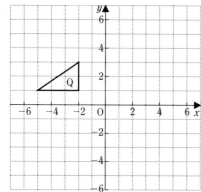

Copy the diagram and use your copy to answer part (a).

U is a reflection in the line $x = 1$
V is a reflection in the line $y = -2$
S is a rotation of 180° about the point $(1, -2)$

(a) Draw U(G), V(G), VU(G) and UV(G).
(b) Are VU and UV the same transformation?
(c) Is it true that UV = S?

4. Copy the diagram and use it to answer parts (a) and (b).

   (a) Find Z(M), Z^2(M), XZ(M), YZ(M), WZ(M), and IZ(M).

   (b) Complete the following statements with a single letter.

       (i) Z^2 =   (ii) XZ =   (iii) YZ =   (iv) WZ =   (v) IZ =

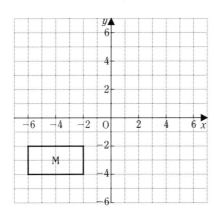

AVERAGES

It is sometimes necessary to describe how a set of data is distributed. For example, the distribution of the weights of two thousand people could be described by a value representative of most of these weights, i.e. an average value, together with an indication of how far the weights are spread about this value.

The Shape of a Distribution

It is possible to get an impression of the distribution of a set of data by looking at a bar chart.

Consider these two bar charts; they show the scores obtained in a general knowledge quiz by two different groups of 250 people.

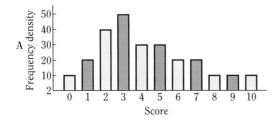
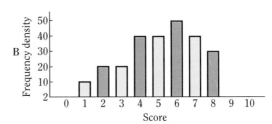

From the charts it is apparent that the bulk of the scores of group A is lower than the bulk of scores of group B. It is also clear that the spread of scores for group B is less than that for group A. We will look at this aspect of distributions later in this chapter.

Both 'average' and 'bulk' are vague ways of referring to the centre of a distribution. There are three more precise ways of giving a central value for a set of numbers and we will define each in turn.

Mode

The mode is the number that occurs most often.

For example, for the set   1, 3, 3, 5, 6, 7, 8, 8, 8   the mode is 8.

For the scores for group A, the modal score is 3 and for group B, the modal score is 6.

Sometimes there are two or more numbers that occur equally often; in this case there are two or more modes. When the numbers are all different, there is no mode.

Median

 When numbers are arranged in order of size, the median is the number in the middle.

There are nine numbers in the set   1, 3, 3, 5, 6, 7, 8, 8, 8,   so the middle number, or median, is the 5th number, i.e. the $\dfrac{9+1}{2}$ th   number. Hence the median of this set is 6.

If there is an even number of numbers in the set, then the median is the value halfway between the two middle values.

Find the median of these sums of money: £2.50, £1.85, £3.54, £2.60

First the items must be arranged in ascending size order.

$$£1.85, \ £2.50, \ £2.60, \ £3.54$$

There are four items here, so the middle ones are £2.50 and £2.60

The median sum of money is halfway between £2.50 and £2.60, i.e. £2.55

In general, if there are n numbers in a set, the median is the value of the $\dfrac{(n+1)}{2}$ th number. when the numbers are arranged in size order.

The Mean

 The mean, or arithmetic average, of a set of n numbers is the sum of the numbers divided by n.

For example, the mean of the set   1, 3, 3, 5, 6, 7, 8, 8, 8   is

$$\frac{1+3+3+5+6+7+8+8+8}{9} \ = \ \frac{49}{9} \ = \ 5\frac{4}{9}$$

To give an interpretation of the mean, suppose that the numbers in this set are the scores obtained from 9 balls on a pinball machine. If it were possible to even out the scores, i.e. to get an equal score from each ball to give the same total, then this equal score would be the mean; we would say that the average score is $5\frac{4}{9}$. The mean value does not have to be one of the given values or even, as in this case, a possible value.

The mean is the most frequently used central measure, so much so that the mean value is often called 'the average'.
However, each of the mean, mode and median has advantages in different situations.

Consider, as one example, a shoe retailer who records the size of each pair of shoes sold. The modal size (i.e. the most common size) would be of most interest in this case because it would be sensible to stock most of that size.

On the other hand suppose that the following sums of money are the daily earnings of a group of people in a small company: £5, £52, £58, £59 £60

The mean sum is £46.80 which is lower than all but one of these sums. This is because one very low sum has affected the mean and in this case the mean sum of money does not give a fair impression of the daily earnings. It would be better to use the median sum of £58 as representative of these daily earnings.

In general, if the median is greater than the mean then more than half the numbers are greater than the mean. Conversely, if the median is less than the mean then more than half of the numbers are less than the mean. In the context of a set of test marks with mean 6.3 and median 5, we can say that more than half the students got a mark below the mean.

Exercise 36a

1. Find the mean, median and mode of each of the following sets of numbers. Give answers correct to three significant figures where necessary.

    (a) 3, 6, 2, 5, 9, 2, 4

    (b) 1.6, 2.4, 3.9, 1.7, 1.6, 0.2, 1.3, 2

    (c) 4, 3, 4, 5, 2, 5, 4, 3

    (d) 0.8, 0.7, 0.6, 0.7, 0.8, 0.8, 0.9, 0.5

2. A small firm employs nine people. The annual salaries of the employees are £60 000, £25 000, £20 000, £12 000, £10 000, £10 000, £10 000, £9 000, £8 000.
   Find the mean, modal and median salaries. Which of these three figures would you be most interested in if you were involved in negotiating salary increases and were
   (a) the boss   (b) a union official.
   Give brief reasons for your answer.

3. Five students got mean marks of 52, 45.5, 63, 73.6 and 85.7 respectively for ten tests. Find the total marks obtained by each student.

4. The mean daily takings in a shop from Monday to Friday were £580, while the mean daily takings from Monday to Saturday were £680.50.

    (a) How much was taken over the five days Monday to Friday?

    (b) How much was taken over the six days Monday to Saturday?

    (c) How much was taken on Saturday?

In a game of darts, three throws make one turn. On 15 turns, John had a mean score of 25. How much does he need to score on his next turn to raise his mean score to 26?

The total made for the first 15 turns is
$$15 \times 25 = 375$$

To get a mean score of 26 on 16 turns, John needs to make a total score of
$$16 \times 26 = 416$$

Therefore John needs to score $416 - 375$, i.e. 41   on his 16th turn.

5. In a boat race the average weight of the eight oarsmen was 75.3 kg and the average weight of the crew was 73.2 kg. How heavy was the cox?

6. The average weight of the fifteen players in a rugby team was 81.9 kg, while the average weight of the team plus a reserve was 82.7 kg. How heavy was the reserve?

7. In five visits to a dart board, a dart player's average score was 65. After a further visit his average fell to 61. What did he score on his sixth visit?

This bar chart shows the scores obtained by a group of people (Group A, p. 562) in a quiz. Find the mean score.

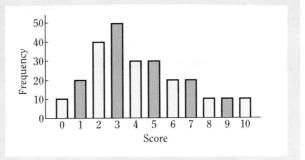

To find the mean score, we first have to find the total value of all the scores, i.e. to find $10 \times 0 + 20 \times 1 + 40 \times 2 + \ldots$ and so on. It is easier to keep track of these calculations if we first make a frequency table from the histogram, and add an extra column to accommodate 'frequency $\times$ score'. Using f for frequency and x for the score gives

x	f	fx
0	10	0
1	20	20
2	40	80
3	50	150
4	30	120
5	30	150
6	20	120
7	20	140
8	10	80
9	10	90
10	10	100
Total	250	1050

From the table, we see that 250 people got a total score of 1050.

Therefore the mean score is $\dfrac{1050}{250} = 4.2$

8. Use these bar charts to find the mean value of the distribution.

(a)

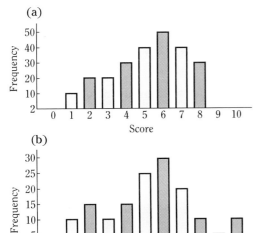

(b)

9. An ordinary dice was thrown 50 times. The table gives the number of times each score was obtained.

Score	1	2	3	4	5	6
Frequency	7	8	10	8	5	12

Find the mean score per throw.

10. Three coins were tossed together 30 times and the number of heads per throw was recorded.

Number of heads	0	1	2	3
Frequency	3	12	10	5

Find the mean number of heads per throw.

It is also possible to find the median from a frequency distribution. This is illustrated in the next worked example.

Use the bar chart from the worked example on page 565 to find the median score.

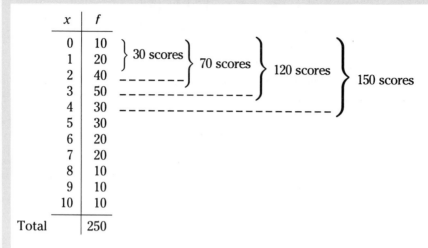

x	f
0	10
1	20
2	40
3	50
4	30
5	30
6	20
7	20
8	10
9	10
10	10
Total	250

There are 250 scores so the median score is halfway between the 125th and 126th score when they are arranged in order of size.

By adding the frequencies, as shown above, we see that the 125th and 126th score are both in the 5th row of the table.

The median score is 4.

11. This table gives the distribution of marks obtained in a test. Find the median mark.

Mark	0	1	2	3	4	5
Frequency	1	5	9	12	15	8

12. Find the median of the distribution given in question 9.

FINDING AVERAGES FROM GROUPED FREQUENCY TABLES

This frequency table shows the results of asking some men to count the number of items in their pockets.

Number of items	0–4	5–9	10–14	15–19	20–24
Frequency	6	11	6	4	3

Mode and Median

Because the number of items have been placed in groups, some detail is lost. We do not know how many men had 3 items in their pockets so, although it is possible that more men had 3 items than any other number, we cannot give the mode as a single figure. It is clear, however, that more men had 5 to 9 items in their pockets than any other group; this is called the *modal group*.

It is also possible to find the group in which the median of the distribution lies, by counting up frequencies as before. The distribution shows, in order of size, the number of items in the pockets of 30 men, so the median is the average number of items in the pockets of the 15th and 16th men. These are both in the second group, so the best that we can say at this stage is that the median number of items is in the 5–9 items group.

Mean

As we have seen, we do not know the exact number of items that each man had so it is not possible to find the total number of items exactly. However if we *assume* that the mean number of items per group is the halfway value of the group, we can find an approximate total.

Consider, for example, the first group; assuming that the mean number of items is 2, there is an approximate total of 12 items in that group.

Doing the same calculation for the other groups and arranging the results in a table gives

No. of items	f	x (halfway values)	fx
0–4	6	2	12
5–9	11	7	77
10–14	6	12	72
15–19	4	17	68
20–24	3	22	66
Total 30			Total 295

Therefore the mean number of items is approximately $\frac{295}{30} = 9.8$ to 1 d.p.

For continuous data, the calculation is performed in the same way. This table gives the heights of tomato plants four weeks after seeds were planted.

Height, h cm	f	Halfway value, x	fx
$0 \leqslant h < 3$	2	1.5	3
$3 \leqslant h < 6$	5	4.5	22.5
$6 \leqslant h < 9$	10	7.5	75
$9 \leqslant h < 12$	3	10.5	31.5
Total 20			Total 132

Therefore the mean height is approximately $\frac{132}{20}$ cm $= 6.6$ cm

Exercise 36b

Estimate the mean value of each distribution.

1. Fifty boxes of oranges were examined and the number of damaged oranges in each box was recorded with the following result.

No. of damaged oranges	0–4	5–9	10–14	15–19
Frequency	34	11	4	1

2. Twenty beans were planted in a seed tray. The table shows the distribution of the heights of the resulting plants three weeks later.

Height, h cm	$1 \leqslant h < 4$	$4 \leqslant h < 7$	$7 \leqslant h < 10$	$10 \leqslant h < 13$
Frequency	2	5	10	3

3. The table shows the distribution of the heights of 50 adult females.

Height, h cm	$149.5 \leqslant h < 154.5$	$154.5 \leqslant h < 159.5$	$159.5 \leqslant h < 164.5$	$164.5 \leqslant h < 169.5$
Frequency	4	21	18	7

4. The bar chart shows the result of an examination of 20 boxes of screws. Start by making a frequency table.

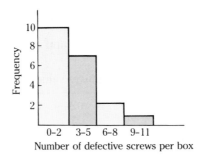

5. This table shows the number of customers entering a supermarket each minute during one day.

No. of customers per minute	0–2	3–5	6–8	9–11	12–14	15–17
Frequency	100	200	150	90	40	20

CUMULATIVE FREQUENCY

In exercise 36a the median of a frequency distribution was found by adding the frequencies to find the value of the middle item. Adding the frequencies in this way gives *cumulative frequencies* which are best set out in a table. Using again the frequency distribution of scores for group A (p. 562) gives this table.

Score x	f	Score	Cumulative frequency
0	10	0	10
1	20	$\leqslant 1$	30
2	40	$\leqslant 2$	70
3	50	$\leqslant 3$	120
4	30	$\leqslant 4$	150
5	30	$\leqslant 5$	180
6	20	$\leqslant 6$	200
7	20	$\leqslant 7$	220
8	10	$\leqslant 8$	230
9	10	$\leqslant 9$	240
10	10	$\leqslant 10$	250

From this table, as well as being able to find the median, we can also find the number of people who got less than, say, a score of 5. The table shows that 150 people got 4 or less, i.e. less than 5.

We can also give the number of people who got a score greater than, say, 6. From the table, 200 people got a score of 6 or less; there were 250 scores altogether, so $250 - 200$, i.e. 50 people, got a score greater than 6.

We can also make a cumulative frequency table for a grouped frequency distribution which, for the number of items in mens' pockets, looks like this.

No. of items	f	No. of items	Cumulative frequency
0–4	6	$\leqslant 4$	6
5–9	11	$\leqslant 9$	17
10–14	6	$\leqslant 14$	23
15–19	4	$\leqslant 19$	27
20–24	3	$\leqslant 24$	30

For the distribution of heights of tomato plants on page 567, the table looks like this.

Height, h cm	f	h	Cum f
$0 \leqslant h < 3$	2	< 3	2
$3 \leqslant h < 6$	5	< 6	7
$6 \leqslant h < 9$	10	< 9	17
$9 \leqslant h < 12$	3	< 12	20

Exercise 36c

1. Make a cumulative frequency table for the distribution of damaged oranges per box given in Exercise 36b, question 1. Use it to find the number of boxes that contained

   (a) at least 10 damaged oranges

   (b) fewer than 15 damaged oranges.

2. Use the information given in Exercise 36b, question 2 to make a cumulative frequency table. Three weeks after planting, how many bean plants were

   (a) at least 7 cm high

   (b) between 4 and 10 cm high?

3. Make a cumulative frequency table for the heights of females as described in Exercise 36b, question 3. How many of the women are less than 159.5 cm tall? Hence find the probability that one of these women chosen at random is less than 159.5 cm tall.

CUMULATIVE FREQUENCY CURVES

Using a grouped frequency distribution and plotting the cumulative frequency against the *upper value* of each group gives a graph. If the points are joined by straight lines, the graph is called *a cumulative frequency polygon.* If a smooth curve is drawn through the points, the graph is called a *cumulative frequency curve.*

The two grouped distributions discussed in the last section give these cumulative frequency curves.

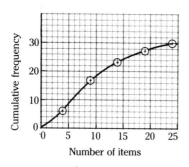

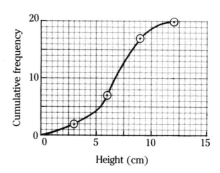

Note that we start the curve at the lower end of the first group. The curve always starts at zero on the cumulative frequency axis.

Finding the Median of a Grouped Frequency Distribution

When we discussed the median number of items in pockets, we said that we could not give a precise value. A good approximation to the median however can easily be read off the cumulative frequency curve. At the middle value of the cumulative frequency, a line is drawn across, to meet the curve, and then down to give the corresponding number of items.

The middle value of the cumulative frequency is the 15.5th value.

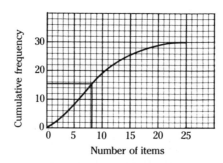

From the graph, the median is approximately 8.

Exercise 36d

1. Use the cumulative frequency tables made in Exercise 36c to draw a cumulative frequency curve for each distribution. Hence give, approximately, the median of each of these distributions.

2. This cumulative frequency curve illustrates the journey times to college of some students.

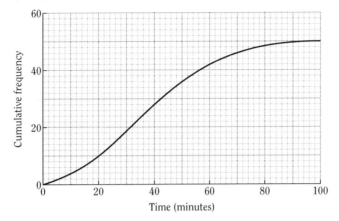

Use the curve to find

(a) the number of students who took part in the survey

(b) the median journey time

(c) the number of students who took less than 10 minutes to get to college

(d) the number of students who had journey times greater than 30 minutes

(e) the number of students who took between 40 minutes and one hour to get to college

(f) the probability that a student chosen at random had a journey time of between 20 and 30 minutes.

(g) the percentage of students who took more than 60 minutes to get to college.

3. Using the curve given for question 2, copy and complete this frequency table.

Journey time, t minutes	Number of students, f	Halfway value of t, x	fx
$0 \leqslant t < 10$			
$10 \leqslant t < 20$			
$20 \leqslant t < 40$			
$40 \leqslant t < 60$			
$60 \leqslant t < 80$			
$80 \leqslant t < 100$			

Use the table to

(a) calculate an approximate value for the mean journey time

(b) draw a histogram to illustrate the data.

4. Use your results from questions 2 and 3 to compare the median journey time and the mean journey time.
A student chosen at random from this group is found to have a journey time greater than the mean journey time. Is the probability that this should happen greater or less than 0.5 ?

DISPERSION

An aspect of a set of data that often has to be assessed is the spread of the items in the set. Dispersion is the name for the spread of a distribution and there are several ways of measuring it.

Range

The range of a distribution is defined as the difference between the extreme values. Consider the two distributions of scores at the start of this chapter; for group A, the lowest score is 0 and the highest score is 10, so the range is $10 - 0$, i.e. 10 and for group B, the range is $8 - 1$, i.e. 7.

For a grouped frequency distribution, we do not know the precise extreme values, so in this case we give the range as the difference between the highest and lowest possible values. For the distribution of heights of tomato plants, these extreme values are 0 cm and 12 cm, so the range is 12 cm.

The range is a crude measure of dispersion since it tells us nothing about the intermediate values and it can be distorted by one or two extreme values. Consider a student who scores 8, 52, 56, 60, 68, 70, 75, 77, 80 in nine examinations. The range of marks is from 8 to 80, whereas every mark apart from 8 is over 50.

Inter-Quartile Range

A much better measure of spread is given by using the range of the middle half of the values.

The middle half lies between the value that is one-quarter of the way through a distribution and the value that is three-quarters of the way through. These two values are called the *quartiles.*

If there are *n* values, in ascending order,

then the *lower quartile, Q_1*, is the $\dfrac{(n+1)}{4}$ th value,

and the *upper quartile, Q_3*, is the $\dfrac{3(n+1)}{4}$ th value.

The difference between the upper quartile and the lower quartile is called the *inter-quartile range,* i.e.

the inter-quartile range is $Q_3 - Q_1$

The inter-quartile range can be found easily from a cumulative frequency curve.

The cumulative frequency curve for the heights of tomato plants is shown on the opposite page.

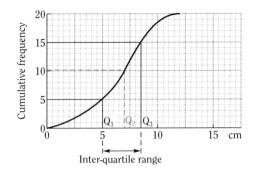

From the graph, the inter-quartile range is $(8.4 - 5)$ cm, i.e. 3.4 cm

Exercise 36e

1. Use the cumulative frequency curves drawn for question 1 in Exercise 36d to find the inter-quartile range of each distribution.

2. The cumulative frequency curve given below shows the weekly earnings, in pounds, of a group of teenagers.

   Use the graph to find

   (a.) the median

   (b) the upper and lower quartiles.

   Hence find the inter-quartile range.

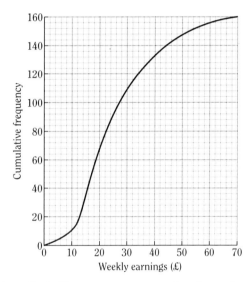

3. Two brands, X and Y, of AA batteries were investigated by a consumer magazine. A sample of 50 of each brand was tested. Each battery was run in a personal cassette player until it failed. The results were

   Brand X: mean life = 20 hours, inter-quartile range = 4 hours
   Brand Y: mean life = 19.5 hours, inter-quartile range = 2 hours

   Which brand of battery was more reliable ?

4. A sample of 50 of another brand of AA batteries was also investigated. The shortest life was 12 hours and the longest life was 24 hours. The lower and upper quartiles were 19 hours and 21.5 hours respectively.

   (a) On graph paper draw a cumulative frequency curve that could represent this information.

   (b) Use your curve to estimate the median life.

   (c) Estimate the probability that one of these batteries will last for less than 15 hours.

STANDARD DEVIATION

Standard deviation is the most useful measure of dispersion. It has the advantage that it uses all the values and it is also the most usually quoted measure of dispersion.

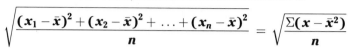

If we have n values, $x_1, x_2, \ldots, x_n,$ and if $\bar{x}$ is the mean value, then the standard deviation is

$$\sqrt{\frac{(x_1 - \bar{x})^2 + (x_2 - \bar{x})^2 + \ldots + (x_n - \bar{x})^2}{n}} = \sqrt{\frac{\Sigma(x - \bar{x}^2)}{n}}$$

This formula can be simplified to

$$\sqrt{\frac{x_1^2 + x_2^2 + \ldots + x_n^2 - \bar{x}^2}{n}} = \sqrt{\frac{\Sigma x^2}{n} - \bar{x}^2}$$

The symbol Σ means 'sum of all such terms'.

The standard deviation is given in the same unit as the original data.

The calculation of standard deviation (s.d.) is best illustrated by an example. Consider these six scores 2, 5, 6, 7, 7, 9.
We need the mean score and then the square of each score.

It is easier to keep track of the calculations if they are set out in a table,

i.e.

x	2	5	6	7	7	9	Total 36
x^2	4	25	36	49	49	81	244

$$\text{Mean, } \bar{x} = \frac{36}{6} = 6 \qquad \text{s.d.} = \sqrt{\frac{244}{6} - (6)^2} = 2.16\ldots$$

For data given in a frequency table, each value of x^2 has to be multiplied by the frequency of x so the formula becomes $\sqrt{\dfrac{\Sigma f x^2}{\Sigma f} - \bar{x}^2}$. For grouped data, the halfway value of the group is used for x (in the same way as it is when calculating the mean value) to give an approximate value for the standard deviation. The calculation for each form of frequency distribution is illustrated in worked examples in the following exercise.

For large quantities of data, the calculation of standard deviation is tedious; there are many computer programs (often included in a spreadsheet) that will calculate both the mean and standard deviation. *Most scientific calculators are also capable of calculating standard deviation. If you have one, it is well worth the effort to learn how to use it (consult the manual).*

Exercise 36f

1. Find the standard deviation of each of the following sets of data.

   (a) 2, 4, 5, 5, 6 and 8 people.

   (b) marks of 24, 46, 57, 68 and 80.

   (c) 2 kg, 5 kg, 6.6 kg, 7 kg.

   (d) 10 h, 12.2 h, 8 h, 6 h, 7.5 h

This bar chart illustrates the scores obtained in a quiz by a group of people. Find the mean score and the standard deviation of the scores.

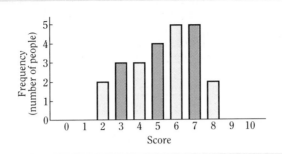

We start by making a frequency table and finding the mean. Then we can extend the frequency table.

x (score)	f	fx	x^2	fx^2
2	2	4	4	8
3	3	9	9	27
4	3	12	16	48
5	4	20	25	100
6	5	30	36	180
7	5	35	49	245
8	2	16	64	128
Totals	24	126		736

Mean, $\bar{x} = \frac{126}{24} = 5.25$ Standard deviation $= \sqrt{\frac{736}{24} - 5.25^2} = 1.76$

Note that if the mean value is given, the third column of the table is not needed.

2. Find the standard deviation of each of the following frequency distributions. The mean value is given in each case.

(a)

x	f
2	2
3	3
4	4
5	3

$\bar{x} = 3.67$

(c)

x	f
0.15	10
0.17	12
0.20	15
0.25	11
0.26	6

$\bar{x} = 0.2$

(b)

x	f
0	1
1	4
2	3

$\bar{x} = 1.25$

(d)

x	f
1.29	51
1.54	68
3.27	45

$\bar{x} = 1.94$

Find the standard deviation of the distribution of the heights of tomato plants given on page 567, using the mean value $\bar{x} = 6.6$ cm.

(halfway value) $\bar{x} = 6.6$

Height, h cm	f	x	x^2	fx^2
$0 \leqslant h < 3$	2	1.5	2.25	4.5
$3 \leqslant h < 6$	5	4.5	20.25	101.25
$6 \leqslant h < 9$	10	7.5	56.25	562.5
$9 \leqslant h < 12$	3	10.5	110.25	330.75
Totals	20			999

Standard deviation $= \sqrt{\frac{999}{20} - 6.6^2} = 2.53$ to 3 s.f.

3. Use the information given and found for questions 1 and 2 in Exercise 36b to find the standard deviation of each distribution. Use the statistical functions on your calculator.

Using Standard Deviation

Standard deviation can be thought of as a measure of average dispersion about the mean. Hence the smaller the value of the standard deviation, the closer most of the data is to the mean, i.e. a small standard deviation means that the values do not vary much whereas a large standard deviation indicates that individual values are more variable.

For example, these frequency polygons show the results of testing a sample of Brand A and Brand B light bulbs to find out how long they last.

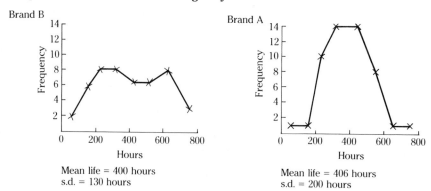

Mean life = 400 hours
s.d. = 130 hours

Mean life = 406 hours
s.d. = 200 hours

Each of these distributions is roughly symmetrical, i.e. the mean is approximately in the middle of the distribution. The mean and range of both samples are very nearly the same, but the standard deviation of the Brand B sample is much smaller than that of Brand A. This means that more Brand B bulbs have a life closer to the mean than Brand A bulbs, and that fewer Brand B bulbs are likely to fail after a short time, than Brand A bulbs, i.e. Brand B bulbs are more reliable. This can be confirmed from the frequency polygons: one Brand B bulb failed before 150 hours whereas five Brand A bulbs failed by the same time.

The range of a distribution can be expressed as a number of standard deviations. This gives a way of measuring the complete spread in terms of the average spread.

Consider, for example, this bar chart, which illustrates the results of a test taken by a group of students.

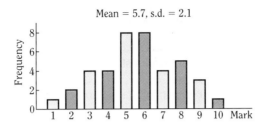

Mean = 5.7, s.d. = 2.1

The range of the marks is $10 - 1$, i.e. 9, and $\dfrac{\text{range}}{\text{s.d.}} = \dfrac{9}{2.1} = 4.3$

Hence the range is 4.3 standard deviations.

The Effect of Changing All Values by the Same Amount

Sometimes all the values in a distribution are increased (or decreased) by the same amount.

Suppose that all the students who took the test above had their marks increased by 2 (because one question was added and they all did it correctly).

The effect of this on a frequency polygon is to shift it by 2 units to the right,

i.e.

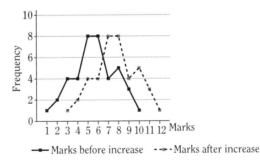

—■— Marks before increase   - -■- - Marks after increase

The shapes of the two distributions are the same so there has been no change in the variability of the marks, i.e. the standard deviation is not altered.

This means that when *all* the values in a distribution are increased (or decreased) by the *same* amount,

the standard deviation is unchanged.

However the shift has clearly changed the mean value. As each mark has increased by 2, the mean mark has also increased by 2.

This can be proved from the formula for the mean:
if $\bar{x}$ is the mean of the original marks and $\bar{y}$ is the mean of the increased set of marks then,

$$\bar{x} = \frac{\Sigma fx}{\Sigma f} \qquad \text{and} \qquad \bar{y} = \frac{\Sigma fy}{\Sigma f} = \frac{\Sigma f(x+2)}{\Sigma f} = \frac{\Sigma fx}{\Sigma f} + \frac{\Sigma 2f}{\Sigma f} = \bar{x} + 2$$

Comparing Distributions

As we saw at the start of this chapter, we can compare two distributions by looking at their shape. This method is fine for showing up obvious differences, but we can now use means and standard deviations to make more detailed comparisons.

Suppose, for example, that the crop of apples from one tree has
a mean mass of 90 grams and a standard deviation of 10 grams,
whereas the crop from another tree has
a mean mass of 110 grams and a standard deviation of 20 grams.

Although the apples from the first tree are, on average, lighter than those from the second, their masses are more consistent. (This could make them more valuable for commercial sale where variability in size is not usually wanted.)

Exercise 36g

1.

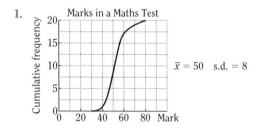

$\bar{x} = 50$ s.d. $= 8$

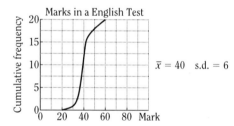

$\bar{x} = 40$ s.d. $= 6$

The curve in the first diagram illustrates the results from a test in mathematics and the curve in the second diagram illustrates the results from a test in English. Both tests were taken by the same group of students. Use the given information to determine whether there are any substantial differences in the two sets of results.

2. A mathematics examination was marked out of 60 and an English examination was marked out of 95. The mean mark for mathematics was 28 and for English it was 51.
Explain how these mean marks can be written in a form which allows them to be compared.

3. The mean and standard deviation masses of potatoes grown under normal conditions are 100 g and 18 g respectively.
The mean and standard deviation masses of potatoes grown under a variety of experimental conditions were

A: 150 g, 40 g   C: 120 g, 18 g

B: 80 g, 10 g   D: 100 g, 34 g

(a) Compare each distribution with the potatoes grown under normal conditions.

(b) State, with reasons, whether you consider any of the experimental conditions offer an improvement, as far as the masses of the potatoes grown is concerned.

4. These are the masses of ten letters as weighed by an automatic franking machine.

26 g, 30 g, 42 g, 70 g, 36 g,

29 g, 84 g, 56 g, 71 g, 48 g

(a) Find the mean and the standard deviation of these masses.

(b) After the letters had been weighed, it was discovered that the machine was set incorrectly; each mass should be 10 g greater than the mass recorded.
Write down the mean and the standard deviation of the correct masses.

COMPARING THEORETICAL AND PRACTICAL DISTRIBUTIONS

Sometimes we need to look for similarities in two distributions. Consider this situation: four coins are tossed 64 times. Each toss will give either no heads, 1 head, 2 heads, 3 heads or 4 heads. We can work out how many times each of these possibilities should theoretically occur, using a probability tree.

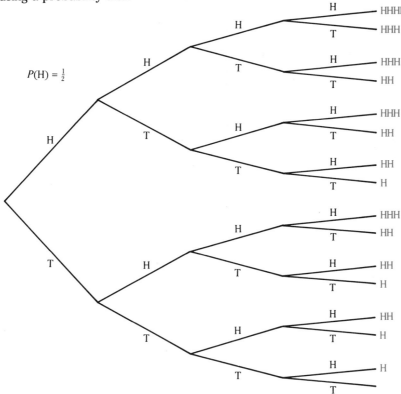

$P(H) = \frac{1}{2}$

From the probability tree, we see that

$$P(0 \text{ heads}) = \tfrac{1}{16}, \quad P(1 \text{ head}) = \tfrac{4}{16}, \quad P(2 \text{ heads}) = \tfrac{6}{16},$$
$$P(3 \text{ heads}) = \tfrac{4}{16}, \quad P(4 \text{ heads}) = \tfrac{1}{16}$$

So if the coins are tossed 64 times, *in theory* we will get this frequency table.

Number of heads	0	1	2	3	4
Frequency	4	16	24	16	4

Tossing 4 *real* coins 64 times gave this frequency table.

Number of heads	0	1	2	3	4
Frequency	5	16	28	14	1

Comparing the frequencies from the real coins with the theoretical frequencies we can see that the numbers are a little different, and n the case of 4 heads, very different. If we draw the bar charts of both of these distributions we get a clearer picture of how they compare.

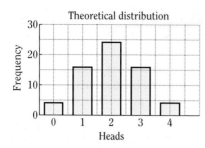

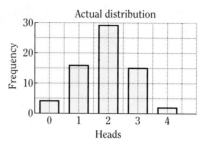

We can see that the overall shape of the two bar charts is similar. If we also find the mean and standard deviation of each distribution, we find

that for the theoretical case, $\bar{x} = 2$ and   s.d. $= 1$
and for the experimental case, $\bar{x} = 1.8$ and   s.d. $= 0.91$

These agree fairly closely so it is reasonable to say that the real coins are probably unbiased and so was the tossing.

Note that actually tossing four real coins is unlikely to give the theoretical frequencies. However, if the coins are tossed properly and they are not bent or otherwise biased, we are likely to get a fairly close match. It *is* possible to get 4 heads 64 times under these conditions, but that is very unlikely to happen and if it did, we would be inclined to doubt that the tossing had been done properly with unbiased coins.

Note the use of the words 'probably', 'likely' and 'unlikely' in the sentences above; no particular outcome in circumstances of this kind is either certain or impossible.

Exercise 36h

1. The frequency table shows the number of telephone calls received per minute by a theatre box-office over a two-hour period.
Copy and complete the table.

| | | (halfway value) | | | | | |
calls/min	f	x	fx	x^2	fx^2	cumulative f
0–4	1					
5–9	2					
10–14	15					
15–19	42					
20–24	45					
25–29	16					
30–34	3					
35–39	0					

Totals

Mean $\bar{x} =$ Standard deviation $=$

Construct a cumulative frequency curve and use it to estimate the percentage of the distribution that lies within

(a) 1 standard deviation of the mean

(b) 3 standard deviations of the mean.

(c) From the cumulative frequency curve, what can you conclude about the shape of the actual distribution?

2. The first table shows the scores that are obtained in theory when a dice is tossed 60 times. The second table shows the scores obtained when an actual dice is tossed 60 times.

Score	1	2	3	4	5	6
Frequency	10	10	10	10	10	10

Score	1	2	3	4	5	6
Frequency	8	10	12	11	8	11

Draw bar charts to illustrate each set of data. Find the mean score and the standard deviation of the theoretical distribution of scores and of the actual distribution. Use these, together with the shapes of the two charts, to compare the two distributions, giving reasons for any conclusions that you draw.

Investigation

You need access to a computer database and a statistical package for this investigation.

Many questions vary; any list of values of a variable, such as times, prices, etc., can be investigated statistically and the shape of the distribution examined. Large quantities of data are stored in computer databases and the functions built into the database and/or spreadsheets can be used to sort and group information, draw charts and cumulative frequency curves, and to find means and standard deviations.

Find some data from a database and investigate it, comparing it if possible with other similar data. A few examples of data that may be available are: weights of machine-packed goods, examination results, birthdates, sales figures, times taken to cover a fixed distance in athletics, stock exchange prices.

Self-Assessment 36

1. Find the mode, the median and the mean of this set of numbers.

$$2, 4, 4, 5, 6.5, 6.8, 7, 7, 7, 8, 9.5$$

2. The table shows the number of employees working overtime each day for a period of one month.

Number of employees	0	1	2	3	4	5	6
Frequency	3	4	8	9	4	2	1

(a) Find the mean number of employees working overtime each day.
(b) Calculate the standard deviation.
(c) Draw a cumulative frequency curve and use it to find the median and the inter-quartile range.

3. This frequency table shows the distribution of lengths of screws made by a machine.

Length, l mm	$4.5 \leqslant l < 5.0$	$5.0 \leqslant l < 5.5$	$5.5 \leqslant l < 6.0$	$6.0 \leqslant l < 6.5$	$6.5 \leqslant l < 7.0$
Frequency	5	20	14	3	2

(a) Find the mean length.   (b) Find the standard deviation.
(c) How many standard deviations span the range of this distribution ?

VARIATION

DIRECT VARIATION

Throughout this book we have used several different ways of expressing the relationships between quantities, and the ways in which they vary one with another.

The form of variation most frequently encountered is that when two quantities are in direct proportion, i.e. when one quantity doubles or trebles so does the other. The relationship between two quantities, x and y say, that are directly proportional can be expressed in various ways; these are now summarised and extended.

Either   (a) x is to y as   3 is to 2

   or   (b) $x : y = 3 : 2$

   or   (c) $\dfrac{x}{y} = \dfrac{3}{2}$ or $\dfrac{x}{3} = \dfrac{y}{2}$ or $\dfrac{y}{x} = \dfrac{2}{3}$ or $y = \dfrac{2}{3}x$

The third version (c), in any of its forms, is the one to use in calculations.

Ratio is used when dealing, for example, with similar triangles. Corresponding sides of similar triangles are in the same ratio, and the areas of similar triangles are in the same ratio as the squares of corresponding sides.

Graphs

A graph shows the connection between variables; for example, the ratio $\dfrac{y}{x} = \dfrac{2}{3}$ can be written $y = \frac{2}{3}x$ and a graph can be drawn to represent this.

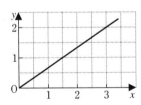

Quantities that are in direct proportion, such as two different currencies, are sometimes represented by such a graph. In such a case the graph is often called a conversion graph.

Values of x have to be multiplied by $\frac{2}{3}$ to give corresponding values of y, so $\frac{2}{3}$ is sometimes called the conversion factor.

Scales

Maps or scale drawings use scales, which can be given either as a ratio, e.g. $1 : 10\,000$, or in the form $1\,\text{cm} = 100\,\text{m}$.

The Symbol for Direct Proportion

The symbol $\propto$ means 'is directly proportional to', so the phrase 'volume is proportional to mass' can be written 'volume $\propto$ mass' or '$V \propto m$'.

As an abbreviation, the symbol $\propto$ is neat but it is not useful in calculations. Instead we write $V = km$ where k is the constant of proportion. Alternatively k can be thought of as a conversion factor.

Exercise 37a

Use any appropriate concise method to answer the following questions.

1. If $\dfrac{x}{y} = \dfrac{4}{5}$, find

   (a) x when $y = 9$
   (b) y when $x = 6$

2. If $x : y = 7 : 5$, find
   (a) x when $y = 3$
   (b) y when $x = 2$

3. Write the statement $a : b = 3 : 4$ in as many different forms as possible.

4. A man lays 250 bricks in 3 hours in laying a driveway. If he continues to work at the same rate, how long does he take to lay the next 175 bricks ?

5. If the exchange rate is 12 kroner to the £ and 320 drachma to the £, how many drachma are equivalent to 17 kroner ?

6. If $y : x = 3 : 4$, give an equation for y in terms of x and sketch a graph to show this.

7. (a) Draw a currency conversion graph to show the connection between pounds and lire when the exchange rate is 2200 lire to the pound. (Consider amounts up to £ 20.)
   (b) Use the graph to find how many lire can be exchanged for £ 8.60

8. $\triangle$s $\begin{smallmatrix} \text{PQR} \\ \text{ABC} \end{smallmatrix}$ are similar. AB $= 8$ cm, AC $= 10$ cm, PQ $= 10$ cm and RQ $= 6$ cm. Find BC and PR.

9. A scale is marked on a map in the form $1 : 50\,000$
   (a) Give the scale in the form 1 cm represents . . . km.
   (b) What is the length on the map of a road 6 km long ?

10. A line AB is divided at C into two parts in the ratio $2 : 3$,
    Give the vector $\overrightarrow{\text{AC}}$ in terms of
    (a) $\overrightarrow{\text{AB}}$ (b) $\overrightarrow{\text{CB}}$.

11. Write the statement '$y \propto x$'
    (a) in a more useful algebraic form
    (b) in words.

The following questions do not involve quantities that are in direct proportion but they do involve ratios.

12. Two quadrilaterals are similar and corresponding sides measure 4 m and 5 m. The area of the smaller one is 20 m^2. What is the area of the other ?

13. Two similar statuettes are of heights 12 cm and 20 cm. The volume of the larger one is 775 cm^3. What is the volume of the smaller statuette ?

RELATIONSHIPS AND GRAPHS

Information about the relationships between variables can be given in the form of a table. This enables us to draw a graph and possibly find an equation connecting the two variables.

The table below gives information about corresponding values of x and y.

x	1	3	6	7	10
y	2	6	12	14	20

The relationship is easy to spot; we can see that $y = 2x$.
We used a table of related values when a sequence was given. Corresponding values of n and of the nth term, u_n, were tabulated in order to find a formula for u_n in terms of n.

For the sequence 2, 5, 10, 17, 26, ... the table is

n	1	2	3	4	5
u_n	2	5	10	17	26

Comparing n^2 with u_n, we see that $u_n = n^2 + 1$

Sometimes we know the *form* of the equation connecting the two quantities.
For instance, if we know that y is directly proportional to x then we know that $y = \text{constant} \times x$. If we also know that $y = 12$ when $x = 3$, then we can find the equation.

We write $y = kx$

When $x = 3$, $y = 12$ so $12 = k \times 3$

$\therefore k = 4$ and the equation is $y = 4x$

In the graphs given below, one quantity is directly proportional to the other. The line always passes through the origin if the quantities are directly proportional.

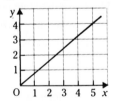 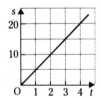

Dependent and Independent Variables

Usually one of the quantities varies because of a change in the other.

If T pence is the cost of several kilograms of potatoes and C pence is the cost of 1 kilogram, then T goes up because C goes up, i.e. T *depends* on C.
T is the *dependent* variable while C is the *independent* variable.

When graphs are drawn, the independent variable is usually marked on the horizontal axis and the dependent variable on the vertical axis. We saw this in the kinematics chapter when drawing velocity–time graphs; time is the independent variable and velocity the dependent variable; time is plotted on the horizontal axis.

Exercise 37b

In each question from 1 to 4, write down the equation connecting the variables. The relationship should be easy to spot but plot the points on a graph if you cannot see them from the information given.

1.

x	2	5	7	8
y	1	2.5	3.5	4

2.

x	3	5	6	10
y	9	25	36	100

3.

t	2	4	5	8	10
s	6	4	3	0	−2

4.

t	1	3	4	7	8
v	0	4	6	12	14

5. A triangle varies in size in such a way that its height, h cm, is always equal to its base. Its area is A cm^2.
   Give the equation connecting A and h and complete the table.

h	2	3	4	6	10
A	2	4.5			50

6. The first three terms of a sequence are 5, 7 and 9 and the tenth term is 23. Form a table from the information about n and the nth term and find the formula for the nth term in terms of n.

7. Copy and complete the table so that y is directly proportional to x.

x	2	6		9
y	6		21	27

   Give the equation connecting x and y.

8. Copy and complete the table so that $A \propto b$

b	1	2.4	7	10
A			10.5	15

   Give the equation connecting A and b.

9. Complete the table so that $C \propto x$

Number of kg, x	1.2	4	5	7.2
Total cost in £, C	0.3		1.25	

   Give the equation connecting C and x. What meaning can you give to the constant of proportion ?

Two variables, x and y, are such that $y \propto x$ and $y = 22$ when $x = 4$. Find x when $y = 12$

First find the equation connecting x and y

$y \propto x$ i.e. $y = kx$

When $x = 4$, $y = 22$

$\therefore$ $22 = k \times 4 \Rightarrow k = \frac{11}{2}$

$\therefore$ $y = \frac{11}{2}x$

When $y = 12$, $12 = \frac{11}{2}x$

i.e. $24 = 11x \Rightarrow x = \frac{24}{11}$

10. If y is directly proportional to x and $y = 200$ when $x = 25$, find
    (a) the equation connecting x and y
    (b) y when $x = 6$
    (c) x when $y = 8$

11. C is proportional to p and $C = 16$ when $p = 5$.
    (a) Find the equation connecting C and p.
    (b) Find C when $p = 8$.
    (c) Find p when $C = 8$.

12. Given that $y \propto x$ and $y = 9$ when $x = 2$, find
    (a) y when $x = 6$
    (b) x when $y = 3$

13. Find y when $x = 12$ given that y varies directly with x and that $y = 9$ when $x = 7$

14. Which of the following graphs show direct proportion ? For each graph that does, give the equation relating x and y.

 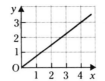 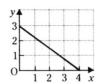

Other Forms of Variation

Not all related quantities are directly proportional. The area of a circle, for example, can be found from the formula $A = \pi r^2$. Thus, although it is correct to say that $A \propto r^2$, A is *not* directly proportional to r. We say that A varies with the square of r.

Notice that the words 'varies with' mean the same as 'is directly proportional to'. Hence 'y varies with the cube of x' can be written '$y \propto x^3$'.

INVERSE PROPORTION

Another form of variation is called inverse proportion. Consider the time taken by a car to cover a fixed distance at various speeds. It is clear that as the speed goes up the time taken goes down. The speed is not directly proportional to the time taken; instead $\text{speed} \propto \dfrac{1}{\text{time}}$

In all cases of inverse proportion, one quantity decreases as the other increases.

 If the product of the two quantities is constant then one is *inversely* proportional to the other.

For example, if a bowl of trifle is to be shared equally among p people so that each gets v grams then, as p increases, v decreases.
The product vp is constant (vp grams is the mass of trifle in the bowl).

We say that v varies inversely with p (and vice versa)

i.e. $v \propto \dfrac{1}{p}$

This is more usefully written as $v = k \times \dfrac{1}{p}$, i.e. $v = \dfrac{k}{p}$

The graph of $v = \dfrac{k}{p}$ is not a straight line. It is a hyperbola.

Neither p nor v can be zero.

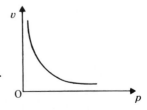

On the other hand be aware that when $y = 4 - x$, y decreases as x increases but in this case x and y are not inversely proportional because xy is not constant.

The portions of graphs below show various cases where y decreases as x increases but where x and y are *not* inversely proportional.

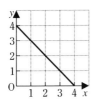

$$y = 4 - x$$

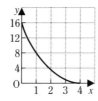

$$y = (x - 4)^2$$

$$y = 16 - x^2$$

Exercise 37c

If y varies as the square root of x and $y = 4$ when $x = 25$, find y when $x = 81$

$y \propto \sqrt{x}$, so $y = k\sqrt{x}$

When $x = 25$, $y = 4$, so $4 = k \times 5$

$$k = \tfrac{4}{5}$$

$\therefore$ $\qquad\qquad y = \tfrac{4}{5}\sqrt{x}$

When $x = 81$, $y = \tfrac{4}{5} \times 9 = 7.2$

1. If z is proportional to the cube of t and $z = 24$ when $t = 2$,

   (a) find the equation connecting z and t

   (b) find z when $t = 10$

2. If $A \propto w^2$ and when $w = 3$, $A = 144$,

   (a) find A when $w = 1$

   (b) find w when $A = 100$

3. If v varies as the square root of t and $v = 4$ when $t = 4$, find

   (a) v when $t = 16$ (b) t when $v = 6$

4. The area of a quadrilateral PQRS, which changes size but not shape, is proportional to the square of the length of the side PQ. When $PQ = 5\,cm$, the area is $16\,cm^2$. Find the area when $PQ = 8\,cm$.

5. In which of the following tables is y inversely proportional to x? In each case sketch a graph.

   (a)

x	2	3	9	11
y	3.6	5.4	16.2	19.8

   (b)

x	1	4	5	7
y	17	14	13	11

   (c)

x	3	4	6	10
y	16	12	8	4.8

6. For each part of question 5, write down the equation connecting x and y.

If y is inversely proportional to x and $x = 6$ when $y = 7$, find an equation connecting x and y.

$$y \propto \frac{1}{x} \qquad \therefore y = \frac{k}{x}$$

When $y = 7$, $x = 6$,

so $7 = \dfrac{k}{6}$

hence $k = 7 \times 6 = 42$

The equation is $y = \dfrac{42}{x}$

It could also be written as

$xy = 42$ or $x = \dfrac{42}{y}$

---

7. If y is inversely proportional to x and $y = 6$ when $x = 4$

(a) find an equation connecting x and y and give two other forms of the equation

(b) find x when $y = 2$

8. If y varies inversely with x and $y = 5$ when $x = 60$

(a) find y when $x = 12$

(b) find x when $y = 15$

9. If $y \propto \dfrac{1}{x}$ and $y = 16$ when $x = 9$,

(a) find x when $y = 36$

(b) state what happens to y if x is doubled

(c) give two forms of the equation connecting x and y.

10. For a certain fixed sum of money, M pence, I can buy s stamps costing c pence each.

(a) Give an equation connecting s, c and M.

(b) If $s = 24$ when $c = 25$, find M.

(c) How many stamps can I buy at 20 p each ?

(d) Sketch a graph to show the connection between s and c.

11. The wavelength, λ m, of a radio wave varies inversely with its frequency, f kHz. When the frequency is 400 kHz, the wavelength is 750 m.

(a) Find the frequency when the wavelength is 500 m.

(b) Find the wavelength when the frequency is 360 kHz.

(c) Sketch a graph to show the connection between f and λ.

12. In an electrical circuit, the resistance, R ohms, is inversely proportional to the square of the current, I amps. When the resistance is 4 ohms, the current flowing is 6 amps.

(a) Find the resistance when the current is 7 amps.

(b) Find the current when the resistance is 3 ohms.

13. If y varies inversely with x^2 and $y = 12$ when $x = 3$, find y when $x = 1.2$

14. If $y \propto \dfrac{1}{x^3}$ and $y = 3$ when $x = 4$, find y when $x = 2$

15. A plank rests in a horizontal position on two supports one at each end. A mass, m kg, placed on the centre of the plank causes the centre to sink down d cm. If m varies with d^2 and if $d = 0.8$ when $m = 12$, find

(a) m when $d = 0.6$ (b) d when $m = 10$

16. Find the equation linking the two quantities for each of the graphs shown below. State in each case whether the graph shows direct variation, inverse variation or neither.

(a)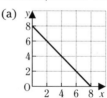

(b)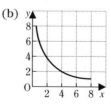

(c)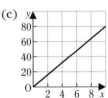

(d)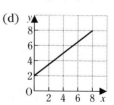

THE INVERSE SQUARE LAW

We have seen that some everyday quantities are directly proportional to each other and others are inversely proportional. There are, however, other relationships between quantities. For example, the gravitational pull of the earth on an object depends upon the distance of that object from the earth's centre in the following way:

> if the distance, d metres, is doubled
> the gravitational pull, g newtons, is divided by 4 (i.e. 2^2)
> if the distance is trebled, the pull of gravity is divided by 9 (i.e. 3^2).

These two cases illustrate the general relationship between g and d which is

$$g = \frac{k}{d^2}, \text{ where } k \text{ is a constant}$$

We say that g is inversely proportional to the square of d.

This kind of relationship is known as the *inverse square law*.

Exercise 37d

The distance between a subject being photographed and the intensity of light from the flash falling on it are related by the inverse square law, such that the intensity of light is inversely proportional to the square of the distance. If the flash is moved from 2 m to 2.5 m from the subject, what happens to the light falling on the subject?

The distance has increased by a factor $\frac{2.5}{2}$, i.e. 1.25

Therefore the light falling on the subject is divided by $(1.25)^2 = 1.56$ (3 s.f.)

1. Two quantities, x and y, obey the inverse square law such that x is inversely proportional to the square of y. When x is 10, y is 4. If y is increased to 8, what happens to x and what is its new value?

2.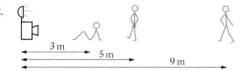

The diagram shows Carla being photographed in three different positions. The light from the flash that falls on Carla and her distance from the flash obey the inverse square law as described in the worked example.

What fraction of the light that falls on Carla when she is nearest the camera, falls on her when she is (a) furthest from the camera (b) in the middle position?

3. The gravitational pull of the earth on an object is inversely proportional to the square of the distance of the object from the centre of the earth. The orbit of a satellite is changed from 6000 miles above the centre of the earth to 5000 miles above. What happens to the gravitational pull on the satellite?

4. The signal strength received from a radio transmitter is inversely proportional to the square of the distance from the transmitter. Stella is 6 kilometres from the transmitter and Scott is 8 kilometres from it. How many times stronger is the signal strength where Stella lives than where Scott lives?

5. The capacity of a cylindrical tank is fixed. Show that the height is inversely proportional to the square of the radius.

   (a) If the height is increased what happens to the radius?

   (b) If the radius is reduced what happens to the height?

EXPERIMENTAL DATA

In science many experiments are conducted in which one quantity is measured for various values of another quantity. If these values are plotted on a graph, the points often lie on what appears to be a smooth curve or even a straight line.

If the points lie more or less on a straight line we can find the equation of that line and hence find the likely connection between the two quantities.

Suppose that a marble is rolled down a groove and its velocity is v m/s after t seconds. Corresponding values of v and t are measured and recorded in the table.

t	1	3	4.4	5	6.8	9.6
v	2	5.9	11	7	15	20

From the table we can draw a graph.

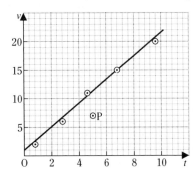

The point marked P is probably the result of an error in measurement. If we ignore it we can draw by eye a line of best fit through the other points.

The equation of the line will be of the form $v = mt + c$ where m is the gradient and c the intercept on the v-axis. From the graph, $c = 1$ and $m = 2$

The equation is therefore $v = 2t + 1$ and this is the likely relationship between v and t.

The values of m and c have significance: $v = 1$ when $t = 0$, i.e. the initial velocity is 1 m/s, and v changes by 2 m/s every second so the acceleration is 2 m/s^2.

Exercise 37e

1. A water container is being emptied by a tap in the bottom. The amount taken out, v cm^3, is measured after t s, and the information recorded in the table.

t	2	5	8	9	11	14
v	40	91	145	169	205	254

   (a) Plot the points, using scales of 1 cm to 1 s and 4 cm to 100 cm^3. Draw the line of best fit.

   (b) Find the gradient of the line and hence find the equation connecting v and t.

   (c) Use first the graph and then the equation to find the volume after 10 s. Do your answers agree ?

2. Ink was dropped on to absorbent paper and the radius of the resulting circular stain measured at various times. The area, A cm^2, was calculated for each time, t s, and the information is given in the table.

t	1	2	4	7	8	9	10
A	0.5	0.8	1.75	1.9	3.6	3.9	4.45

   (a) Plot the points, using scales of 1 cm to 1 s and 2 cm to 1 cm^3. Has there been any obvious error in measuring or calculating ? Draw the line of best fit.

   (b) What was the area of the stain after 6 s ?

   (c) Find the equation connecting A and t.

3. A spring is stretched using a force of F newtons and the length, L cm, is recorded.

F	3	4	7	10	13	15
L	30	32.5	37	42.5	48	51.5

(a) Plot the points, using scales of 1 cm to 1 newton and 4 cm to 10 cm, starting the L scale at 20. Draw the line of best fit.

(b) Find the gradient of the line and hence give its equation.

(c) What force is needed to make the length 41 cm?

(d) How long is the spring when unstretched?

4. M is the magnification produced by a convex lens when the the distance of the lens from the image is v m.
Corresponding values of M and v are given in the table.

v	30	37	40	50	58	65
M	1.2	1.7	1.8	2.6	3.1	3.7

(a) Draw a graph (start the M scale at -2) and find the equation relating M to v.

(b) The focal length of the lens is given by the reciprocal of the gradient of this graph. What is the focal length of this lens?

5. Which of the experiments in questions 1 to 4 have shown that one of the quantities is directly proportional to the other?

Using Functions as Models

For a science experiment, Flora measured the mass, y milligrams, of vitamin C in fresh orange juice, at various times, x hours after squeezing the oranges. Her results are shown in the table.

Time, x hours	0	8	24	48	72	96
Mass, y milligrams	120	119	114	95	65	30

The mass is related to the time by the equation $y = ax^2 + b$ and Flora has to use her results to obtain estimates for the values of a and b.

These values could be plotted on a graph, which we know from the equation should look like part of a parabola (if it doesn't, the results may be faulty). The coordinates of two points on the graph can then be used to calculate estimates for a and b. There are two disadvantages however; drawing a curve freehand through a set of points is not easy and, because the range of values for x and for y is large, a fairly coarse scale has to be used. Both of these factors mean that values read from such a graph are likely to be very inaccurate.

Greater accuracy can be obtained when the points to be plotted fall (more or less) on a straight line.

Now if, in $\quad y = ax^2 + b,\quad$ we replace x^2 by X, the relationship becomes

$\qquad y = aX + b,\quad$ which is represented by a straight line.

Therefore, if values of y are plotted against values of X,

i.e. $\qquad$ if values of y are plotted against values of x^2,

we should get a straight line.

We add another line to the table, and then plot the points.

Time, x hours	0	8	24	48	72	96
Mass, y grams	120	119	114	95	65	30
x^2 (X)	0	64	576	2304	5184	9216

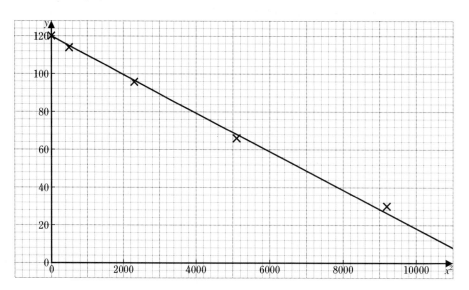

Now we can use the fact that, for the line $y = mx + c$,

m gives the gradient and c is the intercept on the y-axis.

Comparing $y = mx + c$

with $y = aX + b$

we see that b is the intercept on the vertical axis, therefore $b = 120$
and a is the gradient, i.e. $a = -0.01$.

At this level, the relationship between the two variable quantities is usually given, but sometimes we have to guess what the relationship might be. To do this we have to rely on our knowledge of the shapes of curves that represent different relationships.

Exercise 37f

1. Ball-bearings of various diameters were weighed and the following results obtained.

Diameter in mm, d	2	3	4	5	6
Masses in grams, m	0.26	0.89	2.11	4.13	7.13

(a) By plotting m against d^3 verify that the relation between these quantities is of the form $m = ad^3$ and find the value of a.

(b) Use your formula to find the mass of a ball-bearing with a diameter of (i) 3.5 mm (ii) 5.7 mm.

(c) What is the diameter of a ball-bearing whose mass is (i) 3 g (ii) 6.5 g?

(d) Can you suggest a meaning for a? Justify your answer.

2. Two variables P *and* Q are known to be connected by a law of the form $Q = aP^3 + b$, where a and b are constants.

   In an experiment the following values of P and Q were obtained:

P	5.5	6.8	8	11.3	12	13.6	14
Q	650	870	1170	2560	2990	4170	4520

   Draw a graph of P^3 against Q, taking $6\,\text{cm} \equiv 1000$ units on both axes and use your graph to find the values of a and b.

   Find (a) Q when $P = 10$ (b) P when $Q = 3500$.

   (Give your answers correct to two significant figures.)

3. The number of bacteria in a culture were counted at hourly intervals and the results recorded in a table.

Time in hours, t	0	1	2	3	4	5	6
Number of bacteria, N	3	6	12	24	48	96	192

   (a) Plot this data on 2 mm graph paper using scales of 2 cm for 1 unit on the t-axis and 4 cm for 50 units on the N-axis. Draw a smooth curve to pass through the points.

   (b) It is thought that the relation between t and N is either   (i) $N = a + bt^2$ (ii) $N = a + bt^3$ or (iii) $N = ab^t$. Draw the graphs of N against t^2 and N against t^3.

   From the information you have so far, decide which of the three relations is the most likely. Give reasons for dismissing the other two.

   (c) Substitute the values $t = 0$ when $N = 3$ and $t = 1$ when $N = 6$ into the relation between t and N you think most likely. Hence find the values of a and b.

   What is the relation between t and N?

   Check that the other values in the table satisfy this relation.

   (d) How many bacteria would you expect to find in the culture after

   (i) 7 hours   (ii) 12 hours   (iii) $5\frac{1}{2}$ hours?

   (You will need to use the x^y button on your calculator. Give any value that is not a whole number correct to the nearest whole number.)

4. At a road testing centre a prototype car was driven round bends of different radii and varying speeds to determine the maximum speed at which it could round each bend safely. The results are given in the table.

Radius of bend, R metres	45	53	72	84	100
Maximum safe speed, S m.p.h.	34	36	42	46	50

   (a) Plot this information on a graph to determine which is the more likely relationship between S and R: $S = kR^2$ or $S = k\sqrt{R}$ or $S = kR$.

   (b) Draw a suitable straight line graph to verify your choice and use it to determine the value of k.

   (c) Use your formula to find the maximum safe speed that this car can round a bend of radius

   (i) 60 m   (ii) 150 m.

5. Two variables x and y are found by experiment to have the following values:

x	1.2	2.5	3.6	4.2	6.7
y	7.2	31.3	64.8	88.2	224.5

Choose your own scales for parts (a) and (b)

(a) Plot values of y against the corresponding values of x.
   Does your graph suggest that the connection between x and y is of the form $y = ax$?
   If it does, justify your answer and give the value of a.

(b) Plot values of y against the corresponding values of x^2.
   Does your graph suggest that the connection between x and y is of the form $y = ax^2$?
   If it does, justify your answer and give the value of a.

(c) When the experiment was repeated George recorded the following results

x	1.4	2.6	3.3	4.8	5.2
y	9.8	33.8	54.5	105.2	135.2

Do all but one of these values confirm the relation between x and y you found above?
Which pair of values suggest that an error has been made? What would you expect the value of y to be for the given value of x?

(d) Use your formula to find
   (i) y when $x = 2.8$ (ii) x when $y = 100$.

Self-Assessment 37

1. In which of the following equations is y directly proportional to x?

   (a) $\dfrac{y}{x} = \dfrac{1}{2}$ (c) $y = \dfrac{2}{x}$

   (b) $y = 3x$ (d) $y = 4x^2$

2. If y is proportional to x and $y = 20$ when $x = 6$,

   (a) find the equation connecting x and y
   (b) find y when $x = 7$
   (c) find x when $y = 2.4$

3. If y is inversely proportional to x and $y = 6$ when $x = 5$,

   (a) find the equation connecting x and y
   (b) find y when $x = 1.8$
   (c) find x when $y = 2.4$

4. The following table contains experimental data on two quantities z and r. Draw a graph and find the equation connecting z and r.

r	2	4.2	6	8	10.2	12
z	6	14	20	25	32	39

What would you expect the value of z to be if r is 7.2?

5. State which of the following graphs show direct proportion, which show inverse proportion and which neither. Where possible, give the equation connecting the variables.

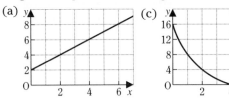

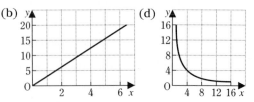

6. Which of the following tables shows that y is inversely proportional to x?

(a)

x	3	6	9
y	12	6	4

(b)

x	3	6	9
y	12	9	6

7. The time for one swing of a pendulum of length L m is T seconds and T varies as the square root of L. When the length is 1.44 m the time for one swing is 2.4 seconds.

   (a) If the time of one swing is 1.8 seconds, how long is the pendulum?

   (b) If the length is 0.5 m what is the time for one swing?

8. In an experiment Sara found the maximum load, W tonnes, that could be suspended on a steel rope of diameter d cm, before the rope snapped. Her results are given below.

Diameter of rope, d cm	1.3	1.7	2.8	3.3	3.8
Maximum weight the rope will support, W tonnes.	0.68	1.16	3.14	4.36	5.78

   (a) It is assumed that the relation between these variables is of the form $W = a + kd^2$.

   By drawing a graph of values of W against values of d^2 determine whether or not the assumption is correct. If it is write down the values of a and k.

   (b) Use your formula to find

   (i) the maximum weight that can be supported by a steel rope of diameter 3 cm before it snaps.

   (ii) the diameter of a rope that is about to snap when a load of 5 tonnes is suspended from it.

ANSWERS

Where answers are given correct to a number of significant figures, you may find a difference between the last figure of your answer and that given here. This situation can arise when a calculated value is used in its corrected form to calculate a further value. Wherever possible uncorrected values should be used for further calculation.

When answers come from measurements from drawn diagrams, it is not possible to give exact answers, nor is it sensible to expect complete agreement with answers given here.

Some diagrams are included in these answers. They are small and not fully labelled and are only intended to provide a check on shape. Your diagrams should be fully labelled and very much larger.

CHAPTER 1

Exercise 1a page 3

5. (a) 54
   (b) 1200
   (c) 99
   (d) 2100
   (e) 8000
   (f) 132
   (g) 7
   (h) 63
   (i) 50
   (j) 108
   (k) 8
   (l) 25
   (m) 80
   (n) 62
   (p) 40
   (q) 55
   (r) 1440
   (s) 51
   (t) 7
   (u) 45

6. (a) 85
   (b) 246
   (c) 96
   (d) 722
   (e) 650
   (f) 105
   (g) 24
   (h) 260
   (i) 60
   (j) 21
   (k) 128
   (l) 12
   (m) 69
   (n) 29
   (p) 12
   (q) 126
   (r) 442
   (s) 138
   (t) 27
   (u) 21

7. (a) 3
   (b) 1
   (c) 1
   (d) 1
   (e) 3
   (f) 6
   (g) 1
   (h) 1
   (i) 4
   (j) 1
   (k) 4
   (l) 4
   (m) 5
   (n) 11
   (p) 8
   (q) 3

8. (a) 8
   (b) 14
   (c) 6
   (d) 3
   (e) 4
   (f) 8
   (g) 14
   (h) 41
   (i) 29
   (j) 13
   (k) 22
   (l) 5

9. (a) 45
   (b) 910
   (c) 22
   (d) 35
   (e) 8
   (f) 16
   (g) 6000
   (h) 2500

10. (a) 2, 4
    (b) 11, 4
    (c) 5, 7
11. (a) 6, 3
    (b) 11, 1
    (c) 11
12. 102
13. 18p
14. 122
15. 27
16. The end result is 99 or 0.

Exercise 1b page 5

1. 13 284
2. 18 078
3. 53 710
4. 6840
5. 23 352
6. 112 194
7. 144 432
8. 240 165
9. 31, r 10
10. 31, r 17
11. 11, r 24
12. 18, r 4
13. 32, r 9
14. 389, r 9
15. 31, r 117
16. 15, r 235

Exercise 1c page 7

1. (a) 1, 2, 3, 6
   (b) 1, 2, 4, 8
   (c) 1, 3, 7, 21
   (d) 1, 2, 3, 5, 6, 10, 15, 30
   (e) 1, 2, 4, 8, 16
   (f) 1, 2, 4, 5, 10, 20
   (g) 1, 11
   (h) 1, 5, 25
   (i) 1, 2, 3, 6, 9, 18
   (j) 1, 2, 3, 4, 6, 9, 12, 18, 36
   (k) 1, 3, 9, 27
   (l) 1, 3, 5, 9, 15, 45

2. 2, 3, 5, 7, 11, 13, 17, 19, 23, 29, 31, 37, 41, 43, 47, 53, 59, 61, 67, 71, 73, 79, 83, 89, 97

3. (a) 2, 4, 6, 8
   (b) 4, 8, 12, 16
   (c) 5, 10, 15, 20
   (d) 3, 6, 9, 12
   (e) 12, 24, 36, 48
   (f) 8, 16, 24, 32

4. (a) 1
   (b) 2
   (c) 4
   (d) 9
   (e) 3
   (f) 13
   (g) 3
   (h) 6
   (i) 6
   (j) 2
   (k) 13
   (l) 6

5. (a) 6
   (b) 12
   (c) 15
   (d) 36
   (e) 30
   (f) 20
   (g) 60
   (h) 72
   (i) 90
   (j) 72
   (k) 36
   (l) 48

6. (a) 27
   (b) 32
   (c) 125
   (d) 1
   (e) 64
   (f) 16
   (g) 9
   (h) 81
   (i) 11
   (j) 81
   (k) 64
   (l) 196
   (m) 153
   (n) 192
   (p) 729
   (q) 4

7. (a) $2^3 \times 17$
   (b) $2^4 \times 3^2 \times 5$
   (c) $2^3 \times 3^3$
   (d) $2 \times 3^2 \times 5^2$
   (e) $2^2 \times 3 \times 7$
   (f) $2^4 \times 3 \times 11$
   (g) $2 \times 3 \times 11^2$
   (h) 2×157
   (i) $2^4 \times 7^2$
   (j) $3^4 \times 5$

8. (a) 3, 5, 11, 17
   (b) 3, 6, 15, 21, 27
   (c) 1, 3, 4, 5, 6, 10, 15

9. 24 m
10. 60 s
11. 50 cm
12. £100
13. 45 cm
14. 110 cm

Exercise 1d page 11

1. (a) <
   (b) >
   (c) <
   (d) >
   (e) >
   (f) >
   (g) >
   (h) >
   (i) >
   (j) <
   (k) <
   (l) >

2. (a) -7 (e) 3 (i) 0 (m) 8
(b) -1 (f) 1 (j) -5 (n) -14
(c) 1 (g) -3 (k) -3 (p) -4
(d) -9 (h) -13 (l) 3 (q) -9
3. (a) -6 (d) -1 (g) 2 (j) 10
(b) 4 (e) -9 (h) 15 (k) -6
(c) 7 (f) 5 (i) -3 (l) 1

Exercise 1e   page 12

1. (a) 10 (d) 1 (g) -4 (j) 12
(b) -8 (e) 7 (h) -6 (k) 16
(c) 2 (f) 23 (i) -8 (l) -288
2. (a) -26 (c) 1 (e) -8
(b) 1 (d) 17 (f) -22
3. 5 and -5
4. -7
5. One number is -3 times the preceding number.
6. (a) One number is -2 times the preceding number.
(b) $-1, 2, \ldots, 128, -256$
7. (b) $5 - (-2) = 7$ (e) $-1 + (-2) = -3$
(c) $2 + 3 = 5$ (f) $5 - (-4) = 9$
(d) $2 - (-2) = 4$
8. e.g. $8 - (-2) = 5 \times 2$

Exercise 1f   page 14

1. (a) $5, 6$ (c) $15, 21$
(b) $5, 7$ (d) $13, 17$
2. (a) natural numbers   (c) triangular numbers
(b) odd integers   (d) prime numbers
3. (a) $1, 0, -1, -2$ (b) $13, 17, 19, 23$
4. (a) $1, 3, 5, 7, 9$ (e) $1, 4, 9, 16, 25$
(b) $1, -2, 4, -8, 16$ (f) $3, 6, 9, 12, 15$
(c) $96, -48, 24, -12, 6$ (g) $1, 2, 2, 4, 8$
(d) $1, 3, 4, 7, 6$ (h) $2, 3, 5, 10, 20$

Self-Assessment 1   page 15

1. (a) 27 (b) 22
2. (a) 6 (b) 36
3. (a) 17 (b) 72
4. 13
5. $162, -486$
6. (a) 36 (b) 37 (c) 235
and other possible answers
(d) 62
7. $38\,430$
8. 37
9. (a) 3600 (b) 40 (c) 12
10. $14, 10$ **12.** $-3, 9, -12, 21, -33$
11. 51 **13.** $3\,\text{cm}$

CHAPTER 2

Exercise 2a   page 19

1. (a) $\frac{4}{8}$ (b) $\frac{2}{8}$ (c) $\frac{6}{8}$
2. (a) $\frac{6}{12}$ (b) $\frac{8}{12}$ (c) $\frac{9}{12}$ (d) $\frac{10}{12}$
3. $\frac{2}{5} = \frac{4}{10} = \frac{6}{15} = \frac{10}{25} = \frac{40}{100}$
4. (a) $\frac{1}{3}$ (d) $\frac{2}{7}$ (g) $\frac{3}{4}$
(b) $\frac{1}{3}$ (e) $\frac{3}{4}$ (h) $\frac{5}{23}$
(c) $\frac{1}{12}$ (f) $\frac{4}{7}$

5. (a) $2\frac{1}{2}$ (d) $7\frac{2}{5}$ (g) $5\frac{3}{8}$
(b) $1\frac{2}{3}$ (e) $5\frac{3}{10}$ (h) $6\frac{3}{11}$
(c) $2\frac{1}{4}$ (f) $6\frac{3}{4}$
6. (a) $\frac{5}{4}$ (d) $\frac{13}{4}$ (g) $\frac{17}{5}$
(b) $\frac{7}{3}$ (e) $\frac{8}{3}$ (h) $\frac{27}{4}$
(c) $\frac{7}{5}$ (f) $\frac{15}{8}$
7. (a) $6\frac{1}{4}$ (d) $4\frac{1}{6}$ (g) $4\frac{1}{5}$
(b) $4\frac{1}{3}$ (e) $4\frac{1}{8}$ (h) $1\frac{8}{9}$
(c) $7\frac{1}{5}$ (f) $4\frac{1}{2}$
8. $\frac{5}{7} = \frac{15}{21}, \frac{2}{3} = \frac{14}{21}, \frac{5}{7}$
9. $\frac{2}{3} = \frac{10}{15}, \frac{4}{5} = \frac{12}{15}; \frac{2}{3}$
10. (a) $\frac{1}{60}$ (b) $\frac{1}{6}$ (c) $\frac{5}{6}$
11. $\frac{1}{5}$ **12.** $\frac{1}{4}$ **13.** $\frac{9}{16}$
14. (a) $\frac{11}{30}, \frac{1}{2}, \frac{3}{5}, \frac{2}{3}$ (b) $\frac{3}{8}, \frac{2}{5}, \frac{7}{10}, \frac{17}{20}$
15. (a) $\frac{5}{6}, \frac{7}{12}, \frac{1}{2}, \frac{1}{3}$ (b) $\frac{3}{4}, \frac{7}{10}, \frac{17}{25}, \frac{3}{5}$
16. (a) $\frac{14}{5}, \frac{17}{6}, 2\frac{7}{8}, 3$ (b) $\frac{12}{7}, \frac{27}{14}, 2\frac{1}{6}, \frac{7}{3}$

Exercise 2b   page 23

1. (a) $\frac{13}{20}$ (c) $\frac{1}{5}$ (e) $\frac{8}{15}$ (g) $\frac{1}{6}$
(b) $\frac{19}{20}$ (d) $\frac{1}{6}$ (f) $\frac{11}{12}$ (h) $\frac{13}{56}$
2. (a) $\frac{5}{6}$ (c) $\frac{5}{6}$ (e) $4\frac{9}{20}$ (g) $3\frac{1}{20}$
(b) $2\frac{5}{6}$ (d) $3\frac{1}{4}$ (f) $1\frac{5}{6}$ (h) $\frac{7}{12}$
3. (a) $\frac{17}{20}$ (c) $\frac{1}{2}$ (e) $\frac{3}{5}$ (g) $\frac{1}{8}$
(b) $\frac{53}{100}$ (d) $\frac{29}{30}$ (f) 0 (h) $6\frac{7}{15}$
4. (a) £6   (e) £32   (i) $27\,\text{cm}$
(b) $20\,\text{min}$ (f) $34\,\text{kg}$ (j) $22\frac{1}{2}\,\text{ft}$
(c) £7   (g) $2\,\text{days}$ (k) $219\,\text{days}$
(d) $3\,\text{cm}$ (h) $40\,\text{s}$ (l) £72
5. (a) $\frac{2}{15}$ (e) $\frac{9}{14}$ (i) $\frac{2}{9}$
(b) $\frac{5}{24}$ (f) $\frac{6}{25}$ (j) $\frac{1}{7}$
(c) $\frac{1}{6}$ (g) $\frac{6}{49}$ (k) $1\frac{3}{4}$
(d) $\frac{4}{7}$ (h) $\frac{1}{15}$ (l) $11\frac{1}{5}$
6. (a) $1\frac{2}{3}$ (e) $4\frac{1}{2}$ (i) $\frac{2}{5}$
(b) $2\frac{1}{2}$ (f) $2\frac{2}{5}$ (j) $\frac{4}{13}$
(c) $1\frac{2}{7}$ (g) $\frac{1}{4}$ (k) $\frac{4}{11}$
(d) $1\frac{1}{3}$ (h) $\frac{1}{6}$ (l) $\frac{2}{3}$
7. (a) $\frac{3}{4}$ (e) $\frac{2}{3}$ (i) $32\frac{1}{7}$
(b) $\frac{1}{12}$ (f) $\frac{9}{30}$ (j) $\frac{5}{6}$
(c) $\frac{2}{5}$ (g) 6 (k) $\frac{4}{27}$
(d) $\frac{2}{3}$ (h) 5 (l) $4\frac{5}{6}$
8. (a) 1 (c) $\frac{3}{2}$
(b) $\frac{8}{15}$ (d) $\frac{27}{50}$
9. (a) $\frac{9}{20}$ (c) 10
(b) $\frac{4}{5}$ (d) $\frac{5}{13}$
10. (a) $1\frac{1}{18}$ (d) $\frac{7}{12}$ (g) $\frac{21}{40}$
(b) $\frac{5}{24}$ (e) $2\frac{9}{14}$ (h) $1\frac{1}{2}$
(c) $1\frac{5}{8}$ (f) $\frac{7}{10}$ (i) $\frac{21}{34}$

11. 6

12. $\frac{3}{4}$

13. £135

14. $2\frac{2}{5}$

15. (a), (b)

16. 23, $\frac{1}{2}$ cm

17. $1\frac{1}{4}$ seconds

18. $7\frac{1}{2}$ minutes

Exercise 2c   page 28

1. (a) $\frac{7}{100}$ (c) 70   (e) $\frac{7}{100}$

(b) $\frac{7}{10}$ (d) 7   (f) $\frac{7}{1000}$

2. (a) $\frac{1}{5}$ (e) $\frac{1}{1000}$ (i) $1\frac{1}{20}$

(b) $\frac{1}{2}$ (f) $\frac{7}{10}$ (j) $\frac{1}{400}$

(c) $\frac{1}{4}$ (g) $1\frac{2}{5}$ (k) $2\frac{3}{50}$

(d) $\frac{2}{25}$ (h) $\frac{1}{8}$ (l) $5\frac{1}{200}$

3. (a) 1.9   (e) 2.8

(b) 1.8   (f) 1.4

(c) 4.5   (g) 11.7

(d) 1.3   (h) 3.2

4. (a) 1.94   (e) 2.77   (i) 8

(b) 0.46   (f) 0.18   (j) 2.47

(c) 1.64   (g) 5.67   (k) 2.331

(d) 1.66   (h) 0.7   (l) 1.437

5. (a) 250   (e) 0.0035

(b) 0.66   (f) 4.4

(c) 2.44   (g) 0.032

(d) 1.2   (h) 2660

6. (a) 90   (e) 0.03

(b) 0.08   (f) 0.12

(c) 36   (g) 240

(d) 140   (h) 0.021

7. (a) 3   (e) 10

(c) 10   (f) 0.2

(c) 20   (g) 40

(d) 0.3   (h) 500

8. (a) 0.12   (e) 0.125

(b) 0.01   (f) 0.25

(c) 0.45   (g) 0.21

(d) 0.0001   (h) 0.008

9. (a) 3.072   (e) 0.126

(b) 0.266   (f) 0.63

(c) 0.135   (g) 0.32

(d) 4.41   (h) 0.2

10. (a) 4   (e) 12

(b) 30   (f) 30

(c) 3   (g) 0.012

(d) 0.07   (h) 2220

11. (a) 0.55   (f) 3.7

(b) 1.08   (g) 900

(c) 110   (h) 19.8

(d) 23.7   (i) 4.69

(e) 0.00032   (j) 1480

12. (a) 0.0002   (f) 3240

(b) 45.01   (g) 2.81

(c) 12   (h) 0.0054

(d) 2.07   (i) 0.064

(e) 1.25   (j) 5.1

13. (a) 0.2   (f) 0.25

(b) 0.125   (g) 0.875

(c) 0.75   (h) 0.24

(d) 0.6   (i) 0.075

(e) 0.15

14. 6.4

15. 0.251 m

16. 3.68

Exercise 2d   page 30

1. (a) $0.1\dot{6}$ (c) $0.\dot{2}$ (e) $0.\dot{1}4285\dot{7}$

(b) $0.\dot{6}$ (d) $0.8\dot{3}$ (f) $0.0\dot{3}$

2. (a) $\frac{5}{9}$ (c) $\frac{2}{11}$ (e) $\frac{44}{111}$

(b) $\frac{3}{11}$ (d) $\frac{11}{37}$ (f) $\frac{41}{303}$

3. (a) $0.0666\ldots = \frac{1}{10} \times 0.666\ldots$ (b) $\frac{2}{30} = \frac{1}{15}$

4. (a) $\frac{1}{450}$ (b) $\frac{7}{110}$ (c) $\frac{1}{180}$ (d) $\frac{11}{222}$

5. (a) $0.2\dot{5} = 0.2 + 0.0\dot{5}$ (b) $\frac{23}{90}$

6. (a) $\frac{11}{90}$ (b) $\frac{11}{30}$ (c) $\frac{8}{55}$ (d) $\frac{1051}{4995}$

Exercise 2e   page 32

1. (a) 2180   (e) 21   (i) 140

(b) 2600   (f) 0   (j) 910

(c) 27   (g) 300   (k) 13

(d) 4000   (h) 400   (l) 400

2. (a) 0.69   (d) 2.253   (g) 40.38

(b) 13.5   (e) 0.058   (h) 77.998

(c) 1.00   (f) 28.8   (i) 0.05077

3. (a) 2200   (e) 21   (i) 140

(b) 2600   (f) 0.48   (j) 910

(c) 27   (g) 300   (k) 13

(d) 3500   (h) 440   (l) 380

4. (a) 0.694   (d) 2.25   (g) 40.4

(b) 13.5   (e) 0.0581   (h) 78.0

(c) 1.00   (f) 28.8   (i) 0.0508

5. (a) 0.667   (d) 0.222   (g) 0.385

(b) 0.143   (e) 0.0909   (h) 0.778

(c) 0.167   (f) 0.267   (i) 0.0652

6. and **7.** It is not possible to give definitive answers but your approximations should, in general, agree with the answers for question 8 as far as the first significant figure.

8. For question 6

(a) 17.5   (d) 0.368   (g) 5.03

(b) 5.46   (e) 0.00212   (h) 2.15

(c) 19.2   (f) 0.00776

For question 7

(a) 5.77   (d) 1.04   (g) 0.0162

(b) 1.37   (e) 0.309   (h) 0.535

(c) 0.0274   (f) 0.0841

9. $1\frac{2}{7}, \frac{15}{11}, 1.49, 1.57, \frac{5}{3}$

10. $\frac{6}{25}, \frac{3}{16}, \frac{2}{13}, 0.105, 0.05$

11. 49.6 m

12. 0.15 m

13. 566

14. 1.72

15. 14

16. £8.19

17. 29 kg (29 000 g)

18. 540 cm

19. 6804 kg

Exercise 2f   page 36

1. (a) 16   (e) $\frac{1}{2}$ (i) $\frac{1}{25}$

(b) $\frac{1}{16}$ (f) 729   (j) $\frac{1}{64}$

(c) 1   (g) 1   (k) $\frac{1}{27}$

(d) $\frac{1}{32}$ (h) $\frac{1}{3}$ (l) 1

2. (a) 1200   (e) 907 040

(b) 0.0314   (f) 0.0007605

(c) 317 000   (g) 0.000 000 000 115

(d) 0.00955   (h) 2 800 000 000 000

3. (a) 4 (c) 1 (e) $\frac{3}{2}$
(b) $\frac{4}{25}$ (d) $\frac{64}{27}$ (f) 1

4. (a) 5 (e) 3 (i) 4
(b) 3 (f) 5 (j) 11
(c) 2 (g) 7 (k) 5
(d) 2 (h) 25 (l) 12

5. (a) 9 (d) 27 (g) 25
(b) 8 (e) 1000 (h) 216
(c) 0.1 (f) 0.5

6. (a) 3 (d) 1000 (g) 2
(b) $\frac{1}{100}$ (e) $\frac{1}{25}$ (h) $\frac{1}{27}$
(c) $\frac{5}{4}$ (f) $\frac{1}{4}$

7. (a) 24.1 (g) 1.48
(b) 1.71 (h) 1.36
(c) 0.0514 (i) 38.7
(d) 2.29 (j) 2.41
(e) 0.135 (k) 0.000 005 69
(f) 1.78 (l) 0.708

8. (a) 2.65×10^4 (e) 2.21×10^{-3}
(b) 8.23×10^{-3} (f) $1.070\,03 \times 10^6$
(c) 2.04×10^5 (g) 6.2×10^0
(d) 5.099×10^{-2} (h) 4.788×10^3

9. (a) 6.36×10^{10} (d) 5×10^2
(b) 1.08×10^0 (e) 1.92×10^3
(c) 3×10^2 (f) 7.47×10^{-1}

10. (a) 8.64×10^{12} (d) 6×10^2
(b) $6.\dot{6} \times 10^{-3}$ (e) 1.44×10^{10}
(c) 3.624×10^7 (f) -3.576×10^7

11. (a) 64 (c) 216
(b) 1 (d) 64

12. (a) 4 (e) 7776 (i) 1
(b) $\frac{1}{6}$ (f) 64 (j) $\frac{9}{4}$
(c) 8 (g) 27 (k) $\frac{1}{27}$
(d) 8 (h) 72 (l) 5

13. (a) 6.738×10^9 km (b) 5.162×10^9 km

Exercise 2g   page 39

1. $2\sqrt{2}$ 17. $5\sqrt{3}+9$
2. $2\sqrt{3}$ 18. $\sqrt{30}-5$
3. $4\sqrt{2}$ 19. $6\sqrt{3}-12$
4. $3\sqrt{3}$ 20. $8\sqrt{2}-12$
5. $5\sqrt{2}$ 21. $\frac{3\sqrt{2}}{2}$
6. $3\sqrt{5}$ 22. $\frac{\sqrt{5}}{5}$
7. $10\sqrt{2}$ 23. $\frac{\sqrt{2}}{4}$
8. $4\sqrt{3}$ 24. $\frac{\sqrt{10}}{5}$
9. $6\sqrt{2}$ 25. $\frac{\sqrt{6}}{2}$
10. $10\sqrt{5}$ 26. $\frac{\sqrt{2}}{2}$
11. $5\sqrt{10}$ 27. $\frac{2\sqrt{6}}{3}$
12. $3\sqrt{2}$ 28. $\frac{\sqrt{15}}{5}$
13. $2\sqrt{2}-2$ 29. $\sqrt{15}$
14. $3\sqrt{5}+5$ 30. $\sqrt{3}$
15. $4-\sqrt{2}$ 31. $\sqrt{2}$
16. $7-\sqrt{14}$ 32. $\frac{5\sqrt{2}}{3}$

33. (a) $3\sqrt{3}$ (c) $3\sqrt{2}+3\sqrt{3}$
(b) $2\sqrt{5}$ (d) $\sqrt{3}$

34. $\frac{2\sqrt{3}-3}{3}$ **37.** $\frac{\sqrt{2}-12}{4}$

35. $\frac{\sqrt{5}+5}{5}$ **38.** $\frac{5\sqrt{14}+7\sqrt{2}}{28}$

36. $2\sqrt{2}-\sqrt{6}$ **39.** $\frac{3+\sqrt{2}}{3}$

40. (a) $\frac{3\sqrt{2}}{2}$ (c) $\frac{5\sqrt{3}}{3}$
(b) $\frac{5\sqrt{3}}{3}$ (d) $\frac{11\sqrt{5}}{10}$

41. (b), (c), (e), (f), (g) and (i)

Self-Assessment 2   page 41

1. (a) $\frac{4}{3}$ (b) $\frac{2}{3}$
2. (a) 6 (b) $1\frac{1}{9}$ (c) $3\frac{1}{2}$
3. $\frac{3}{14}$ **5.** $\frac{5}{9}$, 0.65, $\frac{2}{3}$, 0.7
4. $\frac{6}{35}$, 60   **6.** $2\frac{13}{14}$
7. (a) $10\sqrt{2}$ (b) $\frac{5}{3}\sqrt{3}$
8. 0.25
9. (a) 1.62 (c) 10 (e) 0.09
(b) 0.35 (d) 2.33 (f) 0.05
10. (a) 64 (c) $\frac{1}{16}$ (e) 9
(b) 1 (d) $2\frac{1}{2}$
11. (a) 4.5×10^6 (b) 2.4×10^{-3}
12. (a) 12.7 (b) 0.004 71 (c) 9.98
13. (a) $\frac{121}{999}$ (b) $\frac{3}{110}$ (c) $\frac{43}{90}$

CHAPTER 3

Exercise 3a   page 44
1. (a) 180° (c) 720°
(b) 270° (d) 240°
2. (a) 30° (c) 36°
(b) 180° (d) 153°
3. (a) 30°, acute (b) 270°, reflex
4. (a) (i) acute, 15° (iv) obtuse, 111°
(ii) acute, 60° (v) acute, 26°
(iii) reflex, 230°
5. $a = 48°$, $b = 132°$ **8.** $x = 80°$
6. $c = 36°$ **9.** $y = 148°$
7. $p = 180°$, $q = 145°$ **10.** $z = 147°$

Exercise 3b   page 48
1. (a) b (b) g (c) d (d) h
2. (a) b (b) c (c) c (d) b
3. (a) c and f, b and e (c) e and d, c and f
(b) c and g, b and d (d) c and g, b and h
4. $a = 100°$, $b = 80°$
5. $c = 105°$, $d = 105°$, $e = 105°$, $f = 105°$
6. $g = 110°$, $h = 110°$, $i = 120°$, $j = 60°$
7. $k = 45°$, $l = 135°$
8. $m = 28°$, $n = 118°$
9. $p = 75°$, $q = 105°$
10. $p = 70°$
11. $r = 42°$, $s = 38°$
12. $q = 18°$

Exercise 3c   page 51
1. $a = 60°$, $b = 60°$, $c = 60°$
2. $d = 68°$, $e = 68°$, $f = 112°$
3. $g = 90°$, $h = 90°$, $i = 117°$
4. $j = 75°$, $k = 105°$, $l = 150°$
5. $m = 120°$
6. $n = 60°$
7. $p = 50°$
8. $x = 55°$, $y = 125°$
9. $q = 34°$, $r = 34°$, $s = 112°$
10. $t = 72°$, $u = 43°$, $v = 115°$
11. $w = 64°$, $x = 52°$, $y = 52°$, $z = 76°$
12. $a = 149°$, $b = 31°$
13. $c = 55°$, $d = 35°$, $e = 29°$
14. $f = 67°$, $g = 46°$, $h = 23°$
15. $i = 51°$
16. $j = 122°$, $k = 78°$, $l = 102°$
17. (a) (i) 64°   (ii) 76°   (iii) 28°
    (b) $\triangle$ACE   (c) right-angled $\triangle$ (d) no
18. (a) (i) 68°
    (ii) $B\widehat{C}D = 60°$, $C\widehat{B}D = C\widehat{D}B = 60°$
    (b) equilateral
19. (a) $z = 65°$, $w = 115°$
    (b) $y = 56°$, $z = 72°$
    (c) $x = 56°$, $w = 126°$
    (d) $x = 66°$, $z = 56°$
20. (a) $2x = 84°$, $3x = 126°$, $y = 108°$, $z = 72°$
    (b) $x = 37°$, $2x = 74°$, $3x = 111°$, $z = 42°$
    (c) $y = 114°$, $x = 41°$, $2x = 82°$, $3x = 123°$
    (d) $x = 36°$, $2x = 72°$, $3x = 108°$, $y = 144°$, $z = 36°$
21. 78°, 22°   **22.** 108°
23. 90°, 66°, 24°
24. (a) 30°
    (b) 150°, 15°, 15°
    (c) 75°, 30°, 75°
    (d) Not possible. $A\widehat{E}D = 105°$

Exercise 3d   page 56
1. 5.07 cm
2. DE $= 5.65$ cm, DF $= 3.36$ cm
3. 9.63 cm
4. 70°
5. 4.31 cm
6. $\widehat{A} = 56°$, $\widehat{B} = 40°$, $\widehat{C} = 84°$
7. $\widehat{D} = 45°$, $\widehat{E} = 52°$, $\widehat{F} = 83°$
8. 5.92 cm
9. Two triangles are possible for part (a), one only for part (b) and none for part (c).
   When two sides and an angle are given and the angle is not the included angle, there may be one or two triangles satisfying the given data or it may be impossible to draw any triangle at all.
10. AC $= 7.4$ cm
11. PR $= 7.4$ cm
12. WZ $= 6.4$ cm, YZ $= 6.0$ cm
13. BC $= 5.2$ cm, DC $= 8.1$ cm

Exercise 3e   page 58
3. The line divides $\triangle$LMN into 2 triangles, one of which is the reflection of the other in this line.
4. The shape on one side is not a reflection of the shape on the other side of the line.
5. The perpendicular bisector of AB.
8. 90°   9. 45° each   11. parallel

Self-Assessment 3   page 59
1. 150°
2. (a) $p = 53°$ (b) $q = 72°$
3. (a) c (c) c and f
   (b) d and h (d) f and h
4. (a) $a = 37°$, $b = 74°$, $c = 32°$
   (b) $d = 44°$, $e = 56°$, $f = 80°$, $g = 136°$
5. BC $= 5.5$ cm
6. QR $= 7.8$ cm
7. $\widehat{D} = 41°$, $\widehat{E} = 56°$
8. $x = 57°$, $2x = 114°$, $y = 66°$
9. Measuring $\widehat{C}$ (it should be 75°)

CHAPTER 4

In this chapter, re means reflection, ro means rotation and tr means translation

Exercise 4a   page 61
1. A(1, 3) B(−2, 1) C(6, 2) D(2, −3)
   E(−5, −4) F(0, −2) G(4, 0)
2. (4, 48°), (2, −30°)
3. (5, 100°), (3, −156°)
4.

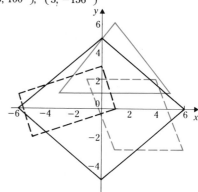

(a) black outline; rhombus
(b) black broken outline; rectangle
(c) green outline; isosceles triangle
(d) green broken outline; parallelogram

Exercise 4b   page 63
1. (a)

(d)

(c)

(f)

2. (a)

(c)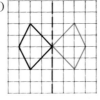

(b)

(d)

3. (a) 2   (b) 2   (d) 4

4. (i) (e)
   (ii) (a), (c), (d)
   (iii) (b), (f)

5.

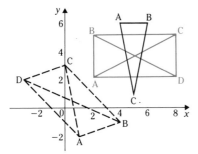

(a) black outline; (i)
(b) green outline; (iii)
(c) black broken outline; (ii)

6. (a) $(-1, -3), (6, -1)$ or $(8, -1), (8, -3)$ etc.
   (b) $(4, -3), (6, 4)$

Exercise 4c   **page 65**
1. (a)

(c)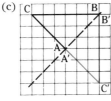

(b)

(d)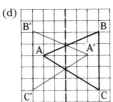

2. and **3.**

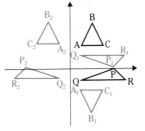

4.

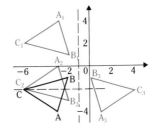

5. (d) re in x-axis

6. (a)

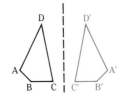

(b)

(c)

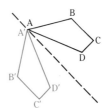

7.

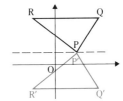

Exercise 4d   page 67

1. (a) re
   (b) tr
   (c) re
   (d) tr
   (e) tr
   (f) re

2.

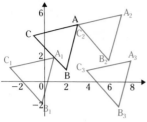

3. (a) 3 right, 3 down
   (b) 4 left, 2 down
   (c) 2 left, 8 down

4.

   (c) tr; distance equal to BC in the direction BC

5. (d) tr; 5 left, 1 up

Exercise 4e   page 68

1. (a) $90\circlearrowright$
   (b) $90\circlearrowright$
   (c) $180°$
   (d) $90\circlearrowright$

2. (a) A'(3, 2), B'(3, −2)
   (b) A'(−2, −1), B'(1, 2)
   (c) A'(1, 2), B'(−1, 2)
   (d) A'(1, −1), B'(−3, −3)

3. (a)

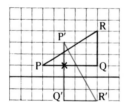

   (b)

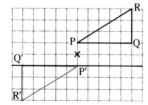

   (c)

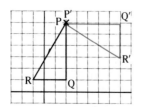

(d)

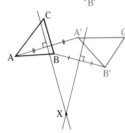

Exercise 4f   page 70

1.

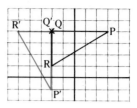

2.

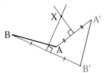

3. tr; 4 left 2 up
4. re in horizontal line through (0, 1)
5. re in line through (1, 2) and (2, 3)
6. tr; 3 left
7. re in line through (3, 2) and (5, 0)
8. ro of 180° about (3, 2)
9. re in y-axis, tr 8 right, ro of 180° about (0, 1½)
10. re in y-axis, ro of $90\circlearrowright$ about O
11. re in y-axis, tr 4 left, ro of $90\circlearrowright$ about O, ro of 180° about (0, 2), ro of $90\circlearrowright$ about (0, 4)
12. re in y-axis, tr 4 right, ro of $120\circlearrowright$ about O, ro of $120\circlearrowright$ about X

Exercise 4g   page 73

1. yes, re
2. no
3. yes, ro
4. yes, ro
5. no
6. no
7. (a) tr or re or ro   (b) yes
8. (a) ro   (b) yes
9. (a) ro   (b) yes
10. (a) re   (b) yes

Self-Assessment 4   page 75

1. (a) line, 1   (e) both, 3, 3
   (b) rotational, 2   (f) both, 5, 5
   (c) rotational, 3   (g) rotational, 2
   (d) neither   (h) neither

2. (a) yes, AC and BD
   (b) yes, (1½, 2½)
   (c) no line symmetry; yes, (2½, 2½)

3. (a) (2, 138°)   (b)

4. (1) tr; 7 left
   (2) re in horizontal line on which $y = 5$
   (3) ro about $(15, 3)$

5. (a)

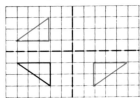

   (b)

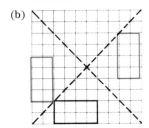

6. The vertical line through $(5, 0)$
7. (a) no   (b) yes   (c) yes
8. reflection
9. 90° clockwise; (1.0)

10.

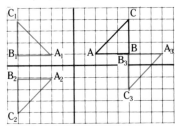

   (b) ro of 180° about O
   (c) tr; 10 right, 2 up

CHAPTER 5

Exercise 5a   page 79
1. (a) 4000 g   (g) 21 000 kg
   (b) 8.1 cm   (h) 0.121 g
   (c) 210 cm   (i) 3.5 cm
   (d) 2.024 kg   (j) 5.67 t
   (e) 5000 m   (k) 1.4 m
   (f) 7300 mg   (l) 23 000 mm
2. (a) 35 mm   (d) 3.45 km
   (b) 3250 kg   (e) 7.88 m
   (c) 8036 m   (f) 9.077 g

Exercise 5b   page 81
1. (a) 24.8 cm   (b) 2.84 m
2. (a) 15 m   (b) 34.2 mm
3. 40 cm
4. 35 m
5. 52 cm
6. (a) 21.9 m   (b) 1.68 cm
7. 144 cm   **9.** 44 cm
8. 42 cm   **10.** 420 mm

Exercise 5c   page 83
1. (a) 27 squares   (c) 24 squares
   (b) 16 squares
2. (a) 28 squares   (c) 15 squares
   (b) 12 squares   (d) 33 squares

Exercise 5d   page 85
1. 81 cm²   **3.** 8.41 cm²
2. 28 mm²   **4.** 5.76 m²
5. (a) 3.84 m² or 38 400 cm²
   (b) 14.26 cm² or 1426 mm²
6. 864 cm²   **9.** 92 m²
7. 1664 cm²   **10.** 2.88 m²
8. 415 mm²   **11.** 164 cm²
12. (a) 0.3 m² and 0.175 m² or 3000 cm² and 1750 cm²
   (b) 1.205 m² or 12 050 cm²
   (c) 220 cm and 170 cm

Exercise 5e   page 90
1. 8
2. (a) 6   (b) 6
3. (a) 128   (b) 16   (c) 2
4. 4 cm by 6 cm or 2 cm by 12 cm
5. (a) 60 mm³   (b) 21.96 m³   (c) 64 cm³
6. (a) 420 000 cm³   (c) 6300 cm³
   (b) 0.292 cm³   (d) 0.0731 cm³
7. (a) 6200 mm³   (c) 430 mm³
   (b) 92 000 000 mm³   (d) 43 000 mm³
8. 840 000 cm³   **10.** 17.5 cm³
9. 60 mm³   **11.** 0.28 m³

Exercise 5f   page 92
1. (a) 2400 cm³   (b) 1600 cm³
2. (a) 864 000 cm³   (b) 864 litres
3. yes, 370 mℓ   **6.** 4128 g
4. 122 g (3 s.f.)   **7.** 13.8 g
5. 980 g

Exercise 5g   page 94
1. 40 miles   **4.** 4 h
2. 16 km/h   **5.** 42 km
3. 5 h
6. (a) 1.2 miles/minute   (b) 32 400 m.p.h.
7. (a) 1200 metres/minute   (b) 7.56 km/h
8. 60 m.p.h.   **9.** 9 m.p.h.
10. (a) 105 m.p.h.   **12.** (a) 21 m.p.h.
   (b) 32 miles   (b) 40 m.p.h.
   (c) 96 m.p.h   (c) 28.9 m.p.h. (3 s.f.)
11. 10.5 m.p.h. (3 s.f.)   (d) 41.4 m.p.h. (3 s.f.)

Self-Assessment 5   page 95
1. (a) 5.88 m   (d) 0.495 t
   (b) 5880 mm   (e) 80 000 cm²
   (c) 3200 mg   (f) 5000 mm³
2. (a) 17.2 cm   (b) 14.6 cm or 146 mm
3. (a) 18.49 cm²
   (b) 11.22 cm² or 1122 mm²
4. (a) 560 miles
   (b) 3 hours 15 minutes
5. (a) 1500 m²   (b) 1100 m²   (c) 1080 m²
6. (a) 0.0909 miles/minute ($\frac{1}{11}$)
   (b) 5.45 m.p.h. ($5\frac{5}{11}$)
7. 104 cm³ (3 s.f.) (103.823 cm³)
8. (a) 162   (b) 6

9. (a) 0.39 m³ or 390 000 cm³
   (b) 0.2444 m³ or 244 400 cm³
10. (a) yes   (c) 450 mℓ
11. 0.815 g/cm³ (3 s.f.)

CHAPTER 6

Exercise 6a   page 98

1. 0.38, $\frac{19}{50}$ 7. 90%, 0.9
2. 7%, $\frac{7}{100}$ 8. 0.175, $\frac{7}{40}$
3. 150%, 1.5   9. 77%
4. 61%, $\frac{61}{100}$ 10. 33%
5. 0.05, $\frac{1}{20}$ 11. 14%
6. 235%, $2\frac{7}{20}$ 12. 21%

Exercise 6b   page 99

1. 117   7. 0.07 m = 7 cm
2. 2 m   8. £1935.20
3. 92.5 kg   9. £58.25
4. 5000   10. £650
5. £2.65   11. 4.41 m²
6. 156   12. 77, 49
13. £175
14. (a) £17.40   (b) £162.40
15. (a) 92 000   (b) 98 500
16. Jane, by 36 p
17. (a) £116   (b) £53.60
18. Jim's store, by 64 p
19. 29.75 cm by 42 cm
20. (a) £621   (b) £558.90
21. (a) £131.20   (b) £141.04
22. A by £2.30
23. 27 300

Exercise 6c   page 102

1. £735.55   4. £332.35
2. £11.28   5. £188; £195.20
3. £6627
6. (a) £644   (b) no
   (d) He calculated the extra $2\frac{1}{2}$% on £644 instead
   of on £560; £658
7. £6.21
8. (a) £4370   (i) £908.80   (ii) £961
   (iii) 987.10
   (b) £4540   (i) £949.60   (ii) £1012
   (iii) £1043.20
   (c) £2390   (i) £478   (ii) £478
   (iii) £478
9. (a) £877   (c) £820
   (b) £6876   (d) £13478
10. £78.80 per month
11. NIL
12. £505.56
13. £2112 per year

Exercise 6d   page 106

1. (a) £448   (b) £449.44   (c) £450.20
2. (a) £1081.60   (b) 8.16%
3. Account (i) by £1.12
4. £49.50
5. (a) £33.28   (b) £165.50   (c) £47.42
6. £1756.92   8. £2382.03
7. £957.77   9. £480

Exercise 6e   page 108

1. (a) 1.262   (c) 0.4336   (e) 2.488
   (b) 1.874   (d) 0.6983
2. (a) £1500   (b) £1100 (to nearest £100)
3. (a) £44 995   (b) £54 743 (to nearest £)
   (c) £87 645
4. 3 700 000
5. £13 (to nearest £)

Exercise 6f   page 109

1. £12.60   4. 22 600
2. £25.30   5. (a) 120   (b) 445
3. 3100   6. £140, £330

Exercise 6g   page 111

1. (a) (i) £325   (ii) £715   (b) £45 000
2. (a) £510   (b) £6120   (c) £153 000
3. £45 600, £2400
4. (a) £56 000   (b) £705.60   (c) £225 680
5. £13 (to nearest £)
6. (a) £340   (b) £2158   (c) £458
7. (a) £1168.50   (b) £1434
8. (a) £600   (b) £2160   (c) £180
9. bank loan by £638
10. £9.68
11. no; only £131 credit left.

Exercise 6h   page 114

Non-exact answers are given to 3 s.f.
1. 60%   3. 60%
2. 67.2%   4. 26%
5. (a) 2.7%   (b) 4.76%   (c) 3.88%
6. (a) 70%   (c) 74%
   (b) 85%   (d) 70%
7. 10.3%
8. (a) 90%   (b) 10%
9. 27.27%
10. 78.3%   14. 57.1%
11. 40%   15. 15%
12. 75%   16. 18.2%
13. (a) 3.57%   17. 5%
    (b) 3.57%   18. 29.2%

Exercise 6i   page 115

1. 80   3. 9
2. 25   4. £210
5. (a) 25   (b) 76%
6. 72
7. (a) £900   (d) £80
   (b) £495   (e) £240
   (c) £800   (f) £2000
8. £7
9. £7000
10. (a) £1200
    (b) (i) 1.15   (ii) 1.175   (iii) 1.22
11. 15 km/litre
12. 250 cm³
13. £240

Self-Assessment 6   page 116

1. (a) 350%   (c) 0.37
   (b) 283%   (d) $1\frac{7}{20}$
2. (a) £6.40   (b) 14 355
3. Right Tools, by 21 p
4. 12.5%

5. (a) £298.45 (b) £309.88
6. £1276.50
7. £406; £10.15; £395.85; £69.27; £465.12
8. 62.9%
9. (a) £5704 (b) £4828
10. (a) 70% (b) 46.2%
11. £56
12. (a) (i) £575 (ii) £6900 (iii) £172500
(b) 375%
13. Reliant West (£4 better)
14. (a) £5646 (b) 37.5%
15. Corner Shop by £1200

CHAPTER 7

Exercise 7a   page 120
1. (a) $7x+5$ (c) $x+5y$ (e) $2-8p$
(b) $7a+4$ (d) $3t-5$ (f) $4a-4b$
2. (a) $2-5x$ (d) $3s+t+6$
(b) $7-12y$ (e) $4p+q$
(c) $2b-4a$ (f) $5x-y-z$
3. (a) $3x-9$ (c) $6x-4$
(b) $6x+8$
4. (a) $5x-5$ (c) $3a-6b$
(b) $12-4x$
5. (a) $25x+12$ (g) $2-2t$
(b) $3x-5$ (h) $23b-8$
(c) $8-7p$ (i) $10-9x$
(d) $4x-2$ (j) $-5x-1$
(e) $3a-16$ (k) $20-10c$
(f) $2b-5$
6. (a) p^3 (f) x^2
(b) $6a^2$ (g) a^2
(c) $2x^3$ (h) y^{-1}
(d) $3b^4$ (ii) 1
(e) $12xy$ (j) $2x$
7. (a) $\dfrac{4x}{y}$ (f) a^6
(b) $2x^2$ (g) x
(c) $-b^2$ (h) 1
(d) $4x^2$ (i) c^2
(e) $\dfrac{3y^2}{2x}$ (j) $\dfrac{1}{x^2}$
8. (a) $5x+x^2$ (g) x^2
(b) $a^2+2ab-b^2$ (h) $bc-ac$
(c) $2x-x^2$ (i) x^2-x-6
(d) $-ac-c$ (j) $2pq+6pr$
(e) $4x^2-12x$ (k) x^4+x^2
(f) $2x^2-x^4-x$
9. (a) $\dfrac{7x}{6}$ (g) $\dfrac{(x^2-x)}{6}$
(b) $\dfrac{3a}{20}$ (h) $\dfrac{2x}{(3x-3)}$
(c) $\dfrac{y^2}{6}$ (i) $\dfrac{5z}{2}$
(d) $\dfrac{8x^2}{75}$ (j) $\dfrac{2}{3a}$
(e) $\dfrac{(5x-3)}{6}$ (k) $\dfrac{y}{2x}$
(f) $\dfrac{(7-x)}{6}$ (l) $\dfrac{(2x^2+x^3)}{4}$
(m) $\dfrac{x^5}{8}$ (p) $\dfrac{(8a-3a^2)}{12}$
(n) $\dfrac{2}{x}$ (q) $\dfrac{(-5x-4)}{6}$
10. (a) 14 (b) -7
11. (a) 5 (b) 2
12. (a) 3 (b) -3
13. (a) $\frac{1}{6}$ (c) $\frac{1}{6}$
(b) $\dfrac{x-1}{6}$
14. (a) $\dfrac{x}{2}$ (d) $\dfrac{x^2-x}{12}$
(b) $\frac{2}{3}$ (e) $\dfrac{7x-4}{12}$
(c) $\dfrac{3x^2}{50}$ (f) $\dfrac{4-x}{12}$

Exercise 7b   page 124
1. (a) 3 (e) 3 (i) -2
(b) 7 (f) 1 (j) 0.55
(c) 2 (g) 1 (k) 0.6
(d) -1 (h) 2 (l) -0.4
2. (a) $-\frac{3}{2}$ (e) $\frac{13}{7}$ (i) $\frac{1}{2}$
(b) -1 (f) $\frac{19}{9}$ (j) -3 .
(c) 1 (g) -3 (k) 1.3
(d) 10 (h) $\frac{1}{4}$ (l) -1
3. (a) $\frac{15}{2}$ (e) $\frac{8}{5}$ (i) 7
(b) $\frac{3}{8}$ (f) -2 (j) $\frac{8}{7}$
(c) $\frac{3}{10}$ (g) $\frac{11}{7}$ (k) $\frac{3}{2}$
(d) $\frac{60}{11}$ (h) 10 (l) $\frac{35}{4}$
4. $\dfrac{x}{3} = 15$; 45 people
5. $3x = 81$; 27 cm
6. $\dfrac{20x}{100} = 27$; £135
7. $\dfrac{x}{3} = x-2$; 3
8. $2x+2(2x) = 60$; 10 m
9. $10x = 8x+36$; 18 cm^3
10. $x+10 = 2x$; 10 years old
11. e.g. $4x-12 = 48$; 15 cm

Exercise 7c   page 129
1. (a) $\vdash\!\!\bullet\!-\!\oplus\!\!\dashv$ 11.5 12.5 (b) 7.5 8.5 (c) 99.5 100.5
2. (a) 2.65 2.75 (b) 34.35 34.45 (c) 4.95 5.05
(d) 1.05 1.15
3. (a) 2.15 2.25 (b) 0.145 0.155 (c) 115 125
(d) 9.55 10.5
4. (a) $x > 2$ (g) $x \geqslant 1$
(b) $x < 1$ (h) $x \leqslant 3$
(c) $x < 2$ (i) $x \leqslant -3$
(d) $x > -\frac{1}{2}$ (j) $x \leqslant \frac{2}{3}$
(e) $x > -2$ (k) $x \leqslant 8$
(f) $x > 1$ (l) $x < \frac{4}{5}$

5. (a) 3   (b) 2
6. (a) 3   (b) 2
7. (a) $x \leqslant 1$ (e) $-5 \leqslant x \leqslant 2$
  (b) $1 \leqslant x \leqslant 2$ (f) $1 \leqslant x \leqslant 5$
  (c) $1 < x < 4$ (g) $2 < x < 5$
  (d) $-9 \leqslant x \leqslant -4$ (h) $-1 \leqslant x \leqslant 2$
8. (a) none, 1   (e) $-5, 2$
  (b) 1, 2   (f) 1, 4
  (c) 2, 3   (g) 3, 4
  (d) $-9, -4$ (h) $-1, 2$
9. (a) $-4, 0$ (c) 3, 4
  (b) 2, 2   (d) no values
10. $w \geqslant 15$, w kg is weight of popcorn
11. $0 \leqslant n \leqslant 56$, n is an integer (the number of passengers)
12. $t > 0$, $t\,°C$ is the temperature
13. $2x + 2 < 100$, x is the number
14. $6n + 1.5 \leqslant 50$, n is an integer (the number of books)
15. 254
16. 352.5 cm

Exercise 7d   page 131
1. $T = F + P$ **6.** $N = S - T - R$
2. $m = x + y$ **7.** $T = 35p + 30$
3. $A = a^2$ **8.** $W = Np + x$
4. $d = st$ **9.** $N = L - np$
5. $p = a + b + c$ **10.** $T = 20x + y$
11. $K = \dfrac{(nW + c)}{1000}$
12. $C = \dfrac{nx}{100}$
13. $t = s + \dfrac{v}{60}$
14. $A = 100\,lc$
15. $K = L - \dfrac{nl}{100}$
16. $N = 2s + c$
17. $n = p + q + r$
18. $u_n = n^2$
19. $C = 2n + 5m$, where n and m are the numbers of small and large posters sold, respectively.
20. $P = 3n$, n is the number of hours worked.
21. $u_n = 2u_{n-1}$

Exercise 7e   page 133
1. (b) 15 cm   (d) 77 mm
  (c) 18.4 cm   (e) 359 cm
2. (a) 150 km   (d) 0.833 km (to 3 s.f.)
  (b) 360 miles   (e) $7\frac{1}{2}$ nautical miles
  (c) 15 km   (f) 283 m
3. (a) 92 p   (c) £1.08
  (b) £12.86   (d) 11 p
4. (a) 54   (b) 8   (c) 5.04
5. (a) 25   (b) 8.65   (c) 169
6. (a) 3.87   (b) 0.173   (c) 2.51
7. (a) 0.103   (b) 3.25   (c) 0.231
8. (a) 1   (b) 1   (c) 2   (d) 0.7
9. (a) $4\frac{1}{2}$ (b) -5.1
10. (a) 4   (b) $\frac{14}{3}$ (c) -1.5 (d) $-\frac{123}{4}$
11. 2.13
12. 4.7 cm   **14.** 4.5 cm
13. 7 cm   **15.** 3.8 cm, 12.8 cm
       16. 12 mm, 13.2 cm

17. 25.4 mm, 457.2 mm^2 **19.** 12 mm
18. 0.02 cm   **20.** 4 cm

21. $C = \dfrac{nx}{100}$ (a) £12.50   (b) 40

22. $C = S + \dfrac{np}{100}$ (a) £61.85   (b) 5000

23. $p = nq + r$

Exercise 7f   page 137
1. (a) $x = c - y$ (d) $u = r - t$
  (b) $s = V + t$ (e) $x = py$
  (c) $T = \dfrac{C}{r}$
2. (a) $a = s - 2b$ (c) $u = v - rt$
  (b) $p = b - q - r$ (d) $m = Ln$
3. (a) $x = y - d$ (e) $y = \dfrac{4x}{3}$
  (b) $t = \dfrac{(S + d)}{2}$ (f) $I = 10A - 10P$
  (c) $a = 2b - c$ (g) $R = \dfrac{VI}{2}$
  (d) $t = \dfrac{(u - v)}{3}$ (h) $r = 5p - 5q$
4. (a) $x = \dfrac{(c - y)}{2}$ (e) $a = \dfrac{(c + d)}{b}$
  (b) $q = \dfrac{p}{2} + r$ (f) $x = \dfrac{c}{a} - b$
  (c) $t = 4p - s$ (g) $P = \dfrac{R}{3} - Q$
  (d) $r = \dfrac{C}{2\pi}$ (h) $R = \dfrac{100I}{PT}$
5. (a) $S = 3n + 3$ (c) 111
  (b) $n = \dfrac{(S - 3)}{3}$
6. (a) $C = P + nS$ (c) 40
  (b) $n = \dfrac{(C - P)}{S}$
7. (a) $P = \dfrac{zx}{100} - y$ (c) $y = \dfrac{zx}{100} - P$
  (b) $x = \dfrac{100P + 100y}{z}$

Self-Assessment 7   page 139
1. $16x - 2y$ **3.** $\frac{2}{3}$
2. -5 **4.** ⊶ 5
5. $2.555 \leqslant x < 2.565$
6. (a) $6b^2$ (b) 2   (c) $5x - x^2$
7. $-1 < x < 1$
8. $\dfrac{5x}{12}$
9. (a) x^4 (b) w^{-4}
10. $W = c + d$
11. 30
12. $-\frac{1}{2}$
13. $p = \dfrac{r}{a} - q$

14. (a) $P = \dfrac{nd}{100}$ (b) $d = \dfrac{100P}{n}$

15. $y = 125 - x, A = x(125 - x)$

CHAPTER 8

Exercise 8a   page 140

1. (a) £176   (c) £218, £42
(b) £194   (d) £254.40
2. (a) £182   (d) £11
(b) £7.80   (e) George, by £14.10
(c) £214.50
3. (a) 8.00 a.m.   (e) Thursday
(b) 4.30 p.m.   (f) $36\frac{1}{2}$h
(c) 1 h   (g) £175.20
(d) (i) 4 h   (ii) $3\frac{1}{2}$h
4. (a) £400   (b) £130   (c) £390
5. £260   **6.** £259.50   **7.** £555
8.

	(a)			(b)		(c)
	No. plugs	(i)	(ii)			
Mrs A	188	100	88	£107.20		
Mr B	158	80	78	£ 90.70		
Ms C	192	100	92	£109.80		
Mr D	220	100	120	£128		

(d) Thursday, 169
9. 270, 15   **10.** £64.30   **11.** 1602

Exercise 8b   page 143

1. £98.94   **3.** £13.34   **5.** £168.28
2. £12.10   **4.** £38.60

Exercise 8c   page 145

1. £79.79   **2.** £113.65   **3.** £115.16
4. (a) 39 141, 39 487, 202, 40 704   (c) £31.51
(b) £96.48   (d) £288.85
5. £75   **7.** £130.54
6. £183.75   **8.** £231.94
9. Domestic Prepayment tariff by £4.65
10. Credit tariff by £3.05
11. Credit tariff by 16 p
12. £49.35   **15.** £76.09
13. £58.60   **16.** £145.95
14. £118.61

Exercise 8d   page 148

1. 48 in   **9.** 6 in
2. 8 oz   **10.** 288 sq in
3. 3 ft   **11.** 12 oz
4. 5 yd   **12.** 3 miles
5. 91 lb   **13.** 480 pints or 60 gallons
6. 20 pints   **14.** 20 sq yd
7. $1\frac{1}{4}$lb   **15.** $2\frac{1}{2}$ fluid oz
8. $1\frac{1}{2}$gall   **16.** 1 mile (1760 yd)

Exercise 8e   page 149

All answers are approximate.
1. 54 ℓ   **3.** 16 mm
2. 47 p   **4.** 12
5. 350 acres
6. 360 cm (390 required to be certain)
7. 10 (to use 9.09 kg)
8. The department store by 67 p per m^2

Exercise 8f   page 151

1. 25 m.p.h.
2. 112 km/h
3. 1 800 000 litres/h
4. 18 km/l
5. 2400 sq ft/gallon
6. 55 lb/sq in
7. 194 miles
8. 1600 m^2
9. 1.23 lb/sq in
10. 3 min
11. 2 h 8 min (approx)
12. (a) 0.083 (2 s.f.)   (b) 0.071 (2 s.f.)
13. 11.1 oz/in^3

Exercise 8g   page 152

1. (a) 0830   (c) 0542
(b) 2030   (d) 1436
2. (a) 3.00 a.m.   (c) 8.51 a.m.
(b) 7.42 p.m.   (d) 10.43 p.m.
3. (a) 11 h 48 min   (c) 13 h 5 min
(b) 6 h 12 min   (d) 21 h 12 min
4. (a) 0835, 2 h 3 min
5. 11.35, 1 h 23 min
6. The 0835 and the 1035 both take 2 h 3 min. Both are through trains.
7. The 0905 and the 1105 both take 1 h 26 min.
8. 1 h 12 min
9. (a) Reading, 6 min   (b) Bristol Parkway

Exercise 8h   page 155

1. (a) 77 p   (b) £3.80
(b) 47 p   (e) £10.95
(c) £1.00
2. (a) 29 p   (c) £1.45
(b) 52 p   (d) 20 p
3. £6.55   **4.** £12.96   **5.** 12
7. (a) 120 p   (c) 340 p
(b) 165 p   (d) 760 p
8. (a) £4.64   (c) make 21 copies
(b) 29
9. (a) 72 p   (b) 30.6 p   (c) 18 p
10. (a) 14.85 p   (b) 44.1 p   (c) 26.1 p
11. £1.19   **12.** 33.47 p

Exercise 8i   page 157

1. £420   **2.** £240
3. (a) £78   (b) piano, ring
4. (a) £251.40   (b) £243.78
5. (a) £525   (b) £252   (c) 60%
6. £2088, £40.15   **7.** £158.42

Exercise 8j   page 159

1. (a) £25   (b) £26.18   **6.** (a) £250   (b) £257.73
2. (a) £7.50   (b) £7.85   **7.** (a) £1.20   (b) £1.22
3. (a) 20 p   (b) 22 p   **8.** (a) £625   (b) £700.79
4. (a) £19   (b) £20.93   **9.** (a) 20 p   (b) 18 p
5. (a) 40 p   (b) 37 p

10. 4.2 Ff   **13.** 14.7 Ff
11. 7 pta   **14.** 66.9 Ff
12. 10 780 L   **15.** 2.93 pt

16. 6.6 Dm   **19.** £4.09
17. 5.5 Dm   **20.** £5.45
18. 9.68 Dm   **21.** £1.14

Exercise 8k   page 161
1. 221.3 Dm
2. £ 103.65
3. £ 423.91
4. £ 307.50
5. 92 500 pta
6. £ 99.33
7. £ 533.69
8. £ 9.71
9. £ 53.52
10. £ 218
11. less by £ 8.96

Self-Assessment 8   page 163
1. (b) by £ 40.10
2. £ 72.97
3. (a) 49p   (b) (i) 144 km/h   (ii) 90 m.p.h.
4. 165 seconds
5. (a) £ 519.20   (b) £ 498.94
6. £ 28.70

CHAPTER 9

The answers for marked angles are given in alphabetical order.

Exercise 9a   page 166
1. (a) general   (b) 90°
2. (a) parallelogram   (b) 57°, 123°, 123°
3. (a) isosceles trapezium   (b) 64°, 116°, 116°
4. (a) general   (b) 54°
5. (a) kite   (b) 98°, 57°
6. (a) trapezium   (b) 90°, 58°
7. parallelogram, trapezium; 55°, 55°, 55°, 125°, 125°
8. kite; 94°, 94°, 115°
9. isosceles trapezium, general; 66°, 66°, 114°
10. trapezium; 25°, 15°, 105°
11. parallelogram, trapezium; 37°
12. parallelogram, two trapeziums; 75°, 40°, 65°, 75°, 50°
13. (a) 36   (b) since $5x = 180$
14. (a) 55°   (b) 55°, isosceles
15. (a) 60°   (c) 15°
    (b) 150°   (d) 75°
16. (a) parallelogram   (c) trapezium
    (b) kite   (d) rhombus
17. (a) 122°, 116°, 58°, 64°, 58°
    (b) isosceles
    (c) isosceles trapezium, parallelogram
    (d) not possible; position of F is not fixed by the given information
18. (a) 24°, 24°, 132° in each triangle
    (b) isosceles
    (c) trapezium
    (d) isosceles

Exercise 9b   page 169
1. 115°
2. 60°
3. 75°
4. 52°

Exercise 9c   page 170
1. 80°
2. 60°
3. 108°
4. 135°
5. (a) n (b) $180n°$ (c) 360°

Exercise 9d   page 171
1. (a) 72°   (c) $51\frac{3}{7}°$ (e) 20°
   (b) 60°   (d) 36°   (f) 18°
2. (a) 140°   (c) 165°
   (b) 150°   (d) 170°
3. (a) 12   (b) 18   (c) 15
4. (a) 6   (b) 15   (c) 20
5. (a) yes   (c) yes
   (b) no   (d) no
6. (a) yes   (c) yes
   (b) yes   (d) no
7. 160°
8. 110°
9. 60°
10. 35°
11. 54
12. 75
13. 72
14. 30
15. 72°, 72°, 36°
16. (a) (i) 60°   (ii) 120°
    (b) (i) 30°   (ii) 90°   (iii) 60°   (iv) 30°
17. $x = 65, y = 130, z = 115$
18. $\widehat{OAB} = \widehat{OBA} = 67.5°$, $\widehat{AOB} = 45°$
19. (a) 36°   (b) 36°
20. $\widehat{CDI} = \widehat{DCI} = 45°$, $\widehat{CID} = 90°$
21. (a) 135°   (d) 45°
    (b) 22.5°   (e) 45°
    (c) 67.5°   (f) 90°   right-angled isosceles

Exercise 9e   page 175
1. (a)   (c)

(b)   (d)

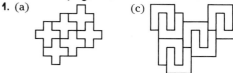
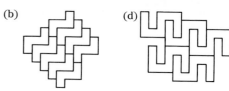

2. yes
3. yes
4. (a) yes   (c) no   (e) yes
   (b) yes   (d) yes   (f) yes

Self-Assessment 9   page 176
1. (a) 54°, 54°, 72°   (b) 63°, 117°
2. 140
3. 24
4. (a) no   (b) yes
5. $\widehat{AEC} = \widehat{EAC} = 72°$, $\widehat{ACE} = 36°$
6. All except (c) will tessellate.
   (a)   (d)

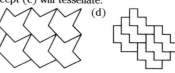

   (b)

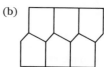

CHAPTER 10

Exercise 10a   page 178
1. (a) (i) 174.2   (ii) 3.633
   (b) (i) 582 200   (ii) 27.62
   (c) (i) 0.81   (ii) 0.9487
   (d) (i) 0.000 004 529 (ii) 0.082 04
2. (a) (i) 3215   (ii) 7.530
   (b) (i) 11 360 000   (ii) 58.05
   (c) (i) 0.6724   (ii) 0.9055
   (d) (i) 0.000 000 25 (ii) 0.022 36
3. 16.3 cm   5. 16.7 cm
4. 9.39 cm   6. 23.6 cm
7. AC = 25 cm, DC = 9 cm
8. RS = 4.47 cm, PR = 6.71 cm
9. (a) 6.26 cm   (b) 5.50 cm
10. (a) yes, A   (c) no
    (b) yes, X   (d) yes, Q
11. (a) 35.8 cm   (c) 14.3 cm
    (b) 28.6 cm
12. 7.48 cm
13. (a) 6.71   (c) 11.4   (e) 15
    (b) 11.4   (d) 13   (f) 12.5

Exercise 10b   page 180
1. 42.8 nautical miles
2. 24.0 cm
3. 13 cm
4. AB = 3.96 m, BC = 9.12 m
5. 997 m to nearest m
6. 18.8 m
7. (a) 1.04 cm   (b) 0.693 cm^2
8. 8.28 m, 7.71 m
9. (a) (i) 5   (ii) 12   (iii) 7
   (b) (ii) $a = 11, c = 61$
       (iii) 13, 84, 85; 15, 112, 113
10. (a) 212.7 cm or 2127 mm
11. (a) 30 cm, 42.4 cm   (b) 47.4 cm

Exercise 10c   page 183
1. (a) 11.7 cm   (b) 14.7 cm, equal to AG
2. (b) (i) EF, DC, HG   (ii) FB, GC, HD
       (iii) AD, EH, FG
   (c) 12.6 cm   (d) 13 cm
3. (a) 12.4 cm   (b) 14.4 cm   (c) 17.3 cm
4. (a) 8.49 cm   (c) 6.71 cm
   (b) 10.4 cm   (d) 9 cm
5. (a) (i) 8.54 cm   (ii) 17.3 cm
   (b) AC, $C\widehat{A}E < C\widehat{B}E$
6. (a) AC = 5.66 cm, AX = 2.83 cm
   (b) 4.12 cm
7. PQ = 5 units, PR = 9 units, QS = 29 units

Self-Assessment 10   page 185
1. (a) (i) 4.24 cm   (ii) 6.75 cm
   (b) no
2. 7.21
3. 32 cm
4. (a) 4.47   (b) 8.06   (c) 8.31
5. 6.04

CHAPTER 11

Exercise 11a   page 187
1. 84 cm^2 7. 36 cm^2
2. 38.88 cm^2 8. 180 cm^2
3. 352 cm^2 9. 192 m^2
4. 12 cm^2 10. 288 cm^2
5. 456 mm^2 11. 4.8 cm^2
6. 63 cm^2 12. 480 mm^2

Exercise 11b   page 189
1. 48 cm^2 4. 21 cm^2
2. 22.2 cm^2 5. 540 cm^2
3. 64 cm^2 6. 30 cm^2
7. (a) 1.89 m^2 (b) 18 900 cm^2
8. (a) 0.152 m^2 (b) 1520 cm^2
9. (a) 0.0874 m^2 (b) 874 cm^2
10. 1.69 m^2, 16 900 cm^2
11. 0.002 64 m^2, 26.4 cm^2
12. 0.0032 m^2, 32 cm^2
13. 12 cm^2 18. 28 cm^2
14. 9 cm^2 19. 28 cm^2
15. 20 cm^2 20. 47.5 cm^2
16. 79 cm^2 21. 6 mm
17. 45 cm^2 22. 36 cm
23. 0.5 cm or 5 mm
24. 4 m or 400 cm

Exercise 11c   page 192
1. 353, 349   7. 91, 83
2. 3.56, 3.52   8. 8.8, 7.7
3. 0.477, 0.471   9. 0.032, 0.031
4. 514 000, 512 000   10. 0.95, 0.81
5. 1.2, 1.1   11. 1200, 1300
6. 5.1, 4.7   12. 27, 30
13. (a) 3.605 cm $\leqslant$ length < 3.615 cm;
        2.565 cm $\leqslant$ width < 2.575 cm
    (b) 9.308 625 cm^2, 9.246 825 cm^2
    (c) 9.25 cm^2 $\leqslant$ area < 9.31 cm^2
14. (a) 25.55 mm $\leqslant$ height < 25.65 mm;
        19.25 mm $\leqslant$ base < 19.35 mm
    (b) 248.163 75 mm^2, 245.918 75 mm^2
    (c) 246 mm^2 $\leqslant$ area < 248 mm^2
15. (a) 8.425 cm $\leqslant$ side < 8.435 cm;
        5.205 cm $\leqslant$ base < 5.215 cm
    (b) 43.988 525 cm^2, 43.852 125 cm^2
    (c) 43.9 cm^2 $\leqslant$ area < 44.0 cm^2
16. (a) 4.065 cm $\leqslant$ side < 4.075 cm
    (b) 16.605 625 cm^2, 16.524 225 cm^2
    (c) 16.5 cm^2 $\leqslant$ area < 16.6 cm^2

Exercise 11d   page 194
1. 20 cm^2
2. 2200 mm^2
3. 157.5 cm^2

Exercise 11e   page 196
1. (a) 60 cm^2 (b) 1.98 cm^2
2. (a) 39 cm^2 (b) 3.105 m^2
3. 13 cm   8. 0.84 m^2
4. 10 cm   9. 84 mm^2
5. 20 cm   10. 33.02 m^2
6. 101.5 cm^2 11. 9.92 m^2
7. 18 cm^2 12. 74.75 m^2
13. (a) 72.2 m^2 (b) 16205

Exercise 11f   page 200

1. 94 cm², 60 cm³
2. 102 cm², 63 cm³
3. 122 cm²
4. 65.5 cm²
6. (b) F and J   (c) BC
7. (a) 13 cm   (d) 26.2 cm (3 s.f.)
     (b) 37 cm   (e) 23.9 cm (3 s.f.)
8. (b) 151 mm (3 s.f.)

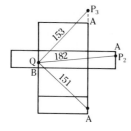

     (c) (b)
9. (a) and (c)

Exercise 11g   page 204

1. 720 cm³   **4.** 1242 cm³
2. 2160 cm³   **5.** 1120 cm³
3. 660 cm³   **6.** 1600 cm³
7. (a) 6.175 m³   (b) 23.1 m² (3 s.f.)
8. 0.3726 m³
9. 5 cm
10. 3 cm
11. (b) 244 cm²
12. (b) 248 cm²
13. 81.7 cm³ (3 s.f.)
14. 48 cm³ (3 s.f.)
15. 90 cm³
16. 8 cm³
17. (a) 134 cm² (3 s.f.)   (b) 31.7 cm² (3 s.f.)
18. (a) 12, 6, 8   (d) 6, 4, 4
     (b) 9, 5, 6   (e) 12, 6, 8
     (c) 8, 5, 5
19. (b) $E = F + V - 2$
     (c) 6, a pentagonal pyramid
     (d) no; yes
20. (a) 8, 18, 12   (b) yes

Self-Assessment 11   page 208

1. (a) 166 cm² (3 s.f.)
     (b) (i) 12 cm   (ii) 252 cm²
2. (a) 1.73 cm² (3 s.f.)
     (b) 178.5 cm²
3. 19 cm²
4. 39 cm²
5. (a) 4 cm   (b) 24 cm²
6. 21 cm², 20 cm²
7. (a) 28.6 cm²   (b) 22.62 m²
8. (b) 62 cm²
9. (a) 35 cm   (c) 17.7 cm (3 s.f.)
     (b) 24.5 cm (3 s.f.)
10. 10.9 cm³ ⩽ volume < 11.1 cm
11. prism: 144 cm³, 200 cm² (3 s.f.)
     pyramid: 48 cm³, 104 cm² (3 s.f.)

12.

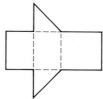

13. (b) Each 8.49 cm (3 s.f.)   (c) 31.2 cm² (3 s.f.)
14. (a) 18 cm²   (b) 36 cm³

CHAPTER 12

Exercise 12a   page 211

1. (a) 36 cm   (d) 33 cm
     (b) 19.2 mm   (e) 24 cm
     (c) 18 m   (f) 12 mm
2. (a) 239 mm   (c) 66.0 cm
     (b) 27.6 m   (d) 1.57 m
3. (a) 176 cm   (c) 19.8 cm
     (b) 44.0 m   (d) 30.8 mm
4. (a) 10.3 cm   (c) 22.8 cm
     (b) 18.3 cm   (d) 45.1 cm
5. 4.71 m; £ 32.50
6. (a) 176 cm   (c) 200
     (b) 176 cm   (d) 15
7. 94.2 cm

8. 62.8 m
9. 6.28 seconds, 9.55
10. 47.1 m
11. (a) 1 m   (c) 1.57 m
     (b) 0.5 m   (d) 6.57 m
12. (a) 6 cm   (c) 9.42 cm
     (b) 11 cm   (d) 31.4 cm
13. (a) 2.79 cm   (b) 20.1 cm
14. 45.7 cm
15. (a) 12.2 cm   (c) 104 cm
     (b) 40.2 cm
16. (a) 20.9 cm   (b) 80.9 cm
17. (a) 7.85 cm   (c) 155 cm
     (b) 47.1 cm
18. (a) 7.00 cm   (d) 87.5 m
     (b) 19.3 mm   (e) 5.76 mm
     (c) 132 cm   (f) 4.77 cm
19. 61.1 m
20. 20 m

Exercise 12b   page 216

1. (a) 13.9 cm²   (c) 4.52 m²
     (b) 254 mm²   (d) 1260 cm² or 0.126 m²
2. (a) 3 m   (b) 14.1 m²
3. 1.77 cm²
4. (a) 900 m²   (c) 1253 m²
     (b) 353 m²
5. (a) 36 cm²   (c) 64.3 cm²
     (b) 28.3 cm²
6. 278 cm²

7. (a) $2340\,\text{cm}^2$ (c) $603\,\text{cm}^2$
(b) $374\,\text{cm}^2$
8. (a) $12.8\,\text{cm}^2$ (c) $75.4\,\text{cm}^2$
(b) $131\,\text{cm}^2$ (d) $7370\,\text{cm}^2$
9. area B $=$ area C $= 576\,\text{cm}^2$; area A $= 489\,\text{cm}^2$
$1640\,\text{cm}^2$
10. (a) $38.5\,\text{m}^2$ (b) 13
11. (a) $12\,\text{m}^2$ (c) $7.48\,\text{m}^2$
(b) $4.52\,\text{m}^2$ (d) $7.54\,\text{m}$
12. (a) $615\,\text{cm}^2$
(b) $\pi(15.1^2 - 14^2)\,\text{cm}^2 = 101\,\text{cm}^2$
13. (a) $118\,\text{cm}^2$ (b) $137\,\text{cm}^2$
14. $992\,\text{cm}^2$
15. (a) $1352\,\text{cm}^2$ (c) $36.3\,\%$
(b) $9.97\,\%$
16. $190°$

Exercise 12c   page 220

1. (a) $75.4\,\text{cm}^2$ (c) $1700\,\text{cm}^2$
(b) $91.1\,\text{cm}^2$ (d) $255\,\text{cm}^2$
2. $347\,\text{cm}^2$
3. $3.92\,\text{m}^2$
4. (a) $132\,\text{cm}^2$ (c) $160\,\text{cm}^2$
(b) $13.9\,\text{cm}^2$
5. (a) $24\,100\,\text{cm}^2$ (b) $27\,900\,\text{cm}^2$
6. (a) $2.90\,\text{m}^3$ (c) $4.42\,\text{cm}^3$
(b) $14.1\,\text{m}^3$
7. (a) $57\,900\,\text{cm}^3$ (b) $57.9\,\text{litres}$
8. (a) $80.4\,\text{cm}^3$ (b) $844\,\text{g}$
9. (a) $2.69\,\text{cm}$ (c) $2\,\text{m}$
(b) $16.8\,\text{mm}$ (d) $2\,\text{cm}$
10. $1.99\,\text{m}$
11. (a) $1.2\,\text{m}^3$ (b) $101\,\text{cm}$
12. $1.62\,\text{m}$
13. $18.8\,\text{cm}$
14. $185\,\text{cm}^3/\text{s}$ or $0.185\,\ell/\text{s}$
15. $398\,\text{cm}^3$; $10.3\,\text{cm}$
16. (a) $138\,\text{mm}^3$ (c) $8\,\text{g/cm}^3$
(b) $415\,\text{mm}^3$

Exercise 12d   page 223

1. (a) (i) $19\,200\,\text{cm}^3$ (ii) $3980\,\text{cm}^2$ (iii) $4660\,\text{cm}^2$
(b) (i) $490\,\text{cm}^3$ (ii) $270\,\text{cm}^2$ (iii) $383\,\text{cm}^2$
(c) (i) $2570\,\text{cm}^3$ (ii) $844\,\text{cm}^2$ (iii) $1150\,\text{cm}^2$
2. $10.1\,\text{cm}^3$ **4.** $527\,\text{cm}^3$
3. $1470\,\text{cm}^3$ **5.** $2940\,\text{cm}^3$
6. (a) $524\,\text{cm}^3$, $314\,\text{cm}^2$ (c) $3.05\,\text{m}^3$, $10.2\,\text{m}^2$
(b) $7240\,\text{mm}^3$, $1810\,\text{mm}^2$
7. $5750\,\text{mm}^3$ ($5.750\,\text{cm}^3$)
8. $64\,500\,\text{cm}^3$
9. (a) $24.8\,\text{cm}$ by $12.4\,\text{cm}$ by $18.6\,\text{cm}$
(b) $2995\,\text{cm}^3$ (c) $52.4\,\%$
10. (a) $392\,000\,\text{cm}^3$ (c) 200
(b) $1960\,\text{cm}^3$
11. (a) (i) $2\pi r$ (ii) $2\pi l$

Exercise 12e   page 225

1. (a) length   (e) length
(b) volume   (f) volume
(c) area   (g) length
(d) area   (h) length

2. (a) length   (c) volume
(b) area
3. (a) length   (c) area
(b) volume
4. (a) cm   (c) cm^2 (e) cm
(b) cm^2 (d) cm^3 (f) cm^3
5. (a) area   (e) area
(b) length   (f) volume
(c) area   (g) area
(d) volume   (h) length
6. (c) b^3 is volume, others are area
(e) $V(\text{vol})$, $a(\text{length})$, $B(\text{area})$
7. $2\pi r$ is a length, not measured in cm^2
8. 2
9. (a) area   (b) none   (c) length   (d) volume

Self-Assessment 12   page 226

1. $47.8\,\text{cm}$
2. (a) $804\,\text{cm}^2$ (b) $73.1\,\text{cm}^3$
3. (a) $26.2\,\text{cm}^2$ (c) $37.7\,\text{cm}^2$
(b) $56.5\,\text{cm}^2$
4. (a) $10.5\,\text{cm}$ (c) $18.8\,\text{cm}$
(b) $12.6\,\text{cm}$
5. (a) $12.0\,\text{m}$ (c) $8.89\,\text{m}^2$
(b) $£55.20$ (d) $498\,\text{g}$
6. (a) $905\,\text{cm}^2$ (c) $4.98\,\text{kg}$
(b) $2110\,\text{cm}^3$
7. $3170\,\text{cm}^3$, $531\,\text{cm}^2$
8. (a) $62.8\,\text{cm}^3$ (c) $39\,\%$
(b) $103\,\text{cm}^3$
9. (a) $96.5\,\text{cm}^2$ (c) $8.19\,\text{cm}$
(b) $25.7\,\text{cm}^3$
10. (a) $11\,\text{cm}$ (c) $10.6\,\text{cm}$
(b) $704\,\text{cm}^3$

CHAPTER 13

Exercise 13a   page 228

1. (a) $16\,\text{m} : 24\,\text{m} = 2 : 3$
(b) $12\,\text{p} : 48\,\text{p} = 1 : 4$
(c) $8\,\text{kg} : 14\,\text{kg} = 4 : 7$
2. (a) $36\,\text{p}$ compared with $18\,\text{p}$ is the same as 2
compared with 1.
(b) $18\,\text{g}$ compared with $20\,\text{g}$ is the same as 9
compared with 10.
(c) 240 compared with 180 is the same as 4
compared with 3.
3. (a) $1 : 3$ (c) $4 : 7$
(b) $1 : 3$ (d) $9 : 4$
4. (a) $5 : 2 : 8$ (c) $2 : 3 : 5$
(b) $3 : 5 : 9$ (d) $2 : 5 : 7$
5. (a) $5 : 6$ (c) $12 : 25$
(b) $3 : 7$ (d) $9 : 7$
6. (a) $3 : 7$ (c) $3 : 1$
(b) $25 : 17$ (d) $3 : 8$
7. (a) $19 : 30$ (c) $1 : 2$
(b) $5 : 2$ (d) $1 : 14$
8. (a) $1 : 4 : 3$ (c) $14 : 9 : 4$
(b) $5 : 3 : 2$ (d) $3 : 25 : 18$
9. (a) $4 : 1$ (c) $4 : 25$
(b) $9 : 4$ (d) $32 : 7$
10. (a) $6 : 25$ (c) $8 : 5$
(b) $7 : 4$ (d) $4 : 3$

11. 43 : 275   **12.** 14 : 9   **13.** 17 : 3
14. (a) 9 : 7   (b) 9 : 16
15. (a) 8 : 7   (c) 25 : 24
    (b) 9 : 10   (d) 36 : 35
16. (a) £92.40   (c) 7 : 8
    (b) £105.60
17. (a) 9 : 41   (c) 8 : 41
    (b) 2 : 3
18. 2 : 3

Exercise 13b   page 230

1. (a) 3 : 4   (c) 2 : 3
    (b) 13 : 8   (d) 4 : 9
2. (a) all equal   (c) $\frac{2}{3} : \frac{3}{4} = 8 : 9$
    (b) all equal   (d) $1\frac{1}{2} : 2\frac{1}{2} = \frac{3}{10} : \frac{1}{2}$
3. (a) 1 : 400   (c) 1 : 7.5
    (b) 1 : 1.6   (d) 1 : 3.13
4. (a) 1 : 2 000 000   (b) 340 km
5. B
6. (a) $2\frac{2}{5}$ (c) $5\frac{1}{3}$ (e) $3\frac{1}{2}$
    (b) $3\frac{1}{2}$ (d) $3\frac{1}{3}$ (f) $4\frac{2}{3}$
7. 450   **8.** 24   **9.** 4.8 cm

Exercise 13c   page 232

1. (a) 40 kg, 8 kg   (b) 24 min, 16 min
2. (a) 64 g, 48 g, 16 g   (b) £24, £24, £36
3. 21 cm   **4.** 4.5 cm, 2 cm
5. (a) 20 cm, 15 cm   (c) 105 cm, 140 cm
    (b) 140 cm, 105 cm
6. Teresa 104 g, Dawn 96 g
7. 9, 15, 21   **8.** £2100   **9.** £124
10. (a) £5600, £6400   (c) £5800, £6200;
    (b) £5700, £6300   never
11. flour 640 g, sugar and butter 320 g, fruit 480 g
12. 48°, 60°, 72°

Exercise 13d   page 234

1. 12   **3.** £12.22
2. 468   **4.** 221 g
5. 6 hours 40 minutes
6. 320 g flour, 80 g marg, 32 g sugar, 53 g sultanas
    (to nearest gram), 100 m of milk, pinch of salt
7. 8640 km   **8.** 24 units; $6\frac{1}{4}$
9. (a) $94\frac{1}{2}$ minutes   (b) 19
10. (a) 412.5 g   (b) 23 m²
11. (a) £138.60   (b) 9 m²
12. Use 1 very large egg.
13. (a) 18 g   (c) 300 g copper, 700 g tin
    (b) 35 g

Exercise 13e   page 236

1. (a) i   (c) i   (e) i   (g) ii
    (b) ii   (d) iii   (f) iii   (h) i
2. 170 to nearest line
3. 400   **4.** $7\frac{1}{2}$
5. (a) $3\frac{3}{4}$ hours   (b) 720 mph
6. (a) 12   (b) 20
7. (a) $16\frac{2}{3}$ days   (b) 350
8. (a) 6   (b) 12 days
9. 60   **10.** 6

11. No link; babies' weight does not increase steadily.
12. (a) £270   (b) 13.5 m²
13. 63   **14.** About 3 hours   **15.** 12
16. No direct link between experience and rate of
    working.

Self-Assessment 13   page 237

1. (a) 5 : 16   (b) 1 : 120   (c) 5 : 2 : 3
2. (a) 3 : 5   (b) 1 : 4
3. (a) 7 : 8
4. (a) 1 : 15   (b) 1 : 2000
5. (a) 21   (b) 38.5
6. 4 hours; no, total time does not increase
7. Nick £300, Winston £360, Gary £180
8. (a) 120   (b) 14 kg
9. (a) 20 days   (b) 40

CHAPTER 14

Exercise 14a   page 240

1. (a) B, N62°E;   C, S35°E;   D, S56°W;   F, N77°E;
       G, N58°W
    (b) B, S62°W; C, N35°W; D, N56°E; F, S77°W;
       G, S58°E
2. (a) B, 062°;   C, 145°;   D, 236°;   F, 077°;   G, 302°
    (b) B, 242°;   C, 325°;   D, 056°;   F, 257°;   G, 122°
3. (a)

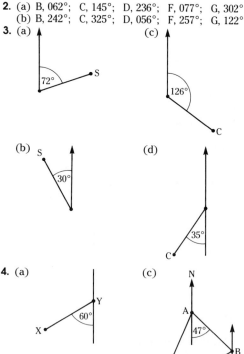

4. (a)

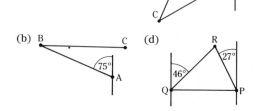

5. 38°
6. A = 46°, B = 44°, C = 90°
7. (a) 6 km on a bearing of 120°
   (b) 8 km on a bearing of 230°
   (c) 5 km on a bearing of 280°
   (d) 4 km on a bearing of 070°
8. (a) 252°   (b) 32°   (c) 036°   (d) 72°

Exercise 14b   page 242
1. (a)

   (b)

2. (a) 1 cm = 1 m   (b) 1 cm = 20 m
   (These are only suggestions; other scales could be chosen.)
3. (a) PQ, 7.6 cm; QR, 10.4 cm   (b) 65 m
4. (a) (i) 80 miles   (ii) 214°
   (b) 75 miles   (c) 067°
5. (a) 9 m   (b) 340 m
6. (a) 35°   (b) 50°   (c) (i) 42 m   (ii) 29 m
7. (b) CN = 7.1 cm, BM = 12.0 cm; 35.5 m and 60 m
   (c) 23 m
8. (a) (i) 043°   (ii) 132°   (iii) 223°
   (c) 109 miles
   (d) (i) 336°   (ii) 156°
9. (a) 2550 m from P and 1810 m from Q
   (b) 1690 m on a bearing of 237°
10. (a) (i) 8.2 cm   (ii) 328 km
   (b) (i) 120 km   (ii) 268 km
   (c) (i) 100°   (ii) 280°
   (d) (i) 232 km   (ii) 56 km
11. (a) 21 mm   (c) 4 mm   (e) 4 mm
   (b) 5 mm   (d) 8 mm

Self-Assessment 14   page 246
1. (a) (i) 078°   (ii) 143°   (iii) 323°   (iv) 258°
   (b) $\widehat{A} = 99°, \widehat{B} = 65°, \widehat{C} = 16°$
2. $\widehat{X} = 8°, \widehat{Y} = 142°, \widehat{Z} = 30°.$
3. (a) AB, 12 cm; AC, 9.5 cm;   (b) 102 m
4. 655 m
5. (b) 19.1 km   (c) 13.1 km

CHAPTER 15

Exercise 15a   page 249
1. (a) $x = 1, y = 1$ (g) $x = 2, y = 4$
   (b) $a = 2, b = 2$ (h) $p = 1, q = 0$
   (c) $a = 3, b = 5$ (i) $a = 9, b = 1$
   (d) $x = 4, y = 2$ (j) $p = 2, q = \frac{1}{2}$
   (e) $x = 3, y = 1$ (k) $a = 1, b = \frac{1}{2}$
   (f) $x = 2, y = 3$ (l) $s = 3, t = 1$
2. (a) $x = 1, y = 4$ (c) $x = 5, y = 1$
   (b) $x = 4, y = -3$ (d) $a = 3, b = 8$
3. (a) $x = 2, y = 1$ (c) $p = 4, q = 3$
   (b) $x = 5, y = \frac{1}{2}$

4. (a) $x = 3, y = -1$ (d) $a = \frac{1}{2}, b = 2$
   (b) $x = 3, y = 4$ (e) $x = \frac{10}{3}, y = 1$
   (c) $p = -\frac{3}{4}, q = \frac{1}{2}$ (f) $f = \frac{7}{2}, r = 1$
5. (a) $a = 5, b = -3$ (d) $s = 5, t = 4$
   (b) $x = 7, y = \frac{3}{2}$ (e) $u = -1, v = 4$
   (c) $p = -1, q = -2$ (f) $c = 2, d = -4$

Exercise 15b   page 251
1. (a) $x = 3, y = 1$ (f) $x = 1, y = 2$
   (b) $x = 1, y = 2$ (g) $a = 1, b = -1$
   (c) $x = \frac{1}{3}, y = 1$ (h) $x = 3, y = -1$
   (d) $a = -12, b = 27$ (i) $r = 3, s = \frac{1}{2}$
   (e) $s = 0, t = 1$
2. (a) $x = 3, y = 2$ (f) $s = 3, t = -1$
   (b) $x = 1, y = 5$ (g) $p = -1, q = 2$
   (c) $x = 3, y = 1$ (h) $x = 2, y = -2$
   (d) $x = \frac{3}{2}, y = 0$ (i) $x = 0, y = 4$
   (e) $a = 0, b = 6$
3. (a) $x = 1, y = 4$ (f) $x = 2, y = 3$
   (b) $x = -1, y = 5$ (g) $p = 0, q = -2$
   (c) $x = 3, y = -2$ (h) $a = \frac{7}{2}, b = \frac{5}{2}$
   (d) $x = 6, y = 28$ (i) $s = 1, t = -2$
   (e) $x = -1, y = -1$
4. (a) $x = 2, y = 4$ (d) $x = 2, y = 6$
   (b) $x = 5, y = 3$ (e) $x = -1, y = 5$
   (c) $x = 1, y = 10$ (f) $x = \frac{9}{2}, y = \frac{15}{2}$
5. 5 p   **8.** 13 and 25
6. 6   **9.** 82.5°
7. $\frac{5}{2}$ **10.** 14.5 cm
11. 6 and 10
12. cup: £1.40, saucer: 65 p
13. 27 years, 9 years
14. 60 m.p.h., 55 m.p.h.

Exercise 15c   page 254
1. (a) 201   (c) ±1.13
   (b) 91.6   (d) ±0.623
2. (a) ±5   (c) ±6.93
   (b) ±2.64   (d) ±2.1 (exactly)
3. (a) 5   (c) ±12
   (b) 2.24
4. (a) ±7.75   (c) ±1.69
   (b) ±24
5. (a) $x = \pm\sqrt{c - y^2}$ (d) $y = \pm\sqrt{2x^2 - g}$
   (b) $b = \pm\sqrt{a^2 - c^2}$ (e) $t = \pm\sqrt{2v/g}$
   (c) $r = \pm\sqrt{p - t}$
6. (a) $r = \pm\sqrt{A/\pi}$ (d) $t = \pm\sqrt{(a^3 - R)/a}$
   (b) $r = \pm\sqrt{V/\pi h}$ (e) $y = \pm\sqrt{x^2 - z^2}$
   (c) $y = \pm\sqrt{5 - x^2}$
7. (a) $q = p^2/2$ (d) $c = b^2 - a$
   (b) $y = 4x^2$ (e) $t = v^2/r$
   (c) $r = q^2/p^2$
8. (a) $c = (b - a)^2$ (d) $c = \pm\sqrt{a^2 - b^2}$
   (b) $t = 3 - V^2$ (e) $z = (x - \frac{1}{2}y)^2$
   (c) $x = \pm\sqrt{H^2 - 4}$

9. (a) 942 cm^3
 (b) $h = V/\pi r^2$
 (c) 0.978
 (d) $r = \sqrt{V/\pi h}$, r cannot be negative, 1.49
10. (a) 8.94
 (b) 1.42 m
 (c) 20 (a cannot be negative)
 (d) $a = \sqrt{d^2 - b^2}$

Exercise 15d   page 256

1. $x = a - b$
2. $x = q - p$
3. $x = a + 2b$
4. $x = a/3$
5. $x = (c - ab)/a$
6. $x = ac/b$
7. $x = rcd/a$
8. $x = q^2/p^2$
9. $x = \pm\sqrt{a - b}$
10. $x = \pm\sqrt{r^2 - y^2}$
11. $x = \pm\sqrt{b/a}$
12. $x = bp^2/a^2$
13. $x = \pm\sqrt{a^2 - v^2/\omega^2}$
14. $x = (c - d - a)^2$

Self-Assessment 15   page 257

1. $x = 10, y = 1$
2. $x = 2, y = 2$
3. $x = (4y + ay)/a$
4. (a) 3.97
 (b) 4.92 seconds
 (c) $g = 4\pi^2 L/T^2$
5. (a) 4.69
 (b) 3.3 m
 (c) 20.4 cm
 (d) $a = \sqrt{(d^2 - b^2 - c^2)}$
6. James £11, Thomas £13

CHAPTER 17

Exercise 17a   page 264

1. 18, 22; add 4 to previous term.
2. 8, 5; take 3 from previous term.
3. 324, 972; multiply previous term by 3.
4. 2, 1; divide previous term by 2.
5. 11, 16; add one more than was added to obtain the previous term.
6. 21, 31; add 2, 4, 6, 8, ... to the previous term.
7. 8, -16, 32, ...
8. 6, 8, 10, ...
9. $1, \frac{1}{2}, \frac{1}{4}, \ldots$
10. 8, 14, 22, ...
11. 6, 10, 16, ...
17. 6, 18, 54, 162, ...
18. 5, 7, 9, 11, ...
19. $-4, -6, -8, -10, \ldots$
20. 3.316 ..., 2.305 ..., 2.075 ..., 2.018, ...
21. $u_{n+1} = u_n + 4$; $u_{n+1} = u_n - 3$; $u_{n+1} = 3u_n$;
 $u_{n+1} = \dfrac{u_n}{2}$
22. nth term $= 3 + 5(n - 1) = 5n - 2$; 23, 28, ..., 48
23. nth term $= n^2$; 25, 36, ..., 100
24. nth term $= 2 \times 3^{n-1}$; 162, 486, ..., 39366
25. nth term $= \dfrac{1}{n}$; $\frac{1}{5}, \frac{1}{6}, \ldots, \frac{1}{10}$
26. nth term $= \dfrac{1}{2^{n-1}}$; $\frac{1}{16}, \frac{1}{32}, \ldots, \frac{1}{512}$
27. n^{th} term $= n(n + 1)$; 30, 42, ..., 110
28. n^{th} term $= 6(11 - n)$; 36, 30, ..., 6
29. n^{th} term $= 2n^2 + 1$; 73, 99, ..., 201

12. 4, 6, 8, 10, ..., 22
13. 2, 4, 8, 16, ..., 1024
14. 3, 6, 12, 24, ..., 1536
15. 0, 2, 6, 12, ..., 90
16. 0, 1, 4, 9, ..., 81

Exercise 17b   page 266

1. 46, 62
2. 47, 73
3. 437, 683
4. 6, 28
5. 324, 539
6. e.g. multiply previous term by 3; 54, 162, 486
 or add 8 more than previously added; 38; 66, 102
7. e.g. add 3 times the previous addition; 13, 40, 121
 or nth term $= (n - 1)^2$; 9, 16, 25
8. e.g. multiply previous term by 2; 24, 48, 96
 or add 3 more than previously added; 21, 33, 48
9. 4, 5, 6; n^{th} term $= n$ or add together the previous 2 terms; 5, 8, 13
10. 125, 216, 343, ...; nth term $= n^3$
11. $\frac{5}{6}, \frac{6}{7}, \frac{7}{8}, \ldots$; nth term $= \dfrac{n}{(n+1)}$
12. 16, 27, 43, using a difference table
13. 24, 35, 48; add 2 more than added to obtain previous term.
14. $-241, -1265, -5361$; subtract 4 times the number subtracted to obtain the previous term.
15. 5.7, 6.8, 7.9; add 1.1 to previous term.
16. 6, 2, 7; odd terms are all 2; for even terms add 1 to previous even term.
17. 13, 17, 19; prime numbers.
18. 16, -32, 64; $u_n = (-2)^{n-1}$
19. 37, 50, 65; $u_n = n^2 + 1$
20. 19, 23; add 4 to previous term.
21. nth term $= 4n - 1$
22. $4n$ is even so $4n + 1$ is odd.
23. 21, 77, 165, 285, 437, ...
24. 621, 837
25. 10, 18, 26, 34, 42, ...
26. nth term $= 8n + 2$
27. (a) 3, 10, 21, 36, 55, ...
 (b) 3, 5, 7, 9, 11, ...
 (c) nth term $= 2n + 1$
 (d) nth term $= n(2n + 1)$
28. no
29. yes, 1
30. no
31. no
32. yes, 3.1622...
33. yes, 1
34. yes, 2

Exercise 17c   page 268

1. (a) 1, 3, 4, 7, 11, 18, ...
 (b) 2, 3, 5, 8, 13, 21, ...
 (c) 1, 4, 5, 9, 14, 23, ...
2. 1   3   4   7   11   18
    2   1   3   4   7
 Apart from the first term, 1st differences form the same sequence.
3. (a) 1, 1, 2, 3, 5, 8, 13, 21, ...
 (b) $1, \frac{1}{2}, \frac{2}{3}, \frac{3}{5}, \frac{5}{8}, \ldots$
 (c) 1, 0.5, 0.6667, 0.6, 0.625, 0.6154, 0.6190, ...
 Converges (to 0.6180 ...)
5. 1, 11, 121, 1331, 14641, ...
 Second 10 in sixth line represents number of 100s in 10^5, so 0 appears in hundreds column and 1 must be carried to next column.
6. (a) 81, 9801, 998 001, 99 980 001
 (b) 9 999 800 001

Exercise 17d   page 271

1. (b) 4, 8, 12, 16, 20, ...
 (c) nth term $= 4n$

2. (a) 4, 7, 10, 13, 16, ...
   (c) nth term $= 3n + 1$
3. (b) 1, 3, 6, 10, 15, 21, ...
   (c) nth term $= \frac{1}{2}n(n + 1)$
4. 30, 55; nth term $= 1^2 + 2^2 + 3^2 + \ldots + n^2$
5. 3, 12, 48, 192, 768, ...; $u_1 = 3, u_{n+1} = 4u_n$
   or $u_n = 3 \times 4^{n-1}$
6. 1, 4, 10, 20, 35, ...; $u_1 = 1$,
   $u_n = u_{n-1} + \frac{1}{2}n(n + 1)$
   (u_n = sum of first n triangular numbers.)
7. 2, 4, 6, 8, 10, ...; nth term $= 2n$
8. 2, 4, 7, 11, 16, ...; add 1 more than was added
   to obtain the previous term, or
   nth term $= \frac{1}{2}n(n + 1) + 1$
9. (b) With 2 tiles in the middle of an edge, number
   of tiles along an edge must be even. 4 cm is
   the smallest.

   (c)

4	6	8	10	12
12	16	20	24	28

   (d) $2(n + 2)$
   (e) n^2; $n^2 - 2n - 4$

Self-Assessment 17   page 273
1. 35, 48, ...; add 2 more than was added to obtain
   the previous term.
2. 3, 8, 13, 18, ...
3. 7, 15, 31, 63, ...
4. nth term $= 4n - 5$
5. 1
6. 117, 182
7. 0, 2, 5, 9, 14, 20, 27, ...

CHAPTER 18

Exercise 18a   page 275
1. (a) $\sqrt{20}$ (c) $\sqrt{68}$
   (b) 5   (d) $\sqrt{45}$
2. (a) $(4, 4)$ (c) $(6, 5)$
   (b) $(0, 2\frac{1}{2})$ (d) $(-4\frac{1}{2}, -1)$
3. (a) -2 (c) 4
   (b) $-\frac{3}{4}$ (d) -2
4. 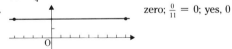   zero; $\frac{0}{11} = 0$; yes, 0

5. 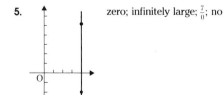   zero; infinitely large; $\frac{7}{0}$; no

6. (a) ‖ to x-axis   (c) ‖ to x-axis
   (b) ‖ to y-axis   (d) not ‖ to either.

Exercise 18b   page 277
1. (a)   (c)

   (b) 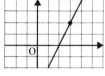   (d)

2. (a) 5   (b) -7 (c) 1   (d) 4
3. (a) -1 (c) 3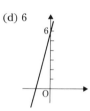

   (b) 3   (d) 6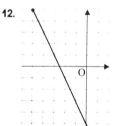

4. (a) $y = 2x + 6$ (c) $y = -3x + 2$
   (b) $y = 4x - 1$ (d) $y = x$
5. (a) (i) $-1, 3$ (ii) $x + y = 3$
   (b) (i) $2, 2$ (ii) $y = 2x + 2$
   (c) (i) $1, -2$ (ii) $y = x - 2$
   (d) (i) $-\frac{1}{2}, -1$ (ii) $2y + x + 2 = 0$
6. (a) 38   (b) -32 (c) -4
7. (a) 2   (b) -1 (c) $\frac{5}{7}$
8. (a) yes   (c) no
   (b) no   (d) yes.
9. (a) 9, 6   (c) 5, $6\frac{2}{3}$
   (b) 15, $-7\frac{1}{2}$ (d) $-3\frac{3}{5}, 4\frac{1}{2}$

10.   **12.**

11.

13. (a) $2y = x + 5$ (c) $y = 3x$
   (b) $y + x = 5$ (d) $2y + x = 14$

Exercise 18c   page 280

1. −1;

2. 1;

3. $4x + 7y = 28$

4. (a) $\frac{1}{3}$, −2

(b) $-\frac{3}{4}$, 2

(c) $-\frac{1}{3}$, 2

(d) 2, −7

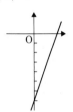

(e) −3, −1

(f) $\frac{1}{4}$, $\frac{1}{2}$

5. (a) $-\frac{3}{4}$

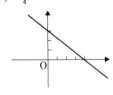

(b) $-\frac{3}{5}$

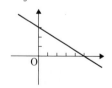

(d) −2

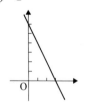

(e) 2

(c) $\frac{1}{2}$

(f) $\frac{3}{4}$

6. (a) $(2, 0)$ and $(0, 4)$ (b) $(12, 0)$ and $(0, -9)$

7. (a) $\frac{x}{6} + \frac{y}{5} = 1$ (b) $\frac{x}{4} - \frac{y}{3} = 1$

8.   ; −1

9. (a) $\frac{x}{3} + \frac{y}{8} = 1$; $m = -\frac{8}{3}$

(b) $\frac{x}{2} + \frac{y}{2} = 1$; $m = -1$

10. (a) $\frac{y}{4} - x = 1$; $m = 4$

(b) $\frac{x}{3} + \frac{y}{7} + 1 = 0$; $m = -\frac{7}{3}$

11. (a) $y = 5x - 21$ (b) $5x + 2y = 19$
12. (a) $5y = x - 6$ (b) $y + x = 3$
13. $y = 2x + 3$ and $y = 4 + 2x$
14. $2x + y = 2$ and $y = 7 - 2x$; $m = -2$
    $3y - 4x = 5$ and $4x = 3y$; $m = \frac{4}{3}$
15. (a) $y = 2x \pm$ any number
    (b) $5x - 2y \pm$ any number $= 0$
    (c) $2x = \pm$ any number $- 3y$
16. (a) $y = 4x + 4$ (c) $2y - x = 8$
    (b) $y + 3x = 4$
17. $y = 5 - 2x$; $m = -2$, $c = 5$; $y = 5x - 2$;
    $m = 5$, $c = -2$; $y + 2x + 2 = 0$
18. $k = 1\frac{1}{2}$

Exercise 18d   page 284

1. $\frac{1}{4}$

2. −1

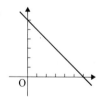

3. $-\frac{3}{5}$

4. 2

5.

6.

7.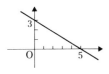

8.

9.

10.

Exercise 18e   page 285

1. $x = 1\frac{1}{2},\ y = 3\frac{1}{2}$ **2.** $x = -\frac{1}{2},\ y = 1\frac{1}{2}$
3. The lines are parallel.
5. e.g. $2 \leqslant x \leqslant 4,\ -1 \leqslant y \leqslant 1$
   ($x \approx 2.7,\ y \approx 0.2$)

Exercise 18f   page 286

1. (a) 84 km/h   (c) 116 km/h
   (b) 62 m.p.h.   (d) 32 m.p.h.
2. (a) £46   (c) £83
   (b) $91   (d) $168
3. (a) 77 °C   (b) 95 °F; 32 °F
4. (a) speed   (c) $3\frac{1}{2}$ hours
   (b) 22.5 km
5. (a) 49%, 88%   (b) 53

Exercise 18g   page 289

1. (a) (i) 9
       (ii) number of francs per pound
   (b) (i) 0.085
       (ii) cost in £/unit
   (c) (i) 17.5
       (ii) rise in temperature per minute
   (d) (i) −0.33
       (ii) number of litres consumed per mile
2. (a) (i) 1 200 000 gallons
       (ii) 5 days
   (b) −100 000; number of gallons used per day
   (c) 1 500 000; number of gallons in reservoir on
       1st day
3. (a) A, 0.055; B, 0.036; cost in £/unit
   (b) A, 12; B, 32; standing charge
   (c) (i) A   (ii) B
4. (a) 0.044, 22   (c) £22
   (b) 4.4 p

Self-Assessment 18   page 290

1. (a) (i) 13   (ii) $(3\frac{1}{2}, 3)$ (iii) $-\frac{12}{5}$
   (b) (i) 10   (ii) $(1, 1)$ (iii) $-\frac{4}{3}$
2. (a)   (b)

 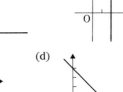

   (c)   (d)

3. (a) −4, 4   (b) $1\frac{1}{2}$, 3   (c) $-\frac{1}{2}$, −2
4. (a) $y = 2x - 9$ (c) $y = 3x$
   (b) $3y + 4x = 12$
5. $3y + 4x = 5$
6. (a) 2   (b) −9   (c) $\frac{5}{3}$
7.

$x = 1, y = 3$

8. (a) 100.64 DM   (b) £72.64
9. (a) £115   (b) $\frac{1}{2}$; cost per page
   (c) production costs before printing

CHAPTER 19

Exercise 19a   page 293

1.   no

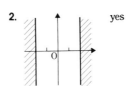

2.   yes

3.   no

4. 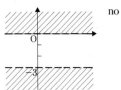 no

5. 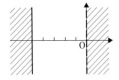 no

6. 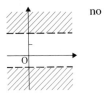 yes

7. $x \leqslant 2$, yes
8. $y < 3$, no
9. $x < -1$, no
10. $-2 \leqslant y \leqslant 2$, no
11. $-\frac{1}{2} < y < 2\frac{1}{2}$, no

12. $-1 \leqslant x < 2$, yes
13. $-3 \leqslant x \leqslant 1$
14. $-4 < y < -1$
15. $3 \leqslant x \leqslant 6$

16.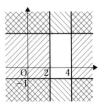

17.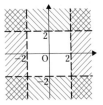

18.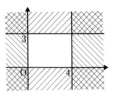

19.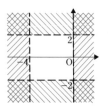

20.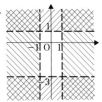

21.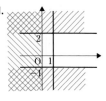

22. $-2 \leqslant x \leqslant 3$, $-1 \leqslant y \leqslant 2$
23. $-2 \leqslant x \leqslant 1$, $y \geqslant -1$
24. $-2 < x \leqslant 2$, $-2 \leqslant y \leqslant 1$
25. $x \geqslant -2$, $y \leqslant -1$

Exercise 19b   page 296

1.

2.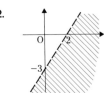

3.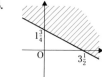

4.

5.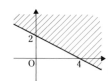

6.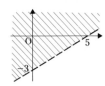

7. $2y - 3x \leqslant 6$

8. $x + y < 2$

9. $x + y > 3$

10. $2x + y + 4 > 0$

11.

12.

13.

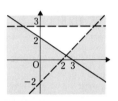

14.

15.

16. Does not exist

17. (a) Region consists of only one point $(1, 2)$.

    (b) Does not exist

Exercise 19c   page 299

1.

2.

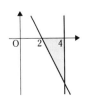

3.

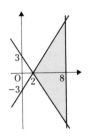

4.

5.

6. $y \geqslant 0,\ \ 2y \leqslant x + 2,\ \ x + y \leqslant 4$

7. $x \leqslant 1,\ \ y \leqslant x + 1,\ \ 3x + y > -3$

8. $y < 3x + 3,\ \ y > 3x - 3$

9. $y \geqslant 0,\ \ y \leqslant x + 2$

10. (a) $x + y + 4 \geqslant 0,\ \ 3y \leqslant x,\ \ y \geqslant x - 4$

    (b) $3y \geqslant x,\ \ y \leqslant x - 4$

    (c) $3y \leqslant x,\ \ y \leqslant x - 4,\ \ x + y + 4 \geqslant 0$

    (d) $x + y + 4 \leqslant 0,\ \ 3y \geqslant x$

    (e) $3y \leqslant x,\ \ y \geqslant x - 4$

    (f) $x + y + 4 \geqslant 0,\ \ y \geqslant x - 4$

11. (a) C   (b) A   (c) B

12. (a) $(2, 2), (-2, 4), (-2, -2)$

    (b) $(2, 3), (-1, 0), (0, -2)$

13. $(-1, 0), (-1, 1), (-1, 2), (-1, 3), (0, -1),$

    $(0, 0), (0, 1), (0, 2), (0, 3), (1, 0), (1, 1), (1, 2),$

    $(2, 1)$

14. $(2, -1), (2, 0), (2, 1), (2, 2), (3, 1), (4, 0),$

    $(5, -1), (4, -1), (3, -1)$

Exercise 19d   page 302

1. (a) $(-2, 5), (-2, 2), (4, 1)$

    (b) $(-2, 5)$

    (c) $(-2, 2)$

    (d) $(-2, 3), (-2, 4), (-1, 2), (-1, 3), (-1, 4),$

        $(0, 2), (0, 3), (1, 2), (1, 3), (2, 2)$

    (e) no

    (f) no

2. (a) $(-2, -1), (0, 3), (3, -1), (3, 3)$

    (b) $(3, 3)$

    (c) $(-2, -1)$

    (d) $(-1, -1), (0, -1), (1, -1), (2, -1),$

        $(-1, 0), (0, 0), (1, 0), (2, 0), (3, 0),$

        $(-1, 1), (0, 1), (1, 1), (2, 1), (3, 1), (0, 2),$

        $(1, 2), (2, 2), (3, 2), (1, 3), (2, 3)$

    (e) no

    (f) no

3. $(1, 2)$ **5.** $(2, -1)$

4. $(2, 2)$ **6.** $(0, 3)$; no

Exercise 19e   page 304

1. $2x + 2y \leqslant 20$, $xy \geqslant 12$

2. $x \geqslant 2y$, $x + \frac{1}{2}y < 100$

3. $3x + 4y < 45$, $y \leqslant x$

4. Barbara p years old, Christa q years old.
  (a) $p = 3q$, $p + q < 20$
  (b) 1, 2, 3 or 4 years old

5. (a) $x \geqslant 100$, $y \geqslant 200$; $\frac{3}{2}x + y \leqslant 600$ or
    $3x + 2y \leqslant 1200$
  (b) 550

6. $x > 2y$, $y \geqslant 2$, $30x + 40y \leqslant 500$
  (a) 4 pens, 9, 10 or 11 pencils
    (points on $2y = x$ are not in the region)
  (b) 14 pencils and 2 pens

7. b bungalows and m maisonettes
    $5b + 4m \leqslant 80$, $2b + m \geqslant 15$, $b \geqslant 5$;
    18 (5 or 6 or 7 or 8 bungalows)

8. (c) 58 spectacular and 20 super

Self-Assessment 19   page 307

1. (a) $y \geqslant 2$ (b) $x < -2$ and $x \geqslant 1$

2. (a)   (b)

3. (a) $-4 \leqslant x \leqslant 3$ and $-2 < y < 3$
  (b) $x > -2$ and $-1 \leqslant y \leqslant 2$

4.

5.

6. $y + 2x > -3$, $y + x \leqslant 0$, $3x - 2y \leqslant 6$

7. $(-2, 2), (-1, 0), (-1, 1), (0, 0), (0, -1),$
    $(0, -2), (1, -1)$

8.

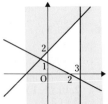

9. 21; 3

10. (a) $8x + 5y \leqslant 500$, $x \geqslant 2y$, $x \geqslant 20$
  (c) 88

CHAPTER 20

Exercise 20a   page 309

1. 0.7536	**7.** 2.3°	**13.** 60.6°
2. 3.1910	**8.** 75.7°	**14.** 43.0°
3. 0.1139	**9.** no	**15.** 42.0°
4. 0.6346	**10.** 35.0°	**16.** 49.4°
5. 36.9°	**11.** 40.6°	**17.** 43.1°
6. 55.5°	**12.** 53.1°	**18.** 1

Exercise 20b   page 311

1. 4.69 cm	**6.** 3.70 cm
2. 3.56 cm	**7.** 4.41 cm
3. 0.918 cm	**8.** 43.3 cm
4. 13.9 cm	**9.** 9.60 cm
5. 9.02 cm	**10.** 30.4 m

11. (a) about 570 m (±30 m)   (b) (ii)

12. 24.0°   **15.** 39.8°

13. 36.9°   **16.** 5.96 cm, 29.8 cm²

14. 10.2 km   **17.** 112.6°

18. (a) 3.16, 6.32, 7.07   (c) 26.6°
  (b) $\hat{B} = 90°$

Exercise 20c   page 314

1. (a) 0.9703   (b) 0.1959   (c) 0.3827

2. (a) 0.4384   (b) 0.8517   (c) 0.9986

3. (a) 47.0°   (b) 67.8°   (c) 17.5°

4. (a) 83.1°   (b) 67.4°   (c) 63.6°

5. (a) $\frac{6}{10}$; 36.9°   (b) $\frac{12}{13}$; 67.4°

6. (a) $\frac{16}{20}$; 36.9°   (b) $\frac{8}{17}$; 61.9°

7. (a) sine   (c) cosine
  (b) sine   (d) sine

8. (a) 44.4°   (c) 49.5°
  (b) 54.3°   (d) 64.8°

9. Between 0 and 1 for angles in right-angled
    triangles.

10. (cos) 53.1°   **13.** (sin) 48.2°

11. (tan) 49.1°   **14.** (sin) 45.6°

12. (cos) 60°   **15.** (tan) 50.3°

16. $\tan A = \frac{3}{4}$, $\sin A = \frac{3}{5}$, $\cos A = \frac{4}{5}$

17. (a) $\sin 30° = \frac{1}{2}$, $\cos 30° = \frac{\sqrt{3}}{2}$, $\tan 30° = \frac{1}{\sqrt{3}}$
  (b) $\sin 60° = \frac{\sqrt{3}}{2}$, $\cos 60° = \frac{1}{2}$, $\tan 60° = \sqrt{3}$

18. 47.6°

Exercise 20d   page 316

1. 6.71 cm	**10.** 6.16 cm
2. 2.10 cm	**11.** 15.8 cm
3. 2.94 cm	**12.** 7.77 cm
4. 4.72 cm	**13.** 7.21 cm
5. 12.5 cm	**14.** 14.9 cm
6. 2.55 cm	**15.** 8.15 cm
7. 84.9 cm	**16.** 15.1 cm
8. 2.90 cm	**17.** 10.3 cm
9. 18.1 cm	

Exercise 20e   page 318

1. 112.6°   **2.** (a) 5.22 cm (b) 7.95 cm

3. (a) 24°
  (b) (i) 2.23 cm (ii) 5.47 cm
  (c) (i) 90°, 42° (ii) 4.07 cm
  (d) 4.07 cm, yes

4. 112 m   **5.** 23.6°

6. (a) 56.3°   (b) 7.21 miles   (c) 348.7°
7. 24.4 m
8. (a) 44.4°   (b) 105.6°
9. (a) 32.0 km   (c) N26.3°W
     (b) 64.6 km   (d) 72.1 km
10. (a) 9.42 cm   (b) 10.2 cm   (c) 7.36 cm
11. (a) 17.4 ft   (b) 12.2 ft   (c) 38.1 ft
12. 79.7°   **13.** 0.75 m
14. (a) 2.61 m   (b) 1.49 m
15. (a) 104°   (b) 7.88 miles   (c) 073°
16. (a) 18.5 m, 29.5 m, 11 m
     (b) 23.6 m, 5.21 m, 28.8 m
     (c) 69° with the horizontal
17. (a) 32.0°   (b) 63.4°
18. (a) 14.14 cm, 7.07 cm
     (b) 53.9°
     (c) yes, to 4 s.f.; 9.695 cm
     (d) 62.7°
19. (a) 8.06 cm   (d) e.g. FB
     (b) 29.7°   (e) e.g. BE or AF
     (c) 19.3°

Exercise 20f   page 324

1. (a) $E\hat{A}F$ (b) $E\hat{G}F$ (c) 55.6°, 64.1°
2. (a) $D\hat{F}H$ (b) $F\hat{D}E$
3. (a) $F\hat{A}C$ (b) $A\hat{E}B$ (c) 23.2°, 50.2°

Exercise 20g   page 326

1. 51.3°   **3.** 39.8°   **5.** 62.7°
2. 33.7°   **4.** 38.7°   **6.** 120°

Self-Assessment 20   page 327

1. 0.8517, 0.5240, 1.625
2. (a) 67.5°   (b) 47.8°
3. 49.7°   **4.** 9.40 cm   **5.** 64.6°
6. (a) 35.4 miles   (c) 258.7°
     (b) 7.07 miles
7. (a) 21.8°   (b) 63.4°
8. (a) 4.60 cm   (b) (i) 1.93 cm   (ii) 1.07 cm
     (c) 130°   (d) OA = OC (radii)   (e) 5.44 cm
9. 1.44 cm

CHAPTER 21

Exercise 21a   page 329

1. (a) $x^2 - 2x$ (g) $4s^2 + 10s$
     (b) $6x - 3x^2$ (h) $-x^2 - 2xy$
     (c) $10x - 6x^2$ (i) $2x^2 + 2xy$
     (d) $2a^2 - 5a$ (j) $-2pq + 3p^2$
     (e) $2p - 2p^2$ (k) $2a^2 - 4ab$
     (f) $10a - 15a^2$ (l) $12st - 8s^2$
2. (a) $x^2 - x + 6$ (d) $2ab + 2ac - 2b - 4c$
     (b) $3x^2 - 17x - 24$ (e) $-3x$
     (c) $2x - x^2$ (f) $4x - 3x^2$
3. (a) $x^2 + 5x + 6$
     (b) $x^2 + 2x - 8$
     (c) $2x^2 - 7x - 15$
     (d) $6x^2 + 14x + 4$
     (e) $2x^2 - 17x + 21$

     (f) $a^2 + ab - ac - bc$
     (g) $ps - pt + qs - qt$
     (h) $x^2 - 2xz - xy + 2yz$
     (i) $x^2 - 5xy + 6y^2$
     (j) $a^2 + ab - 2b^2$
     (k) $4p^2 - q^2$
     (l) $6x^2 + 3xz + 4xy + 2yz$
4. (a) $x^2 + 5x + 4$ (e) $t^2 + 10t + 21$
     (b) $x^2 + 3x + 2$ (f) $p^2 + 7p + 10$
     (c) $a^2 + 6a + 5$ (g) $x^2 + 14x + 48$
     (d) $a^2 + 8a + 15$ (h) $x^2 + 13x + 30$
5. (a) $x^2 - 5x + 6$ (e) $s^2 - 9s + 20$
     (b) $x^2 - 7x + 12$ (f) $x^2 - 13x + 42$
     (c) $x^2 - 7x + 10$ (g) $p^2 - 10p + 24$
     (d) $a^2 - 5a + 4$ (h) $t^2 - 12t + 32$
6. (a) $x^2 + 4x - 12$ (f) $p^2 - 2p - 15$
     (b) $x^2 + x - 6$ (g) $a^2 - 4a - 21$
     (c) $x^2 - x - 12$ (h) $x^2 + 5x - 36$
     (d) $x^2 + 2x - 15$ (i) $x^2 + 4x - 21$
     (e) $t^2 - 2t - 48$ (j) $y^2 - y - 2$

Exercise 21b   page 330

1. (a) $x^2 + 9x + 20$ (e) $a^2 + 12a + 35$
     (b) $y^2 + 10y + 9$ (f) $x^2 - 8x + 12$
     (c) $p^2 - 10p + 24$ (g) $s^2 + 11s + 24$
     (d) $x^2 - 10x + 21$ (h) $x^2 + 16x + 63$
2. (a) $x^2 + 4x - 21$ (e) $x^2 - 2x - 8$
     (b) $a^2 + a - 20$ (f) $s^2 + 4s - 45$
     (c) $t^2 - 3t - 18$ (g) $b^2 + 4b - 5$
     (d) $x^2 + 2x - 48$ (h) $x^2 - 7x - 8$
3. (a) $x^2 - 3x - 54$ (e) $x^2 - 5x - 36$
     (b) $b^2 + 4b + 3$ (f) $a^2 + 11a + 30$
     (c) $y^2 - 14y + 48$ (g) $t^2 - 12t + 35$
     (d) $x^2 + x - 30$ (h) $x^2 + 11x + 24$
4. (a) $2x^2 + 7x + 3$ (f) $12y^2 - 23y + 5$
     (b) $6a^2 + 13a + 5$ (g) $20x^2 + 23x + 6$
     (c) $2t^2 - 7t + 6$ (h) $7t^2 + 19t + 10$
     (d) $3x^2 - 23x + 30$ (i) $6x^2 - 31x + 40$
     (e) $2x^2 - 17x + 35$
5. (a) $3x^2 - x - 10$ (f) $14x^2 - 3x - 5$
     (b) $6x^2 - 19x - 7$ (g) $35x^2 - 2x - 1$
     (c) $4s^2 - 4s - 15$ (h) $15x^2 + 2x - 1$
     (d) $8x^2 + 22x - 21$ (i) $4a^2 - 25$
     (e) $9x^2 - 1$
6. (a) $15t^2 + 19t + 6$ (f) $5 + 7y + 2y^2$
     (b) $12x^2 + 23x - 24$ (g) $24 - 34x - 3x^2$
     (c) $16x^2 - 38x - 5$ (h) $10 + x - 2x^2$
     (d) $10a^2 - 41a + 21$ (i) $24 - 38y + 15y^2$
     (e) $6 - 5x + x^2$
7. (a) $10x^2 - 79x + 132$ (c) $10a^2 + 115a - 60$
     (b) $6p^2 + 11p - 30$ (d) $18 + 89x + 36x^2$

Exercise 21c   page 331

1. (a) $x^2 + 2x + 1$ (e) $x^2 + 2xy + y^2$
     (b) $x^2 + 4x + 4$ (f) $a^2 + 2ab + b^2$
     (c) $y^2 + 8y + 16$ (g) $p^2 + 2pq + q^2$
     (d) $a^2 + 14a + 49$ (h) $x^2 + 16x + 64$

2. (a) $x^2 - 2x + 1$
(b) $x^2 - 10x + 25$
(c) $t^2 - 18t + 81$
(d) $p^2 - 12p + 36$
(e) $x^2 - 2xy + y^2$
(f) $a^2 - 2ab + b^2$
(g) $y^2 - 14y + 49$
(h) $x^2 - 18x + 81$

3. (a) $x^2 - 1$
(b) $x^2 - 16$
(c) $c^2 - 4$
(d) $y^2 - 25$
(e) $x^2 - y^2$
(f) $a^2 - b^2$
(g) $x^2 - 49$
(h) $t^2 - 36$

4. (a) $9x^2 + 6x + 1$
(b) $25x^2 - 20x + 4$
(c) $9y^2 + 12y + 4$
(d) $4x^2 - 4x + 1$
(e) $4a^2 - 12a + 9$
(f) $9x^2 - 6x + 1$
(g) $16x^2 + 24x + 9$
(h) $25p^2 + 20p + 4$

5. (a) $4x^2 - 49$
(b) $9x^2 - 1$
(c) $16x^2 - 25$
(d) $4a^2 - 49$
(e) $16t^2 - 9$
(f) $4a^2 - 25b^2$

6. (a) $2x^2 + 9x + 8$
(b) $3x^2 + x + 4$
(c) $2x^2 - 4$
(d) $7x^2 + 22x + 1$

7. (a) $6 + x - x^2$
(b) $7x - 3 - 2x^2$
(c) $9 - 6x + x^2$
(d) $9x - 2x^2 - 4$
(e) $28 + 2t - 6t^2$
(f) $4 - 12a + 9a^2$
(g) $9 - 4x^2$
(h) $12a - 3a^2 - 12$
(i) $4 - 9x^2$
(j) $6xy - y^2 - 5x^2$
(k) $s^2 - st - 6t^2$
(l) $4xy - 4x^2 - y^2$

8. (a) $x^2y^2 - 2xyz + z^2$
(b) $p^2 + 2pqr + q^2r^2$
(c) $p^2q^2 - 2pqr + r^2$
(d) $a^2 - 2abc + b^2c^2$
(e) $x^2y^2 - z^2$
(f) $a^2b^2 - c^2$
(g) $a^2b^2 + 2abcd + c^2d^2$
(h) $x^2y^2 - w^2z^2$

9. (a) $18 - 8\sqrt{2}$ (c) 1
(b) $7 + 4\sqrt{3}$ (d) -4
(e) $8 + \sqrt{7}$

10. (a) $9x^2 - 6ax + a^2$ (b) $a = 2, q = -12$

11. $p = 3, q = 2$ (or -2)

Exercise 21d   page 333

1. (a) $3(x + 2)$
(b) $4(y - 2)$
(c) $3(2a - 3)$
(d) $2(a + 2b)$
(e) $5(2p - 1)$
(f) $4(2 - 3x)$
(g) $3(2 - 5a)$
(h) $2(a + 2b)$
(i) $3(4x - 3y)$
(j) $2(4q - 9p)$

2. (a) $x(x + 3)$
(b) $b(b + 6)$
(c) $y(y - 2)$
(d) $x(3x + 2)$
(e) $a(4 - a)$
(f) $x(x - 4)$
(g) $b(4b - 1)$
(h) $p(1 - p)$

3. (a) $3(x^2 + 2x + 3)$
(b) $5(2x^2 - x - 4)$
(c) $4(4 - 3x - 5x^2)$
(d) $x(5y - 2z + 3)$
(e) $a(b - 2c + 4d)$
(f) $3y(y^2 + 2y - 3)$

4. (a) $2x(x - 2)$
(b) $5x(y + 2z)$
(c) $x^2(1 + x)$
(d) $4bc(2a - 3d)$
(e) $3y(x + 2y - 3)$
(f) $5b(a + 2c - d)$
(g) $x^2(a - b)$
(h) $\frac{1}{2}h(a - b)$
(i) $r(\pi r + 4 + r)$
(j) $ax(x + a)$

5. (a) $m(g - a)$
(b) $\pi r(2 + h)$
(c) $\pi(R^2 - r^2)$
(d) $2r(h_1 - h_2)$
(e) $\frac{1}{2}m(u^2 - v^2)$
(f) $\pi r(2h + r)$
(k) $P\left(1 + \dfrac{RT}{100}\right)$
(l) $m(gh - \frac{1}{2}v^2)$

Exercise 21e   page 335

1. (a) $(x + 1)(x + 2)$
(b) $(x + 1)(x + 4)$
(c) $(x + 3)^2$
(d) $(x + 2)(x + 6)$
(e) $(x + 1)(x + 7)$
(f) $(x + 1)(x + 15)$
(g) $(x + 3)(x + 6)$
(h) $(x + 10)((x + 2)$

2. (a) $(x - 1)(x - 3)$
(b) $(x - 1)(x - 5)$
(c) $(x - 1)^2$
(d) $(x - 1)(x - 6)$
(e) $(x - 3)(x - 4)$
(f) $(x - 3)(x - 5)$
(g) $(x - 5)(x - 6)$
(h) $(x - 9)(x - 2)$

3. (a) $(x - 3)(x + 2)$
(b) $(x + 3)(x - 2)$
(c) $(x - 4)(x + 1)$
(d) $(x + 5)(x - 4)$
(e) $(x + 5)(x - 2)$
(f) $(x + 3)(x - 4)$
(g) $(x - 6)(x + 4)$
(h) $(x - 10)(x + 2)$
(i) $(x + 9)(x - 2)$
(j) $(x + 12)(x - 5)$

4. (a) $(x - 7)(x - 2)$
(b) $(x + 6)(x - 3)$
(c) $(x + 5)(x + 4)$
(d) $(x + 6)(x - 1)$
(e) $(x - 5)(x + 2)$
(f) $(x + 1)(x + 5)$
(g) $(x - 7)(x + 2)$
(h) $(x - 5)^2$
(i) $(x - 2)(x - 13)$
(j) $(x + 3)(x + 8)$

Exercise 21f   page 336

1. (a) $(2x - 1)(x - 1)$
(b) $(3x + 2)(x + 2)$
(c) $(3x - 2)(x - 1)$
(d) $(4x + 3)(x + 1)$
(e) $(x - 3)^2$
(f) $(5x - 2)(x - 3)$
(g) $(2x + 1)(x - 2)$
(h) $(3x + 4)(x - 1)$
(i) $(7x + 2)(x - 3)$
(j) $(6x + 5)(x - 2)$
(k) $(x - 7)^2$
(l) $(4x - 3)(x + 5)$

2. (a) $(x - 5)(x + 5)$
(b) $(x - 1)(x + 1)$
(c) $(x - 4)(x + 4)$
(d) $(2x - 5)(2x + 5)$
(e) $(6 - x)(6 + x)$
(f) $(x - y)(x + y)$
(g) $(3x - 2)(3x + 2)$
(h) $(3a - 1)(3a + 1)$
(i) $(1 - 6x)(1 + 6x)$
(j) $(4a - b)(4a + b)$
(k) $(3x + 5)(3x - 5)$
(l) $(6 - 5x)(6 + 5x)$

3. (a) $(3x + 2)(2x + 1)$
(b) $(5x - 2)(7x - 2)$
(c) $(3 - 5x)(3 + 5x)$
(d) $(2x - 3)(4x + 1)$
(e) $(7x - 4)(3x + 2)$
(f) $(1 - 3x)(1 + 3x)$
(g) $(2x + 3)^2$
(h) $(2 - 7x)(2 + 7x)$
(i) $(5x + 3y)(x - 2y)$
(j) $(5x - 2)^2$
(k) $(5x - 3)(3x - 7)$
(l) $(8x - 3)(10x + 3)$

Exercise 21g   page 338

1. (a) $(x + 1)(x + 8)$
(b) $(x - 3)^2$
(c) $(x + 7)(x + 3)$
(d) $(4 - x)(5 + x)$
(e) no factors
(f) $(x - 5)(x - 3)$
(g) $(x - 7)(x - 1)$
(h) $(x + 2)^2$

2. (a) $3(x - 1)(x - 8)$
(b) $4(x - 3)^2$
(c) $x(x - 3)^2$
(d) $5(x - 1)^2$
(e) $4(x - 1)^2$
(f) $2(x - 11)(x + 2)$
(g) $2(x - 1)(x - 8)$
(h) $a(x^2 + 3x + 4)$

3. (a) $(5 - x)(x - 6) = (6 - x)(x - 5)$
(b) $2(x^2 - x + 3)$
(c) $2(x - 2)(x + 2)$
(d) $2(x^2 + 2)$
(e) no factors
(f) $(2 - x)(14 + x)$
(g) no factors
(h) $2x(2x - 1)(x - 1)$
(i) $(x + 9)(x + 2)$
(j) $(2x + 1)(3x + 1)$
(k) $(4x + 1)(2x - 1)$
(l) $3(2 - 3x + 2x^2)$
(m) $2(2x - 3)(2x - 1)$
(n) no factors

4. (a) $(a - b + c)(a + b - c)$
(b) $y(2x - y)$
(c) $(3x - 7)(x - 8)$
(d) $(xy - 1)^2$
(e) $3x(x^2 - 2x + 8)$
(f) $(b - c)(2a + b + c)$

5. 1, 10

6. $53.4^2 - 46.6^2 = (53.4 + 46.6)(53.4 - 46.6)$
$= 100 \times 6.8 = 680$

7. Evaluate $(x - 3)(x - 2)$; y: 20, 15.75, 13.8125, 13.0725

8. $a = 70$, $b = 69$

(j) $\sigma = \dfrac{16\rho(r - x)}{(8x + 3r)}$

(k) $a = \pm l \sqrt{\dfrac{(4w^2 - R^2)}{(3w^2 - R^2)}}$

Exercise 21h   page 338

1. (a) $p = \dfrac{T}{(2 + h)}$

(b) $C = \dfrac{M}{(n - 3)}$

(c) $r = \dfrac{(hl - g)}{\pi h}$

(d) $r = \dfrac{V}{(a^2 + \pi ah)}$

(e) $a = \dfrac{(vh - r^2)}{v}$

(f) $h_1 = \dfrac{(A + 2\pi rh_2)}{2\pi r}$

2. (a) $x = \dfrac{b}{(a + c)}$

(b) $x = \dfrac{(q + r)}{(a - b)}$

(c) $x = \dfrac{(a - c)}{(b + d)}$

(d) $x = \dfrac{b}{(b - a - c)}$

(e) $x = \dfrac{(a + ab)}{(a + b)}$

(f) $x = \dfrac{ab}{(2a - b)}$

3. (a) $x = \dfrac{2ab}{(a + b)}$

(b) $a = \dfrac{b}{(bT - 1)}$

(c) $p = \dfrac{1}{(r - R)}$

(d) $P = \dfrac{100A}{(100 + RT)}$

(e) $x = \dfrac{(b^2 - a^2)}{(a - b)} = -(a + b)$

(f) $c = \dfrac{ab}{(b + a)}$

(g) $m = \dfrac{(h - hrt)}{r}$

(h) $v = \dfrac{(2s - ut)}{t}$

4. (a) $h = \dfrac{(A - \pi r^2)}{\pi r}$

(b) $u = \pm\sqrt{(v^2 - 2as)}$

(c) $a = \dfrac{(2s - 2ut)}{t^2}$

(d) $H = \dfrac{Th}{(2h - T)}$

(e) $h = \pm\dfrac{\sqrt{(A^2 - \pi^2 r^4}}{\pi r}$

(f) $u = \pm\left[\dfrac{(mv^2 - 2E)}{m}\right]$

(g) $x = \dfrac{ac}{(a - b)}$

(h) $l = \pm\dfrac{\sqrt{(v^2 - w^2 h^2)}}{w}$

(i) $\sin A = \dfrac{(a \sin B)}{b}$

Exercise 21i   page 340

1. (a) $\dfrac{a}{2}$

(b) $\dfrac{a}{b}$

(c) $\dfrac{b}{2c}$

(d) $\dfrac{p}{2}$

(e) $\dfrac{2}{3y}$

(f) $\dfrac{m}{k}$

(g) $\dfrac{s}{4t}$

(h) $\dfrac{1}{x}$

(i) $\dfrac{t}{(s - t)}$

(j) 2

(k) $\dfrac{1}{(a - 4)}$

(l) $x + y$

2. (a) $\dfrac{2a}{(4a - 3b)}$

(b) $\dfrac{2q}{(p - q)}$

(c) $\dfrac{1}{a}$

(d) $\dfrac{3}{a}$

3. (a) $\frac{1}{3}$

(b) $\frac{1}{3}b$

(c) x

(d) $\dfrac{a}{3}$

(e) $\dfrac{1}{(x - 2)}$

(f) $\dfrac{1}{(a - 4)}$

(g) $\dfrac{b}{(a - 2)}$

(h) $\dfrac{t}{(s + 2)}$

(i) $\dfrac{2}{(x - 4)}$

(j) $x + 6$

(k) $\dfrac{3}{(x - 4)}$

(l) $\dfrac{y}{(x - 2)}$

4. (a) $\dfrac{(x + 3)}{(x + 1)}$

(b) $\dfrac{(2 - x)}{y}$

(c) $\dfrac{4}{(x + 2)}$

(d) $-a$

(e) $\dfrac{(2x - 1)}{(x - 2)}$

(f) $\dfrac{(y + 3)}{(2y + 1)}$

(g) $\dfrac{1}{(2 - x)}$

(h) $\dfrac{(x - 3y)}{x}$

(i) $\dfrac{(a + b)}{(a - b)}$

(j) $\dfrac{(4y + 1)}{4y}$

(k) $\dfrac{-1}{(1 + a)}$

(l) $\dfrac{(x - y)}{(3x - 2y)}$

5. (a) $2(x - 2)$

(b) $4(x + 3)$

(c) $\dfrac{11}{4x}$

(d) $\dfrac{(x^2 - 2)}{xy}$

(e) $\dfrac{10}{(x + 3)(x - 2)}$

(f) $\dfrac{5(x - 2)}{2(x + 3)}$

(g) $\dfrac{(7x - 4)}{(x + 3)(x - 2)}$

(h) $\dfrac{(3x - 8)}{2x(x - 2)}$

(i) $\dfrac{(x - 2)}{2(x - 3)}$

(j) $\dfrac{(4 - x)}{2x(x - 2)}$

6. (a) $\dfrac{1}{(x - 1)}$

(b) $\dfrac{1}{(x - 4)}$

(f) $\dfrac{2}{(x + 4)}$

(g) $\dfrac{1}{(x + 1)(x + 2)}$

(c) $\dfrac{1}{(2x+1)}$

(h) $\dfrac{3}{(x+2)(x+5)}$

(d) $\dfrac{2}{(x-3)(x+1)}$

(i) $\dfrac{-(p^2-p+2)}{(p-1)^2(p+1)}$

(e) $\dfrac{-4}{2x+1}$

(j) $\dfrac{M(2M-1)}{(M^2-4)(M-3)}$

Self-Assessment 21   page 343

1. (a) $12x-8x^2$
   (b) $6+6x-x^2$
   (c) $6x^2+x-12$
   (d) $4x^2-12x+9$
   (e) $4a^2-b^2$
   (f) $48-32x-3x^2$
   (g) -1

2. (a) $3y(x-3z)$
   (b) $2\pi(r_1-r_2)$
   (c) $(x-4)(x-2)$
   (d) $4(x-3)(x+3)$
   (e) $(2-x)(x-1)$
   (f) $(3x-5)^2$

3. (a) $v=\dfrac{(d+Tu)}{T}$
   (b) $v=\dfrac{at}{(2t-a)}$
   (c) $v=\dfrac{uf}{(u+f)}$

4. (a) $\dfrac{(6x+8)}{(x-2)(x+2)}$
   (b) $\dfrac{3(x+2)}{2}$
   (c) $\dfrac{1}{(2x-1)(3x+1)}$

CHAPTER 22

Exercise 22a   page 345

1. (a) (i) £166.5   (ii) £254.7
   (b) about 6 yr 1 month
2. (a) 200 t   (b) 3.16 cm
3. (a) 3   (b) (i) 59   (ii) 76.5

Exercise 22b   page 347

1. (a) 84 m   (b) 6.25 s
2. All have the same shape. The vertex is at $(0,C)$.
3. (a) 2.1   (b) 1.3
4. (a) 23.7   (b) 3.3   (c) 0.6   (d) -3.2
5. (a) 2.25 when $x=1.5$ (c) 0.38 and 2.62
   (b) 0 and 3
6. (a) $-1, 1, 3$
   (b) (i) $-0.9, 0.75, 3.1$ (ii) -1.6
   (c) 3.1 when $x=-0.15$
   (d) any value of x greater than 3.31
7. (a) 2
   (b) 8/0 is indeterminate
   (c) (i) 1.9   (ii) -2.35
   (d) (i) 1.90   (ii) -2.35
8. (a) $(0,1)$ (b) No, 3^x is never negative
   (c) (i) 5.2   (ii) 0.2
   (d) (i) 0.4   (ii) -0.6
9. (a) $(0,1)$ (b) No, 2^{-x} is never negative
   (c) (i) 0.4   (ii) 2.8
   (d) (i) -0.6 (ii) 1
   (e) Similar shape, reflected in y-axis.

Exercise 22c   page 352

1. (a) $\smile$ through $(3,0)$, $(6,0)$ and $(0,18)$
   (b) $\smile$ through $(-4,0)$, $(6,0)$ and $(0,-24)$

(c) $\frown$ through $(0,0)$ and $(5,0)$

(d) $\smile$ through $(0,2)$

(e) $\smile$ through $(-4,0)$, $(-3,0)$ and $(0,12)$

(f) $\frown$ through $(-3,0)$, $(5,0)$ and $(0,15)$

(g) $\smile$ through $(\frac{1}{2},0)$, $(6,0)$ and $(0,6)$

(h) $\smile$ through $(2,0)$, $(6,0)$ and $(0,12)$

2. $\smile$ vertex at $(0,0)$;
   $\smile$ through $(-2,0)$, $(2,0)$ and $(0,-4)$;
   $\frown$ through $(-2,0)$, $(2,0)$ and $(0,4)$
   (a) a translation 4 units vertically downward
   (b) reflection in the x-axis

3. (a) $A(-2,0)$, $B(4,0)$, $C(1,-9)$
   (b) $y=3(x-4)$

4.

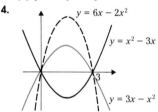

5. (a)

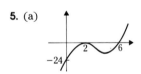

(b) $\sim$ through $(-4,0)$, $(0,0)$ and $(4,0)$

(c) $\sim$ through $(-2,0)$, $(0,0)$ and $(2,0)$

(d) $\sim$ through $(-3,0)$, $(0,0)$ and $(3,0)$

6. $A(-4,0)$, $B(3,0)$
7. $p=12$, $q=1$
8. $A(4,0)$, $B(2,0)$, $C(0,16)$
9. (a) $y \to 0$ (b) no   (c) no
10.

$$y=-\dfrac{8}{x} \qquad y=\dfrac{8}{x}$$
$$y=\dfrac{8}{x} \qquad y=-\dfrac{8}{x}$$

11. B
12. C
13. (a) 1   (b) 3   (c) 4   (d) 2   (e) 5

Exercise 22d   page 355

1. (a) −1.45, 3.45   (d) 0.29, 1.71
   (b) −2.32, 4.32   (e) −0.41, 2.41
   (c) −0.73, 2.73
2. (a) 0, 3   (c) −0.8, 3.8
   (b) 1, 2   (d) −0.3, 3.3
3. (a) (i) 0.84   (ii) 0.72, 2.78
   (b) The graph does not cross the x-axis
       i.e. $2x^2 − 7x + 7$ cannot be zero.
4. From −1.74 to 5.74, $x^2 − 4x − 10 = 0$
5. (a) −0.67, 0.46, 3.2   (c) −0.53, 0.65, 2.88
   (b) −1.21, 1.54, 2.68
6. (a) 1.17, 6.83   (b) $x^2 − 8x + 8 = 0$
7. $y = 2 − 5x$, −5.37 and 0.37
8. (a) $y = x + 2$
   (c) No, there is also a negative solution.
9. $y = 3x − 1$
   The graphs show three intersections, two of
   which are for positive
   values of x.

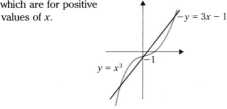

10.

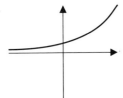

   (a) $y = x$ (b) 2, both positive
11. 2 solutions ≃ −2 and ≃ 0.8

Exercise 22e   page 360

1. (a) 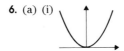 symmetrically through $(0, 4)$

   (b) symmetrically through $(0, −4)$

   (c) symmetrically through $(0, −\frac{1}{2})$

   (d) symmetrically through $(0, 8)$

2. (a) vertex at $(4, 0)$

   (b) vertex at $(−3, 0)$

   (c) vertex at $(−\frac{1}{2}, 0)$

3. (a) vertex at $(6, 0)$

   (b) vertex at $(0, 6)$

   (c) vertex at $(6, 6)$

4. (a) with the × at the origin

   (b) with the × at $(1, 0)$
   (c) with the × at $(0, −3)$
   (d) with the × at $(−3, 0)$
   (e) with the × at $(0, 4)$

   (f) i.e. shallower than the previous ones

5. (a)  with the × at $(0, 5)$

   (b) with the × at $(0, −4)$

6. (a) (i)   (ii)

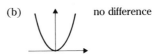

   (iii)

   (b)   no difference

7.

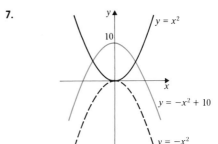

8.

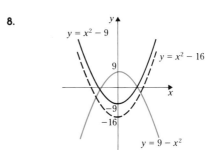

9.

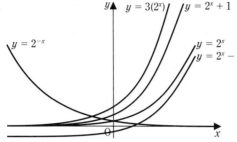

10. (a)   (c)

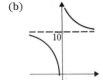

(b)   (d)

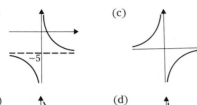

11. (a) $3x^2 - 20x + 12 = 0$
(b) $0.67 < x < 6$ and $x < 0$

12.

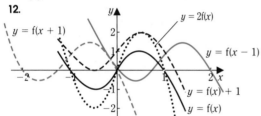

Self-Assessment 22   page 361
1. (a) (i) -16.25 when $x = -2.5$
(ii) $-5.85, 0.85$
(b) $y = x + 1$, one
2. one; 1 and 2

3. (a)  with the × at the origin

(b) with the × at $(2, 0)$ and passing through $(0, -8)$

(c) with the × at the origin

(d) with the × at $(3, 0)$ and passing through $(0, 27)$

4. B

CHAPTER 23

Exercise 23a   page 362
1. (a) $(30 - 2x)$ cm and $2(30 - 2x)$ cm
$= (60 - 4x)$ cm
(c) 4000 cm^3 when $x = 5$
(d) $6\frac{2}{3}\%$
2. (a) (i) 12.6 cm   (ii) 16.7 cm
(b) (i) 0.75ℓ (ii) 4.03ℓ
3. (a) $6.5, 7$
(c) (i) 7.19 m   (ii) 1.29 m or 0.31 m
(d) 0.63 m
4. base 4.16 m by 4.16 m, depth 2.08 m
5. (a) Beginning of wk 1 to end of wk 3, and from
beginning of wk 7 to the early part of wk 11.
(b) Beginning of wk 4 to the end of wk 6 and
from the middle of wk 11 on.
(c) (i) end of wk 6   (ii) early in wk 11
(d) probably a fall in price
(e) false

Exercise 23b   page 365
1. $x \leqslant -1, \ x \geqslant 1$
2. $-\frac{1}{2} < x \frac{1}{2}$
3. $x < -3, \ x > 3$
4. $-2 < x < 2$
5. $1 \leqslant x \leqslant 3$
6. $x \leqslant -1, \ x \geqslant 2$
7. $-1 < x < 4$
8. $-2 \leqslant x \leqslant 1$
9. $x < 1, x > 4$
10. $-3 < x < 1$ and $x > 2$

Exercise 23c   page 367
1. (a) 1, 1 or 2   (c) 1, 1 or 2
(b) 2, 0 or 1   (d) 2, 1 or 2
2. 1.52, 0.618, 1.85, 1.12
3. -1.41

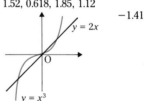

4.   0.5

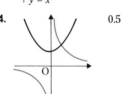

5. (a) 1.9   (b) 2.8

Exercise 23d   page 369
1. 0.653 to 3 s.f.
2. (b) $x_{n+1} = \dfrac{(x_n^2 + 6)}{9}$ (c) 0.73
3. (a) $x = 7 - \dfrac{2}{x}, \ x = \dfrac{(x^2 + 2)}{7}, \ x = \sqrt{(7x - 2)},$
$x = \dfrac{2}{7 - x}$

(b) $x = 7 - \dfrac{2}{x}$, 6.7

4. (a) $2, \frac{y}{2}, \frac{20}{7}, \frac{61}{20}, \frac{182}{61}, \frac{547}{182}, \frac{1640}{547}, \frac{4921}{1640}$; 3

(b) $0, -\frac{3}{2}, -\frac{6}{7}, -\frac{21}{200}, -\frac{60}{61}, -\frac{183}{182}, -1$

(c) $x^2 - 2x - 3 = 0$

5. $-3.45, 1.45$

6. (a) 2   (b) $x_4 = 2.080$

Exercise 23e   page 371

1. (a) 3   (b) 0   (c) $-\frac{1}{2}$ (d) 1

2.

x	3	4	5	6	7	8
y	0.9	1.6	2.5	3.6	4.9	6.4

(a) 0.6   (c) $\frac{1}{5}, \frac{4}{5}, \frac{6}{5}$

3.

x	5	6	7	8
y	2	1.7	1.4	1.3

(a) -1 (b) $-2.5, -0.4$ (c) -1.1

Exercise 23f   page 372

1. (a) (i) 29   (ii) 33

(b) 33 or 34 (must be a whole number)

(c) $\frac{21}{4}$; the number of ripe raspberries is increasing by $5\frac{1}{4}$ a day on average.

(d) -6; the number of ripe raspberries is falling at 6 per day.

(e) Friday   (f) ≈ 194

2. (a) -7.2; from 1910 to 1940, the population decreased by an average of 7.2 people per year.

(b) -11; in 1910, the population was decreasing by 11 people a year.

3. (a) 800; in month 2, sales increased by 800 jars a month.

(b) 1800; in month 4, sales increased by 1800 jars a month.

4. (a) 3   (b) 27

Exercise 23g   page 374

1. 12 sq units

2. 36 sq units

3. 9 sq units

4. 78 sq units

5. 60 sq units

6. 33.75 sq units

Exercise 23h   page 376

1. (a) 26 sq units   (b) 27 sq units

The answer to (b) is probably nearer the true value

2. 14 sq units

Using 2 strips gives 12.5 sq units: less accurate because the second strip leaves out a larger area than the extra included by the first trapezium.

3. 11.5 sq units

4. 26 sq units: this is greater than the true value.

5. (a) 28.5 sq units   (b) 27.375 sq units

6. (b) 183.75 m^2 (c) 46 000 000 litres

Self-Assessment 23   page 377

1. (a) £732

(b) 10.5 m.p.h. and 28.5 m.p.h.

(c) 17.3 m.p.h.

2. $-3 < x < 2$

3. (a) 2.54   (b) $x = \sqrt{9 - x}$

4. (a) (i) 0   (ii) -3 (iii) -6

(b) 30 sq units

CHAPTER 24

Exercise 24a   page 379

1. (a) 7 m/s   (b) 18 m.p.h.

2. (a) 72 m   (b) 59.5 km

3. (a) 3 s   (b) 4.72 h (3 s.f.)

4. (a) 280 miles

(b) 56 m.p.h.

(c) No, the speeds are not equally important.

5. (a) 0.1 m s^{-1} (c) 8.33 m s^{-1} (3 s.f.)

(b) 167 m/min (3 s.f.)   (d) 32.4 km/h

6. (a) Steady speed of 0.75 m/s, distance 6 m.

(b) Steady speed of 0.5 m/s, distance 4 m.

(c) At rest 4 m from A.

Exercise 24b   page 381

1. (a) speed   (d) displacement

(b) distance   (e) velocity

(c) velocity   (f) speed

2. (a) Starts from A and moves 6 m in 8 s at 0.75 m/s, then returns to A in 3 s at 2 m/s, i.e. with velocity -2 m/s.

(b) Starts 2 m from A and moves 3 m in 3 s at 1 m/s then 1 m in 5 s at 0.2 m/s.

(c) Starts 2 m from A and moves 4 km in 4 h at 1 km/h, is then stationary 6 km from A for 4 h.

(d) Starts 30 m from A and moves 20 m back towards A in 3 h at 6.67 m/h then remains at rest for 3 h before moving 10 m back to A in 2 h with velocity -5 m/h.

3. (a)   (b)

4. 1st train: leaves A at 12 noon, travels 60 km in 1 h 48 m at 33.3 km/h; rests 1 h 12 m; returns to A in 2 h with velocity -30 km/h.

2nd train: leaves A at 1 p.m., travels 20 km in 1 h at 20 km/h; rests 12 m; continues in same direction, travelling 40 km in 1 h 48 m at 22.2 km/h. They pass travelling in opposite directions.

5. (b) 40 km/h

(c) At about 1.50 p.m., 33 km from A

(d) 100 km/h

Exercise 24c   page 385

1. (a) (i) 9 m   (ii) 19.7 m   (iii) 13 m

(b) after 2 s

(c) at the start

(d) 4 s

2. (b) 3.1 m   (c) 2 m/s   (d) 3.5 m/s

3. (b) 0.4 m

(c) (i) 0.4 m/s downward

(ii) 0.75 m/s downward

Exercise 24d   page 387
1. (a) 0.25 m/s^2
   (b) 0.5 m/s^2
   (c) 5 m/s
   (d) (i) 50 m   (ii) 25 m
   (e) 225 m
2. (a) 4 m/s
   (b) 2 m/s^2
   (c) It comes to rest.
   (d) 4 m
   (e) It returns down the groove.
3. (a) (i) 1.8 m/s   (ii) 2.8 m/s   (iii) 1.8 m/s
   (b) after 35 s
   (c) after 20 s
   (d) −2 m/s; it is moving backwards.
4. (a) 56.7 m
5. (b) 2 m/s^2 (c) 253 m   (d) about 6.2 s

Exercise 24e   page 389
1. (a) Population increasing at constant rate.
   (b) Population increasing, slowly at first then faster, i.e. rate of growth is increasing.
   (c) Population decreasing, slowly at first then faster then more slowly again. Rate of decay small, increasing, then decreasing to zero.
   (d) Population decreasing fast at first, then rate of decay decreasing to zero.
2. (b) 1960
   (c) 1900
   (d) 2.6 thou/year, 0.8 %
3. (b) 7° per min   (c) 3.7° per min
4. (b) 113 cm^3/s
5. (b) Between 15 and 20 points per year; about 11 to 14 %.
   (c) About 8 points per year; 4.7 %
   (d) Decrease. No, prices are still increasing, but at a slower rate.
6. (b) 1 g/year; 1.7 %
   (c) 0.7 g/year; 1.7 %
   (d) Same percentage rate of decay. Percentage rate of decay is constant. No.

Self-Assessment 24   page 391
1. 40 km/h
2. (a) velocity   (b) speed
3. (a) Starting from A it travels at a steady speed for 1 h. It is stationary for $\frac{3}{4}$ h, then travels back, fast to start with, then gradually slowing down to come to rest after $1\frac{1}{4}$ h, 20 km from A.
   (b) 60 km/h
4. (a) It starts at 3 m/s, accelerates at 1.5 m/s^2 for 2 s, moves at a constant speed for 2 s, then slows down to 2 m/s after another 2 s.
   (b) 21 m
   (c) −2.4 m/s^2
5. (b) Gradient gives rate of change.
   (c) Decrease of about 55 per year or 4.6 per month.

CHAPTER 25

Exercise 25a   page 396
1. (a) 9
   (b) 5
   (c) dog 9; cat 8; bird 5; other pet 7
   (d) 29
   (e) not possible to know

2. (a) M 10; W 9; B 6; G 7
   (b)

   (c) 16 of each
   (d) 1
   (e) 32
3. (a) $3\frac{1}{2}$–4   (b) $1\frac{1}{2}$–2   (c) no   (d) 40
4. (a) 30, 89
   (b)

30–39	40–49	50–59	60–69	70–79	80–89
8	11	18	13	8	12

   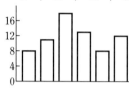
   (d) 50–59 (18)
   (e) 4

Exercise 25b   page 399
1. (a) discrete   (e) continuous
   (b) continuous   (f) continuous
   (c) discrete   (g) continuous
   (d) continuous   (h) discrete
2. (a) 1   (b) 7   (c) 20   (d) no
3.
4. (a) 13   (c) $140 < h \leqslant 145$
   (b) 25   (d) cannot tell from bar chart
5. (a) 47 kg
   (b) $59.5 \leqslant w < 60.5$
   (c) 20, 61, 13, 6: Total 100
   (d) 81
   (e) Because 100 kg is in the middle of a group.

Exercise 25c   page 402
1. 96°, 132°, 60°, 42°, 30°
2. 128°, 152°, 48°, 24°, 8°
3. 108°, 180°, 40°, 18°, 14°
4. (a) $\frac{1}{4}$ (c) £45   (e) £120
   (b) $\frac{1}{12}$ (d) £15
5. car $\frac{13}{120}$, cycle $\frac{2}{15}$, bus $\frac{63}{180}$, walk $\frac{49}{120}$
   (b) 441   (d) 84
   (c) 189   (e) 10.8 %
6. (a) (i) 10 %   (ii) 14 %
   (b) under 10 and 10–19 years
7. (a) 2.6 million, 4.3 million, 65 %
   (b) 600, 1300
   (c) 16–24 year-olds, 20 year-old male
   (d) 3.3 %, 142 000
   (e) 4.5 %
   (f) Northern Ireland
   (g) theft from person

Exercise 25d page 408

1. 3, + or − 1 orange
2. (a) no (?)   (b) about 1800 g
   (c) No, because koi don't grow indefinitely at the same rate.
3. (a) fairly good
   (b) His height is likely to be between 160 cm and 175 cm, but this is a wide range so the information is not very useful.
4. Too much scatter to give an opinion.
5. about 165 cm to 174 cm

Exercise 25e page 411

1. (a) 10 units   (b) 5 units   (c) 10 units
2.

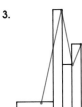

3.

4.

Age, n years	$0 \leqslant n < 3$	$3 \leqslant n < 4$	$4 \leqslant n < 5$
Frequency	15	15	18

5.

Time, t minutes	Frequency
$0 \leqslant t < 5$	10
$5 \leqslant t < 15$	18
$15 \leqslant t < 20$	11
$20 \leqslant t < 25$	6

6.

Height, h cm	Frequency
$10 \leqslant h < 30$	14
$30 \leqslant h < 40$	11
$40 \leqslant h < 50$	16
$50 \leqslant h < 70$	8

Exercise 25f page 415

1. (a) 27, 28   (b) 608, 278   (c) 843, 2263
2. Numbering the students from 1 to 450 and then using random numbers to give 45 numbers from 1 to 450.
4. Numbers 1 to 23 have a greater chance than numbers 24 to 76.

Exercise 25g page 417

1. Catering 59, Academic 28, Engineering 77, Sport 6, Technology 52.
2. 3 from Yr 1, 3 from Yr 2, 3 from Yr 3, 3 from Yr 4, 4 from Yr 5, 2 from Yr 6.
3. (a) A: 357 kg, B: 314 kg C: 200 kg D: 129 kg
   (b) Simple random sampling from the total yield as the numbers damaged in individual fields is not relevant.

4. A stratified sample of about 10 %. Stratified into year groups and male and female because both age and gender are likely to influence attitudes. 10 % because this is likely to be a manageable number, although the size depends on the number in the school.

The answers to questions 5 and 7 are brief and intended to get you thinking; you are welcome to disagree with them. The best way to approach these questions is to discuss them with other people.

5. (a) No, because many religious schools have names beginning with 's' (e.g. St Agnes).
   (b) No, because the population has different characteristics and these are not evenly distributed across the country.
   (c) Yes, if the list is in alphabetical order; no, if it is in order of education authority.
   (d) It does not fairly represent the proportion of schools in each category (some systems change at 11, some at 13 and some at 14 and some at both 11 and 16).
6. (a) The categories can be chosen so that there is no overlap.
   (b) Some categories may include fewer than 10 schools.
   (c) Those pupils whose birthdays are on the 10th, 20th and 30th of each month can be chosen.
7. (a) 1
   (f) 0.42 (this is a theoretical answer, and your answer should be close to this)
   (h) 0.56 (this is a theoretical answer)

Self-Assessment 25 page 420

1.

Number of heads	0	1	2	3	4	5
Frequency	4	5	11	11	4	3

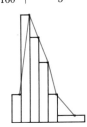

2.

Time, t sec	Frequency
$0 \leqslant t < 20$	4
$20 \leqslant t < 40$	15
$40 \leqslant t < 60$	12
$60 \leqslant t < 80$	8
$80 \leqslant t < 100$	4
$100 \leqslant t < 160$	3

3.

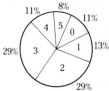
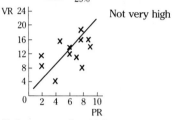

4. (a)

Not very high

(c) She is likely to score 6 or higher.

5. (a) 538   (b) A 193, B 102, C 241
(c) Any acceptable reason. For example: a representative sample is needed because machines vary in the quality of component they produce.

CHAPTER 26

Exercise 26a   page 423

1. (a) 1, 3   (d) 3, -1 (g) $-3, -5$
(b) 0, 2   (e) 0, 7   (h) 0, $-\frac{4}{3}$
(c) $\frac{1}{2}, 4$ (f) $\frac{2}{3}, -2$ (i) $\frac{3}{2}, -\frac{3}{2}$

2. (a) 1, 4   (d) $-4, -3$ (g) 8, -3
(b) 5, 2   (e) $-7, 1$ (h) 0, 3
(c) $-1, -2$ (f) $-3, 2$ (i) 3, -3

3. (a) $-\frac{1}{2}, -8$ (c) $\frac{2}{3}, -\frac{1}{2}$ (e) $-\frac{2}{5}, -5$
(b) $\frac{2}{3}, 3$ (d) $\frac{3}{2}, -4$ (f) $2, -\frac{1}{6}$

4. (a) 2, 3   (c) $-\frac{2}{3}, -1$ (e) $\frac{1}{2}, -3$
(b) 0, 3   (d) 1, 2   (f) $0, \frac{1}{2}$

5. (a) 6, -5 (c) 2, 5   (e) $-4, 3$
(b) $\frac{5}{2}, \frac{5}{2}$ (d) 3 (twice)   (f) 7, -4

6. (a) 5, -4 (d) 0, 4   (g) $2, -\frac{1}{7}$
(b) 2, 2   (e) $\frac{1}{2}, -\frac{1}{2}$ (h) $\frac{5}{2}, -\frac{5}{2}$
(c) $\frac{1}{3}, -\frac{1}{3}$ (f) $-\frac{4}{3}, -\frac{1}{2}$ (i) 3, -1

7. (a) $x + 4$ (c) 14 years
(b) $x(x + 4) = 140$; 10, -14

8. (a) $x + 3$ (c) $x(x + 3) = 54$; 6, -9
(b) $x(x + 3)$ (d) 9 cm

Exercise 26b   page 425

1. (a) $(x - 3)^2 = 13, a = 3, b = 13$
(b) 6.61, -0.606

2. (a) 1, -5 (c) 0.55, 5.45
(b) $\frac{1}{2}, -\frac{3}{2}$ (d) $-4.33, 1.33$

3. (a) $-5, 1$ (c) $-0.394, -7.61$
(b) 7, -1 (d) 3.73, 0.268

4. It is not possible to find the square root of a negative number; none.

Exercise 26c   page 427

1. (a) $-0.55, -5.45$ (e) 1.19, -4.19
(b) 0.65, -4.65 (f) 0.27, -7.27
(c) 4.73, 1.27   (g) $-0.30, -6.70$
(d) $-1.63, -7.37$ (h) 5.61, -1.61

2. (a) 3.41, 0.586   (e) $-0.260, -1.54$
(b) 5.85, -0.854 (f) 2.78, 0.719
(c) $-0.314, -3.19$ (g) 1.59, 0.157
(d) $-0.566, -1.77$ (h) 0.468, -2.14

3. (a) 2.76, 0.24   (d) 0.22, -1.55
(b) 1.86, -0.36 (e) 1.21, -0.21
(c) 3.27, -0.77 (f) 0.28, -1.78

4. (a) 0.5, -2 (f) 3, -0.33
(b) $-0.42, -1.58$ (g) 3, 1.67
(c) $-0.5, -0.67$ (h) no real roots
(d) no real roots   (i) 0.5, -5
(e) 2.39, 0.28   (j) 9.22, -0.22

Exercise 26d   page 429

1. (a) $-1, 4$ (f) $-\frac{3}{4}, 2$
(b) $-5, -2$ (g) $-\frac{2}{3}, 3$
(c) $-3, 5$ (h) $-1, 5$
(d) $-1, 4$ (i) $-2, 1\frac{1}{2}$
(e) $-1, 8$

2. (a) 10.82, 0.18   (d) $-0.70, -4.30$ (g) 8.65, 0.35
(b) 4.19, -1.19 (e) 2.80, -4.55 (h) $-2.69, 0.19$
(c) 6.70, 0.30   (f) 0.59, -0.84 (i) $-1.77, 0.23$

3. 5 cm
4. 5 cm and 8 cm
5. 8.46 cm
6. 13.8 cm
7. 6 years
8. 8.89 or 0.113

9. 450 g
10. -0.54, 0.70, 4.30, 5.54
11. 42
12. 60 km/h
13. 2 cm or $3\frac{1}{7}$ cm

Exercise 26e   page 432

1. (a) $x = 1, y = 2$; $x = 2, y = 1$
(b) $x = 5, y = 1$; $x = 1, y = 5$
(c) $x = 3, y = -1$; $x = -1, y = 3$

2. (a) y (b) x

3. (a) $x = -1, y = -12$; $x = 6, y = 2$
(b) $x = 2, y = 4$; $x = 12, y = \frac{2}{3}$
(c) $x = 0, y = 0$; $y = 4, y = 4$

4. (a) $x = 2.41, y = 0.59$; $x = -5.41, y = 8.41$
(b) $x = 0.89, y = 2.11$; $x = 10.11, y = -7.11$

5. (a) $x = 1, y = -2$; $x = -\frac{1}{3}, y = -\frac{26}{9}$
(b) $x = \frac{5}{4}, y = \frac{15}{4}$; $x = 3, y = 2$
(c) $x = 1, y = 2$; $x = 3, y = -2$

6. 13
7. 12 m, 9 m

Self-Assessment 26   page 433

1. (a) 1, 4   (b) 5, -2 (c) $-1, -2$
2. (a) 1.08, -5.58 (b) 6.12, -2.12
3. (a) 9   (b) $\frac{25}{16}$ (c) $\frac{81}{4}$ (d) $\frac{1}{16}$
4. $a = 4$, $b = 6$; 6.45, 1.55
5. $x = \frac{5}{2}, y = 2$; $x = -1, y = -5$
6. 3.766
7. 5 cm, 12 cm, 13 cm
8. 0.70, 0.18
9. 21.8 cm, 18.8 cm, 28.8 cm
10. (a) 1.57, -9.57 (b) $a = 4, b = -31$
(c)

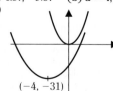

$(-4, -31)$

CHAPTER 27

Exercise 27a   page 435
1. (a) 3   (b) 2

2.

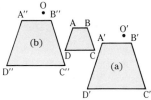

5. (a) $A_1(3, 8)$, $B_1(9, 2)$, $C_1(3, -4)$, $D_1(-3, 2)$
    (b) $A_2(5, 3)$, $B_2(6, 2)$, $C_2(5, 1)$, $D_2(4, 2)$
    (c) $A_1D_1 = 6 A_2D_2$
6. $(-7, -2)$, 3
7. $(2, -2)$, $\frac{1}{3}$
8. $(1, 3)$, the centre of enlargement

Exercise 27b   page 438
1. Yes, sides containing equal angles in the same ratio.
2. Yes, corresponding sides in the same ratio.
3. No, sides containing equal angles not in the same ratio.
4. Yes, sides containing equal angles in the same ratio.
5. No, sides containing equal angles not in the same ratio.
6. Yes, corresponding sides in the same ratio.
7. yes, 2.5 cm   **9.** 7.5 cm
8. yes, 6.3 cm   **10.** 4.5 cm
11. (b) each ratio is $\frac{1}{2}$ (c) (i) 90°   (ii) 10 cm
15. (c) 57°
16. 66 ft
17. 8 m, 8.25 m
18. (b) BC = 12 cm, AC = $10\frac{2}{3}$ cm   (c) both 3 : 5
19. (b) ST = $4\frac{1}{2}$ cm, TR = $\frac{1}{4}$ cm
20. $7\frac{1}{2}$ cm

Exercise 27c   page 443
1. 3 cm   **4.** 1 cm
2. 7.5 cm   **5.** 2 cm
3. $2\frac{2}{3}$ cm   **6.** 6 cm

Exercise 27d   page 444
1. (a) 1 : 2 : 3 : 4
    (b) 1 : 2 : 3 : 4
    (c) 1 : 4 : 9 : 16; yes; $1 : 4 : 9 : 16 = 1^2 : 2^2 : 3^2 : 4^2$
    (d) 1 : 2 : 3 : 4
2. (a) (i) 6 units   (ii) 4 units
    (b) 12 square units
    (c) (i) $\frac{1}{2}$ (ii) $\frac{1}{4}$ (iii) $\frac{1}{4}$
    (d) (i) $\frac{3}{8}$ (ii) $\frac{9}{64}$ (iii) $\frac{9}{64}$
    $\triangle GHI = 21\frac{1}{3}$ sq units, HZ = $5\frac{1}{3}$ units
3. 7 cm, area ABCD = 32 cm², area EFGH = 98 cm²

Exercise 27e   page 445
1. (b) $\dfrac{\text{area ABCD}}{\text{area PQRS}} = \dfrac{9}{25}$
    (c) $\dfrac{\text{area large circle}}{\text{area small circle}} = \dfrac{9}{4}$
    (d) $\dfrac{\triangle ABC}{\triangle PQR} = \dfrac{64}{25}$
2. $\frac{1}{1600}$
3. (b) $\frac{4}{3}$ (c) $\frac{7}{4}$ (d) $\frac{3}{5}$
4. 8 cm²
5. 14.7 cm²
6. 32 cm²
7. (a) 1 : 2 500 000 000   (c) 250 000 m²
    (b) 500 m   (d) 625 000 m²
8. 12 cm²
9. (a) 1000 m²   (b) 3000 m²
10. 30 000 m²
11. (a) $1\frac{4}{5}$ cm   (b) $\frac{9}{64}$ (c) $\frac{9}{55}$
12. $\frac{4}{9}$; 2 : 3
13. (a) (i) 9 m   (ii) 12 m   (iii) $\frac{1}{16}$ (iv) $\frac{9}{16}$
    (b) (i) $16x$ m²   (ii) $9x$ m²
14. (a) 90 m, 50 m, 150 m
    (b) (i) $\frac{1}{16}$ (ii) $\frac{9}{16}$
    (c) $\frac{3}{1}, \frac{1}{3}$, no

Exercise 27f   page 449
1. (a) 1 : 2 : 3
    (b) 1 : 8 : 27; yes; $1 : 8 : 27 = 1^3 : 2^3 : 3^3$
2. (a) (i) 2 : 3   (ii) 2 : 3   (iii) 2 : 3
    (b) 64 and 216; yes $\dfrac{64}{216} = \dfrac{8}{27} = \dfrac{2^3}{3^3}$
3. (a) (i) 4 : 5 : 7   (ii) 4 : 5 : 7
    (b) $46 080\pi : 90 000\pi : 24 960\pi = 64 : 125 : 343$
      $= 4^3 : 5^3 : 7^3$
4. 8 : 125
5. (a) 4 : 3   (b) 4 : 3
6. $\frac{1}{2}$ pt and $1\frac{11}{16}$ pt
7. 27 p
8. 80 kg
9. (a) 1 : 50   (c) 4.8 cm
    (b) 1 : 125 000   (d) 15 000 cm²
10. (a) 156 %   (b) 310 %
11. (a) 26 %   (b) 26 %   (c) 58.7 %
12. 58 %
13. 1370 cm³ (3 s.f.)

Self-Assessment 27   page 452
1. $(-1, 3)$, 3
2. (a) no   (b) yes
3. (a) yes   (b) yes
4. CD = 9 cm, DE = 10.5 cm
5. (a) 1.5   (b) 5.4 cm
6. (a) (i) 4 : 9   (ii) 8 : 27   (c) 121.5 cm²
    (b) 8 cm   (d) 32 cm³

CHAPTER 28

Exercise 28b   page 459
1. yes; SSS   **5.** yes; SAS
2. yes; AAS   **6.** no

3. no   **7.** yes; SSS
4. yes; RHS   **8.** yes; AAS

Self-Assessment 28   page 463
1. C and E; F and H
2. (a) $60°$ (b) $70°$ (c) 10   (d) 14.7

CHAPTER 29

Exercise 29a   page 466
1. PQ   **5.** PR
2. $\widehat{PQS}$ or $\widehat{PRS}$ **6.** $\widehat{RPS}$, $\widehat{RQS}$
3. no   **7.** AC
4. major   **8.** BD
9. ED
10. (a) $\widehat{CAB}$ (b) $\widehat{EAC}$ or $\widehat{EBC}$ or $\widehat{EDC}$
11. (a) $\widehat{EAB}$ (b) $\widehat{DEA}$ or $\widehat{DCA}$
12. $\widehat{AEB}$, $\widehat{ACB}$
13. they are equal
14. $\widehat{AOB} = 2\widehat{APB}$

Exercise 29b   page 468
1. $42°$ **7.** $\widehat{x} = 20°$, $\widehat{y} = 40°$
2. $85°$ **8.** $45°$
3. both $90°$ **9.** $\widehat{x} = 90°$, $\widehat{y} = 40°$
4. $100°$ **10.** $\widehat{x} = 50°$, $\widehat{y} = 60°$
5. $54°$ **11.** $155°$
6. $120°$ **12.** $20°$

Exercise 29c   page 471
1. 24 cm   **4.** 14 cm
2. 20 cm   **5.** 10 cm
3. $2\sqrt{3}$ cm   **6.** $35°$
7. $\widehat{x} = 30°$, $\widehat{y} = 60°$
8. $\widehat{x} = 30°$
9. $\widehat{x} = 67\frac{1}{2}°$, $\widehat{y} = 45°$
10. $\widehat{A} = \widehat{B} = 60° \Rightarrow AB = 5$ cm;
     $OC = \sqrt{4^2 - 2^2} = 3.46$ cm
12. $056°$

Exercise 29d   page 473
1.

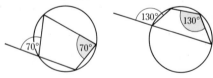

2. $122°$
3. $\widehat{x} = 101°$, $\widehat{y} = 131°$
4. $\widehat{x} = 84°$, $\widehat{y} = 60°$
5. $\widehat{x} = 86°$, $\widehat{y} = 40°$
6. $\widehat{x} = 100°$
7. $\widehat{x} = 42°$, $\widehat{y} = 96°$

Exercise 29e   page 475
1. $x = 30$, $y = 60$
2. $x = 24$, $y = 66$
3. $x = \sqrt{27} = 3\sqrt{3}$, $y = 30$
4. $x = 24$
5. $x = 62$, $y = 28$, $z = 62$
6. $x = 30$
7. $x = 100°$
8. $x = 50°$, $y = 70°$

Exercise 29f   page 478
1. $x = y = 60$; equilateral
2. $x = 122$, $y = 61$
3. $\widehat{a} = 31° = \widehat{c}$, $\widehat{b} = 118°$, $\widehat{x} = 59° = \widehat{y}$
4. 75
5. (a) 5 cm   (b) $180° - 2x°$
6. (a) $37°$ (b) 12 cm

Exercise 29g   page 480
1.

2.

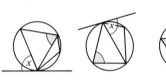

3. (a) $\widehat{d} = 73°$, $\widehat{e} = 26°$, $\widehat{f} = 81°$
     (b) $\widehat{p} = 57° = \widehat{q}$
4. (a) $\widehat{k} = 64°$, $\widehat{l} = 64° = \widehat{m}$, $\widehat{n} = 52°$
     (b) $\widehat{e} = 54° = \widehat{f} = \widehat{g}$, $\widehat{h} = 72°$
5. (a) $\widehat{x} = 28°$, $\widehat{y} = 62°$, $\widehat{z} = 62°$
     (b) $\widehat{x} = 60°$, $\widehat{y} = 61\frac{1}{2}°$, $\widehat{z} = 58\frac{1}{2}°$

Self-Assessment 29   page 482
1. C   **3.** C
2. D   **4.** $x = 40$, $y = 80$, $z = 50$
5. $90°$ anticlockwise; no, the same
6. $x = 135$, $y = 90$; CA subtends a rt angle at O
     so if CA is a diameter of a circle, that circle must
     pass through O.
7. (a) $32°$ (b) $16°$ (c) 1.6 m
8. (a) $60°$ ($\widehat{PTO} = 90°$)
     (b) $30°$ ($\angle$ at circum $= \frac{1}{2} \angle$ at centre)
     (c) $60°$ ($\widehat{OTR} = \widehat{ORT} = 30°$, $\widehat{OTQ} = 90°$)
9. $\widehat{x} = 28°$, $\widehat{y} = 56°$, $\widehat{z} = 34°$
10. $2\sqrt{21}$ cm $= 9.17$ cm

CHAPTER 30

Exercise 30a   page 485
1. a circle
2. (a) vertical straight line
(b)

3. arc of a circle
4. (a) straight line parallel to road
(b)

(c)

5.

6.  circle and its interior, radius 6 m

7.

8. perpendicular bisector of AB
· A   · B

9. pair of parallel lines

10. pair of angle bisectors

11. arc of a circle

12.

Exercise 30b   page 487
1. circle centre C radius 4 cm
2. diameter perpendicular to AB

3. interior of circle centre A radius 4 cm

4. boundary is perpendicular bisector of AB
· A   · B

5. bisector of BÂC
6. circle centre A radius 6 cm
7. circle on AB as diameter
8. boundaries are parallel lines

9. 4.6 cm
10. 8.1 m, 13.8 m
11. (a) 6.4 m
(b) less than 8.9 m

12. (a) semicircle centre A
(b) semicircle centre B
(c) semicircle centre midpoint of AB
(d) semicircle centre midpoint of AB, radius 5 cm
13. Square, four times the size of the original drawing
14. (a) and (b) Q  P

(c) 15 and 5 cm

Exercise 30c   page 490
1. horizontal arc of 80°, radius 1 m
2. plane parallel to the floor, 1 m up
3. hemisphere centre Q, radius 80 cm
4. pair of planes parallel to given plane
5. (a) sphere centre Q, radius 10 cm
(b) two spheres centre Q, radii 6 and 2 cm
(c) sphere centre Q, radius 8 cm, and point Q
6. curved surface of cylinder with same axis as tube and radius 3 cm
7. part of sphere, centre the hive, between the ground and a plane parallel to the ground and 1 m from it
8. plane perpendicular to line joining the nests, through the midpoint
9. (a) line through T perpendicular to fixed line
(b) circle centre T, radius 5 cm
10. (c) DA = DB = DC; radius of circumcircle is 6 cm
11. (a)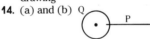
arcs of circles of radii WX and WY
(b)
arcs of circles of radius XY

12. (a) (b) (c)

13. (a) part of a helix

(b)

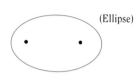

(c) 12 cm

(d) It is the same.

14.

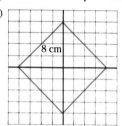

(Ellipse)

15. (a) spheres centres A and B, radius 10 cm
    (b) circle centre midpoint of AB, radius 6 cm

16. (a)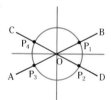

8 cm

(b)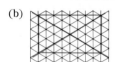

17. (a) 90°

(b) 8, 16 and 13.9 cm

Self-Assessment 30   page 492
1. square of side 2 cm
2. (a)   (b)

3. 3.6 cm
4. (a) sphere, centre B, radius 5 cm
    (b) plane through C perpendicular to AB
    (c) circle, centre C, radius 3 cm
5. Part of a circle with
    (a) centre B, radius 4 cm
    (b) centre D, radius 4 cm
    (c) centre B, radius 8 cm
    (d) centre midpoint of BD, radius 2 cm.

CHAPTER 31

Exercise 31a   page 494
1. (a) 0.5   (b) 0.5
2. (a) 0.7771   (b) −0.7771
3. (a) 0.6428   (d) 0.3090
    (b) −7.115   (e) −2.747
    (c) −0.9511   (f) −0.7880
4. (a) 0.866   (c) 0.707
    (b) −0.309   (d) 0.6691
5. (a) 0, 1, 0   (c) 0, −1, 0
    (b) 1, 0, no value
6. (a) $\frac{3}{5}$ (c) $\frac{3}{5}$
    (b) $\frac{4}{5}$ (d) $-\frac{4}{5}$
7. (a) 53.1°   (c) 137.3°
    (b) 107.5°   (d) 42.7°
8. (a) 30°, 150°   (b) 49.9°, 130.1°
9. (a) 159.8°   (b) 139.5°
10. (a) 2   (c) 2
    (b) 1

Exercise 31b   page 496
1. 7.20 cm   **4.** 5.79 cm
2. 9.32 cm   **5.** 5.89 cm
3. 12.7 cm   **6.** 4.98, 3.62 cm
7. (a) 67.6 m   (c) 46.0 m
    (b) 55.7 m

Exercise 31c   page 498
2. $b^2 = a^2 + c^2 - 2ac \cos B$
3. $m^2 = l^2 + n^2 - 2ln \cos M$
3. $d^2 = e^2 + f^2 - 2ef \cos D$
5. 4.31 cm
6. 10.7 cm
7. 17.1 cm
8. 1.26 cm
9. 132 m
10. $\cos A = \dfrac{b^2 + c^2 - a^2}{2bc}$ $\cos B = \dfrac{a^2 + c^2 - b^2}{2ac}$

Exercise 31d   page 499
1. 58.4°   **3.** 145.8°
2. 31.6°   **4.** 110.7°
5. (a) 38.9°   (b) 84.8°
6. 29.0°
7. 034.8°
8. $\widehat{P} = 81.7°$, $\widehat{Q} = 54.8°$, $\widehat{R} = 43.5°$

Exercise 31e   page 501
1. 2; $\dfrac{e}{\sin E} = \dfrac{c}{\sin C}$; 8.47 cm
2. 3; $l^2 = m^2 + n^2 - 2mn \cos L$; 7.86 cm
3. 4; $\cos Q = \dfrac{p^2 + r^2 - q^2}{2pr}$
    or $q^2 = p^2 + r^2 - 2pr \cos Q$; 35.3°
4. 1; 3.04 cm
5. none of these; use tan; 3.75 cm
6. (b) $\dfrac{g}{\sin G} = \dfrac{f}{\sin F}$; 7.24 cm
7. 24.5 km

8. (a) 94.5°   (b) 12.7 cm
9. (a) 10.9 m   (b) 6.69 m
10. (a) 21.3 km   (b) 076.4°
11. (a) 5 cm   (e) 69.4°
    (b) 6.40 cm   (f) 45.7°
    (c) 6.40 cm   (g) △s PBA and PGC
    (d) 7.55 cm
12. (a) 69.3°   (c) 9.60 cm
    (b) 8.85 cm   (d) 51.2°
13. 19.0 m, 56.2 m
14. (a) 37.1 m   (b) 31.5 m

Exercise 31f   page 503
1. (a) 36.9°, 143.1°   (c) 30.8°, 149.2°
   (b) 26.7°, 153.3°
2. 29.8°
3. 58.1° or 121.9°
4. 96.6°
5. 46.7° or 133.3°
6. (a) no, 83.3° or 96.6°
   (b) No. At least one measurement must be
       wrong.
7. 56.0°
8. Two triangles are possible, one with $\widehat{C} = 66.6°$
   and one with $\widehat{C} = 113.4°$

Exercise 31g   page 505
1. 11.1 cm^2
2. 51.4 cm^2
3. 12.5 cm^2
4. (a) 4.80 cm   (b) 8.91 cm^2
5. 43.3 cm^2
6. (a) 086.3°   (c) 337.7°
   (b) 2240 km^2
7. 10.5 cm^2
8. (a) PA = 5 cm, AQ = 6.32 cm, PQ = 5.39 cm
   (b) 55.3°
   (c) 13 cm^2 (exact), 13.0 cm^2 (3 s.f.)

Self-Assessment 31   page 506
1. (a) 0.8387   (b) −0.7071
2. (a) 153.1°   (b) 102.3°
3. 5.88 cm
4. 7.84 cm
5. 5.87 cm
6. 115.4°
7. 21.0 cm^2
8. 4.76 cm
9. Two triangles; 63.1°, 116.9°

CHAPTER 32

Exercise 32a   page 509
1. (a) scalar   (e) scalar
   (b) vector   (f) scalar
   (c) vector   (g) vector
   (d) vector   (h) vector
2. $\mathbf{a} = \begin{pmatrix} 3 \\ 4 \end{pmatrix}$, $\mathbf{b} = \begin{pmatrix} 3 \\ -3 \end{pmatrix}$, $\mathbf{c} = \begin{pmatrix} -2 \\ 4 \end{pmatrix}$,

   $\mathbf{d} = \begin{pmatrix} -5 \\ -3 \end{pmatrix}$, $\mathbf{e} = \begin{pmatrix} -4 \\ 0 \end{pmatrix}$, $\mathbf{f} = \begin{pmatrix} 0 \\ 4 \end{pmatrix}$

3.
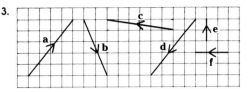

4.
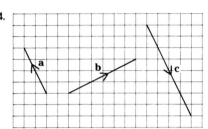

(a) **a** and **c**   (b) **a** and **b**, **b** and **c**
(c) (i) **a, c**   (ii) none   (iii) **a, c**
    (iv) none   (v) **b**   (vi) none

5. (a) 5   (c) 6   (e) $\sqrt{5}$
   (b) 4   (d) 13   (f) $\sqrt{13}$

Exercise 32b   page 511
1.
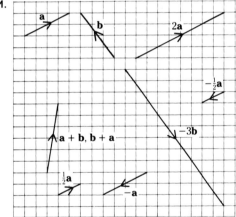

2. (a) parallel vectors: **a**, **e** and **f**, **c** and **d**, **b** and **g**
      c and **d** are perpendicular to **a**, **e** and **f**
      a = −**e**, **d** = 2**c**, **g** = 2**b**, **f** = 3**e**
   (b) **a**, **b**, **c** and **e**; **d** and **g**
   (c) $\mathbf{a} = \begin{pmatrix} 3 \\ -1 \end{pmatrix}$, $\mathbf{b} = \begin{pmatrix} -1 \\ 3 \end{pmatrix}$, $\mathbf{c} = \begin{pmatrix} 1 \\ 3 \end{pmatrix}$,

      $\mathbf{d} = \begin{pmatrix} 2 \\ 6 \end{pmatrix}$, $\mathbf{e} = \begin{pmatrix} -3 \\ 1 \end{pmatrix}$, $\mathbf{f} = \begin{pmatrix} -9 \\ 3 \end{pmatrix}$,

      $\mathbf{g} = \begin{pmatrix} -2 \\ 6 \end{pmatrix}$

3. (g) **a** + **c** = **c** + **a**; **a** + **b** + **c** = **a** + **c** + **b**
      = **b** + **c** + **a** = **c** + **b** + **a**; order does not
      matter when adding vectors.
   (h) **b** + **a** + **c**, **c** + **a** + **b**; yes

4. (a) $\begin{pmatrix} 4 \\ -6 \end{pmatrix}$ (f) $\begin{pmatrix} -1 \\ -1 \end{pmatrix}$

(b) $\begin{pmatrix} 4 \\ 4 \end{pmatrix}$ (g) $\begin{pmatrix} -2 \\ 3 \end{pmatrix}$

(c) $\begin{pmatrix} -2 \\ -7 \end{pmatrix}$ (h) $\begin{pmatrix} -26 \\ -31 \end{pmatrix}$

(d) $\begin{pmatrix} 2 \\ -13 \end{pmatrix}$ (i) $\begin{pmatrix} -8 \\ -28 \end{pmatrix}$

(e) $\begin{pmatrix} 12 \\ 12 \end{pmatrix}$

5. (a) $\begin{pmatrix} 5 \\ 3 \end{pmatrix}$ (d) $\begin{pmatrix} 9 \\ -3 \end{pmatrix}$

(b) $\begin{pmatrix} -5 \\ -3 \end{pmatrix}$ (e) $\begin{pmatrix} 12 \\ 3 \end{pmatrix}$

(c) $\begin{pmatrix} -3 \\ 15 \end{pmatrix}$ (f) $\begin{pmatrix} 1 \\ -5 \end{pmatrix}$

Exercise 32c   page 512

1. (a)   (b)

(c)   (e)

(d)   (f)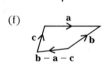

2. (a) $\mathbf{a} - \mathbf{b}$ (or $-\mathbf{b} + \mathbf{a}$)   (b) $\mathbf{b} - \mathbf{a}$
3. (a) $\mathbf{b} - \mathbf{a}$ (b) $\mathbf{c} - \mathbf{b}$ (c) $\mathbf{c} - \mathbf{a}$
4. (a) $\mathbf{b} - \mathbf{a}$ (d) zero vector
5. (a) $\frac{2}{3}(\mathbf{c} - \mathbf{b})$ (b) $\frac{1}{3}\mathbf{b} + \frac{2}{3}\mathbf{c}$
6. (a) $\mathbf{b} - \mathbf{a}$ (d) $\mathbf{a} - \mathbf{b}$

(b) $\frac{1}{2}(\mathbf{b} - \mathbf{a})$ (e) $\frac{1}{2}(\mathbf{a} - \mathbf{b})$

(c) $\frac{1}{2}(\mathbf{a} + \mathbf{b})$ (f) $\frac{1}{2}(\mathbf{a} + \mathbf{b})$

7. (a) $\frac{1}{3}$ (b) $\overrightarrow{AC} = \begin{pmatrix} 2 \\ -3 \end{pmatrix}$, $\overrightarrow{CB} = \begin{pmatrix} 4 \\ -6 \end{pmatrix}$

8. $\frac{1}{2}\mathbf{a} + \frac{1}{2}\mathbf{b}$

9. (a) $\frac{1}{2}(\mathbf{a} + \mathbf{b})$ (c) $\frac{1}{4}\mathbf{b}$

(b) $\frac{2}{3}\mathbf{a}$ (d) $-\frac{2}{3}\mathbf{a} + \frac{1}{4}\mathbf{b}$

Exercise 32d   page 514

1. (a) $\overrightarrow{QS} = \mathbf{a} - \mathbf{b}$, $\overrightarrow{SO} = \mathbf{a}$ (b) parallelogram
(c) Yes, $\overrightarrow{PS}$ & $\overrightarrow{SO}$ are parallel vectors with a point in common.
2. (a) $\frac{1}{4}\mathbf{q}$ (d) $\frac{5}{4}\mathbf{p}$

(b) $\mathbf{p} + \mathbf{q}$ (e) lines are parallel

(c) $\frac{1}{4}(\mathbf{p} + \mathbf{q})$

3. (a) $\mathbf{c} - \mathbf{d}$
(b) $\frac{1}{2}\mathbf{c}$
(c) $\frac{1}{2}\mathbf{b} + \frac{1}{2}\mathbf{c} - \mathbf{d}$
(d) $\frac{1}{2}(\mathbf{b} - \mathbf{d})$
(e) $\frac{1}{2}(\mathbf{b} - \mathbf{d})$
(f) One pair of opposite sides equal and parallel.
4. B is the midpoint of AC
5. (a) $h = 6$, $k = -2$ (c) $h = 3$, $k = 4$
(b) $h = 0$, $k = -3$ (d) $h = -24$, $k = -6$
6. (a) $\frac{3}{8}$ (c) $\frac{3}{5}$

(b) $-\frac{9}{4}$ (d) $h = 2$ or -2

7. (a) $\frac{1}{3}\mathbf{b}$
(b) $\frac{1}{3}\mathbf{b}$
(c) $\mathbf{b} - \frac{1}{3}\mathbf{a}$
(d) $\mathbf{a} - \frac{1}{3}\mathbf{b}$
(e) $h(\mathbf{b} - \frac{1}{3}\mathbf{a})$
(f) $k(\mathbf{a} - \frac{1}{3}\mathbf{b})$
(g) $\frac{1}{3}\mathbf{a} + h(\mathbf{b} - \frac{1}{3}\mathbf{a})$
(h) $\frac{1}{3}\mathbf{b} + k(\mathbf{a} - \frac{1}{3}\mathbf{b})$
(i) $h = k = \frac{1}{4}$, $AD:DE = 3:1$
8. (a) $\frac{1}{2}\mathbf{q}$
(b) $\mathbf{p} - \frac{1}{2}\mathbf{q}$
(c) $k(\mathbf{p} - \frac{1}{2}\mathbf{q})$
(d) $-\mathbf{p} - \mathbf{q}$
(e) $h(-\mathbf{p} - \mathbf{q})$
(f) $-\mathbf{p} + k(\mathbf{p} - \frac{1}{2}\mathbf{q})$
(g) $h = \frac{1}{3}$, $k = -\frac{2}{3}$
(h) $1:2$
9. (a) $\frac{1}{2}\mathbf{b}$
(b) $\frac{1}{2}\mathbf{c}$
(c) $\frac{1}{2}\mathbf{c} - \mathbf{b}$
(d) $\frac{1}{2}\mathbf{b} - \mathbf{c}$
(e) $k(\frac{1}{2}\mathbf{b} - \mathbf{c})$
(f) $h(\frac{1}{2}\mathbf{c} - \mathbf{b})$
(g) $\mathbf{c} + k(\frac{1}{2}\mathbf{b} - \mathbf{c})$
(h) $\mathbf{b} + h(\frac{1}{2}\mathbf{c} - \mathbf{b})$
(i) $h = k = \frac{2}{3}$; $2:1$

Exercise 32e   page 518

1. (a) $\begin{pmatrix} 8 \\ 2 \end{pmatrix}$ (c) $\begin{pmatrix} 4 \\ 1 \end{pmatrix}$ (e) $\begin{pmatrix} 6 \\ 3 \end{pmatrix}$

(b) $\begin{pmatrix} 4 \\ 4 \end{pmatrix}$ (d) $\begin{pmatrix} 2 \\ 2 \end{pmatrix}$

2. (e) parallelogram   (f) $\begin{pmatrix} 2 \\ 2 \end{pmatrix}$

3. (a) $\begin{pmatrix} 3 \\ -4 \end{pmatrix}$ (c) $\begin{pmatrix} -3 \\ -4 \end{pmatrix}$

(b) $\begin{pmatrix} -3 \\ 4 \end{pmatrix}$ (d) $\begin{pmatrix} 2 \\ 0 \end{pmatrix}, \begin{pmatrix} 5 \\ 4 \end{pmatrix}, \begin{pmatrix} 2 \\ 0 \end{pmatrix}$

(e) $\begin{pmatrix} 3.5 \\ 2 \end{pmatrix}$ $\overrightarrow{OO_1} = \overrightarrow{AA_4} = \overrightarrow{BB_1} = \begin{pmatrix} 2 \\ 0 \end{pmatrix}$

4. (a) $\begin{pmatrix} 3 \\ 4 \end{pmatrix}$ (c) $\begin{pmatrix} -3 \\ 1 \end{pmatrix} - \begin{pmatrix} 3 \\ 4 \end{pmatrix} = \begin{pmatrix} -6 \\ -3 \end{pmatrix}$

(b) $\begin{pmatrix} -6 \\ -3 \end{pmatrix}$

5. (a) $A_1\,(5,3)$, $B_1\,(8,4)$, $C_1\,(7,8)$

(b) $A_2\,(-5,2)$, $B_2\,(-2,3)$, $C_2\,(-3,7)$

(c) $A_3\,(1,-3)$, $B_3\,(4,-2)$, $C_3\,(3,2)$

(d) $\begin{pmatrix} -10 \\ -1 \end{pmatrix}$

3. (b) and (c)

4. first and third

5. $\begin{pmatrix} 1 \\ 4 \end{pmatrix}$

6. $(2,4),(-5,5)$

7. $5\mathbf{i}+\mathbf{j}$, $-\mathbf{i}+9\mathbf{j}$

8. 13

9. (a) $\frac{1}{2}(\mathbf{a}+\mathbf{c})$

10. 7.2 N, 36°

11. 3.29 km/h

Exercise 32f   page 520

1. (a) $6\mathbf{i}+3\mathbf{j}$ (d) $5\mathbf{i}$

(b) $7\mathbf{i}-4\mathbf{j}$ (e) $4\mathbf{j}$

(c) $-\mathbf{i}-3\mathbf{j}$ (f) $-5\mathbf{j}$

2. (a) $(2,-4)$ (c) $(-7,0)$

(b) $(6,4)$ (d) $(0,3)$

3. (a) $13\mathbf{i}-4\mathbf{j}$ (d) $4\mathbf{i}+\mathbf{j}$

(b) $15\mathbf{i}-18\mathbf{j}$ (e) $3\mathbf{i}-22\mathbf{j}$

(c) $\mathbf{i}-6\mathbf{j}$

5. $-\mathbf{i}-3\mathbf{j}$, $3\mathbf{i}+\mathbf{j}$, $-4\mathbf{i}+4\mathbf{j}$

6. (a) $3\mathbf{n}+4\mathbf{e}$ (b) $-3\mathbf{n}-4\mathbf{e}$

7. (a) $2\mathbf{b}+\mathbf{a}$ (c) $3\mathbf{a}$

(b) $3\mathbf{a}+\mathbf{b}$ (d) $2\mathbf{a}+\frac{1}{2}\mathbf{b}$

Exercise 32g   page 521

1.

2. (a)

(b) 10 N

3. (a)

(b) 3 N   (c)

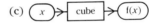

4. (a) 5 m/s   (b) 36.9° (calculated value)

5. (a) 9.27 at 82.6° to the +ve direction of the x-axis.

(b) (i) 52.0° to the +ve direction of the x-axis.

(ii) 10.2

6. 7.21 N, at 46.1° to the resultant.

7. (a) At 79.1° to the downstream bank.

(b) At 48.2° to the upstream bank.

(c) 1.5 m/s

8. 322.8°

Self-Assessment 32   page 523

1.

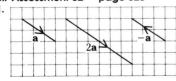

2. $\begin{pmatrix} -1 \\ 6 \end{pmatrix}$, $\begin{pmatrix} 7 \\ 4 \end{pmatrix}$

CHAPTER 33

Exercise 33a   page 526

1. (a) treble

(b) take the reciprocal of

(c) add 1

2. (a)

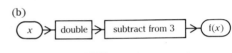

(b)

(c)

3. (a) 4   (b) 25   (c) 0   (d) 16

4. (a) 0   (c) 6   (e) 4

(b) -20 (d) -126 (f) 5.625

5. (a) $\frac{1}{3}$

(b) 100

(c) $-\frac{1}{4}$

(d) it is not possible to divide by 0

6. (a) 5   (c) 5 and -5

(b) $\frac{1}{8}$ (d) 1

7. (a) 7, 5, 2   (c) decrease

(b) 5

Exercise 33b   page 527

1

2.

3.

4.

5.

6.

7.

8.

9.

10. (b)

Exercise 33c   page 529

1. (a) least -1 at $x = 4$

(b) least -4 at $x = 1\frac{1}{2}$

(c) greatest $\frac{49}{4}$ at $x = -\frac{1}{2}$

(d) least $-\frac{9}{8}$ at $x = -\frac{11}{4}$

(e) least 0 at $x = 3$

(f) greatest $\frac{529}{12}$ at $x = \frac{31}{6}$

2. (a) $(x-\frac{3}{2})^2 - \frac{1}{4}$

(b) $(x+\frac{3}{2})^2 - \frac{1}{4}$

(c) $(x+\frac{3}{2})^2 - \frac{17}{4}$

(d) $3(x+1)^2 + 2$

(e) $3(x-1)^2 - 8$

(f) $2(x-\frac{1}{4})^2 + \frac{47}{8}$

(g) $6 - (1+x)^2$

(h) $6 - (1-x)^2$

(i) $15 - 2(x-2)^2$

3. (a) least $-\frac{1}{4}$ at $x = \frac{3}{2}$

(b) least $-\frac{1}{4}$ at $x = -\frac{3}{2}$

(c) least $-\frac{17}{4}$ at $x = -\frac{3}{2}$

(d) least 2 at $x = -1$

(e) least -8 at $x = 1$

(f) least $\frac{47}{8}$ at $x = \frac{1}{4}$

(g) greatest 6 at $x = -1$

(h) greatest 6 at $x = 1$

(i) greatest 15 at $x = 2$

4. (a) $f(x) = (x+\frac{3}{2})^2 + \frac{19}{4}$ so $f(x)$ has a least

value of $\frac{19}{4}$ at $x = -\frac{3}{2}$

(c) $f(x) > 0$ for *all* values of x

Exercise 33d   page 530

1. $a = 1, b = 4$ **2.** $a = 4, b = -3$

3. (a) D   (b) C   (c) B   (d) A

Exercise 33e   page 533

1.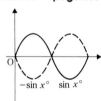

2.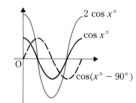

The curves $y = \sin x°$ and $y = \cos(x° - 90°)$
are the same.

3.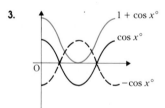

4. (b) 0, 180, 360

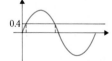

5. (b) 90, 270

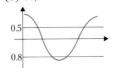

6. (a) $-1 \leqslant \sin x° \leqslant 1$
(b) $-1 \leqslant \cos x° \leqslant 1$

8. The curve $y = \cos x°$ is a translation of the curve $y = \sin x°$ by 90 to the left.

9.

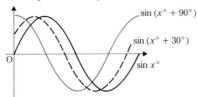

10. (c) a sin wave
11. (b) one-way reduction by a factor 2 parallel to Ox
(c) one-way reduction by a factor 3 parallel to Ox
(d) one-way stretch by a factor of 2 parallel to Ox
12. (b) $-1 \leqslant \sin x° \leqslant 1$
13. (b) $-1 \leqslant \cos x° \leqslant 1$

Exercise 33f   page 535
1.

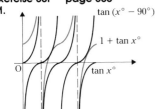

2. 2; 38, 142
3. (b) tan $x°$ increases from 0 to 1 as x increases from 0 to 45
(c) tan A increases, getting very large indeed as $\widehat{A}$ approaches 90°
4. These answers are given to the nearest tenth of an hour
(a) 7.5 h, 10.5 h   (b) 1.6 h, 10.4 h
5. (a) 0, 180, 360   (b) 90, 270
6. (a) 45
(b) ≈ 60 (62 to nearest unit)
7. (a) 9.85   (b) one
8. 45.2
9. (a) $y = 50 \cos x°$ and $y = x - 10$
(there are other possible graphs)
(b) $x - 1 + 100 \cos x° = 0$
10. (a) (i) 14.75   (ii) 14.75   (iii) 8.8   (iv) 13
(b) 90; 270   (c) 16 Feb, 24 Oct.
(d) Only allows for 360 days in 1year.

Self-Assessment 33   page 537
1. 6, −2, −3
2. $-\frac{1}{2}$
3. 3, 1
4. $a = 1, b = 3$
5.

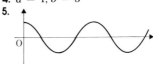

6.

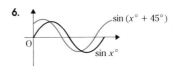

7. 1

8.

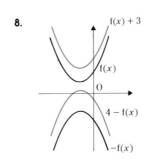

CHAPTER 34

Exercise 34a   page 539
1. (a) $\frac{1}{3}$
2. (a) $\frac{11}{18}$ (b) 1
3. (a) $\frac{1}{4}$ ($\frac{92}{365}$ is better!)
4. (a) $\frac{5}{26}$ (b) $\frac{1}{2}$ (c) $\frac{9}{26}$
5. (a) $\frac{2}{5}$ (b) $\frac{3}{5}$
6. (a) $\frac{4}{9}$ (b) $\frac{5}{9}$
7. $\frac{3}{5}$
8. (a) $\frac{1}{75}$ (b) $\frac{74}{75}$
9. (a) $\frac{1}{10}$ (b) $\frac{3}{10}$ (c) $\frac{2}{5}$ (d) $\frac{7}{10}$
10. (a) $\frac{15}{22}$ (b) $\frac{7}{22}$ (c) $\frac{1}{22}$ (d) $\frac{3}{11}$
11. (a) $\frac{5}{12}$ (b) $\frac{1}{3}$ (c) $\frac{3}{4}$
12. $\frac{2}{5}$
13. $\frac{1}{3}$
14. (a) $\frac{1}{6}$ (b) $\frac{7}{30}$
15. (a) $\frac{5}{18}$ (b) $\frac{13}{36}$ (c) $\frac{7}{12}$

Exercise 34b   page 542
1. (a) 30   (b) 90   (c) 90
2. (a) 20   (b) 65   (c) 130   (d) 10
3. 4
4. (a) 69   (b) 115
5. 16
6. 450 milk, 750 cola and 600 squash
7. (a) 0.36   (b) (i) 7 200 000   (ii) 1 500 000

Exercise 34c   page 543
1. (a) $\frac{1}{26}$ (b) $\frac{1}{26}$ (c) $\frac{1}{13}$
2. (a) $\frac{1}{6}$ (b) $\frac{1}{3}$ (c) $\frac{1}{2}$
3. (a) $\frac{1}{6}$ (b) $\frac{1}{6}$ (c) $\frac{1}{3}$
4. (a) $\frac{8}{9}$ (b) $\frac{1}{9}$
5. (a) $\frac{5}{7}$ (b) $\frac{11}{14}$
6. (a) $\frac{24}{35}$ (b) $\frac{15}{28}$ (c) $\frac{131}{140}$ (d) $\frac{9}{140}$
7. (a) $\frac{1}{2}$ (b) $\frac{1}{2}$ (c) $\frac{5}{6}$

Exercise 34d   page 544
1. (a) $\frac{1}{6}$ (b) $\frac{2}{9}$ (c) 0
2. (a) $\frac{7}{12}$ (b) $\frac{5}{6}$ (c) $\frac{17}{36}$
3. (a) $\frac{1}{4}$ (b) $\frac{3}{4}$ (c) $\frac{1}{2}$
4. (a) $\frac{1}{2}$ (b) $\frac{1}{4}$ (c) $\frac{3}{4}$
5. (a) $\frac{1}{4}$ (b) $\frac{3}{4}$

Exercise 34e   page 545
1. (a) $\frac{1}{2}$ (b) $\frac{26}{51}$
2. (a) (i) $\frac{2}{5}$ (ii) $\frac{3}{5}$ (b) (i) $\frac{4}{9}$ (ii) $\frac{5}{9}$
3. (a) (i) $\frac{4}{11}$ (ii) $\frac{7}{11}$ (c) (i) $\frac{8}{21}$ (ii) $\frac{13}{21}$
   (b) (i) $\frac{1}{3}$ (ii) $\frac{2}{3}$

Exercise 34f   page 547
1. (a) $\frac{5}{11}$ (b) $\frac{3}{5}$ (c) $\frac{3}{11}$ (d) $\frac{3}{11}$
2. (a) $\frac{4}{9}$ (c) $\frac{5}{18}$ (e) $\frac{5}{18}$
   (b) $\frac{1}{6}$ (d) $\frac{5}{18}$ (f) $\frac{5}{9}$
3. (a) $\frac{8}{13}$ (b) $\frac{7}{12}$ (c) $\frac{5}{39}$
4. (a) $\frac{2}{5}$ (b) $\frac{9}{14}$ (c) $\frac{18}{35}$ (d) $\frac{4}{91}$

Exercise 34g   page 549
1. $\frac{5}{9}$ (b) $\frac{4}{9}$
2. (a) $\frac{77}{306}$ (b) $\frac{77}{153}$ (c) $\frac{76}{153}$
3. $\frac{20}{39}$
4. (a) $\frac{3}{8}$ (b) $\frac{3}{8}$ (c) $\frac{7}{8}$
5. (b) (i) $\frac{1}{3}$ (ii) $\frac{4}{45}$ (iii) $\frac{16}{675}$ (iv) $\frac{64}{3375}$
6. (a) $\frac{9}{20}$ (b) $\frac{7}{10}$ (c) $\frac{13}{60}$
7. (a) $\frac{1}{12}$ (b) $\frac{3}{8}$ (c) $\frac{5}{12}$
8. (a) (i) $\frac{27}{100}$ (ii) $\frac{9}{100}$ (iii) $\frac{1}{5}$
   (b) (i) $\frac{9}{1000}$ (ii) $\frac{43}{250}$
9. (a) $\frac{1}{4}$ (b) $\frac{1}{6}$ (c) $\frac{1}{3}$

10. (a) $\frac{1}{5}$ (c) $\frac{506}{1015}$
    (b) $\frac{24}{145}$ (d) $\frac{509}{1015}$
11. (a) $\frac{4}{9}$ (b) Cath
12. (a) $\frac{1}{10}$ (c) $\frac{1}{50}$ (e) $\frac{8}{125}$
    (b) $\frac{4}{25}$ (d) $\frac{1}{20}$ (f) $\frac{1}{1000}$
13. (a) (i) $\frac{1}{9}$ (ii) $\frac{4}{45}$ (b) (i) $\frac{1}{18}$ (ii) $\frac{7}{90}$
14. $\frac{126}{625} = 0.20$ (2 s.f.)

Exercise 34h   page 552
1. relative frequency
2. equally likely outcomes
3. relative frequency
4. equally likely outcomes
5. equally likely outcomes
6. relative frequency
7. relative frequency

Self-Assessment 34   page 554
1. (a) $\frac{1}{26}$ (b) $\frac{1}{52}$
2. (a) $\frac{7}{10}$ (b) $\frac{3}{10}$
3. (a) $\frac{1}{2}$ (b) $\frac{13}{36}$ (c) $\frac{1}{3}$ (d) $\frac{1}{3}$
4. (a) 60   (b) 120
5. (a) (i) $\frac{4}{11}$ (ii) $\frac{7}{11}$ (b) (i) $\frac{1}{3}$ (ii) $\frac{2}{3}$
6. (a) $\frac{7}{26}$ (b) $\frac{7}{13}$

CHAPTER 35

Exercise 35a   page 555
1.
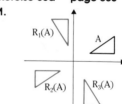

2.
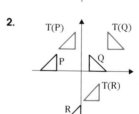

3.
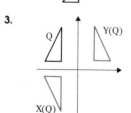

4.

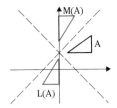

5.

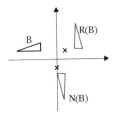

Exercise 35b   page 557

1.

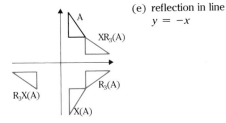

(e) reflection in line
$y = -x$

2.

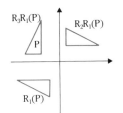

(d) R₃
(e) R₂

3.

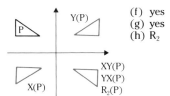

(f) yes
(g) yes
(h) R₂

4.

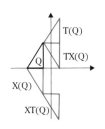

(e) translation defined by
vector $\begin{pmatrix} 2 \\ -3 \end{pmatrix}$

(f) translation defined by
vector $\begin{pmatrix} 0 \\ 6 \end{pmatrix}$

Exercise 35c   page 558

1.

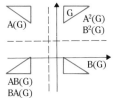

(b) AB = BA = rotation of 180° about (−1, 2)
(c) A² = B² = I

2.

(b) yes
(c) yes

3. (a) $R_1^2 = R_2$, $R_2R_1 = R_3$
   (b) $R_3^2 = R_2$, $R_2R_3 = R_1$, $R_3R_2 = R_1$
4. (a) $R_1R_3 = R_3R_1 = I$
   (b) $R_2^2 = I$, $R_2R_3 = R_1$, $R_1R_2 = R_3$
5. (b) (i) $X^2 = I$ (ii) $XY = R_2$
6. (b) (i) $WZ = R_2$ (ii) $Z^2 = I$ (iii) $XZ = R_3$
      (iv) $YZ = R_1$ (v) $IZ = Z$
7. (b) (i) $X^2 = I$ (ii) $XR_1 = W$ (iii) $R_1X = Z$
   (c) false
8. (b) $XI = X$, $YI = Y$, $IX = X$, $IY = Y$
9. (b) $ZI = Z$, $WI = W$, $W^2 = I$
10. (b) $R_2R_1 = R_3$, $R_1R_2R_1 = I$
   (c) yes   (d) first

Self-Assessment 35   page 560

1.

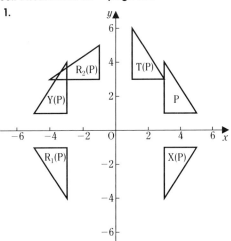

2. (a)

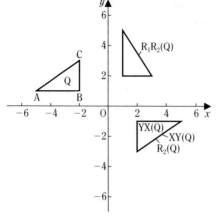

(d) yes   (e) yes   (f) yes

3. (a)

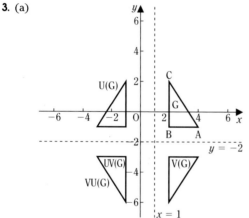

(b) yes   (c) yes

4.

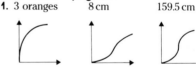

(b) (i) I   (ii) R_3 (iii) R_1 (iv) R_2 (v) Z

CHAPTER 36

Some of these answers are taken from graphs and some others calculated using statistical functions on a calculator. In these cases your answers may vary slightly from those given here.

Exercise 36a   page 564
1. (a) 4.43, 4, 2   (c) 3.75, 4, 4
     (b) 1.84, 1.65, 1.6   (d) 0.725, 0.75, 0.8
2. £18 200, £10 000, £10 000
     (a) mean (shows employees' pay is high)
     (b) median or mode (shows a lower figure for
         employees' pay)
3. 520, 455, 630, 736, 857
4. (a) £2900   (b) £4083   (c) £1183
5. 56.4 kg
6. 94.7 kg
7. 41
8. (a) 5.21   (b) 5.33
9. 3.64
10. 1.57
11. 3
12. 3.5

Exercise 36b   page 567
1. 4.2
2. 7.6
3. 159.8
4. 3.1
5. 6.15 customers per minute

Exercise 36c   page 569
1. (a) 5   (b) 49
2. (a) 13   (b) 15
3. (a) 25   (b) 0.5

Exercise 36d   page 571
1. 3 oranges   8 cm   159.5 cm

2. (a) 50   (d) 32   (g) 16 %
     (b) 38 minutes   (e) 14
     (c) 4   (f) 0.16
3. (a) 39 minutes   (b)
     (b)

4. median is less than mean; greater then 0.5

Exercise 36e   page 573
1. 4 oranges, 3.3 cm, 6.5 cm
2. (a) £22   (b) £16, £34; £18
3. Brand Y; three-quarters of the sample is greater
     than 18.5 h whereas three-quarters of Brand X is
     not
4. (b) $\simeq$ 20.2 hrs   (c) $\simeq$ 0.05

Exercise 36f   page 574
1. (a) 1.83 people   (c) 1.97 kg
   (b) 19.2 marks   (d) 2.15 h
2. (a) 1.03   (c) 0.04
   (b) 0.661   (d) 0.826
3. 3.63 oranges, 2.53 cm

Exercise 36g   page 578
1. In each case the ranges are the same and about two thirds of each distribution lies within 1 s.d. of the mean. The mean English mark is higher than the mean maths mark.
2. By writing each as a percentage of the total possible mark (maths 47%, English 54%).
3. (a) A: higher mean but much more variable
      B: lower mean but more consistent masses
      C: higher mean, same variability
      D: same mean but much more variable masses
   (b) B offers an improved consistency of mass but with a lower mean mass
      C offers an improvement in mean mass without producing more variable masses
4. (a) $\bar{x} = 49.2$, s.d. $= 19.3$ (b) 59.2, 19.3

Exercise 36h   page 580
1. $\bar{x} = 19.6$, s.d. $= 5.2$ (a) 69%   (b) 99.2%
   (c) It is a very symmetrical distribution.
2. theoretical: $\bar{x} = 3.5$, s.d. $= 1.7$
   practical: $\bar{x} = 3.6$, s.d. $= 1.7$
   A very good match, so it is reasonable to assume that the dice is unbiased and fairly tossed.

Self-Assessment 36   page 581
1. 7, 6.8, 6.1
2. (a) 2.55   (b) 1.46   (c) 2.1, 1.8
3. (a) 5.49 mm
   (b) 0.47 mm
   (c) 5.3

CHAPTER 37

Exercise 37a   page 583
1. (a) 7.2   (b) 7.5
2. (a) 4.2   (b) 1.43 (3 s.f.)
3. $\frac{a}{b} = \frac{3}{4}$, $\frac{b}{a} = \frac{4}{3}$, $\frac{a}{3} = \frac{b}{4}$, $4a = 3b$
4. 2.1 hours
5. 453 to nearest drachma
6. $y = \dfrac{3x}{4}$
7. (a) 44 000

   (b) 19 000 approx. (18 920 exact)
8. 4.8 cm, 12.5 cm
9. (a) 1 cm represents $\frac{1}{2}$ km   (b) 12 cm
10. $\overrightarrow{AC} = \frac{2}{5}\overrightarrow{AB} = \frac{2}{3}\overrightarrow{CB}$
11. (a) $y = kx$
    (c) y is proportional to x
12. 31.25 cm²
13. 167 cm³ (3 s.f.)

Exercise 37b   page 585
1. $y = \frac{1}{2}x$
2. $y = x^2$
3. $s = 8 - t$
4. $v = 2t - 2$
5. 8, 18; $A = \frac{1}{2}h^2$
6. nth term $= 2n + 3$
7. 18, 7; $y = 3x$
8. 1.5, 3.6; $A = \frac{3}{2}b$
9. 1, 1.8; $C = \frac{1}{4}x$; cost of 1 kg in £
10. (a) $y = 8x$ (b) 48   (c) 1
11. (a) $C = \frac{16}{5}P$ (b) 25.6   (c) 2.5
12. (a) 27   (b) $\frac{2}{3}$
13. 15.4 (3 s.f.)
14. (b) $y = \frac{3}{4}x$

Exercise 37c   page 587
1. (a) $z = 3t^3$ (b) 3000
2. (a) 16   (b) 2.5
3. (a) 8   (b) 9
4. 40.96 cm²
5. (c); (a)

6. (a) $y = 1.8x$ (b) $y = 18 - x$ (c) $y = \dfrac{48}{x}$
7. (a) $y = \dfrac{24}{x}$, $xy = 24$, $x = \dfrac{24}{y}$
   (b) 12
8. (a) 25   (b) 20
9. (a) 4
   (b) y is halved
   (c) $y = \dfrac{144}{x}$, $x = \dfrac{144}{y}$, $xy = 144$
10. (a) $sc = M$ (c) 30
    (b) 600   (d)

11. (a) 600   (c)
    (b) 833 (3 s.f.)

12. (a) 2.94 (3 s.f.)   (b) 6.93 (3 s.f.)
13. 75
14. 24
15. (a) 6.75   (b) 0.730 (3 s.f.)
16. (a) $y = 8 - x$ (c) $y = 8x$
    (b) $y = \dfrac{8}{x}$ (d) $y = 2 + \dfrac{3x}{4}$

Exercise 37d   page 589
1. x decreases by a factor 4, 2.5
2. (a) $\frac{1}{9}$ (b) $\frac{9}{25}$
3. increases by a factor 1.44
4. $1.78 \left(\frac{16}{9} \right)$
5. (a) decreases to 0.87 of the original radius
   (b) increases to 4 times the original height

Exercise 37e   page 590
Because drawing a line of best fit is a matter of judgment, your answers may not agree exactly with those given here but they should be close.
1. (b) $v = 18.5\,t$
   (c) 185
2. (a) (7, 1.9) looks out of place.
   (b) $2.65\,\text{cm}^2$
   (c) $A = 0.44\,t$
3. (b) 1.75, $L = 1.75\,F + 25$
   (c) 9.1 N
   (d) 25 cm
4. (a) $M = 0.075\,v - 1$
   (b) 14 m
5. Qu. 1 and 2

Exercise 37f   page 592
1. (a) $a = 0.033$
   (b) (i) 1.41 g   (ii) 6.11 g
   (c) (i) 4.5 mm   (ii) 5.8 mm
   (d) 0.033 g is the mass of $1\,\text{mm}^3$ of the material
2. $a = 1.5$, $b = 400$ (a) 1900   (b) 13
3. (a) and (b) $N = ab^t$. Plotting N against t^2 and N against t^3 do not give straight lines. Therefore, if one of the three given relations is correct it must be (iii)
   (c) $a = 3$, $b = 2$ i.e. $N = 3 \times 2^t$. The other values satisfy this.
   (d) (i) 384   (ii) 12288   (iii) 136

4. (a) The shape of the curve is

which suggests the equation
$S = k\sqrt{R}$
   (b) Plot S against $\sqrt{R}$. This gives a straight line $k = 5$. i.e. $S = 5\sqrt{R}$
   (c) (i) 39 m.p.h.   (ii) 61 m.p.h., each correct to the nearest whole number
5. (a) and (b) The relationship between x and y is $y = 5x^2$.
   (c) yes. If $x = 4.8$, $y = 115.2$ not 105.2 as in the table.
   (d) (i) 39.2   (ii) 4.5 (to 1.d.p.)

Self-Assessment 37   page 594
1. (a) and (b)
2. (a) $y = \frac{10}{3}x$
   (b) 23.3 (3 s.f.)   (c) 0.72
3. (a) $y = \frac{30}{x}$
   (b) 16.7 (3 s.f.)   (c) 12.5
4. $z = 3.2r$, 23
5. (a) Neither; $y = 2 + x$
   (b) Direct; $y = 3x$
   (c) Neither
   (d) Probably inverse, in which case $y = \frac{16}{x}$
6. (a)
7. (a) 0.81 m   (b) 1.41 s (3 s.f.)
8. (a) Plot W against d^2. This gives a straight line passing through the origin. Therefore $a = 0$. The gradient of the line is 0.4 $\left(\frac{2}{5} \right)$ i.e. W and d are related by the equation $W = 0.4d^2$.
   (b) (i) 3.6 t   (ii) 3.5 cm (each correct to 1 d.p.)

INDEX